Twentieth-Century Music

ELLIOTT ANTOKOLETZ

University of Texas, Austin

PRENTICE HALL   Englewood Cliffs, New Jersey 07632

Library of Congress Cataloging-in-Publication Data

ANTOKOLETZ, ELLIOTT.
  Twentieth-century music / Elliott Antokoletz.
      p.   cm.
  Includes bibliographical references and index.
  ISBN 0-13-934126-9
  1. Music—20th century—History and criticism. I. Title.
ML197.A63 1992
780'.9'04—dc20

                                        90-19651
                                        CIP
                                        MN

In Memory of My Father, Jack Antokoletz

Editorial/production supervision: Michael R. Steinberg
Interior design: Arthur Maisel
Cover design: Patricia Kelly
Prepress buyer: Herb Klein
Manufacturing buyer: Patrice Fraccio
Acquisitions editor: Bud Therien

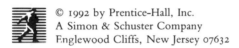

© 1992 by Prentice-Hall, Inc.
A Simon & Schuster Company
Englewood Cliffs, New Jersey 07632

Printed in the United States of America

10 9 8 7 6 5 4 3 2 1

ISBN 0-13-934126-9

PRENTICE-HALL INTERNATIONAL (UK) LIMITED, *London*
PRENTICE-HALL OF AUSTRALIA PTY. LIMITED, *Sydney*
PRENTICE-HALL CANADA INC., *Toronto*
PRENTICE-HALL HISPANOAMERICANA, S.A., *Mexico*
PRENTICE-HALL OF INDIA PRIVATE LIMITED, *New Delhi*
PRENTICE-HALL OF JAPAN, INC., *Tokyo*
SIMON & SCHUSTER ASIA PTE. LTD., *Singapore*
EDITORA PRENTICE-HALL DO BRASIL, LTDA., *Rio de Janeiro*

Contents

Preface

An unprecedented departure from established musical traditions characterizes much of the music composed during the first decade of the twentieth century. Despite the passage of more than three quarters of a century, many works written around 1910 are still referred to as "modern." No changes of musical style or technique have ever produced such a sense of historical discontinuity as those that gave rise to our own era. This condition may be traced directly to the radical change in the basic premises of the musical language itself, a revolutionary transformation stemming most prominently from the works of Ives, Scriabin, Debussy, Bartók, Stravinsky, and members of the Vienna Schoenberg circle.

The prevailing political conditions that surrounded both World Wars contributed to the isolation and divergency of the new musical idioms. Pre–World-War-I conflicts between the Triple Alliance (Prussia, the Austro-Hungarian Empire, and, temporarily, Italy) and the Triple Entente (Russia, France, and England) led to a weakening of the Germanic musical sphere of influence in Europe. While German late-Romantic music continued to exert an influence primarily in Germany and Austria in the early twentieth century, many non-Germanic composers turned fervently toward new sources for their musical languages and styles. Nationalistic demands induced composers to look toward Eastern Europe, France, and their own national treasures in literature, the arts, and folklore as the basis for new sources for composition. Thus, in the late nineteenth and early twentieth centuries, three conflicting musical forces were prevalent: German late Romanticism, national styles first evident in Russia and spreading to other countries, and new French styles as manifested in the distinctive approaches of Debussy and Satie.

Motivation by many composers to break away from the German musical hegemony of the late nineteenth century led to two extremes of tonal orientation in the early twentieth century. The ultrachromaticism of Wagner, Bruckner, and Mahler, evolved into the more dissonant chromaticism of Richard Strauss and the expressionistic atonality of the Vienna Schoenberg circle, while the pentatonic-diatonic modalities of folk music were to serve as the basis for transformation into new kinds of scale systems found in the music of Debussy, Scriabin, Stravinsky, Bartók, Kodály, and other composers of diverse national backgrounds. The most significant of these modal transformations are the various hybrid modal types and "cyclic-interval" scales, for instance, whole-tone and octatonic (the latter, an eight-note symmetrical scale based on alternating whole-steps and half-steps, or vice versa, is formed by joining any two of the three diminished-seventh chords, i.e., "minor-third cycles"). Stemming from these two opposing sources, German ultrachromaticism and the modal sources of folk music, it was inevitable that the new music would reveal irreconcilable differences in details of phrase, rhythm, pitch organization, and large-scale formal construction.

Despite their fundamental differences, the special premises that underlie each of these two broadly polarized categories could only have been established by the liberation of meter and rhythm permitted by the disappearance of traditional tonal functions in the early twentieth century. In the major-minor scale system, the basic concepts of consonance and dissonance were tied inextricably to the regular barline, but the emergence of new systems of pitch organization was to foster the new autonomy in meter, rhythm, and the other musical parameters. Many composers who drew from folk-music sources, especially from outside of Western culture (Eastern Europe, Russia, Asia, and Africa), introduced unequal-beat patterns from both dynamic dance rhythms in strict style ("tempo giusto") and free vocal style ("parlando rubato") into their contemporary idioms. Thus, certain musical divergencies in the twentieth century can be traced to the basic split in the late nineteenth century between Germanic and non-Germanic political, social, and musical spheres.

Traditional Italian operatic styles, like the German sources, also permeated various musical cultures, including those of Eastern Europe (for instance, Hungary) and Latin America (for instance, Mexico and Argentina). Although the musical cultures of Italy and Germany are as "national" as any other musical culture, their historical influences and global dissemination point to their essential international role in the course of early twentieth-century musical developments. However, by the end of World War I, the German and Italian influences were superseded largely by new international sources, which had emerged originally as part of the early twentieth-century tendency toward national individuation. Of the new sources, the impressionism of Debussy and the primitivism of the Russian works of Stravinsky were among the most prominent aesthetic and stylistic models to be absorbed by composers world wide, the influence of Debussy having already been in evidence since the first decade of the century and that of Stravinsky by the early 1920s. To these sources must be added the influence of Bartók, Webern, and several others of varied national backgrounds, all of whom also contributed to international musical developments. The organization of the chapters in this book is intended partly to reflect these changing emphases.

ORGANIZATION

This text is organized in two large sections, which reflect the two fundamental waves of modernism in the twentieth century. The first wave, which appears to have grown out of the reaction to the Romantic era, became evident entirely by the first decade of the century. The second wave, which gained momentum after World War II with the revival of serialism and the disappearance of censorship of the avant garde, blossomed fully by the early 1950s. *Part I: Music to the Late 1940s* is organized as follows: Chapters 1-3 explore chromaticism both within and beyond the limits of tonality in Germany and Austria; Chapters 4-8 cover diverse national developments, which include the new folk-music orientation and other aesthetic and stylistic assumptions that arose from the increasing awareness of national and cultural identity; Chapters 9-12 discuss various facets of the Neoclassical ideal, which also includes a strong tendency toward a national sense in some cases; Chapter 13 is based on early interests in color, noise, and new sonorities, which appear to have resulted from dissolution of the traditional major-minor scale system and the need to establish new means of expression and structural organization; and Chapter 14 provides a history of the extensions of the twelve-tone system both in and outside of Vienna from the mid-1920s through the 1940s. *Part II: Music Since the Mid-1940s* explores both the continuation and development of trends that were established prior to World War I as well as the newer trends that began to emerge in the decades between the wars: Chapters 15-17 explore the multiplicity of atonal and twelve-tone techniques that became widespread after World War II; Chapters 18-19 deal with the contrasting compositional assumptions that were emerging prominently in the musique concrète, electronic, and aleatoric movements; and Chapter 20 provides discussions of many composers who continued, in varying degrees, to absorb elements from their own national idioms as well as other early twentieth-century trends. All of these post–World-War-II musical developments are viewed in the context of the new political, social, and economic conditions—these include the aftermath of the Nazi holocaust, reaction to the political conditions and life styles of the interwar years, advent of the atomic and space age, and new electronic and computer technologies—all of which were to contribute either directly or indirectly to the increasing multiplicity in all areas of the arts.

Major book-length studies of twentieth-century music have been proliferating over the past several years. Notwithstanding the important contributions that many of these studies have made to our understanding of the music, the tendency has been to provide either an encyclopedic historical overview, i.e., with little or no in-depth theoretic-analytical discussion of the compositions themselves, or to provide a compendium of compositional techniques, i.e., with limited or no emphasis on historical aspects. The intention of this text is to provide as thorough and balanced a perspective of the music of our century as possible. Thus, detailed theoretic-analytical studies from a broad spectrum of musical idioms form a significant part of this study within larger discussions of the political, social, and cultural framework.

Certain composers have received greater attention than others in these chapters according to criteria not always based on artistic merit. Such determinations may have been dictated by the following factors: impact of a composer on his own and/or future generations; contribution to the development of a particular theoretical principle; role in the dissemination of prevalent aesthetics, styles, and techniques through teacher-pupil or other types of associations; stature as a national figure; popularity as reflected in the number of score publications and recordings; and so on. At the same time, relatively unknown composers are given more attention than certain more established ones occasionally because of the intrinsic quality of their music, which is deserving of this opportunity for public exposure.

Because of the extraordinary number of composers and the diversity of music that one must contend with in producing a history of twentieth-century music, it seems impossible to provide an entirely fair or balanced representation in the discussions. Several early twentieth-century composers as well as many younger ones of true artistic worth could not be given more than brief mention or, in some cases, had to be excluded altogether. Decisions for inclusion were made on the basis of what might best contribute to a coherent historical understanding of the general aesthetic, stylistic, and technical principles that characterize the music of our century. Such decisions have been based on my own intensive study and intimate contact with the music itself, these experiences having come from over fifteen years of teaching a variety of courses in twentieth-century music, personal contact with composers, and participation in contemporary music ensembles in performances of much of the string quartet literature and other genres.

This text is based on both in-depth and brief analyses of a variety of compositional idioms, which have been selected for their relevance and comprehensiveness in demonstrating the basic principles of a particular musical language and in reflecting a given historical tendency. At the same time, the analytical discussions are by no means intended to cover every aspect of a composer's style or technique, but rather to point to the most salient features that might pave the way for more comprehensive and detailed studies of individual compositions and, ultimately, the larger output of a given composer or group of composers. Musical discussions range from contexts based on both traditional (sometimes even harmonically functional) pitch constructions and less traditional modal (often folk-music-derived) forms to the most abstract melodic and harmonic constructions as well as materials organized by means other than pitched sounds. Where pitch relations are removed from traditional tonal means of organization, new terms and labels, many of which have by now become standard, are employed in order to avoid the conceptual implications of the traditional tonal system, which may no longer be relevant to the new idiom. The introduction of the relevant terminology in this textbook will facilitate students' awareness and understanding of fundamental twentieth-century compositional approaches, since the terminology is connected inextricably to the concepts themselves.

Primary instances of such terminological issues are found in the twelve-tone serial idiom as well as in music based on non–twelve-tone pitch-sets, in which alphabetical names of pitch classes have been replaced in analytical studies by numerical nomenclature (numbers 0 through 11 being assigned to the twelve pitch classes, with the octave designated by either 0 or 12). While such numerical substitution has been in use since the first half of the century, the present text employs numbers for pitch classes according to a principle that has not yet been adopted universally. In order to establish a more unified analytical approach to the vast array of compositions based on pitch-sets, we arbitrarily assign 0 (=12) to pitch-class C. Transposition numbers of pitch collections will also be designated by numbers from 0 to 11. We will assume a referential order (as we do for triads and the major and minor scales in the traditional tonal system) in assigning a transposition number to a scale or pitch collection: the pitch-class number of the "first" note will designate that collection. If a referential collection is "based" on C, its transposition number is 0 (=12). If the collection is transposed so that its "first" note becomes C♯, its transposition number becomes 1 (=13).

The logic of the latter is the same as that in naming tonalities or keys in traditional tonal music, in which the alphabetical nomenclature is fixed. For instance, we know immediately what is meant when we say a piece is in B♭ major or G♯ minor—it would be absurd to assign "A major" or "A minor" to the first (or basic) key of every tonal piece simply because "A" is the first letter of the alphabet. Nevertheless, such designations have been standardized in analyses of serial or pitch-set compositions, in which "0" is assigned automatically to the initial pitch-class of the first (or basic) statement of the twelve-tone row regardless of that pitch-class. Thus, if we say that the basic row statement in Schoenberg's *Fourth String Quartet* is "P-2," we would like to know that the first note of that "prime" form of the row is D. Such fixed designations (with C=o) are applied consistently to non–twelve-tone (serial or nonserial) as well as twelve-tone sets throughout the present study. For compositions based on the church or folk modes, the standard terminology (Dorian, Phrygian, Lydian, etc.) will be used. These and other terms and concepts will be defined more explicitly in the course of the analytical discussions. In order for the reader to derive maximum benefit from the musical analyses, it would be helpful to supplement the illustrative musical examples within the text by keeping in hand the musical score of the work under discussion.

ACKNOWLEDGMENTS

I wish to express my gratitude to Professors Malcolm Gillies (Musicology, Melbourne University), Malena Kuss (Musicology, North Texas State University at Denton), Jann Pasler (Musicology, the University of California at San Diego), George Perle (Professor Emeritus of Composition and Theory, City University of New York), and Dr. Benjamin Suchoff (Former Successor-Trustee of the Estate of Béla Bartók and Head of the New York Bartók Archive), for their careful reading of specific chapters and for their invaluable suggestions concerning either scholarly or editorial matters. Thanks are also due to Professor Michael von Albrecht (Klassische Philologie, Universität Heidelberg) for providing me with historical information on the music of his father, Georg von Albrecht. I am grateful to composers Luis Jorge González (University of Colorado at Boulder), Karl Korte, Russell Pinkston, and Dan Welcher (University of Texas at Austin), and Barton and Priscilla McLean (MLC Publications, R.D. 2, Box 33, Petersburg, N.Y.), for having made valuable suggestions in reference to those sections dealing with their own music.

I am pleased for this opportunity to thank Prentice Hall for requesting that I write this book. Special appreciation is expressed to the Executive Editor, Norwell F. Therien, Jr., for his confidence in my work and for his guidance from the time of the book's inception, and to the Production Editor, Michael Steinberg, for his expertise in the careful preparation of the final manuscript for publication. For aid in proofreading bibliographic data, I am indebted to my student, Bashar Lulua. To Don W. Tharp, Library Assistant of the Performance Library at the University of Texas at Austin, I must express thanks for providing me with data on publishers in preparation of the musical examples. Finally, I should like to express my gratitude and affection to my wife, Juana Canabal Antokoletz, for having read large portions of the text and for providing me with invaluable editorial suggestions, and to my son, Eric Antokoletz, for his aid in proofreading the entire set of page proofs.

Breitkopf & Härtel, Wiesbaden, Germany, for excerpts from:
  Sibelius: *Fourth Symphony*.

Edizioni Suvini Zerboni, Milano, Italy, for excerpts from:
  Dallapiccola: *Il Prigioniero*.

European American Music Distributors Corporation, Valley Forge, Pennsylvania, for excerpts from:
  Bartók: *Fourth String Quartet;* Berg: *String Quartet,* Op. 3; Berg: *Lyric Suite;* Berg: *Wozzeck;* Boulez: *Piano Sonata No. 3;* Boulez: *Structure Ia;* Boulez: "Zur Meine 3. Klaviersonate" from *Darmstaedter Beitrage zur Neuen Musik III;* Hindemith: *Mathis der Maler;* Hindemith: *Quintet for Wind Instruments,* Op. 24, No. 2; Kodály: *Sonata for Violoncello and Piano,* Op. 4; Ligeti: "Boulez" from *Die Reihe,* Volume 4; Penderecki: *Fluorescences;* Schoenberg: *Three Piano Pieces,* Opus 11, Nos. 1 and 2; Schoenberg: *Quintet,* Op. 26; Schoenberg: *Piano Piece,* Op. 33a; Stockhausen: *Studie II;* Webern: *Bagatelle for String Quartet,* Op. 9, No. 5; Webern: *Five Pieces for Orchestra,* Op. 10, No. 3; Webern: *Cantata No. 1,* Op. 29.

Luis Jorge González, Longmont, Colorado, for excerpt from:
  Harawi.

GunMar Music, Inc., Newton Centre, Massachusetts, for excerpt from:
  Perle: *Thirteen Dickinson Songs,* Vol. II, No. 5.

Hal Leonard Publishing Corporation, Milwaukee, Wisconsin, for excerpts from:
  Sessions: *Sonata for Solo Violin.*

McGinnis & Marx Music Publishers, New York, N.Y., for excerpt from:
  Davidowsky: *Synchronism No. 1.*

MLC Publications, R.D. 2, Box 33, Petersburg, N.Y., for excerpts from:
  McLean: *Dimensions I.*

Music Associates of America, Englewood, New Jersey, for excerpts from:
  Babbitt: *Three Compositions for Piano, No. 1;* Krenek: *Lamentio Jeremiae Prophetae,* Op. 9.

North/South Editions (BMI), New York, N.Y., for excerpt from:
  González: *Voces II.*

Österreichische Nationalbibliothek, Musik-Sammlung, Wien, for excerpt from:
  Douglas Jarman: *The Music of Alban Berg* (1979).

Oxford University Press, Oxford, for excerpts from:
  Reginald Smith Brindle: *The New Music.*

Peer Southern Concert Music, New York, N.Y., for excerpts from:
  Ives: *The Cage;* Ponce: *Concierto Del Sur;* Thomson: *Symphony on a Hymn Tune.*

C.F. Peters Corporation, New York, N.Y., for excerpts from:
  Cage: *Concert for Piano;* Cage: *Music of Changes;* Feldman: *Intersection I;* Ligeti: *Volumina.*

Ricordi Americana S.A.E.C., Buenos Aires, for excerpts from:
  Ginastera: *Malambo.*

Schirmer Books, Macmillan Publishing Co., New York, N.Y., for excerpts from:
  David Ernst: *The Evolution of Electronic Music* (1977).

E.C. Schirmer Music Co., Boston, Massachusetts, for excerpt from:
  Perle: *Eighth String Quartet ("Windows of Order").*

G. Schirmer, Inc., New York, N.Y., for excerpts from:
  Babbitt: *Composition for Twelve Instruments;* Brown: *Available Forms II;* Carter: *Etude VII* of *Eight Etudes and a Fantasy;* Carter: *Second String Quartet;* Chávez: *Sinfonía India;* Falla: *El Amor brujo;* Granados: *Danzas españolas,* Op. 37; Griffes: *Piano Sonata;* Griffes: "The White Peacock" from *Roman Sketches,* Op. 7; Honegger: *Pacific 231;* Poulenc: *Sonata* for horn, trumpet, and trombone; Prokofiev: *Fifth Symphony;* Schoenberg: *Five Piano Pieces,* Op. 23, No. 1; Schuman: *Symphony No. 3;* Shostakovich: *Fifth Symphony;* Stravinsky: *Histoire du Soldat;* Vaughan Williams: *Mass in G Minor;* Villa-Lobos: *Chôros No. 10.*

Seesaw Music Corp., New York, N.Y., for excerpts from:
  Wolpe: *Form* for piano.

The University of California Press, Berkeley, California, for excerpts from:
Elliott Antokoletz: *The Music of Béla Bartók: A Study of Tonality and Progression in Twentieth-Century Music* (1984); Jann Pasler: *Confronting Stravinsky: Man, Musician, and Modernist* (1986); George Perle: *Serial Composition and Atonality.* 6th edition, revised (1991).

Theodore Presser Co., Bryn Mawr, Pennsylvania, for excerpts from:
Ives: *Psalm 24*; Messiaen: *Modes de Valeurs et d'Intensités;* Perle: *Fifth String Quartet;* Ruggles: *Men and Mountains;* Welcher: *String Quartet No. 1.*

Yale University Press, New Haven, Connecticut, for excerpt from:
Pieter C. van den Toorn: *The Music of Igor Stravinsky* (1983).

1 Toward expressionism and the transformation of nineteenth-century chromatic tonality

Transformation of German late-Romantic musical styles into more concentrated expressionistic idioms in the early twentieth century was concomitant with, and to an extent dependent upon, certain new tendencies in literature and psychology. Reaction by many turn-of-the-century dramatists against the naturalistic tendencies of nineteenth-century theatre appears to have been based on a new interest in psychological motivation and the projection of spiritual rather than naturalistic actualities. Some of the most prominent among these new dramatists were Strindberg, Yeats, Ibsen, Chekhov, Toller, Joyce, and other figures of diverse national backgrounds. In Vienna, these new literary assumptions were primarily manifested in the dramas and novels of Hugo von Hofmannsthal, Jacob Wassermann, and Arthur Schnitzler, who founded the group known as "Young Vienna" in 1900 in opposition to the German naturalist school of drama. These writers were to reveal new psychological insights into the pathology of their individual characters. As the seat of the Austro-Hungarian Empire and a scientific and cultural center, Vienna had also attracted such musical figures as Brahms, Bruckner, Mahler, Richard Strauss, and Schoenberg.

STRAUSS, HOFMANNSTHAL, AND THE VIENNA OF SIGMUND FREUD

Between 1906 and 1908, Hofmannsthal and Strauss began their collaboration with the operatic setting of *Elektra*.[1] In many of his librettos, Hofmannsthal approached the subject of love and hate from a profound human perspective, concerning himself with psychological motivation, more lucid character delineation, and the symbolic transcendence of external reality. It was during this time in Vienna that Freud was developing his theory of psychoanalysis in *Studien über Hysterie* (1895; *Studies in Hysteria,* 1955) and *Die Traumdeutung* (1899; *The Interpretation of Dreams,* 1953). These psychoanalytic studies were instrumental in establishing the premise of subconscious domination over the conscious mind. The connection between Hofmannsthal's psychological approach to *Elektra* and Freud's theories is a direct one.[2] When the Austrian theatre director Max Reinhardt expressed to Hofmannsthal his disinterest in what he considered to be the dullness of the ancient Greek dramatic style, Hofmannsthal was impelled to turn to a study of Rohde's *Psyche* as well as

---

[1] See *Richard Strauss und Hugo von Hofmannsthal: Briefwechsel: Gesamtausgabe,* ed. Franz and Alice Strauss, rev. Willi Schuh (Zurich: Atlantis Verlag AG, 1952, enlarged 2/1955; Eng. tr. Collins, 1961), letters from 1906 through 1909 passim.

[2] See William Mann, *Richard Strauss: A Critical Study of the Operas* (Cassell and London: Cassell & Company Ltd., 1964), p. 68.

Freud's *Studien über Hysterie* before producing his version of the *Elektra* play in 1903. These psychoanalytic influences obviously led Hofmannsthal to his more intense and powerful version of the original Sophocles model.

In conjunction with these developments in literature and psychology, composers sought new technical means to express the more profound psychological states underlying emotions. The ultrachromaticism of Wagner, Bruckner, and Mahler reached its most intensive stage in the dissonant chromatic tonality of *Elektra,* a landmark in Strauss' operatic development that epitomizes late Romantic music on the threshold of the new chromatic idiom. While the expressionistic quality as well as certain "nontonal" aspects of *Elektra* predate the *free-atonality* of Schoenberg's *Erwartung* (1909) and Berg's *Wozzeck* (1914–1922), Strauss never crossed that threshold. After *Elektra,* in his operas *Der Rosenkavalier* and *Ariadne auf Naxos* (1911–1912), he reverted to classical techniques and forms. *Elektra* foreshadowed certain characteristics of the new idiom, especially in its overall tonal organization based on a specific scheme of chromatic relations. The trend toward equalization of the twelve semitones of the chromatic scale and the dissolution of traditional tonal functions in the compositions of the Vienna Schoenberg circle were already suggested in *Elektra,* where traditional triadic roots are symmetrically distributed around the central tonality of D.[3] For instance, Elektra's leitmotif is based on two triads a tritone apart (mm. 12–15), the B and F roots of which are symmetrical to D (B–D–F). As part of this scheme, the symmetrical polarization of the tonalities (B♭, at No. 36, mm. 6ff., and F♯, No. 130, mm. 3ff.) of Agamemnon and Klytaemnestra on either side of the B–F motif of the child (F♯/B–F/B♭) is essential both to the psychological structure of the opera and the more chromatic harmonic conception. In Classical harmonic progressions, the derivation of triads from common or closely related diatonic scales permits maximal intersection of triadic content, whereas in Strauss' opera the symmetrical organization of triadic roots produces maximal chromatic and dissonant relations between the triadic constructions themselves. Strauss' approach to harmonic progression, dissonance, and the overall symmetrical tonal scheme in *Elektra* represents a radical departure from nineteenth-century chromaticism, the new musical principles providing expanded possibilities for expressing the psychological symbolization of the drama.[4]

Ethan Mordden places *Elektra* in proper perspective: "a monumental nexus of revenge tragedy, psychological study, and classical reinvestment— the regeneration of old themes via modern interrogation . . . the heroine's

---

[3] This tonal organization is outlined by Elliott Antokoletz in "Strauss' *Elektra:* Toward Expressionism and the Transformation of Nineteenth-Century Chromatic Tonality," *Musik und Dichtung* (Frankfurt am Main: Verlag Peter Lang, 1990): 449.

[4] These musico-dramatic relations are discussed in detail in Antokoletz, "Strauss' *Elektra*" (see note 3 above).

monologue, a case for Freud not merely in word-pictures, but in sounds as well, insatiable natterings, outbursts, screaming; Elektra's confrontations with her sister and her mother, the latter scene presaging the expressionism of atonal opera."[5]

EARLY POST-ROMANTIC PERIOD OF THE VIENNA SCHOENBERG CIRCLE

Whereas Strauss' *Elektra* approached the extreme limits of chromatic harmony, the early works of the Viennese composers Arnold Schoenberg, Anton Webern, and Alban Berg were only the beginning of a new chromaticism. Through Schoenberg, Vienna became the center for the transformation of classical tonality. It was primarily with the disappearance of the triad itself, when Shoenberg subsequently turned to free-atonality in 1901 that any suggestion of traditional harmonic functions was to be entirely dissolved. While Schoenberg's works prior to 1909 remained within the chromatic tonal sphere of Wagner, certain works of this early Post-Romantic period already suggested his inclination toward a more subjective, dissonant, and atonal idiom and the tendency toward an increased delay of tonal resolution. Several works written between 1897 and 1900 achieved a degree of acceptance, especially the string sextet *Verklärte Nacht* (1899), composed in the chromatic idiom of Wagner's *Tristan und Isolde*. However, his early songs, Opp. 1–3 (1896–1898), which reveal a more individual style, produced outbursts of protest in 1900 that foreshadowed the general opposition that Schoenberg was to receive throughout his life.

Around 1900, Schoenberg conducted several amateur choral groups in the suburbs of Vienna, increasing his interest in vocal composition. At this time, he began work on his choral piece, the *Gurrelieder* ("Songs of Gurre," "Gurre" being a castle in Scandinavian mythology), after a poem by the Danish writer, Jens Peter Jacobsen. This work, which surpasses the formidable orchestral dimensions of Mahler and Strauss, is scored for five solo voices, speaker, three male choruses, eight-part mixed chorus, and large orchestra. While the first two parts of the work were completed in the spring of 1901, the final chorus remained in sketch until 1910; since the possibility of performance was remote, there was no reason to meet a deadline for completion.

In the *Gurrelieder,* Schoenberg exploited all the possibilities of the German late-Romantic orchestra, further including such coloristic devices as *col legno* and *sul ponticello* effects in the strings, the interplay of various solo instruments, and some of the earliest uses of *sprechtstimme* in certain vocal passages. In contrast to Strauss and Debussy, we find more self-contained melodic structures as well as wide melodic skips that foreshadow Schoenberg's later work. In contrast to the free form of the music drama of

[5] Ethan Mordden. *Opera in the Twentieth Century: Sacred, Profane, Godot* (New York: Oxford University Press, 1978), pp. 116.

Wagner, the distinct forms of the separate poems in this huge song cycle outline an overall construction that appears to have a closer connection to the more abstract structural conceptions of Brahms.[6] Nevertheless, while the poems are each self-contained musically, together they form a continuous organic whole and are further linked by common thematic associations.

In July 1903, after Schoenberg returned to Vienna from Berlin where he had formed an *überbrettl* (artistic cabaret) with Frank Wedekind, Ernst von Wolzogen, and O. Bierbaum at Wolzogen's Buntes Theatre, he began to receive some recognition through Mahler's influence. In autumn 1904, both Webern and Berg came to Schoenberg for private study. Schoenberg and his pupils generally worked in intimate and esoteric situations, conditions largely formed by the conservative tastes of the Viennese public. Since it was difficult to find public support for new works, Schoenberg and his teacher, Alexander von Zemlinsky, established the *Vereinigung Schaffender Tonkünstler* (Society for Creative Musicians) in March 1904, in which Mahler held the position of honorary president. Performances often included works of Mahler, Strauss, and Zemlinsky. Under the auspices of this society, Schoenberg had the opportunity to conduct the first performance of his *Pelléas* in 1905, the same year in which the *Vereinigung* ended.

In the remaining works of Schoenberg's first style period, marked changes began to occur on all levels of composition. In his *String Quartet No. 1* in D major, Op. 7 (1905), and the *Kammersymphonie,* Op. 9 (1906), a greater sense of delayed tonal resolution is felt within more complex and dense contrapuntal textures. The latter work, which marks the climax of Schoenberg's first period, establishes "a very intimate reciprocation between melody and harmony, in that both connect remote relations of the tonality into a perfect unity," thereby making "great progress in the direction of the emancipation of the dissonance."[7] While these extremely chromatic works are still set within the limits of tonality, delayed resolution of dissonance seems to have perplexed audiences at first performances of the *Quartet* in Vienna and Dresden in 1906, and *Kammersymphonie* in 1907. While departures from traditional tonal harmony (by the use of whole-tone formations, chords built on fourths, and other symmetrical constructions) in the latter work primarily have linear rather than harmonic importance, such constructions apparently contributed to the scandalous audience reactions. Schoenberg felt that the true cause of audience resistance to his works, especially in his first period, was to be found in his "tendency to endow every work with an

[6] Philip Friedheim, "Tonality and Structure in the Early Works of Schoenberg" (Ph.D. dissertation, New York University, 1963), p. 142. For the most extensive analysis of the work, see Alban Berg, *Arnold Schönberg: Gurre-Lieder Fuehrer* (Vienna: Universal Edition, grosse Ausgabe 1913; Kleine Ausgabe 1914).

[7] Schoenberg, "My Evolution (1949)," in *Style and Idea,* ed. Leonard Stein (London: Faber and Faber, Ltd., 1975), p. 84.

extravagant abundance of musical themes . . . It was, of course, the tendency of the Wagnerian and post-Wagnerian epoch."[8]

Schoenberg knew that he could reduce the length of works by the restriction of such techniques, and felt that this could be achieved by two methods: condensation and juxtaposition. He believed that it was in the principle of *developing variation* that one found greater aesthetic merit than in the use of either the unvaried phrase repetitions or the unvaried sequences of earlier works, even though this new technique of *developing variation* barely reduced the length of the *First Quartet*. Nevertheless, Schoenberg's interest in generating all material from basic germ ideas as part of this new technique in the *Quartet* and *Kammersymphonie* was significant in that it led to his use of motivic (or pitch-cell) transformations in the contrapuntal textures of the atonal idiom. Pervasive use of cellular or motivic construction is basic to the cyclic form of the *Quartet* and, as we have already observed, to that of earlier works such as the *Gurrelieder*.

Webern's studies with Schoenberg continued from 1904 until 1908, during which time such works as his *String Quartet* (1905) revealed a significant post-Romantic influence of Schoenberg's *Verklärte Nacht* . His use of varied recurrences of a three-note motif was intended to solidify the structure. This attempt was more successful in his *Piano Quintet* (1907), which shows a greater unity and economy of material in its structural design. This sonata movement in C major now reveals influences of Brahms and Reger, in addition to Schoenberg. All three stylistic influences are seen in his *Passacaglia,* Op. 1, for orchestra (1908), written at the end of this period of study with Schoenberg. While the orchestration is at times extremely rich and colorful, similar to Mahler, or Schoenberg in his *Pelléas,* the first variation for flute, trumpet, harp, violas, and cellos, marked ***pp,*** foreshadows Webern's unique qualities of the delicate and reduced textures subsequently found in his atonal works.

Webern's development during these years paralleled that of Schoenberg's, especially in his tendency towards employing greater continuity in developing variation. Webern began to move towards atonality in his set of *Five Songs* (1906–1908), based on the poetry of Richard Dehmel. The use of a key signature in each of these songs seems almost superfluous, as his use of symmetrical formations (e.g., diminished triads and whole-tone constructions) obscures a sense of clear tonality. Similarly, in his *Entflieht auf leichten Kähnen,* Op. 2, for a cappella chorus (1908), the tonality is obscured by constantly shifting harmonies. While this four-part canon still uses a key signature, the text by Stefan George elicits a similar meaning to the George text ("the air of another planet") used by Schoenberg in his *Second String Quartet* (also 1908), in which the key signature is discarded in the last movement. Also similar to Schoenberg's works of these years is Webern's increas-

---

[8] Schoenberg, "A Self-Analysis (1948)," in ibid., pp. 76ff.

ing tendency towards concentrated material and reduced structural length, especially in his two groups of *Five Songs,* Opp. 3 and 4, with piano (1909). In these works, Schoenberg's technique of developing variation can be observed in Webern's greater emphasis on motivic (or cellular) generation of the material. Furthermore, we get variety within unity by means of vertical projection of the linear elements. These techniques and characteristics were basic to Webern's atonal compositions.

Berg came to Schoenberg at a time when the latter was undergoing some of the most significant developments in his early career. Berg's *Seven Early Songs,* with piano (1905–1908), that were produced during early years of study with Schoenberg, reflect stylistic influences from the German late-Romantic *lied* tradition as well as certain characteristics from his teacher's early post-Romantic style. Schoenberg's and Webern's tendency towards contrapuntal writing, in which small motifs or cellular components generate the melodic and harmonic fabric in a more concentrated structural plan, is reflected in Berg's *Piano Sonata,* Op. 1 (1908). At the same time, this one-movement work also reveals the influence of Debussy, as reflected for instance in Berg's use of whole-tone and other nontraditional configurations in a context that articulates tonal priorities at prominent structural points. It is in Berg's *Four Songs,* Op. 2 (1909), that the influence of Wagnerian harmonies and touches of Debussy are evidenced, and we see Berg's first strong inclination towards atonality. The key signature of the second song is not a true indication of the suggested tonality; the piece may be analyzed almost entirely as a chain of French–6th chords. The final song of this opus is clearly Berg's first atonal piece.

We see in the evolution of the works of the Vienna Schoenberg circle to 1909, a common inclination towards reduction of content and structure, a focus on singular pitch constructions as the primary generators of the contrapuntal fabric according to Schoenberg's technique of developing variation, and the replacement, by new types of harmonic constructions, of those normative elements that were basic to the establishment of traditional tonal functions and resolutions in the preceding century.

SUGGESTED READINGS

ELLIOTT ANTOKOLETZ.   "Strauss' *Elektra:* Toward Expressionism and the Transformation of Nineteenth-Century Chromatic Tonality," *Musik und Dichtung* 23 (Frankfurt am Main: Verlag Peter Lang, 1990): 443–467.

ALBAN BERG.   *Arnold Schönberg: Gurre-Lieder Fuehrer* (Vienna: Universal Edition, grosse Ausgabe 1913; kleine Ausgabe 1914).

NORMAN DEL MAR.   *Richard Strauss* Vol. I (Ithaca, New York: Cornell University Press, 1962, 1986), pp. 287–333 (on *Elektra*).

PHILIP FRIEDHEIM.   "Tonality and Structure in the Early Works of Schoenberg" (Ph.D. dissertation, New York University, 1963).

ERNEST HUTCHESON.   *Elektra by Richard Strauss: A Guide to the Opera* (New York: G. Schirmer; Boston: Boston Music Co., 1910).

WILLIAM MANN.   *Richard Strauss: A Critical Study of the Operas* (Cassell and London: Cassell and Company Ltd., 1964).

ETHAN MORDDEN.   *Opera in the Twentieth Century: Sacred, Profane, Godot* (New York: Oxford University Press, 1978), pp. 115–117 (on *Elektra*); pp. 155–157 (on *Erwartung*).

LEONARD STEIN, ed.   *Style and Idea, Selected Writings of Arnold Schoenberg,* trans. Leo Black (London: Faber and Faber Ltd.; Los Angeles: Belmont Music Publishers, 1975; Berkeley and Los Angeles: University of California Press, 1984), including: "A Self-Analysis (1948)," pp. 76–79; "My Evolution (1949)," pp. 79–92.

FRANZ AND ALICE STRAUSS, ed.   *Richard Strauss und Hugo von Hofmannsthal: Briefwechsel: Gesamtausgabe,* rev. Willi Schuh (Zürich: Atlantis Verlag AG, 1952, enlarged 2/1955; Eng. tr. Collins, 1961), references to *Elektra* in letters from 1906 through 1909 passim.

2 Vienna Schoenberg circle: Free atonality and expressionism

EXPRESSIONISM By the end of the first decade of the century, the ultrachromatic late-Romantic styles of Wagner and Strauss were transformed into the atonal and expressionistic idiom of the Viennese composers Schoenberg, Webern, and Berg. The more intensely subjective attitude of the Viennese composers was foreshadowed in Romantic inclinations toward extreme emotionalism as well as the strangeness and grotesqueness of subjects. In contrast to the nineteenth-century German Romantics such as E. T. A. Hoffmann, Weber, Schumann, Wagner, and others, Schoenberg belonged to an era of strong reaction to Romantic aesthetics, as artists from various countries sought new ways to represent external reality. The term *expressionism,* which originated in the early part of the century as an antithesis to *impressionism,* was used to describe any modern art work, in which representation of nature was subordinated to the expression of emotion induced by the spontaneous distortion of form and color. In painting, Van Gogh is often considered to be the precursor of expressionism; this tendency was developed further by the Norwegian Edvard Munch and the Germans E. L. Kirchner and Schmitt-Rottluff, who belonged to the group called *die Brücke.*

Painting and literature also provided momentum for the expressionist movement in music. During a period of crisis and change in his musical style and language between 1907 and 1910, in which he moved toward increasing concentration of expression, Schoenberg turned to painting and eventually became associated with the Munich *Der Blaue Reiter* group, which included the Russian-German abstract painter Wassily Kandinsky, Paul Klee, and Franz Marc. In a letter to Schoenberg dated January 18, 1911, Kandinsky expressed a vital kinship to Schoenberg, embracing his music and general aesthetic ideas, which led to a joint exhibition of their paintings and a life-long friendship.[1]

In the Vienna of Freud, these aesthetics were more intensively developed in the paintings and writings of Oskar Kokoschka and the poetry of Stefan George and Richard Dehmel, with whom Schoenberg had artistic connections. Interest in the subconscious and irrational led to the use of distorted forms on expressionistic canvases, which resulted in more intense expression of the artist's emotions and underlying psychological states. Such images provided a new concept of reality that had little to do with conven-

---

[1] See *Arnold Schönberg—Wassily Kandinsky: Briefe, Bilder und Dokumente einer aussergewöhnlichen Begegnung* (Salzburg and Vienna: Residenz Verlag, 1980); in English as *Arnold Schoenberg—Wassily Kandinsky: Letters, Pictures, and Documents,* ed. Jelena Hahl-Koch, trans. John C. Crawford (London and Boston: Faber and Faber Ltd., 1984), pp. 21ff.

tional notions of aesthetics. Musical expressionism was based on the adoption of new conceptions of melody, harmony, tonality, rhythm, timbre, and form. While Schoenberg's musical language took as its point of departure the ultraemotional chromatic idiom of Wagner's *Tristan*, his expressionistic assumptions, as manifested in such works as his opera *Erwartung* (1909), were based on subjects of nightmare, shock, and bizarre actions. To this end, the expressionist composer exploited the possibilities of distorted word accentuation, athematicism and nonrepetition, harmonic dissonance in conjunction with wide and angular melodic leaps, unconventional uses of instrumental timbre and register, and more concentrated and uniform use of materials in contexts of relentless intensity, in an effort to induce increased emotional intensity.

FREE-ATONALITY

Shortly after Schoenberg turned to painting, he began to compose in the *free-atonal idiom*.[2] New works, which were more dissonant and subjective, were to be subsumed eventually under the expressionist label. In 1907–1908, he foreshadowed the new development in his *String Quartet* No. 2, Op. 10, in F♯ minor, in which the third and fourth movements include a soprano setting of the poems of Stefan George. While the work begins within the bounds of chromatic tonality and thematic construction, it proceeds toward linear chromaticism, where motifs and intervals come to define the structure as they replace tonal functions. The final cadence of the fourth movement is in F♯, but Schoenberg found no general need for a key signature in this movement, since such indication no longer served any practical tonal purpose. Regarding his evolution toward the concept of atonality, Schoenberg stated that "there are many sections in which the individual parts proceed regardless of whether or not their meeting results in codified harmonies . . . The key is presented distinctly at all the main dividing points of the formal organization. Yet the overwhelming multitude of dissonances cannot be balanced any longer by occasional returns to such triads as represent a key."[3] In the same year, he wrote his first freely dissonant work, *Das Buch der hängenden Gärten*, Op. 15, a song cycle for high voice based on fifteen poems of George. Schoenberg felt that these songs showed a style different from anything he had written thus far, and considered it a first step towards the atonal idiom.[4] New sonorities as

[2] While Schoenberg preferred the term "pantonal," meaning the "inclusion of all tonalities," the negative term "atonal" has become the standard designation for the new idiom.

[3] See Willi Reich, *Schoenberg, a Critical Biography*, trans. Leo Black (London: Longman; New York: Praeger, 1971), p. 31. See also Paul Lansky and George Perle, "Atonality," *The New Grove Dictionary of Music and Musicians*, ed. Stanley Sadie (London: Macmillan Publishers Ltd., 1980), pp. 669ff.

[4] See Leonard Stein, ed., *Style and Idea, Selected Writings of Arnold Schoenberg*, trans. Leo Black (London: Faber and Faber Ltd.; Los Angeles: Belmont Music Publishers, 1975; Berkeley and Los Angeles: University of California Press, 1984), pp. 49–50.

well as new kinds of melody were introduced. According to Schoenberg, these songs were not revolutionary as many had considered them, but grew logically out of existing musical resources.

PRINCIPLES OF ATONAL ORGANIZATION

The first consistently atonal works of the Viennese composers were written in 1909. Webern and Berg also turned toward the new idiom shortly after Schoenberg. Free atonality originated in an attempt to equalize the value of the twelve notes of the chromatic scale, so that they would no longer form a hierarchy of functions so fundamental to the chromaticism of the traditional tonal system. The "free-atonal" works of the Viennese composers may be grouped according to two general organizational principles[5]—*variation* based on the *intervallic cell,* which serves as the identifiable referential unit and as the means of integrating the musical fabric, and *nonrepetition,* which may produce an "athematic style, a kind of musical stream of consciousness wherein the thread of continuity is generated by momentary associations."[6]

With regard to the first category, a *cell* may be defined as a small collection of pitch-classes, that may be exploited equally and simultaneously on both the melodic and harmonic levels. This technique does not permit any significant intervallic differentiation between these two contextual dimensions. (In contrast to works in the atonal idiom, harmonic structures in the major-minor scale system are usually distinguished from linear thematic formations—while triads in the traditional tonal system contain the fundamental elements of harmonic and melodic construction, the intervals of the triad on the melodic level, in contrast to the harmonic level, are often diatonically or chromatically filled in by step.) In the earliest atonal compositions of the Schoenberg School, e.g., in the first piece of Schoenberg's *Drei Klavierstücke,* Op. 11 (1909), and in the fourth piece of Webern's *Fünf Sätze,* Op. 5, for string quartet (1909), the elements of the cell do not have a consistent ordering.

Despite accusations of anarchy and revolution by critics of his new style in Op. 11, Schoenberg asserted that "a centralizing power comparable to the gravitation exerted by the root is still operative in these pieces," and that "a composer's only yardstick is his sense of balance and . . . belief in the infallibility of the logic of his musical thinking."[7] This is exemplified in the logic of Op. 11, No. 1, which depends significantly on the generation of the musical content from a basic cell. This content unfolds within the framework of a traditional formal scheme, in which we find (by analogy to tradition) modulations away from and back to the original pitch levels of the respective

[5] See George Perle, *Serial Composition and Atonality* (6th ed., rev., Berkeley and Los Angeles: University of California Press, 1991), pp. 9–39.

[6] Ibid., p. 19.

[7] See Schoenberg, *Style and Idea,* n. 4, above, pp. 86–87, where he points to his original discussion of this "centralizing power" in his *Harmonielehre* (1911).

themes. It is in the replacement of the triad by the cell as the basic harmonic premise that we find the primary means by which tones are liberated from their traditional tonal functions.[8]

While the intervallic content of the basic cell remains unchanged in many of its statements, we also find an extremely free treatment of the cellular intervals in this early atonal work, where the cell generates larger thematic lines: consequently, the intervallic content as well as rhythm and contour of the cell are frequently altered. The basic three-note cell, B–G♯–G, which initiates the opening theme (mm. 1–3), consists of interval-classes 1, 3, and 4 (i.e., minor second or major seventh, minor third or major sixth, and major third or minor sixth) (Ex. 2–1). This three-note segment is established as a cellular unit of the theme by the immediate linear and harmonic context: the cadential notes of the theme (F–E–D♭) and two of the chords (A–G♭–F and D♭–B♭–A) are varied manifestations of the same cellular structure. The cell is then projected into the structure of each of the next two theme groups: at each of the cadential points of theme 2 (mm. 4–8), the referential transposition of the cell (B–G♯–G) is partitioned into its interval-classes B–G and B–G♯; and the opening of theme 3 (m. 12) is initiated by a permutation of transposition E♭–C–B. Near the end of the development section (mm. 46–47), the last transposed statement of theme 1 is accompanied by material based exclusively on transpositions of the inverted form of the initial cell (Ex. 2–2).

From the outset of the work, we also find a process of thematic generation, in which the cellular intervallic structure itself is radically altered. The cadential-segment A–F–E of theme 1 (mm. 2–3) retains interval-class 1 of the basic cell, but expands interval-class 3 to interval-class 4. At the first modified return of theme 1 (mm. 9–11), interval-classes 1 and 3 of the basic cell are both expanded now to interval-classes 2 and 4 OF F♯–D–C. This expanded form of the cell generates the larger thematic statement, which, together with its accompanying harmony, now bases itself on one of the complete whole-tone collections (with one "odd" note, A, at m. 11). This form of the cell in the modified statement of theme 1 provides evidence that an earlier whole-tone figure, E–C–B♭ (at mm. 4–8), that had initiated each phrase of theme 2, is also a transformation of the basic cell.

The significance of such cellular transformation is three-fold: (1) it permits unifying relationships between contrasting thematic areas; (2) the

---

[8] According to Philip Friedheim, "Tonality and Structure in the Early Works of Schoenberg" (Ph.D. dissertation, New York University, 1963), p. 471, the movement is in a sort of rondo (A–B–A–C–A') or quasi-sonata form: Principal section in A–B–A (mm. 1–24); development, transition (mm. 25–33); Middle section C (mm. 34–47); Transition (mm. 48–52); Recapitulation A' (mm. 53–64). Perle's analysis, in *Serial Composition,* n. 5, above, pp. 10–15, suggests a sonata form of a somewhat different interpretation, suggesting that the development begins with a transposed statement of theme 2 (mm. 20ff.), the recapitulation beginning with a modified statement of theme 3 at its original pitch level (mm. 49ff.).

EXAMPLE 2–1. Schoenberg, *Three Piano Pieces,* Op. 11, No. 1, mm. 1–12

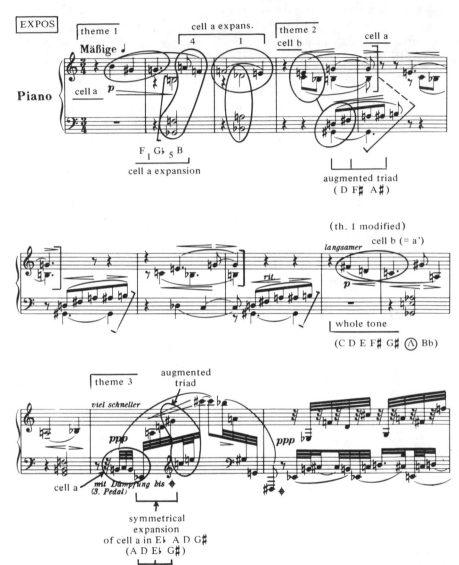

original cell is transformed into a whole-tone cyclic segment, which in turn generates the larger symmetrical whole-tone cycle; and (3) other symmetries are also generated from the initial nonsymmetrical cell as part of the developmental process. The last is significant in the large-scale unfolding of the piece: the initial three-note cell is ultimately transformed by means of intervallic expansion and literal inversion into a four-note symmetry, E♭–A/D–G♯ (last

EXAMPLE 2-2. Schoenberg, *Three Piano Pieces,* Op. 11, No. 1, mm. 46–47

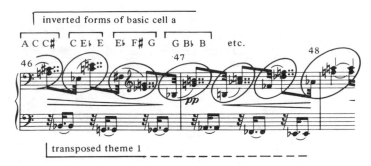

chord of the piece).[9] This final symmetrical chord, which is based on two tritones a minor-second or perfect-fourth apart, first appears at the same transpositional level at the opening of theme 3 (m. 12), where it is elided with E♭ of the transposed basic-cell, E♭–C–B. Construction E♭–A/D–G♯ is foreshadowed by the first chord of the piece, ([]–G♭/B–F), which forms a transposed segment of the latter symmetry. This opening chord may also be understood as an expansion of the basic cell structure, in which interval-class 1 of B–G♯–G remains unchanged, while interval-class 3 is expanded to interval-class 5. Thus, expansion and symmetrization of the cell appears to be a primary goal of organic development in the work.[10]

In this as well as other twentieth-century compositions, symmetrical pitch constructions are also a significant means of progression for the transposition of themes or cells away from, and back to, original pitch-levels. In this piece, the (symmetrical) augmented triad functions on the local level as a primary thematic pivot. The augmented triad D–F♯–A♯, which first occurs at mm. 4–5, lower staff, as an unobtrusive structural element of theme 2, returns as a local foreground detail in the recapitulation (at mm. 51–54, left hand) in three successive rotations: F♯–B♭–D, A♯–D–F♯, and D–F♯–A♯), the last of which restores the second theme to its original pitch level (Ex. 2–3).[11] The augmented triad first appears as transposition A–F–D♭ at the cadence of theme 1 (mm. 2–3), the F–D♭ of which is reinterpreted immediately as part of the cadential statement of cell a (F–E–D♭) (see Ex. 2–1). Similarly, the

[9] See Elliott Antokoletz, *The Music of Béla Bartók: A Study of Tonality and Progression in Twentieth-Century Music* (Berkeley and Los Angeles: University of California Press, 1984), pp. 16–17.

[10] Perle states, in *Serial Composition,* n. 5, above, p. 26, that "Because of its self-evident structure such a [symmetrical] chord tends to have a somewhat stable character."

[11] See Perle, ibid., p. 15; see also Antokoletz, *The Music of Béla Bartók,* n. 9, above, pp. 17–18.

EXAMPLE 2–3. Schoenberg, *Three Piano Pieces*, Op. 11, No. 1, mm. 51–54

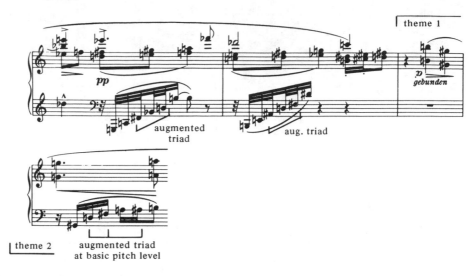

theme-2 occurrence of augmented-triad D–F♯–A♯ also has one of its major thirds (F♯–A♯) forming part of a basic-cell statement, F♯–A–A♯ (mm. 4–5). In theme 3 (m. 12), another augmented triad, G♯–C–E, appears for the first time as a figure linearly intact, though one of its major thirds (C–E) is again reinterpreted immediately as part of the basic cell (C–C♯–E). A new transposition of theme 2 (E♭–G–B♭–B–C, at mm. 20ff.) is introduced by three chords: the first two are forms of the basic cell, the third an augmented triad, E–A♭–C. Then (at m. 24, right hand), a permutation of the pitch content of this theme-2 transposition yields an intact foreground statement of its augmented triad, G–E♭–B. Thus, the (symmetrical) augmented triad, which is the primary means of returning theme 2 to its original pitch-level in the recapitulation, is derived initially from both the basic cell of theme 1 and the structure of theme 2. In later atonal compositions, the elements of the cell sometimes have a fixed order, i.e., are serialized, as in the first piece of Schoenberg's *Fünf Klavierstücke*, Op. 23 (1923). Here, the cell is distinguishable in four transformations: *prime, inversion, retrograde, and retrograde-inversion* (Ex. 2–4).[12] The use of an ordered cell in this otherwise nontwelve-tone piece of Schoenberg's foreshadows his twelve-tone serial idiom immediately; the fifth piece of this opus is one of the earliest works to be based on a twelve-tone series.

[12] See Perle, ibid., p. 10, for a detailed study of the serial procedures in the opening measures. See also Chap. 3, n. 10, below, for transposition numbers in serial composition.

EXAMPLE 2–4. Schoenberg, *Five Piano Pieces,* Op. 23, No. 1: (a) two cells and their transformations; (b) opening, overlapping set-forms

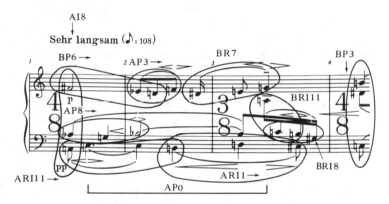

With regard to works in the second category of atonal organization, repetition is minimized, so the material proceeds in an ever-changing, more or less *athematic continuum.* In this style, any identifiable repetition generally occurs in the form of local sequences or ostinato patterns. Schoenberg, who originated this concept, stated that:

> I . . . immediately and exhaustively explained to him [Webern] each of my new ideas . . . but failed to realize that he would write music of this kind sooner than I would . . . . It was like that when I had just completed the first two of the Three Piano Pieces, Op. 11. I showed him them and told him I was planning a cycle (which I never wrote), among which would be a very short piece, consisting of only a few chords. This he found most surprising, and it was obviously the cause of his extremely short compositions. I also discussed what would be

essential if a short piece were not to be merely a "shortened" one: concentration of the expression and of the phrases.[13]

The second piece of Schoenberg's Op. 11, while no shorter than the first, nevertheless reveals a certain tendency towards nonrepetition and concentration of expression. Set within a sort of sonata form, most of the "thematic" ideas are primarily related to each other by their similarity of contour, resulting in a general uniformity of material. Contrasting rhythmic patterns are the basic means by which "thematic" groups are differentiated from one another, coherence within a given "thematic" section being achieved by local use of modified repetitions or sequences.[14] While certain pitch-cell patterns are implied in linear adjacency, e.g., three-note, gapped whole-tone segments (in reordered spelling, A–[]–Db–Eb, Ab–[]–C–D, and Eb–Db–[]–A, at mm. 2–4), their varied intervallic permutations as well as irregular rhythms tend to produce an amorphous continuum, in which any clear sense of surface pitch-cell reiteration is obscured (Ex. 2–5). Furthermore, the pervasive ostinato figure, which is the most obvious unifying element of the entire structure, is itself ambiguous rhythmically and metrically. The ostinato, which may be heard either as triplets or duplets, begins on the beat, then shifts away from the barline (at m. 3); the ambiguous metric character of the theme, which contradicts the 12/8 time signature, further obscures the rhythmic character of the ostinato. Direction in this ambiguous and continually changing fabric is primarily achieved by movement from an amorphous rhythmic state to a more clearly defined motif in theme B. The latter expands in several varied repetitions above the now more metrically defined ostinato, culminating on more stable duple chords at the cadence (mm. 11–13). The return of A' (m. 13) brings us back to the amorphous character of the opening, the sense of rounding out being supported by the reinterpreted relationship of ostinato to theme (i.e., the ostinato now begins after the start of theme A', entering where it originally dropped out in m. 3). While themes reappear at their original pitch level in the Recapitulation, their order is varied above the more sustained and metrically reinterpreted ostinato. The third piece of Op. 11 is a more significant example of athematic materials, which unfold in fragmentary rhythmic motion. Here, the interval replaces form and tonality as a basic organizing factor; the series of "major thirds" in the upper part at the beginning acquire a structural function as they

---

[13] Schoenberg, *Style and Idea,* n. 4, above, pp. 484–485.

[14] Friedheim, in "Tonality and Structure," n. 8, above, p. 453, gives the following thematic-formal outline: Exposition (mm. 1–19), A (mm. 1–4), B (mm. 4–13), A' (mm. 13–15), C (mm. 16–19); Transition (last two notes of m. 19); Development (mm. 20–28), A' (mm. 20–26), B' (mm. 26–28); Mid Section (mm. 29–54), D–C' or B″ in three statements (mm. 29–39), mutated A (mm. 39–44), climax at reappearance of B (mm. 45–50), D (mm. 51–54); Recapitulation at original pitch level (mm. 55–66), A (mm. 55–58), C (mm. 59–62), D–C' (mm. 63–65), B (mm. 65–66).

EXAMPLE 2–5. Schoenberg, *Three Piano Pieces,* Op. 11, No. 2, opening

Used by permission of Belmont Music Publishers.

recur in varied contexts (e.g., see the recurrence of thirds in descending form at m. 5).[15]

These principles of structural concentration and reduction, nonrepetition and athematicism, as well as cellular variation and transformation, the basis of Schoenberg's new expressionistic and symbolic idiom, continued to be developed in the remainder of his atonal compositions prior to the First World War. His works composed during this time include his *Five Orchestral Pieces,* Op. 16 (1909), the operas *Erwartung,* Op. 17 (1909), and *Die Glückliche Hand,* Op. 18 (1910–1913), the *Sechs kleine Klavierstücke,* Op. 19 (1911), *Herzgewächse* for soprano, celesta, harmonium, and harp, Op. 20 (1911), *Pierrot Lunaire,* Op. 21 (1912), and the *Four Orchestral Songs,* Op. 22 (1913–1916). *Erwartung,* a monodrama in four continuous scenes on a text by Marie Pappenheim, represents Schoenberg's first major breakthrough in transforming the chromatic idiom of Wagner's *Tristan* into an expressionistic and atonal musical language.[16] In the Vienna of Freud, writers and artists turned with greater awareness to the subconscious and the irrational. According to Adorno, "the concept of shock is one aspect of the unifying principle of the

[15] Perle, *Serial Composition,* n. 5, above, p. 21.

[16] Part of the following discussion of *Erwartung* is taken from Elliott Antokoletz and George Perle, *Erwartung and Bluebeard,* program note for the performance by the New York Metropolitan Opera (January 16, 1989).

epoch. It belongs to the fundamental level of all modern music . . . Through such shocks the individual becomes aware of his nothingness."[17] Schoenberg's monodrama includes one character in an extreme of convulsive expression. The Woman enters the forest to keep a rendezvous with her lover, but the lover has been murdered, and in the dark stumbles over his corpse. All of nature seems to reflect her anxiety and absorb her innermost feelings. The work is highly symbolic, metaphoric, and ambiguous in that we do not know whether what we see on the stage is supposed to be a representation of a series of events or of a dream. And if a dream, whose dream?

Erwartung is unified by means of related sonorities. Most of the chords have six notes, which generally combine two three-note chords each encompassed by a major-seventh.[18] For instance, the symmetrical construction, Gb–C–F/B–E–Bb, alternates tritones and perfect-fourths, which pervade the texture in various transpositions, permutations, transformations, and combinations. However, the work is entirely athematic (i.e., without motivic development, repetition, or transformation) to produce an amorphous stream of consciousness. This is due to the dissociation of the sonorities from any recognizably consistent rhythms, thematic contours, or registers, and the result is an ever-changing contrapuntal fabric that supports the relentless unfolding of psychological drama. The opera lasts half an hour, but its singular mood in a context of perpetually *developing variation* (Schoenberg's term) induces a sense of extreme psychological condensation of the entire action into a single moment or, stated in reverse, a single moment based on an anxiety or state of mind expanded to half an hour. There is no real sense of past, present, or future, since psychological time relies, of necessity, on our perception of the temporal ordering of distinguishable events. Schoenberg has concealed the sectional premise of traditional operatic construction, stating that *Erwartung* represents "in *slow motion* everything that occurs during a single second of maximal spiritual excitement."[19]

In 1912, Schoenberg again moved further away from traditional principles of melodic and harmonic construction. His *Pierrot Lunaire*, Op. 21, which sets twenty-one poems (in three groups of seven) by the French Symbolist Albert Giraud in German translation, is scored for five instruments (flute, clarinet, violin, cello, and piano, the first three of which alternate with piccolo, bass clarinet, and viola, respectively). Here, we find a completely new approach to text, as the half-speaking, half-singing voice (*Sprechstimme*) is instructed to move in a sort of *glissando* between two designated pitches. The result is a feeling of improvisation and the removal of any sense of dissonance, which was traditionally produced by intersection of the melodic

---

[17] Theodor Wiesengrund-Adorno, *Philosophy of Modern Music,* trans. Anne G. Mitchell and Wesley V. Blomster (New York: The Seabury Press, 1973), pp. 155–156.

[18] See Charles Rosen, *Arnold Schoenberg* (Princeton, New Jersey: Princeton University Press, 1975), pp. 41ff.

[19] Schoenberg, *Style and Idea,* n. 4, above, p. 105.

and harmonic levels. This brought about a crisis in traditional concepts of melodic and harmonic organization. Any harmonic sense seems to come from the linear configuration within each individual instrument.[20] This new idiom is removed from the convulsive inner feelings of *Erwartung*.

Between the time Schoenberg composed *Erwartung* and *Pierrot Lunaire*, he taught theory and composition at the Royal Academy of Music and Dramatic Art in Vienna (1910). Because of the anti-semitic attacks that he sustained, he transferred to Berlin in 1911, where he took up his old position as lecturer at the Stern Conservatorium. Perhaps influenced by these academic affiliations, he turned in his spare time to writing *Harmonielehre* (1910–1911). In this treatise he provided a traditional exposition of chords and progressions as well as a detailed theoretical discussion of his new ideas, which were evolving in his compositions. The latter discussions primarily dealt with cyclic-symmetrical pitch constructions,[21] which included functions of the whole-tone scale (as derived from traditional sources) and fourth chords. He discussed the aesthetics of chords with six or more tones, and evaluated his radically new concept of *Klangfarbenmelodien* (a "melody" organized by timbre or "tone color" rather than pitch). It was also in Berlin (in February 1913) that the *Gurrelieder*, under the direction of Franz Schreker, had its first performance. Though the work was a considerable success, Schoenberg refused to acknowledge the reception, as a result of the long-standing critical reactions to his works.

While Schoenberg moved toward increasing concentration of material during these years of atonal composition, Webern produced the most radical examples of nonrepetition. In certain movements of Webern's *Five Pieces for String Quartet*, Op. 5 (1909), we already observe his tendency towards extreme reduction of texture and structure, his concept of "theme" and "development" often being reduced to just a single sound or event. In Op. 5, No. 4, for example, the pizzicato chord of m. 2 and its recapitulation at m. 11 serves as a referential element. In the sparseness of the contrapuntal fabric, Webern's delicate and classically controlled approach reveals the antithesis of both the dense expressionistic idiom of Schoenberg and the full Romantic textures of Berg's works of the same period. After his Op. 5, in which only the first piece incorporates thematic development in a sonata form based on several motivic ideas, he produced both the *Six Pieces*, Op. 6, for orchestra and the *Four Pieces*, Op. 7, for violin and piano (1910). In his *Two Songs*, Op. 8, with eight accompanying instruments (1911–1912), Webern consistently avoided octave doublings as both a reductive technique and means of denying a sense of pitch-class priority. In his next three works—the

[20] See Rosen, *Arnold Schoenberg,* n. 18, above, pp. 50–51.
[21] Any pitch formation derived from or forming a segment of one of the interval cycles, which may be defined as a series based on a single recurrent interval, such as the whole-tone scale or cycle of fourths. A collection of notes is symmetrical if one half of its intervallic structure maps into the other half through mirroring, i.e., literal inversion.

Six Bagatelles for String Quartet, Op. 9 (1911–1913), *Five Pieces for Orchestra,* Op. 10 (1913), and *Three Little Pieces,* Op. 11, for cello and piano (1914)— Webern went even further than before in terms of structural and textural concision. One instance, the fourth piece of Op. 10, is a mere six measures and extremely sparse in its instrumental texture. Another, the last piece of Op. 11, consists of only twenty notes.

One of the primary means of progression in the athematic atonal context of the second piece of Op. 5 is found in fluctuations between *nonsymmetrical* and *symmetrical pitch collections.*[22] In the fifth of the *Six Bagatelles,* Op. 9, symmetrical pitch relations more profoundly pervade the overall structure.[23] This piece exemplifies Webern's early development toward a new concept of content in relation to form. The latter is largely determined by the development of material according to the principle of symmetrical unfolding in various parameters. The rounded binary form is primarily determined by: (1) the symmetrical scheme of dynamics (section A, mm. 1–7) ***ppp–pp–ppp,*** (section B, mm. 8–10) ***pp–pp,*** (section A′, mm. 11–13) ***ppp–pp–ppp;*** (2) corresponding subdivisions of these three large sections according to complete rests or cadences, into 3, 2, and 3 smaller sections respectively; and (3) the departure from and return to a primary "axis of symmetry."[24] The opening section (A) symmetrically unfolds from the initial chord C–C♯–D♯–E, which is based on an implied axis of D–D (Ex. 2–6). Three new notes (B–D–F) are added at the opening of the second phrase (mm. 2–3, vnI and va), symmetrically expanding the pitch content to B–C–C♯–D–E♭–E–F. In the last two measures of this phrase (mm. 4–5), vnI further expands this symmetry by the addition of its double-stop, B♭–G♭. In the final phrase of this section (mm. 6–7), the latter interval (in enharmonic spelling, F♯–B♭) is chromatically filled by the remaining tones, giving us the symmetry F♯–G–A♭–A–B♭ around the dual axis A♭. In other words, D–D and its tritone, A♭–A♭, represent the two intersections of the same symmetry (Ex. 2–7a).[25] In the middle section, B (mm. 8–10), the entire pitch content (B–C–C♯–D–E♭–E–F–G♭) produces a "modulation" to a new set of symmetrical relations with a dual axis of expressed D–E♭ and implied G♯–A (Ex. 2–7b).[26] The modified return (A′) at m. 11 is initiated by dyad G♯–A, which,

[22] See Bruce Archibald, "Some Thoughts on Symmetry in Early Webern; Op. 5, No. 2," *Perspectives of New Music* 10/2 (Spring-Summer, 1972): 159ff.

[23] A detailed analysis of these relations in this piece is given by Antokoletz, in *The Music of Béla Bartók,* n. 9, above, pp. 17–20.

[24] Any collection of two notes is symmetrical, since they are equidistant from an imaginary axis. If we add other pairs of notes to the first pair so that the two notes in each pair are equidistant from the same axis of symmetry, larger symmetrical collections result. The real axis, as opposed to the imaginary one, is represented by the pair of notes, either expressed or implied, that form the center of the larger symmetrical construction.

[25] See Antokoletz, *The Music of Béla Bartók,* n. 9, above, Ex. 18, inversional symmetry based on axial intersections D–D and A♭–A♭; for a fuller explanation of this principle, see ibid., Chapter IV, Exx. 77–79 and the corresponding discussion.

[26] Ibid., Ex. 19.

EXAMPLE 2–6. Webern, *Fifth Ragatelle for String Quartet,* Op. 9, mm. 1–4, symmetrical unfolding around D–D (or A♭–A♭) axis

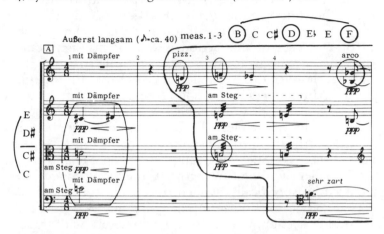

EXAMPLE 2–7. Webern, *Fifth Ragatelle,* Op. 9: (a) inversional symmetry based on axial intersections D–D and A♭–A♭; (b) shift to new axis (D–E♭ or G♯–A) in section B, mm. 8–10

(a)

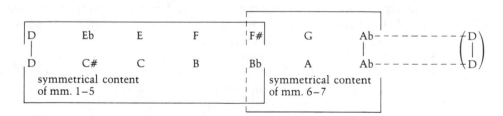

(b)

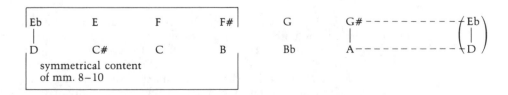

while maintaining the preceding axis, also serves as a pivot point back to the original axis (D–D or A♭–A♭); this dyad, with the following one (G–A♭), forms a four-note symmetry, G–A♭/G♯–A, based on the original A♭–A♭ axis.

Webern's special use of instrumental techniques and timbres in this and other pieces of this period is one of his significant contributions in expanding the means for defining large-scale structure in the atonal idiom. The final chord of this bagatelle (B/C♯–D–E♭–E), though nonsymmetrical, appears to function as part of a long-range symmetrical relation. Three of its notes (B–C♯–D), played *pizzicato,* are a literal inversion of the first three pizzicato notes of the piece (D–E♭–F) in vnI. Together, these two pizzicato segments form a long-range symmetry (B–C♯–D/D–E♭–F) around the primary D–D axis. (Such long-range inversional relationships are also significant in other works of Webern.) Other long-range associations are also produced by specifically defined timbres in this chord. While three of the notes are pizzicato (B–C♯–D), the remaining two (E–E♭) are played *am steg.* The middle section, B (m. 8) begins precisely with these two pitch-classes (E–E♭), played *am steg* in contrast to a pizzicato F. Other such timbral relations also appear to have structural significance. The pizzicato-dyad G♯–A (at m. 11), one of the two axial intersections (D–E♭ explicitly and G♯–A implicitly) of the entire pitch collection of the middle section, B–C–C♯–D–E♭–E–F–G♭ (mm. 8–10), is immediately preceded by the two pizzicato notes G♭–B (at m. 10). Both these pizzicato dyads are symmetrically related: G♭/G♯–A/B. Another structural function of a prominent timbral element occurs in the last phrase of section A (mm. 6–8). The basic axis of symmetry (A♭) is the one note played pizzicato (vc, at m. 8). (Other such structural uses of timbre are discussed later in connection with Webern's works based on the technique of *klangfarbenmelodien.*)

Berg's atonal compositions generally do not fall exclusively into either category, *variation* or *nonrepetition,* but rather combine both techniques in extremely complex textures. While Schoenberg's tonal and early atonal compositions were to exert an influence on Berg,[27] a significant degree of originality was manifested in Berg's atonal works, especially after his studies with Schoenberg ended in 1911 and he began to produce his first independent compositions.[28] The *String Quartet,* Op. 3 (1910), was Berg's last work to be written under the supervision of Schoenberg. This highly personal and expressive work, aesthetically and stylistically removed from that of his colleagues, contains unresolved tonal motions that result from a complex of linearly unfolding motifs and themes. Whereas the earlier *Piano Sonata,* Op.

[27] See Perle, "Berg, Alban," *The New Grove,* p. 526, where he discusses the influences of *Gurrelieder* on both *Wozzeck* and *Lulu.*

[28] According to Hans F. Redlich, *Alban Berg: Versuch einer Würdigung* (Vienna: Universal Edition, 1957); Eng. trans. abridged as *Alban Berg: The Man and His Music* (London: John Calder; New York: Abelard-Schumann, 1957), p. 222, the year 1911 begins the second of four periods into which Berg's life can be subdivided.

1, had set such motions ambiguously within a tonal frame of B minor, the *Quartet* borders more closely on an atonal harmonic context, though it too does not dispense ultimately with a sense of tonal settling. Structural coherence is primarily produced by the pervasive use of motivic elements and their transformations as well as permutations of underlying referential pitch collections (i.e., unordered, or nonserialized sets). The work is in two movements, the second of which is a development of the first. The main themes and their transformations in the first movement, as well as five different cellular components of the opening theme, are outlined in Ex. 2–8.[29] Two melodic patterns, including the cadential figure of the first subject and the second theme of the second subject group, are both derived from the descending whole-tone contour of the initial head motif of the first theme. Different figures, all of which are based on the second cell (ii) of the main theme, may also be demonstrated. This cell is reiterated in inversion within the second theme of the first subject group. Other thematic transformations in the first movement join different cells of the opening themes, and there are also thematic and cellular links between movements.

Other special techniques of structural significance, in addition to the integration by means of motivic, cellular, and thematic development, are basic to this and the remaining works of Berg.[30] In the *Quartet,* the opening figure consists of a five-note segment of one whole-tone scale plus a note (C) from the other whole-tone scale (Ex. 2–8a). The resultant semitone, B–C, then appears as the *nucleus,* or *axis* of the next motivic segment. The latter symmetrically expands around this axis (B–C) by means of inversionally related semitonal scalar segments (or *cyclic interval* segments). At the same time, the combined cells, iii and iv, form two aligned descending cyclic segments, one of semitones, and the other of perfect-fourths. The use of such symmetrical pitch relations contributes to the dissolution of traditional tonal functions and progressions. In support of this cyclic expansion, we get an arithmetically expanding rhythmic progression of one, two, and three articulations, another significant technique in many of Berg's works.

Berg's dependence on and admiration for Schoenberg was demonstrated in 1912 by his contribution to a book produced by Schoenberg's pupils and published in Munich by Piper-Verlag. The book includes essays on Schoenberg as composer, theoretician, teacher, and painter, includes contributions by Kandinsky and Paris von Gütersloh, and reproductions of five paintings by Schoenberg. In Berg's essay, he states that Schoenberg is "the teacher, the prophet, and the messiah; and the spirit of language . . . gives the creative artist the name 'master,' and says about him that he 'starts a school.' "[31] During this year, Berg was completing his first independent

---

[29] See Douglas Jarman, *The Music of Alban Berg* (Berkeley: University of California Press, 1979), pp. 32–34.

[30] See Perle, "Berg, Alban," n. 27, above, p. 525.

[31] Willi Reich, *Alban Berg* (Zürich: Atlantis Verlag AG, 1963); trans. Cornelius Cardew (New York: Vienna House, 1974), pp. 36–37.

EXAMPLE 2–8. Berg, *String Quartet,* Op. 3, Mov. I, main themes and transformations, five cellular components of main theme (Jarman, p. 33)

work, the *Fünf Orchesterlieder nach Ansichtskartentexten von Peter Altenberg,* Op. 4. Schoenberg conducted two of these songs in a concert in Vienna in 1913, which resulted in a scandal and censorship by the critics.[32] Within each of these tightly constructed songs, the huge orchestral forces are exploited to produce a coherent interaction of timbre and texture within a complex linear fabric based on motivic interplay. It is also significant that the main theme of this work is the first example of a twelve-note series.[33]

In various ways, each of Berg's earlier atonal works prepared the way for the first of his two operas, *Wozzeck.* In May 1914, the same year that he completed the *Three Orchestral Pieces,* op. 6, Berg saw several performances of Georg Büchner's dramatic fragment *Woyzeck* at the Vienna Chamber Theatre. Shortly thereafter he decided to set the work as an opera and began to arrange the text, while continuing his work on the *Three Orchestral Pieces.* Later in the year, he completed a fair copy of the score of the Praeludium from Scene 1 and the Military March from Scene 3, which he sent to Schoenberg. During the next year or so, Schoenberg's teaching came to a halt as his pupils were selected for military duty. Berg spent more than three years in the Austrian army, so the entire short score of *Wozzeck* was not completed until 1919, the final orchestration in 1922.

Büchner's drama, although written in the first half of the nineteenth century, anticipated the morbid reality of Berg's own era. *Wozzeck* can be considered real twentieth-century drama, imbued further by Berg's musical setting of a highly expressionistic quality, in which the emotional and psychological state of the protagonist seems to be projected into every external object, action, and musical fiber. The work has not only become one of the cornerstones of expressionism, but is also an historical document of the War years, and a highly personal, autobiographical expression of the composer. Wozzeck, who is a symbol of the oppressed man, refers to himself as "wir arme Leut." He is a poor soldier who is exploited by his superiors and "tormented by *all the world.*"[34] Fatalistically driven by unconscious forces, he eventually murders his unfaithful mistress and drowns himself. In his preoccupation with *Wozzeck* during a short leave in 1918 from his own military duties, Berg wrote a letter to his wife (dated August 7), in which he revealed his sense of identity with Büchner's character.[35]

One of Berg's main concerns in composing *Wozzeck* was the means by which both local and large-scale structural unity could be achieved in the

[32] See George Perle, *The Operas of Alban Berg,* Vol. I. *Wozzeck* (Berkeley and Los Angeles: University of California Press, 1980), p. 8.

[33] See Perle, "Berg, Alban," n. 27, above, p. 526.

[34] Letter from Berg to Webern, dated August 19, 1918. See Redlich, *Alban Berg: Versuch einer Würdigung,* n. 28, above, p. 365n205. See also Reich, n. 31, above, pp. 43 and 45.

[35] See Alban Berg, *Letters to His Wife,* trans. Bernard Grun (New York: St. Martin's Press, 1978), p. 229; see also George Perle, *The Operas of Alban Berg,* Vol. I. *Wozzeck,* n. 32, above, p. 20.

atonal idiom. He could neither rely on the Büchner text for such coherence because of its fragmentary nature, nor on the organizational principles of tonal form and development. In part, Berg's solution lay in the use of a series of diverse but coherent traditional forms, which were to "correspond to the diversity in the character of the individual scenes."[36] For the libretto, Berg first reduced Büchner's twenty-five scenes (based on the Franzos-Landau edition of twenty-six scenes of the text) to fifteen, then organized them in three acts of five scenes each. Each scene has a "rounded off" and individual character, yet contributes to the overall unity. While the musical forms are classical and clearly defined, Berg's main accomplishment lay in his ability to draw audience attention away from the "various fugues, inventions, suites, sonata movements, variations, and passacaglias," to the "vast social implications of the work which by far transcend the personal destiny of Wozzeck."[37] Furthermore, in place of traditional tonal relations for support of the structure and psycho-dramatic currents, Berg provided a complex set of musical inter-relationships and transformations based on recurrent motifs as well as referential pitch collections, all of which unfold in an extremely colorful and varied orchestration.

Berg suggested an outline of the scenes based on the main dramatic and musical events.[38] The large three-act form is determined by the dramatic structure and based on a corresponding temporal symmetry in the musical architecture: the three acts form an arch, in which the longer and more complex middle section (Act 2) forms a bridge between the symmetrically balanced outer sections (Acts 1 and 3). According to Reich's outline of Berg's chart, Act I ("Wozzeck in his relation to the world around him") is a dramatic *exposition* of the main characters and their relationship to the protagonist. These different character sketches are represented by a series of older musical forms of distinctly different styles. The dramatic "development" of the plot, however, which begins at the end of Act I (where Marie is embraced by the Drum Major), actually unfolds in Act 2, where the succession of scenes represents Wozzeck's gradual realization of Marie's infidelity. Here, a closed symphonic shape of five movements (scenes) is the developmental as well as unifying musical structure. The "catastrophe" and final outcome of the plot are the basis of Act 3. The scenes of Act 3 are now individual situational sketches (each in the form of an invention on a single musical idea) that balance the character sketches of Act 1. Regarding these abstract and clearly

---

[36] See n. 34, above.

[37] See "Postscript by Alban Berg, 1931," in Reich's *Wozzeck: A Guide to the Text and Music of the Opera* (New York: G. Schirmer, Inc., reprinted from the monograph originally published by The League of Composers, *Modern Music*, 1927, 1931, 1952), p. 22.

[38] See Reich, *Alban Berg*, n. 31, above, pp. 120–121; see also Perle's discussion of "The Text and Formal Design," in *The Operas of Alban Berg*, Vol. I. *Wozzeck*, n. 32, above, pp. 38ff.

organized musical forms, Perle points out that:

> The musical coherence that the opera has, independently of the staged events, reflects an objective order whose irrelevance to the subjective fate of Wozzeck poignantly emphasizes his total isolation in an indifferent universe . . . this is not to say that the assignment of a specific "absolute" musical form to a given scene is made without reference to specific dramaturgical considerations.[39]

The "Passacaglia" (Act 1, scene 4), for instance, provides a rigid musical structure which can be seen as reflecting the strict diet that the Doctor has forced upon Wozzeck, in his use of him as "guinea pig" for his medical experiments. The opera is pervaded by musical details of structural or local textual significance, such details having either *Leitmotivic* or *nonLeitmotivic* functions.[40]

The opera generally belongs to the atonal idiom, but there seems to be no single system to which all the pitch relations and harmonic constructions are accountable. Whereas traditional tonal works are based on a priori functional associations of the major–minor scale system, with the triad as the single harmonic referent, in *Wozzeck* we find a diversity of constructions that are given both musical and literary significance primarily by the immediate musical context within which they occur. Differing views regarding this question of the existence of a large-scale, unified system of pitch relations in *Wozzeck* are expressed in several major studies.[41]

Certain pitch constructions do seem to have a referential function in the overall working out of the material. In the "Murder scene" (Act 3, scene 2), which is one of the primary dramatic focal points in the opera, Wozzeck's obsession is reflected by an insistent "Invention on a Tone B." At the same time, reminiscences of the earlier musical ideas associated with Marie seem to flash through her mind as she is about to die. Underlying these reminiscences, tone B occurs in various temporal, registral, and timbral positions. It is introduced at the end of the preceding scene (No. 71f.), where it occurs as a "dissonant" pedal against the bitonal combination of major triads on D and E♭. At Marie's first words in the "Murder Scene," the sustained notes (No. 73, m. 1) harmonically extend the B pedal to a whole-tone tetrachord, B–C♯–E♭–F, encompassed by tritone B–F. The upper boundary tone of this

---

[39] George Perle, "Representation and Symbol in the Music of *Wozzeck*," *Music Review* 33/4 (November 1971): 281; see also Perle, ibid., p. 93.

[40] For a systematic outline and description of the main associative themes, motifs, and figures, see Reich, *Wozzeck,* n. 37, above, pp. 8–21; see also Perle, *The Operas of Alban Berg,* n. 32, above, pp. 94ff.

[41] See Jarman, *The Music of Alban Berg,* n. 29, above, p. 22; Perle, *The Operas of Alban Berg,* n. 32, above, p. 130; and Janet Schmalfeldt, *Berg's Wozzeck: Harmonic Language and Dramatic Design* (New Haven: Yale University Press, 1983), pp. ix–x.

collection (F, in the horn) is also marked by Marie's entry pitch. The first two phrasal segments of Wozzeck's entry, based on F–G–A–[]–C♯ (No. 75), together with the B pedal, provide the remaining notes of this whole-tone collection. Again, the vocal entry pitch is F, the tritone of B. This whole-tone cycle is completed by the C♯–D♯ of vnI, while the ending of Wozzeck's line secondarily unfolds a segment (F♯–[]–B♭–C–D) of the other whole-tone collection. The basic tritone, B–F, which emerges more prominently in the double bass (at m. 84), is further manifested as a primary structural element in subsequent passages approaching the murder.

Cyclic-interval fillings of the main tritone, B–F, establish an essential principle of musical progression and dramatic association in the earlier sections of the opera. In the Praeludium of the opening Suite, the cadential tone (D♭) of the Captain's Leitmotif (mm. 4–6) overlaps his statement, "Easy, Wozzeck, easy," as Wozzeck shaves his superior officer (Ex. 2–9). In correspondence with the Captain's apparent need for control, the reiterated D♭ moves from a "dissonant" (or odd-note) position against whole-tone segment C–D–E (No. 5) to a "consonant" position within a gapped segment B–[]–E♭–F of the other whole-tone collection. This completes the basic whole-tone tetrachord B–D♭–E♭–F. While the two whole-tone segments are

EXAMPLE 2–9. Berg, *Wozzeck*. Act I, Scene 1, mm. 4–6, whole-tone segments

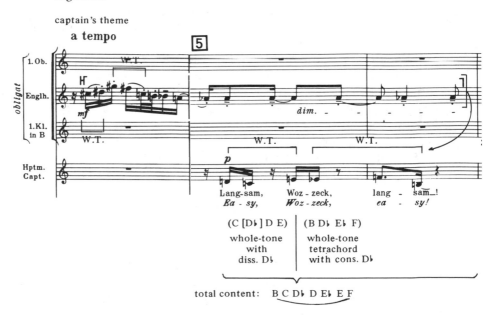

distinct in the linear partitioning, the entire pitch content of the voice and English horn forms a semitonal filling of tritone B–F (B–C–D♭–D–E♭–E–F); this basic tritone appears as a cadential focal point. The Captain's theme itself opens with two juxtaposed whole-tone segments, F♯–G♯ and C♯–B–F (m. 4), the latter (B–C♯–[]–F) foreshadowing the basic whole-tone tetrachord B–D♭–E♭–F immediately.

At the reprise of the Praeludium (A′, mm. 24ff.), these musico-dramatic relations are more explicit. While the Captain's thematic material from the very opening of the Praeludium returns slightly varied in the winds at this point, D♭ is reiterated as the basis of both Wozzeck's first explicit "Jawohl" statement and, as before, as the cadential tone of the Captain's theme (mm. 28–30). Whereas D♭ was absorbed into the whole-tone tetra-chord B–D♭–E♭–F in the original statement of the Captain's theme (mm. 5–6), it is now part of an expanded whole-tone segment (D♭–E♭–F–[]–A–B), which is sustained in the winds in the final measures of the Praeludium (mm. 27–29). This collection is anticipated (at m. 26) in the combined "Jawohl" statement and pizzicato chord (D♭–E♭–F–[]–A–B, with one odd note, C). Thus, priority is given to one of the whole-tone cycles (i.e., that which contains the main tetrachord, B–D♭–E♭–F), as it pervades, and then ends the reprise exclusively.

The Pavanc begins with the Captain's words, "It makes me afraid for the world to think of eternity" (No. 30f.), further revealing an obsessive fear of his inability to control the objective world. In this connection, the section is based on a more complex interaction of the interval cycles. The first six triplets of the Captain's transformed Leitmotif repeat the whole-tone pitch content of the cadence, the odd note (C) this time being expanded to a tritone (G♭–C) from the other whole-tone cycle. While the prevailing interval-class of this thematic segment (D♭–E♭–[]–G–A–B) and the accompanying triplet figure (D♭–E♭) in the harp and horn is whole tone (No. 30), the sustained chord of the winds reinterprets the whole-tone dyad D♭–E♭ as part of a four-note segment of the cycle of fourths, or fifths (D♭–A♭–E♭–B♭); the entire accompaniment in this measure is based on the larger cyclic segment, G♭–D♭–A♭–E♭–B♭. (Whereas the earlier combination of whole-tone seg-ments, C–D–E and B–D♭–E♭–F, at the cadence of the Captain's theme, mm. 5–6, implied the content of a semitonal cyclic segment, B–C–D♭–D–E♭–E–F, the combination of whole-tone elements in this passage outlines a segment of the cycle of fourths/fifths.) Then, at mm. 33–34, a seemingly endless descent of fourths, F–C–G–D–A–E–B–F♯–C♯, appears to symbolize "eter-nity." On another level, increased complexity can also be noted in the absorption of Wozzeck's "Jawohl" rhythm into the Captain's vocal line, at the words "as I think of eternity. 'Eternal, that's eternal.'"

Strictness, and an obsessive need for control, is manifested even more obviously in the megalomaniacal character of the Doctor, who uses Wozzeck for his medical experiments. Scene 4 is appropriately based on a strict ostinato pattern in the form of a twelve-tone Passacaglia theme, which underlies a set of twenty-one variations. These are organized into three main sections:

Variations 1–12, the Doctor's increasing insistence on an ascetic diet for his medical subject and Wozzeck's objections; Variations 13–18, the Doctor's psychological exploitation of Wozzeck as a "guinea pig" for his dietary experiments; and Variations 19–21, the height of the Doctor's conceit and his cry for immortality, after which there is a return to the dialogue of the opening. At the climax of the scene, beginning at Variation 19, the Doctor's conceit is musically represented by extreme control of the material. As the Doctor reviews Wozzeck's strict diet, "Eat your beans then, and mutton to follow," his vocal line systematically unfolds two descending whole-tone tetrachords, D♯–C♯–B–A and G–F–E♭–D♭, which together complete the primary whole-tone cycle. Both tetrachords are interlocked by an intersecting segment of the cycle of fourths, A–D–G.[42] At the same time, the Doctor's obsession is supported by a strict three-part canon in the strings, the contrapuntal texture increasing in density as his obsession intensifies, "Don't slacken, and the Captain you'll shave, and cultivate your idée fixe further." The vocal line (at mm. 615–616) also provides a complete descending statement of the other whole-tone cycle. At the climax of the Doctor's conceit, "Oh! my hypothesis!" (beginning of Variation 20), the vocal line presents a more emphatic statement of an expanded, descending five-note segment of the primary whole-tone cycle (Ex. 2–10). The strings support this statement by a more dense six-part canon, now entirely based on an array of linearly and vertically intersecting cyclic collections. While each string line unfolds both whole-tone cycles in tetrachordal segments as well as complete scales, all the strings are contrapuntally aligned in such a way as to permit a harmonic sequence of perfect-fourth cyclic segments. Furthermore, the sequence of canonic entry pitches outlines the major-third cycle, F♯–A♮–D–F♯–[F]–B♭–D. Overlapping this canon, the winds unfold a series of chords (at mm. 623–637), the outer voices of the winds (piccolo 1 and bass tuba) expanding in inversional motion in connection with the Doctor's most grandiose exclamations, "Oh my fame! I shall be immortal! Immortal! Immortal!" These chords, most of which are built on fourths, lead to the chorale-like final variation (marked *fortissimo*) and the Doctor's last cry for immortality.

These final variations, with their systematic and strict presentation of the interval cycles, are a focus for earlier cyclic-interval development in connection with the trend of the drama. The structure of the twelve-tone Passacaglia theme itself serves as an essential unifying link in this development. The row can be partitioned into alternating segments of the two whole-tone collections: E♭–B–G–C♯/C–F♯–E–B♭/A–F/A♭–D. However, the concluding three-note segment (F–A♭–D), which forms an incomplete cycle of minor thirds, often functions as a refrain element, a connecting link between variations, and as a disruption of unfolding whole-tone succes-

---

[42] The significance of this cyclic interlocking is established more prominently in connection with the six-part canon that begins Variation 20 (mm. 620–623).

EXAMPLE 2–10. Berg, *Wozzeck,* Act I, Scene 4, mm. 620ff., five-note segment of whole-tone cycle supported by six-part canon based on array of interlocking cyclic collections

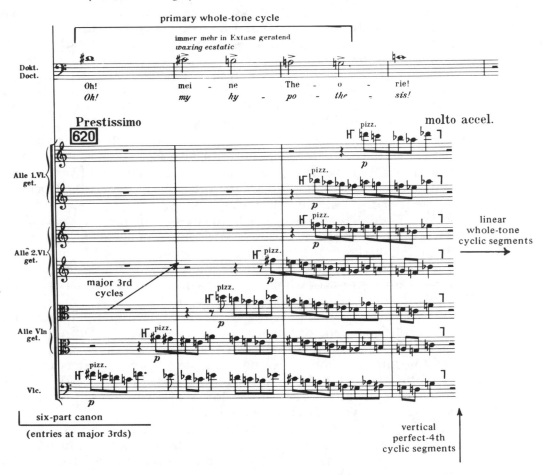

sions. The scene opens (mm. 488ff.) with a cello recitative statement of the Passacaglia theme, which is obscured by the lengthy pitch reiterations in rubato style. This accompanies the Doctor's irregular speech-like vocal line, in which he scolds Wozzeck. The refrain element (F–Ab–D) is first brought out at the Doctor's declamatory "Eh, Eh, Eh!", which refers to his having caught Wozzeck coughing. A recognizable structure within the otherwise irregular phrases is the "Jawohl" rhythm at Wozzeck's "What sir? What,

Doctor?" and at the Doctor's words, "you howled like a dog." Then, the Doctor's conceit begins to be revealed in his statement, "You do not get paid every day for such antics, Wozzeck!", which, in contrast to the preceding statements, is based on the first systematic occurrence of descending whole-tone tetrachords (G–F–E♭–D♭ and B–A–G–F). These are interlocked by a perfect-fourth cyclic segment (D♭–G♭–B). In the remainder of the Doctor's moralizing statements (to m. 495), vocal pitch adjacencies form whole-tone extensions of the corresponding cyclic segments in the Passacaglia theme (e.g., B–A–G–F of the voice cyclically extends G–C♯, then G♯–F♯–D extends C–F♯–E–B♭ to form the entire whole-tone collection, B♭–C–D–E–F♯–G♯, at the words, "This is bad! The world is bad, so bad!"). Wozzeck's reference to his own lack of control, "When forced to that [coughing] by nature!", is then punctuated by the disruptive cadential tones of the row in the cello (F–A♭–D). The latter association is established further by the recurrence of this refrain figure in the viola (mm. 496 and 497), where the Doctor refers to "your nature!" and "ridiculous superstition."

The Doctor then proceeds to the first of his explicitly grandiose statements (in the second half of Variation 1, mm. 498ff.), "Have I not proved quite clearly that the muscles are subject to the human will?" This obvious reference to the need for strictness and control is manifested in the accompanying *stretto* of whole-tone tetrachords (Ex. 2–11). Tritone G–C♯ of the Doctor's vocal line is cyclically extended by one of these tetrachords, D♭–C♭–B♭♭–G (bassoon), which is bounded by the same tritone. The next stretto of whole-tone tetrachords (mm. 500–502) is then disrupted by the cadential figure, F–A♭–D, as the Doctor scolds Wozzeck for coughing. As the Doctor shifts to a more "scientific" attitude toward the dietary experiments (Variations 2–3), the more "learned" character of the text is reflected in the voice. Here begins what Perle refers to as "Berg's secret art," in which linear symmetries pervade the entire vocal line.[43]

In connection with the Doctor's growing conceit and his obsession with his strict medical experiments, which reach a peak in the final variations, cyclic and symmetrical collections emerge from unobtrusive positions in irregularly organized contexts to being more systematic, local, foreground events. The most prominent of these is the whole-tone cycle, especially its derivative tetrachordal segments. As discussed earlier, the basic transpositional level of the whole-tone tetrachord (B–D♭–E♭–F) is significantly manifested in the "Murder" scene in connection with Wozzeck's obsession, or *idée fixe*.

The foregoing discussion of Berg's opera is intended, on the one hand, to outline only some of the dramatic functions of the formal organization, and several representative thematic constructions. On the other hand, the detailed discussion of one aspect of pitch organization and progression (albeit an essential one) in connection with the psychological development of

---

[43] See Perle, "Representation and Symbol," n. 39, above, p. 304.

EXAMPLE 2–11. Berg, *Wozzeck,* Act I, Scene 4, mm. 498ff.

certain characters is intended to provide some basic insights into Berg's musical thinking. It should be made clear that this work is based on a multiplicity of melodic and harmonic pitch constructions, rhythms, and styles, which defy any single approach to Berg's idiom. While unity is provided by pervasive use of Leitmotive, strictly organized forms, and prominent interactions of certain cyclic-interval formations (especially whole-tone formations), the work also includes such contrasting features as mixed-interval and triadic constructions, atonal and tonal passages (though without the hierarchy of functions found in the major–minor scale system), juxtaposition of *Sprechtstimme* and lyric vocal lines (e.g., as in Marie's Bible-reading scene), *parlando* and *arioso* vocal styles, instrumental writing in both chamber and large orchestral textures, irregular, atonally organized phrasal constructions in contrast to folk-like symmetrical phraseology, and traditional classical forms that are often mathematically strict in proportions in contrast to freely organized passages and sections.

 Wozzeck represents a confluence of divergent historical tendencies, in part reflected in these juxtapositions of differing styles and techniques. Composed during a period in which established principles of musical organization were being profoundly altered by Berg and his colleagues, the composer of *Wozzeck* also leaned toward a reconciliation of the principles of pitch organization and rhythm of the new musical language, with certain structural and thematic principles basic to the older Austro-German tradition. It is significant, however, that Berg himself never intended either to reform or revolutionize opera through *Wozzeck,* but instead "simply wanted to compose good music."[44] The technical and stylistic means of composition were obviously secondary to the expression of the poetic text, and, due to Berg's personal circumstances during these bitter war years, the text was deeply colored by his intense personal involvement with the subject matter. Many details of Berg's life during his military service parallelled those of Wozzeck. We have only to cite Berg's exploitation by superiors and assignment to guard duty in Vienna after his complete physical breakdown in November, 1915. This incident serves to remind us of the suffering of the opera's tormented soldier, under quite similar conditions; Berg had, indeed, described his own duties as "imprisonment" or "slavery." The tendency of Viennese expressionism to move toward one of its most intensive stages of development in this opera was inextricably tied to the political, social, cultural, as well as personal circumstances of Berg during the First World War. However, this connection is not so much manifested in the literal historical and autobiographical correlations that one can find in the work, but rather in the emotional and psychological correspondences between composer and subject. It is the latter which prominently contributes to the unity of purpose and mood, permitting the composer to exploit the possibilities existing in the multiplicity of strict classical forms, as well as in both older and newer techniques, for their special character and logic in the creation of a new idiom.

SUGGESTED READINGS

THEODOR WIESENGRUND-ADORNO.   *Philosophy of Modern Music,* trans. Anne G. Mitchell and Wesley V. Blomster (New York: The Seabury Press, 1973).

[44] Reich, *Wozzeck,* n. 37, above, p. 21.

ELLIOTT ANTOKOLETZ AND GEORGE PERLE. *Erwartung and Bluebeard,* program note in *Stagebill* for the performance by the New York Metropolitan Opera (January 16, 1989).

BRUCE ARCHIBALD. "Some Thoughts on Symmetry in Early Webern; Op. 5, No. 2," *Perspectives of New Music* 10/2 (Spring-Summer, 1972): 159–163.

MOSCO CARNER. *Alban Berg: The Man and the Work* (London: Duckworth, 1975).

DONALD CHITTUM. "The Triple Fugue in Berg's Wozzeck," *Music Review* 28 (February 1967): 52–62.

PHILIP FRIEDHEIM. "Tonality and Structure in the Early Works of Schoenberg" (Ph.D. dissertation, New York University, 1963).

JELENA HAHL-KOCH, ed. *Arnold Schönberg—Wassily Kandinsky: Briefe, Bilder und Dokumente einer aussergewöhnlichen Begegnung* (Salzburg and Vienna: Residenz Verlag, 1980); *Arnold Schoenberg—Wassily Kandinsky: Letters, Pictures, and Documents,* Eng. trans. John C. Crawford (London and Boston: Faber and Faber Ltd., 1984).

ROSEMARY HILMAR. *Alban Berg: Leben und Wirken in Wien bis zu seinen ersten Erfolgen als Komponist,* Wiener Musikwissenschaftliche Beiträge, Band 10 (Wien: Hermann Böhlaus Verlag, 1978).

DOUGLAS JARMAN. *The Music of Alban Berg* (Berkeley: University of California Press, 1979).

ETHAN MORDDEN. *Opera in the Twentieth Century: Sacred, Profane, Godot* (New York: Oxford University Press, 1978), pp. 158–162 (on *Wozzeck*).

GEORGE PERLE. "Berg's Master Array of the Interval Cycles," *Musical Quarterly* 63/1 (January 1977): 1–30.

———. "Representation and Symbol in the Music of *Wozzeck*," *Music Review* 33/4 (November 1971): 281–308.

———. *Serial Composition and Atonality: An Introduction to the Music of Schoenberg, Berg, and Webern* (6th ed., rev., Berkeley and Los Angeles: University of California Press, 1991).

———. "The Musical Language of *Wozzeck*," *The Music Forum* I (1967): 204–259.

———. *The Operas of Alban Berg,* Vol. I. *Wozzeck* (Berkeley and Los Angeles: University of California Press, 1980).

HANS F. REDLICH. *Alban Berg: Versuch einer Würdigung* (Vienna: Universal Edition, 1957); Eng. trans. abridged as *Alban Berg: The Man and His Music* (London: John Calder; New York: Abelard-Schumann, 1957).

WILLI REICH. *Alban Berg* (Zürich: Atlantis Verlag AG, 1963); trans. Cornelius Cardew (New York: Vienna House, 1974).

———. *Schoenberg, a Critical Biography,* trans. Leo Black (London: Longman; New York: Praeger, 1971).

———. *Wozzeck: A Guide to the Text and Music of the Opera* (New York: G. Schirmer, Inc., reprinted from the monograph published originally by The League of Composers, *Modern Music,* 1927, 1931, 1952).

CHARLES ROSEN. *Arnold Schoenberg* (Princeton, New Jersey: Princeton University Press, 1975).

JANET SCHMALFELDT. *Berg's Wozzeck: Harmonic Language and Dramatic Design* (New Haven: Yale University Press, 1983).

ARNOLD SCHOENBERG. *Harmonielehre* (Vienna: Universal Edition, 1911); *Theory of Harmony,* Eng. trans. by Roy E. Carter (Berkeley and Los Angeles: University of California Press, 1978).

LEONARD STEIN, ed.   *Style and Idea, Selected Writings of Arnold Schoenberg,* trans. Leo Black (London: Faber and Faber Ltd.; Los Angeles: Belmont Music Publishers, 1975; Berkeley and Los Angeles: University of California Press, 1984), including: "New Music: My Music (c. 1930)," pp. 105–106 ("4. Opera"); "How One Becomes Lonely (1937)," pp. 30–53.

The International Alban Berg Society Newsletter, including: "An Alban Berg Bibliography 1966–1968," compiled by Christine Berl and Paul Lansky, No. 1 (December 1968): 7–9; "An Alban Berg Bibliography 1969–1977," compiled by Mary Lou Humphrey, No. 6 (June 1978): 14–15 (on *Wozzeck*); "An Alban Berg Bibliography 1978–1980," compiled by Stephen W. Kett, No. 11 (Spring 1982): 9–17.

3 Vienna Schoenberg circle: The twelve-tone idiom

During the First World War, musical activities in Vienna were curtailed as Schoenberg and his pupils were called up for military service. By the end of the war, Vienna was the capital of an Austria devastated by revolution and reduced to a small republic. Schoenberg began the post-war era in severe financial circumstances. While his efforts to complete his oratorio *Die Jakobsleiter* were to no avail, he was able to develop his new ideas on musical pedagogy and to make progress with his Seminar for Composition at the Schwarzwald School from 1917 to 1920, during which time he presented some of his earliest lectures on his twelve-tone method.[1]

As an outgrowth of the Seminar, Schoenberg founded his *Verein für Musikalische Privataufführungen* (Society for Private Musical Performances; 1918–1921) for the purpose of promoting modern music, with Schoenberg as president and Berg and Webern as supervisors of the programs. By this time, other pupils had joined the Schoenberg circle, including Paul Pisk (secretary of the *Verein*), Edward Steuermann (pianist), Rudolf Kolisch (violinist and leader of a string quartet known for its performances of Schoenberg's chamber music), Hanns Eisler (who became the leading composer of East Germany), and others. Esoteric circumstances surrounded the *Verein*—no activities could be published in newspapers or periodicals, no applause was permitted, and critics were excluded from performances. There were neither symposia nor lectures at the *Verein,* so Schoenberg's twelve-tone system was never discussed in this framework. Among the most significant events that took place was the first performance of Webern's *Passacaglia*, Op. 1, arranged for two pianos (six hands). Later, there were the well-known *Walzerabend,* in which Schoenberg, Berg, and Webern transcribed Johann Strauss waltzes for chamber orchestra. These chamber orchestra performances were important because, at that time, large orchestral works by contemporary composers were prevented from being performed by economic conditions. The arrangement of such works in the *Verein,* especially those by Reger and Mahler, were therefore made to acquaint the public of the *Verein* with them, but works by composers of other nationalities were also included. (Schoenberg's *Pierrot Lunaire* was performed only later, since he did not allow performances of his own works in the first two years.)[2]

---

[1] See Elliott Antokoletz, "A Survivor of the Vienna Schoenberg Circle: An Interview with Paul A. Pisk," *Tempo* 154 (September 1985): 18.

[2] Ibid., p. 17.

NONREPETITION AND EARLY OCCURRENCES OF TWELVE-TONE GROUPINGS

By 1915, the free-atonal compositions of Schoenberg, Webern, and Berg had evolved toward a musical synthesis based on the new workings of content in its relationship to form. With the disappearance of traditional harmonic functions, it was questionable whether a basic tone asserted at prominent structural points could still have large-scale significance as a referential "tonal center" for harmonic construction and progression. In "free-atonal" works, this loss of "tonic" function, together with the move toward equalization of all twelve tones (what Schoenberg called the *emancipation of the dissonance*), led to a radical change of compositional technique.[3] The "extreme emotionality" of such pieces had to be "counterbalanced with extraordinary brevity." Also, because of the unknown constructive chord potential of the new idiom, "it seemed at first impossible to compose pieces of complicated organization or of great length."[4] Formal brevity was a consequence of the principle of nonrepetition, which served as the basic source for the gradual evolution toward the twelve-tone conception. In his *Harmonielehre* (1911), Schoenberg recommended both the avoidance of octave doublings and pitch-class repetitions, since these would produce an emphasis on a tone, which, in turn, could be interpreted as a tonic.[5] While such doublings and repetitions of tones still occurred occasionally in the early atonal compositions, the nonsystematic circulation of all twelve tones within a short span of time was prevalent, especially in Webern's works.

As early as 1910, Webern had already avoided octave doublings in his *Two Songs,* Op. 8. In 1932, he lectured to students in a German university on his early *Bagatelles,* Op. 9 (1911–1913), suggesting that nonrepetition was the source for his later twelve-tone thinking: "Here I had the feeling, 'when all 12 notes have gone by, the piece is over.' Much later I discovered that all this was a part of the necessary development. In my sketchbook I wrote out the chromatic scale and crossed off the individual notes. . . . In short, a rule of law emerged; until all 12 notes have occurred, none of them may occur again.'"[6] Strict adherence to this principle in his later works was to result in a consistent (systematic, or serial) ordering of the twelve notes in their successive unfoldings. Whereas pitch order is also a distinguishing feature of traditional melodic themes, independence of pitch order from rhythm, contour, and tonal function is special to the atonal idiom and must be considered, in addition to the principle of nonrepetition, as essential to the development

---

[3] See Leonard Stein, ed., *Style and Idea, Selected Writings of Arnold Schoenberg,* trans. Leo Black (London: Faber and Faber Ltd.; Los Angeles: Belmont Music Publishers, 1975; Berkeley and Los Angeles: University of California Press, 1984), p. 216.

[4] Ibid., p. 217.

[5] See Schoenberg's reasons for the necessity of avoiding tonic emphasis, in ibid., p. 219.

[6] Anton Webern, *Der Weg zur neuen Musik,* ed. Willi Reich (Vienna, 1960); Eng. trans., *The Path to the New Music* (Bryn Mawr, Pa., 1963), p. 51.

of the serial concept.[7] The closest Webern had come, in his early works, to systematic twelve-tone composition was the fourth of the *Five Orchestral Pieces,* Op. 10 (1913). Although the piece is not serially composed, the entire chromatic is unfolded in the first twelve notes. While many free-atonal pieces had included unordered (nonserial) collections of the twelve notes, some ordered statements could already be found as the basis of isolated themes in Berg's *Altenberg Lieder,* Op. 4 (1912), in which a twelve-tone series forms one of the main themes, and in *Wozzeck,* Act I, Scene 4, which is based on a twelve-tone Passacaglia theme (see Chapter II, above).

BEGINNING OF SCHOENBERG'S "METHOD OF COMPOSING WITH TWELVE TONES"

In 1915, Schoenberg took his first decisive step toward replacing the structural functions of harmony. While he published no new works between 1915 and 1923, he began to sketch a symphony in 1915, in which the theme of the scherzo accidently consisted of twelve tones. The next important step occurred in 1917 with his unfinished *Die Jakobsleiter,* which was originally intended as the last movement of the symphony. All the main themes of this movement were to be built from a row of six tones: C#–D–F–E–A♭–G, the remaining six tones entering gradually. However, the order of the six tones was not maintained in the themes, so Schoenberg had not yet arrived at a methodical application of a *set.* Nevertheless, he later felt that "this beginning was a real twelve-tone composition," based on a procedure which he called "Method of composing with twelve tones which are related only with one another."[8]

Schoenberg first used rows of twelve tones in 1921 in his "Praeludium" from the *Piano Suite,* Op. 25, all six movements of which were completed in 1923. Since he felt that confusion would arise if he were to make this method publicly known at the time of its composition, he remained silent until 1923, when, according to his own statement, he finally explained it to twenty of his pupils.[9] In his *Five Piano Pieces,* Op. 23, and the *Serenade,* Op. 24 (both completed in 1923), only certain parts were based on strict twelve-tone serial procedures. The last piece of Op. 23—this was his first twelve-tone movement to be composed after his "Praeludium"—has a twelve-tone row that serves as the basis for all the pitch relations. Twelve-tone operations are limited here, however, since the row appears neither transformed, except for two retrograde statements at the end, nor transposed. The only twelve-tone serial piece of Op. 24 is the "Sonett" (No. 4), the row now appearing in all four of its transformations (prime, inversion, retrograde, and retrograde-

[7] See George Perle and Paul Lansky, "Twelve-Note Composition," *The New Grove Dictionary of Music and Musicians,* ed. Stanley Sadie (London: Macmillan Publishers Ltd., 1980), p. 287.

[8] Schoenberg, *Style and Idea,* n. 3, above, pp. 247–248 and 218.

[9] Ibid., p. 213.

inversion), but still not transposed. Most other pieces in these two opuses represent more rudimentary stages in the development toward the twelve-tone system; for example, the first piece of Op. 23 is serial, but only employs three-note sets. Opus 25 is Schoenberg's first work in which all the movements are based on twelve-tone serial procedures, a single series of which is common to all the movements. This is Schoenberg's first opus in which the twelve-tone series is presented not only in all four of its transformations (P, I, R, and RI), but also at two different transpositional (T) levels as separated by the tritone (P–0, I–0, R–0, RI–0 and P–6, I–6, R–6, RI–6).[10] Since tritones occur as surface details within the row (as at notes 3–4, G–D♭), transposition of the series by the tritone (T–6) or in inversion at T–0 or T–6 permits the local tritone component to remain unchanged in all these set forms (Ex. 3–1). (This is due to the principle of *tritone equivalence,* in which the tritone remains invariant under transposition or inversion by itself.)

SCHOENBERG AND "TWELVE-TONE TROPING"

Since 1919, the Viennese composer/theorist Josef Mathias Hauer had also been moving toward a formulation of his own "law of the twelve notes." However, while Schoenberg presented some of Hauer's compositions at his *Verein* in this year, it did not appear that Hauer's compositions or his theories had any significant influence. Hauer and Schoenberg were in contact during the early 1920s and Schoenberg suggested they collaborate on a series of pamphlets,[11] but conflicts arose between the two because of Hauer's claim that he, himself, had discovered twelve-tone composition. Each composer had in fact arrived at his own twelve-tone formulation independently of the other. In 1920, Hauer worked out certain formulations in order to distinguish different twelve-note groupings. A significant aspect of this twelve-tone method is the principle of partitioning the total chromatic into two mutually exclusive groups of six notes each, three groups of four, four groups of three, six groups of two, or various uneven groupings such as 7 + 5 notes, etc.

---

[10] Transposition numbers of prime (P) and inverted (I) set-forms are determined by their first notes, while retrograde (R) and retrograde-inversion (RI) forms are determined by their last notes in order to identify these retrograde forms with their original forms. Thus, the retrograde of P–0 is R–0, and the retrograde of I–0 is RI–0. In all subsequent analytical discussions, where pitches or pitch classes are designated by numbers, we arbitrarily assign 0 (= 12) to pitch-class C, 1 (= 13) to C♯, 2 (= 14) to D, 3 (= 15) to E♭, and so on through 11 to B. Transposition numbers of pitch collections or sets will also be designated by numbers from 0 to 11. We will assume a referential order in assigning a transposition number to a collection: the pitch-class number of the "first" note (or "last" note in the case of retrogrades of serialized sets) will designate that collection. If a referential collection is "based" on C, its transposition number is 0 (= 12). If the collection is transposed so that its "first" note becomes C♯, its transposition number becomes 1 (= 13).

[11] *Arnold Schönberg: Ausgewählte Briefe* (Mainz: B. Schotts Söhne, 1958); Eng. *Arnold Schoenberg Letters,* ed. Erwin Stein (London: Faber and Faber, 1964), pp. 103–106.

EXAMPLE 3–1. Schoenberg, *Suite for Piano*, Op. 25, basic row forms

(or: P-10 if C=0)											or: R-10 of C=0
P-6 →	B♭	B♮	C♯	G	C	A	D	G♯	F	G♭	E♭	E♮ ←R-6
	1	2	3	4	5	6	7	8	9	10	11	12

	1	2	3	4	5	6	7	8	9	10	11	12
P-0 →	E	F	G	D♭	G♭	E♭	A♭	D	B	C	A	B♭ ←R-0
(or: P-4 if C=0)									(or: R-4 if C=0)		

(or: I 4 if C=0)									(or: RI 4 if C=0)		
I-0 →	E	E♭	D♭	G	D	F	C	F♯	A	G♯	B	B♭ ←RI-0
	1	2	3	4	5	6	7	8	9	10	11	12

	1	2	3	4	5	6	7	8	9	10	11	12
I-6 →	B♭	A	G	D♭	A♭	B	F♯	C	E♭	D	F	E ←RI-6
(or: I-10 if C=0)									(or: RI-10 if C=0)		

Hauer's formulations, however, were based only on the possibilities of partitioning the twelve pitch-classes into two mutually exclusive hexachords. Since only the pitch content and not the ordering of the notes within each hexachord was maintained, Hauer referred to such a set and all of its transpositions as a *trope*.

Although Hauer's is the earliest known general theoretical formulation of this principle, Schoenberg had already employed a *hexachordal twelve-tone trope* as the thematic basis in *Die Jakobsleiter* several years earlier. The "Tanzscene" (No. 5) of Schoenberg's Op. 24 is also based on such a hexachordal trope. Originally composed in 1920, the piece was based on an unordered six-note motif. In 1923, Schoenberg revised this piece, adding the remaining six notes in newly composed sections, so that the juxtaposition of both hexachords (F–G–A♭–B–C♯–D/A–B♭–C–D♯–E–F♯) formed a twelve-tone trope; that is, while the pitch content of each hexachord was maintained, the order of notes was not. Since the tritone complement of each note is present within the same hexachord, either hexachord may be transposed by a tritone without alteration of pitch-class content. The hexachordal pitch content of the opening measure (G–D–F–C♯–B–G♯) is retained as it is transposed by the tritone and reordered in the "Valse" section accompaniment, C♯–G♯–B–D–G–F (at m. 59).[12] In the alternate measures of this accompaniment, we get a slightly varied ordering of the latter, as the first two notes are reversed (G♯–C♯–B–D–G–F). This new ordering is then literally transposed by the tritone to D–G–F–G♯–C♯–B (at m. 65). Again (at m. 66), Schoenberg employs the analogous procedure of reversing the first two notes of the last hexachordal form to give us G–D–F–G♯–C♯–B. Because of the altered rhythm (at mm. 65 and 66), which now vertically aligns the final two motivic segments, the ordering of hexachordal notes 4–6 is ambiguous. One interpretation (G♯–C♯–B) relates the intervallic ordering of the entire hexachord, D–G–F–G♯–C♯–B (at m. 65), to the preceding tritone-related statement, G♯–C♯–B–D–G–F (at m. 64), while another interpretation (C♯–B–G♯) refers the entire hexachord, G–D–F–C♯–B–G♯ (at m. 66), back to the original transpositional level and exact ordering of the opening measure. The clarinet adds the remaining six tones to the hexachord of the accompaniment (at mm. 63ff.). Thus, the hexachordal trope concept permits variety in hexachordal pitch and intervallic ordering, while maintaining invariance of hexachordal content.

SCHOENBERG AND THE "TWELVE-TONE SERIES": SEGMENTATION AND PERMUTATION

Schoenberg also employed hexachordal partitioning of the twelve tones in his *Quintet for Winds,* Op. 26 (1924). However, while the hexachords of the "Tanzscene" were part of a twelve-tone trope, the hexachords in the *Quintet* function as part of a twelve-tone series. Thus, in this more complex work, the concept of segmentation is joined with the *serial principle*. In the *Quintet* , the first large-scale composition of the twelve-tone idiom, a wide variety of thematic and harmonic materials is derived from the hexachordal properties of the basic series.

The four set forms (P, I, R, and RI) and their transpositions, "like the modulations in former styles, serve to build subordinate ideas."[13] The hexachordal partitions of the set are used in such a way as to produce classical phrasal and thematic contrasts and to distinguish "tonal" areas within the traditional forms, the movements being *sonata, scherzo, ternary,* and *rondo* types. At the same time, these segmental relations contribute to the organic unification of the large-scale forms. Maximal associations among the various forms of the set are primarily produced by the almost identical structures of the two hexachords. While the second hexachord is a perfect-fifth transposition of the first and differs only in its final interval, both hexachords

---

[12] See Schoenberg, *Style and Idea*, n. 3, above, p. 90.
[13] Ibid., p. 227.

analogously contain five-note segments representing the two whole-tone collections, respectively (Ex. 3–2).

The antecedent and consequent phrases of the main theme (at mm. 1–6, flute) are differentiated, in the classical sense, by the contrasting contours of the otherwise maximally equivalent hexachords (Ex. 3–3). The antecedent phrase for the most part moves stepwise (mm. 1–4), while the consequent is extremely disjunct and angular (mm. 5–6). These differing hexachordal contours are also the basis for producing contrast between this conjunct opening flute phrase and the simultaneously unfolding disjunct accompaniment. Since both hexachords are equally based on mutually exclusive whole-tone constructions, whole-tone clarity is permitted in their simultaneous statement only by the distinctiveness of the wind timbres; in more homogeneous instrumental combinations, the whole-tone properties would tend to be obscured in such a dense contrapuntal unfolding of all twelve tones. The phrase structure of theme 2 (mm. 42–47, oboe) is also defined by the same conjunct-disjunct contour relationship of hexachordal members, now in I–7 (G–E♭–D♭–B–A–B♭ and C–A♭–G♭–E–D–F). The conjunct antecedent phrase of theme 2 (as with theme 1) is also opposed by a disjunct hexachordal accompaniment. Here, however, the accompaniment (played by the bassoon) is based on the first hexachord of the retrograde form, RI–7 (F–D–E–F♯–A♭–C); as in the complementary relation between the two hexachords of P–3 at the opening of theme 1, this hexachord of RI–7 complements the first hexachord of I–7 of the oboe to produce all twelve tones.

Segmental partitioning of the series also contributes to structural delineation as well as unity and development within each theme group. While the entire first-theme group (mm. 1–28) is exclusively based on a single transpositional level (T–3) for the four set-forms, these forms are juxtaposed and segmented in such a way as to establish classical phrase and period relationships. Set within the context of gradually increasing rhythmic activity and textural density, mirror forms of the series delineate the periods symmetrically (see Ex. 3–3). The first period of the flute theme (mm. 1–6) unfolds P–3 in two hexachordal phrases. This is temporally mirrored in the continuing flute line by R–3, which now unfolds in half the number of measures to speed up the *serial rhythm* (mm. 7–9). The second period is completed (mm. 10–14, first beat) now, by the simultaneous statement of the inverted form and its retrograde, I–3 and RI–3 (in flute and horn/bassoon, respectively), thereby increasing the *serial density*. At each cadential point, segmentation

EXAMPLE 3–2. Schoenberg, *Quintet for Winds,* Op. 26, hexachordal properties of the basic twelve-tone series

EXAMPLE 3–3. Schoenberg, *Quintet,* Op. 26, Mov. I, opening

into smaller subcollections contributes to the phrasal articulation. At the P–3 cadence (m. 6), the last three notes (10–11–12 in the flute) simultaneously complete linear and vertical statements of the series. The vertical statement is based on an instrumental distribution of the row into four three-note partitions. Here, notes 7–8–9 (horn) also form an intersection with the linear unfolding of P–3 in the accompaniment. At the opening of the R–3 statement (m. 7), we get double-row functions of both trichordal and hexachordal segments, as the flute unfolds the first hexachord against notes 7–8–9–10–11–12 (horn) and notes 6–5–4/7–8–9 (bassoon). At the R–3 cadence (m. 9), the linear statement of the second hexachord in the flute serves a similar, though more complex double function as it again intersects with two accompanying R–3 segments. The opening of the I–3/RI–3 phrase (mm. 10–14) presents overlapping three-note segments in the RI form (horn and bassoon, then bassoon and clarinet). Thus, these row partitionings contribute to phrasal articulation as well as an increasing serial density and rhythmic activity for organic growth.

Transposition produces a sense of "modulation" from one theme group to the next, similarly to the tonal schemes of classical practice. However, no traditional harmonic functions are assigned the components of the row forms. Within the theme–1 group (mm. 16–17), a false sense of modulation is produced as the oboe unfolds the second hexachord of P–3 (B♭–D–E–F♯–G♯–F). Since the originally disjunct character of this hexachord is replaced here by the conjunct character of the first hexachord, we get the impression that P–3 has "modulated" by the perfect fifth (from E♭–G–A–B–C♯–C to B♭–D–E–F♯–G♯–F). In this case, however, the final hexachordal interval (G♯–F) is crucial to identifying this oboe statement as hexachord 2 of basic P–3, rather than hexachord 1 of a new transposition (P–10). The first significant "modulation" is suggested at the Transition (m. 29), where the bassoon initiates I–7; this form is subsequently established as the basis of theme 2 (mm. 42ff., oboe). Another allusion to traditional tonality is suggested. I–7 (on G) is a major-third transposition of P–3 (on E♭), and the first two notes of I–3 (G–E♭) reverse the first two of P–3. The inversion produces duplication of a basic interval of the "E♭ major tonic triad." Again, the nonfunctional serial context defies any traditional tonal perception, so these tonal allusions in the transpositional relations provide no more than a formal anchor. However, by analogy with traditional classical key relations, in which the new key area has a maximal number of tones in common with the original one, I–7 and P–3 are also maximally related in terms of their hexachordal pitch content. Five of the six notes of their corresponding hexachords belong to the same whole-tone cycle; at the same time, corresponding hexachords are maximally invariant in pitch content (five notes are the same) (Ex. 3–4).

Segmentation is also employed as a means of permuting elements of the series, which results in a variety of thematic shapes and harmonic constructions in the different movements. The Scherzo opens with an entirely

EXAMPLE 3–4. Schoenberg, *Quintet,* Op. 26, hexachordal relations between set forms: P–3 and I–7

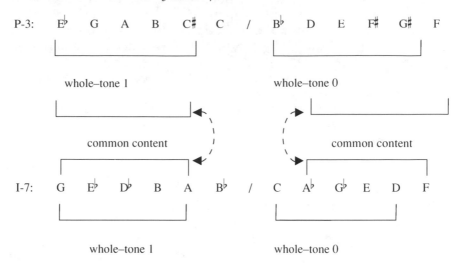

new theme, yet is based on original P–3. This theme, which reverses the original conjunct-disjunct contours of the thematic hexachords at the opening of Movement I, is also segmented more prominently into both trichordal and hexachordal components from the outset. The accompaniment introduces notes 1–3 of the series, the oboe "Hauptstimme" unfolding notes 4–12. This segmental distribution creates an impression of a new transpositional level, since the theme begins with pitch-class B (note 4) while actually unfolding within the serial confines of P–3.

At theme b of the Scherzo (m. 28), the harmonic projection of the four trichordal segments of P–3 results in a linear permutation of the row elements (Ex. 3–5). (The rhythmically distinct eighth-note figure in the horn is not considered here, since it outlines the last three notes of a different, overlapping row form, I–3.) The linear pitch adjacencies in the oboe, F–E♭–C–B♭, which form the new thematic idea (*Hauptstimme*), are a foreground statement of the P–3 hexachordal boundary notes (12–1–6–7). This serial permutation is part of an overall process in the work, in which cyclic-interval components of the series become increasingly prominent. That is, isolation of these P–3 hexachordal boundary notes (E♭–G–A–B–C♯–C/B♭–D–E–F♯–G♯–F), which form two whole-steps (E♭–F/B♭–C) or a segment of the cycle of fourths/fifths (E♭–B♭–F–C), leaves two equivalent, mutually exclusive whole-tone tetrachords remaining (2–3–4–5 and 8–9–10–11). This cyclic-interval partitioning of the series is prominently established, at the *frei* (*langsam*), as the cadential focal point of section c of the Trio (m. 142). Here, the P–3 hexachordal boundary tones are sustained,

EXAMPLE 3–5. Schoenberg, *Quintet,* Op. 26, Scherzo, m. 28

while the two whole-tone tetrachords are linearly stated in the piccolo. At the corresponding point of the Trio return (m. 359), a slight modification in the piccolo establishes the tritone boundary of the first whole-tone tetrachord as a local foreground detail. This foreshadows the first cadence of Movement III (m. 21), where I–3 is partitioned (in the flute) into the tritone boundaries, B–F/E–B♭ (2–5/8–11), of its whole-tone tetrachords as well as into its hexachordal boundary notes, A♭–E♭–D♭–G♭ (7–1–12–6), above the held internal whole-steps, A–G and D–C (3–4/9–10), of the row (Ex. 3–6).

Thus, the *Quintet* is a remarkable example of a combination of various twelve-tone techniques, which, together, contribute to overall structural articulation and thematic definition as well as to the unity and organic development of the material. These techniques include serialism (based on the four P, I, R, and RI set transformations and their transpositions), segmenta-

EXAMPLE 3–6. Schoenberg, *Quintet,* Op. 26, Mov. III, m. 21, special partitioning of I–3

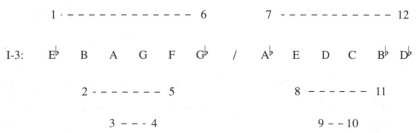

tion, and permutation of the components of the row, the latter of which permits cyclic-interval reinterpretations of the variously derived subcollections.

SCHOENBERG AND SEMICOMBINATORIALITY

In the late 1920s, following his *Four Pieces for Mixed Chorus,* Op. 27 (1925), *Three Satires for Mixed Chorus,* Op. 28 (1925), *Suite,* Op. 29, for septet (1927), and *Third String Quartet,* Op. 30 (1926), Schoenberg began to modify certain basic principles of his original twelve-tone conception. As part of his expressionistic aesthetic, he moved toward a greater systematization of serial relations, which resulted in a more extreme sense of "atonality" as well as a greater "transparency of clear-cut ideas."[14] In this connection, Schoenberg worked out the hexachordal substructures of a given series in such a manner that, if the basic form of the set (P–0) is contrapuntally combined with its inversion at the lower fifth (I–5), then the corresponding aligned hexachords of both set-forms will have no duplicated tones between them. That is, the antecedent hexachords of P–0 and I–5, together, produce all twelve tones, and the same is true for the combined consequent hexachords. This principle was later referred to by Milton Babbitt as *combinatoriality.*[15]

In the Op. 26, discussed above, the relationship between the basic set and its inversion a fifth below does not yet meet the "combinatorial" requirement, and so is not employed in the work. In this case, the first six tones of P–3 and the first six tones of I–8, together, yield only ten different tones, and the same is true for their consequents; notes C and B appear twice in the antecedent hexachords, notes F and F♯ twice in the consequent ones (Ex. 3–7). In his continued efforts to achieve a clarity of texture and ideas, Schoenberg further developed special relations between set-forms to maintain strict avoidance of octave doublings in the harmony. While he had not yet arrived at a pervasive use of the combinatorial principle in either of his next two

EXAMPLE 3–7. Schoenberg, *Quintet,* Op. 26, quasi-combinatorial relation between P–3 and its inversion at the lower fifth, I–8

	antecedent hexachords						consequent hexachords					
P-3:	E♭	G	A	*B*	C♯	*C*	/	B♭	D	E	*F♯*	*G♯*	*F*
I-8:	A♭	E	D	*C*	B♭	*B*	/	C♯	A	G	*F*	*E♭*	*F♯*

[14] Ibid., p. 235.

[15] See Milton Babbitt, "Set Structure as a Compositional Determinant," *Journal of Music Theory* (1961): 72–94. Since this procedure in Schoenberg's works is limited to set-forms related inversionally and separated by the perfect fifth, Babbitt assigned the term "semi-combinatoriality" here more specifically. The principle of "all-combinatoriality" will be discussed below in connection to later serial composers.

opuses, the *Variations for Orchestra,* Op. 31 (1927–1928), and the one-act opera *Von Heute auf Morgen*, Op. 32 (1929), one of the set relations in the former work suggests an interest in this principle. Schoenberg asserted that "most orchestral combinations do not promote what the artist calls unmixed, unbroken colours."[16] His training in chamber-music performance and composition had led him already in these early years to the use of thinness and transparency of style in his orchestral works. One of the means of achieving this in the *Variations* (Ex. 3–8) was to construct the basic set (P–10) "so that its antecedent hexachord, starting a minor third below [as the first hexachord of I–7], inverted itself into the remaining six tones" of basic P–10, permitting no hexachordal pitch-class duplication.[17] This was only one of several associations between set-forms that produced local variety within overall serial unity in the work.

Consistent semicombinatorial associations between set-forms was first employed by Schoenberg in his *Two Piano Pieces,* Op. 33a/b (1928–1931). Here, the principle is maintained throughout by the contrapuntal alignment of the basic set (P or R) with its corresponding inversion (I or RI) at the lower fifth. The large-scale formal structure of Op. 33a, which once again reveals Schoenberg's reliance upon the classical sonata-allegro model, serves as the framework for the unfolding of a more intensely expressionistic and atonal sound world.[18] The classically distinct theme-groups and their smaller antecedent-consequent phrase members provide, by means of rhythmic differentiation, segmentation, and thematic contour, a variety of material that is otherwise entirely unified by rigidly systematic operations on a single series. The main theme of the exposition is based on a group of three ascending and three descending chords, an arch shape that suggests a telescoping of the large-scale form. The ambiguous serial ordering of the four notes in each of these opening "simultaneities" is unequivocally established in subsequent linear statements of the row; for instance, the modified recapitulation (mm. 32–33) unfolds linearly the first three chords in the right hand. At this point, the order of the last three chords of the original thematic statement is reversed and presented simultaneously with the first three, so the basic set, P–10, with

EXAMPLE 3–8. Schoenberg, *Variations for Orchestra,* Op. 31, non-repetition of hexachordal content between P–10 and I–7

P-10:   B♭   E   F♯   Eb   F   A   /   D   C♯   G   G♯   B   C

I-7:   G   C♯   B   D   C   A♭   /   E♭   E   B♭   A   F♯   F

[16] Schoenberg, *Style and Idea,* n. 3, above, p. 235.

[17] Ibid., p. 236.

[18] See George Perle, *Serial Composition and Atonality* (6th ed., rev., Berkeley and Los Angeles: University of California Press, 1991), pp. 111–116, for formal outline and detailed analysis.

its inversion at the lower fifth, I–3, forms a combinatorial association (Ex. 3–9). The original statement of six chords juxtaposes P–10 and I–3 successively, but the last three chords actually unfold the latter (I–3) in retrograde order as RI–3, thereby permitting a type of "temporal mirror."

Schoenberg's concern for phrase and period symmetry is confirmed in the remaining passages of the first-theme group (mm. 1–11) (Ex. 3–10). The consequent phrase (mm. 3–5) is distinguished from the antecedent by its contrasting thematic contour and rhythm, and increased number of articulations per measure. It balances the antecedent symmetrically by employing a simultaneous statement of the corresponding retrograde forms, R–10 (left hand) and RI–3 (right hand). While the second period provides further contrast to the first by employing a similarly varied contour and increased number of articulations per measure, the specific pairing of combinatorially related set-forms in the latter further contributes to the still larger architectural balance of the first period: P–10 of the antecedent phrase (m. 6) is mirrored temporally by I–3 (i.e., RI–3 forward), while the consequent phrase (mm. 8–9) now contrapuntally inverts and retrogrades the pair of set-forms of the earlier consequent (R–10 and RI–3) by unfolding them as P–10 and I–3. The first-theme group is then rounded out by a modified return of the opening chords to provide sectional unity. At the same time, this return is more serially dense than the opening, since the original temporal mirror that was produced by P–10/I–3 (i.e., RI–3) is now reinterpreted as a simultaneous mirror, in which RI–3 is now reversed to unfold I–3 explicitly.

The second-theme group is established (mm. 14ff.) by a new thematic contour, based on an angular melody (left hand) with static accompaniment. This contrast of theme is further supported by a change of the rhythmic segmentation of each set form, from groupings of 3×4 notes throughout theme 1 to 2×6 notes in the second-theme group. While the result is sectional variety, the combinatorial pairings of set-forms continue to be retained at their original transpositional level. At the modified return of theme 2 (mm. 21–22), melody and accompaniment are inverted contrapuntally, providing a larger architectural balance within this theme group. Thus, we get endless variety of thematic materials in the exposition, while unity is provided by a single twelve-tone row, whose combinatorially paired set-forms have remained at a constant transpositional level.

The row is initiated by two consecutive perfect-fourths/fifths (B♭–F–C). This cyclic-interval–5/7 segment is projected into the large-scale formal plan as the basis for moving away from the basic pitch level in the

EXAMPLE 3–9. Schoenberg, *Piano Piece,* Op. 33a, mm. 32–33, combinatorial association between P–10 and its inversion at the lower fifth, I–3

P-10:   B♭   F   C   B   A   F♯   /   C♯   D♯   G   A♭   D   E

I-3:   D♯   G♯   C♯   D   E   G   /   C   B♭   G♭   F   B   A

EXAMPLE 3–10. Schoenberg, *Piano Piece*, Op. 33a, mm 1–11

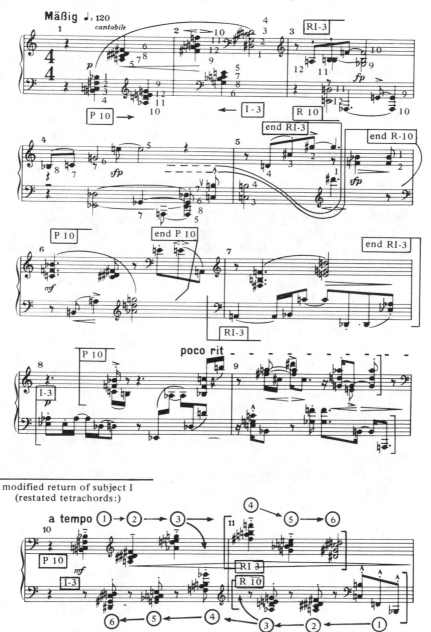

development section and back again in the recapitulation. This intervallic projection of a basic property of the set suggests a correspondence with the tonal relations of the traditional sonata plan. In traditional schemes, the principle of modulation entails tonal motion by the components of the triad. That is, if we were to move from the tonic area of the first-theme group to the dominant area of the second-theme group and development section, the motion would have its reference in the root and fifth degrees of the tonic triad. The same principle is demonstrated in minor keys where the tonality shifts by way of the root, to the third degree of the tonic minor-triad.[19] To draw an analogy, motion from the exposition to the opening of the development section in the present work is based on a projection of the initial interval 5/7s of the row. This should not be construed to mean that the inherent functional significance of the perfect fifth in the major-minor scale system is to be assumed in Op. 33a. Perle states that "the compositional importance of the interval of a fifth in Opus 33a is a consequence of the structure of the set, not of any quality inherent in the interval itself."[20] A codetta and transition follow (middle of m. 23 through middle of m. 27), in which the rhythmic grouping for the first time changes to 4 × 3 notes. The development section, which now presents various types of row segmentation, establishes a new transpositional level (at end of m. 28f.) based on the combinatorial pairing of P–0 (right hand) and its inversion at the lower fifth, I–5 (left hand). Then (from middle of m. 29 through middle of m. 31), two successive pairings are both based on P–5 (left hand) and I–10 (right hand), after which the basic pitch level of the combinatorial pairings is reestablished in the recapitulation (mm. 32ff.). The entire scheme is given in Ex. 3–11. The combinatorial relationship between the two inversionally related set-forms in each pairing remains unchanged by maintaining the constant difference (perfect-fifth, or interval 7) between their T-nos. That is, by subtracting the I or RI number from the corresponding P or R number, we can express the combinatorial relationship as shown in Ex. 3–11b.[21] Thus, the transpositional scheme represents a large-scale unfolding of the initial interval 5/7s of the set: the development transposes to the second fifth above B♭, then to the first fifth above, and the recapitulation descends by a fifth to reestablish the original "key."

After Hitler came to power in 1933, Schoenberg was dismissed from the Prussian Academy of Arts in Berlin, where he had headed the master class in composition since 1925. He then moved to the United States, where he taught at the University of California at Los Angeles until his death in 1951. His last works written in Europe were the *Begleitmusik zu einer Lichtspielszene,*

---

[19] See Elliott Antokoletz, *The Music of Béla Bartók: A Study of Tonality and Progression in Twentieth-Century Music* (Berkeley and Los Angeles: University of California Press, 1984), p. 119.

[20] Perle, *Serial Composition,* n. 18, above, p. 116.

[21] Where a P or R number is smaller than the I or RI number, add modulus 12 to the first number.

EXAMPLE 3–11. Schoenberg, *Piano Piece,* Op. 33a: (a) entire scheme of paired, combinatorially related row transpositions; (b) constant difference of a perfect fifth maintained between successive combinatorial pairs

(a)   Exp: P/R-10 (B♭)   Dev: P-0 (C), P-5 (F)   Recap: P/R-10 (B♭)
            I/RI-3 (E♭)   I-5 (F), I-10 (B♭)   I/RI-3 (E♭)

(b)   (12)   (17)

T-no.:	10		0	5		10
	-3		-5	-10		-3
interval:	7		7	7		7

Op. 34, or *Accompaniment to a Film Scene,* for orchestra (1929–1930), the first two acts of his opera *Moses und Aron* (1930–1932), the religious text written by Schoenberg himself (1928), *Six Pieces for Male Chorus,* a cappella (1930), an unpublished set of *Three Songs,* with piano accompaniment (1933), and the *String Quartet Concerto* after Händel, which he composed in France in the summer of 1933.

Some of Schoenberg's American works reveal certain tendencies characteristic of the works of many other composers in the 1930s and '40s. These tendencies include an infusion of tonal elements into twelve-tone writing, greater stylistic accessibility, and religious (*Kol Nidre* for reciter, chorus, and orchestra, Op. 39, 1938) as well as political protest elements (*A Survivor of Warsaw*, Op. 46, 1947). While he continued to use strict twelve-tone serial techniques in the *Fourth String Quartet* (1936), the *Violin* and *Piano Concertos* (1936, 1942), *String Trio,* Op. 45, and *Phantasy* for violin and piano, Op. 47 (1949), all of which are based on a variety of partitioning procedures and manipulations of the twelve-tone materials, other works such as the *Ode to Napoleon* (1942) along with *A Survivor of Warsaw* reveal an infusion of tonal elements into twelve-tone writing. The *Suite* for string orchestra (1934), the second *Kammersymphonie,* Op. 38 (1906–1940), *Variations on a Recitative* for organ, Op. 40 (1941), and *Theme and Variations* for band, Op. 43b (1943), tend toward greater accessibility of style and are yet more prominently tonal. In all of these works, we find a sense of extreme fluidity in the use of "developing variation," in which the material is varied, yet continuous, logical, and unified.

BACKGROUND AND DEVELOPMENT OF WEBERN'S FIRST SERIAL WORKS

In the mid-1920s, Webern and Berg continued to follow their teacher by turning to twelve-tone serial composition. It was primarily Webern, however, who began to extend the serial concept into the realm of dynamics, register, and all parameters beyond pitch organization. At the same time, he also adhered more closely to certain basic principles of Schoenberg's teachings than did Berg, and for that matter, even Schoenberg himself, who asserted the premise that only one row should be used in a composition. Webern observed this principle "unambiguously," while Berg consistently employed two or more independent sets in a single movement, use of cyclic permutation, and frequent incorporation of nontwelve-tone or nonserial episodes into the twelve-tone sections.

Webern began the postwar era by returning in 1918 to Vienna and settling in the suburb of Mödling, where he remained close to Schoenberg and taught composition. From 1918 to 1921, he served with Berg as supervisor in Schoenberg's *Verein für Musikalische Privataufführungen.* Webern's public musical activities between 1922 and 1934 were in keeping with the political and social developments in Vienna. In 1922, the city became an autonomous province of Austria and, under the successful Social Democratic city government headed by Karl Seitz, new social programs were started. Public housing projects included model apartments for workers (e.g., at the Karl Marx hof), which replaced the urban slums and general decay of prewar Vienna. Following the dissolution of Schoenberg's *Verein* in 1921, Webern began to conduct various groups in Mödling and Vienna and encouraged a popular interest in new music. In conducting the Vienna Workers' Symphony Concerts (1922–1934) and the Vienna Workers' Chorus (1923–1934), he demonstrated his kindness, warmth, and patience in explaining musical details to lay performers, in spite of his great intensity and meticulous approach as conductor.[22]

Webern's attempts to bridge the gap between the popular musical movement of workers' groups and the new esoteric compositional developments during this period have some connection, at least in the attitude if not in the actual musical style of his own compositions, with the "Gebrauchsmusik" (useful or practical music for amateur performances) and "Proletarian" movements in Germany, Russia, and elsewhere in the 1920s, and in the 1930s especially. The intention of these larger movements was to create accessible and socially functional music for nonprofessionals and the masses in general.

After Hitler came to power in 1933, Webern's conducting and composing were seriously disrupted. Tensions arose between the Viennese Socialists and the clerico-fascistic government under Chancellor Dollfuss, which caused severe civil disturbances, including damage to the workers' apartments in the civil war of February 1934. The Nazis dissolved the Workers' associations in this same year. The Nazis regarded Webern's music as Bolshevist, censoring the performance of his works, destroying his writings, and forcing the teachings of the Schoenberg circle underground. The

---

[22] Antokoletz, "A Survivor of the Vienna Schoenberg Circle," n. 1, above, p. 18.

final blow came on March 15, 1935, when Hitler entered Vienna, and Austria was annexed to Germany.

WEBERN'S TWELVE-TONE SERIAL COMPOSITIONS

All of Webern's works from Op. 12 through Op. 19 (written between 1915 and 1927) were for solo voice and piano or instrumental accompaniment. In his last pre–twelve-tone work, the *Five Canons on Latin Texts,* Op. 16, for voice, clarinet, and bass clarinet (1924), we find a greater strictness in counterpoint, phraseology, and formal structure. In the same year, he experimented for the first time with the rudimentary use of a series in his miniature *Kinderstück* for piano, a logical extension of the strictness that was manifested in his earlier canonic writing. Then, in his *Drei Volkstexte,* Op. 17 (1924–1925), for voice, clarinet, bass clarinet, and violin, based on sacred texts, the second and third pieces each have their own row, but without serial transformation or transposition. In the *Drei Lieder,* Op. 18, for voice, piccolo, clarinet, and guitar (1925), a different series is used for each song: No. 2 uses the series for the first time in its four transformations (P, I, R, and RI), while No. 3 unfolds all four transformations in each of the contrapuntal lines. The *Zwei Lieder,* Op. 19, based on Goethe's "Chinesisch-deutsche Jahres- und Tageszeiten," for mixed chorus, violin, two clarinets, celesta, and guitar (1926), is Webern's first opus to demonstrate all of the fundamental assumptions of the twelve-tone system, both songs employing the same row in all four transformations and in transposition. A sketch of a third song reveals Webern's first attempt at a twelve-tone canon, a procedure which was to dominate most of his later works. It was in his instrumental work, the *String Trio,* Op. 20 (1926–1927), that Webern first used serial techniques in a relatively lengthy work. While the two movements are based on traditional forms, rondo and sonata, the numerous time-signature changes as well as extreme registral, dynamic, rhythmic, and timbral variations of the rondo theme at each of its recurrences tend to obscure the classical formal outline, producing variety within unity.

WEBERN AND STRICT INVERSIONAL SYMMETRY

Schoenberg's tendency toward extreme atonality was fulfilled by the principle of combinatoriality, in which the mutually exclusive content of corresponding P and I hexachords was to be maintained by the strict pairing of a given series with its inversion at the lower fifth. The opposite concept, which permits the establishment of a kind of "tonality," or pitch-class priority, is based on the principle of *strict inversional symmetry.* While the combinatorial relationship is maintained by moving the two set-forms in each P/I pairing in parallel motion (i.e., maintaining the constant difference of a perfect-fifth in all pairs of set-forms, as expressed by subtracting the T–no. of I from that of P), strict inversional symmetry is conversely maintained by transposing the two set-forms in each P/I pairing in opposite directions by an equivalent number of semitones (i.e., consistently maintaining the same "sum of complementation," or "axis of symmetry," in all the pairs of set-forms, as expressed by adding the T—nos. of P and I).[23]

Inversionally symmetrical procedures prominently appear as the basis of many of Webern's twelve-tone serial compositions written since 1928. In the first movement of both the *Symphony*, Op. 21 (1928), and *Saxophone Quartet*, Op. 22 (1930), the second movement of the *Variations for Piano*, Op. 27 (1936), and the first movement of the *Cantata No. 1*, Op. 29, for chorus and orchestra (1938–1939), contrapuntal alignments of prime and inverted forms of the twelve-tone row (i.e., successive pairings of inversionally related set-forms) strictly maintain a common axis of symmetry throughout. The *Symphony*, for chamber orchestra, represents not only the peak of Webern's canonic technique, but also the most prominent early twelve-tone example of his use of symmetry. In movement I, for instance, each of the three sections (mm. 1–26, 25–44, 43–66) unfolds a double canon for two pairs of voices, the answering pair imitating the leading pair in contrary motion. In the first and third sections, the successive P/I pairings all have a common axis of symmetry, A–A or E♭–E♭; given that C = 0, this axis has a sum of 6, as expressed in the equation $9 + 9 = 3 + 3 = 6$ (or 18).[24] In other words, the P and I set-forms of each pair are transposed in opposite directions by an equivalent number of semitones in relation to the preceding pair (Ex. 3–12a). Any pair of simultaneous pitch-classes within each of these P/I pairings can be found in the alignment of inversionally related semitonal cycles specifically intersecting, in this case, at A–A and its dual axis, E♭–E♭ (Ex. 3–12b).

In contrast to Schoenberg's, and Berg's writing especially, Webern's twelve-tone compositions reveal more prominently a strict control of the many varied elements in the sparse and transparent textures. In movement II of the *Variations for Piano,* Op. 27, a canon at the eighth note also unfolds alignments of P and I forms of the twelve-tone row that strictly maintain a common axis of symmetry throughout. Specific registral positioning of all tones is strictly maintained in each of the two canonic lines respectively, and certain dynamics and articulations are generally associated with specific tones or tone groups.[25] In the *Cantata,* Op. 29, varied, distinct vocal and instrumental timbres (including four-part mixed chorus, soprano solo, woodwinds, brass, percussion, celesta, harp, mandolin, and strings) are used in connection with the word painting and symbolism of its text, written by Hildegarde Jone. At the same time, these timbres are exploited by Webern to produce a kaleidoscopic textural distribution of the strictly serialized row elements, thereby generating a context of seemingly endless variations of the

---

[23] The establishment of "tonal centricity," or "axes of symmetry," through operations upon inversionally complementary interval cycles is a basic premise of what George Perle has referred to as "twelve-tone tonality"; see Chapter 17, below.

[24] According to the modulus of 12, $18 - 12 = 6$.

[25] For a detailed study of these principles in this piece, see Peter Westergaard, "Webern and 'Total Organization,'" *Perspectives of New Music* I/2 (Spring, 1963): 109.

EXAMPLE 3–12. Webern, *Symphony,* Op. 21, mm. 1–26: (a) axis of sum 6 maintained between P and I forms; (b) inversionally related semitonal cycles intersecting at dual axis A–A and E♭–E♭

(a)   section 1 (mm. 1-26), based on row pairings of sum 6:

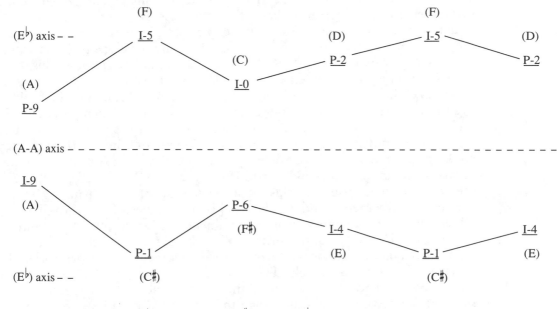

(b)   series of sum-6 dyads:

    A   B♭   B   C   C♯   D   E♭ - - - - - - - A

    A   G♯   G   F♯   F   E   E♭ - - - - - - - A

serial writing. These serial procedures, which are based on strict inversionally symmetrical relations between paired set-forms, together with the movement's overall cyclic form and symmetrical phraseology, also provide a controlled and balanced framework to serve the poetic meaning—the seasonal cycle of birth, death, and resurrection. The form of movement I is organized around two poetic lines, each equally divided into two clauses:

1a. Zün- den- der Licht- blitz des Le- bens schlug
      Light- ning, the kind- ler of be- ing, struck,

1b. ein   aus   der Wol- ke des Wor- tes.
      flashed from the word in the storm cloud.

2a. Don- ner der Herz- schlag folgt nach,
      Thun- der, the heart- beat, fol- lows,

2b. bis er in Frie- den ver- ebbt.
      at last dis- solv- ing in peace.

These a cappella vocal statements are framed by an instrumental Prelude, two Interludes, and a Postlude, so the formal scheme is cyclic and symmetrical, except for one deviation—while line 1b follows line 1a without interruption, lines 2a and 2b are separated by the second Interlude (Ex. 3–13). This second Interlude is the one disruptive and expansive component of the form, perceived as such in light of the otherwise symmetrical format that underlies the movement. This formal expansion seems to correspond with the poetic meaning of the statements, in which life develops (the "heartbeat follows"). The expanded distance between lines 2a and 2b supports this sense of growth. The poetic reference is also reflected in the local relationship of the voices in each of the four poetic lines (Ex. 3–14). At "Zundender Lichtblitz" (lightning) and "Donner" (thunder), the voices move *homorhythmically*. In each case, the voices diverge in correspondence with the text, which refers first to the "kindler" of life and then to the following of "the heartbeat." They reconverge at the end of lines 1b, 2a, and 2b. (Furthermore, the only simultaneous statement of voices and instruments occurs on "Schlug," or "struck," the *sf* chord being used for this significant detail of word painting.) This convergent-divergent trend is supported by the shapes of the vocal lines, in which the successive intervals of each gradually widen, a technique common to many of Webern's vocal works. As life dissolves in peace, the Postlude quietly rounds out the cyclic form of the movement, as witnessed by the reversal of the dynamic levels of the Prelude.

Symmetrical construction of the row, as well as the consistent inversionally symmetrical relations among the row transformations and transpositions, provide a further means for symbolizing poetry, at the same time contributing to the articulation and control of the work's formal structure. The row itself is completely symmetrical. Each three-note segment contains intervals 1, 3, and 4, the intervallic ordering within the last two cells retrograding the ordering within the first two. The retrograde-inversion (RI–1) of the entire set-form is equivalent to the original (P–1) in one transposition (Ex. 3–15). These three-note segmental properties are motivically exploited as a means of defining sectional and overall formal symmetry. For instance, the four row forms (P–8, I–7, P–1, I–2) that simultaneously unfold in part I of the Prelude (mm. 1–6) each maintain their notes 1–3 in a single instrument (Ex. 3–16). The next two three-note segments of both P–8 and I–7 each have

EXAMPLE 3–13. Webern, *Cantata* No. 1, Op. 29, form of Mov. I

Movement I form

Prel	line 1a, line 1b.	Interl	line 2a,	Interl	line 2b.	Postl
I / II /	/	/	/	/	/	/ I / II
2-note orch. elision	2-note vocal elision	3-note vocal-orch. elision	3-note orch-vocal elision	2-note vocal-orch. elision	3-note orch-vocal elision	2-note vocal-orch elision

EXAMPLE 3–14. Webern, *Cantata* No. 1, Op. 29, Mov. I, choral entry, lines 1a and 1b

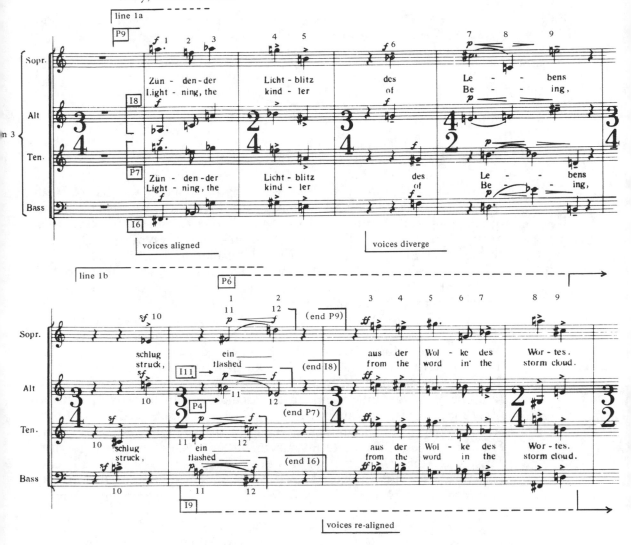

an irregular distribution of notes 4–5 in one instrument and note 6 in another, the same occurring with notes 7–8 and 9 in P–1 and I–2. Each of the four forms returns to a single instrument for its last three notes, thereby cyclically rounding out this opening passage. This principle of departure and return in terms of segmental and timbral synchronization reaffirms the priority of the basic three-note rhythmic motif. On a higher architectonic level of the move-

EXAMPLE 3–15. Webern, *Cantata* No. 1, Op. 29, equivalence of RI–1 and P–1 in one transposition

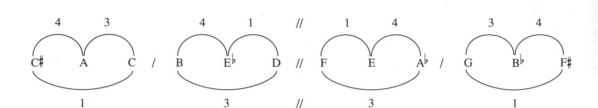

ment, this motivic structure also serves as the referent for departure and return, i.e., of alternating between two- and three-note elisions in the linearly overlapping row forms (see Ex. 3–13). The greatest elisions (three-note groups) occur toward the center of the movement's symmetrical form in connection with the cyclic structure and meaning of the text.

A special poetic as well as essential musical function is assigned to the consistent inversionally symmetrical organization of the row forms around a single axis of symmetry. In a letter to Jone, dated January 16, 1940,[26] Webern finally decided that the movement he composed last had to be in that position after all: "Musically it has to be the ending. It was so in the plan and has turned out exactly so. Musically there is not a single center of gravity in this piece. The harmonic construction (resultant of the individual voices) is such that everything is floating." Webern's reference to "floating" is expressed in the first line of the text in Movement II, "Kleiner Flügel Ahornsamen schwebst im Winde." This text alludes to the little winged maple seed floating in the wind, falling to earth, and rising again to the daylight and air of spring. Significantly, with regard to his statement "not a single center of gravity in this piece," the principle of an axis of symmetry, so essential to the entire structure of the first movement, is correspondingly dropped from the last two movements. Movement I is based on consecutive groupings of simultaneously stated set-forms, each group based on two pairs of P/I. All these groupings strictly maintain inversionally symmetrical relations around the single axis of sum 3 (C♯–D, or its dual intersection, at G–G♯) (Ex. 3–17).

The Op. 29 is the second of Webern's three cantatas. The other two, *Das Augenlicht,* Op. 26 (1935), and *Cantata No. 2,* Op. 31 (1941–1943), are also based on the poems of Jone, with whom he was in constant correspondence during this period. Her poetry offered him, among other things, a view of nature that was always so important to him. The remaining vocal works of

[26] See Anton Webern, *Briefe an Hildegard Jone und Josef Humplik,* ed. Josef Polnauer (Vienna: Universal Edition, A. G., 1959); English edition, trans. Cornelius Cardew (Bryn Mawr: Theodore Presser Company, 1967), p. 40.

EXAMPLE 3–16. Webern, *Cantata* No. 1, Op. 29, Mov. I, opening

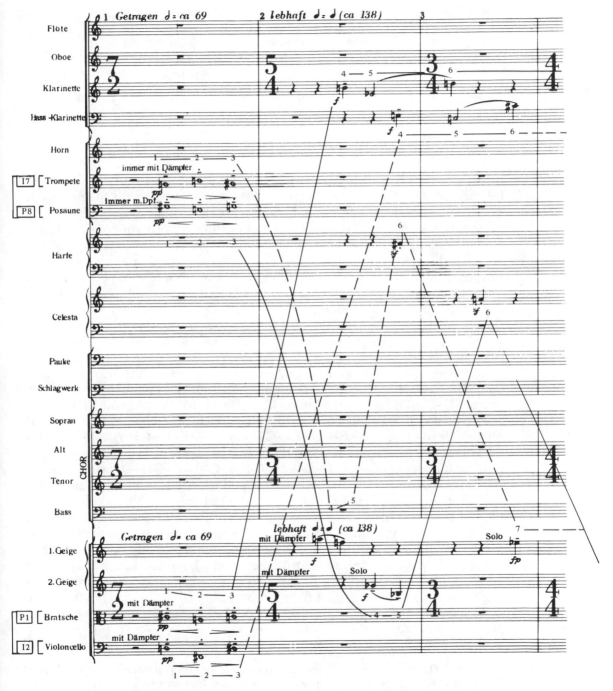

EXAMPLE 3–17. Webern, *Cantata* No. 1, Op. 29, strict inversional symmetry around Axis of Sum 3

Prel		voices		Interl. v.		I. v.	Postl.
mm. (1-6)	(6-13)	(14-19)	(19-24)	(24-31)	(30-36)	(36-41)	(41-47)
1-7	I-10	P-9	P-6	P-3	I-5	P-7	P-6
P-8	P-5	I-8	I-11	I-2	P-10	I-8	P-4
P-1	P-10	P-7	P-4	P-1	P-0	I-6	I-11
I-2	I-5	I-6	I-9	I-0	I-3	P-9	I-9

this period, *Drei Lieder*, Op. 23 (1933–1934), and *Drei Lieder*, Op. 25 (1934), are also based on Jone's poetry beginning with the second song of Op. 23. All these vocal works employ serial techniques, formal constructions, and timbral relations that are highly descriptive and expressive of the texts. Particularly notable is his special serial construction of the vocal lines for expressive purposes: in the Op. 25, No. 1, "Wie bin ich froh" (How happy I am), the vocal intervals and ranges in the successive phrases gradually widen through octave displacements, expressing the words of the song text: "all around me grows green . . . once more I am at the center of becoming."

Of the remaining instrumental pieces of this period, the *Concerto for Nine Instruments,* Op. 24 (1934), is perhaps the most progressive in terms of its tendency toward integration and serialized control of the various parameters. The basic series is derived from permutations of a single three-note cell: prime (B–B♭–D), retrograde-inversion (E♭–G–F♯), retrograde (G♯–E–F), and inversion (C–C♯–A). In four different set-forms (and, of course, their retrogrades)—P-11 (B–B♭–D–E♭–G–F♯–G♯–E–F–C–C♯–A), I-0 (C–C♯ –A–G♯–E–F–E♭–G–F♯–B–B♭–D), P-5(F–E–G♯–A–C♯–C–D–B♭–B–F♯– G–E♭), and I-6 (F♯–G–E♭–D–B♭–B–A–C♯–C–F–E–G♯)—these three-note cells each maintain their internal content and ordering, while changing their positions relative to each other. Structural functions of these cells are exploited by means of systematic assignments of the register, timbre, rhythm, and dynamics of the individual pitches.[27] At the same time, especially in the instrumental pieces of this period, including the *Symphony*, Op. 21 (1928), *Variations for Piano*, Op. 27 (1936), the *String Quartet*, Op. 28 (1938), and *Variations for Orchestra*, Op. 30 (1940), Webern became more oriented toward traditional, classically abstract forms. These are manifested in sonata as well as ternary forms, which also include distinct antecedent and consequent phraseology.

[27] The *Concerto* was to serve as a model for certain Darmstadt composers after World War II, in their tendency toward the total serialization of all the parameters; see Chapter 15.

BACKGROUND AND DEVELOPMENT OF BERG'S FIRST SERIAL WORKS

Radical political and social changes had taken place in Austria since 1918, which affected Berg's health as well as his general lifestyle. During his military service (1915–1918), his health had seriously deteriorated, worsened by the political, social, and economic conditions during the Austrian Revolution.[28] During a period of postwar readjustment, Berg established himself in Vienna as a teacher of composition, an independent composer, and one of Schoenberg's supervisors at the *Verein*. Because of his health, Berg did not participate in performing activities as did Schoenberg and Webern, and this restricted his compositional activity to some extent as well. During the last period of his life, he generally remained in Austria, spending his time working at his home in the Trauttmannsdorfgasse in Vienna, the Berghof family estate in Carinthia, and at the estate of the Nahowski's (his wife's parents) in southwestern Styria. However, during the 1920s, there were increasing professional trips to other countries in connection with performances of *Wozzeck,* the first taking place in Berlin in 1925 at the International Society for Contemporary Music (ISCM) festival. It was during this final creative period of Berg's life that he turned, in the mid-1920s, to twelve-tone serial composition. While his creative inspiration found support in his relationship with Schoenberg, to whom he had always remained a loyal follower, his technical as well as stylistic approach to composition in this period was nevertheless quite different (as it had already been in his earlier atonal works) from that of either Schoenberg or Webern.

After Berg independently published the vocal score of *Wozzeck* (1922), and after his "Praeludium" and "Reigen" from the *Three Orchestral Pieces,* Op. 6, premièred on June 5, 1923, in Berlin as part of an Austrian Music Week, Berg focused his energies on an entirely different type of work—a *Chamber Concerto* for piano, violin, and thirteen wind instruments (1923–1925). Berg's inclination toward use of extramusical numerical schemes with symbolic or psychological meaning could already be observed in certain metric and metronomic relationships in *Wozzeck.* The main melodic motifs of the *Concerto* form a three-part subject based on the musical letters in the names of "Arnold Schönberg" (A–D/E♭–C–B–B♭–E–G), "Alban Berg" (A–B♭–A/B♭–E–G), and "Anton Webern" (A/E–B♭–E). In an open letter from Berg to Schoenberg,[29] in which the work is dedicated to his former teacher on the latter's fiftieth birthday, Berg stated that "that in itself already suggests a *trinity of events.* . . . The three parts of my concerto, which are joined in one movement, are characterized by the following three headings, or rather tempo indications. . . . Formally, too, the trinity or multiples

---

[28] See Berg's letter to Webern, in Hans F. Redlich, *Versuch einer Würdigung* (Vienna: Universal Edition; New York: Abelard-Schumann, 1957), pp. 220–221.

[29] This letter was first printed in the Viennese musical magazine *Pult und Taktstock* (February 1925); see *The Berg-Schoenberg Correspondences: Selected Letters,* ed. Juliane Brand, Christopher Hailey, and Donald Harris (New York and London: W. W. Norton, 1987), pp. 334–337.

therefore keep recurring."[30] As with certain works of Schoenberg and Webern in this period, Berg was also turning to more classically oriented forms with distinct sectional returns, as seen in the more objective neoclassical styles that were emerging in the works of foreign composers since the end of the war. Schoenberg showed Berg how one could co-mingle the new rules of twelve-tone organization with traditional forms, as Schoenberg had been doing with dance pieces (e.g., the *Piano Suite*) and the sonata–allegro plan. In like fashion, Berg also began to move toward stricter control of the twelve-tone system in the *Chamber Concerto*, with occasional occurrences of twelve-tone collections in the four transformations (P, I, R, and RI).

BERG'S TWELVE-TONE SERIAL COMPOSITIONS

Berg's "first attempt at strict twelve-note serial composition" was his second setting of the poem by Theodor Storm, *Schliesse mir die Augen beide* (1925), for voice and piano.[31] Berg had originally given the same poem a traditional tonal setting (in C major) in 1907. While the earlier version was written for his new love and future wife, Helene, the 1925 version was written for another woman, Hanna Werfel-Fuchs-Robettin. Berg's secret love for her was to serve as an inspiration for his creative work throughout his life. The twelve-tone version of the song anticipated the first movement of the *Lyric Suite* for string quartet (1925–1926). Based on the same twelve-tone series as the song, the quartet was also secretly written for Hanna.[32] Here, the extramusical (programmatic) associations, based on Berg's relationship with Hanna, are systematically meshed within the details of the musical fabric; this inclination toward symbolic musical representation had already been manifested in earlier works of Berg. The composition of the *Lyric Suite* had its origins in 1925, when Berg prepared his trip from Vienna to Berlin to attend a rehearsal of *Wozzeck* for the ISCM, the trip requiring him to stay overnight in Prague. Alma Mahler-Werfel, his wife's close friend, suggested to Berg that he stay with her sister-in-law, Hanna, then married to the industrialist, Herbert Fuchs. Thus began Berg's relationship with the woman who inspired his score.

Berg had written the complete text of Stefan George's translation of Baudelaire's "De Profundis Clamavi" into the sketch of the finale of the *Lyric Suite*, revealing the deeper meaning of the musical quotations, use of *Leitmotiv*, and recurrent use of number symbolism (e.g., in the metronomic markings and their multiples, sectional proportions, etc.) throughout the

---

[30] For Berg's outline of these numerical schemes, see also his letter to Schoenberg, in Willi Reich, *Alban Berg* (Zürich: Atlantis Verlag AG, 1963); trans. Cornelius Cardew (New York: Vienna House, 1974), pp. 143ff.

[31] See Berg's letter to Webern of October 12, 1925, in Redlich, *Versuch einer Würdigung,* n. 28, above, p. 177.

[32] See George Perle, "The Secret Program of the *Lyric Suite*," and Douglass Green, "Berg's De Profundis: The Finale of the *Lyric Suite*," *International Alban Berg Society Newsletter* 5 (June 1977): 4–12 and 13–23.

entire work. Berg's personal use of twelve-tone techniques permitted him "the freedom to quote from the opening bars of Wagner's *Tristan und Isolde*" (finale, mm. 26–27). Berg connected this by an arrow to the following statement in the annotated score: "It has also, my Hanna, allowed me further freedoms! For instance, I have secretly inserted our initials, H. F. and A. B., into the music, and have related every movement and every section of every movement to our numbers of fate, ten and twenty-three."

These details provide a significance that goes far beyond the programmatic associations, in that they play an essential role in the generation, interactions, and associations of the materials of the musical language itself. The initials H. F./A. B., in German notation, B–F/A–B♭, form a basic musical cell in the work. Two of the notes, A–F, initiate the *Tristan* quote, while the remaining two, B♭–B, end it, establishing an association between their unrequited love and that of the two characters of Wagner's opera. The scheme of the six movements and their titles, as well as the thematic connections from one movement to the next, are all part of the "larger development (mood intensification) in the Suite as a whole ('suffering destiny')," as Berg told the violinist, Rudolf Kolisch.[33] In the annotated score, Berg referred to the moods of each of the movements, the scheme of tempi which outline a "wedge shape"—the fast movements, 1, 3, and 5, show an increase in speed, while the slow movements, 2, 4, and 6, show a decrease (Ex. 3–18).

Berg also wrote that "this first movement, whose almost inconsequential mood gives no hint of the tragedy to follow, continually touches on the keys of H and F Major. The principal theme [the twelve-tone row that, with variations, governs the whole work] is likewise enclosed by your ini-

EXAMPLE 3–18. Berg, *Lyric Suite* for String Quartet, overall formal wedge-shape based on tempo relations of the six movements

V. Presto delirando
A B A B A coda
(A free) (B "tenebroso" 12 tone)

III. Allegro misterioso
Scherzo/Trio estatico/S.
A　　　B　　　A retro
(12 tone) (free)

I. Allegretto gioviale
binary
(12-tone, 3 rows)

II. Andante amoroso
rondo ABACA' + B
+A+ A beginning coda
(non - 12 - tone, free)

IV. Adagio appassionato
non - 12 - tone
(free)

VI. Largo desolato
free form
(12 tone, 4 rows)
(has Tristan
quote (mm.26-7)

[33] See Berg's analysis for Kolisch in facsimile in Reich, *Alban Berg: Bildnis in Wort* (Zürich: Peter Schifferlei, Verlag "Die Arche," 1959), pp. 45–46.

tials, F and H." Special serial techniques are basic in the development of the series throughout the movement and, at the same time, emphasize and vary the position of Hanna's initials. The basic row, P–5 (F–E–C–A–G–D/A♭–D♭–E♭–G♭–B♭–B), which forms the main theme in vnI at the opening, is harmonically and tonally defined by its contour and hexachordal content (Ex. 3–19).[34] The first "white-note" hexachord prominently contains an outline of the F major triad, while the second, almost exclusively "black-note" hexachord prominently contains an outline of the H or B major triad. Berg mixes these tonal implications with complex serial relationships throughout. The basic twelve-tone row of Movement I can be referred to as a *cyclic set*,[35] its alternate tones outlining inversionally related segments of the cycle of fifths (or fourths). These complementary cyclic segments within each of the two hexachordal partitions generate a complete succession of symmetrically related dyads (F–E, C–A, G–D/A♭–D♭, E♭–G♭, B♭–B) that intersect at the dual axis (E–F and B♭–B) a tritone apart (Ex. 3–20). At mm. 33–36 (closing theme

EXAMPLE 3–19. Berg, *Lyric Suite,* Mov. I, opening, hexachordal permutation of initials "H.B."

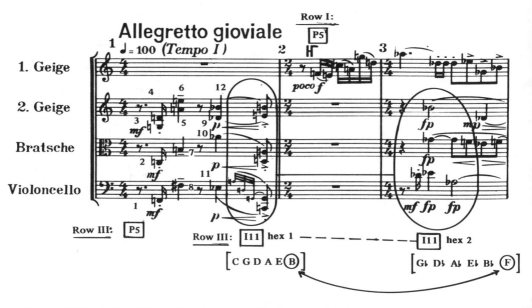

[34] Douglas Jarman, *Alban Berg* (Berkeley and Los Angeles: University of California Press, 1979), p. 82.

[35] Perle, *Twelve-Tone Tonality* (Berkeley and Los Angeles: University of California Press, 1977), p. 19.

EXAMPLE 3–20. Berg, *Lyric Suite,* Mov. I, symmetrically related dyads of the basic cyclic set, P–5

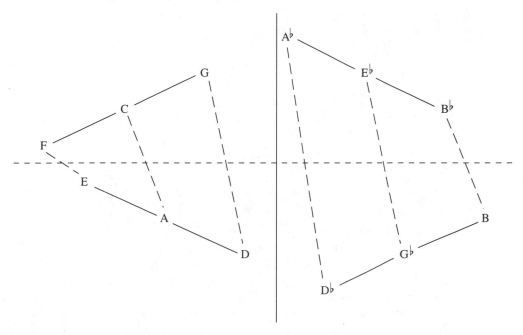

and opening of the recapitulation), the cello part successively unfolds two new forms of the twelve-tone row, C–D–E–F–G–A/F♯–G♯–A♯–B–C♯–D♯ and F–C–G–D–A–E/B–F♯–C♯–G♯–D♯–A♯. Both are derived from the basic set (i.e., these are referred to as *derivative sets*), in that the original hexachordal pitch content is maintained, though in a revised ordering. This relates the three sets to each other according to Hauer's (and Schoenberg's) principle of *twelve-tone hexachordal troping.* Due to the cyclic-interval properties, the elements within each of the hexachords appear symmetrically reorganized around the original axial dyads (E–F and B♭–B), respectively (Ex. 3–21). (Row III unfolds the hexachords explicitly in their cyclic ordering of consecutive perfect fifths.) Thus, we have observed several principles of twelve-tone technique, which are combined in a programmatic context. These include the use of a cyclic set, serialism, hexachordal troping, strict inversionally symmetrical relations around an axis of symmetry, and the use of derivative sets, the first and third of which are generated or bounded by Hanna's initials (H–F, or B–F).

Hanna's initials are more profoundly integrated within the twelve-tone unfolding as part of yet another serial principle, which is based on the permutation or rotation of certain components of the set (see Ex. 3–19). The first three chords (m. 1) unfold the entire cycle of fifths in the Row–III form of P–5 (see Ex. 3–21). The final chord of the measure repeats a six-note segment of the cycle (C–G–D–A–E–B). This hexachord, together with the

EXAMPLE 3–21. Berg, *Lyric Suite,* Mov. I, hexachordally related derivative sets: "twelve-tone hexachordal tropes"

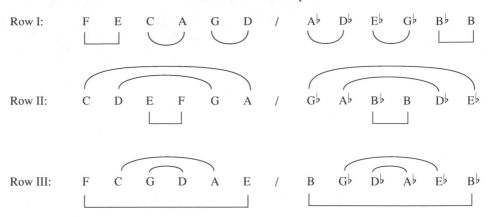

first six notes in the accompaniment at m. 3 (G♭–D♭–A♭–E♭–B♭–F), represents a Row–III cyclic ordering of I–11 (i.e., Row I of I–11, B–C–E–G–A–D/A♭–E♭–D♭–B♭–G♭–F, appears here in its Row–III form, C–G–D–A–E–B/G♭–D♭–A♭–E♭–B♭–F). Then (at m. 4, beginning in vnI and continuing in vc), the last note of P–5 (B) simultaneously serves as the first note of I–11, Row I, the next two measures contrapuntally and harmonically overlapping both set forms. Basic P–5 (F–E–C–A–G–D/A♭–D♭–E♭–G♭–B♭–B) and this inversion at the tritone transposition, I–11(B–C–E–G–A–D/A♭–E♭–D♭–B♭–G♭–F), are related by their maximal invariance of hexachordal content. The difference is that the boundary notes (F–B) of P–5 are reversed in I–11, so Hanna's initials are switched between the hexachords. I–11 subsequently appears as the basis of the second theme (mm. 23ff., third beat, vnII), where it is aligned with P–11; both begin with the same note (B), with P–11 continuing in the va. (P–11 is simply a retrograde of P–5, so it contains the original position of Hanna's initials in contrast to I–11.) Both P–11 and I–11 prominently continue throughout this theme group. Hanna's initials are joined for the first time as a local detail in a canon based on a serial rotation of the theme (at mm. 7ff.). Violin I initiates this canon, in which the notes of P–5 are rotated (or cyclically permuted) in relation to the original thematic rhythm: the canonic subject begins with the last four notes of P–5, which linearly connect with the original permutation (E♭–G♭–B♭–B/F–E–C–A–G–D–A♭–D♭ . . .).

   The cyclic-interval properties of the series are essential in providing basic associations among certain transpositions of the four set transformations, P, I, R, and RI. P–5 is based on an alignment of two inversionally related segments of the interval–5/7 cycle (F–C–G . . . and E–A–D . . .). If we realign these cycles (Ex. 3–22), so the descending perfect-fifth cycle begins the series (on E), the inversion (I–4) is produced (E–F–A–C–D–G/

EXAMPLE 3–22. Berg, *Lyric Suite,* Mov. I, primary and secondary sums

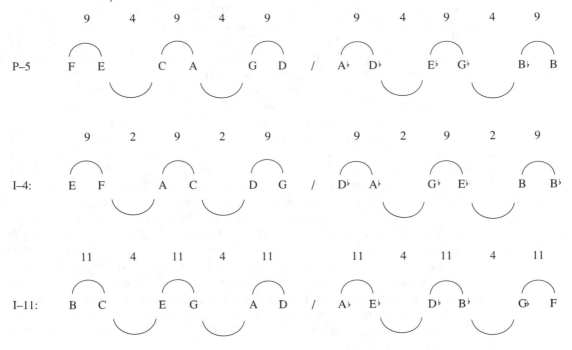

Db–Ab–Gb–Eb–B–Bb). While the succession of sum–9 dyadic adjacencies remains unchanged between P–5 and I–4, the original secondary dyadic adjacencies of sum 4 in P–5 are changed to a series of sum–2 dyads in I–4. However, it is the inversion at the tritone (I–11), rather than at I–4, that is employed in Movement I. In this case, the secondary dyadic sum of 4 remains invariant between P–5 and I–11, rather than the primary dyadic sum of 9. Thus, "modulations" between these set-forms are permitted by the *cognate* (common sum) relation.

Variety within unity is also permitted by the systematic permutation of the basic series in subsequent movements. P–5 of Movement I (F–E–C–A–G–D/Ab–Db–Eb–Gb–Bb–B) is transposed, in the nonserial context of Movement II (mm. 24–28, va), to P–8, but with an interchange of notes 4 and 10 (Ab–G–Eb–[A]–Bb–F/B–E–F#–[C]–C#–D). This brings Alban's and Hanna's initials (A–Bb and F–B, at notes 4–7) into adjacency for the first time. In turn, the latter ordering of the series is maintained in the P–10 transposition (Bb–A–F–B–C–G/Db–Gb–Ab–D–Eb–E) at the opening of Movement III (mm. 2–3, vnI), the reordered initials remaining invariant in notes 1–4. In the serial context of the scherzo section of this movement, the tetrachord remains invariant in several transpositions of the row. At the opening, we get three different orderings of the tetrachord (Bb–A–F–B, A–Bb–B–F, and

A–B♭–F–B), suggesting a nonserial context. However, toward the ending of the scherzo (mm. 45ff.), a stretto is initiated by I–3, P–10, and P–8, each of the three orderings of the tetrachord appearing as an invariant segment within the respective set-forms. The series in the serial context of the two Tenebroso sections of Movement V is again transposed and more radically permuted (D♭–C–A♭–D–F–A/E–B♭–B–D♯–F♯–G). This foreshadows the form of the series underlying the serial context of Movement VI (F–E–C–F♯–A–C♯/G♯–D–E♭–G–B♭–B). In both cases, the initials no longer appear together. The successive alterations of the series, which culminate in complex derivations of several "half series" in movement VI ("Largo desolato"), have programmatic significance according to Berg, i.e., in terms of the characters—"submitting to fate."[36] The basic permutations of the series in Movements I, III, V, and VI are outlined below, the brackets pairing the tones according to the basic sum of a given row transposition to indicate the successive systematic permutations of the original series (Ex. 3–23).

In addition to these serial techniques, Movement III provides an early example of a serially derived rhythmic set. This set unfolds in the "Hauptstimme" and "Nebenstimme" (mm. 10–12, va and vnI), where it is subdivided into two rhythmic subsets. The latter are derived by partitioning the pitch set according to the registral distribution of elements. These subsets are independently developed in the following measures, several occurrences appearing in rhythmic diminution: subset 1 (mm. 12–13, vnII; mm. 13–14, vnI; and mm. 22–24, vnI), subset 2 (mm. 13–14, vc), and both subsets (mm. 30–31, vns) (Ex. 3–24).

EXAMPLE 3–23. Berg, *Lyric Suite,* permutations of the series in Movs. I, III, V, and VI

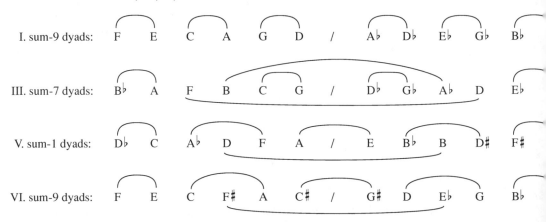

I. sum-9 dyads: F   E   C   A   G   D   /   A♭   D♭   E♭   G♭   B♭

III. sum-7 dyads: B♭   A   F   B   C   G   /   D♭   G♭   A♭   D   E♭

V. sum-1 dyads: D♭   C   A♭   D   F   A   /   E   B♭   B   D♯   F♯

VI. sum-9 dyads: F   E   C   F♯   A   C♯   /   G♯   D   E♭   G   B♭

---

[36] See Reich, *Alban Berg,* n. 30, above, p. 149.

EXAMPLE 3–24. Berg, *Lyric Suite,* Mov. III, serially derived rhythmic sets, mm. 10–12

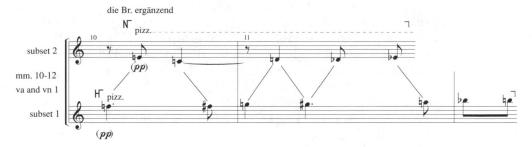

BERG'S LAST WORKS

By late 1928, Berg had already composed a portion of his second opera, *Lulu,* but early work on the opera was interrupted in 1929 by a commission for a concert aria, *Der Wein,* which was finished by the summer of the same year. The Aria is based on three Baudelaire poems in Stefan George's German translation: "Die Seele des Weines" ("The soul of the wine"), "Der Wein der Liebenden" ("The wine of lovers"), and "Der Wein der Einsamen" ("The wine of the lonely"). This piece served as a kind of preparation for *Lulu,* the libretto of which Berg derived from two plays, *Der Büchse der Pandora* (Pandora's Box) and *Der Erdgeist* (Earth Spirit), by the German dramatist Frank Wedekind (1864–1918).

Berg's operatic setting provides a deeper understanding of the social implications of the Wedekind play, based on the tragic destruction of Lulu as *femme fatale*. In the highly complex, expressionistic musical idiom of the opera, Berg's profound musical perception is evidenced in his assignment of specific vocal styles to the individual characters, use of associative orchestral material, recapitulative episodes that have both psychological and dramatic significance, assignment of multiple roles to individual performers, and special pitch-set materials.[37] These include twelve-tone rows and derived chords as well as specific cellular subcollections. One instance is a four-note double-tritone segment, referred to by Perle as "Basic Cell I."[38] This cell begins the opera as the generator of the initial twelve-tone tetrachordal trope: Bb–Eb–E–A/G♯–C♯–D–G/F♯–B–C–F. In the course of the opera, the first form of the cell comes to be identified with the Countess Geschwitz, the

---

[37] For the most extensive study of the musical symbolism as well as musical language of the opera, see Perle, *The Operas of Alban Berg.* Vol. II: *Lulu* (Berkeley and Los Angeles: University of California Press, 1984).

[38] See Perle, *Lulu,* n. 37, above, p. 87.

second with Dr. Schoen, and the third with Lulu.[39] All of these features form part of a highly integrated network of musico-dramatic relationships.

Political developments in the early 1930s had a direct bearing on Berg's spiritual well-being as well as on his creativity. He felt that the Nazi move toward power in Germany meant the ruin of his own life as well as the ruin of all Austrians. This feeling became most pronounced in 1933, when Hitler became chancellor and Austria became unified with Germany.[40] At the Brahms festival in Vienna, which began on May 17, 1933, Berg was dismayed to hear Nazi-inspired speeches that "betrayed the whole of post-Brahmsian music, especially Mahler and the younger generation (like Hindemith). There was no reference to the Schoenberg circle as even existing." Both he and Webern were particularly worried about the fate of Schoenberg, whom they were never to see again after the latter left Austria for the United States in this year. Soon afterwards, Berg's music was censored throughout Nazi Germany as decadent and performances of his works had to be cancelled. Resulting financial problems soon interfered with Berg's work, but even if he had been able to finish *Lulu* during the 1933–34 season, prospects for its performance were grim. Nevertheless, he forged ahead during the next several years with the composition of the opera. After Furtwängler informed Berg that the opera could not be performed, Berg decided to introduce the work as a concert suite, *Symphonische Stücke aus der Oper "Lulu"* for voice and orchestra, which was finished in 1934 and performed in Berlin. Despite official policies of the Nazis, many in the audience responded to the work with enthusiasm. Long after the composer's death, an unfortunate series of events continued to obstruct the production and correct publication of the opera. Although Berg had completed the preliminary score of *Lulu,* leaving only the orchestration unfinished, Erwin Stein's arrangement of the vocal score of Acts I and II was all that was published in 1936, and Stein's promise to prepare an arrangement of Berg's short score of Act III for future publication remained unfulfilled. It was only in 1979, with the completion of the orchestration of Act III by the Austrian composer Friedrich Cerha, that we have been provided finally with the publication of a complete and "authentic" edition.[41]

By way of a commission from the American violinist Louis Krasner, Berg abandoned work on *Lulu* to write a *Violin Concerto* in 1935, which was to be his last completed work. His original intention was to compose a work of "absolute music," but this changed at the untimely death of Manon Gropius, the eighteen-year-old daughter of Alma Mahler and her second husband. Berg himself died on December 24 without ever hearing the *Con-*

[39] See Douglas Jarman, "Countess Geschwitz Series: A Controversy Resolved?" *Proceedings of the Royal Musical Association* 107 (1980–1981); 111–118. See also Perle, ibid.

[40] See Hans F. Redlich, *Alban Berg: The Man and His Music* (London: John Calder, 1957, pp. 239ff.; see also Perle, *Lulu,* n. 37, above, p. 239.

[41] See Perle, "The Cerha Edition," *International Alban Berg Society Newsletter* 8 (Summer 1979): 5–7.

certo. As in most of Berg's works, the *Concerto* was based on a clearly constructed, purely musical, formal framework as well as a descriptive emotional expression. The two movements portray the life and death of the young girl, Movement I (representing her life) divided into two sections, slow–fast, and Movement II (her death and transfiguration) into two sections, fast–slow, the tempi of which mirror those of the two sections in Movement I. In addition to the explicit program, there is evidence that the *Concerto,* similarly to the *Lyric Suite,* is also based on a secret one of an autobiographical nature.[42]

In the *Concerto,* as in *Der Wein* and the *Lyric Suite,* complex serial procedures were integrated with seemingly traditional elements. The work is developed from two basic elements—the first a twelve-tone row, the second a folk song from Carinthia. Most striking is the inclusion of the chorale "Es ist genug" by Johann Ahle, which was used by J. S. Bach in his *Cantata No. 60* "O Ewigkeit, du Donnerwort," in the last section. The chorale is integrated into the work and is related to the basic series. However, the chorale was a later addition to the *Concerto* and Berg expressed his pleasure in seeing that the whole-tone tetrachord of the chorale matched the last four notes (B–C♯–E♭–F) of the basic row. The row unfolds as a succession of triads and a concluding whole-tone tetrachord (G–B♭–D–F♯–A–C–E–G♯–B–C♯–E♭–F). The cyclic-interval components of this basic P–7 form initially unfold in the first two arpeggiated figures of the solo violin (mm. 2–4). While the first (G–D–A–E) is a segment of the perfect-fifth cycle, the second (F♯–G♯–B♭–C) is a segment of one of the whole-tone cycles. We get the first

EXAMPLE 3–25. Berg. *Violin Concerto,* Mov. I, cyclic tetrachords of the twelve-tone series, mm. 15–18, violin

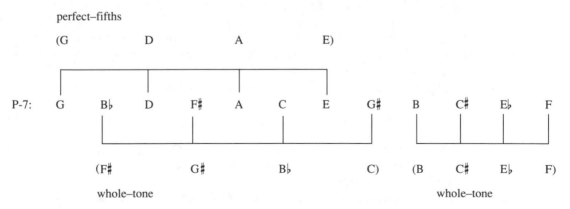

[42] See Douglas Jarman, "Alban Berg, Wilhelm Fliess and the Secret Programme of the Violin Concerto," *Newsletter of the International Alban Berg Society* 12 (Fall–Winter 1982): 5–11. See also Perle, *Lulu,* n. 37, above, pp. 254–257.

explicit statement of P–7 beginning in the fifth measure of section A (mm. 15–18, solo violin). The first eight notes of the row unfold both of these four-note cyclic segments alternately, while the remaining four notes (B–C♯–E♭–F) unfold a four-note segment of the other whole-tone cycle. Thus, the row is formed by a systematic joining of these three cyclic tetrachords (Ex. 3–25).

Thus, the music of all three Viennese composers has contributed to the replacement foundations of the traditional tonal system by its incorporation of new sets of a priori compositional assumptions. Each of the composers, within his own stylistic and technical sphere, had joined traditional means of formal and tonal organization with the principles of the new idiom, and this fusion is most apparent in Berg's oeuvre. All three composers had laid the groundwork for the path that most composers followed, and diverged from, after the Second World War.

SUGGESTED READINGS

ELLIOTT ANTOKOLETZ.   "A Survivor of the Vienna Schoenberg Circle: An Interview with Paul A. Pisk," *Tempo* 154 (September 1985): 15–21.

MILTON BABBITT.   "Set Structure as a Compositional Determinant," *Journal of Music Theory* (1961): 72–94.

JULIANE BRAND, CHRISTOPHER HAILEY, AND DONALD HARRIS. ed.,   *The Berg-Schoenberg Correspondences: Selected Letters* (New York and London: W. W. Norton, 1987).

DOUGLAS JARMAN.   *The Music of Alban Berg* (Berkeley and Los Angeles: University of California Press, 1979).

———.   "Countess Geschwitz Series: A Controversy Resolved?" *Proceedings of the Royal Musical Association* 107 (1980–1981): 111–118.

———.   "Dr. Schön's Five-Strophe Aria: Some Notes on Tonality and Pitch Association in Berg's *Lulu*," *Perspectives of New Music* 8/2 (Spring-Summer 1970): 23–48.

DAVID LEWIN.   "Inversional Balance as an Organizing Force in Schoenberg's Music and Thought," *Perspectives of New Music* 6/2 (Spring-Summer 1968): 1–21.

GEORGE PERLE.   "Berg's Master Array of the Interval Cycles," *Musical Quarterly* 63/1 (January 1977): 1–30.

———.   *Serial Composition and Atonality* (rev. 6th ed., Berkeley and Los Angeles: University of California Press, 1991).

———.   *The Operas of Alban Berg.* Vol. II: *Lulu* (Berkeley and Los Angeles: University of California Press, 1984).

HANS F. REDLICH.   *Versuch einer Würdigung* (Vienna: Universal Edition, 1957); Eng. trans. abridged as *Alban Berg: The Man and His Music* (London: John Calder; New York: Abelard-Schumann, 1957).

WILLI REICH.   *Alban Berg* (Zürich: Atlantis Verlag AG, 1963); Eng. trans. Cornelius Cardew (New York: Vienna House, 1974).

———.   *Alban Berg: Bildnis in Wort* (Zürich: Peter Schifferlei, Verlag "Die Arche," 1959).

ARNOLD SCHOENBERG.   *Ausgewählte Briefe* (Mainz: B. Schotts Söhne, 1958); *Arnold Schoenberg Letters,* ed. Erwin Stein (London: Faber and Faber, 1964).

LEONARD STEIN, ed. *Style and Idea, Selected Writings of Arnold Schoenberg,* trans. Leo Black (London: Faber and Faber Ltd.; Los Angeles: Belmont Music Publishers, 1975; Berkeley and Los Angeles: University of California Press, 1984), including: "Composition With Twelve Tones (1941)," pp. 214–249.

The International Alban Berg Society Newsletter, including: Douglass Green, "Berg's De Profundis: The Finale of the *Lyric Suite,*" No. 5 (June 1977): 13–23; Douglas Jarman, "Alban Berg, Wilhelm Fliess and the Secret Programme of the Violin Concerto," No. 12 (Fall-Winter 1982): 5–11; Anna Maria Morazzoni, "Berg and Italy in the Thirties," No. 13 (Spring-Summer 1985): 10–31; George Perle, "The Secret Program of the *Lyric Suite,*" No. 5 (June 1977): 4–12.

ANTON WEBERN. *Briefe an Hildegard Jone und Josef Humplik,* ed. Josef Polnauer (Vienna: Universal Edition, A.G., 1959); Eng. trans. Cornelius Cardew (Bryn Mawr: Theodore Presser Company, 1967).

———. *Der Weg zur neuen Musik,* ed. Willi Reich (Vienna, 1960); Eng. trans., *The Path to the New Music* (Bryn Mawr, Pa., 1963).

PETER WESTERGAARD. "Webern and 'Total Organization': An Analysis of the Second Movement of Piano Variations, Op. 27," *Perspectives of New Music* I/2 (Spring, 1963): 107–120.

4 Musical reactions to the ultra-chromaticism of the Wagner-Strauss period: Rise of national styles

Around the turn of the century, the interaction between elements of non-Western folk music and the new harmonic vocabulary of Russian and French composers laid the basis for a musical language very different from the ultrachromaticism of the Wagner-Strauss period. Pre-World War I political conditions contributed to these non-Germanic national developments. After the Franco-Prussian War of 1871 and the defeat of Napoleon III by Bismarck, Prussia became a unified empire. New political alliances were formed and international hostilities became polarized between the Triple Alliance (Prussia, the Austro-Hungarian Empire, and Italy) and the Triple Entente (Russia, France, and England). From the time of the rule of Peter the Great in the eighteenth century, Russia had looked toward Germany for her political and cultural models, but with increasing tensions in the late nineteenth century, she now began to look toward France for new and reciprocal political and cultural relationships. The long-established German musical hegemony in Europe was then challenged by the growing nationalistic sentiment in Russia and by a new era of artistic change in France. (France had undergone rapid return to prosperity under her new Republic.) This surge in national interests eventually led to a weakening of the German musical sphere of influence in Europe.

While German late-Romantic musical styles continued to exert an influence in Germany and Austria in the twentieth century, reaction to the ultrachromatic idiom of German late-Romantic music caused many non-German composers to turn vehemently toward new sources for musical languages and styles. Nationalistic demands induced composers to look toward Eastern Europe as well as France, and also toward their own national treasures of literature, the arts, and folklore. Thus, in the late nineteenth and early twentieth centuries, three divergent musical forces were prevalent: *German late-Romanticism,* as exemplified in the styles of Wagner, Bruckner, Mahler, and Richard Strauss; new *national styles,* first evident in Russia and spreading to other countries; and new *French styles* of composition, seen in the distinctive approaches of Debussy and Satie.

The pentatonic and modal phrases found in Debussy's music have been attributed to the indirect influences of Russian folk music by way of Russian nationalists, Mussorgsky especially. Similarly, Stravinsky's early works reveal an origin in Russian folk music as well, partly by way of the Russian nationalists, but with more direct roots in folk sources (than did Debussy's works).[1] Documentary evidence reveals Stravinsky's direct con-

---

[1] See Béla Bartók, "Selbstbiographie," appearing originally in *Musikblätter des Anbruch* (Vienna) 3/5 (March 1921): 87–90, where Bartók discusses common influences of

nections to musical ethnology: that "Stravinsky's jottings can be related to known classified folksong prototypes whose aptness to the scenario demonstrates both their authenticity and Stravinsky's unsuspected sensitivity to matters ethnological."[2] There appeared a common bond in the inclination toward the pentatonic and modal constructions of folk music, such constructions forming a nonfunctional basis on which a new kind of tonality was to be established.[3]

The break from German musical dominance led to two extremes of tonal orientation in the early twentieth century. The ultrachromaticism of Wagner, Bruckner, and Mahler was transformed into the more dissonant chromaticism of certain works of Strauss and ultimately into the expressionistic atonality of the Vienna Schoenberg circle. At the same time, the pentatonic-diatonic modalities that were basic to the folk music of many nations were transformed into new kinds of scale constructions, primarily modal, whole-tone, and octatonic, the interactions of two or more of these commonly found in the music of Debussy, Scriabin, Stravinsky, Bartók, Kodály, Ives, and other composers of diverse national backgrounds.[4]

The emergence of these new systems of pitch organization fostered a new autonomy of metric and rhythmic approaches. With the dissolution of traditional tonal functions, where the basic concepts of consonance and dissonance had been tied inextricably to the regular barline, greater freedom in metric/rhythmic organization was permitted. Composers using folk music sources, especially from the borders of Western culture (Eastern Europe, Russia, Asia, and Africa), introduced *unequal beat patterns* both from dynamic dance rhythms in strict style (*tempo giusto*) and free vocal style (*parlando rubato*). Thus, certain musical divergencies in the twentieth century can be traced, to a large extent, to the fundamental split between Germanic and non-Germanic political, social, and musical spheres.

DEVELOPMENT AND TRANSFORMATION OF DIATONIC MATERIAL

The free use of the semitoneless pentatonic scale (represented by any one of five rotations on the piano's black-key collection) as well as the heptatonic modal permutations of the diatonic scale (as represented by any one of seven modal octave segments on the piano's white-key collection) led to a weaken-

---

Russian folk music on the works of Debussy and Stravinsky; see also *Béla Bartók Essays,* ed. Benjamin Suchoff (New York: St. Martin's Press, 1976), p. 410.

[2] See Richard Taruskin, "Russian Folk Melodies in *The Rite of Spring,*" *Journal of the American Musicological Society* 33/3 (1980): 501–543 and 509.

[3] See Elliott Antokoletz, *The Music of Béla Bartók: A Study of Tonality and Progression in Twentieth-Century Music* (Berkeley and Los Angeles: University of California Press, 1984), pp. 8 and 13.

[4] See Ex. 4–8, below, and corresponding discussion for a definition and outline of the octatonic scale and its "Models."

ing of the hierarchical pitch relations inherent in the traditional dominant-tonic progressions. What emerged was a new conception of diatonicism based on equalization of the modal scalar degrees, i.e., the elimination of any tendency by one pitch to gravitate to another. This trend within the diatonic spectrum appears to have paralleled a similar one in late-Romantic chromatic music, so composers of divergent stylistic backgrounds began evolving a new concept of relations contained within the chromatic continuum.

The tendency to equalize the tones of the chromatic continuum and weaken tonal motion was foreshadowed in the nineteenth century by the infusion of symmetrical pitch relations, most prominently as the basis of harmonic root progression, into traditional triadic contexts. In the music of Schubert, Chopin, Berlioz, Liszt, Glinka, and others, chordal root progressions often outlined consecutive motions by a single interval, commonly by the minor third, major third, or major second. Symmetrical pitch relations in this century were manifested in vertical constructions as well as linear progressions. Due to the dictates of the traditional tertian system, however, symmetrical harmonic construction was limited to the dominant-ninth, diminished-seventh, and French augmented-sixth chords.[5] A prominent example of symmetrical harmonic construction and progression would be a passage from Mussorgsky's *Boris Godunov,* Act II, Clock Scene (p. 155), based on the alternation of two transpositions of the symmetrical dominant-ninth chord, with the common axial tritone held as an ostinato in the bass and reiterated in the voice (Ex. 4–1).[6] Such progressions resulted in subdivisions of the octave into "cycles" of intervals in contexts otherwise based on traditional triadic harmony.

These practices led to pervasive use of symmetrical and cyclic-interval constructions in many twentieth-century compositions, as the primary means of integrating large-scale compositional structure. While symmetrical properties emerged from the chromatic tonality of late nineteenth-century Romantic music in the works of certain German and Viennese composers, the concept of symmetry was to a large extent commonly derived, by French, Russian, and Hungarian composers, from the pentatonic and modal materials of Eastern European folk-music sources. Pentatonic and modal scales often

---

[5] For some of these manifestations of symmetrical construction and progression in chromatic tonal music of the nineteenth century, see: George Perle, "Symmetrical Formations in the String Quartets of Béla Bartók," *Music Review* 16 (November 1955); 301; Philip Friedheim, "Radical Harmonic Procedures in Berlioz," *Music Review* 21/4 (November 1960): 286; Felix Salzer and Carl Schachter, *Counterpoint in Composition: The Study of Voice Leading* (New York McGraw-Hill, 1969): 215–221; Gregory Proctor, "Technical Bases of Nineteenth-Century Chromatic Tonality: A Study in Chromaticism" (Ph.D. diss., Princeton University, 1977); Elliott Antokoletz, *The Music of Béla Bartók,* n.3, above, 323–325; and Richard Taruskin, "Chernomor to Kashchei; Harmonic Sorcery; Or, Stravinsky's 'Angle,'" *Journal of the American Musicological Society* 38/1 (Spring 1985): 79ff.

[6] See ibid., Perle, p. 302, and Antokoletz, pp. 4–5.

EXAMPLE 4–1. Mussorgsky, *Boris Godunov*, Act II, "Clock Scene" (p. 155), alternation of two transpositions of the symmetrical dominant–ninth chord, with common axial tritone held as ostinato in bass and reiterated in voice

(a)

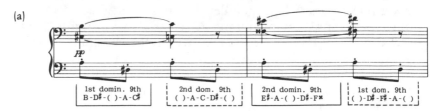

| 1st domin. 9th | 2nd domin. 9th | 2nd domin. 9th | 1st dom. 9th |
| B -D♯-( )-A-C♯ | ( )-A-C-D♯-( ) | E♯-A-( )-D♯-F✕ | ( )-D♯-F♯-A-( ) |

(b)

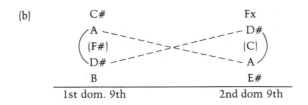

| 1st dom. 9th | 2nd dom 9th |

generate symmetrical pitch constructions in works of the latter group of composers, these scales themselves being transformed into *cyclic* (symmetrical) *collections*. The pentatonic scale (for example, the black keys of the piano) is often employed explicitly in its symmetrical permutation, E♭–G♭–A♭–B♭–D♭, with two of its whole steps encompassed by its two minor thirds (the only form of the scale found in Hungarian folk music). A distinction between the scalar and cyclic-interval forms of the same collection is often made, the scalar content of which can be reordered as a segment of the cycle of fifths: G♭–D♭–A♭–E♭–B♭. Larger diatonic collections are also often exploited as both scale and cycle within the same composition. For instance, the Dorian form of the white keys of the piano (D–E–F–G–A–B–C–D) is the one symmetrical modal permutation of the diatonic scale, which is also often found to be compositionally ordered as a seven-note (symmetrical) segment of the cycle of fifths: F–C–G–D–A–E–B.

Other types of symmetrical pitch collections, some of which are often associated with or derived from *pentatony* or *diatony,* have come to be associated with certain composers. Debussy, Bartók, Stravinsky, and others have prominently employed the whole-tone scale, while Rimsky-Korsakov, Scriabin, Bartók, and Stravinsky have been generally the most singled out for their extensive exploitation of the octatonic scale. These varied types of symmetrical collections (whole-tone, octatonic, and permuted forms of the pentatonic and diatonic scales) are all often revealed explicitly as part of a larger uniform field of pitch relations based on the interval cycles. While we may find extremely contrasting aesthetic and stylistic ideals in the music of composers coming from divergent national backgrounds, common approaches to the use of multifaceted types of pitch constructions reveal a new kind of unity in the early twentieth century, the significance of which lies in the growth toward a new tonal system and new means of progression. A more relevant view of established concepts of pitch construction (including *bitonality, polytonality, pandiatonicism, extended tonality, "wrong-note" intrusions into diatonic spheres,* etc.) is suggested by principles of the equal-division system, to which belongs the concept of *nonfunctional diatonicism.* These national approaches to aesthetics, styles, and compositional techniques in the context of historical developments form the basis for the following discussions.

DEBUSSY: SYMBOLISM AND IMPRESSIONISM IN FRANCE

After the Franco-Prussian War (1871), France returned to former material prosperity, and to a foreign policy of continuing colonial expansion, now in Africa and Asia, in the years before 1914. As Paris once again, in the last quarter of the nineteenth century, became an important cultural and artistic center, a new era in French art emerged. Certain poets under the influence of Baudelaire began to react to realism and naturalism in the literature of the preceding era. As forerunners of the *symbolist movement,* these poets, including Verlaine, Mallarmé, and Rimbaud, rebelled against the writings of such authors as Flaubert, Taine, and Renan, and all others influenced by the Positivist philosophy of Auguste Comte, whose objective and calculated approach to reality was replaced by symbolic representation. Moods and impressions were now simply suggested by sounds and rhythms of the poetic text. The new aesthetics were further developed in the poetry of LaForgue, Moréas, Regnier, and the dramas of Maeterlinck, as well as in the writings of later symbolists, including Claudel, Valéry, Jammes, and Fort. This symbolist trend in France, which was further developed in the discursive style of Proust, also led to similar developments in all the arts.

The aesthetic principles of the impressionists in the visual arts are also based not on historically realistic subjects, but instead focused on the atmospheric effects of light and color in nature. The most consistently impressionistic were the painters Monet, Sisley, and Pissarro, although Renoir, Degas, Manet, and Cézanne were also associated with this movement. Through impressionistic technique, representative form and line were sacrificed as small planes of color became juxtaposed to create vibrant surfaces.

The musical correlation to impressionist painting has been observed in the static tonal planes of Claude Debussy (1862–1918). Musical impressionism was begun by Debussy in the late nineteenth century as a conscious reaction to the romanticism of Wagner. In a lecture, Erik Satie had claimed the following: "I explained to Debussy the need a Frenchman has to free himself from the Wagnerian venture, which didn't respond to our natural aspirations. . . . Why could we not use the means that Claude Monet, Cézanne, Toulouse-Lautrec and others had made known? Why could we not transpose these means into music?[7] While there is no evidence that Debussy was affected consciously by the impressionist painters, Satie's statement draws our attention to this fundamental stylistic parallel as well as to Debussy's reaction to the highly emotional, ultrachromatic counterpoint of German late-Romantic music.[8] This reaction appears to have been part of Debussy's more general negative attitude toward the Germanic sphere of influence.[9] Debussy's impressionism was to become one of the strongest influences in the first decades of the twentieth century, as evidenced in the music of other French composers: Paul Dukas and Albert Roussel, as well as the Spanish composers Isaac Albéniz and Manuel de Falla, the Austro-German Franz Schreker, the English composers Frederick Delius, Cyril Scott, and Arnold Bax, and the Americans Charles T. Griffes, Charles Martin Loeffler, and John Alden Carpenter. Maurice Ravel was also inclined to some extent toward impressionistic textures, though rarely at the expense of clear classical forms and intact linear themes.

Debussy's early compositions, including his choral works, *L'Enfant prodigue* (1884) and *La Damoiselle élue* (1888), and the slow movement of the *String Quartet* (1893), reveal Massenet's influence, characterized by a highly personal, intimate lyrical melodic style also found in the music of Gounod. However, new sources of influence first became manifested in Debussy's works of the early 1890s. The delicate textural planes, figurations, and shifting timbres, as well as an increasing preoccupation with individual harmonic sonorities (nonfunctional seventh and ninth chords) in his *String Quartet* (1893) and orchestral *Prélude à l'Aprés-midi d'un faune* (1894), inspired by a poem of Mallarmé, now reveal his debt to the impressionist painters and symbolist poets. His first large-scale work, in which the elusive impressionist and symbolist styles predominate, was his opera *Pelléas et Mélisande* (1893–1902), a setting of the Maeterlinck play.

The Russian influence began to pervade Debussy's musical language as early as 1891 in his *Ballade, Mazurka,* and *Rêverie.* At the same time that he began to reject Wagner's efforts to "overwhelm" the listener (after his second visit to Bayreuth in 1889), he heard Rimsky-Korsakov conduct two concerts of Russian music at the Exposition Universelle of 1889 in Paris. This historical moment began what has been referred to as the *Franco-Russian musical alliance.*[10] In the early 1880s, Debussy had only come into limited contact with music of the Russian nationalists during his visits to Moscow.[11] Af-

---

[7] Edward Lockspeiser, *Debussy* (New York: McGraw-Hill, 1936; rev. J. M. Dent & Sons Ltd., 1963), p. 47.

[8] Ibid, p. 48.

[9] See Debussy's letter to Stravinsky, in Igor Stravinsky and Robert Craft, *Conversations with Igor Stravinsky* (Berkeley and Los Angeles: University of California Press, 1980), pp. 54–55.

[10] See Lockspeiser, *Debussy,* n.7, above, p. 41.

[11] Ibid, pp. 16–17.

ter 1889, the Russian idiom became an increasingly decisive influence on Debussy's musical language, though his initial interest in pentatonicism was apparently inspired by the music of the Javanese *gamelan* orchestra at the Exposition. (Although he had seen the score of Mussorgsky's *Boris Godunov* as early as 1889 in Paris, his full appreciation of the opera did not come until 1896, several years after he began *Pelléas*.[12])

While Mussorgsky captured the essence of his Russian peasant music through pervasive modal coloring and folk-inspired rhythms, he was to remain within the limits of traditional tonality and harmonic construction. His musical idiom, with all its leanings toward folk music, therefore, essentially belongs within the Western European art-music tradition. The pentatonic and modal characteristics that Debussy acquired, largely through the influences of the Russian nationalists, are the basis for a more significant tendency toward the breakdown of the traditional tonal system and the formation of a new one based on new scale formations. While Debussy was only indirectly influenced by folk music, he went beyond the precepts of tradition in his extensive employment of pentatonic/modal themes and harmonies as well as whole-tone constructions often derived from the latter. As a result, traditional chord functions were either minimized or dissolved altogether, as in his orchestral *Nocturnes* (1893–1899); the disappearance of the leading tone in these new scalar constructions, or the omission of either the third or fifth degrees of the seemingly traditional tertian chords, led to a chordal staticism that acquired a *coloristic* rather than *functional* meaning. Instead, some sense of motion was achieved by means of gently insistent rhythms, changes of timbre, and harmonic changes that are often produced by parallel chord motion.

One of the fundamental dramatic premises of Debussy's *Pelléas* is that of polarity, which is manifested in two dramatic concepts—one in which the individual characters are symbols of fate, the other in which they are real human beings capable of love, hate, and jealousy. The Maeterlinck libretto is paradoxically reminiscent of the *Tristan* plot. Golaud finds Mélisande lost in the forest, falls in love with her and marries her. He later becomes jealous of his half-brother Pelléas, who has been secretly meeting with Mélisande. After killing Pelléas, Golaud drags Mélisande by her hair, but she forgives him just before she dies at childbirth. Mélisande perhaps signifies the seductive siren, who draws Pelléas as well as herself toward inevitable destruction. Events seem preordained as the introverted characters move quietly and without resistance toward their fate. Maurice Emmanuel recalls Debussy's conversation in October 1889 with his Paris Conservatoire professor, Ernest Guiraud, in which Debussy, revealing his opposition to the Wagnerian approach, prophetically anticipated his discovery of the Maeterlinck play: "I dream of texts which will not condemn me to perpetrate long, heavy Acts, but will

[12] Ibid, p. 50.

provide me, instead, changing scenes, varied in place and mood, where the characters in the play do not argue, but submit to life and fate."[13] Dramatic direction is suggested not by the underlying musico-dramatic action, which is permeated by orchestral descriptions of the forest, fountains, and general atmosphere, but rather by plot alone. Debussy's static musical language, based on parallel seventh and ninth chords, modal and whole-tone melodies and harmonies, and chromatic fragments, as well as his mosaic-like handling of repeated motivic, phrasal, and periodic constructions, provides an ideal medium for the absorption of worldly objects into the fatalistic realm. All these musical features are most evident in the orchestra, the vocal line always unfolding in a kind of "measured" recitative style that is sensitive to the French language. The orchestra, which always carries the melodic phrase, suggests emotion, while the vocal line, often dwelling upon a single note, serves to express the characters' intentions.

The static phrasal planes provide the structural foundation upon which certain musical elements interact to reflect dramatic polarity. First, a general outline of the prelude: the prelude's rounded form is entirely built on successive pairings of repeated phrase segments as part of larger binary periods, each pair of segments based on a different thematic motif. The opening antecedent phrase (mm. 1–4, divided and muted cellos, double basses, and bassoons) introduces the "Forest" motif in two almost identical halves, followed by a consequent phrase (mm. 5–6, oboes, English horn, and clarinets) that introduces the "Fate" motif, also in two almost identical halves.[14] After a modified repeat of the entire period (at mm. 8–13), one of Mélisande's motifs (mm. 14–15, oboe over a tremolo in the divided strings) is presented in two identical segments to form an antecedent phrase to her closely related "Naïveté" motif (p. 2, mm. 1–2). Just prior to the recapitulation of the "Forest" motif at the end of the prelude, we get a more complex texture, rhythmically, of thematic layers by a simultaneous combination of the "Naïveté" and "Fate" motifs (p. 2, mm. 3–4), which are distinguished from each other by the contrasting woodwind and brass timbres. This phrase is balanced by a consequent (p. 2, mm. 5–8), which now presents both motifs in succession (a skeletal form of the "Naïveté" motif ends the period). In this penultimate passage, the usual consecutive repetitions of the motifs are replaced by their inversions, which are now stated simultaneously with their basic forms to produce a sense of fusion.

On this mosaic structural foundation, special relationships are established between the contrasting diatonic and whole-tone sets that reflect the fundamental interactions between the polarized dramatic spheres of the

---

[13] For the original French text, see Maurice Emmanuel, *Pelléas et Mélisande de Claude Debussy: Étude et Analyse* (Paris: Éditions Mellottée, 1926, 2/1950), p. 36

[14] For a description of the basic motifs of the opera, see Lawrence Gilman, *Debussy's Pelléas et Mélisande: A Guide to the Opera* (New York: G. Schirmer, 1907). Cited page and measure numbers refer to the piano-vocal score of the opera (New York: Edwin F. Kalmus, n.d.).

opera. From the outset, pentatonic/diatonic collections are identified with those motivic figures that come to represent the natural or human sphere, whole-tone collections with the "Fate" motif. In the prelude, the two whole-tone collections are generated from the whole-step components of the pentatonic scale in connection with the symbolic meaning of the drama, i.e., the gradual permeation and transformation of the natural or human realm by "Fate." The opening "Forest" motif, which is based exclusively on a D–pentatonic collection, D–E–G–A–C, registrally polarizes two of the pentatonic whole-steps, C–D and G–A. This motif is immediately absorbed or transformed by "Fate" (Ex. 4–2) as the pentatonic C–D linearly moves to A♭ (m. 5) to draw this whole-step into the whole-tone sphere (A♭–C–D). This foreshadows the subsequent transformation of the diatonic "Awakening Desire" motif, A–C–D (in Act II, p. 77, mm. 4ff., oboe), into the linearly implied whole-tone form, A♭–C–D (p. 86, m. 2), as Mélisande refers to fate, "C'est quelque chose qui est plus fort que moi" ("But this is something that's stronger than myself"). In the prelude (m. 5), the pentatonic C–D is also harmonically reinterpreted as the axis of the larger symmetrical French-sixth chord, A♭–C–D–F♯, which is established as a substructure of the complete

EXAMPLE 4–2. Debussy, *Pelléas et Mélisande,* (a) "Forest" theme, mm. 1–4; (b) "Fate" theme, mm. 5–6

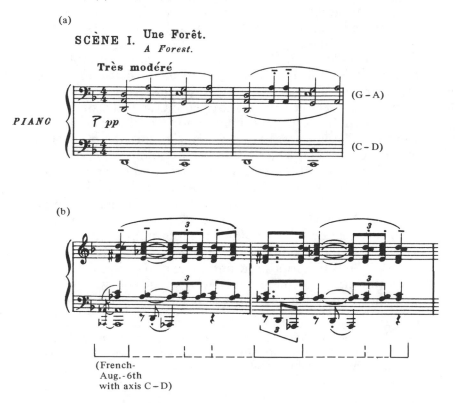

(a)

SCÈNE I. **Une Forêt.**
A Forest.

Très modéré

PIANO

(G – A)

(C – D)

(b)

(French-
Aug.-6th
with axis C – D)

whole-tone collection, A♭–B♭–C–D–E–F♯.[15] Subsequently, at Golaud's entrance (p. 3, m. 1), the upper pentatonic whole-step (G–A) from the opening "Forest" theme is also drawn into the whole-tone sphere, where it analogously appears as the axis of the other whole-tone collection (E♭–F–G–A–C♭–D♭) in the initial ascending triplet ordering.

Mélisande's main motif is based on a new pentatonic segment (mm. 14–15, oboe), in enharmonic spelling, A♭–B♭–C♯, suggesting the tritone transposition of the opening pentatonic "Forest" motif (D–E–G–A–C). In a context based on increased figural activity, this passage more intensively draws the human element into the fatalistic realm by simultaneously transforming this pentatonic construction into the whole-tone set. The harmony of the accompanying strings forms the French-sixth chord B♭–D–E–A♭, a whole-tone transposition of the original one, A♭–C–D–F♯ (m. 5). The specific harmonic position of the chord, as it unfolds in the thirty-second-note figures (A♭–B♭–D–E), provides a whole-tone expansion of the "Mélisande" motif (A♭–B♭–C♯ to A♭–B♭–D) in the three lower notes. The larger, symmetrical French-sixth chord can be interpreted as a joining of the latter whole-tone segment (A♭–B♭–D) with its inversion (B♭–D–E), both whole-tone forms of which occur throughout the opera. This "influence" of fate on "Mélisande" produces a single "pungent" dissonance between C♯ and D. Thus, all the themes presented at this point are drawn into the atmosphere of the forest and fatalistic realm through a progressive integration of the contrasting pentatonic and whole-tone sets in a growing continuum of thematic and textural planes. Segments common to both sets are the basic links between these planes.

The dominant-ninth chord (originally appearing on D, p. 2, mm. 3–4, as an expanded melodic variant of the half-diminished-seventh "Naïveté" motif) also serves as a prominent hybrid construction in transformations between the naturalistic (diatonic) and fatalistic (whole-tone) realms. Act II, Scene 1 opens (p. 55) with a form of the "Pelléas" motif, C♯–E–F♯, which is a diatonic variant of its original occurrence (p. 33, mm. 10–11). This variant (C♯–E–F♯), which is a literal inversion of the basic pentatonic "Mélisande" motif (A♭–B♭–C♯), is based on the "Fate" rhythm, played by the flute in the C♯-Aeolian mode. Transformation from diatonic to whole-tone spheres begins at the first statement of the "Fountain" motif (p. 55, mm. 10ff.), in anticipation of the loss of Mélisande's ring. At this focal point, the motif is based on a new dominant-ninth transposition, C–E–G–B♭–D, its four whole-tone components separated timbrally from the fifth degree (G/B♭–C–D–E). After some unfolding of modal and pentatonic scales in the orchestra and vocal line, respectively, we get a new statement of the "Fountain" motif (p. 57, m. 1) as Mélisande begins her flaunting before the foun-

---

[15] The term "French-sixth chord" and other such traditional designations in this discussion are to be understood only as convenient labels, since such traditional chord constructions are nonfunctional in this context.

tain, "Oh! what clear water" (Ex. 4–3). The motif is based on a timbrally partitioned C dominant-ninth chord, its whole-tone segment B♭–C–D–E (in divided violins and violas) transposed to F♯–G♯–A♯–B♯ (p. 57, m. 2) to complete the whole-tone set (B♭–C–D–E/F♯–G♯–A♯–B♯). The latter transposition of the motif, which accompanies Pelléas' words, "Yes, and always colder than ice," is harmonized not by an expected G♯ dominant-ninth chord (G♯–B♯–D♯–F♯–A♯, or D♯/F♯–G♯–A♯–B♯), but rather by a whole-tone transformation of it by the replacement of the fifth degree (D♯) by D. The resulting whole-tone segment (D–[ ]–F♯–G♯–A♯–B♯) is completed by the whole-tone scale in the voice (D–E–F♯–G♯–A♯). Thus, the alteration of a single note (fifth degree) of the dominant ninth produces an almost "magical" quality as it transforms the diatonic (human) into the whole-tone (fatalistic) realm.

The elusiveness of Debussy's impressionistic textures in a musical language based on the nonfunctional interactions of pentatonic, modal, whole-tone, and other types of pitch sets is further manifested in the three seascapes of *La Mer* (1905), *Images* (1912), the ballet *Jeux* (1912), songs, piano works such as *Pour le piano* (1901), *Estampes* (1903), *Suite bergamasque* (1905), *Images* (1905 and 1907), *Children's Corner* (1908), *Préludes* (book i, 1910; book ii, 1914), and the choral work *Le Martyre de Saint Sebastien* (1911). During these years, Debussy continued to discover new sonorities, which were

EXAMPLE 4–3. Debussy, *Pelléas,* Act II, Scene 1, "Fountain" motif, p. 57, mm. 1–2, transformation of dominant-ninth into whole-tone cycle.

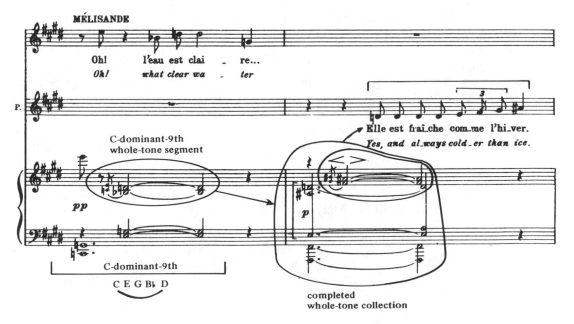

imbued with increasingly imaginative textures. Despite fleeting moods and a sense of formal vagueness, these new sonorities were actually set within carefully calculated formal constructions.[16]

Debussy's second prélude for piano, *Voiles* (1910), provides us with a primary example of his impressionist aesthetics. The ambiguous title can be translated either as "sails" or "veils," the latter invoking a mood of vagueness or concealment especially, as in a "veil" of mist. Both suggest delicate layers, which appear to be reflected significantly in the mosaic-like musical textures of the piece. As in *Pelléas,* thematic ideas are constantly presented in paired statements, which provide a local structural framework within which the more vague thematic contours and rhythms can unfold. At the same time, these phrasal repetitions contribute to the overall sense of staticism and singularity of the musical imagery that is primarily established by the non-directional, exclusively symmetrical pitch relations.

The entire harmonic and melodic fabric is based on a single whole-tone set, A♭–B♭–C–D–E–F♯–G♯, with the exception of the brief central section (mm. 42–47), which unfolds the pentatonic black-key collection of the piano in its symmetrical ordering, E♭–G♭–A♭–B♭–D♭. The common "reference" of these two symmetrical pitch sets to a single "pitch center" (axis) within the symmetry of the overall ternary (ABA) form significantly contributes to the work's staticism and uniformity of mood. At the same time, this piece exemplifies the move toward a new concept of content in its relationship to form.[17] The opening whole-tone descent is registrally bounded by the octave G♯–A♭, which, together with its tritone, D, at the midpoint of this symmetrical scale, forms the dual axis (any symmetrical formation has two points of intersection separated by the tritone, in this case, G♯–G♯ and D–D). The first prominent cadential point (m. 5), on C–E, further establishes the priority of the D–D axis. A B♭ pedal, which provides a new rhythmic layer that underscores the entire piece, represents a disruption of the opening symmetry. However, it is immediately absorbed into the second thematic idea, A♭–B♭–C (mm. 7ff.) as the new axis of symmetry, or secondary "key" area. At m. 15, after a restatement of theme 1, which has now departed from its original metric position to produce some sense of tension, the simultaneous statement of the two themes (i.e., in an additive construction of thematic layers) vertically juxtaposes the two axes. Theme 1 is then expanded (mm. 17–21) by an ascent back to the initial octave position of G♯, after which the axis D–D is for the first time expressly stated as a primary foreground event. At mm. 31ff. the D–D axis appears as the octave boundary of the sixteenth-note figure, both primary axial pitches, D and A♭ (m. 41), ending

[16] Roy Howat, in his in-depth study, *Debussy in Proportion: A Musical Analysis* (Cambridge: Cambridge University Press, 1983), discusses proportional structure and the Golden Section in various orchestral and piano works, including some discussion of their associations with symbolism.

[17] See Antokoletz, *The Music of Béla Bartók,* n.3, above, pp. 6–8.

the first large whole-tone section. The six-measure middle section shifts to a new symmetrical formation, the pentatonic scale Eb–Gb–Ab–Bb–Db, which retains the original axis of symmetry, G#–Ab, of theme 1.[18] It should also be noted that this scale systematically interlocks representative segments from the two whole-tone cycles (Gb–Ab–Bb and Eb–Db), as was observed earlier in *Pelléas*. At the return of the basic whole-tone scale in the final section (m. 48), the three-note pentatonic whole-tone segment Gb–Ab–Bb is cyclically extended to five notes (in enharmonic spelling, F#–G#–Bb–C–D); the entire cycle is completed by the following transposition of this segment (Ab–Bb–C–D–E). This modified recapitulation (mm. 48ff.), which brings back the two main whole-tone themes in reversed order to produce an overall symmetrical three-part form, progresses correspondingly in reversed order from the secondary axis of symmetry (Bb–Bb) through a passing axis, C–C, to the primary one, D–D (or G#–Ab), at m. 58. (The passing axis, C–C, originally connected the basic ones in the first section, at mm. 11–12, lower staff.) The return of theme1 at the end of the overall mirror form also reestablishes the theme in its original metric position. After some alternating between the primary (D–D, or G#–G#) and secondary (Bb–Bb, or, in this case, E–E) axes, the final cadence on C–E establishes the priority of the primary axis. Thus, the work is exclusively based on two unordered non-twelve-tone sets (the whole-tone and pentatonic scales), linked by a common axis of symmetry, which provides a more systematic example of pitch-set relations, as connected to the dramatic symbolization of *Pelléas*.

Debussy's late works, written during the war years, reveal a marked change of style that is exemplified in his three *Sonatas,* the first for cello and piano (1915–1916), the second for flute, viola, and harp (1916), and the third for violin and piano (1917). During this time, Debussy became more vehemently nationalistic, so that, although he was exhausted by serious illness and the attrition of war, he forced himself to begin composing in order to preserve the spirit of French music—the title page of the three *Sonatas* proudly contains the inscription "musicien français." The style of these works, much like his earlier impressionistic musical language, also had a new approach to texture. The works were almost "neoclassical" in their clarity and economy of melodic and harmonic construction. The specific handling of the instrumentation further contributed to the elegance, sparseness, and austerity of the sonorities, suggesting certain roots in the French "Galante style" of the eighteenth century; these works were originally planned as a set of six sonatas for various instrumental combinations. For instance, a fourth sonata had been planned for oboe, horn, and harpsichord. With regard to his extreme concern for clarity of detail, he wrote, in a letter to Godet, that the second *Sonata* was "so terribly melancholy that I can't say whether one should laugh or cry. . . . The further I go, the more I am horrified by a deliberate

[18] See Perle, "Symmetrical Formations," n.5, above, 301.

disorder, which is nothing but aural bluff, and also by those eccentric harmonies which amount to nothing but flirting with fashion. How much has to be explored, and discarded, before reaching the naked flesh of emotion!"[19]

RAVEL: IMPRESSIONIST AND NEOCLASSICAL TENDENCIES

Similar to Debussy, Maurice Ravel (1875–1937) also worked outside of the German musical sphere of influence. Ravel too was influenced by Borodin and Mussorgsky as well as by the exotic music of the Javanese gamelan. He was first exposed to this music at the Paris Exposition Universelle in 1889. The Exposition Concerts of Russian music presented by Rimsky-Korsakov were to have a bearing on Ravel's brilliant and colorful orchestral development especially. Chabrier and Satie, both of whom he met in 1893, were additional sources of influence on his early works, as seen in his *Sérénade grotesque* for piano and the song *Ballade de la reine morte d'aimer*. Influenced by these composers, Ravel absorbed certain elements for his harmonic language, exploiting especially parallel chord progressions, ninth and eleventh chords in particular. In his earliest years at the Paris Conservatoire, he studied counterpoint and orchestration with André Gédalge, and in 1896 entered the class of Gabriel Fauré, whose refinement of detail and economy of means exerted important influence on him. Fauré's sympathetic support for Ravel's music replaced the earlier negative, " official" views at the Conservatoire. At the same time, he assimilated the literary aesthetics of the symbolist poets Baudelaire and Mallarmé as well as Poe, the absorption of all these sources leading to a unique stylistic synthesis in the music that, exoticisms aside, remains peculiarly French. Certain impressionistic precedents were established in such piano works as Chopin's *Nocturne in Db* as well as Liszt's *Années de Pèlerinage,* book III, and in other compositions.

Impressionistic sonorities and techniques were employed by Ravel in some of his early works, but his enthusiasm for French harpsichord music, the brilliant orchestration of Rimsky-Korsakov, and a general inclination toward use of clear, intact melodic shapes with well-defined rhythmic patterns generally contributed to his divergence from the aesthetic principles of Debussy. The distinct linear features of Ravel's music are often provided with some functional harmonic basis (e.g., triads with added tones), set within clearly defined, large-scale formal constructions. While his harmonies are often as delicate and "exotic" as Debussy's, he generally provided a more prominent sense of sharp dissonance by means of diatonically oriented seconds and sevenths. Ravel's classical orientation is apparent in a number of his works, including such piano compositions as his *Menuet antique* (1895) and *Pavane pour une Infante défunte* (1899), the *String Quartet* (1903), *Sonatine* (1905), and *Trio* for piano, violin, and cello (1914). In the later works, such as the *Duo Sonata* for violin and cello (1922), *Sonata* for violin and piano (1927),

---

[19] See Lockspeiser, *Debussy,* n.7, above, pp. 179–180.

the opera-ballet *L'Enfant et les sortilèges* (1920–1925), the two *Piano Concertos* (1931), including one for left hand alone, and *Don Quichotte à Dulcinée* for baritone and chamber orchestra (1932–1933), he tended toward an even greater clarity, precision, and economy of means. Even in some of his most impressionistic contexts, his classical orientation is still evident in the clear thematic contours, the recognizable framework of the external structures, and the cadentially articulated tonal organization. Cadences serve as a focus for nonfunctional modal contexts containing ninths and elevenths, free use of parallel harmonic motion, and chromatic tones. Representative of this impressionistic/neoclassical category are his piano pieces *Jeux d'eau* (1901), *Miroirs* (1905), and *Gaspard de la nuit* (1908), the orchestral suite *Rapsodie espagnole* (1907–1908), the comic opera *L'heure espagnole* (1910), and the ballet *Daphnis et Chloé* (1909–1912).

Divergent national characteristics were absorbed into Ravel's compositional idiom, which is ultimately "French" in style. One influence came by way of Diaghilev and the *Ballets Russes,* for which he was commissioned to write *Daphnis et Chloé.* This led to his acquaintance with Stravinsky, who was to be particularly influential on Ravel; Stravinsky's first Russian ballet *The Firebird* was soon to be premièred in Paris (1910). During this time, Ravel was involved in the harmonization of folk songs as well as in the preparation of a new performance version of Mussorgsky's *Khovanshchina* in collaboration with Stravinsky. One also finds characteristics of the Viennese waltz in his "choreographic poem" *La Valse* (1920), the influence of jazz in the *Piano Concerto for Left Hand* (1931), the influence of the "Blues" movement in the *Sonata* for violin and piano (he had met Gershwin in the United States), and Spanish characteristics in many of his works (which is reflected in their titles). To the last is added his *Bolero* (1927–1928), brilliantly orchestrated with accompanying castanets in a set of variations based on a long orchestral crescendo. One distinct melody of about seventy-two measures, in a dance rhythm based on moderate triple time, is repeated without development or change of key almost until the end of the work. A sense of variety is almost entirely dependent upon contrast and development of the orchestration and instrumental timbres and a change of the mode of C major (to Phrygian) by means of flatting certain notes of the scale (D, E, A, and B).

Ravel's colorful use of timbre is also essential to the impressionistic moods of many of his works, of which the ballet *Daphnis et Chloé* is a primary example. The work opens with a quiet chromatic figure in the lowest strings, above which the divided flutes and clarinets hover with delicately wavering figures. Against the harp glissandi, the horns hold pianissimo chords. In the first section ("The Break of Day"), the mood is suggested by the fluid figure initiated by the double basses, which then ascends through the orchestral texture. The following pastoral section, marked "Lent," unfolds parallel inverted triads and seventh chords. The sound of the flute is heard in the next section, which is based on a slow, then a fast dance. A special "exotic" timbral quality is invoked by the addition of celesta and piccolo.

Another striking and consistent feature of Ravel's music is his use of ostinato-like repetitions of a single musical figure or note, as in *Bolero* and especially in the piano music (e.g., *Miroirs, Gaspard de la nuit,* and the earlier *Menuet antique*)—this technique is most relevant to the mechanical and layered writing of the French neoclassical style. The *String Quartet* also reveals Ravel's use of pedal and ostinato in characteristic passages combining modal melody and super-tertian (seventh- and ninth-chord) harmonic construction (Ex. 4–4). Thus, the music of Ravel, while absorbing numerous features from composers of various national backgrounds, primarily joins techniques from the two main contrasting aesthetic and stylistic spheres of early twentieth-century French music: impressionism and neoclassicism.

STRAVINSKY'S RUSSIAN PERIOD WORKS

The most important foreign artists associated with the international cultural scene in Paris during the early years of the century were Russian—a situation fostered by the favorable political ties between Russia and France at this time. Glazunov had conducted his *Second Symphony* in Paris as early as the 1889 Exposition, while Scriabin performed in that city on his second Western tour in 1896. The great impresario, Sergey Diaghilev, made his first visits to the West with five concerts at the Paris Opera in 1907, which were followed the next year by his production of Mussorgsky's *Boris Godunov* (with Chaliapin in the leading role). The early visits of Diaghilev's *Ballets Russes* (since 1909) included dance performances of the brilliant and colorful orchestral scores of Borodin and Rimsky-Korsakov. With the poster-color costume designs of Leon Bakst, the powerful choreography of Mikhail Fokine, and the dancing of Vaslav Nijinsky, Paris was provided with a special Russian vitality and exotic flavor.

It is in this international artistic context that the early Russian ballets of Igor Stravinsky—*The Firebird* (1910), *Petrushka* (1911), and *The Rite of Spring* (1912)—had been created for Diaghilev's *Ballets Russes*. Stravinsky's

EXAMPLE 4–4. Ravel, *String Quartet,* Mov. I, No. 6, mm. 1ff., modal melody and super-tertian harmonic construction, pedal and ostinato

arrival on the French musical scene in 1910 resulted from Diaghilev's chance hearing of two of the composer's orchestral pieces (*Scherzo fantastique* and *Fireworks*) at one of the Siloti Concerts at St. Petersburg on February 6, 1909. Impressed by the brilliant and colorful orchestration of these two short works, Diaghilev commissioned Stravinsky to orchestrate two Chopin pieces for a forthcoming ballet production of *Les Sylphides* as well as Grieg's *Kobold* for a suite of divertissements under the title *Le Festin*. Diaghilev soon turned to Stravinsky for the score of *The Firebird* ballet. Stravinsky interrupted work on his opera *Rossignol* for this important commission, delaying the opera's completion until 1914. The impact created by *The Firebird* at its Paris Opera première on June 25, 1910, clearly established his reputation.

In Stravinsky's earliest compositions, we find an obvious awareness of the music of the Russian masters. The *Sonata* of 1903–1904 clearly reveals the presence of Tchaikovsky, while his *Symphony No. 1, in E♭*, Op. 1 (1905–1907), suggests influences of Borodin and Glazunov as well as Rimsky-Korsakov. His first important works, however, were primarily written under the influence of Rimsky-Korsakov, with whom he studied (mostly orchestration) privately in St. Petersburg from 1903 to 1906.[20] It was also from Rimsky-Korsakov's Russian folk music collection, *One Hundred Russian Folk Songs* (St. Petersburg, 1877), as well as those of early twentieth-century Russian ethnomusicologists such as Evgeniya Linyova and Anton Juszkiewicz, that Stravinsky derived much of the folk source material that was manifested in his early Russian ballets.[21]

The new technical and aesthetic principles of Debussy's musical language, as well as the characteristics of Russian art and folk music, were also to have a profound influence on the Stravinsky idiom. From 1910 on, Stravinsky found himself enmeshed in the artistic developments of Paris (becoming a self-imposed exile in French Switzerland between 1914 and 1920, after which he moved to Paris). It was just prior to the war that he established his friendship with Debussy.[22] While the styles of Debussy and Stravinsky are very different from one another—the colorful, exotic sonorities of Debussy's scores are absorbed and transformed within the violent Russian rhythmic-accentual idiom of Stravinsky's *The Rite of Spring* —Debussy's exploitation and transformation of traditional modal and pentatonic constructions into new kinds of harmonic formations within his static isolated sound patterns can be found in Stravinsky's mosaic forms and block juxtapositions. Rimsky-Korsakov pointed to certain modernistic characteristics of Debussy in Stravinsky's *Faun and Shepherdess* (1906) and French influences are still more

[20] See Stravinsky and Craft, *Conversations*, n.9, above, p. 39.
[21] See Taruskin "Russian Folk Melodies," n.2, above, 501–543. Also see Taruskin, "From Subject to Style: Stravinsky and the Painters," in *Confronting Stravinsky: Man, Musician, and Modernist,* ed. Jann Pasler (Berkeley and Los Angeles: University of California Press, 1986), especially pp. 28ff.
[22] See letters from Debussy, in Stravinsky and Craft, *Conversations,* n.9, above, pp. 48–56.

decisive in the *Scherzo fantastique* and the *Fireworks* (1907–1908). While the middle section of *Fireworks* contains an obvious allusion to Dukas' *L'apprenti sorcier,* the most definite influence is that of Debussy's *Nocturnes,* which Stravinsky heard at a Siloti concert in St. Petersburg. In most of the works of his Russian period—including especially the three early ballets (1910–1912), the song games *Pribaoutki* (1914), and the dance-cantata *Les Noces* (1917, orchestrated 1923)—Stravinsky covers the broad expanse ranging from pentatony and diatonic folk modes to the new constructions of his contemporary musical language. Although Stravinsky himself stated that he could never share Bartók's lifelong enthusiasm for his native folklore, and, in fact, deplored it in Bartók, these works appear most prominently to be direct outgrowths of Russian folk music.[23] Bartók cites *Pribaoutki* as a typical example:

> The vocal part consists of motives which . . . throughout are imitations of Russian folk music motives. The characteristic brevity of these motives, all of them taken into consideration separately, is absolutely tonal, a circumstance that makes possible a kind of instrumental accompaniment composed of a sequence of underlying, more or less atonal tone-patches very characteristic of the temper of the motives.
>
> Even the obstinate clinging to a tone or group of tones borrowed from folk motives seems to be a precious foothold: it offers a solid framework for the compositions of this transition period and prevents wandering about at random.[24]

THE MUSICAL LANGUAGE OF STRAVINSKY'S RUSSIAN BALLETS— *THE RITE OF SPRING*

The above description by Bartók points to the folk-music source of Stravinsky's block juxtapositions, planes, and ostinato-based layers. At the same time, these blocks can be viewed as a hardening of the delicate mosaic constructions so fundamental to Debussy's impressionist contexts. The exotic orchestral colors, harmonies, and rhythms of *The Firebird* and *Petrushka* had only provided a glimpse of the violent harmonic and rhythmic idiom that was to emerge in *The Rite of Spring.* In this highly ritualistic ballet, we find the most thorough-going use of narrow-range melodies, based on nonfunctional diatonic modality, and constant repetition of short rhythmic motives or phrases in the typically irregular meters of Russian folk music. A sense of motion in otherwise static modal contexts is produced by means of constant overlappings and reinterpretations of accent, meter, rhythm, and phrase. Each structural plane or block that forms a piece within the larger mosaic

---

[23] See ibid., p. 74.
[24] Béla Bartók, "The Influence of Folk Music on the Art Music of Today," *Melos* (Berlin) I/17 (October 1920): 384–386; No. 2 (February 1930): 66–67. See also *Béla Bartók Essays,* n.1, above, p. 318.

scheme, whether a motif, theme, phrase, or section, is delimited not only by its own special instrumentation or texture, but also by an interrelationship of elements that "round it off" as a closed form. The opening rhapsodic folk tune (to No. 1, bassoon), which Stravinsky had taken from Juszkiewicz's anthology of Lithuanian folk songs originally,[25] is an example of a complete and closed entity, established as such primarily by means of its rhythmic structure (Ex. 4–5).[26] The tune is comprised of four differentiated rhythmic segments,[27] which mechanically encircle the tonic of the A–Aeolian mode. These segments are related in such a way as to create a sense of structural balance. The first rhythmic segment, based on a held note and several short ones, is retrograded by the fourth segment, while the third segment of 3 × 2

EXAMPLE 4–5. Stravinsky, *The Rite,* opening, closed structure of rhapsodic Lithuanian folk tune

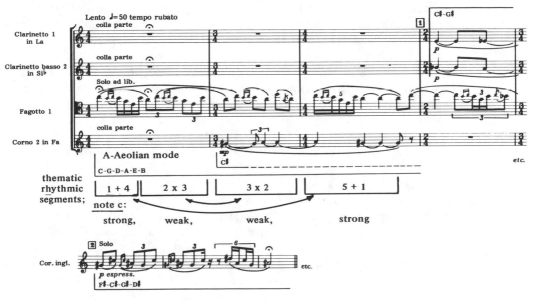

[25] Anton Juszkiewicz, *Melodje ludowe litewskie* [Lithuanian folk songs] (Cracow, 1900); in German, *Litauische Volks-Weisen* (Krakau: Verlag der Polnischen Akademie der Wissenschaften, 1900), No. 157.

[26] Specific associations of highly individualized instrumental colors, as in this unusually high bassoon theme, to the various motivic and thematic layers throughout the work suggest a debt to certain orchestral works of Debussy.

[27] See discussion of the cellular rhythmic structure of this theme in Pierre Boulez, "Stravinsky Remains," *Notes of an Apprenticeship,* trans. Herbert Weinstock (New York: Alfred A. Knopf, 1968), pp. 80–81.

eighths forms a converse of the second one, based on 2 × 3 triplets, to produce an internal balance. This balance is supported by the departure from, and return to, the strong placement of pitch C in the successive segments, the first and fourth of which are the only ones to place C at the barline. Three more statements of this bassoon theme follow. While a sense of repetition is produced by these recurrences, there is actually no repetition in the growing continuum of short phrases, since each modified melodic statement changes its point of entry and cadence through rhythmic displacement. The second statement (at No. 1), which is reduced simply to a sustained note and triplet figure, begins before the barline. The third statement (No. 1, m. 4), which includes conversely all the segments except for the triplet figure, also begins before the barline. A sense of growth is produced as the triplets are increasingly projected into the surrounding contrapuntal lines. The fourth statement (No. 3), which begins on D of the third rhythmic segment, brings us back to the barline, thereby reflecting the principle of departure and return on a higher architectonic level. Through constant rhythmic and metric reinterpretation, Stravinsky produces, paradoxically, a "closed off" and proportionally balanced, yet developmental, formal scheme.

The generation of material from the opening Lithuanian folk tune establishes the musical criteria for the dramatic premise (i.e., pagan ritual) associated with the fertility of spring. It is in this connection that Stravinsky transforms and expands the Russian folk-music properties into an abstract set of pitch relations to form his own personal contemporary musical language.[28] Interactions between the folk- and art-music sources are basic to each of the dance movements of the ballet. The initial folk-tune statement (to No. 1) (see Ex. 4–5) unfolds six notes of the white-key diatonic collection, the Aeolian modal permutation (A–B–C–D–E–[ ]–G) being suggested by the priority of A at each of the local cadential points. The modal properties, mechanical thematic contour, and rhapsodic rhythmic quality of the tune establish the folk character as a basic stylistic premise at the outset, while structural properties of the tune itself contain the seeds for modal transformation into abstract intervallic formations. The tune is registrally bounded by the minor-seventh, E–D. The low note (E) and the high note (D) of the two middle rhythmic segments together encompass symmetrically the modal tonic, A, by forming a perfect fourth below and above it (E–A–D). This interval-5/7 (perfect fourth/perfect fifth) thematic structure lends support to the interpretation that the white-key content of the tune can be conveniently viewed as an unordered six-note segment of the interval-5/7 cycle, C–G–D–A–E–B, generated from the note C, which initiates each of the four rhythmic segments of the tune.

A major-minor conflict is introduced (at m. 2) by the entry of the horn on C♯, the major-third variant of the A mode. This single entry pitch of

[28] See Elliott Antokoletz, "Interval Cycles in Stravinsky's Early Ballets," *Journal of the American Musicological Society* 39/3 (Fall 1986): 578–614.

the horn, of which the second note (D) is simply an upper neighbor, represents the first disruptive element outside the white-key collection (C–G–D–A–E–B), or A–Aeolian mode. At No. 1, the C♯, now in clarinet I, is joined with its fifth, G♯, to introduce the first cyclic expansion of the complementary black-key interval-5/7 (pentatonic) collection—C♯–G♯ initiates and ends a pair of parallel descending semitonal scales. A counter-theme is introduced (at No. 2) in the English horn, the pitch content of which expands the black-key partition to a four-note segment of the interval-5/7 cycle, F♯–C♯–G♯–D♯. While the pitch content of each of these interval-5/7 segments, C–G–D–A–E–B and F♯–C♯–G♯–D♯ (to No. 3), is registrally contained within a one-octave range, so that a diatonic thematic contour is expressly outlined in each case, interval 5/7 becomes increasingly explicit.[29]

The tritone separation of these two interval-5/7 segments, which are generated from C and F♯, respectively, is reflected locally in the structure of the theme. At the bassoon cadence (No. 1, m. 2), G♭ and C together form a new, chromatic boundary, which is a symmetrical contraction of the original diatonic boundary (E–D). Both boundaries (E–A–D and G♭–A–C) maintain the modal tonic A as the structural axis of the tune. This chromatic registral contraction to tritone G♭–C is a fundamental step in the transformation of the folk-tune structure into other cyclic-interval formations as well. The four varied bassoon statements of the folk tune are outlined structurally by minor thirds and tritones.[30] The initial statement is a diatonic embellishment of the prominently placed modal tonic (A) and minor third (C), the thematic contour establishing a background-level descent from C to A. At No. 1, mm. 1–2, this descent is chromatically filled in and occurs within a shorter temporal span. In turn, the tonic A descends at a cadence to the minor third below to give us an important foreground statement of A–G♭. The cadential tritone, G♭–C, is, by this, subdivided into its two interval-3 components (G♭–A–C) as a prominent foreground event. In the final thematic variant (No. 3, mm. 1–3, bassoon I), the structural descent is further extended to complete the cyclic collection, C–A–F♯–D♯. While the cadence, at No. 1, m. 2, establishes the priority of tritone G♭–C, the chromatic descent of the last statement establishes the other tritone (A–D♯) of this interval-3 cyclic partition as a basic background-level thematic structure.

A significant link between the black-key diatonic counter-theme in the English horn (No. 2f.) and the bassoon (at No. 3, m. 3) on the minor third F♯–D♯ is established by a symmetrical relationship between them: the counter-theme is exclusively based on the interval-5/7 segment,

---

[29] For detailed discussions of the cyclic-interval-5/7 interpretation of diatonic collections, see Antokoletz, "Principles of Pitch Organization in Bartók's Fourth String Quartet" (Ph.D. diss., City University of New York, 1975), Chap. 5; more extensively in Antokoletz, *The Music of Béla Bartók,* Chaps. 3, 7, and pp. 314–316, in connection with *Le sacre;* also see George Perle's discussion of *Le sacre,* in "Berg's Master Array of the Interval Cycles," *The Musical Quarterly* 63 (1977): 10–12.

[30] See Perle, ibid., pp. 11–12.

F♯–C♯–G♯–D♯, which is encompassed precisely by the cadential interval-3, F♯–D♯, of the bassoon. Furthermore, both interval-5/7 segments, C–G–D–A–E–B and F♯–C♯–G♯–D♯, which have thematically unfolded thus far, are symmetrically defined by the background-level interval-3 cycle, C–A–F♯–D♯ (Ex. 4–6). Thus, at the outset of the ballet, a transformation of the folk material into abstract (cyclic) formations, which are symmetrically interlocked to each other, begins by means of registral, durational, and temporal emphases on significant structural tones.

The cyclic intervals that are either implied or embedded in the opening folk-tune statements are further abstracted and developed as more foreground events in subsequent sections of the work. One instance is the "Jeu du rapt" (Nos. 45–46), where all three interval-3 cycles, C–A–F♯–D♯, A♭–F–D–B, and D♭–B♭–G–E, appear simultaneously in descending order against an interval-5/7 segment, A–E–B–F♯–C♯–G♯–D♯–A♯–F.[31] Prior to this passage, the entire pitch content (at Nos. 42–43) is based exclusively on the octatonic collection C–C♯–E♭–E–F♯–G–A–B♭, which interlocks two of the three interval-3 cycles, C♯–E–G–B♭ and C–E♭–F♯–A.[32] A new combination of two interval-3 cycles, C–E♭–F♯–A and D–F–A♭–B (exclusive content at Nos. 44–45), forms another octatonic collection, C–D–E♭–F–F♯–A♭–A–B. This precedes the linear statements of all three interval-3 cycles immediately (at No. 45). The cyclic partition common to both these octatonic collections is C–A–F♯–D♯, which, if only by coincidence, is the basic structure of the opening thematic statements of the bassoon solo. This common cyclic partition, which serves as link between the two octatonic collections (Ex. 4–7), is isolated in the oboes and English horns (No. 44, mm. 4–5) as a prominent foreground event. This is foreshadowed by the roots of the arpeggiated pizzicato triads (Nos. 42f.), which outline this basic cyclic parti-

EXAMPLE 4–6. Stravinsky, *The Rite,* m. 1 through No. 3, m. 3: segmental relation between the ten-note interval–5/7 cyclic segment and the basic interval-3 cycle

---

[31] See Perle, ibid., p. 12.

[32] "Octatonic" refers to an eight-note symmetrical scale based on alternating half- and whole-steps or whole- and half-steps. See Arthur Berger, "Problems of Pitch Organization in Stravinsky," *Perspectives of New Music* 2 (1963): 27–28, for the first use of the term "octatonic," and for his identification of the octatonic collection in this passage. Certain principles set forth originally by Berger regarding octatonic-diatonic interactions in Stravinsky's music have been developed further by Pieter C. van den Toorn, *The Music of Igor Stravinsky* (New Haven: Yale University Press, 1983), as discussed below in connection with Ex. 4–8.

EXAMPLE 4–7. Stravinsky, *The Rite,* "Jeu du rapt," Nos. 42 and 44, interval-cycle-3 link between two octatonic collections

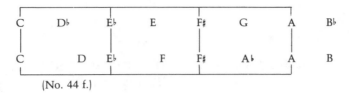

(No. 44 f.)

tion. Thus, the interlocking of interval-5/7 and interval-3 cyclic partitions at the opening of the work and their subsequent interaction within the larger compounded spheres (diatonic and octatonic, respectively) are basic to the dynamic and structural development of the ballet.

Van den Toorn's two octatonic "Models," shown in Ex. 4–8, refer to special rotational and partitioning schemes of the set. "Model A" contains the 1, 2, 1, 2, 1, 2, 1, 2 ordering of each of the three collections, "Model B" the 2, 1, 2, 1, 2, 1, 2, 1 ordering (reading downward in the scale). The symmetrical disposition of the octatonic scale in both "Models" permits intervallically equivalent transpositions of nonsymmetrical diatonic subcollections at 0, 3, 6, and 9. For instance, the "Model A" partitionings into major and minor triads (0–3–7/0–4–7, etc.) remain equivalent at T–0, T–3, T–6, and T–9. Similarly, the "Model B" partitionings into minor tetrachords (0–2–3–5, etc.) remain equivalent at these transpositions. The "Model B" partitioning into 0–2–3–5 minor tetrachords, which provide a folk-like

EXAMPLE 4–8. "Octatonic Models" (van den Toorn, pp. 50–51)

	i		ii		iii		iv		v		vi		vii		viii		(i)
						Model A											
Collection I:	E		f		G		a♭		B♭		b		D♭		d		(E)
Collection II:	F		f♯		A♭		a		B		c		D		e♭		(F)
Collection III:	F♯		g		A		b♭		C		d♭		E♭		e		(F♯)
pitch numbers:	0		1		3		4		6		7		9		10		(0)
intervals:		1		2		1		2		1		2		1		(2)	

	i		ii		iii		iv		v		vi		vii		viii		(i)
						Model B											
Collection I:	E		d		C♯		b		B♭		a♭		G		f		(E)
Collection II:	F		e♭		D		c		B		a		G♯		f♯		(F)
Collection III:	F♯		e		E♭		d♭		C		b♭		A		g		(F♯)
pitch numbers:	0		2		3		5		6		8		9		11		(0)
intervals:		2		1		2		1		2		1		2		(1)	

modal quality, is largely confined to Stravinsky's Russian works. In *The Rite,* the 0–2–3–5 tetrachord generally serves as a link between the "white-key" modal permutation on D (D–C–B–A/G–F–E–D, or 0–2–3–5/7–9–10–0) and octatonic "Model B."

SCRIABIN: LATE ROMANTIC AND RUSSIAN STYLISTIC AND TECHNICAL SOURCES

In the first fifteen years of the century, the Russian composer and pianist Alexander Scriabin (1872–1915) contributed to, as did his great contemporaries in Vienna and Paris, the dissolution of the traditional tonal system, and the establishment of a new musical language. In contrast to Stravinsky, Scriabin's musical language was not rooted in Russian national folk sources, but rather in various art-music traditions. His extensive concert tours as pianist took him to musical centers throughout Europe and to the United States, so that from the outset of his career we can observe a cosmopolitan compositional orientation.

Scriabin's music may be generally viewed as a fusion of Eastern- and Central-European sources, which eventually led him to a highly original approach that became increasingly evident in later works. His early training in composition and piano came from his Russian background. When Scriabin was twelve, Taneyev recommended him to Zverev's class, where he met Rachmaninov. In 1888, he became a student at the Moscow Conservatory, studying theory first with Taneyev and then Arensky, and piano with Safonov. In 1898, Scriabin joined the faculty of the Conservatory, where he remained until 1903. Prior to this appointment, however, he had also come into contact with musical developments outside Russia. His publisher, Belaiev, sent him on two tours of Europe, the first in 1895 to Germany, Switzerland, Italy, and Belgium, and the second in 1896 to Berlin, Paris, Brussels, Amsterdam, The Hague, and Rome. During these early years, he composed many works primarily for piano, including seven sets of *Préludes,* three *Sonatas,* the *Piano Concerto*, Op. 20, and other piano music, as well as two symphonies. Although Scriabin absorbed much from his Russian teachers, none of the compositions reveals any significant stylistic connection to the music of his Russian contemporaries, but were written instead under the influence of Chopin. This could be seen in his use of distant modulations, as well as rhythmic and pianistic configurations. Influences of Liszt and Wagner are also in evidence in these early works.

As Scriabin's style developed after 1903, the earlier Romantic models began to be replaced by the more dissonant chromaticism of Schoenberg and prominent tinge of Debussy's impressionism. Scriabin's experiments with new types of scalar and harmonic constructions, including the alteration of certain degrees of the dominant-seventh chord (especially the lowering of the fifth), and the formation of super-tertian, whole-tone, and quartal harmonies, were coupled with an increasingly mystical, highly subjective interest in the relationship between color and musical sound. This was apparently sparked by his discussions with Rimsky-Korsakov in 1907, his thought already influenced by the theosophical ideas of Madame Blavatsky in 1905.

The highly personal developments in his musical language, which began to be manifested clearly in such works as his *Symphony No. 3 "Le divin poème"* (1902–1904), became most evident in *Le poème de l'extase* for orchestra (1905–1908), as well as in seven more *Sonatas,* eight more sets of *Préludes,* and many other piano works. During this period, we find a more decisive move away from tonality toward a focus on individual sonority. In his *Prométhée, le poème du feu* (1908–1910), which is based on a large and colorful orchestration, such tonal developments appear in conjunction with the increased tendency toward a synthesis of the arts. The score includes the use of a *color organ,* in which the colors are to be projected simultaneously onto a screen. The ultimate realization of this fusion was the intended goal of his unfinished *Mysterium.*

From 1910 on, Scriabin came to focus on the harmonic rather than linear constructions in his works, his harmonies generally being derived from his so-called "mystic chord" of *Prométhée.* This chord approximates the seventh to thirteenth partials of the overtone series (C–D–E–F♯–G–A–B♭), and can be constructed in fourths, C–F♯–B♭–E–A–D–[]. In his late sonatas, Scriabin added the seventh tone G (eleventh harmonic partial), expanding this chord to C–F♯–B♭–E–A–D–G. The linear arrangement (C–D♭–E–F♯–G–A–B♭) of the basic set of the *Sonata No. 7 "Messe blanche,"* Op. 64 (1911), is closely related to this segment of the overtone series, the latter (C–D–E–F♯–G–A–B♭) manifesting itself as one of several variants of the basic set in the course of the composition when the second degree (D♭) is raised to D.[33] Scriabin's employment of the set as both chord and scale represents a significant adumbration of serial procedures.

The basic set of the *Sonata* (C–D♭–E–F♯–G–A–B♭), which alters one note of the "mystic chord" (D to D♭), forms a seven-note segment of an octatonic scale (C–D♭–[E♭]–E–F♯–G–A–B♭). The latter, which already appeared as an autonomous and uniform set of intervallic relations as early as 1867 in Rimsky-Korsakov's symphonic poem *Sadko,* Op. 5, and as we have seen, in Stravinsky's Russian works, plays a more systematic role as a compound cyclic set (i.e., interlocking any two of the three minor-third cycles or four of the six tritone cycles) in a large number of Scriabin's works.[34] His *Prelude for Piano,* Op. 74, No. 3 (1914), is exclusively based on a single octatonic set, A♯–B♯–C♯–D♯–E–F♯–G–A, in which one chromatic passing tone (e.g., G♯ in m. 1) occurs in each of the two-measure thematic statements.[35] In this nonfunctional octatonic context, we may first observe how rhythm plays a primary and independent role in producing motion, as well as demarcating the formal structure. The piece is in four sections (A–B–A–B), the rhythmic relationships of the varied thematic transpositions

---

[33] See George Perle, *Serial Composition and Atonality* (6th ed., rev., Berkeley and Los Angeles: University of California Press, 1991), p. 41.

[34] See Nicolai Rimsky-Korsakov, *My Musical Life,* ed. Carl Van Vechten, trans. Judah A. Joffe (New York: Alfred A. Knopf, 1923), p. 72.

[35] See the analysis of this piece in Antokoletz, *The Music of Béla Bartók,* n. 3, above, pp. 10–11.

establishing the closed form of section A (mm. 1–8) and separation of the latter from section B (mm. 9–12). The initial thematic statement, on A♯ (T–10), begins with a broken major seventh at the barline. The next statement, at the tritone on E (T–4), now begins with the broken major seventh an eighth note after the barline. Original T–10 returns at m. 5, again presenting its major seventh at the barline, but now as an unbroken interval. Analogous to the second statement (at m. 3), the next partial thematic statement, on G (T–7), begins an eighth note after the barline, but its major seventh again presented as an unbroken interval. Although the final partial statement (m. 8) is at the tritone transposition, on E (T–4), the original rhythmic disposition of the major seventh, i.e., in its broken form, is once again at the barline to round out the A section.

Thematic transposition by tritones and minor thirds (A♯–E–A♯–G–E) permits the pitch content of all the statements to remain exclusively within the single larger octatonic collection. These equal (cyclic) subdivisions of the octave are further reflected on all levels of the contrapuntal fabric. In the opening section, the accompaniment is linearly partitioned into two equivalent cyclic subcollections of the octatonic set: the alto and tenor lines each unfold one of two diminished-seventh chords (A♯–C♯–E–G), while the bass unfolds the other (B♯–D♯–F♯–A). The latter further appears partitioned into its two tritone cycles (B♯–F♯ and D♯–A). This cyclic partitioning of the octatonic scale into equivalent subcollections is illustrated in Ex. 4–9. Since the tritone complement of each note is present in the octatonic set (producing four tritones altogether), and in each of the symmetrical subcollections, the exact return of the first two sections (mm. 1–8 and 9–12) at the tritone transposition (mm. 13–20 and 21–24) permits total invariance both of the set and of each of its segments. (This is due to the principle of *tritone equivalence*: the tritone remains invariant at its own transposition or in its complementary inversion.) It should be noted that in this context, a seemingly traditional tertian chord, the held dominant seventh A–C♯–E–G (m. 2), is no more than a nonsymmetrical substructure of the octatonic set, since each of its tones has

EXAMPLE 4–9. Scriabin, *Prelude* for piano, Op. 74, No. 3, symmetrical partitioning of the octatonic set into equivalent subcollections

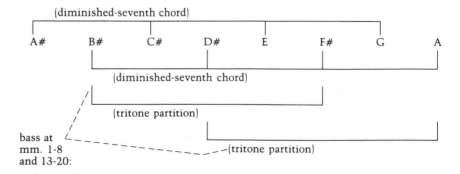

exclusive cyclic meaning in the linear voice-leading. Similarly, the nonsymmetrical chord at the opening of section B (D♯–A–C♯–E) also represents a contrapuntal convergence of cyclic-interval components (D♯–A and C♯–E), these having been independently established in the two lower lines in section A. Thus, the concept of invariance of the total octatonic content as well as of the more local interval/pitch structures (interval-3 and -6 cycles) of the individual lines under transposition establishes a new means of thematic association, progression, and unity within this limited symmetrical context.

In studies of Eastern-European folk music, Bartók and Kodály found certain nondiatonic modes that were previously unknown in modal art music.[36] One instance is E–F♯–G–A–B♭–C–D, a permutation of Scriabin's "mystic chord" (in the scalar ordering according to the overtone series, C–D–E–F♯–G–A–B♭). This modal form was also extensively exploited by Bartók, Stravinsky, Szymanowsky, and other composers from Eastern Europe. As with the seven modal permutations of the diatonic scale, this special mode is also used in its seven permutations by these composers. In two of these permutations, the implied presence of certain cyclic segments becomes evident. The lower six notes of Ex. 4–10a form an octatonic segment, E–F♯–G–A–B♭–C, while the lower five notes of Ex. 4–10b form a whole-tone segment, B♭–C–D–E–F♯. In a third permutation (Ex. 4–10c), the lower six notes outline a segment of the G–Dorian mode, G–A–B♭–C–D–E, while the entire scale outlines G melodic-minor. This special scale is therefore an

EXAMPLE 4–10. Three permutations of a special nondiatonic mode

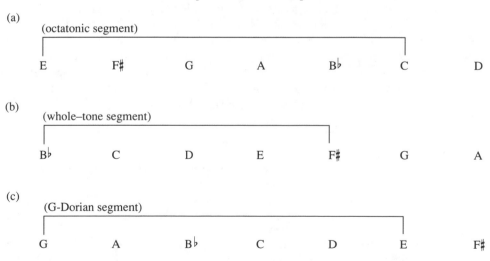

(a)

(octatonic segment)

| E | F♯ | G | A | B♭ | C | D |

(b)

(whole–tone segment)

| B♭ | C | D | E | F♯ | G | A |

(c)

(G-Dorian segment)

| G | A | B♭ | C | D | E | F♯ |

[36] See *Béla Bartók Essays*, n. 1, above, p. 363, the original publication appearing in the "Harvard Lectures," *Journal of the American Musicological Society* (Richmond) 19/2 (Summer 1966): 232–243.

important source for the simultaneous generation of traditional nonsymmetrical scalar structures as well as symmetrical cyclic formations.

Cyclic extensions of this special nondiatonic mode are discussed by George Perle in connection with Scriabin's *Seventh Sonata*.[37] Perle refers first to Scriabin's use of a seven-note segment derived from the octatonic scale, such derivation having practical advantages as compared to the octatonic. Since the octatonic scale remains unchanged at its successive minor-third (T–3) transpositions, there are only three different octatonic collections. A derived seven-note segment is permitted to modulate to four (T–3) transpositions within a given octatonic scale, so that a single pitch-class in each seven-note group differs in relation to each of the other groups. For instance, segments A♯–B♯–C♯–D♯–E–F♯–G, C♯–D♯–E–F♯–G–A–B♭, E–F♯–G–A–B♭–C–D♭, and G–A–B♭–C–D♭–E♭–F♭, from the octatonic scale (A♯–B♯–C♯–D♯–E–F♯–G–A) give us four transpositions of slightly varied content. Perle states that "Scriabin provides a source of contrast through a variant form of the derived scale, the final degree of which is occasionally raised by a semitone" and that this produces "a striking change of harmonic color by converting a five-note segment of the scale into a whole-tone collection."[38] This variant form is the special nondiatonic mode discussed above.

French and Russian composers of the late-nineteenth and early twentieth centuries were the first to break away significantly from the pervasive influence of German music, which dominated European musical developments for at least a century and a half prior to 1900. The basic seeds for these national developments were to lead to new assumptions of harmonic construction and progression that were largely removed from the ultrachromaticism of the German late-Romantic composers. In the following chapters, these national divergencies are more fully revealed by means of a study of those developments that were to grow out of the earliest extensive scientific investigations of national folk idioms. Two extremes become apparent between the ultrachromaticism of German late-Romantic music and the pentatonic–diatonic modality of peasant folk-songs.

SUGGESTED READINGS

ELLIOTT ANTOKOLETZ. "Interval Cycles in Stravinsky's Early Ballets," *Journal of the American Musicological Society* 39/3 (Fall 1986): 578–614.

BÉLA BARTÓK, *Essays,* ed. Benjamin Suchoff (New York: St. Martin's Press, 1976), including: "Autobiography (1921)," p. 408–411. Published originally as "Selbstbiographie," in *Musikblätter des Anbruch* (Vienna) 3/5 (March 1921): 87–90; "The Influence of Folk Music on the Art Music of Today," pp. 316–319. Published originally as "Der Einfluss der Volksmusik auf die heutige Kunstmusik," *Melos* (Berlin) I/17 (October

---

[37] George Perle, "Scriabin's Self-Analyses," *Music Analysis* (August 1984): 103–104.

[38] Ibid., p. 104.

1920): 384–386; No. 2 (February 1930): 66–67; "Harvard Lectures," 354–392. MSS of four lectures given during February 1943. Published originally in *Journal of the American Musicological Society* (Richmond) 19/2 (Summer 1966): 232–243.

ARTHUR BERGER.   "Problems of Pitch Organization in Stravinsky," *Perspectives of New Music* 2 (1963): 27–28.

PIERRE BOULEZ.   "Stravinsky Remains," *Notes of an Apprenticeship,* trans. Herbert Weinstock (New York: Alfred A. Knopf, 1968, pp. 72–145.

MAURICE EMMANUEL.   *Pelléas et Mélisande de Claude Debussy: Étude et Analyse* (Paris: Éditions Mellottée, 1926, 2/1950).

LAWRENCE GILMAN.   *Debussy's Pelléas et Mélisande: A Guide to the Opera* (New York: G. Schirmer, 1907).

ROY HOWAT.   *Debussy in Proportion: A Musical Analysis* (Cambridge: Cambridge University Press, 1983).

EDWARD LOCKSPEISER.   *Debussy* (New York: McGraw-Hill Book Company, 1936; rev. J. M. Dent & Sons Ltd., 1963).

JANN PASLER, ed.   *Confronting Stravinsky: Man, Musician, and Modernist* (Berkeley and Los Angeles: University of California Press, 1986), including: Jann Pasler, "Music and Spectacle in *Petrushka* and *The Rite of Spring*," pp. 53–81; Richard Taruskin, "From Subject to Style: Stravinsky and the Painters," pp. 16–38.

———.   "*Pelléas* and Power: Forces Behind the Reception of Debussy's Opera," *19th Century Music* 10/3 (Spring 1987): 243–264.

GEORGE PERLE.   "Scriabin's Self-Analyses," *Music Analysis* 3 (August 1984): 101–122.

———.   *Serial Composition and Atonality* (6th ed., rev., Berkeley and Los Angeles: University of California Press, 1991), p. 40–44 (on nondodecaphonic serial composition in Debussy, Scriabin, and Roslavets).

NICOLAI RIMSKY-KORSAKOV.   *My Musical Life*, ed. Carl Van Vechten, trans. Judah A. Joffe (New York: Alfred A. Knopf, 1923), p. 72.

BORIS DE SCHLOEZER.   *Scriabin: Artist and Mystic,* Eng. trans. by Nicolas Slonimsky (Berkeley and Los Angeles: University of California Press, 1987).

IGOR STRAVINSKY AND ROBERT CRAFT.   *Conversations with Igor Stravinsky* (Berkeley and Los Angeles: University of California Press, 1980), including: Claude Debussy letter to Igor Stravinsky, pp. 54–55.

RICHARD TARUSKIN.   "Chernomor to Kashchei: Harmonic Sorcery; Or, Stravinsky's 'Angle,'" *Journal of the American Musicological Society* 38/1 (Spring 1985): 79–142.

———.   "Russian Folk Melodies in *The Rite of Spring*," *Journal of the American Musicological Society* 33/3 (1980): 501–543.

PIETER C. VAN DEN TOORN.   *The Music of Igor Stravinsky* (New Haven: Yale University Press, 1983), pp. 1–177 (on the Russian period).

———.   *Stravinsky and The Rite of Spring* (Berkeley and Los Angeles: University of California Press, 1987).

ERIC WALTER WHITE.   *Stravinsky: The Composer and His Works* (Berkeley and Los Angeles: University of California Press, 1966).

5 Béla Bartók in Eastern Europe and the United States

BASIC SOURCES OF BARTÓK'S STYLE Béla Bartók (1881–1945) was born in the town of Nagyszentmiklós in the Torontál district of Hungary. When two-thirds of Hungarian territory was distributed among Rumania, Yugoslavia, and Czechoslovakia after the signing of the Treaty of Trianon in June of 1920, Bartók's birthplace was absorbed into the western tip of Rumania and renamed Sînnicolau Mare. This national tragedy was to have great psychological ramifications for Bartók in the course of his personal and musical development. He expressed recurrently his grief and pessimism, and advocated a philosophy based on desire for brotherhood among nations. The evolution of his musical aesthetics is a direct reflection of this philosophy, and as a result of his broad international interests and activities, he was to absorb both divergent folk- and art-music sources, and he ultimately created a highly original musical language and style.

In the late nineteenth and early twentieth centuries, several conflicting musical forces became evident in Europe, the most prominent of which were *German late Romanticism, French impressionism,* and the *folk music of Eastern Europe.* Increasing nationalist demands during the decades of international tension prior to the First World War contributed to the independent developments of these forces. Non-Germanic composers began to react against the ultrachromaticism of the Wagner-Strauss period as they turned away from the long tradition of German musical hegemony toward the new spheres of influence in France and Eastern Europe. These conditions served as the social and musical framework from which Bartók's art was to emerge.

Bartók's pioneering musical role is best understood in the context of international political developments. As part of a dual monarchy, Hungary was absorbed into the German political sphere as a member of the Triple Alliance (which included Germany, the Austro-Hungarian Empire, and Italy); in 1918, Hungary suffered defeat along with Germany and Austria. Ruled by the "Germanized" Magyar aristocracy, the Hungarian peasants and national minorities (especially Rumanians, Serbo-Croatians, and Slovaks) opposed the domination of their country by the Austrian Hapsburgs. Intense nationalistic sentiment had already burst forth in the Hungarian Revolution of 1848, which was led by the patriot Lajos Kossuth. While the Hungarians achieved independence, this autonomy was short-lived. In 1849, Austria, with the aid of Russia and the rebellious Slavic and Rumanian minorities, ruthlessly suppressed Kossuth's nationalist regime.

GERMANIC MUSICAL INFLUENCES FROM 1897 TO 1902

Bartók ardently felt the nationalist spirit, but his musical training and knowledge were deeply rooted in the Germanic tradition. His early compositions, dating from the 1890s in Pozsony (now Bratislava, Czechoslovakia), reveal a distinctly Brahmsian style, which was developed during his student days at the Royal Academy of Music in Budapest (1899–1903) by his intensive studies of the chromatic scores of Wagner (particularly *Tristan und Isolde*). However, Bartók soon became discouraged with the possibilities of further evolving his style in the Germanic tradition. This problem was temporarily resolved when he heard a performance of Richard Strauss' symphonic poem, *Also sprach Zarathustra*, by the Philharmonic Orchestra on February 2, 1902, which led Bartók out of a period of stagnation: the Strauss work contained "the seeds for a new life."[1] In the same year, Bartók transcribed Strauss' *Ein Heldenleben*, for piano solo: his memorized, virtuoso performance made a profound impression both in Budapest, and later, at the Tonkünstlerverein in Vienna on January 26, 1903.

His own compositions began to reveal the harmonic, tonal, and motivic influences of Strauss. This idiom guided him toward the creation of a new type of chromatic melody, later exemplified in such works as movement I of his *First String Quartet* (1908–1909).[2] Although the chromatic line of the quartet evokes the romantic restlessness expressed in the musical thread of Wagner's *Tristan und Isolde*, Bartók's freer tonality (largely achieved by sudden major-minor mixtures) and almost continuously dissonant texture (based on pervasive use of appoggiaturas and sevenths) may be primarily associated with the more daring harmonic fabric of Strauss' works, for example, his opera *Elektra* (1906–1908).[3] Both the Bartók quartet and Strauss opera are based on the assumptions of triadic harmony, but their constantly shifting tonalities frequently result in polytonal relations.

Straussian characteristics can also be observed in other works of the same year. Both the early *Concerto for Violin and Orchestra,* Op. posth., and *Two Portraits* for orchestra are based on the same leitmotif, D–F♯–A–C♯, which is also recognizable in the *First String Quartet* as well as No. XIV of the *Fourteen Bagatelles for Piano,* Op. 6. This leitmotif has programmatic significance, symbolizing the violinist Stefi Geyer with whom Bartók was in love. In addition to the romantic feature, these works are also structurally related: Bartók had incorporated the first movement of the then unpublished *Con-*

---

[1] See Bartók's "Selbsbiographie," which appeared originally in several versions, the first in *Musikblätter des Anbruch* (Vienna) 3/5 (March 1921): 87–90; see also *Béla Bartók Essays,* ed. Benjamin Suchoff (New York: St. Martin's Press, 1976), p. 410.

[2] Elliott Antokoletz, *The Music of Béla Bartók: A Study of Tonality and Progression in Twentieth-Century Music* (Berkeley and Los Angeles: University of California Press, 1984), p. 14.

[3] This relationship should not be construed to mean that the quartet is influenced by the opera but, rather, that they demonstrate parallel developments. While the general impact of Strauss' idiom on Bartók was decisive, he expressed a specific dislike for *Elektra* in an essay written in 1910; see "Elektra. Strauss Richard operája," *A zene* (Budapest) 2/4 (April 1910): 57–58. See also *Béla Bartók Essays,* n.1, above, p. 446.

certo[4] into the *Two Portraits,* with some alteration, and combined it with an orchestral version of *Bagatelle No. 14.*[5]

INFLUENCE OF LISZT, THE *MAGYAR NÓTA,* AND FIRST CONTACT WITH AUTHENTIC HUNGARIAN FOLK MUSIC (1902–1905)

In the spring of 1903 resurgent patriotic movements throughout Hungary further roused Bartók's nationalism. He adopted national dress, spoke only Hungarian, and dropped the prefix "von" from his family name (some of his early compositions had been signed "Béla von Bartók"). As a patriotic gesture, he wrote *Kossuth,* a symphonic poem on the life of a revolutionary hero.[6]

Stemming from Bartók's piano studies with István Thomán, one of Liszt's most gifted pupils, we find the influence of Liszt as much in evidence as that of Strauss. Bartók had already given his debut in Budapest in October 1901, with a performance of Liszt's *Sonata in B Minor.* The characteristic style of Liszt's *Hungarian Rhapsodies* is apparent in Bartók's "Fantasy II" and "Scherzo" from *Four Piano Pieces* (1903), *Rhapsody* for piano, Op. 1 (1904), and especially *Kossuth.* At the same time, other works written between 1902 and 1905 had also begun to reveal Bartók's inclination toward the development of a new national style, in particular, the *Four Songs* set to the folk-like texts of Lajos Pósa, the *Sonata* for violin and piano, and the *Piano Quintet.*

This new style, derived from the Hungarian urban folk song (that is, popular art song or *Magyar nóta*), developed in the nineteenth century from a similar type of German urban folk song known as the "Volkstümlichlied." These songs, usually with piano accompaniment, are generally strophic in form with an architectonic (or rounded) ABA structure. Numerous Hungarian imitations were composed by amateurs from the educated classes and disseminated along with the *verbunkos* (recruiting dance) and *csárdás* by urban gypsy bands.[7] (The *Magyar nóta* was not exclusively urban, however, since gypsy bands were invited to peasant gatherings in small villages as well.)

It was in 1904 that Bartók first came into contact with authentic Hungarian folk music. He heard a peasant girl named Lidi Dósa singing a popular art song with modal inflection and attenuated stanza structure. Her rendition was remarkably different from the gypsy-styled café versions,

---

[4] Published by Boosey and Hawkes (London) posthumously in 1958.

[5] Halsey Stevens, *The Life and Music of Béla Bartók* (New York: Oxford University Press, 1953; revised 1964), p. 265.

[6] Béla Bartók Letters, ed. János Demény, trans. Péter Balabán and István Farkas, rev. Elizabeth West and Colin Mason (London: Faber & Faber; Budapest: Corvina Press, 1971), p. 29.

[7] See Béla Bartók, *The Hungarian Folk Song,* ed. Benjamin Suchoff (Albany: State University of New York Press, 1981), pp. xv-xvi; also see Benjamin Suchoff, "Ethnomusicological Roots of Béla Bartók's Musical Language," *World of Music* 29/1 (1987): 43.

which he originally thought, as did Liszt and Brahms, to be the authentic folk music of his country. Thus, Bartók was impelled to investigate the musical repertory of Lidi Dósa's native Transylvanian village and its environs as a new source for his own compositions. Together with Zoltán Kodály (1882–1967), with whom Bartók had formed a lasting relationship, the two young composers visited Hungarian villages in July of 1906 to collect and record peasant music—Bartók in the eastern part of the country, Kodály in the north.

BARTÓK'S FIRST FOLK-MUSIC INVESTIGATIONS, HIS DISCOVERY OF DEBUSSY, AND EARLY COMPOSITIONAL RESULTS (1905 THROUGH WORLD WAR I)

Various composers in the late nineteenth and early twentieth centuries turned to the modalities of their native folk music as the basis for composition, but it was Bartók who most thoroughly and extensively transformed these modes into the materials of a new musical language. In his autobiography, Bartók discussed the influence of these sources:

> The outcome of these studies was of decisive influence upon my work, because it freed me from the tyrannical rule of the major and minor keys. The greater part of the collected treasure, and the more valuable part, was in old ecclesiastical or old Greek modes, or based on more primitive (pentatonic) scales, and the melodies were full of most free and varied rhythmic phrases and changes of tempi, played both *rubato* and *giusto*. It became clear to me that the old modes, which had been forgotten in our music, had lost nothing of their vigor. Their new employment made new rhythmic combinations possible. This new way of using the diatonic scale brought freedom from the rigid use of the major and minor keys, and eventually led to a new conception of the chromatic scale, every tone of which came to be considered of equal value and could be used freely and independently.[8]

In his desire to move away from traditional Western influences, Bartók had to find the means for deriving new pitch structures to harmonize both authentic folk melodies of Eastern origin and his own original inventions, which might include imitations of folk melodies. The folk tunes themselves showed him new ways of harmonization. Using Edison phonograph cylinders, he and Kodály were able to record multiple thousands of melodies on the spot, and later transcribe (notate), analyze, and order them according to a modified classification system developed by the Finnish ethnologist Ilmari Krohn (1867–1960). Later, Bartók independently developed his own methodological approach to the classification of musical folklore. In Bartók's early explorations into the sources of Hungarian peasant music, certain musi-

---

[8] See "Selbstbiographie," n.1, above, 87–90; see also *Béla Bartók Essays,* n.1, above, p. 410.

cal styles became apparent. He found that the peasants, in their oral musical tradition, tended to transform the elements of their music, giving rise to numerous variants of one melody or another.[9] Some peasant groups who had been minimally exposed to outside cultural influences (for instance, segments of the Rumanian population) tended to preserve their old traditions without change. Other peasant groups, having had communication with surrounding tribes and with urban centers, absorbed foreign elements into their existing music, creating a new style that probably began its development only at the turn of the eighteenth century. Bartók found older and newer styles present alongside one another in some nations (for example, Moravian and Slovak nations), while a single homogeneous style several centuries old was preserved in others.

Among the Hungarian peasants, a new style developed in the nineteenth century side-by-side with the older traditions, gradually replacing them. Peasants found it desirable to imitate certain cultural features of the upper classes from the towns, thereby absorbing and transforming them into a new, yet entirely homogeneous style. With greater intercommunication, foreign elements from neighboring peoples (from the Rumanians and Slovaks especially, coming mostly by way of the West) infiltrated Hungarian villages. This acculturation resulted in melodies exhibiting heterogeneous ethnic characteristics. Thus, of the diversely collected folk materials, Bartók distinguished three categories: (1) melodies in the old Hungarian peasant-music style; (2) melodies in the new Hungarian peasant-music style; and (3) a group of diverse melodies exhibiting no unity of style.[10] Bartók considered the old and new styles far more significant than the mixed style, and it is these that pervade his own musical compositions.

In order to understand Bartók's entire compositional output, one must have a fundamental knowledge of the folk-song characteristics. Among the characteristics of the old style is a four-line stanzaic structure based on nonarchitectonic (nonrounded) forms such as ABCD, ABBC, and A^5B^5AB, which are found chiefly to be in a rhythmically free vocal style (*parlando rubato*), while other nonrounded forms generally occur in a rhythmically strict dance style (*tempo giusto*).[11] All four lines consist of an equal number of syllables, the oldest tunes of 8 or 12 syllables per line, the slightly later ones of 6, while others consist of either 7, 9, 10, or 11. Among the characteristics of the new style is an architectonic (rounded) four-line structure such as AA^5BA, AA^5A^5A, and more recently ABBA and AABA. Here, the stanzaic structure usually consists of an unequal and often larger number of syllables per line. These tunes are based on a rhythmic style of *variable tempo giusto,* i.e, in the more complex style of *parlando rubato,* but no longer rubato. The old

---

[9] See Bartók, "Hungarian Peasant Music" *Musical Quarterly* 19/3 (July 1933): 267–289, and *Béla Bartók Essays,* ibid., p. 81.

[10] See *Béla Bartók Essays,* ibid., p. 84.

[11] See Bartók, *The Hungarian Folk Song,* n.7, above, p. 21.

style has a pentatonic scalar basis for the melodies (invariably in the minor-modal form, G–B♭–C–D–F), with occasional transformations of the pentatonic scale into the Dorian, Phrygian, or Aeolian modes.[12] The new style has a heptatonic modal basis for the melodies, including primarily the latter modal forms with strong pentatonic inflections, as well as Mixolydian and major scales—sometimes strongly felt. The Lydian mode, which is strongly characteristic of certain Slovak melodies, is never found in the old Hungarian melodies.[13]

From the pentatonic scale, G–B♭–C–D–F, the basis of the oldest of the Hungarian peasant tunes, Bartók derived special limited possibilities for harmonization. These included two triads, G–B♭–D and B♭–D–F (one major, the other minor), the minor-seventh chord, G–B♭–D–F, and the inversions of these chordal structures. Bartók traced the consonant use of the minor-seventh chord to the old pentatonic melodies, where the seventh appears as an interval of equal importance to the third and fifth. Since these intervals were frequently heard as having equal value in the linear succession, it seemed natural to make them sound equal when used simultaneously. Also, the frequent use of fourth intervals in the pentatonic melodies suggested the use of fourth chords.[14] In December 1906, after Bartók's first expedition with Kodály to collect and to study Hungarian peasant music, the two composers jointly arranged and published *Twenty Hungarian Folksongs* for voice and piano *(Magyar népdalok),* in which the modalities of the tunes already showed a weakening of traditional dominant-tonic relations. For instance, the bass progression of the triads in the first phrase of No. 6 outlines a minor-seventh chord. The latter is a substructure of the pentatonic scale (C–E♭–F–G–B♭), which is prevalent in the C-Aeolian folk tune. Tonal staticism is also produced to some degree by the sustaining of a single third or fourth, as in the harmonization of No. 3. These early investigations culminated in Bartók's many articles and his classic study, *A magyar népdal* (Hungarian Folksong), published in Budapest in 1924.

As Hungarian cultural life became reoriented to that of France, Bartók found yet another source for his musical language in the works of Debussy.[15] Bartók's appointment in 1907 to the Academy of Music in Budapest as teacher of piano was important for his development in both areas. Firstly, it permitted him to settle in Hungary and continue his investigations of folk music. Secondly, at the urging of Kodály (appointed as a composition teacher there), he began to study the music of Debussy thoroughly. According to the contents of Bartók's library (now in the Bartók Archívum in

---

[12] Bartók established the "tonus finalis" of G as the basis of all his modal folk-tune transcriptions.

[13] See Béla Bartók, "La musique populaire hongroise," *Revue Musicale* 2/1 (November 1921): 8–22, and *Béla Bartók Essays,* n.1, above, p. 66.

[14] Each of these pentatonic derivations is discussed by Bartók in "The Folk Songs of Hungary," *Pro Musica* (1928): 28–35, and in *Béla Bartók Essays,* pp. 334–336.

[15] See Béla Bartók, "Hongrie," *La revue musicale* 19/2 (December 1938): 436.

Budapest), Bartók purchased Debussy's *String Quartet* and other works in October of 1907, and, between 1907 and 1911, a number of the piano pieces, including *Pour le piano*, *L'isle joyeuse*, *Images I* and *II*, and *Préludes I*.[16]

Bartók's own *Quatre nénies* (Four Dirges), Op. 9a, reveals significant connections to the Debussy works, not only in the use of French titles but also in the prominent use of pentatonic formations in the *Second Dirge*. Bartók was surprised to find "pentatonic phrases" in Debussy's work similar to those found in Hungarian peasant music, attributing this to influences of folk music from Eastern Europe, particularly Russia. Mussorgsky was a major forerunner of this tendency, and there is evidence that Debussy acquired certain features of folk music primarily from the Russian composer. More extensive similarities between the musical languages of Bartók and Debussy may be seen in the use of modal and whole-tone formations, for example, in Bartók's *First String Quartet* (1908–1909) and his opera, *Duke Bluebeard's Castle* (1911). The latter work is part of the same Maeterlinck trilogy to which Debussy's *Pelléas et Mélisande* belongs, so the pervasive interactions of modal and whole-tone material in these symbolist and impressionist contexts hardly appear to be coincidental.

The *Eight Hungarian Folksongs* for voice and piano (1907–1917) were among Bartók's earliest folk-song arrangements for concert performance. The first five were collected in 1907 during his folk-song expedition to the Csík District of Transylvania. The last three were collected from Hungarian soldiers in 1916–1917, when expeditions to the villages were severely restricted by the war. These were based on soldiers' texts, and both sets were joined in one volume, published in 1922. Six of the eight songs belong to the old style, four of which are exclusively pentatonic, and pentatonic segments are prominent in the vocal lines of two songs that are otherwise modally heptatonic. In addition to the folk tunes of Nos. I, II, IV, and V, which are exclusively E-pentatonic, those of Nos. III (in Eb-Aeolian) and VIII (in D-Aeolian) are cadentially based on pentatonic melodic segments. In contrast, the vocal cadences in Nos. VI (in E-Dorian) and VII (in F-Phrygian) are defined unambiguously in terms of their respective heptatonic modes.[17]

A comparison of the *First* and *Eighth Songs* illustrates the basic differences between the old and new folk styles, respectively, as well as how Bartók derived his harmonic materials from the tunes to transform the folk idiom into an original art-music language. During his 1907 collecting tour, Bartók first became aware of the essential role of pentatony in the oldest of the Hungarian peasant tunes, and in this year also came in contact with the pentatonic phrases and pianistic figurations in Debussy's music. In correspondence with the old style, the four-line stanzaic structure of the *First Song* ("Black is the Earth"), which is an expression of unrequited love, is based on

---

[16] See Anthony Cross, "Debussy and Bartók, *Musical Times* 108 (1967): 126.

[17] All eight songs are discussed in detail by Antokoletz, *The Music of Béla Bartók*, n.2, above, pp. 32–50.

a nonrounded ABAB scheme with an isometric structure of eleven syllables per line. The rhythmic style of the E-pentatonic vocal line is in *parlando rubato,* but the specific rhythmic pattern of each vocal phrase (as manifested unambiguously in the second vocal phrase, mm. 7–8) is actually derived from a still older *tempo-giusto* dance rhythm consisting of eight short notes followed by a short and two long notes. The initial vocal phrase, which is derived from this pattern, reveals how the peasants, by traditionally adding words to the *tempo-giusto* dance rhythm, distorted the lengths of the short notes to produce an irregular and free *rubato* style.

It is in the piano accompaniment that we find a significant point of departure for the development of Bartók's individual harmonic language. The linear pentatonic properties of the folk tune are projected into the harmonic structure, where they serve as the framework for chromatic unfolding of triads and seventh chords that produce expanded modal pitch collections. The E-pentatonic pitch-content is projected into the bass line, where it is expanded into a complete statement of the E-Phrygian mode. The contrapuntal alignment of the E-Phrygian bass against the E-pentatonic vocal line throughout serves, in this otherwise nonfunctional context, to establish the exclusive tonal priority of E: in the first half of the song (Ex. 5–1a), the bass line moves from the tonic (E) to an upper-neighbor sixth (C) at the first cadence (m. 6) and back to the E tonic at the second cadence (m. 8); in the second half (mm. 9ff.), the bass line moves from the fifth degree (B) through the passing fourth degree (A) at the first cadence (m. 13) to the final E-Phrygian descent (G–F–E). The E-pentatonic collection, established in the introduction as a scale figure (E–G–A–B–D) that alternates with its arpeggiated tonic minor-seventh chord (E–G–B–D), forms the harmonic basis (at mm. 3 and 8) of the first and last notes of the tune (seventh degree, D, and tonic, E). While the overall harmonic root progression is determined by the E-Phrygian bass outline, the local harmonic progression between these two pentatonic points expands the E-pentatonic pitch-content to larger E-modal collections. At m. 3, the second-inversion seventh chord, E–G–A–C♯, contains the first chromatic element (C♯) outside the E-pentatonic scale, expanding the latter to an incomplete E-Dorian collection (E–[]–G–A–B–C♯–D). At the cadence of the first phrase (mm. 5–6), a local progression (V_{65}/VI to VI), which microtonicizes the upper-neighbor bass note, C, presents two new notes, F and C. The latter, a chromatic lowering of the second and sixth degrees (F♯ and C♯) of the preceding E-Dorian collection, contributes to the establishment of the E-Phrygian mode (E–F–G–A–B–C–D).

The significance of this harmonic juxtaposition of the E-Dorian and E-Phrygian collections is that together they expand symmetrically around the common E-pentatonic nucleus (Ex. 5–1b). The one nonmodal pitch-class (E♭) of this song (m. 7) is omitted from the analogous point in the second half of the song. Nevertheless, it too belongs to the overall polymodal symmetry, [E♭]–E–F–F♯–G–A–B–C–C♯–D–[E♭]. These modal relations, in an otherwise still tertian harmonic context, are an early development that fore-

EXAMPLE 5–1. Bartók, *First Song:* mm. 3–8; (b) symmetrical polymodal expansion around E-pentatonic nucleus

shadows a new concept of symmetrically filling in musical space. Thus, the pentatonic structure of the folk tune is employed as a new means of harmonic and melodic unification: it serves as a common symmetrical segment between two larger heptatonic modal sets.

In correspondence with the new Hungarian folk-song style, the four-line stanzaic structure of the *Eighth Song* ("Snow is melting"), in which a soldier's pleasure is at an end as he must return to his barracks in Vienna, is based on a rounded AA′BA scheme (with BA refrain) with a heterometric structure of 16, 14, 14, and 16 syllables per line. The rhythmic style of the D-Aeolian vocal line is based on more complex patterns in *variable tempo giusto*. Also characteristic of the new style is a wider vocal range, which spans a minor tenth (from D to F), in contrast to the *First Song* with a range of a minor seventh. Bartók's transformation of the folk-song source is again seen in the piano accompaniment, where melodic and harmonic pentatonic segments serve as a frame of reference for the expansion to larger polymodal chromatic relations. Furthermore, the folk tune itself implies a larger D-Aeolian expansion (D–E–F–G–A–[]–C) of the basic D-pentatonic frame (D–F–G–A–C), an essential melodic characteristic of the new Hungarian style.

EXPANDED FOLK-MUSIC INVESTIGATIONS AND FIRST MATURE COMPOSITIONS

Following his initial investigations of Hungarian folk music in 1906, Bartók also began to explore the folk music of other nations. Unlike Kodály, whose folk-music activities remained limited to the Hungarian villages, Bartók's increasingly international interests led him to collect the melodies of the Slovaks in the autumn of the same year, and the melodies of the Rumanians in the summer of 1909. In 1910, he made his first attempts to collaborate with both Slovaks and Rumanians in a project for the publication of scientific studies for his respective folk-music collections. In 1913, his collecting tours also took him to the Biskra District in Algeria, where he recorded Arab folk music. These as well as other expeditions were to result in the collection, transcription, and analysis of thousands of melodies from Eastern Europe (Bulgaria, Hungary, Rumania, Ruthenia, Slovakia, and Yugoslavia), from North Africa, and from Turkey in 1936. His scholarly contributions to the field of folk-music research have been published in various languages, in many books, and in a substantial number of shorter essays.[18]

Bartók's expanded folk-music research has also resulted in wider influences that were absorbed into his own musical compositions. The Slovak collection provided source material for *Four Slovakian Folksongs* for voice and piano (the first three ca. 1907, the fourth in 1916); the fifth piece of the *Fourteen Bagatelles,* Op. 6, for piano (1908; based on a Slovakian folk song from the province of Gömör); the second volume of piano pieces from *Gyermekeknek* ("For Children," 1908–1909); and, between 1917 and 1924, transcriptions for vocal solo, and male and female choruses.

In the *Bagatelles,* which represented for Bartók "a new piano style that appeared in reaction to the exuberance of the romantic piano music of the nineteenth century," we find, in addition to the general exploitation of progressive compositional techniques (polytonality in No. I, ostinato rhyth-

---

[18] See Elliott Antokoletz, *Béla Bartók: A Guide to Research* (New York: Garland Publishing, Inc., 1988), under "Primary Sources."

mic patterns in Nos. II and V, and fourth chords derived modally in No. XI), experiments with the irregular rhythm (No. V) and tritone (e.g., Nos. VIII, XI, and XIII) of the Slovaks.[19] According to Bartók,

> Rumanian and Slovak folk songs show a highly interesting treatment of the tritone (the first, in a sort of Mixolydian mode with minor sixth, the others, in a Lydian mode). . . . These forms brought about the free use of the augmented fourth, diminished fifth, and of [certain] chords. . . . Through inversion, and by placing these chords in juxtaposition one above the other, many different chords are obtained and with them the freest melodic as well as harmonic treatment of the twelve tones of our present day harmonic system.[20]

Such derivation of tritone-based harmonies as well as melodic segments from the principal tones of the Slovakian Lydian mode (i.e., including the tonic, fourth, and seventh degrees) may be observed, for instance, in No. XI. In No. XI, diatonic considerations dictate that certain intervallic mutations must occur in the harmonic progressions based on perfect-fourth chords. These intervallic mutations include three-note simultaneities in the right hand, each segment of which joins a perfect fourth and a tritone (specific instances include C–F–B at mm. 1, 3, and 8; B♭–E–A at mm. 1 and 3; and F–B–E at mm. 6 and 7). While the perfect-fourth chords are exclusively diatonic, this mutated type can be found in both the diatonic and octatonic sets of the piece.[21] This three-note mutated structure emerges prominently at mm. 30–33 as a melodic cell in a series of linear overlappings. At the Vivo, which immediately precedes the recapitulation (m. 61), overlapping transpositions of the cell appear as the basis of the melodic line, forming the four-note symmetry F–B♭–B–E (Ex. 5–2). This four-note figure represents a transformation of the original three-note modal segment into a larger abstract forma-

EXAMPLE 5–2. Bartók, *Bagatelle No. XI,* Op. 6, mm. 55–60

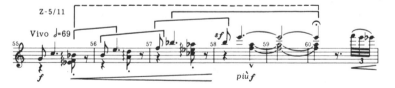

[19] See *Béla Bartók Essays,* n.1, above, pp. 432–433.
[20] See Bartók, "The Folk Songs of Hungary," n.14, above, 28–35; see also ibid., pp. 36–38.
[21] See Antokoletz, *The Music of Béla Bartók,* n.2, above, pp. 206–208.

tion, having little to do with the original diatonic material. The latter double-tritone tetrachordal structure, in all of its transpositions, also pervades the closing measures of No. VIII.[22]

Bartók's Rumanian research also broadened the scope of his compositions, leading to an early arrangement of a Rumanian folk song in the fifth of the *Vázlatok* ("Sketches," 1908–1910) and a number of other transcriptions in 1915, including the *Sonatina, Rumanian Folk Dances from Hungary, Rumanian Christmas Songs (Colinde),* all of which are for piano, *Two Rumanian Folksongs* for a four-part women's chorus, and *Nine Rumanian Songs* for voice and piano (unpublished). Influences from his Arab folk-music research in 1913 are evident in movement III of his *Piano Suite*, Op. 14 (1916), and the *Second String Quartet* (1915–1917). Bartók's plans to expand his sphere of research to Russian folk music were prevented by the outbreak of World War I in 1914, and, two years later, Rumania's military involvement forced discontinuation of further expeditions to Transylvania.

TOWARD SYNTHESIS OF DIVERGENT ART- AND FOLK-MUSIC SOURCES

Despite the reaction against the prevailing Germanic influences in Budapest at the turn of the century, and the search for new sources of artistic inspiration, many of Bartók's compositions continued to manifest certain characteristics prevalent in the Germanic musical tradition. Fundamental features of this tradition were to be absorbed into his compositions and eventually synthesized with those of the peasant melodies and French musical sources. However, in his first, mature works of 1908–1909, these sources were only juxtaposed in a given movement or work, rather than synthesized or transformed.

In terms of the Germanic style, the *First String Quartet,* like Strauss' opera *Elektra,* is historically transitional in its interaction of triadic harmonies with chromatic melodic lines that unfold according to nonfunctional voice-leading patterns.[23] Both works epitomize late Romantic music on the threshold of a new chromatic idiom. While Strauss never crossed that threshold, Bartók's *First Quartet* was only the beginning of his new chromaticism. In the A sections of the ABA form of the opening quasi-fugue movement, the thematically amorphous linear motions appear to determine the nontraditional chromatic progression of triads.

In contrast, the middle section of the movement (No. 6, mm. 5ff.) suddenly moves into a polytonal (or "Phrygian-colored C major") *parlando-rubato* style with a cello drone typical of certain Eastern-European folk music.

---

[22] Ibid., p. 79.

[23] With the disappearance of the traditional triad as the basic harmonic premise in the early part of the twentieth century, greater importance was placed on the interval as a primary means of harmonic and melodic integration.

The diatonic viola theme seems to be a transformation of the chromatic intervallic contour of the A section, so some integration occurs between the Germanic chromaticism and the folk style. The last half of this section (No. 8, mm. 5ff.) abruptly moves into another style change, in which the quiet flow of inverted triads in parallel motion appears to be a direct reference to certain impressionistic passages of Debussy's or Ravel's string quartets. These three divergent sources are also reflected throughout the work by the juxtapositions of chromatic, pentatonic/modal, and whole-tone passages.

The latter two sources (Hungarian folk music and French impressionism) are especially evident in Bartók's opera *Duke Bluebeard's Castle* (1911), based on Maeterlinck. At a competition for a national type of opera, *Bluebeard* was rejected as "unperformable" because its genuine Hungarian qualities seemed unrecognizable to an audience accustomed to hearing Italianate or Germanized settings of Hungarian texts. Bartók strictly preserved the Hungarian language accents in his musical setting of the libretto by Béla Balázs. The archaic syllabic structure is set almost entirely in the old *parlando-rubato* folk-song style, producing a kind of "recitative opera."[24] The Hungarian text—and this is true of the orchestral phrases as well—is appropriately based on eight syllables per line, which is one of the isometric stanzaic patterns that the composer found in the oldest of the Hungarian folk melodies.

Due to the failure of this work as well as of the New Hungarian Musical Association (UMZE), which Bartók and other young Hungarian composers organized to promote new Hungarian music, Bartók withdrew from public musical life in 1912. At the outbreak of World War I in 1914, Bartók also had to give up much of his ethnomusicological fieldwork. He devoted more of his time to the systematic arrangement of the large quantities of folk material he had accumulated. This new stage in work with the folk material and the greater amount of time that he was able to spend in composing account in part for the developments in his compositional creativity.

Bartók's first "products" of this period, in addition to the Rumanian and Slovak settings mentioned earlier, were a ballet, *The Wooden Prince* (1916), the *Piano Suite* (1916), two sets of songs of five songs each, *Öt dal*, Op. 15 (1915), and *Öt dal*, Op. 16 (1916), the latter composed to poems of Endre Ady, and the *Second String Quartet* (1915–1917). The works of this period, especially the *Second Quartet,* reveal a greater fusion of those diverse sources found in his earlier compositions. In these, there is a tendency toward more pervasive manifestations of the folk-music sources, including the influences of Arab folk music. The *Second Quartet* reveals, more than any of Bartók's preceding works, a greater transformation of traditional modal elements into abstract pitch formations, and marks a radical break from the harmonic progression of the *First Quartet*. In the large-scale structure of the *Second Quartet,* pitch cells function both as primary sources of melodic and harmonic

---

[24] Sándor Veress, "Bluebeard's Castle," *Béla Bartók: A Memorial Review* (New York: Boosey and Hawkes, 1950): 42.

integration and as means of associating or transforming thematic statements.[25]

END OF WORLD WAR I TO MID-1920s

The war ended with the defeat of the Alliance, the fall of the Hapsburg Empire, and severe political and economic deterioration. Despite these conditions, Bartók was able to produce several significant works between 1918 and 1920, including the *Three Studies,* Op. 18, for piano (1918), a pantomime *The Miraculous Mandarin*, Op. 19 (1919), and the *Eight Improvisations on Hungarian Peasant Songs,* Op. 20, for piano (1920). All three works reveal remarkable developments in style and musical language.

The *Studies* deal with specific pianistic problems which did not occur in the études of Chopin, Debussy, Stravinsky, or Prokofiev.[26] Although they encompass a smaller range of expression, they are far more advanced technically and tonally than his earlier piano works. Particularly notable is a new concern for the extensions and contractions of the pianist's hand. The *Studies* were premièred with the Ady songs (*Öt dal,* Op. 16) and the *Piano Suite,* Op. 14, at one of the "composer's concerts" arranged for Bartók in 1919, though the *Mandarin* was not to be performed in Budapest during the composer's lifetime, despite the profound and striking quality of the music. Part of the antagonism it aroused was due to the nature of its plot.

After the signing of the Treaty of Trianon in 1920, Hungary had lost much of her prewar territory to surrounding nations, including Rumania, Czechoslovakia, and the Kingdom of Serbs, Croats, and Slovenes (now Yugoslavia). This national loss was also a personal tragedy for Bartók: the severed territories were no longer open to the Hungarian folk-music collector. Conditions since the end of the war had already led Bartók to consider an extended leave of absence from his teaching position at the Academy of Music. This was expressed in a letter by Bartók, dated October 23, 1919.[27]

Although Bartók ultimately remained in Hungary and continued to teach at the Academy, he was forced to shift his activities during this period to composition and also began an intensive concert career. This change of activity can be observed in part in his approach to those compositions that continued to include authentic folk melodies, the approach now best described as *composing with folk song* rather than *folk-song arranging*.

In the *Eight Improvisations on Hungarian Peasant Songs,* Op. 20, for piano (1920), the underlying tunes themselves, which were collected from Felsőiregh (in the District of Tolna), Hottó (Zala), Kórógy (Szerém), Csíkgyimes (Csík), Lengyelfalva (Udvarhely), and Diósad (Szilágy), are

---

[25] For an analysis of these relations, see Antokoletz, *The Music of Béla Bartók,* n.2, above, pp. 93ff.

[26] See Stevens, *The Life and Music of Béla Bartók,* n.5, above, p. 125.

[27] See *Béla Bartók Letters,* ed. Demény, n.6, above, p. 144.

secondary to the added materials: the elements of the tunes are systematically developed, modified, and transformed into highly abstract pitch-sets and interactions. For instance, the closing passage (mm. 69ff.) of the *Eighth Improvisation* is a focal point for pitch-set development throughout the work. The folk tune of this piece, which unfolds linearly in octaves, is accompanied by a harmonic progression (Ex. 5–3a) based exclusively on five of the six

EXAMPLE 5–3. Bartók, *Eighth Improvisation,* Op. 20, mm. 69ff.: (a) folk tune and chordal "cell-Z" accompaniment; (b) five of the six cell-Z transpositions, mm. 69ff.

possible transpositions of "cell Z" (Ex. 5–3b).[28] This symmetrical cell, at first appearing to be unrelated to the underlying diatonic folk-tune statement, is actually derived from the latter. The tune begins in the C-Dorian mode (C–D–Eb–F–G–A–Bb–C), but at m. 74 a lowering of the sixth degree, A, to Ab produces a modal shift to C-Aeolian (C–D–Eb–F–G–Ab–Bb–C). The C-Dorian mode contains one tritone, Eb–A; C-Aeolian contains D–Ab. These two tritones together supply the one Z cell, Z–3/9 (Eb–Ab–A–D), that is missing from the accompanying chords. Thus, in the present context, a nontraditional, symmetrical pitch set (cell Z) is structurally derived from the double-tritone property of the folk tune extended bimodally by Bartók.

The structure of the *parlando-rubato* folk melody in the *Third Improvisation* (strain 1, mm. 3–15, right hand) is also the basis for the derivation and

EXAMPLE 5–3 CON'T.

(b)

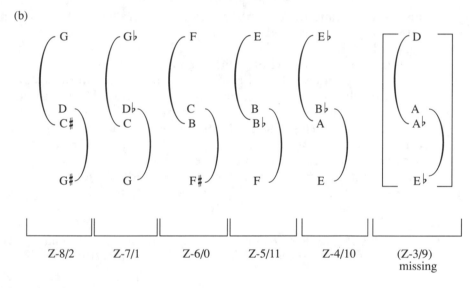

| Z-8/2 | Z-7/1 | Z-6/0 | Z-5/11 | Z-4/10 | (Z-3/9) missing |

[28] See the discussion of this cell, below, in connection with the *Fourth String Quartet*. We will assume a referential order for a given pitch-set, the transposition–number being determined by the "first" note. If we designate pitch-class C as 0 and assign a corresponding number from 0 to 11 for each of the notes of the semitonal scale (C = 0, C♯ = 1, D = 2, Eb = 3 . . . C = 12 or 0), then, for instance, Eb–Ab–A–D will be designated as Z–3. Since Z–3 maintains its pitch content and intervallic order at its tritone transposition, A–D–Eb–Ab (Z–9), we will refer conveniently to it, regardless of its contextual ordering, by both T-nos., hence, Z–3/9.

transformation of abstract symmetrical formations that unfold in the accompaniment. The nondiatonic tune itself, which forms a kind of "mixolydian" variant, D–E–F♯–G–A–B♭–C–D, outlines major and minor (lower and upper) tetrachords, D–E–F♯–G and A–B♭–C–D, which together form a symmetrical scale.[29] In reference to this tune, Bartók stated the following: "Another kind of alteration of the pentatonic scale [D–F–G–A–C] crops up now and then. . . . It is the sharpening of the third degree . . . But even then the pentatonic structure remains so obvious that the origin of all such scales is unmistakable (Nos. . . . 40) . . . The third . . . is sometimes raised and lowered in the course of one tune."[30] A basic symmetrical property (augmented triad, D–F♯–A♯) of this modal variant emerges as an important foreground event in Episode 2 (the quintuplet upbeat to m. 26 through m. 30). The quintuplet figure is initiated by the augmented triad (D–F♯–A♯), which is reiterated throughout the passage. Pitch-class D, the tonality of the basic statement of this modal tune in strain 1, also functions, as does an implied G♯–G♯, as its *axis of symmetry* (D–e–F♯–g–a–B♭–c–D). Throughout episode 2, this augmented triad appears in all three of its harmonic positions (mm. 25–30). These permutations produce a rotating motion around the registrally stable (or invariant) axis tone, D, further establishing the symmetrical connection of this chord with the D-modal variant of strain 1.

The augmented triad D–F♯–A♯ is anticipated in the accompaniment of the first phrase of strain 2 (mm. 19–21) (Ex. 5–4). The succession of major thirds exclusively outlines a five-note segment (D–E–F♯–G♯–A♯) of one of the whole-tone cycles. The pitch content of the latter is constructed symmetrically around D–F♯–A♯, which appears as a local foreground event, for the first time, by the adjacency of the two major thirds, F♯–A♯ and D–F♯. At the quintuplet figure (m. 25), which initiates episode 2, the whole-tone segment (D–E–F♯–G♯–A♯) is explicitly partitioned into the primary augmented triad

EXAMPLE 5–4. Bartók, *Third Improvisation,* Strain 2, mm. 18–21, whole-tone expansion of the symmetrical thematic structure

[29] See Bartók, *The Hungarian Folk Song,* n.7, above, p. 18.
[30] Ibid.

(D–F♯–A♯) and the symmetrically related major third (E–G♯), both of which are held throughout the first phrase of the episode. The whole-tone scale as well as the augmented triad is an abstract transformation of the modal tune.

The significance of Bartók's change of activities in the 1920s can also be seen in his increased contact with international composers and their works. In his two *Sonatas for Violin and Piano* (1921 and 1922), Bartók came closer than in any of his other works to a kind of atonal chromaticism and harmonic serialization typical of the expressionistic works of the Schoenberg school. Bartók once commented that he "wanted to show Schoenberg that one can use all twelve tones and still remain tonal."[31] At about the same time, Schoenberg was producing his first twelve-tone serial works.

In Bartók's works written in the mid-1920s, the transformation of his musical language into further abstractions or fusions of the modal elements of folk music may have been given some direction toward extreme systematization by his contact with his contemporaries and their works: in 1921 he met Ravel and Stravinsky in Paris and in 1922 he participated with members of the Schoenberg circle, as well as Stravinsky, Milhaud, Hindemith, Busoni, and others in the first performances of the International Society for Contemporary Music (ISCM).

In the next few years, Bartók produced little because of his heavy concert schedule and work at the Academy. His most successful work at this time was the *Dance Suite* for orchestra (1923), which was also arranged for solo piano (1925). The work reveals increased economy of material based on a synthesis of a wider variety of folk sources; the first and fourth dances show certain Arab influences, the second, third, and ritornel Hungarian, and the fifth Rumanian. All these sources are synthesized in the finale.[32] Other scholars also point to the combination of modal folk sources in this work.[33]

LAST STYLISTIC PERIOD (1926–1945)

Following *Village Scenes* (1924) for voice and piano, based on five Slovak folk songs, Bartók moved into a new phase of productivity with his piano compositions. In the year 1926 alone, he composed the *Sonata, Out of Doors* cycle of five pieces, *Nine Little Piano Pieces, First Piano Concerto,* and several short compositions that were eventually to become part of the *Mikrokosmos* (completed in 1939), a collection of 153 progressive pieces for didactic purposes.

At the time of the ISCM in London three years earlier (1923), Bartók had met the American composer Henry Cowell. Impressed by the latter's use of tone clusters, Bartók asked him if he could use them in his own composi-

[31] See Yehudi Menuhin, *Unfinished Journey* (New York: Alfred A. Knopf, 1977), p. 165.

[32] See Stevens, *The Life and Music of Béla Bartók,* n. 5, above, p. 270.

[33] Benjamin Suchoff, "The Impact of Italian Baroque Music on Bartók's Music," *Bartók and Kodály Revisited,* ed. György Ránki (Budapest: Akadémiai Kiadó, 1987), pp. 187–188.

tions. Although these piano works of the mid-1920s bear little relationship to the percussive sonorities conceived by Cowell, they nevertheless tended toward greater textural and harmonic density. While Bartók composed these works partly out of the practical necessity to provide himself with a concert repertoire, they also represented in many ways a new stage in the synthesis of his musical language.[34] The *Piano Concerto,* first performed at the ISCM at Frankfurt on July 1, 1927, is representative of this new percussive style, in which the melody is in a simpler folk-like style, while the harmonic dimension is more abstract and dissonant.[35] Another source is also apparent in this, as well as in Bartók's other piano works of 1927. Bartók had toured Italy during 1925, and during this time (in addition to giving performances of Baroque Italian music) he was inspired to investigate contrapuntal techniques in the keyboard works of Benedetto Marcello, Michelangelo Rossi, Azzolino Bernardino della Ciaia, Girolamo Frescobaldi, and Domenico Zipoli, transcribing some of their works for piano.[36]

At the ISCM concert in Baden-Baden on July 26, 1927, Bartók performed his own *Piano Sonata* on the same program as Berg's *Lyric Suite* for string quartet. Shortly afterward, Bartók completed his *Third* and *Fourth String Quartets* (1927 and 1928, respectively). Although the Bartók works show little stylistic resemblance to the lush romantic textures of the *Lyric Suite,* we may observe a superficial yet striking similarity in their common use of exotic instrumental colors as well as certain common assumptions underlying their symmetrical pitch relations. This comparison is not meant to suggest that Bartók was influenced by Berg's use of pitch symmetry, but rather that these quartets of the two composers reveal parallel historical developments; Bartók had already exploited principles of inversional symmetry in No. 2 of his *Bagatelles for Piano,* Op. 6, in 1908, and in many works since that time.

Bartók's move toward ever greater abstraction and synthesis of divergent art- and folk-music sources had reached its most intensive stage of development in the *Fourth Quartet.* The large-scale arch form of the five-movement plan serves as a carefully constructed framework within which Bartók organized diversified melodic, harmonic, and rhythmic formations into a highly systematic network of interrelationships.[37] Despite the more

---

[34] For a detailed study of the stylistic and structural problems in these works, see László Somfai, "Analytical Notes on Bartók's Piano Year of 1926," *Studia musicologica* 26 (1984): 5–58.

[35] See Stevens, *The Life and Music of Béla Bartók,* n.5, above, p. 68.

[36] In addition to a variety of folk sources, the impact of Frescobaldi's toccatas and della Ciaia's Canzone on the *First Concerto* is demonstrated by Suchoff, in "The Impact of Italian Baroque Music," n.33, above, p. 189.

[37] The five movements are related symmetrically, with the first and second mirroring the fifth and fourth, respectively, in tempi and thematic material. The central (slow) movement is enveloped by two scherzo movements. All five movements are in traditional ternary (A–B–A′) forms with codas, the first movement outlining a sonata-allegro plan more specifically: exposition (mm. 1–49), first-theme group (mm. 1–13),

abstract medium, rhythmic and structural properties of folk music are still in evidence nevertheless. Elements from Hungarian and other folk sources provide materials that contribute to the distinctive styles of the different movements. The *tempo-giusto* character of the first movement is balanced by the more complex *variable tempo giusto* of the fifth.[38] In the latter, a motoric Bulgarian ostinato rhythm in a typical unequal-beat dance pattern of 3 + 2 + 3/8 (mm. 11ff.) accompanies the main dance-like theme (mm. 15–18), which is set in an implied, conflicting irregular meter of 4 + 3 + 3/8. This theme is the basis of a folk-like four-line stanzaic structure (unfolding to m. 40). While the successive thematic statements are variants of the initial one, a perfect classical balance is produced by the modified inverted contour relations among them, suggesting a nonrounded form of ABA′B′. The contrasting slow central movement also reveals folk characteristics. The highly embellished *parlando-rubato* cello theme, which is accompanied by a held chord typical of Eastern European dudelsack (bagpipe) drones, suggests a syllabic structure based on one of the old-style *Magyar* rhythmic patterns of eight short notes followed by a cadential figure of a short and two long notes (Ex. 5–5).[39] The rhapsodic melody itself, which appears to derive from the *hora lunga* (long song) that Bartók discovered in Rumanian folk music, has the pastoral quality of the *tárogató,* a Hungarian woodwind instrument shaped like a straight wooden saxophone.[40] Such melodies, common in Bartók's music, are of a "quiet, rather static, but nevertheless florid character, the

---

transition (mm. 14–29), second-theme group (mm. 30–43), closing (mm. 44–49); development (mm. 49–92); recapitulation (mm. 93–134), first-theme group (mm. 93–104), transition (mm. 104–119), second-theme group (mm. 119–126), closing (mm. 126–134); coda (mm. 134–161). Mathematically constructed proportional features of certain movements of the quartet as well as many other works of Bartók are based on the "Golden Section" or "Fibonacci Series," the principles of which have been established and discussed in depth in the theoretical writings of the Hungarian scholar Ernő Lendvai. See his "Einführung in Die Formen und Harmoniewelt Bartóks," in *Béla Bartók, Weg und Werk, Schriften und Briefe,* ed. Bence Szabolcsi (Budapest: Corvina-Verlag, 1957); also see the English translation, *Béla Bartók: An Analysis of His Music* (London: Kahn and Averill, 1971).

[38] *Tempo giusto* refers to the strict rhythm that characterizes the oldest of the Hungarian dance tunes. "Variable" or "adjustable tempo giusto" refers to the more complex strict rhythm of the new Hungarian folk-song style, in which "the crotchet pairs . . . adjust themselves to the quantity, natural or positional, of the sylables of the text." See *Bartók, The Hungarian Folk Song,* n.7, above, pp. xxxvi and 28ff.

[39] See Béla Bartók, "Volksmusik der Rumänen von Maramures," *Sammelbände für Vergleichende Musikwissenschaft* (Munich: Drei Masken Verlag, 1923; also in English translation in *Rumanian Folk Music* V, ed. Benjamin Suchoff, trans. E. C. Teodorescu et al. (The Hague: Martinus Nijhoff, 1975), p. 32–34, for discussion of this type of instrument.

[40] Péter Laki, in "Der lange Gesang als Grundtyp in der internationalen Volksmusik" [The long song as basic type in international folk music], *Studia musicologica* 24/3–4 (1982): 393–400, shows parallels to other international folk-music types (e.g., North African Arab) in terms of melodic structure, mode and tonality, and ornamentation, and refers to Bartók's absorption of this type in the cello melody.

EXAMPLE 5–5. Bartók, *Fourth String Quartet,* Mov. III, mm. 1–10, cello

eight syllables

3-syllable
"Magyar" rhythm

principal notes being surrounded with chromatic embellishments."[41] The tune forms the basis of a folk-like four-line stanza, which runs through the A section (to m. 34).

These folk-music characteristics interact with nontraditional melodic and harmonic constructions to produce a sense of organic expansion within the framework of otherwise traditional forms. Similar to classical phraseology, the first-theme group of the opening sonata-allegro movement is initiated by balanced pairs of phrases that form larger periodic constructions. The initial antecedent phrase is cadenced by the contrary inward motion of the lines (mm. 1–2), balanced conversely in the consequent phrase by an outward linear motion (mm. 3–4).[42] The latter serves as preparation for the systematic intervallic expansions that characterize the rest of the work. The next pair of phrases, each of which now unfolds more systematically in stretto, is initiated by the first basic harmonic expansion of the quartet (mm. 5–6). The held symmetrical tetrachord, C–C♯–D–D♯, a segment of the semitonal (interval-1) cycle, expands to another symmetrical tetrachord, B♭–C–D–E, a segment of one of the two whole-tone (interval-2) cycles (see Ex. 5–10, below). These tetrachords (X–0 and Y–10) are two of three basic cells in the quartet.[43] The last stretto of the first-theme group (mm. 11–13), which

[41] See Stevens, *The Life and Music of Béla Bartók,* n. 5, above, p. 190.

[42] See János Kárpáti, *Bartók vonósnégyesei* [Bartók's string quartets] (Budapest: Zeneműkiadó, 1967; English trans. Fred Macnicol, Budapest: Corvina Press, 1975), p. 211, for a discussion of this period-like relationship between the phrases as part of Bartók's theme-development and form-building technique.

[43] George Perle, in "Symmetrical Formations in the String Quartets of Béla Bartók," *Music Review* 16 (November 1955), was the first to assign the nomenclature *sets X* and *Y* to these two symmetrical tetrachords. See n.28, above, for pitch-class numberings. Transposition numbers of pitch collections will also be designated by numbers from 0 to 11. If a referential collection is based on C, its transposition number is 0 (= 12). If the collection is transposed so that its "first" note becomes C♯, its transposition number becomes 1 (= 13), hence X–0 on C and Y–10 on B♭.

unfolds linear statements of cell X in the basic motif, is preceded by more rapid X–0 to Y–10 expansions. A viola ostinato begins the transition (mm. 14ff.) with a segment of Y–10 ([]–C–D–E), which shifts to the cello and is completed by the addition of B♭ in violin II (at m. 22). At this point, we get a third symmetrical tetrachord, vertically stated as G♯–C♯–D–G (viola and violin I), linearly as D–G–A♭–D♭ (violin I). We shall refer to this combination of two tritone (interval-6) cycles as cell Z–8/2.[44] These two tritones (C♯–G and G♯–D) of Z are anticipated in the preceding canon of the violins (mm. 15ff.), where they form the boundary intervals of the *subject* and *answer,* respectively. Thus, the intervallic expansion in the overall X–Y–Z progression of the first-theme group and transition (shown in Ex. 5–6a) continues the organic developmental process initiated by the outward linear motion of the second phrase (m. 4).

The three cells are also constructed one from the other according to the equal divisions of the octave. The cadential chord of the first-theme group, B♭–B–C–C♯–D–D♯–E (m. 13), represents a joining of two X transpositions (X–10, B♭–B–C–C♯, and X–1, C♯–D–D♯–E), which are separated by a minor third, to produce the tritone boundary of basic Y–10 (B♭–E). This X-cell combination is established explicitly in the linear motivic statements of the preceding stretto (m. 12), where X–10 (violin II and cello) is inverted motivically by X–1 (violin I and viola). Analogously to the construction of the interval-6 boundary of Y from the two conjunct interval-3 X boundaries, the tritone boundaries of Z are formed by a joining of two specific Y cells near the ending of theme 2 (mm. 40–43, violin I) (Ex. 5–7). Here, the boundaries of Y–6 (G♭–A♭–B♭–C) and Y–1 (D♭–E♭–F–G) outline Z–1/7 (D♭–G♭–G–C).

The structural priority of cells X, Y, and Z in the first-theme group and transition is partly established by the principle of metric departure and return to the regular 4/4 barring. Most of the cadential points in the first-theme group (mm. 7, 10, and 13) and the prominent one in the transition (m. 26) conclude stretto passages by vertically aligning the instruments, but all these cadential chords occur on weak beats. At the opening of theme II (m. 30), all the instruments are for the first time aligned on the downbeat of a new Y transposition, A♭–B♭–C–D (one note, E♭, is an accented appoggiatura). The stretto of the third phrase begins a metric shift to an eighth note before the barline and culminates in a vertical alignment of the instruments in the first X-to-Y progression one eighth-note after the barline of m. 6. The stretto

---

[44] Leo Treitler referred to the third set as *cell Z,* in "Harmonic Procedure in the *Fourth Quartet* of Béla Bartók," *Journal of Music Theory* 3/2 (November 1959): 292–298, as a follow-up to Perle's designations of sets X and Y. (The Z nomenclature is not to be confused with that in the theoretical writings of Allen Forte.) All three cells were first discussed in depth and shown to be part of a larger system in Elliott Antokoletz, "Principles of Pitch Organization in Bartók's *Fourth String Quartet*" (Ph.D. diss., The City University of New York, 1975). Cell Z is special in that its pitch content remains unchanged at its tritone transposition (on G♯ and D), and so will be designated by both transposition numbers, 8 (G♯–C♯–D–G) and 2 (D–G–A♭–D♭).

EXAMPLE 5–6. Bartók, *Fourth String Quartet,* Mov. I, X–Y–Z progressions in exposition, mm. 10–23, and development, mm. 49ff.

(a) EXPOSITION

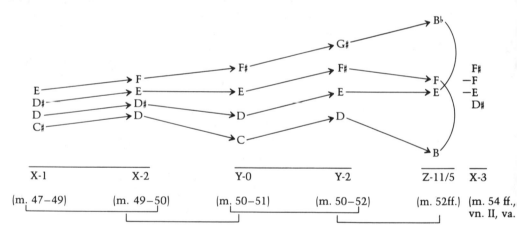

(b) DEVELOPMENT

EXAMPLE 5–7. Bartók, *Fourth String Quartet,* Mov. I, ending of theme 2, mm. 40–42, vnI, Y–Z construction

of the fourth phrase again begins before the barline and culminates (mm. 10–11) in a vertical alignment of the instruments on the second X-to-Y progression, which is removed further from the barline. In the transition (mm. 14ff.), the lines together produce more complex polymetric patterns, each implying an unequal-beat meter against the written barline. At the first foreground occurrence of Z (m. 22), some metric uniformity appears for the first time in this transition. Violin II gives us B♭ of cell Y at the barline; the C–D–E ostinato figure of cell Y in the cello also coincides with the downbeat, and the cell-Z statements in violin I and viola respectively subdivide the measure into 2 + 3 + 3/8 and 3 + 3 + 2/8. At mm. 23–24, the viola establishes regular quarter-notes, while violin I plays a regular syncopation against them.

Of the three basic cells, symmetrical relations may be shown only between X and Z. The basic transpositional levels of X (C–C♯–D–D♯) and Z (G♯–C♯–D–G) share the same axis of symmetry, C♯–D, a principle which forms the basis for a new concept of tonal centricity in Bartók's music. These two symmetrical tetrachords can each be analyzed into dyads that have the same sum—dyads C♯–D (1 + 2) and C–E♭ (0 + 3) of X–0 and dyads C♯–D (1 + 2) and G–G♯ (7 + 8) of Z–8/2 are all symmetrically related at sum 3.[45] These sum dyads can be shown to form part of a series of symmetrically related dyads generated by aligning two inversionally complementary semitonal cycles that intersect at the dual axis C♯–D and G–G♯ (Ex. 5–8). The axis of symmetry is expressed by the sum of the two pitch-class numbers in a dyad.

EXAMPLE 5–8. Alignment of two inversionally complementary semitonal cycles intersecting at a dual axis of symmetry of sum 3

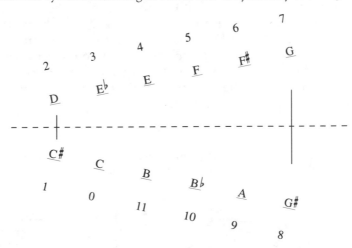

---

[45] Sums 3 and 15 are equivalent according to the present modulus of 12 (i.e., 15 − 12 = 3). Thus, for any number of 12 or above, we may subtract 12.

The basic "key" (axis) of the X–Y–Z progression in the first-theme group and transition is sum 3 (see Ex. 5–6a). The X–Y–Z progressions that begin the development section (see Ex. 5–6b) are analogous to the progressions from X–0 to Y–10 of the first-theme group. The relationship between these two sets of X–Y–Z progressions is analogous to the tonal relations of the traditional sonata plan. In traditional schemes, the common principle of modulation entails tonal motion by the components of the tonic triad. That is, if we move from the tonic area of the first-theme group to the dominant area of the second-theme group and development section, the motion has its reference in the root and fifth degrees of the tonic triad. The same principle is demonstrated in minor keys where the tonality shifts by way of the root to the third degree of the tonic minor-triad. In the present work, tonal motion from the exposition to the opening of the development occurs through the cyclic intervals of the basic chords (i.e., cells): X moves up by semitones, Y by whole tones. At m. 52, Y–2 (D–E–F♯–G♯) expands to Z–11/5 (B–E–E♯–A♯), the minor-third transposition of original Z–8/2 (m. 22). Separation by this interval permits both these Z transpositions to be related to each other symmetrically around either of two different axes of symmetry (Ex. 5–9), in this case, C♯–D (or G–G♯) and E–F (or B♭–B) of sums 3 and 9, so that common-chord (Z-cell) links can be established between these two different "keys" or axes. The common-chord pivot is established at the end of the following canon (mm. 54–60). In m. 53, Z–11/5 is joined with X–3, the final cyclic-interval-1 transposition above the preceding X–2 statement (mm. 49–50). Cell X–3 (D♯–E–E♯–F♯), which becomes the nucleus of the next passage (mm. 54–60, viola and violin II), and Z–11/5 (B–E–E♯–A♯) together establish the new axis of sum 9 (in enharmonic spelling, E–F). Finally, in mm. 56–58, B–B♭ of Z–11/5 in the inverted stretto between the cello and violin I contracts symmetrically around D–G in the two voices to produce a sum–9 permutation of original Z–8/2, C♯–D–G–A♭ (m. 57). Then, G–A♭ in violin I is aligned with D–C♯ in the cello (m. 58), forming a Z–8/2 ostinato (at sum 9) around the X–3 nucleus in the two inner instruments. The long-range modulation from axis C♯–D (sum 3) of the exposition to axis E–F (sum 9) of the development is foreshadowed in the opening interaction of X transpositions at sums 9 and 3 (Ex. 5–10).

EXAMPLE 5–9. Symmetrical relations between two transpositions of cell Z around two common axes of symmetry

EXAMPLE 5–10. Bartók, *Fourth String Quartet,* Mov. I, opening, interaction of cell-X transpositions at sums 9 and 3

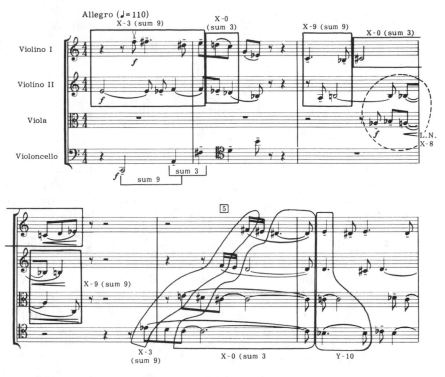

The key of C is acknowledged standardly as the basic tonal frame of the quartet, but it also has special connections with the axial concept of tonality. The dual notion of C as the modal tonic of the cadential quasi-Phrygian segment of Movements I and V and as an axis of symmetry is basic to the fusion concept in Bartók's music: C–C of sum 0 (= 12) is the ultimate axis of the local B♭–B (sum–9) and C♯–D (sum–3) axes. This long-range symmetrical relationship between two of the three X-to-Y progressions in Movement I—X–0 to Y–10 (at mm. 5–6 and 10–11) and its inversion, X–9 to Y–8 (mm. 152–156)—is shown in Ex. 5–11.

In Movement V, Z–1/7 (D♭–F♯–G–C) is basic in generating other larger symmetrical, cyclic sets, for instance the octatonic scale. Against the Z–1/7 ostinato of the lower strings, the nonsymmetrical theme derived from the violin canon in the transition of Movement I is interjected at mm. 15–18. While three notes of the theme (C♯–F♯–G) belong to cell Z, the fourth note (D♯) expands the pitch content of Z to five notes of the octatonic scale C♯–D♯–[ ]–F♯–G–[ ]–[ ]–C. A modified statement of the theme in the violins (Ex. 5–12) further expands Z–1/7 to a six-note segment of the octatonic set, C♯–D♯–[ ]–F♯–G–A–[ ]–B♯, the complete set (C♯–D♯–E–F♯–G–A–B♭–B♯)

EXAMPLE 5–11. Bartók, *Fourth String Quartet,* Mov. I, X-0/Y-10 progression (mm. 10–11) mirrored by X-9/Y-8 (mm. 152–156)

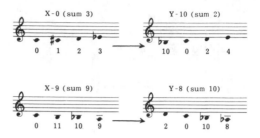

exclusively forming the pitch content of the violins (then with viola) from mm. 44–75. The remaining notes of the octatonic set that complement the original Z–1/7 (C#–F#–G–C) form Z–10/4 (B♭–D#–E–A). This double-Z-cell interpretation of the octatonic set is explicitly confirmed by Z–10/4, B♭–E♭–E–A (violins, m. 45), preceding the complete statement of the larger set immediately. This relationship of two Z cells a minor-third apart is the same as that between Z–8/2 and Z–11/5 of movement I, both of which were subsequently interlocked in the octatonic scale, D–E–F–G–G#–A#–B–C#, in movement II (mm. 243–246, viola).

In movement III, the filling in of each of the two tritones of cell Z by whole tones serves to generate both complementary whole-tone cycles. The tritones of cell Z are produced when the ranges of two specific transpositions of cell Y are joined (Ex. 5–13a). While one whole-tone-filled tritone (cell Y) is a segment of one of the whole-tone cycles, two whole-tone-filled tritones that specifically outline cell Z are respective segments of the two mutually exclusive whole-tone cycles. Measures 1–13 are partitioned into the *parlando-rubato* solo line in the cello and the chordal drone in the other three instruments. This drone unfolds trichords G#–F#–E and C#–B–A, which together form a diatonic hexachord. Through the addition of D and D# in the cello at m. 6, these two trichords are expanded to whole-tone tetrachords D–E–F#–G# (Y–2) and A–B–C#–D# (Y–9) (see Ex. 5–13a). In the drone, the two whole-tone trichords are separated by interval 3 (C#–E), which is

EXAMPLE 5–12. Bartók, *Fourth String Quartet,* Mov. V, mm. 44ff., upper strings, octatonic theme based on two interlocking cell-Z transpositions

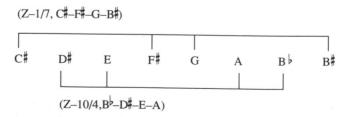

EXAMPLE 5–13. Bartók, *Fourth String Quartet*, Mov. III, mm. 1–6 (a) and mm. 34–39 (b), cellular generation of two whole-tone cycles

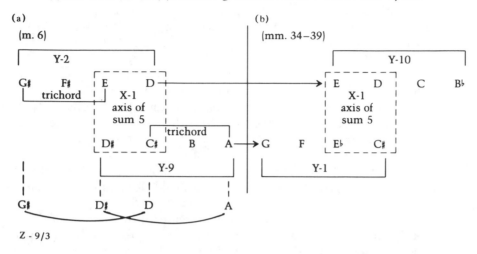

chromatically filled by the axial dyad D–D♯ (cello entrance at m. 6). This establishes a primary axis of sum 5 in this movement. Cell Y–2 (m. 6) is ultimately transposed by interval 4 to Y–10, at the beginning of the middle section (mm. 34–39, four lowest tones of the drone), while the other opening whole-tone tetrachord, Y–9 (m. 6), is analogously transposed by interval 4 to Y–1, in mm. 34–39 (two highest tones of the drone and violin I) (Ex. 5–13b). The transposed collection (Y–10/Y–1) at the opening of the middle section (mm. 34–39) maintains the same axis of symmetry (sum 5) as the initial Y–2/Y–9 collection, and these two passages intersect at the common tones C♯–D–D♯–E (X–1). At the same time, the two passages contain the tetrachordal segments D–E–F♯–G♯ and B♭–C–D–E, respectively, of one of the whole-tone cycles and the tetrachordal segments A–B–C♯–D♯ and C♯–E♭–F–G, respectively, of the other. The transposition from Y–2 to Y–10 adds B♭–C to complete the first whole-tone hexachord, B♭–C/D–E–F♯–G♯, while the transposition from Y–9 to Y–1 adds dyad F–G to complete the other, A–B–C♯–D♯/F–G. In this cyclic generation, the third phrase (mm. 22–29) is transitional. The drone contains five notes of one whole-tone cycle (G♯–B♭–C–D–E) and the cello solo contains five notes of the other (G–A–B–C♯–D♯, completed by F–G at mm. 28–29). The two odd notes (F and F♯) of the respective cycles are interchanged between the lower viola pedal (F) and cello (F♯) at m. 23. Nevertheless, they are in their appropriate registral positions with regard to their respective cycles.

This interchange between F and F♯ is part of a modulatory scheme of axes analogous to that of movement I between sums 3 and 9. Cell Z–9/3 (A–D–D♯–G♯) in the Y–Z construction (at m. 6) is explicitly stated at sum 5, the same sum being reestablished at the opening of section B (mm. 34–39). In the transitional passage (mm. 22–29) between these two points, the interchange of F and F♯ between the respective whole-tone cycles establishes a new axis at sum 11, which is the other axis of symmetry of the opening Z–9/3 (in the implied sum-11 position, D–D♯–G♯–A). The opening section (A) of movement III establishes the two axes (sums 5 and 11) of Z–9/3 analogously to the establishment in movement I of the two axes (sums 3 and 9) of either Z–8/2 or Z–11/5.

The essence of various Eastern European folk-music styles is absorbed into a highly integrated set of abstract principles of pitch organization in the quartet. These principles have included the construction of three symmetrical tetrachords, one from the other, according to the equal subdivisions of the octave, the interaction of the three cells in establishing contrasting "keys" based on the concept of axes of symmetry, and the generation of the larger system of the interval cycles from basic cells to form the primordial material of both the melodic and harmonic fabric within otherwise traditional forms.[46]

The year 1928 was one of the most prolific for Bartók. In addition to the *Fourth Quartet*, he wrote two *Rhapsodies* for violin and piano, both arranged for violin and orchestra, the *First Rhapsody* appearing in a version for cello and piano as well. Both works are founded upon certain folk characteristics, which foreshadow Bartók's renewed interest in folk-music settings. That same year Bartók participated in the International Folk Music Congress in Prague, and his new folk-song arrangements and transcriptions during the next decade reveal his increasing interest in folk texts. The *Twenty Hungarian Folksongs* for voice and piano was composed in 1929, followed by *Four Hungarian Folksongs* for mixed chorus, a cappella (1930), *Transylvanian Dances* for orchestra (1931; a transcription of the *Sonatina* for piano of 1915), *Hungarian Sketches* for orchestra (1931), *Székely Songs* for a cappella male chorus (1932), *Hungarian Peasant Songs* for orchestra (1933; transcriptions of pieces from the *Fifteen Hungarian Peasant Songs* of 1914–1917), *Hungarian Folksongs* for voice and orchestra (1933; transcriptions of pieces from the *Twenty Hungarian Folksongs* of 1929), *Twenty-Seven Choruses* for two- and three-part children's or women's chorus (1935), and *From Olden Times,* on old Hungarian folk- and art-song texts, for a cappella three-part male chorus (1935), and many pieces from the *Mikrokosmos* (1926–1939). As in the *Rhapsody,* Op. 1 (1904), the *Second Sonata* for violin and piano (1922), and *Contrasts* for violin, clarinet, and piano (1938), the two *Rhapsodies* are based on highly ornamented folk materials and are divided into the *conventional lassú* (slow *parlando rubato*) and *friss* (quick *tempo giusto*) of the *Verbunkos* style.[47] The

---

[46] In the present discussion, we have observed the generation of several of these cyclic partitions only, but the entire system, which includes one cycle of minor seconds, two of whole-tones, three of minor thirds, four of major thirds, one of perfect fourths, and six of tritones, is also unfolded throughout the quartet; see Antokoletz, *The Music of Béla Bartók,* n.2, above, Chaps. 4 and 8 especially.

[47] "Verbunkos" (from the German "Werbung"), or "recruiting," was a Hungarian dance that served as a method of enlistment during the imperial wars of the

gypsy association is also evident in the use of the dulcimer-like *cimbalom* in the orchestral version of the *First Rhapsody*.

In the increasingly repressive political atmosphere in Budapest in the 1930s, Bartók withdrew from performing his own works. In 1930 he also composed one of three planned cantatas to express his ideal concerning the brotherhood of neighboring nations—Rumania, Slovakia, and Hungary. The *Cantata Profana,* the only completed work of the group, represents the most explicit musical embodiment of his philosophy.[48] Throughout his life, Bartók felt a deep personal commitment to the principles of national independence and artistic freedom.[49] Stylistically, the *Cantata* reveals a neoclassical approach in its use of earlier forms and procedures, including the canon, fugue, aria, cadenza, turba, and double choruses as well as an orchestral introduction resembling the opening of Bach's *St. Matthew Passion*. The fusion of these familiar features into a highly systematic network of relationships creates one of Bartók's most personal expressions, one in which development and transformation of diatonic and nondiatonic folk modes appear to correspond with the dramatic symbolization.[50]

During the 1930s, Bartók continued his folk-music research, primarily with institutional sources. He attended the International Congress of Arab Folk Music in Cairo in 1932, studied Rumanian folk music at the Bucharest Phonogramme Archives in 1934, began work on the publication of his Hungarian folk-music collection in the same year, became a member of the Hungarian Academy of the Sciences in 1936, and visited Turkey for his last folk-music collecting tour that same year.

---

eighteenth century. The main part of the dance, which consisted of the alternation between slow and quick figures, was performed by a group of hussars led by a sergeant. The musicians, who were mostly gypsies, accompanied them with simple folk tunes and improvised instrumental accompaniments. The idiom has survived primarily in the csárdás; see John S. Weissmann, "Verbunkos," *The New Grove,* pp. 629–630.

[48] In a letter of January 10, 1931, Bartók asserted his ideals of international brotherhood; see *Béla Bartók Letters,* ed. Demény, n.6, above, p. 201.

[49] Serge Moreux, in *Béla Bartók, sa vie, ses oeuvres, son langage* (Paris: Richard-Masse, 1949), p. 81, has suggested that the *Cantata Profana* was a protest against the restrictions of the Regent of Hungary, Miklós Horthy. With regard to Bartók's philosophy and lifelong folk-music endeavors, this work has a special significance; see László Somfai, *Cantata Profana,* preface to the score (Vienna: Universal Edition, 1934; New York: Boosey and Hawkes, 1955). On the title page of the first edition, Bartók wrote "Words from folk songs," which obscured the fact that this is his most individual and poetic work—it is based on his own special translation from Rumanian into Hungarian. The history of the text goes back to April 1914, during a folk-song expedition in Transylvania, where Bartók recorded two versions of a Rumanian *colindâ* text, that is, a Christmas song with many verses. From 1924 through 1926, while writing his book on Rumanian Christmas songs, he outlined a new version of the ballad in Rumanian by combining and rewriting the two original folk ballads.

[50] See Antokoletz, *The Music of Béla Bartók,* n.2, above, Chap. VII, for a detailed discussion of these relations in this and other works of Bartók.

During this period, he composed the *Second Piano Concerto* (1931), *Forty-Four Duos* for two violins (1931), *Fifth String Quartet* (1934), *Music for Strings, Percussion, and Celesta* (1936), which was commissioned by Paul Sacher, whom Bartók met in Basel in 1929, *Sonata for Two Pianos and Percussion* (1937), *Contrasts* (1938), which was dedicated to Benny Goodman and Joseph Szigeti, *Violin Concerto* (1938), and the completion of the *Mikrokosmos* (1939), *Divertimento* for string orchestra (1939), and *Sixth String Quartet* (1939).

Bartók's first performance of the *Second Piano Concerto* in 1933 was his last concert in Germany. In October 1937, he withdrew permission for the broadcasting of his works by the radio stations of Fascist Italy and Nazi Germany and transferred publication of his music from Universal Edition in Vienna (which was under Nazi influence) to Boosey and Hawkes in London in 1937. In April 1938, in a letter to Mrs. Müller-Widman in Switzerland, Bartók expressed his concern about the progress of Nazi power in Eastern Europe, following Germany's unprovoked attack on Austria. Fearful that Hungary, too, would fall under German domination, and contemplating the possibility of emigration, Bartók requested his Swiss friend "give shelter" to his manuscripts.[51]

FINAL YEARS IN THE UNITED STATES (1940–1945)

In October 1940, he and his wife emigrated to New York City. These last years were difficult for Bartók both because of exile from his native national sources and because of the general lack of acceptance of performances of his own music, which led to severe financial straits. However, a grant from Columbia University made it possible for Bartók to work on the Parry collection of Yugoslav folk-music recordings (held at Harvard University) from March 1941 to the end of 1942, while he, at the same time, edited his own Rumanian and Turkish materials.

Bartók's health began to decline in 1942, and he gave his last performance in January 1943, in which he and his wife played the *Concerto* arrangement of his *Sonata for Two Pianos and Percussion*. In the same year, Bartók composed the *Concerto for Orchestra*. Several important events led to its composition: (1) his discovery of a recording of Dalmatian two-part chromatic folk melodies while transcribing Yugoslav folk music at Columbia University; (2) a request from his London publisher Ralph Hawkes in 1942 for "a series of concertos for solo instrument or instruments and string orchestra . . . or combinations of solo instruments and string orchestra"; (3) a broadcast in 1942 of the Shostakovich "Leningrad" *Symphony No. 7*, which Bartók, surprised to hear repetitions of a theme that "sounded like a Viennese cabaret song," was to satirize by using a variant of this theme in the *interrotto* of movement IV of the *Concerto*; and (4) a commission by

---

[51] See *Béla Bartók Letters,* ed. Demény, n.6, above, p. 267.

Koussevitzky in 1943 for an orchestral work to be performed by the Boston Symphony Orchestra.[52] This *Concerto*, which appears to be Bartók's most popular work, is based on the most extensive "synthesis of Eastern folk-music materials and Western art-music techniques."[53]

Diverse international folk-music elements serve as the bases of many of the themes throughout the *Concerto*.[54] The two introductory themes are each in the four-line stanzaic structure of the Hungarian folk song, the opening one of which is pentatonic and in the *parlando-rubato* rhythm of the old style. Theme 1 of the exposition (m. 76f.) is characteristic of Slovak folk music with its *tempo-giusto* rhythm and prominent use of tritone, one of its two contrasting motifs based on a tritone-bounded segment of an octatonic scale (F–G–A♭–B♭–B), the other on an ambiguous segment of either an octatonic or diatonic scale (C–F–E♭–A♭).[55] At the opening of movement II, theme a, played by the bassoons in parallel sixths, is in the style of the Yugoslav *Kolo,* or round dance. Theme c, played by the clarinets in parallel minor-sevenths (m. 52), is in the style of the *sopel* (folk oboe) of Dalmatian folk song. The following flute duet (m. 60), in parallel fifths, major mode, and dotted rhythm, reveals influences from Western Europe. The Trio (m. 123) opens with a chorale-like brass theme, in which the pentatonic lines of the tuba and trombone 2 are harmonized by the other brass in triads. This ends in the progression F♯–A–C♯–E, A–C♯–E–G♯, B–D♯–F♯ (mm. 125–126), the first two chords of which produce a kind of semicadence close of the melody; this is the so-called Yugoslav cadence that infiltrated Rumanian Transylvania.[56] Movement III, which expresses a "lugubrious death song," includes a chromatic viola theme (m. 62f.) in the style of a folk lament.[57] The prominent emphasis on the tritone as well as unequal-beat pattern in the opening oboe theme of movement IV suggests Slovak folk style. A "composed" pseudo-folk song melody of Zsigmond Vincze, "You are lovely, you are beautiful, Hungary," appears as the main viola theme of the middle section (mm. 42–50). The entire finale employs transformed bagpipe motifs that Bartók had collected from Rumanian Transylvania.[58] Finally, the devel-

---

[52] Benjamin Suchoff, "Program Notes for the *Concerto for Orchestra*," *Béla Bartók: A Celebration* (New York: Book-of-the-Month Records, 1981), pp. 6ff.

[53] See ibid. For a detailed analysis of this work in terms of progression and integration, based on the interaction of diatonic, octatonic, and whole-tone sets, as well as the generation of interval cycles, see Antokoletz, *The Music of Béla Bartók,* n.2, above, Chaps. VII and VIII.

[54] See Suchoff, "Program Notes," n.52, above.

[55] For the realization of these modal implications, see Antokoletz, *The Music of Béla Bartók,* n.2, above, pp. 254ff.

[56] See Bartók, *Rumanian Folk Music IV,* n.39, above, p. 20, Bartók's footnote.

[57] See Bartók, "Explanation to *Concerto for Orchestra*," program note for the Boston première, 1944.

[58] Suchoff, in "Program Notes," n.52, above, refers to Bartók's transcription of an *Ardelenescu* ("Transylvanian" or round dance) for comparison.

opment section, introduced by divided violins and harp (mm. 96ff.), suggests the Balinese gamelan (tuned percussion) orchestra. As combined with these divergent folk-music sources, Bartók's own commentary points to certain textural and structural features of traditional art-music:

> The title of this symphony-like orchestral work is explained by its tendency to treat the single instruments or instrumental groups in a *concertant* or soloistic manner. The "virtuoso" treatment appears, for instance, in the *fugato* sections of the Development of the First Movement (brass instruments). . . . As for the structure of the work, the First and Fifth Movements are written in a more or less regular sonata form. . . . Less traditional forms are found in the Second and Third Movements. The main part of the Second Movement consists of a chain of independent short sections, by wind instruments consecutively introduced in five pairs. Thematically, the five sections . . . could be symbolized by the letters "A, B, C, D, E." A kind of "trio"—a short chorale for brass instruments and side-drum—follows, after which the five sections are recapitulated. . . . The structure of the Third Movement likewise is chain-like; three themes appear successively. . . . The form of the Fourth Movement—*Intermezzo interrotto*—could be rendered by the letter symbols "A, B, A— interruption—B, A."[59]

In late 1943 Yehudi Menuhin commissioned the *Sonata for Solo Violin*, which Bartók completed for him in 1944, during a period of temporary improvement in his health. His last two works, the *Third Piano Concerto* and *Viola Concerto*, were composed simultaneously in 1945, the latter work left as an incomplete, fragmented piano version just a few weeks before his death on September 26. This work, commissioned by violist William Primrose, was later reconstructed by Tibor Serly from Bartók's first draft.[60] Thus, in his contributions to the aesthetics and techniques of modern composition and musicological methodology, Bartók was to serve as one of the most influential models for both composers and musical folklorists after World War II.

SUGGESTED READINGS

ELLIOTT ANTOKOLETZ. *Béla Bartók: A Guide to Research* (New York: Garland Publishing, Inc., 1988), especially pp. xvii–xxxi.

———. "Pitch-Set Derivations from the Folk Modes in Bartók's Music," *Studia musicologica* 24/3 (1982): 265–274.

[59] See n. 57, above.

[60] See Tibor Serly, "A Belated Account of the Reconstruction of a 20th Century Masterpiece," *College Music Symposium* 12 (1975): 7–25; see also Sándor Kovács, "Reexamining the Bartók/Serly Viola Concerto," *Studia musicologica* 23 (1981): 295–322.

———. "Principles of Pitch Organization in Bartók's Fourth String Quartet" (Ph.D. dissertation, The City University of New York, 1975).

———. *The Music of Béla Bartók: A Study of Tonality and Progression in Twentieth-Century Music* (Berkeley and Los Angeles: University of California Press, 1984).

———. "The Musical Language of Bartók's 14 *Bagatelles* for Piano," *Tempo* 137 (June 1981): 8–16.

MILTON BABBITT. "The String Quartets of Bartók," *Musical Quarterly* 35 (July 1949): 377–385.

BÉLA BARTÓK. *Essays,* ed. Benjamin Suchoff (New York: St. Martin's Press, 1976), including: "Autobiography (1921)," pp. 408–411. Published originally as "Selbstbiographie," in *Musikblätter des Anbruch* (Vienna) 3/5 (March 1921): 87–90; "Hungarian Peasant Music," pp. 80–102. Published originally in *Musical Quarterly* 19/3 (July 1933): 267–289; "Hungarian Folk Music," pp. 58–70. Published originally as "La musique populaire hongroise," *Revue Musicale* 2/1 (November 1921): 8–22; "The Folk Songs of Hungary," pp. 331–339. Published originally in *Pro Musica* (1928): 28–35; "The Influence of Debussy and Ravel in Hungary," p. 518. Published originally as "Hongrie," *La revue musicale* 19/2 (December 1938): 436.

———. "Explanation to *Concerto for Orchestra,*" program note for the Boston première, 1944.

———. *Letters,* ed. János Demény, trans. Péter Balabán and István Farkas, rev. Elizabeth West and Colin Mason (London: Faber and Faber; Budapest: Corvina Press, 1971).

———. *The Hungarian Folk Song,* ed. Benjamin Suchoff (Albany: State University of New York Press, 1981), pp. xv–xvi.

WALLACE BERRY. "Symmetrical Interval Sets and Derivative Pitch Materials in Bartók's String Quartet No. 3," *Perspectives of New Music* 18 (1979–1980): 287–380.

MALCOLM GILLIES. "Bartók's Last Works: A Theory of Tonality and Modality," *Musicology* 7 (1982): 120–130.

———. *Notation and Tonal Structure in Bartók's Later Works* (New York and London: Garland Publishing, Inc., 1989.

JÁNOS KÁRPÁTI. *Bartók vonósnégyesei* (Budapest: Zeneműkiadó, 1967); *Bartók's String Quartets,* Eng. trans. Fred Macnicol, Budapest: Corvina Press, 1975).

GYÖRGY KROÓ. "Duke Bluebeard's Castle," *Studia musicologica* 1 (1961): 251–340.

ERNŐ LENDVAI. "Einführung in Die Formen und Harmoniewelt Bartóks," in *Béla Bartók, Weg und Werk, Schriften und Briefe,* ed. Bence Szabolcsi (Budapest: Corvina-Verlag, 1957); *Béla Bartók: An Analysis of His Music,* Introduction by Alan Bush (London: Kahn and Averill, 1971).

COLIN MASON. "An Essay in Analysis: Tonality, Symmetry, and Latent Serialism in Bartók's Fourth Quartet," *The Music Review* 18/7 (August 1957): 189–201.

GEORGE PERLE. "Symmetrical Formations in the String Quartets of Béla Bartók," *Music Review* 16 (November, 1955): 300–312.

———. "The String Quartets of Béla Bartók," *Béla Bartók* (New York: Dover Publications, Inc., 1967), pp. 2–8 (program notes for the recordings performed by the Tátrai String Quartet); reprinted in *A Musical Offering: Essays in Honor of Martin Bernstein,* ed. Claire Brook and E. H. Clinkscale (New York: Pendragon Press, 1977), pp. 193–210.

LÁSZLÓ SOMFAI. "Analytical Notes on Bartók's Piano Year of 1926," *Studia musicologica* 26 (1984): 5–58.

————. *Cantata Profana,* preface to the score (Vienna: Universal Edition, 1934; New York: Boosey and Hawkes, 1955).

————. " 'Per finire': Some Aspects of the Finale in Bartók's Cyclic Form," *Studia musicologica* 11 (1969): 391–408.

HALSEY STEVENS. *The Life and Music of Béla Bartók* (New York: Oxford University Press, 1953; revised 1964).

BENJAMIN SUCHOFF. "Ethnomusicological Roots of Béla Bartók's Musical Language," *World of Music* 29/1 (1987): 43–64.

————. *Guide to Bartók's Mikrokosmos* (London: Boosey and Hawkes, 1957, rev. 2/1971); reprint of the rev. 1971 edition (New York: Da Capo Press, 1983).

————. "Program Notes for the *Concerto for Orchestra,*" *Béla Bartók: A Celebration* (New York: Book-of-the-Month Records, 1981), pp. 6ff.

————. "The Impact of Italian Baroque Music on Bartók's Music," *Bartók and Kodály Revisited,* ed. György Ránki (Budapest: Akadémiai Kiadó, 1987), pp. 183–197.

LEO TREITLER. "Harmonic Procedure in the *Fourth Quartet* of Béla Bartók," *Journal of Music Theory* 3/2 (November 1959): 292–298.

SÁNDOR VERESS. "Bluebeard's Castle," *Béla Bartók: A Memorial Review* (New York: Boosey and Hawkes, 1950): 36–53. Reprinted from *Tempo* 13 (1949): 32–38.

6 Diverse national developments in Europe

Twentieth-century musical techniques, styles, aesthetics, and philosophical assumptions appear to be more diverse in this century than in any single era of the preceding ones. Political, social, and economic developments contributed to these divergencies among composers of heterogeneous national backgrounds. Due to the awakening of nationalistic sentiment in the late-nineteenth and early twentieth centuries, composers belonging to cultures that developed largely outside the Central European sphere searched for national identities in their own folklore, literature, and plastic arts, as well as older musical traditions. While national and artistic interests often led to distinct national styles in previous eras, individual features from noncentrally located European countries tended to be absorbed, transformed, and subordinated to those musical forces asserted in the traditional German, French, and Italian idioms.

Nineteenth-century nationalistic inclinations led to an enrichment of the vocabulary of Central European musical traditions, but predisposition toward mood and color for the enhancement of Romantic expression forced these national elements into the conventional molds, so that they were to function as little more than "exoticisms." Such nationalistic composers as Chopin (*Polonaises* and *Mazurkas*), Liszt (*Hungarian Rhapsodies*), Brahms (*Hungarian Dances*), Dvořák (*Slavonic Dances*), Smetana (*The Bartered Bride* and *My Fatherland*), Grieg (*Symphonische Tänze*, Op. 64, based on Norwegian folk-tune arrangements), and others consciously incorporated folk elements into their works. However, even these composers had little understanding of the genuine peasant music of their native lands. Folk elements had often become so thoroughly filtered-down by their incorporation into the sentimental or Romantic idioms of the European composers that folk essence was either distorted totally or lost altogether.

Nationalism in the twentieth century began to acquire a different meaning. This new attitude, based on the first extensive scientific investigations and preservation of national folk idioms by means of recording and transcription, was initiated prior to the research of Bartók and Kodály by such pioneers as the Hungarian folklorist Béla Vikár, the Finnish ethnologist Ilmari Krohn, and the Austrian scholar Erich von Hornbostel, who presented a method for transcribing music from recordings and provided evidence for the use of empirical musicological data in ethnomusicological research. The incorporation and synthesis of national folk idioms as well as other characteristics that are identifiably national in style into art-music composition during the first several decades of the century were basic to the compositional aesthetics, styles, and techniques of composers throughout Europe, Latin America, and the United States.

EASTERN EUROPE: KODÁLY, JANÁČEK, SZYMANOWSKI, AND OTHERS

In contrast to Bartók's broad international interests in the investigation of folk music, Zoltán Kodály (1882–1967) confined his folk-music research almost entirely to the Hungarian villages. In a basic sense, Kodály was more deeply rooted in the folk music of Hungary than was Bartók; while Bartók had been raised in the towns among the lesser gentry and had not come in contact with the authentic Hungarian folk sources before 1904, Kodály had been born from peasant stock and was therefore thoroughly familiar with peasant melodies since his childhood.[1] It was after a thorough study of Kodály's thesis on the stanzaic structure of the Hungarian folk song, which was published in the Budapest journal *Ethnographia,* that Bartók came to initiate the collaboration between the two composers in 1905. Although their early folk-music research experiences and studies of art-music were parallel—Kodály also encouraged Bartók's study of Debussy's music in 1907 when they both became professors at the Academy of Music in Budapest—they diverged in their approaches to the method of folk-song classification as well as in their compositional styles. Following the methodology of the Krohn System, Kodály felt that melody and text were inseparable. He emphasized the rhythmic analysis of text based on the number of syllables per line in either isometric or heterometric stanzaic structures, the text emphasis then, based on the importance that he gave to the social functions of the songs.[2] In contrast, Bartók felt that the melody type was the only logical basis for classification. He, then, grouped together melodies revealing the same construction or style.[3] Both composers were also entirely different in compositional styles. Kodály's Hungarian folk-song arrangements as well as his more abstract compositions, less radical in terms of modal transformation, are set in more traditional contexts of harmonic sonority and tonal progression. The main sources of his style include features from Debussy, Bach, Palestrina, and the Hungarian *verbunkos* style, all of which are united under the pervasive influence of Hungarian folk music.

Kodály produced a number of solo, chamber, and orchestral compositions throughout his life, but solo vocal and choral works were to dominate. This appears to correspond with the composer's basic attitude that singing was the foundation of all music education. In the 1920s, when Kodály's

---

[1] László Eösze, *Zoltán Kodály—His Life and Work,* trans. István Farkas and Gyula Gulyás (Budapest: Corvina Press, 1962), pp. 11–12.

[2] Zoltán Kodály, *A magyar népzene* (Folk Music of Hungary) (Budapest, 1937; enlarged and rev. Lajos Vargyas, trans. rev. Laurence Picken, Budapest: Corvina, 1971), pp. 20ff.

[3] See the "Editor's Preface," in Béla Bartók, *The Hungarian Folk Song,* ed. Benjamin Suchoff (Albany: State University of New York Press, 1981), pp. xxxiii-xlii; see also Betty Devine, "Three Choral Works of Zoltán Kodály: A Study of Folksong Style for Performance Consideration" (D.M.A. treatise, The University of Texas at Austin, 1986), Chap. 2, "The Classification Systems," pp. 29–37.

interest in music education for the young became evident, he turned significantly to choral composition, writing many pieces for children's voices explicitly. Of his best-known compositions—the *Psalmus Hungaricus,* Op. 13, for tenor solo, chorus, and orchestra (1923), the opera *Háry János,* Op. 15 (1925–1926), and the *Missa Brevis* (1944)—two are choral works. Prior to the *Psalmus,* he composed nearly fifty songs (including the folk-song arrangements) and only six choral works. This was reversed after the *Psalmus;* aside from the main body of ten volumes of arrangements in his *Hungarian Folk Music* (1917–1932), he composed only the *Three Songs,* Op. 14 (1924–1929) and a few other works for solo voice with keyboard or orchestra, and produced about one hundred choral works (including some transcriptions). In addition to the pervasive folk influence on these works, Kodály's nationalism was also evident in his opposition to foreign domination, which he expressed in the *Psalmus, Zrínyi's Appeal,* and *Jesus and the Traders.*

One of Kodály's representative folk-song settings for a cappella chorus is the *Székely Keserves* (Transylvanian Lament) (1934). This old-style tune, built on the Hungarian form of the pentatonic scale (E–G–A–B–D), is primarily harmonized by modal tertian constructions.[4] The four lines of the corresponding nonrounded form, ABCD (mm. 1–10), in the irregular rhythmic style of *parlando rubato,* are isometrically organized on twelve syllables per line. The original text, based on a soldier leaving home and lamenting his dying in a foreign country, is extended textually and musically by Kodály to imply a larger succession of theme and three variations interspersed by sections that suggest choral wailing; the latter culminates in a descriptive descent by the seventh and ninth chords in connection to the textual references of burial and lamenting. The E-pentatonic structure of the tune is modally expanded to E-Phrygian (E–F–G–A–B–C–D) by the addition of two new notes, F and C, in the first wailing interlude. In the first variation (mm. 16ff.), F♯ is added to both the tune and accompaniment in place of F, so we also get an E-Aeolian expansion (E–F♯–G–A–B–C–D) of the pentatonic nucleus. With the addition of C♯ in the second interlude (m. 26), a more complex polymodal mixture suggests the combination of E-Phrygian with E-Dorian (E–F♯–G–A–B–C♯–D). The latter then returns (at m. 30) to the simpler Phrygian embellishment of the E-pentatonic nucleus at the opening of the third variation, which is established primarily by the lower voices. New intrusions of chromatic tones into the pentatonic sphere produce increasingly richer and more complex polymodal textures in the remainder of the song, but the fundamental pentatonic quality of the old style is maintained by the general rhythmic deemphasis of the added modal tones, especially in the thematic statements themselves. The pervasivenes of tertian harmonic construction in the fuller and more dense choral writing in many of these

---

[4] For a detailed study of this and two other choral pieces, *Túrót Eszik a Cigány* and *Molnár Anna,* see Devine, "Three Choral Works of Zoltán Kodály," in ibid.

passages is a characteristic that distinguishes Kodály's somewhat more traditional romantic style from the sparser and more dissonant textures of many of Bartók's later folk-song settings.

It is in the folk-like textures of Kodály's more abstract chamber as well as larger choral and orchestral works that modal material is somewhat transformed more radically into a nontraditional musical language. As early as the *Sonata for Violoncello and Piano,* Op. 4 (1910), a folk-like *tempo-giusto* theme in movement II (mm. 19ff.), although harmonized by verticalities that still appear to have some connection to tertian chordal construction, is part of a context based on the nonfunctional interaction of its modal-diatonic properties with nondiatonic collections.[5] Such interaction brings this idiom entirely into the art-music realm of twentieth-century tonality. At mm. 52ff., the octatonic scale, Db–Eb–E–Gb–G–A–Bb–C, is a focal point for the development and interaction of two of its equivalent symmetrical partitions, Db–Gb–G–C and Bb–Eb–E–A, each of which is based on two tritones a perfect fourth (or minor second) apart.[6] The two tritones (Db–G and Gb–C) of the former partition first appear together (m. 24) as unobtrusive boundaries of two gapped whole-tone chords, Db–Eb–[   ]–G and Gb–Ab–[   ]–C (Ex. 6–1a). At the cadence (mm. 31–33, piano part), a partial statement of this octatonic subcollection (Db–Gb–[   ]–C) now emerges as a more prominent foreground event against a partial statement (cello part) of the second octatonic subcollection (Bb–Eb–[   ]–[   ]). In the extension of the theme at mm. 35–36, the latter subcollection appears complete as its two tritones are linearly interlocked (Bb–Eb–E–A). At the same time, a tritone (F♯–C) from the initial partition is vertically stated against the latter partition, giving us six notes of the larger octatonic set ([   ]–Eb–E–F♯–[   ]–A–Bb–C). The octatonic setting of these equivalent double-tritone partitions of the octatonic set is shown in Ex. 6-1b. From the initial partition (Db–Gb–G–C), tritone Gb–C serves as a common link between this octatonic set and the diatonic theme, Gb–Ab–Bb–C–Db–Eb–F (at mm. 18–23, first eighth-note). The single tritone contained in this diatonic collection is Gb–C, which appears expressly as the boundary of the accompanying gapped whole-tone chord, Gb–[   ]–Bb–C. (An inversion, Gb–Ab–[   ]–C, of the latter chord appears at m. 24 of the next thematic statement, in juxtaposition with its inversion, Db–Eb–[   ]–G, the two tritone boundaries together implying the presence of the initial octatonic partition, Db–Gb–G–C.) As early as 1910, we find folk characteristics in Kodály's music as well as references to traditional tertian

[5] Linda Brewer, "Progressions among Non–Twelve-Tone Sets in Kodály's *Sonata for Violoncello and Piano,* Op. 4" (D.M.A. treatise, The University of Texas at Austin, 1978); see also Elliott Antokoletz, *The Music of Béla Bartók: A Study of Tonality and Progression in Twentieth-Century Music* (Berkeley and Los Angeles: University of California Press, 1984), pp. 12–13.

[6] These form the cell-Z tetrachordal construction of Bartók, discusssed in Chap. 5, above.

EXAMPLE 6–1. Kodály, *Sonata for Violoncello and Piano,* Op. 4, Mov. II, (a) mm. 18–36, (b) symmetrical partitioning of octatonic scale

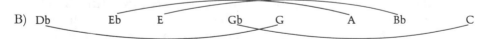

sonority, combined with complex procedures based on invariant segments common to octatonic, diatonic, and partial whole-tone sets.[7]

Other Eastern European composers in the early twentieth century also became reoriented toward their own national idioms, either fusing national elements with nineteenth-century Romantic characteristics or as a

---

[7] Similar relations among these set-forms had appeared two years earlier in some of Bartók's *Bagatelles,* Op. 6, for piano.

means of breaking away from established Central European traditions. In addition to Bartók and Kodály, strong national folk influences also appeared in the music of Czech composers, many of whom had only achieved renown in their own country. Of the more internationally known, Josef Suk continued to absorb national elements into the Romantic tradition of his teacher, Antonin Dvořák, while the Romantic idiom of Vítězslav Novák was more inclined toward the Moravian and Slovak folk styles expressed in his folksong settings. In contrast, the music of Alois Hába was based on an infusion of folk-music elements into a more modernistic idiom. His mother, who was a folksinger, taught him Moravian peasant melodies, which often deviated from traditional Western tuning. In addition to his settings of modal folk tunes that he learned to harmonize from Novák, this experience led to his use of quarter- and sixth-tone microtonality in his operas, *The Mother,* Op. 35 (1927–1929), and *Thy Kingdom Come,* Op. 50 (1932–1942), and in his children's choruses, chamber music, and piano pieces.

The most prominent of twentieth-century Czech composers is Leoš Janáček (1854–1928), who turned to the scientific investigation of his native Moravian folk texts and melodies more than fifteen years before Bartók and Kodály began collecting Hungarian folk tunes. As early as 1888, he collected folk songs in his native region of Northern Moravia; this sparked his reaction to the Romantic idiom of his first opera, *Šárka,* which he was orchestrating at the time. This new interest led to editions of folk-song arrangements, a series of orchestral dances and dance suites, a folk ballet *Rákos Rákoczy* (1891), and a one-act opera, *Počátek románu* ("The Beginning of a Romance," 1891), which was based on folk dances. Janáček originally came out of the tradition of Smetana and Dvořák especially, and, although he never departed entirely from the fundamental principles of nineteenth-century tertian harmonic construction and progression, he infused them prominently within the modality of Moravian folk music. After 1900, his harmonic language also became colored by the whole-tone and ninth-chord formations of the French impressionists. However, he was to depart more radically from the nineteenth century in terms of traditional forms and thematic development, generating the fabric of his compositions by means of varied repetitions of a few basic melodic motifs derived from the rhythm and inflection of his native Czech language. A sense of continual variation in this composed "series of mosaics" was produced by characteristic folk-like rhythmic displacements within the ostinato-like motivic repetitions, which were supported by blocks of contrasting harmonies and directed motion from one local tonal area to another.

Janáček never used actual folk tunes in his compositions, but his interest in their melodic modal structures and texts, combined with his general concern for dramatic truth and realism, led to a type of vocal line lying between recitative and arioso styles. He tended more toward the Russian influences of Mussorgsky than those of his Romantic Czech forebears. His main preoccupation with opera and a cappella choruses throughout his career is perhaps a reflection of these concerns with speech and text, and even his instrumental conceptions generally originated from some programmatic intention. The opera *Jenůfa* (1894–1903) was one of his earliest major works to reveal significant evidence of his speech-like approach to the melodic line, in which the traditional distinctions between recitative and aria were replaced both by motivically generated structures to articulate the form as well as a prominent use of the chorus. His social concerns are also evident in his choice of libretto, which is based on Gabriela Preissovà's powerful drama of Moravian peasant life: Jenůfa's guardian, Kostelnička, murders the illegitimate child of her ward in order to protect the latter from shame.

The successful performance of *Jenůfa* in Prague and Vienna in 1916 opened up new possibilities for the composer at the international level. At the same time, in the wake of new possibilities for national Czech independence, Janáček produced works with strong political and patriotic significance. These included such works as *Mr. Broucek's Excursion to the 15th Century,* dedicated to Masaryk, the first president of the Czechoslovak republic, the symphonic poem, *The Ballad of Blanik* (1920), based on an idea for Czech independence, and later, the five-movement orchestral fanfare, *Sinfonietta* (1926), dedicated in part to the Czechoslovak Armed Forces. Janáček's sympathy for the Russian cause during the war also initiated a period of more intensive interest in Russian literature as well. One of the first results was his three-movement orchestral rhapsody, *Taras Bulba* (1915–1918; orchestrated 1927), after the novel by Gogol. The dramatic power of many of his latest works, which form the foundation upon which his reputation has been established, had been inspired further by the influence of Russian literature: the libretto for his opera *Kátya Kabanová* (1919–1921) is based on Ostrovsky's drama *The Storm;* the inspiration for his *First String Quartet* (1923) coming from Tolstoy's *Kreuzer Sonata;* and the libretto of his last opera, *The House of the Dead* (1928), perhaps his most powerful dramatic work, based on Dostoevsky's memoirs of prison life in Siberia. In addition to the numerous folk-song arrangements, the late vocal and instrumental works are also permeated more prominently by a "speech-like melodic line." These works are now based more subtly on the infusion of the Slavic folk modalities and irregular rhythmic characteristics into a more contemporary idiom. This is based on more extended and flexible modal tonalities without preparatory modulations, the harmonic fabric often colored by pungent dissonances. The discarding of key signatures in the late works also appears to be an indication of his more fluid approach to harmonic and modal-tonal progression. The opera *The Cunning Little Vixen* (1921–1923) is perhaps one of Janáček's most characteristically folk-informed of his late scores. In this fairytale opera, which combines figures from both the animal world and peasant village life, we find the greatest abundance of folk rhythms that underlie the repetitions and variations of the short dance phrases. His *Slavonic* or *Glagolitic Mass* (1926) is among his most brilliantly scored works for both solo voices (of quite unusual ranges) and chorus as well as orchestra, all presented in an objective, archaic style, in connection to the text.

The work of Karol Szymanowski (1882–1937) was central to the development of a national musical style in Poland after the First World War.

Historically, he forms a link in the line of Polish composers stemming from Chopin in the nineteenth century and continuing through the two major national Polish figures after the Second World War, Lutosławski and Penderecki. Szymanowski's early works (*Preludes,* Op. 1, and *Studies,* Op. 4, for piano) reveal a kinship with the Romantic piano styles of Chopin and Scriabin, but he soon began to lean toward the ultrachromatic German idiom of Wagner more heavily. Although he studied harmony and counterpoint in Warsaw, Szymanowski's early German orientation may be attributed to the general lack of a national musical development in Poland in the early years of the century. During his studies in Germany from 1906 to 1908, he moved toward the intense German post-Romantic styles of Strauss and Reger, the influences of which were already apparent in the chromaticism and orchestral resources of his early *Concert Overture* (1904–1905; reorchestrated 1912–1913) and his *First Symphony* (1907).

As early as 1905, Szymanowski's awareness of a need to promote new Polish music led him to found, with several other composers, the *Young Polish Composers' Publishing Company* in Berlin (also known as "Young Poland in Music"), which was also active in Warsaw and other cities in Poland, Germany, and Austria. It was the political conditions of the First World War that were to contribute to his first significant departure from the German late-Romantic sphere. As his visits to Western European countries were curtailed after 1914, he turned to Moscow and Petrograd, where he became more familiar with the impressionism of Debussy. He had already visited Sicily in 1910 and various North African cities (including Algiers, the Biskra district, and other areas) in 1914, having come in contact with both early Christian and Islamic cultures. Together with other non-Germanic musical contacts during this period—he met with Stravinsky and heard Diaghilev's productions of the latter's *Firebird* and *Petrushka*—he developed an original synthesis of various sources. One of the earliest results of this synthesis is his choral *Symphony No. 3* (1914–1916), which joins the more static impressionistic harmonies of Debussy and Scriabin's nonfunctional tonal idiom within the full and colorful orchestration of the German late-Romantic composers. This symphony (entitled "The Song of the Night"), which sets a mystical poem from the second Divan of the Persian poet, Jalál-úd-din Rúmi, for tenor, mixed chorus, and large orchestra, does not employ the melodies or modes of Arab-Persian music, but is rather subtly imbued with its essence. This quality is achieved by imitation of the ornate and chromatic oriental melodic inflections, and by the use of certain percussion instruments and instrumental colors. The continuous and lyrical violin melody, together with intricate wind configurations that introduce a series of motifs, lead to a climactic solo vocal and choral invocation that expresses the impassioned ecstasy of the text. Other works written during this period, including the *Myths* for violin and piano (1915), based on Greek mythology (of which "The Fountain of Arethusa" is particularly striking for its chromaticism as well as impressionistic techniques), the *Songs of a Fairy-Tale Princess* (1915), the opera *King Roger* (1918–1924), coming from his earlier Sicilian experiences, and

Songs of the Infatuated Muezzin (1918), also reveal the synthesis of various sources within the new stylistic orientation.

After the armistice of November 11, 1918, Poland had become an independent state. Szymanowski then became more nationalistic in his political as well as musical attitudes. During the 1920s and 1930s, he began to incorporate Polish national characteristics into his compositions, often quoting Polish folk tunes as well as employing Polish dance rhythms. His *Twenty Mazurkas* (1924–1925), *Four Polish Dances* (1926), and other character pieces for piano, reveal a link with Chopin. Here, we find complex harmonies that are derived from the structures of the folk melodies. The first significant result was his song cycle *Slopiewnie* (1921), based on the text of one of the Skamander poets, J. Tuwim, in which he tried to create a sense of archaic Polish music. A more archaic church-like folk style is the basis of the *Stabat Mater* for solo voices, chorus, and orchestra (1925–1926), which is based on a medieval sequence, and his *Slopiewnie* for solo voice and orchestra (1928). It was in such works as the *Kurpie Songs* for chorus (1928–1929), however, that we find a simpler setting of authentic folk songs. In the 1930s, Szymanowski turned away from the direct influences of folk music as source for his inspiration, maintaining only basic characteristics in an otherwise more subjective compositional idiom. Each of the late works, e.g., the *Veni Creator* for soprano, chorus, orchestra, and organ (1930), the *Litany to the Virgin Mary* (1930–1933) for female chorus and orchestra, the *Fourth Symphony* (1932), and *Second Violin Concerto* (1933), reveals both stylistic features and techniques of his early works combined with those from folk sources influenced by new elements from the style periods of earlier centuries. The basic assumptions underlying Szymanowski's nationalist attitudes and musical characteristics are related to those of other composers outside of Central Europe, in that there was a common desire to move away from the prevailing Germanic musical currents of the late nineteenth century, and to turn toward the new French styles, Eastern sources, and search for one's own national identity.

Other Eastern-European composers of the early twentieth century also looked within their own national boundaries to find new sources for the development of their musical languages. Some of these composers were to absorb and utilize basic elements derived from their own national folk idioms, while others were considered to be "national" in so far as their music reflected the political and social philosophies of their countries. The early Russian works of Stravinsky belong to the first category as does much of the music of the Soviet-trained composer Aram Khachaturian's, who was strongly influenced by the folk music of his Armenian heritage. The musical aesthetics and styles of Khachaturian and several other Soviet-trained composers are more meaningfully discussed in connection with special political and social developments that took place in the Soviet Union after 1917.[8]

---

[8] See Chap. 12, below.

The music of the Russian-born German composer Georg von Albrecht (1891–1976), who studied with Taneyev in Moscow (1914–1915), Glazunov in Leningrad (1918), Straesser in Stuttgart (1922), and later received the Glinka prize in Bonn (1962), reveals the absorption of native Eastern-European folk sources into a personal, native idiom, von Albrecht having collected melodies from the Crimea, Caucasia, and Ural mountains. The composer's folk research is prominently manifested in a number of short piano pieces, including a set of *Baschkiren-Melodien* (1906; arranged 1931), two of which are from his native Kasan, and *Zehn östliche Volkslieder* (1914; 1931), based on Ukrainian, Russian, Lithuanian, Votyakian (Northern-Ural), Tatarian, and Turkish song and dance settings. These diatonic tunes, underscored by traditional harmonic functions, have strong modal, often pentatonic inflection. Von Albrecht's ultimate focus reveals a fusion of divergent sources, including traditional canonic and fugal procedures as well as variation and sonata outlines, which are infused by Romantic features, Russian church music, and more contemporary elements employing polytonality, polymodal chromaticism, nondiatonic modes, and twelve-tone technique. Many of these techniques and procedures are evident in his 24 *Préludes* (in two volumes), Op. 42 and 61 (1934 and 1959), based on his concepts of *Ober- und Untertonreihen* and *Unter- und Obertonreihen,* respectively; in the second cycle, the thirteenth overtone is represented by the "small sixth." While his strong tonal orientation is evident in these cycles of major and minor keys, certain mixed key signatures reveal the composer's contemporary hybrid modal thinking influenced by his folk-music research. For instance, the first piece, in "C-Dur," contains a key signature of F♯ and B♭, which produces one of the permutations (C–D–E–F♯–G–A–B♭–C) of the nondiatonic folk mode commonly used by Bartók, Stravinsky, Szymanowski, and other Eastern European composers. Von Albrecht also associated this mode with the eighth through fourteenth partials of the overtone series.

SCANDINAVIA: CARL NIELSEN, SIBELIUS, AND OTHERS

In the first half of the twentieth century, composers of more or less distinctive national styles emerged in the Northern European countries—Norway, Denmark, Sweden, and Finland. In the nineteenth century, the Norwegian movement toward national independence was reflected in the composition of patriotic songs and in the absorption of Norwegian folk music into art-music composition, the fusion of national and late-Romantic styles having come to fruition in the music of Edvard Grieg and Johan Svendsen. In the field of Norwegian folk-music research, the pioneering work of L. M. Lindeman from 1848 on, was continued in the folksong collections of Sande, Elling, Eggen, and Sandvik after 1900, their work serving as an important source for twentieth-century Norwegian composers. While the followers of Grieg continued in the more traditional Romantic style well into the twentieth century, others attempted to synthesize authentic Norwegian folk music with more modern styles and techniques. After a brief period of impressionist influences on the music of such composers as Alf Hurum and Arvid Kleven in the 1920s, more modernistic tendencies modeled on folk sources became evident in the music of Bjarne Brustad (b. 1895), David Monrad Johansen (1888–1974), Harald Saeverud (b. 1897), and Klaus Egge (b. 1906). Because of his use of more dissonant linear writing in the twelve-tone idiom, Fartein Valen (1887–1952) remained somewhat isolated in Norway. Despite the individual approaches of these composers, their national musical characteristics remained prevalent through World War II.

In Sweden, also, connections to German late Romanticism were established in the emergence of late-nineteenth-century Swedish musical institutions and activities. Strong Wagnerian and Straussian tendencies appeared in the works of Wilhelm Peterson-Berger (1867–1942) and Hugo Alfvén (1872–1960), who also produced nationalistic symphonic poems, and Wilhelm Stenhammer (1871–1927), who turned from a nationalistic style to the broader influences of the German style, and to that of Scandinavian composers—Jean Sibelius and Carl Nielsen. This international tendency, in contrast to that of Norway, became prominent particularly after World War I in the works of Natanael Berg (1879–1957), Oskar Lindberg (1887–1955), and the twelve-tone composer Edvin Kallstenius (1881–1967), many of whom contributed toward the recognition of Swedish composers. The most prominent composers in the first half of the century to develop a more international style further were Hilding Rosenberg (1892–1985), whose style incorporated expressionistic elements, Gösta Nystroem (1890–1966), Moses Pergament (1893–1977), and Dag Wirén (b. 1905), whose style in the 1930s developed along the lines of the French neoclassicists. However, strong Swedish participation in more contemporary international musical styles and techniques came only with the younger generations after World War II.

The earliest Northern European composers to absorb the more modernistic techniques that were developing in Central Europe in the early twentieth century were Danish. Musical developments were extremely varied as new institutions were established to promote contemporary music; among the most important were the *Unge Tonekunstneres Selskab* (1920) and the *Ny Musik Society* (1921), which served as the Danish section of the ISCM since 1923. The most prominent and influential of Danish composers in the early part of the century were Carl Nielsen (1865–1931) and Knud-Aage Riisager (1897–1974), who was influenced by Roussel and French Neoclassicism. Others of the younger generation include Jørgen Bentzon (1897–1951), Finn Hoffding (b. 1899), and Vagn Holmboe (b. 1909).

In the first half of the century, interest in Danish folk music had greatly diminished. This was largely attributed to new industrialization in the late nineteenth century, which began to transform the older agrarian society. These conditions led to the disappearance of folk culture and the replacement of oral musical traditions by mass education and musical commercialization. In this social context, Danish scholars began to preserve folk songs and dance tunes in numerous published volumes since the beginning of the century. As part of the evolving art-music tradition, the music of Carl Nielsen (1865–1931) was decisive in determining the course that Danish music was to follow during the first part of the century. On the one hand, his *Forty Danish Songs* (vol. 1, 1914; vol. 2, 1914–1917), *Ten Little Danish Songs* (1923–1924), sets of *Popular Melodies* (written during and after the war), and other vocal works reveal his increasing interest in moving toward a non-Romantic, folk-like approach in order to reach a larger public. On the other, the stylistic evolution of his instrumental works belongs within the sphere of Central European developments that were to continue along neo-Romantic lines.

Within his varied work, the six symphonies in particular reveal a highly personal approach, the romantic ideal manifested in part by his extension and transformation of late-nineteenth-century harmonic and tonal possibilities, and in his Brahmsian treatment of orchestral color. In his expanded tonal idiom, he employed chromatic materials in rapidly changing, often modal contexts. In this way, he transcended the bounds of late-nineteenth-century chromatic tonality in that all tones and chords came to have meaning not as functional elaborations of secondary scale degrees, but rather as connected to a primary tonal center. This resulted in a tendency toward melodic independence of all degrees of the semitonal scale, in which harmonies are dictated primarily by the linear motion. A sense of linear continuity was further enhanced in the later works by a greater metric freedom. These characteristics of his musical language are organized within the framework of themes, phrases, and forms constructed Classically. By his use of constantly shifting keys, Nielsen created continual variation based on thematic transformation within otherwise clearly defined formal structures. His variational procedures were anticipated as early as his *Second Symphony*, Op. 16 (1901–1902).

The late works also tend toward greater clarity of texture as well as form, in more concise chamber-like textures. In the postwar years, many composers tended to use reduced textures and were interested in the revitalization of the wind quintet medium. The *Wind Quintet,* Op. 43 (1922), reveals Nielson's increased concern for individual instrumental colors. Inspiration for the *Quintet* was sparked by a rehearsal of the Copenhagen Wind Quintet, which Nielsen attended in 1922. This event also led to plans to write a concerto for each of the wind instruments, of which only those for flute and clarinet were completed (1926 and 1928, respectively). The *Quintet* is a lyrical work, in which the inherently distinct wind timbres are suited ideally for representation of the individual personalities of the Copenhagen members—Nielson's intent. This is particularly evident in the final set of *tema con variazione*. The solo variations express the personalities through the precision and sophistication of the flute (variation 2), suavity of the oboe (variation 3), contrast between the quick-temper of the clarinet and controlled objectivity of the bassoon (variation 5), the latter of which is also featured in the steady triplet figuration (variation 7), and the simplicity of the French horn in dotted rhythm (variation 9). The twisting lines of the dark *Preludium* and styles of the remaining variations express wide-ranging moods based on fanfare writing, organ sounds, Scottish drones, and pastorale, march, and chorale-like sections. His Classicism is manifested in the strict Sonata-Allegro and Minuet/Trio forms of the first two movements.

The chamber style of his late years continued in the *Sixth Symphony,* entitled "Sinfonia semplice" (1924–1925), the *Flute Concerto* with chamber orchestra, several chamber works for one or two instruments, and in the controlled counterpoint of such works as the *Three Motets,* Op. 55. Thus, Nielsen's contributions to the development of music in Denmark are characterized by a diversity of national as well as international stylistic characteristics that evolved throughout his career. These are based on an accessible national style in his Danish and popular songs, a neo-Romantic approach in terms of chromatically extended tonal relations, instrumental individuation in his colorful instrumental textures, continual variation and transformation of the thematic material. They are also evidence of a concern for Classical balance and economy in thematic, contrapuntal, and formal construction, and exhibit reduced chamber-like textures.

In Finland, national art-music traditions began to develop in the late-nineteenth century primarily in correspondence with increasing national feeling, as evidenced in the building of new theatres and the establishment of both professional and amateur orchestras and choral groups. In the earlier part of the nineteenth century, Finnish composers were German trained, the later ones adhering primarily to the Wagnerian tradition. The Finnish composer and conductor Robert Kajanus was one of the first to show an interest in Finnish folk music, but it was Jean Sibelius (1865–1957) who was recognized as Finland's leading composer after the première of his nationalistic five-movement choral symphony, *Kullervo* (1892). The latter work was inspired by the *Kalevala,* the national epic of Finland, compiled into its final form in the nineteenth century by Elias Lönnrot from the texts and chant-like melodies of old Finnish folk legends. This epic had been preserved through the oral transmission of folk singers in Eastern Finland, where Lönnrot traveled in 1828 to collect folk songs and poetry of the common people. Its repetitive musical incantations are considered to be the oldest type of Finnish folk song. The *Kalevala* was primary in helping to establish a sense of national identity and pride in the Finnish people, and served as an important textual and musical source for many Finnish composers. Sibelius himself was to travel to Eastern Finland in 1892 to transcribe melodies of the runic singers in Karelia, but tales (rather than the tunes) of the *Kalevala* were to play a more significant role in the inspiration of many of his symphonic compositions. Although Sibelius produced works in various media—songs and choral music, piano pieces, solo string literature, and chamber music—his most characteristic and important "style evolution" is represented by his symphonic music.

While certain twentieth-century Finnish composers reveal prominent influences from contemporary international and traditional European sources, Sibelius imbued traditional Classical and Romantic structures with the essence of the Finnish national spirit. During the 1890s, when Finland's increasing desire for independence from the Russian Empire stirred people toward a new level of national consciousness, Sibelius' music played an important part in the patriotic movements. Although Sibelius did not employ folk tunes in his music, certain stylistic elements tended to evoke the somber, pastoral, or majestic qualities associated with the Finnish landscape, as in his programmatic orchestral tone poems. These Finnish traits were expressed in the modality of the melodies, often played by dark, nostalgic English horn or cello solos, sustained static chords in the brass, full sonorities in the low registers of the winds or strings, and the surging of crescendos to full dynamic climaxes, creating a sense of spaciousness.

Sibelius's style evolution can be traced through four periods: Finnish (1892–1902); Classical (1903–1909); complex and subjective (1911–1915); and mature and synthetic (1924–1957).[9] The early works after *Kullervo* are most significantly represented by the four *Lemminkäinen* legends (1895–1900)—including "Lemminkäinen and the maidens of the island," "Lemminkäinen in Tuonela," "The Swan of Tuonela," and "Lemminkäinen's return"—the symphonic poem *En Saga* (1892, rev. 1902), and the first two *Symphonies* (1899, 1901–1902). Most of these are colorfully scored programmatic works, characterized by the expressive moods of Finnish folklore. Influences are primarily found in Kajanus's symphonic poem *Aino,* the Russian style of Tchaikovsky's *Pathétique* (seen in the slow movement of Sibelius' *First Symphony*), and an originally operatic conception of certain pieces of the *Lemminkäinen* legend coming by way of Wagner. One of his most popular works, *Finlandia* (1899–1900), was written at a time of increasing patriotic fervor.

During a period of extensive international travels (1903–1914), Sibelius' style began to undergo significant changes as he turned away from the Romantic moods of his earlier nationalistic works toward more concise and more objective neoclassicism. The influence of Beethoven was now manifested in a greater economy of means, more classical handling of the orchestration, and in increasing concern with the pervasive development of thematically derived motifs within classically balanced formal structures especially, as seen in the tighter three-movement plan of the *Third Symphony* (1904–1907). Between 1911 and 1915, the outbreak of war and subsequent loss of autonomy to Russia, as well as illness, may have contributed to the more subjective and personal expression of Sibelius' feelings in a still more concentrated and austere approach to form. Tonal direction was often obscured within a more continuous developmental process, as exemplified in the *Fourth* (1911) and *Fifth Symphonies* (1915, rev. 1916 and 1919). By this time, the fusion of contrasting elements was more important than the representation of their individual pictorial qualities.

[9] David Cherniavsky, "Special Characteristics of Sibelius' Style," in *The Music of Sibelius,* ed. Gerald Abraham (New York: W. W. Norton, 1947), pp. 147–152; see also Preston Stedman, *The Symphony* (Englewood Cliffs: Prentice-Hall, Inc., 1979), p. 252.

The *Fourth Symphony* exemplifies Sibelius' more advanced style, where principles of the Classical tradition and the essence of the Finnish spirit are infused in a highly personal idiom. While the four movements are each set within a Classical formal mold, the musical language of the work could only have developed in the twentieth century. This language appears to be somewhat traditional because of the predominating triadic sonorities, but harmonic progression has little to do with the functions of the major-minor scale system. While triads move within the static framework of the diatonic folk modes, which together with ostinato-like thematic patterns and sustained chords contribute significantly to the national flavor of the work, these modes often acquire an exotic coloring through their local transformations into octatonic and whole-tone formations. These nonfunctional pitch-set interactions as well as common motivic rhythmic patterns are basic to the interrelationships among the various thematic ideas that form the sonata–allegro plan of movement I.[10]

The initial idea (a) of the first-theme group unfolds as an ambiguous modal or whole-tone segment, C–D–E–F♯, this ambiguity establishing the basic tension for subsequent development and fulfillment of the dual pitch-set potentialities inherent in the segment. At the same time, the tonality of A minor is obscured initially by the held C, then E–F♯, tritone C–F♯ serving as the melodic and harmonic boundary of this thematic segment. The second idea (b) of the first-theme group (mm. 6ff., solo cello) is initiated by an anacrusic G♯, which momentarily extends the pitch content of idea a to five notes of a whole-tone collection (C–D–E–F♯–G♯). However, the downbeat of the solo (m. 7) immediately draws this collection into A melodic-minor, so that in retrospect the original segment is apparently no more than a whole-tone coloring of this A mode. The E–F♯ ostinato of idea a, now as fifth and sixth degrees of A melodic-minor, continues as an accompaniment to idea b, the latter containing linear fluctuations of the seventh degree (G♯ and G) to produce the A-Dorian mode (A–B–C–D–E–F♯–G). This relatively simple bimodality in the combined ostinato ideas (a and b) is absorbed (at mm. 17ff.) into a more complex and ambiguous mixture of linearly stated diatonic-modal segments, which together imply the presence of a larger octatonic coloring, E–F♯/G♭–G–[   ]–B♭–C–D♭–E♭ (m. 17, beat 3, through m. 19, third eighth-note). The modal-neighbor A♭ of the viola is the only note outside of the octatonic collection (Ex. 6–2). Through further modal shifts (mm. 19–21), new modal mixtures and nondiatonic colorings occur. Cello I, for instance, extends the G♭-Lydian segment linearly (G♭–B♭–C) to five notes

[10] The formal outline of the movement is as follows: Exposition (mm. 1–48), first-theme group (mm. 1–31), a (m. 1), b (m. 6), transition (m. 24), c (m. 29), theme 2 (mm. 31–40, d (m. 31), c (m. 33), d (m. 35), e (m. 37), f (m. 40), closing (mm. 41–53), b (m. 41), a (m. 48); Development (mm. 54–88), b (m. 55), b′ and d (m. 66), a′ (m. 72), b″ (m. 80); Recapitulation (mm. 87–114), a/d (m. 87), c (m. 89), e (m. 93), f (m. 96), closing (mm. 97–114), b (m. 97), a (m. 104). This scheme differs only slightly from that given by Stedman, *The Symphony*, ibid., p. 261.

EXAMPLE 6–2. Sibelius, *Fourth Symphony,* Mov. I, mm. 17ff.

octatonic: E G♭ G [ ] B♭ C D♭ E♭

of the whole-tone scale, G♭–[ ]–B♭–C–D–E. In the following measures (21ff.), the first-theme group is brought to a close by a motion back to C-Lydian.

The octatonic and whole-tone implications within the basic diatonic modality of this section are fully realized in the development section. A stretto, based on a descending form of idea b (mm. 55ff.), outlines the augmented triad B–G–D♯. This whole-tone segment is extended by the addition of C♯–D♯ of idea a (flute and clarinet) to four notes (B–G–D♯–C♯). Cello I (mm. 58–59) then interlocks the augmented triad with an ascending seven-note octatonic segment (D♯–E–F♯–G–A–B♭–[ ]–D♭), the latter in turn interlocking with the whole-tone segment D♭–F–G–B. After a series of transpositions of these interlockings, the whole-tone component is expanded as part of the growth process. The violins (from the middle of m. 68 to the middle of m. 69) give us the first complete whole-tone collection, D–E–F♯–G♯–A♯–C, this time interlocked with diatonic segments. At the center of the development section (mm. 70ff.), the thirty-second-note scalar transformations of the original idea a serve as a focal point in the movement for the realization of both complete whole-tone scales in continuous alternation. At the opening and closing of the Trio section of movement II, mm. 273ff. and mm. 296ff., the low strings unfold a complete ascending octatonic scale, C♯–D–E–F–G–A♭–B♭–B, in counterpoint with the main whole-tone colored modal theme of the Trio.

The earlier ambiguous interlockings of set segments continue to occur in the remaining exposition. The series of short powerful brass crescendi at idea c in the transition (mm. 29–31), which is so characteristic of Sibelius' orchestral writing, leads to idea d of theme 2 in F♯ major. While the descending segment is clearly diatonic, the initial ascending segment, derived from idea a, outlines an ambiguous whole-tone segment, A–B–[ ]–D♯. This is extended to A–B–C♯–D♯ by the second note of the descending segment. Not only do we get a thematic fusion here (a, d, and the crescendo of c), but the chromatic unfolding of tonalities to this point (C, A, and F♯, or G♭) suggests a background-level link to the octatonic rather than diatonic spectrum. The new tritone-boundary A–D♯ of theme 2 is a local extension of this scheme (C–A–F♯–D♯) and is also the minor-third complement of the original C–F♯ boundary of idea a. (The recapitulation of theme 2, at mm. 87ff., cello, now bounded by the original tritone C–F♯, further bears this complementary tritone relationship out; the A tonic is then held as a pedal in place of the F♯.) While theme 2 is a relatively unambiguous diatonic focal point in the exposition, the closing (mm. 41ff.), which returns to ideas a and b, is a preparation for the shift to the central octatonic and whole-tone interactions of the development. Parallel fragments of idea b initiate the section (mm. 41ff.), which are ambiguously modal, whole-tone, and octatonic. In anticipation of the development, the first two segments of the viola (F♯–A♯–C and B–D♯–F) suggest representations of both whole-tone collections, respectively. At the same time, the alignment of each of these with the figure in the cello also implies two octatonic segments: F♯–A♯–C and A♯–C♯–E give us A♯–C–C♯–[ ]–E–F♯[ ]–[ ], while B–D♯–F and D♯–F♯–A give us D♯–F–F♯–[ ]–A–B; the linear progression of A♯–C♯–E and D♯–F♯–A in the cello implies an extension of the first octatonic segment to A–A♯–[ ]–C♯–D♯–E–F♯–[ ]. However, the remaining statements of this closing group establish the primacy of F♯ major, so the initial whole-tone and octatonic implications only serve as chromatic coloring within the diatonic spectrum here. The return of the closing section at the end of the movement establishes the key of A major with some chromatic coloring.

Movement II further develops these pitch-set interactions and modal colorings in a series of thematic unfoldings within a traditional scherzo/trio form, but it is in Movement III that thematic transformation and interaction of modal, whole-tone, and octatonic collections reach their most intensive stage. Within the condensed form and transparent textures, the motivic elements and divergent pitch-set components of the preceding movements now appear to be highly synthesized. For instance, all three pitch-sets are more fully realized in the spinning out of the flute theme and its counterpoint (at mm. 4–6) (Ex. 6–3). The implied octatonic segment (B–C–D–E♭–F) is

EXAMPLE 6–3. Sibelius, *Fourth Symphony*, Mov. III, mm. 4–6, three basic pitch sets in flute theme and counterpoint

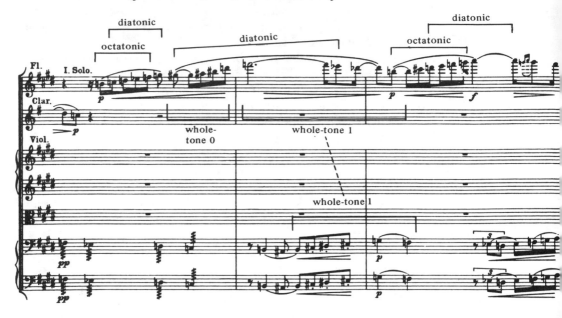

diatonicized by the next note, G, followed by two mutually exclusive wholetone tetrachords (G♯–A♯–B♯–D and F–E♭–D♭–B). The latter wholetone segment is extended to five notes in the low strings (B–C♯–D♯–E♯–G, in enharmonic spelling, B–D♭–E♭–F–G). In turn, the same whole-tone tetrachord in the flute is linearly overlapped by a six-note octatonic segment (B–C♯–D–E–F–G), again diatonicized by the next new note, A. Movement IV, although the longest and most varied of the four in terms of its thematic materials, is highly integrated by means of thematic transformation and is the most unified in terms of its modal-diatonic priorities. Whole-tone and octatonic intrusions into the primarily diatonic contexts are more isolated locally than in the preceding movements and, at the same time, are absorbed for the first time into a directed tonality that is increasingly reliant upon certain basic tonal functions.

Although Finland achieved its independence after the Bolshevik Revolution, conditions worsened as civil war broke out early in 1918. Due to Sibelius' artistic isolation in the following years, during which time he also lacked an affinity with the newest European musical developments, he produced only four major works after the war, including the *Sixth* (1923) and *Seventh Symphonies* (1924), the incidental music to the *Tempest* (1925), and the tone poem *Tapiola* (1926). These late works, based on the most intensive synthesis and development of thematic materials, represent the culmination of his compositional evolution toward extreme formal concentration, which can be seen in the condensation of the traditional four-movement symphonic scheme into the one-movement form of the *Seventh Symphony*.[11] Sibelius has had a direct influence on other Scandinavian composers (Leevi Madetoja from Finland and Wilhelm Stenhammer, Hilding Rosenberg, and Dag Wirén from Sweden) as well as composers from Western Europe and the United States (Bax, Walton, Barber, and Harris).

ENGLAND: VAUGHAN WILLIAMS AND OTHERS

For two centuries after the death of Henry Purcell (in 1695), English music had been dominated first by Italian, then German styles. In the early part of the twentieth century, significant changes became evident in English musical developments; this was characterized by a splintering into divergent experiments, as precipitated by pre-World War I international political conditions. While certain English composers continued to lean toward the German Romantic tradition, an increasing sense of English national identity led others to independence of German late-Romantic styles.

Continuing along Romantic lines were Edward Elgar (1857–1934) and Arnold Bax (1883–1953). Elgar's lengthy symphonic forms, based on the dramatic "working out" of themes, reveal an affinity with the classically oriented but grandiose structural designs of Bruckner and Mahler. Bax tended to blend the chromaticized diatonicism and thematic transformations of Liszt, Strauss, and the Russian Romantics with techniques of the French impressionists and his English contemporaries. Other English composers of Wagnerian and Romantic influences were Hubert Parry (1848–1944), Charles Stanford (1852–1924), Ethyl Smyth (1858–1944), Joseph Holbrooke (1878–1958), Gordon Jacobs (b. 1895), and others. Arthur Bliss (1891–1975) temporarily turned away from German Romantic influences toward French composers, Stravinsky, and Schoenberg in the 1920s, only to return to his earlier kinship with the Romantic style and music of Elgar. Frederick Delius (1862–1934) exhibited a personal style that evolved from the fluid harmonic chromaticism of Wagner, but this was tempered by the more transparent textures and static chromaticism of Grieg and Debussy.

Certain English composers reacted to the aesthetics of Romanticism by leaning more toward individual nationalistic styles. This new orientation evolved by the growth of interest in Tudor church music and English folk song, and through acceptance of the aesthetics, styles, and techniques of the French impressionists. The development of new English musical societies and festivals throughout the century as well as the founding of the School of English Church Music in 1927 provided new opportunities for English composers and performers. Among the many composers who contributed to a distinctive national bent in England, several are notable. Gustav Holst (1874–

[11] Gerald Abraham, "The Symphonies," in *The Music of Sibelius,* ed. Gerald Abraham (New York: W. W. Norton, 1947), pp. 35–36.

1934) was a central figure in English musical life in the first decades of the century, an "antiromantic" who incorporated certain modern techniques including bitonality, nontertian constructions, and multimetric plans into his works. Peter Warlock (alias Philip Heseltine; 1894–1930), whose individual style is best represented by his numerous songs and choral works, exhibits influences of Delius, but was also clearly enriched by his profound knowledge of Elizabethan music and medieval English poetry. Edmund Rubbra (b. 1901) followed both Holst and other contemporary English composers stylistically, and developed a polyphonic style along the lines of the Tudor composers (as seen in his masses, motets, and madrigals).

The most prominent English composer in the first half of the century to combine traditional and contemporary styles into a musical idiom that is distinctively English in spirit was Ralph Vaughan Williams (1872–1958). As with many other English composers of his generation, he was well-versed in the Central European Classical and Romantic styles, having studied with Parry, Wood, and Stanford in England during his college years, Max Bruch in Berlin in 1897, and Ravel in Paris in 1908. These influences, together with his own originality, led him to compose in divergent styles that incorporated twentieth-century technical devices within a tonal context. While his international inclinations are seen in such widely diverging interests as late-Baroque music and French impressionism, his awareness of his own national identity, including an interest in popular traditions and a feeling of kinship with the common man, also led him to absorb characteristics from several of his own national sources. These include English folk music, hymns, the literature of Shakespeare, Tennyson, Blake, Whitman, and others, music of the English Renaissance, Purcell in particular, and that of contemporary English composers. The styles of Parry and Elgar were important influences especially. He had studied Elgar's scores since his youth and expressed great admiration for his choral works as well as for the perfection of his orchestrations.[12] Although he retained an admiration for Wagner's music, the English sources prevailed over his early Romantic tendencies.[13]

The varied activities of Vaughan Williams as composer, teacher, editor, folk song collector, writer, lecturer, and conductor, the last of which included work with amateur singers and instrumentalists throughout his life, were all connected to his humanistic and social attitudes toward people and musical functions. These attitudes were first manifested in his work as ethnographer, resulting in his collection of over 800 English folk tunes during his lifetime. He collected his first folk tune *Bushes and Briars* in 1903, one year

[12] Ralph Vaughan Williams, "What have we learnt from Elgar?" in the memorial issue of *Music and Letters* 16/1 (1935): 13–19.

[13] Vaughan Williams, "Who Wants the English Composer?" *RCM Magazine* IX/1 (1912): 11; reprinted in Hubert J. Foss, *Ralph Vaughan Williams* (London: George G. Harrap and Co., 1950), p. 198, for a statement of his philosophy that music "must grow out of the very life of himself, the community in which he lives, the nation to which he belongs."

before Bartók had discovered the genuine folk music of his native Hungary. He turned, as did Bartók, to the modalities of the folk-song to free his musical language from the tonal functions of the Central European tradition. According to Vaughan Williams, "folk songs seem to take kindly to the harmony of any period at which a skilled musician may happen to treat them harmonically."[14] Among the first compositional results of Vaughan Williams' folk-song studies were his three *Norfolk Rhapsodies* (1905–1906), only the first of which he wanted to have published.[15] The main theme of the latter is introduced by a rhapsodic viola solo exclusively in E-pentatonic (E–G–A–B–D), the strings and flutes adding to the Norfolk atmosphere. The most common modes found among English folk tunes are the Dorian, Aeolian, and Mixolydian, often with emphasis on their pentatonic substructures—only one Lydian and about six Phrygian tunes were discovered by Cecil Sharp.[16] Correspondingly, the Dorian, Aeolian, and Mixolydian modes prevail in many of Vaughan Williams' original compositions as well as in his folk-tune settings. In his ballad opera *Hugh the Drover* (1911–1914), the form of one of the folk tunes, which according to Vaughan Williams are reminiscences of various versions from his own collection and those of others, is set in a rounded quaternary structure of AA'BA' (with refrain) in the mode of B-Aeolian.[17] As in heptatonic modal folk tunes of other nations (for example, Hungary), the underlying pentatonic substructure (B–D–E–F♯–A) in this English tune is also prominently felt. One instance in which the composer simultaneously employs all three modes is the *Kyrie* of the *Mass in G Minor*.

As part of his social philosophy of music, Vaughan Williams also worked as music editor of the new *English Hymnal* from 1904 to 1906, which brought him in contact with old English hymn tunes as well. As a result, he composed a number of his own hymn tunes based on folk tunes, one of which is the famous *Sine nomine* for the hymn *For All the Saints*. Within the G-major structure of the tune, we again find a prevalence of the pentatonic substructure (G–A–B–D–E). His editorial work in 1925 was extended to the hymnal collection *Songs of Praise* and in 1928 to the *Oxford Book of Carols*.

Furthermore, a significant part of his activities from 1905 to 1953 included the conducting of amateur choral and instrumental groups at the annual Leith Hill Music Festivals in performances of the music of Bach and other masters. Many of his own choral works were composed for these occasions, including the *Benedicite* (1930), *A Song of Thanksgiving,* for speaker, soprano, choruses, and orchestra (1945), and choral settings of the cycle *Folk Songs of the Four Seasons* (1950). After 1907, his works were

[14] See Vaughan Williams' lecture on *English Folk Songs* (London, 1912).
[15] Two of the tunes were collected in early 1905 from King's Lynn fishermen.
[16] Michael Kennedy, *The Works of Ralph Vaughan Williams* (London: Oxford University Press, 1964), p. 28.
[17] See this tune in Frank Howes, *The Music of Ralph Vaughan Williams* (London: Oxford University Press, 1954), p. 234.

performed at almost every other English choral festival as well. In the same year, his choral and orchestral setting of Whitman's *Toward the Unknown Region* was heard at Leeds, followed in 1910 by the performance of his *Sea Symphony,* for soprano, baritone, chorus, and orchestra, based on settings of Whitman's *Sea-Drift* and *Passage to India.* Whitman's expression of universal brotherhood in these texts had a special significance for the composer, who continued to use the powerful sea imagery as late as the *Sinfonia antartica,* for soprano, small chorus, and orchestra (1949–1952). At the time of its composition, the *Sea Symphony,* despite its brief quotations of two folk songs in the scherzo and reminiscences of Purcell in other sections, appeared "modern in its elusiveness and tortuous harmonic progressions."[18]

A decidedly original style began to emerge in Vaughan Williams' works at the end of the first decade of the century. At this time, he began to widen his scope with a developing interest in the music of Elizabethan composers. This can be seen in his *Fantasia on a Theme by Thomas Tallis* (1909) for double string orchestra and string quartet, where he employed the Renaissance "polychoral" style as well as long successions of parallel triadic writing in a modal (in this case, Phrygian) context. The latter technique dated back to the Middle Ages and was characteristic of English music. The scholarly musical research of Sir Richard Terry, one of the basic forces in the revival of the polyphonic liturgical music of the English Renaissance composers, was to provide the means for developing a neo-Elizabethan style. It was mainly in his choral works that Vaughan Williams was to absorb and transform this style into a contemporary English idiom by means of a synthesis of other techniques and styles, significantly those of the French impressionists, as in the *Mass* (discussed below).

Following World War I, Vaughan Williams reached a new stage of development in a variety of genres and styles. This ranged from folk-song and Elizabethan text settings for solo voice or chorus to the more profound liturgical choral pieces, and large band and symphonic compositions. Certain works in the latter category reflected an intensified patriotic sense which stemmed from his earlier military experience. This patriotism can be found in the *Pastoral Symphony No. 3* (1916–1921), with its bugle call in the slow movement, and, more significantly, in such works for military band as the *English Folk Song Suite* (1923) and *Toccata marziale* (1924). His liturgical works are particularly significant not only for revealing the composer's more optimistic and visionary expression at this stage of his development, but also for the fusion of the varied sources, including both folk and art music.

The *Mass in G Minor* (1920–1921) is most striking as a pioneering masterpiece in the reestablishment of the a cappella choral style. Through the work of Sir Richard Terry at Westminster Cathedral, the revival of the polyphonic English Renaissance Masses of Byrd and Tallis inspired Vaughan Williams to compose his *Mass,* for four soloists and double chorus. The

---

[18] See the *Yorkshire Post* (October 13, 1910).

techniques and styles of the earlier English composers are manifested here in a variety of ways. The austere and objective liturgical style of the work, based on that of the earlier English composers, corresponds with the dictates set forth in 1903 by Pope Pius X in a document known as the *Motu Proprio* ("on one's own initiative"), an encyclical similar in spirit to the musical reforms of the Church at the Council of Trent during the late Renaissance (1542– 1563).[19] Vatican reaction against eighteenth- and nineteenth-century emotional, sentimental approaches to the liturgy and against use of instrumental accompaniments in the Mass was based on the idea that such forces tended to interfere with the meaning and function of the sacred texts. Among its recommendations was the restoring of Gregorian Chant and Classic polyphony of the Roman School, singing in Latin "as it is in the books, without alteration or inversion of the words, without undue repetition, without breaking syllables, and always in a manner intelligible to the faithful who listen." Also recommended were the maintenance of distinct musical settings for the different sections of the Mass, determination of the length of the musical setting based on the requirements of the liturgy, and the banning of most instruments (winds could be used with permission). As with many composers of sacred compositions in the twentieth century, Vaughan Williams was one of the strongest adherents to these principles, capturing the individual sense of each section without undue emotional emphasis.

In the *Kyrie*, the linear imitative writing is based on a tendency toward chordal style and use of *faburden* (a late-medieval English term describing the use of improvised sixth-chord harmonization in successions of triads moving in parallel motion). Such progressions were also common in the works of the French impressionists. This tendency toward homophonic writing reveals an adherence to the principles of the *Motu Proprio* by permitting greater clarity of the words. Also, since Byrd, a characteristic found frequently in English music was the occurrence of *cross relations,* a device that lent itself to twentieth-century interests in polymodal chromaticism. In the opening *ad lib* organ introduction and *Kyrie* section (at mm. 7–8), linear voice-leading functions result in modal clashes between voices, i.e., through modal mixture (Ex. 6–4). The indication of G-Aeolian in the key signature is altered contextually to form G-Dorian in all the voices except altos (at m. 8). This produces a bimodal conflict between the G-Dorian (raised) sixth-degree E and G-Aeolian sixth-degree E♭. As mentioned above, these two modes, together with G-Mixolydian (suggested at the return of the *Kyrie*), are the three most common modes found in English folk music.

The free and fluid rhythmic style of the Renaissance permits a liberation from the barline and regular phrasal organization as well as from the functional relationships of consonance and dissonance established by the

---

[19] See the translation in Nicolas Slonimsky, *Music Since 1900* (New York: W. W. Norton, 1937; 3rd ed. Boston: Coleman-Ross Company, 1949; rev. 4/1971), pp. 523–529.

EXAMPLE 6–4. Vaughan Williams, *Mass in G Minor, Kyrie*, mm. 7–8, modal mixture

major–minor scale system. The successive imitative entries depart freely from the regular 4/2 barring, reestablishing only momentarily the strong beat at the local G-Dorian tonic cadence on the last syllable of "eleison" (m. 8). Tension is maintained by further departures in the imitative entries until the return to the barline on the last syllable of "eleison" at the final cadence of the section. Similar rhythmic freedom in relation to the barline was achieved by Stravinsky and Bartók by way of Eastern European folk-music sources.

The personal stamp of the composer was manifested in his subtle use of dynamic indications, at certain times *pp* and at others *ff* (as toward the end of the second *Kyrie*). The specific "pianissimo" quality of the opening *Kyrie* in the context of parallel triads also suggests the impressionist influence. This seems more apparent in the shape of the lines, which are often based on static alternations between two tones that produce an undulating linear motion. These influences are increasingly evident in subsequent sections. Both the dynamic indications (including crescendi and decrescendi) and the static linear motions represent twentieth-century infusions into the earlier polyphonic style.

The *Christe* changes to a more brilliant sound through use of solo voices. This new texture produces an antiphonal relationship with the *Kyrie*, which refers us to the polychoral Renaissance style. The brighter and more intense quality one fifth higher (in D) also results from the successive raising of certain degrees (the third and seventh) of the original G-Aeolian/Dorian modes, thereby producing additional polymodal changes with increased occurrences of complex cross relations. The modulation from the opening key of G to the "dominant" in this middle section infuses the more modern tonal principle into the older modal polyphony, a combination which draws the older Elizabethan style into Vaughan Williams' own contemporary approach. While the key signature indicates D-Mixolydian (D–E–F♯–G–A–B–C), the appearance of the low third-degree F (m. 4 of the *Christe*) establishes D-Dorian. The first explicit modal conflict occurs with the raising of the third-degree F to F♯ (m. 6) to produce D-Mixolydian, which then immediately modulates to D-major through the raising of the seventh degree (C) to C♯. At this midpoint, we get a traditional tonal progression of IV–V7–I in the latter key. The weak metric position of this cadence, however, permits a continuation of the contrapuntal flow.

Further contrast is provided by the somewhat more rhythmic character of the *Christe*. The unequal-beat patterns are now derived from the explicit metric changes. In contrast to the departures from and returns to the regular barline in the *Kyrie*, the successive entries of the musical motifs in this section—one associated with the opening statement of "Christe," another with the soprano and alto entries on "eleison" (at mm. 4 and 5)—tend to maintain their respective relationships with the barline, however irregular (compare the tenor entry at m. 3 with the alto entry at m. 7; also compare the alto entry at m. 4 with all the voices at the end of m. 5 and with the soprano and tenor entries at mm. 8 and 9). A greater sense of rhythmic stability and demarcation is felt, albeit in an irregular and more angular multimetric context. The tension is partially resolved by the more stable meter at the homophonic cadence, by the strong metric placement of the V–I cadence, and by the lowering of the third and seventh degrees (F and C) in the return to D-Dorian. The second Kyrie is momentarily brighter than the first. This is due to the overlap of the *Christe* cadence, which produces a G-Mixolydian inflection (raised third degree, B) before returning to G-Dorian/Aeolian.

The music of Vaughan Williams is distinguished from the earlier Renaissance style primarily by means of the composer's synthesis of historically incongruent techniques. Extreme changes in texture, melodic contour, polymodal cross relations, and dynamic level were all employed by Vaughan Williams, in his desire to express his own personal, religious vision. This is more apparent in the *Gloria in excelsis,* with its brilliant contrasts between responsorial (solo vs. chorus) and antiphonal (polychoral) singing. While the extensive use of parallel chord writing is reminiscent of the old English style, rapid chromatic alterations at times appear to obscure the modal identity in a manner that pervades French impressionist compositions. Following the dominant-tonic cadence of the *ad lib* organ, the massive eight-part chordal harmony of the "Et in terra pax" ascends, within a few measures, from G major (perhaps Lydian) to a mixed A-major/minor mode (A–B–C♯–D–E–F–G) by way of a chromatic sequence of secondary dominants (Ex. 6–5).

Each new musical moment continues to present a highly personal expression of the given text. At the "Laudamus te," marked "Allegro," the voices suddenly break into rapid antiphonal alternations. In the successions of parallel triads within the first melismatic passage, at "Benedicimus te," cross-relations now occur between remotely related modes. The linear conflict between G-Mixolydian (G–A–B–C–D–E–F), G-Dorian

EXAMPLE 6–5. Vaughan Williams, *Mass in G Minor, Gloria in excelsis,* "Et in terra pax," chromatic sequence of secondary dominant chords leading to A-major/minor

modal mixture from G to A cadence

(G–A–B♭–C–D–E–F), and G-Aeolian (G–A–B♭–C–D–E♭–F), which are precisely the three most common modes in English folk music, further contributes to the increasing excitement. The original ascent from G to A is temporally expanded in the first ten measures of the Allegro, the second, more expanded melisma in the male voices (at "Glorificamus te") increasing the activity and excitement through imitation and arrival at fortissimo. Further contrast is produced in the succession of antiphonal block structures, each articulated by a change of tonality as well as mode—A-Mixolydian (m. 10), E-Aeolian (m. 16), G-Mixolydian/Dorian (m. 18), E♭-Lydian (m. 22), and a return to G-Dorian/Mixolydian before the entry of the soloists. In terms of tonal and textural relationships, a cyclical reference is made to the opening *Kyrie* both by the establishment of the "dominant" (D-Dorian) at the "Qui tollis" as well as by the brighter responsorial context of this middle section.

The vocal style of the *Sanctus* deserves special mention in terms of the subtle fusion of earlier English styles with French impressionist techniques. The sense of awe, produced by the quiet and fluid melismatic rhythm, is enhanced by the static wavering motion in each of the imitative soprano and alto lines. This undulating motion, atypical of the English Renaissance, is a textural feature of Debussy's music—one need only look to the opening measures of *Pelléas* or to those passages in the *String Quartet* based on alternating parallel triads. The homophonic punctuations by all the voices in the

Sanctus are based on dominant-tonic relations within the otherwise polymodal context. This again reveals the composer's fusion of anachronistic (modal/tonal) techniques. The Andante opens in G-Mixolydian, which is brightened by the raising of the seventh degree (F to F♯) in the dominant chord of the first tutti punctuation, returning to G-Dorian/Mixolydian in the undulating figuration. Toward the end of the *Sanctus* (at "Sanctus Dominus Deus Sabaoth"), another tonally functional motion to the brighter dominant of the dominant (A-major cadence) punctuates the undulating soprano and alto figurations, which are now expanded in range and register. The A-major chord then moves down a step to G-Mixolydian to begin the "Pleni sunt caeli." The overall progression of keys from G to A and back suggests a cyclic return of the same relations that opened the *Gloria.* A remarkable sense of breadth, power, and transformation is produced as the cumulative imitative voices move in crescendo toward the *Osanna.*

During this decade, in which he composed the *Mass,* the oratorio *Sancta civitas* (1923–1925), *Flos Campi* (1925), for solo viola, small wordless chorus, and small orchestra, and edited the *Songs of Praise* and the *Oxford Book of Carols,* we also find other sides to Vaughan Williams' musical personality. Some of his most personal syntheses of English folksong characteristics with styles as wide-ranging as Bach, Debussy, and perhaps even Bartók were created during a time when "English musicians seem, to a later generation, to have been in a kind of vacuum, ignoring the eruptions of musical harmony and language taking place in Europe, suffering what has been termed a 'psychological blockage' and looking to Sibelius as a father-figure rather than to Stravinsky and Schoenberg."[20] The *Concerto for Violin and Strings* (1924–1925) is reminiscent of Bach's contrapuntal writing (as is Holst's *Fugal Concerto*); the *Piano Concerto* (1926–1931) suggests a similarity to the toccata style of Bartók's *First Piano Concerto.* The bitonal opening of the *Flos Campi* is a feature that can be traced to his own *Third Symphony* and *Sancta Civitas.* At the same time, he produced one of his most original expressions in the folk-song idiom, significantly represented in his *Six Studies in English Folksong* for cello and piano (1926). In contrast, Vaughan Williams was also revealing both his comic and lyrical sides in opera. In collaboration with Cecil Sharp's sister Evelyn, he produced *The Poisoned Kiss* (1927–1929), after the last part of Richard Garnett's *Twilight of the Gods* and Nathaniel Hawthorne's *Mosses from the Old Manse.* This comic work, with spoken dialogue, is quite different from *Sir John in Love* (1924–1928), after Shakespeare, and his one-act opera *Riders to the Sea* (1925–1932), an expressive work based on a play by Synge.

Thus, while Vaughan Williams was to synthesize diverse traditional and contemporary techniques and styles in his compositions after World War I especially, all his works were tempered by the fundamental qualities of his own national sources. His music can be placed in two categories, one expressing a profoundly personal quality, and the other intended to be accessible to the performance capabilities of the nonprofessional as well as for the

[20] Kennedy, *The Works of Ralph Vaughan Williams,* n. 16, above, p. 185.

appreciation of the common man. However, the composer's philosophy and aesthetics as manifested in his overall output are not so distinct from one another as these categories might suggest.

In the music of Benjamin Britten (1913–1976), we also sense a deep commitment to the English musical heritage. Whereas Vaughan Williams' debt to specific national sources such as Elizabethan polyphony or English folk song is readily identifiable, the English sources of Britten's style appear to be somewhat more sublimated within a personal idiom based on the most complete synthesis of divergent techniques and styles. Since it is in the post–World War II era that we find the complete ripening of his earlier styles and synthesis with the most diverse international influences in an idiom that may be perceived as thoroughly "English," Britten's music will be discussed later as part of the postwar generation.

SPAIN: GRANADOS, ALBÉNIZ, AND FALLA

The most decisive factors in the development of contemporary Spanish music came from the research and teachings of the musicologist/composer Felipe Pedrell (1841–1922), who began the nationalist revival of Spanish music in 1904. Part of his early musical studies with Juan Antonio Nin y Serra included the transcription of popular songs, which helped him expand his knowledge of folklore and Renaissance music during research in Italy (1876–1877). In his journal *Salterio sacro-hispano,* which he founded in 1882, he published works by earlier Spanish composers and later produced editions of early and contemporary Spanish sacred music. As a composer, he also exhibited an enthusiasm for certain German late-Romantic tendencies, conceiving his operatic trilogy *Los Pirineos* (1890–1891) as a Spanish counterpart to the cycle of Wagnerian music dramas.

Pedrell's nationalistic interests were in part disseminated by way of his pupils, the most celebrated of whom were the Catalan composers Isaac Albéniz (1860–1909) and Enrique Granados (1867–1916), the Sevillan composer Joaquín Turina (1882–1949), and especially the Andalusian composer Manuel de Falla (1876–1946). While some of these composers' works reveal prominent links to mid-nineteenth-century Romantic piano textures, techniques, and harmonic styles, Albéniz, Granados, and Falla all were to transform traditional Spanish folk and popular characteristics into a contemporary idiom by infusing them with the sonorities and figurations of impressionism and other early twentieth-century French sources. In addition to the impressionistic sources, Falla was to draw from the clear, mechanical, and objective textures of Stravinsky's neoclassical works for the creation of a new Spanish style as well.

The *Danzas españolas,* Op. 37 (1892–1900), for piano by Granados, were among the earliest pieces to reveal a new, distinctive style in the development of Spanish art-music. The opening dance theme reveals characteristics common to folk music from all regions of Spain (Ex. 6–6a). One of the common melodic types is represented by a melody consisting of a limited

EXAMPLE 6–6. Granados, *Danzas españolas*, Op. 37, for piano:
(a) folk characteristics of opening dance theme; (b) mm. 34ff.

number of notes (in this case, four) and is typically jagged in contour. Such songs are often built on one or two repeated rhythmic figures (in this case, two in alternation), each of which creates a typical syncopation by deemphasizing the strong beat. Certain modal complexities are also common to the monophonic melodies of modern Spanish folk music.[21] While the ambiguous melodic line, which implies modes on either C or A, remains within the scalar spectrum of G-Ionian, the harmonizations produce bimodal fluctuations between G-Ionian and G-Mixolydian (G–A–B–C–D–E–[F–F♯]) in the opening phrases. The modal quality is firmly established by the minor-dominant

[21] See M. García Matos, *Lirica popoular de la Alta Extremadura* (Madrid: Union musical espagñol, 1944), pp. 194–205 on modal melodic structure especially.

(mm. 5–6) and plagal IV-I (mm. 7–8) cadences in G-Mixolydian. The harmonic cadence at the end of the first section (m. 33) is based on an abrupt shift to G-minor, the middle section (mm. 34ff.) then unfolding harmonic fluctuations among various minor and major modal forms within the key signature of G-Aeolian (Ex. 6–6b). Thus, the polymodally chromatic harmonies, which remain anchored on a common tonic, draw this Spanish dance setting into the twentieth century, its folk-like national quality maintained by the repeated rhythmic figures.

In his six *Piezas sobre cantos populares españoles* (undated), we find a wide variety of polymodal chromatic combinations built on a common tonic. The second piece, "Ecos de la parranda," is interesting especially for its use of certain Spanish folk characteristics that lend themselves to nationalistic, personal expressiveness in a contemporary modal/harmonic idiom. This idiom is often established by simultaneous rather than successive polymodal occurrences. Again, the Spanish dance character is established by the repetition of a basic rhythmic figure that produces a sense of syncopation. The scalar basis of the piece belongs to a larger set of E-Phrygian modal variants found in Spanish folk music. The prevailing modal construction in this piece is the form containing the augmented-second (E–F–G♯–A), but transposed by Granados to the key of F (F–G♭–A–B♭–C). The influence of Arab music is evident in this modal form.

While the tonality of F is established by a static alternation between the tonic and fifth degrees in the bass, variety is produced by fluctuations between the modal variants, F–G♭–A–B♭ and F–G♭–A♭–B♭, or their combination, F–G♭–A♭–A–B♭. A sense of motion (or modulation) occurs at the departure from the basic F-Phrygian source (at m. 15), at the appearance of the raised second-degree G in the ascending thematic line, producing one of the modal permutations of a set of nondiatonic modes, F–G–A–B♭–C–D♭–E♭, found in certain Eastern European sources.[22] While this scale joins lower major and upper Phrygian tetrachords (F–G–A–B♭ and C–D♭–E♭–F), another augmented-second is implied by the appearance of E, first introduced in the cadential modal dominant, C–E–G♭–B♭ (mm. 14–15).[23] This note, E, together with C–D♭–F (at the beginning of m. 16), forms the gapped tetrachord, C–D♭–E–F, now giving us a variant of the upper F-Phrygian tetrachord. Following the return of this theme (mm. 56–61), the superstructure of a new thematic idea is based on the complete content of the implied F-Phrygian source (F–G♭–A♭–B♭–C–D♭–E♭), prominently embellished by the components of the augmented-second tetrachordal variants, F–G♭–A–B♭ (mm. 62ff.) and C–D♭–E–F (mm. 67ff.), in a complex polymodally chromatic context. The entire polymodal content of both thematic ideas (mm.

---

[22] See Béla Bartók, *Rumanian Folk Music,* Vol. IV, ed. Benjamin Suchoff, trans. E. C. Teodorescu et al. (The Hague: Martinus Nijhoff, 1975), pp. 18–20.

[23] The "French-sixth" construction of this chord grows from the original modal properties already evident in the preceding ostinato neighbor-note figuration.

56–73) outlines the chromatic content F–G♭–G–A♭–A–B♭–[ ]– C–D♭–[ ]–E♭–E. Similar polymodal combinations also occur on different tonic degrees in other thematic passages of the overall rondo form. Granados retains a "suggestion" of traditional functional tonality by use of locally asserted perfect-fifth root relations in a context based on tertian harmony. However, the simultaneous as well as successive use of these special Spanish modalities, which unfold in static ostinato rhythmic patterns, produces a chromatic context that is largely dissociated from Romantic as well as Classical tonality.

In addition to the folk sources, we also find both national and international influences in Granados' compositions. For instance, the melodic styles of the songs in the *Colección de tonadillas escritas en estilo antiguo* (1898) are influenced clearly by the Spanish music of the eighteenth century. Granados' favorite painter, Goya, served as an inspiration for his own drawing and painting as well as for the *Goyescas* (1911) for piano, a work based on highly original modulations. This music was later used as the basis of his opera of the same title. The composer's works also exhibit nineteenth-century Central European Romantic traits, often colored by modal elements. The latter tend to weaken traditional tonal relations and, at the same time, suggest a subtle national quality within the Romantic harmonic idiom. The six *Escenas romanticas* (not dated) for piano, which foreshadow the highly original harmonic and melodic style of the *Goyescas,* reveal his affinity with the piano styles of Chopin, Schumann, and Liszt, all of which are absorbed into his distinctive nationalist personality.[24]

Like Granados, Albéniz revealed influences of certain Romantic sources in his early piano music. These influences suggest the virtuoso style of Liszt, his piano teacher of the early 1880s. His six *Mazurkas de salón,* Op. 66 (1887), suggest further his interest in the piano style of Chopin, and an interest in salon music as well. Through his studies with Pedrell, he then began to be drawn increasingly toward Spanish folk music. These national characteristics pervaded his varied compositions, which included mostly piano music, but also a number of songs and, to a lesser extent, theatre and orchestral works. After his move to Paris in 1893, the sonorities of impressionism also became evident in his works. During this time, he established close relationships with such musical personalities as d'Indy, Fauré, Dukas, and Debussy.

Although Albéniz followed French developments, he also contributed to the development of impressionist techniques. His compositions were to serve as an important source for the pianistic styles of both Debussy and Ravel; mutual influences were the result of their personal interactions. When Debussy began to compose his *Iberia,* the second of his three orchestral pieces

---

[24] See Rosa Angelica Lopez, "Granados' *Escenas Romanticas:* Its Romantic Sources and Progressive Features," D.M.A. treatise, The University of Texas at Austin, 1982.

from *Images* (1906–1912), he already knew the first part of Albéniz's *Suite Iberia* for piano, all four books of which were performed in Paris between 1906 and 1909.[25] As early as 1906, Debussy played the piano pieces from the first book and praised them in one of his musical critiques.[26] The fourth part of the Albéniz *Iberia* appeared in February 1909, before Debussy's work was published or performed. Debussy's *Iberia* was "so completely and authentically Spanish that Manuel de Falla hailed it, with *Soirée dans Grenade,* as an example of all that Debussy was able to teach the composers of Spain about a more civilized use of their own folk music."[27]

Written at the peak of Albéniz's career, *Iberia* exemplifies the composer's fusion of styles and techniques in a distinctively nationalistic idiom. The first piece in Book III, "El Albaicin," provides us with an instance in which complex, virtuoso pianistic figurations are joined with both Spanish and impressionistic features.[28] The dynamic ostinato rhythm, characterized by the displaced accents typical of Spanish dance music, forms the framework for the unfolding of the chromatically shifting modal collections built on impressionistic sonorities. The descending portion in one of the *a tempo* passages (mm. 149ff.), for example, unfolds a succession of parallel second-inversion seventh chords that outline the D-Phrygian mode linearly. The cadential point (m. 153) introduces the raised third degree, F$\sharp$, to form that Spanish modal variant (D–E$\flat$–F$\sharp$–G–A) characterized by the augmented-second. The nonfunctional parallel seventh-, ninth-, and other modal harmonies, which frequently color these passages then, together with the use of the characteristic Spanish modal variants within the specific ostinato rhythmic framework, reveal a synthesis of both Spanish and French sources.

The foremost Spanish composer of the early twentieth century is Manuel de Falla. His training and influences were similar to those of his elder countrymen, Granados and Albéniz, who studied with Pedrell, and later became involved in the Parisian musical scene. Falla was to nurture a style and formulate technical underpinnings beyond those acquired from the national folk and French impressionist sources. In Falla's later works, the Spanish characteristics tended to be somewhat sublimated, further absorbed into, and synthesized with other international styles and techniques. Such works move toward a more mechanical, precise Stravinskian neoclassical approach to rhythm and texture, as can be witnessed in the puppet play *El Retablo de Maese Pedro* (Master Peter's Puppet Show, 1919–1922) and the *Concerto for Harpsichord* (1923–1926).

[25] Granados completed little else in the twentieth century.

[26] Léon Vallas, *Claude Debussy: Life and Works,* trans. Maire and Grace O'Brien (London and New York: Oxford University Press, 1933; rep. New York: Dover Publications, Inc., 1973), p. 203.

[27] Edward Lockspeiser, *Debussy* (New York: McGraw-Hill Book Company, 1936), p. 200.

[28] The Gypsy's quarter in Granada.

Although Falla's compositions reflected the results of direct contact with native folk sources—he collected and arranged Spanish folk songs—the compositions in actuality only evoked the essence of folksong; they did not quote them literally. An understanding of Falla's musical aesthetics can be enhanced by an understanding of the composer's basic attitude; he had no interest in achieving popularity or making an appeal to the ordinary person. He did not seek to evoke a sense of national identity or pride as did Kodály, Bartók, Sibelius, Elgar, or Vaughan Williams, but rather aimed only at developing a genuine Spanish art music that would become part of the broader international musical spectrum.[29]

One of Falla's early compositions, typical of the national style, was his Andalusian song, *Tus ojillos negros* (Your little Black Eyes, 1902), a setting of a poem by Cristobal de Castro. In this popular folk-song style, we immediately find traits that characterized the composer's individual approach. While Falla captures the Andalusian atmosphere by use of characteristic Spanish rhythms and folk modes, he also absorbs the folk or popular elements into his own art-music idiom. This is accomplished primarily by means of simultaneous modal combination in addition to the successive unfolding of modal variants common to the folk idiom. The result is a polymodally chromatic context characteristic of the art-music transformations in compositions of other twentieth-century national composers.

Falla's philosophy regarding his subsequent musical development is best expressed in his own comments about Debussy's evocation of Spain in the latter's *Soirée dans Grenade,* a work which, in the final analysis, remains essentially French: "Here we are actually given Andalusia. . . . The truth without the authenticity, as it were, for although not a single measure is taken from Spanish folklore, the whole piece, down to its smallest details, brings Spain to us." This comment, together with a comparison of Falla's music with that of his compatriot, Albéniz, provides further clarification of Falla's aesthetic approach. The brilliant and dynamic lines of Albéniz "offers a real geographical representation," while the textures of Falla provide only an "impression," a word that suggests the influence of Debussy.[30] Falla's absorption of national folk elements and transformation of them through fusion—employing the characteristics of Debussy's impressionism—reveal a direct parallel between Falla's own evolution toward a highly personal style and the evolution of Bartók. Falla's first work which absorbed the essence of Spanish folk music yet was of a completely original style was his lyric drama *La Vida breve* (Life is short, 1904–1905). Having been in Paris since 1907, the

[29] Burnett James, *Manuel de Falla and the Spanish Musical Renaissance* (London: Victor Gollancz Ltd., 1979), p. 63.

[30] Suzanne Demárquez, *Manuel de Falla* (Paris: Flammarion, 1963); trans. from the French by Salvator Attanasio (Philadelphia and New York: Chilton Book Company, 1968), p. 38.

composer revised and reorchestrated the work after his contact with Debussy, Ravel, and Albéniz, and this resulted in a combination of Spanish and
French characteristics. Its first performance at the Opéra-Comique in Paris in
1913 was to establish his international reputation. However, it is primarily in
the *Noches en los jardines de España* (Nights in the Gardens of Spain, 1911–
1915) that a French influence is most clearly evident, the suite of three
symphonic impressions for piano and orchestra begun in Paris in 1909. Here,
we find a more pronounced fusion of Spanish and impressionistic characteristics, along with a strong hint of the Russian orchestral colors of Rimsky-
Korsakov as well.

   While the impressionist influence is less evident in such works as the
one-act ballet with song, *El Amor brujo* (Bewitching Love, 1914–1915), and
the comic ballet, *El Sombrero de tres picos* (The Three-Cornered Hat, 1918–
1919), the Andalusian mood remains prominent in both. The ornamental,
colorful rhapsodic melodies of *El Amor* evoke the atmosphere of the Andalusian gypsies, the ballet having been inspired by the gypsy singer and dancer,
Pastora Imperio. The story by Gregorio Martínez Sierra had a mystical,
symbolic meaning for Falla. A gypsy girl, Candelas, is haunted by the jealous
ghost of her dead lover, who appears whenever she tries to kiss her new lover,
Carmelo. When alive, the former lover had always been attracted to different
women, so Carmelo decides to distract him by bringing another gypsy girl,
Lucia, to his next meeting with Candelas. By this means, the ghost is exor-
cized and Candelas and Carmelo are finally united. Themes such as this are
common in the folklore of many countries.

   The exotic, primitive quality of the Andalusian gypsy songs and
dances is absorbed into the highly original style of the ballet. The source for
many of its passages is the *cante jondo,* a metrically free, ornamented vocal
style found in the melodies of flamenco dances. The two main flamenco
themes, in characteristic 3/4 meter, are established as the basis of the introduction and first scene, respectively (Ex. 6–7). The ostinato-like introductory
theme, played by the upper woodwinds, trumpet, and piano, establishes the
dynamic, intense mood, in which the ghost relentlessly haunts his victim.
The larger formal structure of the introduction is determined essentially by
the contour of this theme: in the first eight measures, the theme encircles E
within the confines of the narrow-ranged figure, D–E–F; in the next seven
measures, the range is extended upwards to F–G, then downwards in the final
flourish (F–E–D–C–B♭); in the final six measures, the theme is narrowed
again, this time to two notes, D–E, so that an overall arch-form is produced.
This arch-form is primarily determined by the thematic motion from the
modal-tonic E to its second-degree F. The shift of metric emphasis from E to
F is effected by a rhythmic diminution at the end of the first portion (m. 7), in
which the E is removed from the barline in preparation for the accented
downbeat on F at m. 9. The general thematic encirclement establishes E as the
linearly expressed tonic of either E-Phrygian (E–F–G–A–B–C–D) or E-
Locrian (E–F–G–A–B♭–C–D). While the latter mode is implied linearly by
the final flourish (m. 15), which contains the diminished-fifth degree (B♭), the

EXAMPLE 6–7. Falla *El Amor brujo,* two main flamenco themes in introduction and first scene

former mode is suggested by the reiterations of the perfect-fifth degree (B) throughout the accompanying figurations. Only in the final tonality of A—the ballet's closing tone—may the theme suggest an encirclement of E as the fifth degree of A-Phrygian, A–B♭–C–D–E–F–G.

Against this E-Phrygian/Locrian theme, the accompaniment unfolds a succession of variant E-modes that produce, in combination with the theme, polymodal chromatic relations that we have found to be common to all the other Spanish works discussed thus far. The first-inversion E-major-triadic arpeggiations in the first and last sections of the introduction, in linear juxtaposition with the first-inversion F-major-triadic arpeggiations of the central portion (mm. 9ff.), suggest the E mode containing the augmented-second in the lower tetrachord, E–F–G♯–A–B–C–[ ]. While this mode is also suggested harmonically between the E-major triad and opening segment of the theme, its combination with the scales of the lower strings outlines another E-modal variant, E–F♯–G♯–A–B–C–D. Under the F-major triad of the middle section (mm. 9ff.), this scale is replaced by the E-Phrygian mode, so that both scales together provide all chromatic tones within the lower tetrachord (E–F–F♯–G–G♯–A–B–C–D).

In the first scene, "En la Cueva," as the gypsies are gathered together at night, the mysterious tremolos of the low strings narrowly encircle the remote tonality of A♭. However, against the three-note tremolo figure (B♭–A♭–G), the clarinet (then oboe and bassoon) echoes the basic interval of the E-Phrygian mode (F–E). This produces a bimodal combination, which forms a larger octatonic segment, E–F–G–A♭–B♭. The three notes (D–A♭–D♭) of the muted horn call (No. 1, m. 12), prominently initiated by a tritone anacrusis, further extend the octatonic segment to seven notes, E–F–G–A♭–B♭–[   ]–D♭–D. The octatonic scale, like the scale with augmented-second, is an example of an oriental source that may have found its way into Spain by way of the North African Arabs.[31]

A new trumpet theme (No. 2), which anticipates the second main theme in the oboe, is based on a segment of C-Aeolian (C–D–E♭–[   ]–G), which is extended by the accompanying G–A♭–B♭ to the larger modal segment (C–D–E♭–[   ]–G–A♭–B♭). While the initial pitch content of the scene absorbs the E-Phrygian mode into the exotic E-octatonic spectrum, the cadential motion (at No. 3, m. 1) from A♭ to G suggests a chromaticized G-Phrygian interpretation (G–A♭–B♭–C–D♭–D–E♭–E–F) for the composite pitch content of the melodic layers after No. 2 (tremolo G–A♭–B♭, trumpet G–C–D–E♭, horn D–A♭–D♭, and woodwind F–E). In this polymodally chromatic context, the Spanish Phrygian form predominates. The original E-Phrygian of the introduction has moved up a minor third to G-Phrygian, the link of which is implied in the E-octatonic collection that opens the scene (E–F–G–A♭–B♭–[   ]–D♭–D). Thus, the composer has created a polymodally chromatic art-music idiom from the Spanish folk modes. The means of progression is based, then, on common contemporary pivotal procedures.

The rhapsodic oboe theme (see Ex. 6–7b) introduces yet another modal layer, now in D-Aeolian. The tonic degree, D, appears at the cadence in juxtaposition with the tritone, A♭; this interval (A♭–D) initiated the earlier horn call. The cadential A♭ transforms the lower modal tetrachord, D–E–F–G, into a segment D–E–F–G–A♭ of the same E- or G-octatonic collection, the presence of which has been implied throughout the scene. A transformation of this theme appears in the oboe melody of the next section, "Canción del Amor Dolido" (Song of Sorrowful Love), the mood of which is appropriately expressed by the lowering of certain degrees (D♭ and A♭) to form the second and sixth degrees of the C-Phrygian mode. The latter then appears in counterpoint with the contralto *soleá* of the gypsy girl, in which she describes the emotional inferno produced by the ghost's jealousy and the sorrows that are killing her.[32] This melody, which combines the repeated dotted rhythm of the introductory theme with the contour of the main "Cueva" theme (No. 3), introduces a dissonant bimodal conflict against the unchanging C-Phrygian accompaniment. The raising of the C-Phrygian sixth degree (A♭) of the accompaniment to A in the vocal line prevents the melody from functioning as a modal variant on the C-Phrygian tonic. That

---

[31] For a reference to this oriental source for the octatonic scale, see Benjamin Suchoff, "Ethnomusicological Roots of Béla Bartók's Musical Language," *World of Music* 29/1 (1987): 59–60.

[32] The *soleá* is a category of the *cante hondo* or *cante flamenco*.

is, the flat-second and raised-sixth degrees, which produce the hybrid construction, C–D♭–E♭–F–G–A–B♭, do not occur together commonly within a
single modal form in the folk idiom. In the first line of each of the two
strophes of the song, the narrow vocal encirclement around the note G
suggests the G-Aeolian mode instead. This conflict is resolved in the cadential
segments (at the *colla voce* and *Piu mosso*) of the first and second strophes,
respectively, where the vocal line descends entirely within the C-Phrygian
mode. Within the second strophe, at the words, "Por querer a otra se orví'a
demi!" ("Because he loves somebody else he forgets me!"), the melodic line
modulates from G-Aeolian to the final C-Phrygian by way of a gradual
lowering of scalar degrees. The first local cadence (at letter C) moves from a
G-Aeolian segment (B♭–A–G) to G-Phrygian (B♭–A♭–G), after which all the
chromatic tones between F and C are unfolded (F–E–E♭–D–D♭–C) to introduce the C-Phrygian cadence. The final vocal punctuation on "Ay!" briefly
reiterates G-Aeolian before the orchestral cadence confirms C-Phrygian,
which is joined typically with the augmented-second variant (C–D♭–
E–F–G–A♭–B♭). Thus, the dissonant modal cross-relations, together with
the melismatic ornamentation of the deep vocal timbres, marked rhythmic
patterns of melody and accompaniment, and the percussive punctuations of
the piano and winds, all contribute to the intense emotional quality of this
Andalusian gypsy ballet. The ritualistic mood of much of the work, in which
such polymodal, rhythmic, and timbral elements continue to unfold in a
series of block-like sectional structures and layered textural patterns, foreshadows the more angular, rigid mechanical textures of Falla's later,
"Stravinskyian" neoclassical works.

One of the few instances of Falla's use of authentic folk materials is his
set of *Seven Spanish Popular Songs* (1914–1915). The significance of these
songs lies more in their role as the first pieces in Falla's repertoire to employ
the principles of his theory of *natural resonance,* which were to become increasingly important in his mature works. The individualized sonorities of later
works owe much to Falla's systematic approach to resonance. Falla referred
to the treatise by Louis Lucas, *L'Acoustic Naturelle,* as the source of his new
harmonic theory. The principles of *natural resonance* are based on the idea that
the harmonics of a fundamental tone are the primary tones of harmonic
construction. The harmonic itself is the new fundamental, thereby expanding
the possibilities of tonal development. The changing emphasis between the
fundamental and the harmonic within the series of "natural resonance" had
already been suggested in some of the shifts and simultaneous combinations
of modal tonalities in *El Amor Brujo.*[33] Ultimately, a fundamental structure is
the initial sonority of the *Concerto,* which consists of a combination of the
tonic E♭-minor-seventh chord (E♭–G♭–B♭–D♭) and a D-major triad (D–

[33] For a more detailed discussion of this theory in connection with Debussy,
Ravel, and Scriabin, as well as Falla, see Burnett James, *Manuel de Falla,* n.29, above, pp.
76–79.

F♯–A). From this apparent polytonal construction, both "Falla, and Halffter after him, built up a harmonic system capable of great force and evocative power."[34]

SUGGESTED READINGS

GERALD ABRAHAM.   "The Symphonies," in *The Music of Sibelius,* ed. Gerald Abraham (New York: W. W. Norton, 1947, pp. 35–36.

BÉLA BARTÓK.   *Essays,* ed. Benjamin Suchoff (New York: St. Martin's Press, 1976), including: "The Influence of Peasant Music on Modern Music," pp. 340–344. Published originally as "A parasztzene hatása az újabb műzenére," in Új idők (Budapest) 37/23 (May 1931): 718–719.

LINDA BREWER.   "Progressions among Non-Twelve-Tone Sets in Kodály's Sonata for Violoncello and Piano, Op. 4" (D.M.A. treatise, The University of Texas at Austin, 1978).

GILBERT CHASE AND ANDREW BUDWIG.   *Manuel de Falla: A Bibliography and Research Guide* (New York: Garland Publishing, Inc., 1986).

DAVID CHERNIAVSKY.   "Special Characteristics of Sibelius' Style," in *The Music of Sibelius,* ed. Gerald Abraham (New York: W. W. Norton, 1947), pp. 147–152.

SUZANNE DEMÁRQUEZ.   *Manuel de Falla* (Paris: Flammarion, 1963); trans. from the French by Salvator Attanasio (Philadelphia and New York: Chilton Book Company, 1968).

BETTY DEVINE.   "Three Choral Works of Zoltán Kodály: A Study of Folksong Style for Performance Consideration" (D.M.A. treatise, The University of Texas at Austin, 1986).

LÁSZLÓ EŐSZE.   *Zoltán Kodály—His Life and Work,* trans. István Farkas and Gyula Gulyás (Budapest: Corvina Press, 1962).

HUBERT J. FOSS.   *Ralph Vaughan Williams* (London: George G. Harrap and Co., 1950).

NANCE LEE HARPER.   "The Piano Sonatas of Rodolpho Halffter: Transformation or New Techniques?" (D.M.A. treatise, North Texas State University, 1985).

FRANK HOWES.   *The Music of Ralph Vaughan Williams* (London: Oxford University Press, 1954).

BURNETT JAMES.   *Manuel de Falla and the Spanish Musical Renaissance* (London: Victor Gollancz Ltd., 1979).

MICHAEL KENNEDY.   *The Works of Ralph Vaughan Williams* (London: Oxford University Press, 1964).

ZOLTÁN KODÁLY.   *A magyar népzene* (Folk Music of Hungary) (Budapest, 1937; enlarged and rev. Lajos Vargyas, Eng. trans. Laurence Picken, Budapest: Corvina, 1971).

EDWARD LOCKSPEISER.   *Debussy* (New York: McGraw-Hill Book Company, 1936).

ROSA ANGELICA LOPEZ.   "GRANADOS' *Escenas Romanticas:* Its Romantic Sources and Progressive Features" (D.M.A. treatise, The University of Texas at Austin, 1982).

M. GARCÍA MATOS, *Lirica popular de la Alta Extremadura* (Madrid: Union musical espaĩol, 1944).

---

[34] Nance Lee Harper, "The Piano Sonatas of Rodolpho Halffter: Transformation or New Techniques?", D.M.A. treatise, North Texas State University, 1985, p. 7.

MINA F. MILLER. *Carl Nielsen: A Guide to Research* (New York: Garland Publishing, Inc., 1987).

PRESTON STEDMAN. *The Symphony* (Englewood Cliffs, NJ: Prentice-Hall, Inc., 1979), pp. 252–268 (on Sibelius symphonies).

ERIK TAWASTSTJERNA. *Jean Sibelius* (Helsinki, 1965–1972); Eng. trans. Robert Layton, Vols. 1 and 2 (Berkeley and Los Angeles: University of California Press, 1976, 1987).

LÉON VALLAS, *Claude Debussy: Life and Works,* Eng. trans. Maire and Grace O'Brien (London and New York: Oxford University Press, 1933; rep. New York: Dover Publications, Inc., 1973).

RALPH VAUGHAN WILLIAMS. *National Music and Other Essays* (2nd ed.; New York: Oxford University Press, 1987; 1st ed., 1963).

———. "What have we learnt from Elgar?" in the memorial issue of *Music and Letters* 16/1 (1935): 13–19.

———. "Who Wants the English Composer?" *RCM Magazine* 9/1 (1912): 11; reprinted in Hubert J. Foss, *Ralph Vaughan Williams* (London: George G. Harrap and Co., 1950), p. 198.

———. lecture on "English Folk Songs" (London, 1912).

7 Music in the United States

THE EMERGENCE OF NATIONAL ART-MUSIC STYLES IN THE UNITED STATES Popular-, folk-, and art-music idioms had provided the basic sources from which the first American art-music styles were to emerge in the late-nineteenth and early twentieth centuries. The main influences in the formation of modern American music came from European Classical and Romantic traditions, which had found their way to the United States in the nineteenth century, and from the tunes of the American Indian and Afro-American Negro. In the early nineteenth century, elements from these sources were absorbed already into the works of the American composer-pianist Louis Moreau Gottschalk (1829–1869), who had studied in Paris since 1842 and had performed in various cities of Europe and the Americas. His eclectic compositional approach, which included musical quotations, as well as his use of special rhythmic techniques (syncopation, etc.) foreshadowed the music of Charles Ives and the jazz movement. Particularly striking was his absorption of the tunes of Stephen Foster, Negro minstrels, and other African-influenced folk materials which found their way into his piano and orchestral works. In the middle of the nineteenth century, another prominent musical figure, the internationally known Bohemian composer Anthony Philip Heinrich (1781–1861), had also infused his Classical-Romantic European style with experiences he acquired from travels across the American frontier. These styles were evident in his first major publication of vocal and instrumental pieces, *The Dawning of Music in Kentucky, or The Pleasures of Harmony in the Solitudes of Nature* (1820), which also incorporated popular musical quotations such as *Yankee Doodle* into his often elaborate and complex forms. In his first orchestral piece, *Pushmataha, a Venerable Chief of a Western Tribe of Indians* (1831), and other works, he revealed what may be considered the earliest influences of American Indian music on the classical repertoire.

Further infusion of Indian and Negro tunes (including spirituals) into the Romantic national idiom came from another Czech composer, Antonin Dvořák, as well. His invitation to the United States from 1892 to 1895 was based on the interest of Mrs. Jeannette Thurber, who was in the process of founding an American school of composition; she was also interested in the creation of works on American subjects. The result was Dvořák's *Symphony No. 9* in E minor ("From the New World") and the *String Quartet No. 12* in F major ("The American"). During the next four decades, the inclination toward absorption of all these ethnic elements as the basis for an American nationalism gathered momentum. This movement was part of a worldwide trend toward the search for national identity and the "splitting" from Central European (especially Germanic) musical domination.

The music of the American composer Arthur Farwell (1872–1952) was also rooted in the European Romantic tradition. After having studied in Germany and France in the 1890s, his opposition to German hegemony led him, like many European composers, to French and Russian sources. Based on his interest in the diversity of his national heritage, he moved toward infusing American Indian, Negro, Spanish-American, Anglo-American, and cowboy songs with his new Romantic idiom, which contained certain modernistic harmonic and tonal practices (polytonality, etc.) unique to the century. In 1901, after his inability to find a publisher for his *American Indian Melodies,* Op. 11, for piano (1900), Farwell established the Wa-wan Press (from 1901 to 1911 in Newton, Massachusetts) as the basis for promoting an American musical tradition. What followed were both arrangements and original compositions revealing his interest in generating materials derived from American folk sources, as in his *Impressions of the Wa-Wan Ceremony of the Omahas,* Op. 21, for piano (1905), *String Quartet* "The Hako," Op. 65 (1922), *Symphonic Song on "Old Black Joe,"* Op. 67, for audience and orchestra (1923), *Four Indian Songs,* Op. 102, for chorus (1937), and other works.

The absorption of American musical folklore into the Romantic tradition was further exemplified in the music of Henry F. B. Gilbert (1868–1928). He contrasted with his European-trained teacher, Edward MacDowell, "the great American composer" of the late nineteenth century who was actually opposed to composing a specifically American music. Gilbert himself was particularly inclined to use Negro spirituals, minstrel and ragtime tunes, and became associated with Farwell and the Wa-Wan Press in 1902. Some of his compositions revealing one or another of these sources were his orchestral *Humoresque on Negro-Minstrel Tunes* (1913, originally as *Americanesque,* 1902–1908), *Comedy Overture on Negro Themes* (1905), the symphonic poem *The Dance in Place Congo* (c. 1908, rev. 1916) with its creole tunes, and *Negro Rhapsody* (1912). Other folk or popular elements, which he derived from Indian, Celtic, South American Gypsy, and jazz sources, were also incorporated into his orchestral, piano, and vocal compositions. After Gilbert was introduced to the folk-influenced music of the Russian nationalists at the Chicago World's Fair in the early 1890s, he had become one of the first American composers to turn away from German Romanticism (though he admired Wagner's music) toward that of the Russian and French composers. He was drawn to Paris in 1901 to hear the première of Charpentier's opera *Louise,* its strong popular flavor leaving an indelible impression on him. He also turned to the folk-imbued Romanticism of the Bohemian and Scandinavian composers in his more mature works, in which he was to reveal an increasing diversity of sources within his highly original "American" idiom. His national orientation was also reflected in his interest in actively collecting folk songs. Gilbert edited *One Hundred Folk Songs from Many Countries* (1910) and wrote articles on folk music in art music, jazz, and Indian music as well.

These pioneering composers had set the pace for the development of music in the United States during the first several decades of the twentieth century. Other American composers also tended toward highly varied and eclectic approaches stemming from the infusion of numerous folk sources into European-derived (primarily French, Russian, and other non-Germanic), impressionistic, and Romantic styles. For instance, the new interest in French styles was transferred, by way of the teachings of Edward Burlingame Hill at Harvard, to the younger generation of American composers that included Walter Piston and Virgil Thomson. Others, too, showed strong early leanings toward Russian and French sources. In 1896, Homer Norris published his *Practical Harmony on a French Basis* in Boston, where the Alsatian-American composer Charles Martin Loeffler was, at the time, intensively involved in a highly refined musical impressionism characteristic of contemporary French tastes, despite his experience with German, Russian, and Ukrainian folk- and art-music cultures.

One of the first major American composers to move away from German Romantic influences toward French impressionism and Russian exoticism and mysticism was Charles T. Griffes (1884–1920) who, like other American composers, was also absorbing exotic Eastern Asian elements into an original and homogeneous compositional language. As early as 1910, Griffes heard a band performance of "American ragtimes with such a swing that they really sound[ed] quite fine," but he did not feel a compositional inclination toward the popular medium, despite his appreciation of Scott Joplin's works.[1] In his late period, however, he did draw from American Indian sources for his *Two Sketches Based on Indian Themes* for string quartet (1918–1919, published posthumously as *Two Indian Sketches*). Following his early period of study in Berlin from 1903 to 1907 and his gradual transition away from his German style during the next several years, Griffes turned exclusively to English texts, a change that resulted in his early song settings of Oscar Wilde's poetry in 1912. He also drew from authors of the new American poetry movement. Most significant was his new musical interest in the impressionism of Debussy which he had had since 1911, as manifested in his use of descriptive titles, freer approach to form, sensitivity to instrumental color, parallel harmonic progressions, the whole-tone scale, and fluidity of rhythm. Both his French and Russian influences were qualified by the English critic Norman Peterkin (in the *Chesterian*), who stated that "unlike some of his younger American *confrères* . . . he was never enslaved by these influences, but was able to extract from them precisely those elements he needed to set free, and to express his own personality."[2] This description of his eclecticism, individuality, and freedom in drawing from various sources for his own expressive purposes points to what can be considered a hallmark of the early twentieth-century American approach.

Prominent among Griffes' impressionistic works are several sets of piano pieces: *The Three Tone Pictures,* Op. 5, including "The Lake at Evening" (1911), "The Vale of Dreams" (1912?), and "The Night Winds" (1912), the titles of which are suggestive of the atmospheric titles of Debussy;

---

[1] Edward M. Maisel, *Charles T. Griffes, The Life of an American Composer* (New York: Alfred A. Knopf, 1943), pp. 115–116.
[2] Ibid., p. 113.

EXAMPLE 7–1. Griffes, "The White Peacock," from *Roman Sketches,*
Op. 7, for piano, opening, motivic blocks and figural layers

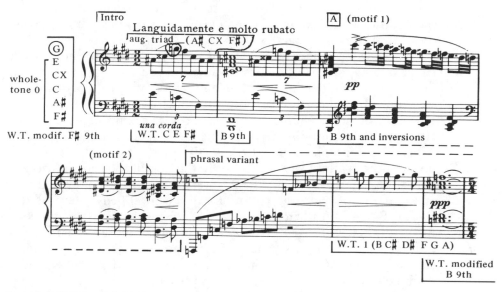

and *Roman Sketches,* Op. 7, including "The White Peacock" (1915), "Night-fall" (1916), "The Fountain of Acqua Paola" (1916), and "Clouds" (1916), several of which he subsequently orchestrated. Equally striking for their refined impressionistic quality are his song settings, most of which are based on Wilde's poetry: *Tone-Images,* Op. 3, including "La fuite de la lune" (1912), "Symphony in Yellow" (1912?), and "We'll to the Woods and Gather May" (1914, on a Henley poem); and *Four Impressions,* including "Le Jardin" (1915), "Impression du matin" (1915), "La mer" (1912, newly set in 1916), and "Le réveillon" (1914). The composer's individual approach to the subtle moods and colors of his impressionistic style is exemplified in "The White Peacock," which is one of his most popular pieces. Both the structural and harmonic schemes are similar to those which characterize the impressionistic forms of Debussy, though the more defined, intact melodic contours are more suggestive of Ravel's. The overall structure of the piece is generated from two types of contrasting motivic configurations (arpeggiations and chords in dotted rhythm), the local phrasal and periodic pairings of which produce somewhat disconnected mosaic textures.[3] At the same time, each local moti-

---

[3] The ternary form is outlined as follows: introduction (mm. 1–3, beat 1); section A (mm. 3–17), transition (mm. 14–17); section B (mm. 18–34), transition (mm. 31–34); section A' (mm. 35–60), part 1 (mm. 35ff.), transition (mm. 41ff.), part 2 (mm. 47ff.); and Coda (mm. 59–66), based on return of the introduction. This scheme differs slightly from that given in Robert E. Weaver, "The Piano Works of Charles T. Griffes" (Master's thesis, The University of Texas at Austin, 1956), p. 9.

vic block is often comprised of two contrasting, simultaneously stated figural layers (Ex. 7–1). The static quality is further established by the nonfunctional harmonic progressions based almost exclusively on dominant-ninth chords, the occasional alterations of which lean either toward whole-tone sonorities or local color dissonances.

Motivic repetition is evident from the outset of the piece, in which two exact statements of the seven-note introductory figure of the upper line unfold contrapuntally against the contrasting triplet layer of the lower line. The fundamental harmony of this introductory statement is the punctuating B-dominant-ninth chord, B–D♯–F♯–A–C♯, a kind of *tonic sonority* which alternates with a modified F♯-dominant-ninth construction in the combined triplet and septuplet arpeggiations, F♯–A♯–C–C×–E–G. Four of the five notes of the B-dominant-ninth imply the presence of one of the whole-tone collections (A–B–C♯–D♯), an interpretation which is confirmed by the alteration of the fifth degree, F♯ to F, at the modified return of this chord, B–D♯–F–A–C♯ (cadence at mm. 7–8), to form the larger whole-tone segment, A–B–C♯–D♯–F. Five of the six notes of the opening altered F♯-dominant-ninth form a segment of the complementary whole-tone collection (E–F♯–[   ]–A♯–C–C×).[4] The latter is manifested simultaneously as two distinct linear segments, C–E–F♯ and the augmented-triad A♯–C×–F♯. Such interactions between diatonic and whole-tone spheres in nonfunctional harmonic contexts are also pervasive in the music of Debussy.

Structural fluidity as well as structural formulization of impressionist music is achieved similarly in this piece by means of the variation process, in which successive pairings of the two contrasting motivic members result in variants of the same idea throughout.[5] The initial pairing of motivic segments in section A (mm. 3–4) may be identified as a single phrase by means of the common dotted rhythm and the uniform harmonization, which is based simply on inversions of the B-dominant-ninth chord. This is followed by four consecutive phrasal variants. In each variant, the original descending chromatic motif is replaced by an ascending arpeggio, while the dotted character of the second motif is retained, and the B-dominant-ninth is part of the cadential articulation of each pairing. The basic motif of Section B (mm. 18ff.) is also a variant of the dotted motif of Section A, but is stated contrapuntally rather than successively, the arpeggiated idea producing a sense of increased activity.[6] The dotted motif is paired successively with the original chordal idea (see the accompaniment to the chromatic motif in m. 3), the latter of which is now extended to produce nonsymmetrical phrase lengths as

---

[4] According to Arnold Schoenberg, in his *Theory of Harmony,* trans. Roy E. Carter (Berkeley and Los Angeles: University of California Press, 1978), p. 392, such six-tone chords result from the simultaneous raising and lowering of the fifth degree of the dominant-ninth, the significance of which lies in the transformation of these traditional tertian constructions into the symmetrical whole-tone scale.

[5] A similar example of this procedure is the opening movement of Debussy's *Sonata* for flute, viola, and harp, composed at about the same time.

[6] The same procedure may be observed in the motivic pairings in the prelude to Debussy's *Pelléas et Mélisande.*

a means of development. While the harmony shifts in blocks from one dominant-ninth to another, the basic B-dominant-ninth and F♯-dominant-ninth constructions are placed at prominent structural points within this section (mm. 18–19 and first chord of 25). At this midpoint of the section (m. 25), the original chromatic motif is transformed so that it acquires the dotted rhythm of the second motif (left hand) as well as the appoggiatura outline of the introductory idea now in sixteenths (right hand). Section A′ (mm. 35ff.) brings back the chromatic motif at the tritone, and is accompanied by more active arpeggiations outlining an F-dominant-ninth ([ ]–A–C–E♭–G), the tritone transposition of the original B-dominant-ninth chord. This transposed recapitulation permits further structural fluidity as well as identity. The second part of the recapitulation (mm. 47ff.) returns to the original pitch level of the chromatic motif, the more active arpeggiations now anchored on one position of the B-dominant-ninth ([ ]–D♯–F♯–A–C♯). The coda (mm. 59ff.) is a return to the introduction, but extended so that the original triplet whole-tone cell, C–E–F♯, has priority at the cadence.

The style and language of impressionism, based on symmetrical dominant-ninth and whole-tone constructions, was to remain essential to Griffes' contemporary American idiom. However, toward the end of the First World War, his compositional sources became more diversified, and his musical language moved toward greater abstraction, formal definition, dissonance, and melodic angularity. Shortly after composing his Oriental works, of which the *Five Poems of Ancient China and Japan,* Op. 10, for voice and piano (1917), *The Pleasure-Dome of Kubla Khan* (piano, 1912; orchestrated, 1917), and the *Poem* for flute and orchestra (1918, originally for flute and piano) are an example, he showed a marked change, and became more modern in style. This style was akin to that of Scriabin and Schoenberg. (Griffes never had much of an interest in the music of either Farwell or MacDowell.) By 1915, he had become familiar with Schoenberg's *Six Little Piano Pieces,* Op. 19, which he found no more revolutionary than the music of Debussy or Ravel.

Griffes' short three-movement *Piano Sonata* (1917–1918; revised, 1919) and the *Three Preludes* for piano (1919) represent his most daring harmonic experiments, although he never crossed the threshold into atonality. The traditional form of the *Sonata* reveals a structural logic similar to Schoenberg's atonal and twelve-tone pieces. Griffes' individually contoured, chromatic themes also underwent a process similar to Schoenberg's "developing variation," in which the individual thematic identities as well as interrelations were dependent upon common intervallic constructions.[7] As shown in each of the themes of Movement I (Ex. 7–2), six or more of the twelve chromatic tones unfold within a short time span, Ex. 7–2a unfolding eight different pitch-classes with few repetitions. The prevailing intervals are the semitone and (exotic) augmented-second, with occasional octave displacements producing an angular melodic contour. Varied segments based on these intervals are embedded within each of the longer thematic lines. In Ex.

[7] See Maisel, *Charles T. Griffes,* n.1, above, pp. 273–287.

EXAMPLE 7–2. Griffes, *Piano Sonata,* Mov. I, intervallic construction and interrelations of themes

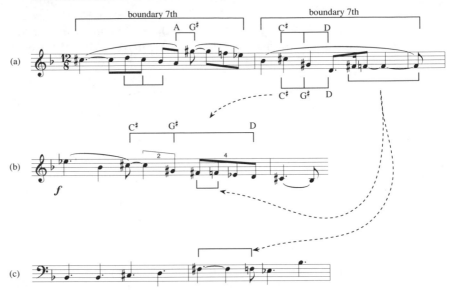

7–2a, the two halves of the theme reveal structural pitch relations, but in highly varied arrangements. The first half is bounded by the angular major-seventh A–G♯, the second half by the major-seventh D–C♯. Segment D–C♯–B♭–A–G♯ in the first half, which contains the primary intervals (semi-tone and augmented-second), is reordered in the second half as B♭–C♯–G♯–D (i.e., D–C♯–B♭–[   ]–G♯). The new adjacencies in the latter, i.e., perfect fourth and tritone (C♯–G♯–D), become structural elements (in Ex. 7–2b) in the figure C♯–G♯–[F♯–F–E♭]–D, two of the "filling-in" elements (F♯–F) playing the same role in a different placement in Ex. 7–2a. The pitch-class content of the theme in Ex. 7–2c (B♭–C♯–D–E♭–F–F♯–[   ]) is based on a permutation of that of Ex. 7–2b exclusively, with a metric and registral emphasis on the F♯–F, which had a cadential, "filling-in" role in the two preceding thematic forms.

Such thematic/motivic permutations of common pitch and interval-lic constructions in the *Sonata* were foreshadowed in the atonal compositions of Schoenberg as well as the dissonant octatonic piano preludes of Scriabin. This quality is also evident in the opening of the first of Griffes' *Three Preludes,* where linearly overlapping octatonic (D–D♯–F–F♯) and aug-mented-second segments (in enharmonic spelling, B♭–B–C×–D♯) unfold over tertian harmonies in a mechanical, anti-Romantic context. Thus, Grif-fes' absorption of numerous sources in an evolution moving toward an increasingly angular and dissonant anti-Romantic style, based primarily on nonfunctional intervallic relations, provides us with a significant glimpse of the new American music.

CHARLES IVES: EXPERIMENTAL MUSIC AND TRANSCENDENTALISM

Among the most eclectic yet original of the early twentieth-century American composers was Charles Ives (1874–1954). For his compositional style and language, he drew from virtually every source available to him—American folk, popular, sacred, secular, and European Classical and Romantic traditions—and transformed them into a cohesive musical language that could only belong to the twentieth century. The essence of Ives' independent, innovative musical thinking digs deeper than any of the sources that he either quoted from, imitated, or transformed in his compositions. His basic aesthetic assumptions can be traced back to the "self-reliant" attitude of composers from the period of the American Revolution on, as well as to his more direct connections with nineteenth-century American musical life and thought.[8] According to Ives, "Many American composers . . . have been interested in working things out for themselves to a great extent, but it seems to be the general opinion that, unless a man has studied most of his life in a European conservatory, he has no right (and does not know how) to throw anything at an audience, good or bad."[9] Ives' own skeptical attitude toward such a critical opinion, according to which an American composer had to study abroad before he could create "unusual harmonies, rhythms, or original ideas," was evident in his reluctance to follow the approach of his conservative German-trained teacher Horatio Parker, with whom he studied at Yale from 1894 to 1898.

Ives did acquire a secure, traditional, technical foundation from Parker, and was also influenced to some extent by the latter's espousal of the individualistic precepts inherent in the traditional Romantic musical model. However, he also developed a more flexible and open-minded attitude, the basic assumptions of which did not emerge spontaneously, but which had certain roots in a family tradition connected with *Transcendentalism,* a philosophical strain prevalent throughout New England during the mid- and late nineteenth century. This philosophy was founded upon the notion of the immanence of God in nature, which had developed into the religious conviction which stated that man is individual and self-reliant. These theories were expressed in the writings of Ralph Waldo Emerson, Henry David Thoreau, Bronson Alcott, Margaret Fuller, and others. Consequently, these writers adhered to the idea that all of human creation is equally important, since man himself is part of God. Enthusiasm for the Transcendental aesthetics, especially those of Emerson and Thoreau, can be traced back through several generations of the Ives family. Ives' grandmother, Sarah Hotchkiss Wilcox Ives, had become an advocate of the Transcendental philosophy by the early 1850s, after having attended Emerson's lectures.[10] Transcendentalism and the

---

[8] See Gilbert Chase, *America's Music from the Pilgrims to the Present* (New York: McGraw-Hill Book Co., 1955; 2nd ed., 1966), p. 427.

[9] Charles E. Ives, ed. John Kirkpatrick (New York: W.W. Norton and Company, Inc., 1972), p. 32.

[10] Ibid., p. 245.

writings of Emerson and Thoreau were to be part of Ives' broad interest in religion, philosophy, and social justice.[11]

In keeping with the Transcendental idea, art is to be considered a means of achieving a higher goal. In Emerson's hierarchical ordering of the arts, he places poetry, dance, and music at the highest level because they are "intellectual, transcendent, and abstract" and, at the same time, fundamental to human expression.[12] For Ives, the inextricable connection between artistic transcendence and human experience was basic to the creation of a purely American musical idiom. The idea of the uniqueness, individuality, and importance of all things under God was already reflected in the extreme diversity of his father's musical interests and activities. Following the Civil War, George Ives returned to his home town of Danbury, Connecticut, where he continued his work as a band conductor, played piano at barn dances and organ in church. He was also well-versed in music theory and taught the standard European musical repertory. However, his concerns went far beyond the fairly typical activities of a town musician in New England. He experimented with contraptions that could produce quarter-tones, and also found beauty in the "polytonal" results of several instrumental ensembles playing different pieces simultaneously. He placed a higher artistic value on the "substance" manifested in the fervent out-of-tune singing heard at camp meetings and church services, rather than simply on the "manner" or technical polish of a professional performance. All this was to become the basis of Charles' own musical activities and the freedom of thought he was to exhibit in his search for a personal and distinctively American idiom.

After graduating from Yale in 1898, Ives went into the life-insurance business rather than the music profession. According to his father's belief, this would provide him with the financial security necessary for developing an uncompromising musical originality and freedom, which might otherwise be sacrificed to the pressures of having to meet the usual practical demands. Furthermore, experience taught him that his music should not be separated from the rest of his life's activities and "that to be thrown with people of all conditions all day long, for a good part of a man's life, widens rather than cramps up his sensibilities, etc."[13] His business experience brought him into contact with people from many walks of life, which strengthened his interest and confidence in the average human being. His self-reliant attitude toward both his business and his music, plus the idea that one's art cannot be isolated from life itself, permitted him to develop a musical ideal that was rooted both realistically and philosophically in his native soil. The notion of a transcendental art, for all its abstraction, was for Ives a part of his New England culture.

[11] Peter Burkholder, *Charles Ives, The Ideas Behind the Music* (New Haven and London: Yale University Press, 1985), p. 33.

[12] Régis Michaud, *L'esthétique d'Emerson* (Paris: Libraire Felix Alcan, 1927), p. 22n; also see Laurence Wallach, in "The New England Education of Charles Ives" (Ph.D dissertation, Columbia University, 1973), p. 292–293.

[13] See Ives, *Memos*, n.9, p. 131.

Ives' compositional originality had already emerged by 1898, and by 1902 the composer devoted his energies to business and composition equally. Although Ives lived well into the post–World War II period, his intense compositional activities were curtailed after a heart attack in 1918. He no longer composed after 1926, and in 1930 retired from his business. Nevertheless, within the first quarter of the century, Ives had produced a varied spectrum of original compositional styles and techniques in virtually all genres, including solo song and choral settings, as well as keyboard, chamber, and orchestral music. Between 1897 and 1902, he had written, as part of a larger body of early works, the forward-looking *Fugue in Four Keys* (1897) for flute, cornet, and strings, the *Pre-First Violin Sonata* (1899–1902), *Second Symphony* (1900–1902), and *From the Steeples and Mountains* (1901–1902?) for trumpet, trombone, and four sets of bells, a work that included some of his most experimental sonorities to that date.

During this period, Ives also began to set a number of psalms for chorus. In his setting of *Psalm XXIV,* "The Earth is the Lord's" (1894), we find a new approach to sonority and progression that lends itself to the religious fervor of congregational singing. Set to five stanzas of four lines each, the cumulative form is a reflection of the excitement found in the increasing references "Lift up your heads" and "The King of Glory." While the work is framed in the tonality of C major, the entire fabric is based on horizontal and vertical intersections of expanding interval cycles, the resulting sonorities tending to neutralize any harmonic or tonal sense. What is apparent is a uniform *mass of sound* that transcends traditional musical notions, focusing on the human feeling or "substance" instead.

The opening textual description of the earth's "fullness thereof" is supported musically by the outward inversional motion of semitonal cycles between the upper and lower voices within the first half of Stanza 1. A sense of expansion is produced further by metric emphasis on the interval-3 cycle, C–D♯–F♯–A–C, and its inversion, C–A–G♭–E♭–C, which unfold simultaneously in the sopranos and basses (mm. 1–6). Interval expansion is also established in the opening harmonic progression, which moves from an interval-0 chord on C to interval-classes 1 (B–C–C♯) and 2 (B♭–C–D) chords. The cyclic intervals of the following, more complex chords have noncyclic notes added (e.g., first chord of m. 2, where the vertical cycle-3 segment, A–C–D♯, is joined by the alto's F), such sonic irregularities invoking perhaps a sense of amateur congregational singing. Nevertheless, the trend is toward systematic expansion of harmonic intervals, the cadential chord (m. 6) of which is based on the perfect-fifth, C–G–C–C. In the remainder of Stanza 1 (mm. 6–11), the inversionally related outer voices expand the original linear statements of the semitonal cycle to the whole-tone cycle, and octave displacements within the ascending whole-tone line of the soprano produce sevenths and ninths to heighten the agitation. Virtually all the chords are segments of the whole-tone cycle, the first two (in m. 7) expanding from G♯–B♭–C–D to the cyclic-interval-4 segment, A♭–C–E, analogous to the original expansion (in m. 1) from intervals 0 through 2. In Stanza 2, at the words "Who shall ascend unto the hill of the Lord?," all

EXAMPLE 7–3. Ives, *Psalm XXIV,* "The Earth is the Lord's," mm. 28–34, linearly consecutive tritones in outer voices moving by interval-class 1 in implied contrary motion

voices, in still wider leaps through octave displacements, unfold an interval-3 cycle linearly, C–D♯–F♯–A–C, which is also projected vertically throughout. Further expansion occurs in the linear unfolding of minor and major thirds (mm. 16ff.).

Stanza 3 begins with unison chords in parallel motion, the voices then diverging to build pure fourth chords and linear segments of the cycle of fourths supporting the sublime mood of the text, "He shall receive the blessing from the Lord, and righteousness from the God of his salvation." This stanza closes (mm. 28–34) with inversional motion between soprano and bass, each based on alternating tritones and fourths. A double bar and C-major cadence then ends this central portion of the piece. While the primary cyclic interval of this passage is the tritone, a reinterpretation of the semitonal opening is suggested. The original linear statements of semitonal cycles in the soprano and bass had moved outward in opposite directions. In this central section (Ex. 7–3), the consecutive tritones in each of the outer lines move inward inversionally by interval-class 1. The manifestation of the semitonal cycles as major-seventh cycles, however, establishes paradoxically a sense of further intervallic expansion. Beginning at "Lift up your heads," the basic process is reversed (though wide intervallic leaps are maintained through octave displacements). Contraction of the original inversionally related semitonal cycles occurs in the sopranos and altos, the lower voices encircling irregularly the basic cadential fifth, C–G. Thus, the humanistic quality is manifested in a new concept of tonality and progression.

Following his *Third Symphony* "The Camp Meeting" (1904), the three movements entitled "Old Folks Gatherin'," "Children's Day," and "Communion," Ives' music became increasingly experimental, due in part to his courtship of Harmony Twitchell that had begun in 1905. Twitchell provided inspiration for Ives' personal musical inclinations, and also influenced his literary tastes. Among the first works composed at this time was the *Three-Page Sonata* (1905) for piano, which Ives indicated in a memo as "made mostly as a joke to knock the mollycoddles out of their boxes and to kick out the softy ears!"[14] The first of the three sections, marked "Allegro Moderato," is based on transformations of the B–A–C–H motif. There are parodistic references to elements of the traditional sonata form in the margins of the manuscript, but his approach to tonality and sonority are unique.[15]

Ives moved toward an even more innovative approach in the next several years. In 1906 alone, he composed the *Set for Theatre Orchestra, Over the Pavements,* and his *Two Contemplations* for orchestra, including his famous *The Unanswered Question* and *Central Park in the Dark,* which are performed by two independently conducted orchestras that mix both tonal and atonal materials. In 1907, he began his *Emerson Overture/Concerto* ("the orchestra was the world and people hearing, and the piano was Emerson"), that remained unfinished. His main period of composition encompassed the years 1908 to 1917, which began with his marriage to Harmony in 1908. In addition to his *Fourth Symphony* (1910–1916), in which he continued to use unusual devices along the lines of *Contemplations,* he produced many other orchestral works, such as the *First Orchestral Set (A New England Symphony; Three Places in New England)* (1911–1914), which included "The Saint-Gaudens in Boston Common," "Putnam's Camp, Redding, Connecticut," and "The Housatonic at Stockbridge." To this period also belongs the *Second String Quartet* (1911–1913), which reveals the most extreme variety of contrasting quoted and original materials in three programmatic movements, entitled "Discussions," "Arguments," and "The Call of the Mountains," plus other varied chamber works.

Among the most important works of this period is the *Second Piano Sonata "Concord, Mass., 1840–60"* (1911–1915), which reveals his deep involvement with American literature and the Transcendentalists, as indicated in the titles of the "Emerson," "Hawthorne," "The Alcotts," and "Thoreau" movements. Ives' eclectic approach was reflected in the incorporation of material from his earlier unfinished *Orchard House Overture* (1904), the *Emerson Concerto* (1907), and the *Hawthorne Concerto* (1910), as well as in the quote "Here comes the bride" from the "Alcotts" movement and motif of Beethoven's *Fifth Symphony,* hidden near the very opening of the "Emerson" movement and elsewhere in the piece. The Transcendental significance of the latter musical quote is exposed by Ives' own statement:

[14] Ibid. p. 155.

[15] For a basic discussion, See H. Wiley Hitchcock, *Ives: A Survey of the Music* (London: Oxford University Press, 1977), pp. 44–48. For an in-depth study of various aspects of pitch relations in this work, including a kind of twelve-tone tonal system, analyses of referential collections, segmentation, interval cycles, tonal priorities and tonal motion, etc., and their relevance to the extra-musical dimensions of Ives' aesthetics, see Carol Baron, "Ives on His Own Terms: An Explication, A Theory of Pitch Organization, and a New Critical Edition for the *3-Page Sonata,*" (Ph.D dissertation, The City University of New York, 1986).

There is an "oracle" at the beginning of the *Fifth Symphony*—in those four notes lies one of Beethoven's greatest messages. We would place its translation above the relentlessness of fate knocking at the door, above the greater human-message of destiny, and strive to bring it towards the spiritual message of Emerson's revelations—even to the "common heart" of Concord—the Soul of humanity knocking at the door of the Divine mysteries, radiant in the faith that it *will* be opened—and that the human will become the Divine![16]

The varied moods used to capture the essence of the New England writers were the results of freely changing stylistic and technical musical elements, as in the improvisatory succession of events reflecting Emerson's writing: "Emerson wrote by sentences or phrases, rather than by logical sequence . . . based on the large unity of a series of particular aspects of a subject, rather than on the continuity of expression."[17] Ives' musical successions included contrasting textures of extreme density and transparency, frequent changes of tempi and dynamics, and irregular meters in juxtaposition with nonmetric (unbarred) passages. Dissonant counterpoint often results from the simultaneous unfolding of contrasting types of pitch-sets, as in the inversional alignment of the complete whole-tone (A♯–C–D–E–F♯–G♯–A♯) and partial octatonic (B–A–A♭–[ ]–F–D♯–[ ]–[ ]) scales at the very opening, while polytonal harmonies and huge tone clusters pervade the score—one of the passages in the "Hawthorne" movement alternates wide-ranging white- and black-key clusters in an unmeasured rhapsodic style. The *Sonata* reveals Ives' concern for freedom over formal construction and tonal definition, in keeping with his philosophy of *substance* over *manner*.

Ives was extremely prolific in choral and solo vocal composition especially, having produced almost 200 songs between his first and last ones, *Slow March* (1887?) and *Sunrise* (1926). Although many of the songs were choral works originally, hardly a year went by in which he did not compose songs, and it is in this genre that we find his most varied approach to musical styles, techniques, and literary subjects. As his compositional activities waned after his heart attack of 1918, Ives began to turn more toward literary expression. The result was his *Essays Before a Sonata,* which dealt with the literary basis of the *"Concord" Sonata,* and the penning of many short articles.[18] As he began to "clean house" in preparation for the publication of his compositions, his increased literary interests were also manifested in the selection, rearrangement, and compilation of a large number of songs which he composed between 1887 and 1921 and published at his own expense in a volume entitled *114 Songs* (1922). These songs were grouped, according to their diverse text sources, into several general categories, which included settings of Italian, German, and French poets, hymn tunes, songs of war,

[16] Charles Ives, *Piano Sonata No. 2* (New York: Associated Music Publishers, 1947), preface.

[17] Ibid.

[18] See Charles Ives, *Essays Before a Sonata and Other Writings,* ed. Howard Boatwright (New York: W. W. Norton and Co., 1961, 1962).

street songs, sentimental ballads, as well as songs from a cantata (*The Celestial Country*). In his song *Charlie Rutlage,* we also find cowboy melodies of frontier origins. The subjects of the songs range from nostalgia and biography, to nature, philosophy, religion, politics, humor, sentimentality, literature, and Americana, in either lyrical or dramatic contexts.[19] Musical styles and techniques range appropriately from the simple diatonic settings of *A Christmas Carol* (1897?) and the more pungent and lively triadic tonality of *The Circus Band* (1894), which consists of syncopated ragtime rhythms and "piano-drumming," to the atonal vocal style and dissonant harmonic clusters of *Majority* (1921) and the wide-ranging but more serene atonal harmonies of *Thoreau* (1915), which also includes spoken narrative and an unmeasured speech-like vocal line.

Between these tonal and sonic extremes lies songs such as *The Cage* (arranged in 1920 from his 1906 *Set for Theater or Chamber Orchestra*), in which some sense of nonfunctional tonality was infused into an otherwise atonal context. This combination of contradictory tonal notions suggests a Transcendental musical significance. The atonal distortion of a sort of E major/minor, which becomes evident in the last two vocal phrases (Ex. 7–4), seems to invoke the musical quality of an out-of-tune amateur performance that Ives and his father had viewed as part of life. At the same time, the symmetrical disposition of the atonal pitch constructions (whole-tone vocal phrases and quartal harmonies) produces a sense of harmonic and tonal indeterminacy that supports the meaning of the text. According to Ives, the text was "a result of taking a walk one hot summer afternoon in Central Park with Bart Yung (one-half Oriental). . . . Sitting on a bench near the menagerie, watching the leopard's cage and a little boy (who had apparently been a long time watching the leopard) . . . aroused Bart's Oriental fatalism. . . . Technically this piece is but a study of how chords of 4ths and 5ths may throw melodies away from a set tonality."[20] The philosophical basis of Ives' text, which questions the meaning of life's incessant circuity, is reflected musically by the rounded ABA form and by the systematic, and relentless melodic alternations of the two whole-tone cycles. Ives' instruction to perform the song "evenly and mechanically, no ritard., decresc., accel. etc." seems to imply an almost "fatalistic" acceptance of the monotony of existence. His anti-Romantic intention is further enhanced by the implied irregular meter of the piano against the regular rhythm of the voice in an unbarred scoring. This relation between melody and accompaniment results in chordal articulations that contradict the natural accents of the English language entirely, which produces, in effect, a dissociation of musical sounds from meaning.

The combination of divergent melodic and harmonic elements in this song is transcended by a higher, more systematic musical unity, which draws Ives' innovative techniques into the pitch-set premises of his European con-

---

[19] For a systematic study of the songs according to these subject groupings, see Christina Barnet, "Charles Ives: *114 Songs* and Transcendental Philosophy" (DMA treatise, The University of Texas at Austin, 1986); especially Appendix 2, pp. 77–87.

[20] See Ives, *Memos*, n.9, above, pp. 55–56.

EXAMPLE 7–4. Ives, Song No. 64, "The Cage," from *114 Songs,* entire song, whole-tone vocal phrases, quartal harmonies, and atonal distortion of a sort of E major/minor (last two vocal phrases)

temporaries: Debussy, Scriabin, Bartók, Stravinsky, and the Viennese atonalists. One of the fundamental aspects of pitch-set interaction in their works is the principle of common links between different types of pitch formations—whole-tone, octatonic, and other symmetrical constructions derived from the interval cycles. In Ives' song, such common links are basic to the relation between the two alternating whole-tone cycles of the vocal line as well as between the whole-tone cycles and quartal chords of the piano. In Section A, the vocal line is divided into two melodic phrases, which progress from a five-note segment of one whole-tone cycle, D–E–F♯–G♯–A♯, to a five-note segment of the other, F–G–A–B–C♯, to correspond with the pacing of the leopard. The identical, symmetrical construction of both five-note cyclic segments contributes to the unity of this section, i.e., each is commonly bounded by a minor sixth (in enharmonic spelling, D–A♯ and F–C♯, respectively). Each of these minor-sixth boundaries is divided symmetrically, the D–A♯ boundary of the first phrase by the initial F♯ and the F–C♯ boundary of the second phrase by the cadential A, so that each whole-tone cycle is enframed in a more background-level interval-4 cycle, D–F♯–A♯ and F–A–C♯, respectively. As the leopard's pacing is interrupted "when the keeper came around with meat," the musical form is articulated by a structural revision of the original whole-tone cycle, now expanded to an octave. This expansion, together with the symmetrical partitioning of the octave boundary (E–E) into two tritone (interval-6) cycles by the initial B♭, contributes to the structural definition of the new section. As a boy "began to wonder" if life is "anything like that," a "retransition" is introduced by further alternations of the two whole-tone cycles. At this point, the second whole-tone cycle returns to the original five-note format (G–A–B–C♯–D♯), which is again encompassed by a minor sixth (G–D♯) and enframed by a more background-level interval-4 cycle (G–B–D♯).

At this point in the vocal line, the key of E is suggested, i.e., only one note (E) from the first whole-tone cycle is interpolated to extend the second cycle to an E-minor segment, G–A–B–C♯–D♯–E. Such a linear interaction of whole-tone and diatonic elements, suggested at every juncture between the alternating whole-tone scales of the vocal line, is part of a larger stratification (or layering) of these two types of pitch formations between vocal line and piano melody as well. The linear voice-leading of the chordal accompaniment produces a quartally harmonized diatonic theme, which moves from the F♯-minor melody of the introduction to B minor in the transposed introduction of Section A. Nevertheless, these stratified levels between the vocal and piano parts are unified by special pitch-set relations, in which the melodic whole-tone scales and quartal (cyclic-interval-5/7) harmonies are linked by common elements. Analogous to each of the opening two whole-tone phrases of the voice, each fourth chord also consists of five notes, so the registral boundary is again a minor sixth. Furthermore, as part of an inherent structural relation between the whole-tone and perfect-fourth cycles, each fourth chord is based on a systematic intercalation of components from both whole-tone cycles, e.g., the fourth-chord G♯–C♯–F♯–B–E can be partitioned systematically into the whole-tone segments G♯–F♯–E and C♯–B. Thus, the harmonization of either whole-tone cycle by any fourth chord will permit common pitch elements between them.

The relevance of this cyclic-interval relation is further supported by an analysis of the only three nonquartal (or quintal) chords of the piece (the six-note chord at the end of the introduction, its transposition on the word "side" at the end of the transposed repeat of the introduction, and the eleven-note chord, A–D♯–F–C–D♯–A–C♯–F–B–D♯–G, on the word "wonder" at the end of the expanded and varied repeat of the introduction). The first cadential chord, F–D–A–E–C♯–F♯, is formed by the intercalation of the two whole-tone segments, D–E–F♯ and F–A–C♯, the first of which is projected as the lower three notes of the first vocal whole-tone phrase, the second as the cyclic-interval-4 frame of the second vocal whole-tone phrase. The second cadential chord, B♭–G–D–A–F♯–B, is formed by the intercalation of the two whole-tone segments, B♭–D–F♯ and G–A–B, the first of which is projected symmetrically within the expanded whole-tone octave boundary (E–[F♯]–G♯–[B♭]–C–[D]–E) of Section B, the second of which is projected as the lower three notes of the whole-tone vocal "retransition." The large cadential chord is a vertical projection of one of the whole-tone cycles in its cyclic-interval-4 partitions (reading downward in the chord, G–D♯–B and F–C♯–A) and other significant vocal elements in the lower part of the chord. This expanded chord on "wonder" emphasizes the main philosophical issue as manifested in the boy's question. Thus, the two contrasting cyclic-interval sets of the song are linked by common set segments to form an integrated musical fabric within an otherwise polarized melodic and harmonic context.

Other songs in this collection also significantly include symmetrical cyclic-interval formations as the basis of the individual stylistic contexts. In *Mists* (1910), diatonic melodic segments are reinterpreted as part of one or the other of the two whole-tone collections through the whole-tone harmonizations (e.g., mm. 2–3). In *Like a Sick Eagle* (1913?), the whole-tone boundaries of the vocal segments are filled in chromatically (rather than by perfect-fourths, as in *The Cage*) to produce a sliding motion as the basis for an extra-musical association with the sick eagle. Interval cycles also pervade *On the Antipodes* (1915–1923) and, in *Soliloquy* (1907), they are combined with metrical symmetry as well. Despite his eclectic, diverse, and highly experimental contexts, Ives' compositional approach appears to be more uniform and systematic than has been previously assumed. Due to his originality and apparent diversity, the composer's music came to be understood only gradually, and recognized long after he had stopped composing.

"ULTRAMODERN" AMERICAN COMPOSERS: COWELL, RUGGLES, VARESE, AND OTHERS

In the interwar period, American composers and their European counterparts found it difficult to have their music either published or performed, a situation which was remedied by the formation of several musical institutions in the 1920s for the promotion of modern music. Henry Cowell, who was one of the strongest advocates of the "ultramodern" music of American and European composers, founded the *New Music Society* in Los Angeles in 1925, which was moved to San Francisco the following year. In the original flyer, Cowell stated his aims: "It is seldom that Los Angeles has the opportunity to hear presented the works of the most discussed composers of so-called ultramodern tendencies, such as Stravinsky, Schoenberg, Ruggles, Rudhyar, etc. The New Music Society of California . . . is formed for the purpose of performing such works."[21] In this flyer, Cowell also pointed to the affiliation of this Society with the *International Composers' Guild* of New York, which was founded by the French-American composers Edgard Varèse and Carlos Salzedo in 1921. Among the most modern American composers to be heard at these Guild concerts were Ives, Cowell, Ruggles, and Rudhyar. The Guild also organized the premières of several of Varèse's first American works, including *Offrandes* in 1922, *Hyperprism* in 1923, which caused a scandal in New York, *Octandre* in 1924, and *Integrales* in 1925. In 1928, after the Guild was terminated, Varèse founded the *Pan American Association of Composers,* with Cowell as its acting president from 1929 to 1933. Under its auspices, experimental music was written and performed in the United States, Latin America, and Europe. Premièred at a Pan American Association concert in New York in 1933 was Varèse's percussion piece, *Ionization* (1931), the first work of its kind.[22] It was conducted by Slonimsky and performed by a group of "friendly composers," including Salzedo (on Chinese blocks), Paul Creston (anvils), Riegger (güiro), Cowell (piano), William Schuman (lion's roar), Varèse (sirens), and Harris (in the recording booth).

Cowell had already come into contact with the experimentalism of Carl Ruggles and the dissonant piano music of Leo Ornstein in 1917, and by the early 1920s, both Ruggles and Ornstein as well as Varèse were among his closest associates.[23] In 1927, Cowell initiated the quarterly, *New Music* (*New Music Edition* since 1947), for the publication of "ultramodern" music, which included the compositions of Ives, Cowell, Ruggles, Ornstein, George Antheil, Ruth Crawford Seeger, Dane Rudhyar, and other North American as well as Latin American and European composers.[24] Since the early 1920s, Cowell had also been championing modern music in his writings and in 1933 became editor of the volume *American Composers on American Music,* which was a compilation of the most significant ideas in American music to that date. His own experimentalism was already evident in his *New Musical Resources* (begun in 1919 and published in 1930), which presented the theoretical results of his highly original compositional activities.

Cowell, like Ives, was a highly eclectic and original composer, but was more inclined toward exotic influences from Eastern Asia, and hoped to incorporate these non-European musical sources into an innovative and flexible musical idiom. His numerous compositions range from those based on the dissolution of conventional notions of form and sonority to traditional or folk-like styles. The Eastern Asian influence had a significant bearing on

[21] See Rita Mead, *Henry Cowell's New Music 1925–1936, The Society, The Music Editions, and the Recordings* (Ann Arbor: UMI Research Press, 1981, 1978), p. 32.

[22] For more detailed discussion of Varèse's innovations of the 1920s and 1930s, including an analysis of *Ionization,* see Chapter 13, below, which explores the use of noise, color, and new sonorities. His post–World War II works are discussed in Chapter 18, below, on *musique concrète* and electronic music.

[23] See Mead, *Henry Cowell's New Music 1925–1936,* n.21, above, p. 23.

[24] For a month-by-month listing of the compositional publications from 1927 to 1958, see ibid., Appendix III.

Cowell's idea of *open* or *elastic form,* based on flexibility in the ordering of formal segments, an approach that was to become prominent among American and European aleatoric composers after World War II. Cowell employed tone clusters and other types of unusual sonorities extensively in many of his piano and orchestral works, his *Ostinato Pianissimo* (1934) based on a Balinese gamelan-like percussion ensemble.[25] One of Cowell's most significant contributions to contemporary technique was his notion of *dissonant counterpoint,* in which traditionally dissonant elements were employed as consonances. This reversal of the traditional notions of contrapuntal consonance and dissonance was exemplified in his first two string quartets, written during his greatest period of experimentation (prior to 1935). Cowell stated that "Bach's practice was so poised between consonance as a basis and what was felt to be dissonance that it seemed as though any further progress in the one inevitable direction would result in an actual shifting away from the base of consonant harmony."[26]

Cowell's contrapuntal evolution from the *First* (1915–1916) to the *Second String Quartet* (1928) parallels that of Hindemith's change in the 1930s from an aggressive and freely dissonant counterpoint to one based more on consonant melodic and harmonic intervals. The opening of Cowell's *First Quartet,* which unfolds the basic thematic material of the movement in a highly uniform contrapuntal texture, establishes the metric predominance of major sevenths and other dissonant intervals, while consonances between two or more voices are more evident in appoggiatura motions on weak beats (e.g., F♯–G♭ octave, m. 1, second eighth-note, C-major triad in the three lower voices, m. 1, last eighth-note, and D♭–F between the violins, m. 2, fourth eighth-note, etc.). In his works after 1950, Cowell moved toward a fusion of contrasting traditional and experimental elements. Interest in American folk sources is evident in works like the *Fifth String Quartet,* in which he drew upon eighteenth-century American hymnody and old English and Scottish fuguing tunes that had come to America by way of the settlers. The form of the first movement was modelled on that of the fuguing tune, which moves from homophonic to fugal development and back, and is set in harmonic contexts that use tertian or more dissonant primary harmonies in various passages, with some emphasis on both chromatic and modal melodic structures. In many of these late works, we find mixtures and juxtapositions of folk-like elements from various Western and Eastern nations in contexts that often mix his earlier dissonant counterpoint with more tonal writing.

The Cape Cod–born composer Carl Ruggles (1876–1971) also had an original musical mind, independent and uncompromising in the development of his own personal compositional idiom. In contrast to Ives, whose music was made up of extremely diverse materials often in free forms, Ruggles' music is highly integrated yet distinct both texturally and struc-

---

[25] This and other works of Cowell are discussed in Chapter 13, below, in connection with developments in color, noise, and new sonorities.

[26] Henry Cowell, *New Musical Resources* (New York: Alfred A. Knopf, 1930), p. 37.

turally. His small, compositional repertoire is polyphonic, often exceeding Schoenberg in its use of an intensely dissonant atonal fabric, resulting from a highly angular, chromatic melodic style, in dense, yet brilliant, harmonic combinations. Cowell's concept of "dissonant counterpoint" also can be found in Ruggles' music, in which dissonance replaces consonance in the harmonic demarcation of the strong metric beats. Furthermore, Cowell's melodic lines, which unfold in free-flowing rhythms, often approach a non-serialized twelve-tone style due to the general avoidance of pitch-class repetition. All these features are exemplified in the third movement of *Men and Mountains* for small orchestra (1924). The angular unison line of the upper strings (Ex. 7–5) is based on a succession of all twelve tones, which unfold against the extremely dissonant chromatic counterpoint of the lower strings. The latter are based on linear successions that also contain virtually no note repetitions, and the linear and harmonic adjacencies are pervaded by semitonal, cell-like groupings. Yet, in contrast to many of his American contemporaries, Ruggles never travelled abroad, and despite certain stylistic similarities to the Viennese composers, developed in isolation from other composers during his early career at his home in Vermont to a great extent. As a rugged individualist, he remained uninfluenced by his American colleagues, even though he had been in close contact with their music since the 1920s.

In the 1920s, Ruggles' compositions were among the first to be

EXAMPLE 7–5. Ruggles, *Men and Mountains,* Mov. III, mm. 40–44, angular unison line of upper strings based on a succession of all twelve-tones against extremely dissonant chromatic counterpoint of lower strings

represented in the concerts and publications of the modern American composers. *Men and Mountains* was published in the first issue of Cowell's *New Music* (October 1927), portions of which were performed at the first concerts of the New Music Society in 1925 and 1926. The first San Francisco performance of the Society on October 25, 1927, included, on the same program with Schoenberg's *Quintet for Woodwinds* and Varèse's *Octandre,* wind-ensemble arrangements of "Angels" from his symphonic work *Men and Angels* (1920) and "Lilacs" from the *Men and Mountains* trilogy. His only compositions published prior to that time were the song *Toys* (in 1920) and *Angels* (in 1925) for six muted trumpets. His entire repertoire consists of only eight published works, the most famous of which is *The Sun Treader* (1926–1931) for orchestra, an ideal example of his textural intensity, complexity, and homogeneity, achieved by the relentless doubling of instrumental families within the contrapuntal fabric.[27] Thus, while Ruggles' "Americanism" may be defined primarily by originality and an independent approach, the latter work as well as several others also reveal the literary influence of Romantic English and American poets, and, for a New Englander like Ives, an almost transcendental or religious feeling for nature, as manifested in the musical moods and titles of *Men and Mountains, Men and Angels, The Sun Treader,* and *Vox Clamans in Deserto.*[28]

Many other American composers, whose compositions were published in Cowell's *New Music Quarterly* or performed at New Music Society concerts, further contributed to the "ultramodern" developments in the United States. While innovative approaches to dissonance, timbre, and special sonorities were developed in the divergent works of George Antheil (1900–1959), Wallingford Riegger (1885–1961), and John Becker (1886–1961), the latter two of whom were grouped with Ives, Ruggles, and Cowell as the "American Five," other composers moved away from Central European traditions during the interwar period not only through their individual approaches to contemporary musical language, but also through their interests in promoting the use of either non-Western or American folk sources. The French-American composer Dane Rudhyar (b. 1895), who had lived in Southern California since 1919 and whose music was of fundamental importance to Cowell, turned away from the influences of Liszt, Debussy, and Scriabin after 1924 by identifying himself with the new American music through a style influenced by his studies of tone and acoustics. In the preface to his three dissonant and nontonal piano pieces, *Paeans* (1927), he stated that the music was based on the "building of resonances or complex harmonies which are like vital seed-tones germinating, sprouting into vast trees of harmonics." He was also one of the first in the United States to foster an

---

[27] According to Lou Harrison, in "Ruggles, Ives, Varèse," *Soundings: Ives, Ruggles, Varèse,* ed. Peter Garland (Spring 1974), p. 3, this "may in part be due to the terrific concentration of idea and intergration of style called for by his premise of 'total polyphony' within the new materials."

[28] Virgil Thomson, *American Music Since 1910* (New York: Holt, Rinehart and Winston, 1970, 1971), p. 35.

interest in Asian music. These sources were investigated more systematically by the Canadian-American composer and ethnomusicologist Colin McPhee (1900–1964), who had studied with Varèse and was also part of the new-music movement in New York between 1926 and 1934. McPhee incorporated Indonesian musical stylings into his compositions after his extensive and systematic ethnomusicological field work in Bali and Java in the mid 1930s. One of the most significant results of his cross-cultural musical synthesis during this period was his symphony *Tabuh-Tabuhan* (1936), which was influenced decisively by the *gamelan* orchestra. These inclinations toward the absorption of Eastern Asian music, as evidenced in Cowell's music two years earlier (e.g., *Ostinato Pianissimo*), began to flourish after the late 1930s in the music of John Cage, who studied with Cowell in 1933, and in the music of many other American composers.

Another composer who was supported by Cowell's New Music Society and had her works published for the first time in his *New Music Quarterly* was Ruth Crawford Seeger (1901–1953), a member of the Society's advisory board. Her piano *Preludes* (1924–1928), which were part of the program of October 24, 1928, and the first of her works to be published, are representative of the new harmonic and melodic dissonance based on chromatic, angular, and enormously wide-ranging melodic intervals in improvisatory rhythmic passages (e.g., *Seventh Prelude*). Her notational approach is also unconventional in its use of three staves and the omission of key signatures. The *String Quartet* (1931), the *Andante* of which Cowell felt was "without question the best movement for quartet that any American has written," was recorded on the first *New Music Quarterly Recordings* of 1934.[29] It is based on some of the most novel features in American music prior to World War II in its use of dissonance, numerical systems, and a *spatial,* or *differentiated counterpoint,* including the technique of *contrapuntal dynamics.* (In the third movement, the four instruments are distinguished from each other exclusively within cluster-like contrapuntal densities by their contrasting dynamics.) As another essential aspect of her "Americanism," Crawford began to devote her creative activities to the collection and transcription of American folk songs after her marriage to the musicologist Charles Seeger in 1931. Many of her collected songs were published in her books on *American Folksongs for Children* (1948), *Animal Folksongs* (1950), and *American Folksongs for Christmas* (1953) as well as other collections. She also wrote *Three Songs* (1930–1932) on texts of the American poet Carl Sandburg.

FORGING A NEW AMERICAN MUSICAL IDENTITY:
AARON COPLAND, ROY HARRIS, AND VIRGIL THOMSON

In contrast to the "ultramodernist" aesthetics of Ives, Cowell, and Ruggles, another group of American composers—Aaron Copland, Roy Harris, Virgil

---

[29] Cowell, in a letter to Ives (November 14, 1933); see Mead, *Cowell's New Music 1925–1936*, n.21, above, p. 257.

Thomson, Roger Sessions, Walter Piston, Marc Blitzstein, and others— adhered to a very different notion of what constituted American musical identity from the time of the 1920s. The general stylistic differences of these two groups, one characterized by an experimentalism and individualism that foreshadowed the most extreme developments of the post–World–War–II avant-garde, the other by an inclination toward the more objective, popular, and accessible neoclassical tonalities, represented a global polarity that had been developing in various countries during the interwar period.

The political climate in the United States after World War I led to an increasing antipathy of anything German, so many Americans as well as Europeans were soon inclined toward French culture for their artistic models. In the early 1920s, young American composers were drawn to France, especially to the new American Conservatory in Fontainebleu to study composition with Nadia Boulanger. Grants had been made available for this by major American educational institutions. These American composers were to find in Boulanger an ideal teacher, who could provide them with a strong traditional technical foundation, and at the same time nurture their individual stylistic inclinations. She also had the foresight to realize that a distinctively American music was about to come of age and showed a strong interest in her American pupils. Aaron Copland (b. 1900) was among the first Americans to study with Boulanger in the early 1920s, and it was through these studies that he was introduced to the basic sources that would shape his musical personality. Although he became familiar with various musical styles through his European travels at this time, it was the composers in Paris, including Milhaud, Honegger, Prokofiev, and Stravinsky especially, who attracted him most and were to provide the most viable stylistic models in the development of the new American music. More specifically, in terms of his search for a compositional idiom "that would be immediately recognized as American in character," he also began to show an interest in jazz, a distinctive, uniquely American popular idiom that both Stravinsky and the French composer Satie had already been drawing from as a realistic source for their own more accessible neoclassical styles. Thus, it was this synthesis of syncopated jazz rhythms and bright instrumental colors aligned with the more general stylistic principles of neoclassicism, especially Stravinsky's mechanistic, planed, and layered neo-tonal textures, that was to become the hallmark of Copland's American style after 1920. Copland himself stated that he "was affected by the whole rhythmic side of [Stravinsky's] music, also by its dryness, its non-Romanticism. He dominated the world of music at that time."[30]

Prior to the war, jazz was largely isolated from contemporary art-music idioms, but after 1918 it was increasingly absorbed and transformed in the works of various European and American composers during a time when reaction appeared against the aesthetics of impressionism and Romanticism. Stravinsky's *L'histoire du Soldat* (1918), *Ragtime for Eleven Instruments* (1918),

---

[30] Aaron Copland, in *The Times* (London, November 14, 1970).

and *Octet* (1923) were among his earliest works to be influenced by jazz syncopations, instrumental combinations, and harmonic progressions, while Milhaud's *La Création du Monde* (1923), which prominently incorporates the blues third in a context featuring the saxophone as part of a typical jazz ensemble of the time, resulted from his visit to Harlem in the early 1920s. At the same time, jazz influences became prevalent in the United States through such works as John Alden Carpenter's pantomime *Krazy Kat* (1921) and Gershwin's *Rhapsody in Blue* (1924), so the seeds for a distinctive American musical identity had already been sewn while Copland was still in Paris between 1921 and 1924.

Copland's first work to reveal the anti-Romantic influence of Stravinsky and jazz after his return to the United States was the short five-movement orchestral suite, *Music for the Theatre* (1925). The work combines blues thirds and bitonal progressions, the two tonal levels of which are defined by contrasting timbral layers, with syncopated and irregular multimetric schemes. This was followed by the larger two-movement *Concerto for Piano and Orchestra* (1926–1927). While suggesting the more improvisatory quality of Gershwin's *Rhapsody in Blue* in certain passages, it employs jazz elements in a more aggressively dissonant setting (e.g., second movement), thereby drawing the work into a more modernistic milieu. The movement opens with a highly brittle and accentuated three-note figure, derived from the first movement, and a harmonically static ostinato pattern in the bass which was characteristic of the jazz piano style of the time. In this movement, the piano also unfolds a tonic-dominant ostinato as an accompaniment to a jazz-band type of setting, which includes saxophone, muted brass, and other winds. The instruments then follow with improvisatory solos. At the time Copland composed the *Concerto,* he also wrote two quiet, improvisatory blues works for piano, *Sentimental Melody (Slow Dance)* and one of the *Four Piano Blues* (published in 1949). After the *Concerto,* he began to move away from the symphonic jazz idiom, though the basic stylistic features continued in the scores of the next period. In the late 1920s he turned to a more abstract style in his three-movement *Dance Symphony* (1929; from his earlier ballet score, *Grogh*). Copland's actual relation to the jazz idiom in these works of the French-jazz period has been aptly qualified by Virgil Thomson, who stated that

> [Copland is] largely preoccupied with . . . superficial Americana, characterized by the rhythmic displacements that many in those days took for "jazz" but that were actually, as in George Gershwin's vastly successful *Rhapsody in Blue,* less a derivate from communal improvising, which real jazz is, than from commercial popular music. No wonder the effort to compose concert jazz came to be abandoned, by Copland and by others. . . . Its last appearance in Copland's work is in the otherwise nobly rhetorical *Symphonic Ode* of 1929. . . .[31]

[31] See Thomson, *American Music Since 1910,* n.28, above, p. 52.

As Copland moved toward a more abstract approach to composition in the late 1920s, he became involved more directly in the institutional promotion of modern music. He became a member of the League of Composers, which had earlier commissioned his *Music for the Theatre* and works by other American and European composers, and he chaired and contributed to its quarterly journal, *Modern Music,* where he acknowledged the work of the "ultramodernists": Cowell, Varèse, and others. In 1928, he and Roger Sessions inaugurated the Copland-Sessions Concerts in New York (1928–1931) for the performance of new American music, and it was during this time that he composed his *Piano Variations* (1930), a landmark in his development. The work infused serial elements of the Vienna Schoenberg circle as well as techniques from other European composers into his Stravinskian neoclassicism.[32] Although he was not to use the serial principle again until the 1950s, when he turned to twelve-tone serialism more systematically, this piece heralded Copland's move toward a more abstract, though representative American style in the 1930s. Regardless of Copland's use of programmatic elements in certain works since the 1930s, a more abstract musical plane is evident in his clearly defined, tightly constructed musical forms, as in the orchestral *Statements: Militant, Cryptic, Dogmatic, Subjective, Jingo, Prophetic* (1932–1935).[33] More abstract, however, are the *Short Symphony* (1932–1933), later arranged as a *Sextet for Piano, Clarinet, and Strings* (1937), the *Piano Sonata* (1941), *Sonata for Violin and Piano* (1943), and the serial works since 1950.

With the onset of the economic Depression of 1930, Copland and others had to modify their compositional approaches because of the loss of support from that small, yet special, musical public of the previous decade. In his efforts to reach the more conservative public at large, Copland moved toward a simplified contemporary idiom primarily in orchestral (but also vocal) works composed either for school performance, analogous to Hindemith's *Sing und Spiel* or *Gebrauchsmusik* concepts, or for the more popular media of film, radio, and phonograph, a trend which had also been developing in other countries. The results were his tuneful high school operetta *The Second Hurricane* (1936) and *An Outdoor Overture* (1938) for school orchestra, *Music for Radio* (1937), which also came to be known as *Saga of the Prairie* through requests of the radio audience, and the Hollywood film music for *Of Mice and Men* (1939), *The City* (1939), *Our Town* (1940), *North Star* (1943), *The Cummington Story* (1945), *The Red Pony* (1948), *The Heiress* (1948), and *Something Wild* (1961). The purely musical self-sufficiency of these works has been seen in the performances of some of them as concert suites. In all these works, Copland's prevailingly American quality, as manifested in a simplified harmonic idiom pervaded typically by triads and open fifths as well as frequent use of pandiatonicism, is established not only in the titles, but in the

---

[32] For further reference to this work, which foreshadowed Copland's turn to serialism after World War II, see Chapter 16, below.

[33] See Thomson, *American Music Since 1910,* n.28, above, p. 52.

musical sources themselves. This quality is also evident in his *John Henry* (1940) for chamber orchestra, *Lincoln Portrait* (1942) for speaker and orchestra, in which song quotes from Stephen Foster and folksong materials are juxtaposed with portions of Lincoln's speeches, the *Third Symphony* (1946), which is an abstract work incorporating his earlier patriotic *Fanfare for the Common Man* (1942), and especially his two sets of arrangements of *Old American Songs* (1950, 1954) and pastoral opera *The Tender Land* (1952–1954), based on tunes and dances typical of the American style. He also captured the Latin American quality through his use of popular sources and a brilliant orchestral style in his suite *El Salón Mexico* (1936).

Among the most significant products of Copland's simpler style were the three ballets—*Billy the Kid* (1938), *Rodeo* (1942), and *Appalachian Spring* (1944)—in which he continued to exploit quiet pastoral moods together with angular, vigorous dance rhythms. All three works, which are imbued with Anglo-American folk-music sources as well, are primary examples of Copland's Americanism. The Western mood of *Billy the Kid* is established by the use of several cowboy tunes.[34] The opening scene is divided into two distinct sectional planes, the *Lento Maestoso* establishing the lonely mood of the prairie, the more lively *Moderato* the mood of the frontier town. The first cowboy tune, which initiates the latter section in the piccolo and tin whistle, is derived from the song "Great Granddad." As part of Copland's vivid mood painting, this "nonchalant" tune appears against a transparent harmonic background of nothing but a sustained two-octave E♭ in the upper strings. As the fifth degree of the key, this pitch-class contributes to the open quality of Copland's harmony and forms a contrasting stratum against the lively tune. The symmetrical quatrain structure of the tune also lends itself to Copland's typically delineated approach to phrasal construction and, together with its incessant encirclement of one or two pitches (in this case the fifth degree, E♭, which begins and ends the tune), produces a sense of tonal staticism that contributes further to the uniformity of the melody. All of these Stravinskian characteristics establish the basic premises for generating the distinct textural planes and layers of the larger form.

The tune is reiterated throughout the first half of the *Moderato* (Nos. 6ff.) as a kind of ostinato, its cadential tone (E♭) of which is held at the end of each thematic statement to provide a transparent but dissonant harmonic accompaniment for the entry of the next cowboy tune (No. 7, upbeat to m. 5). The latter, which is derived from the song *The Streets of Laredo*, occurs here in alternation with the first tune, its cadential tone (F) being held conversely as a dissonance against it. The successive statements of these alternating tunes produce a series of contrasting thematic planes, but the close rhythmic and intervallic relations between the tunes contribute to the unity of the larger structure. The sequential rhythmic pattern of the second tune,

---

[34] These folk sources are identified in a concise descriptive survey of the work by Neil Butterworth, *The Music of Aaron Copland* (n.p.: Toccata Press, 1985), pp. 76–79.

based on a metrically articulated half-note and two weak quarter-notes, is derived by the metric displacement of the three-note stretto figure that punctuates the first thematic cadence (No. 6, mm. 9ff.). This episodic figure itself comes from the triadic segment, C–E♭–A♭, embedded near the opening of the first tune (No. 6, m. 2). Both thematic figures are also based on an ascending minor third. Thus, by means of Copland's characteristic metric manipulations, two contrasting but related themes are established as the basis of the larger mosaic formal construction.

While the first part of the *Moderato* is almost exclusively based on open unison/octave sonorities, Copland achieves a sense of development and contrast by means of timbral and harmonic building as well as increasing rhythmic complexity. At the second statement of the first cowboy tune (No. 7), the piccolo line is doubled by the clarinet, to which is also added unison fragments in the violins. All these lines are doubled at the two-octave range originally defined by the held E♭ octaves. A similar doubling procedure occurs in the ensuing thematic alternations until a larger instrumental combination is reached (No. 8, upbeat to m. 6). At this point, the second tune progresses in parallel ninths rather than octaves. The cadential figure of this tune is then extended episodically and broken up into syncopated figures between upper and lower strings.

These syncopations continue against the next entry of the first tune (at No. 9) to produce the first heterophonic juxtaposition between contrasting wind and string planes. The texture is made fuller by the first harmonic occurrence of thirds. At the cadence of this thematic statement (No. 9, mm. 8ff.), the original stretto figure from the end of the first statement is extended in the woodwinds in increased metric displacements and set against two other instrumental planes—one is based on the syncopated grace-note figure in the strings, while the other is based on a replacement of the original E♭ pedal by held, fuller chords that are broken up into a reiterated syncopated rhythm.

The next and fullest sonic statement of the first tune (No. 10, strings) is accompanied by a more active, triadically harmonized waltz rhythm in the winds and piano. The distinction between these simultaneously juxtaposed timbral planes (tune and waltz) is enhanced by the first polymetric conflict of the section, in which the 4/4 meter of the tune is contradicted by the irregular 3 + 3 + 2/4 meter of the waltz, the latter perhaps suggesting a musical reference to the intoxicated cowboys. This trend toward rhythmic complexity and increased textural planing continues in the remainder of the scene, resulting in a succession of thematic layers and timbral planes that interact to produce a cumulative mosaic form. Other folk or popular tunes, which are adapted in various passages, also contribute to the American sound of the ballet. Some of these include allusions to *The Old Chisholm Trail, Git Along Little Dogies, Come Wrangle yer Bronco, Goodbye Old Paint,* and *Oh Bury Me Not on the Lone Prairie.*[35]

---

[35] Ibid.

Appalachian Spring represents another example of Copland's interest in writing American music that would reach the people, but he now focused on the story of a wedding about to take place in rural Pennsylvania in the early nineteenth century. The ballet consists of nine continuous but contrasting sections, with suggestions as well as quotations from American folk sources. The second section (*Allegro*) suggests country-fiddling based on Copland's characteristic use of displaced accents, whereas the seventh section employs a quoted Shaker dance-tune, entitled *'Tis the Gift to Be Simple,* as the basis for a set of dance variations.[36] Copland's American style in this work is a result not only of the pervasive allusions to American folk styles and the use of a quoted authentic folk tune, but of the more conservative handling of open diatonic sonorities that are largely removed from his more dissonant and abstract musical scores. This approach permits a more pastoral quality to be felt. As in the approach to harmony in *Billy the Kid,* the opening harmonizations of the Shaker tune are extremely transparent, focusing on open fifths and octaves both linearly and vertically, and again, the symmetrical quatrain structure of the tune lends itself ideally to Copland's conciseness of structure. The larger set of balanced, contrasting variations, based on clearly articulated changes of texture, key, dynamics, and tempo, is perfectly suited to Copland's inclination toward block juxtaposition as well as timbral and figural layering within each variation. The overall cumulative shape is produced once again by increased doublings toward the full orchestra by the last variation.

An American consciousness was also manifested prominently in the musical styles of Roy Harris (1898–1979) and Virgil Thomson (1896–1989), both of whom were part of the Boulanger group in the 1920s. The most intensive fusion of traditional European forms with American folk-music sources may be found in the large-scale symphonic and choral works of Harris. Much of his music reveals the spirit of his Midwestern background, with a spaciousness that is particularly evocative of the Western landscape, but it was not until the mid 1930s, in his choral work *When Johnny Comes Marching Home* (1935; also for orchestra), that he first used an authentic folk tune. It was also during this time that he came in contact with the American folksong scholars John and Alan Lomax as well as folksingers such as Burl Ives. Many of his works since then had absorbed folk-music materials more extensively, as in his *"Folksong" Symphony No. 4* (1940), for chorus and orchestra, and the later choral *Folk Fantasy for Festivals* (1956), for solo voices, folksingers, choruses, and piano. His roots in the American tradition were already evident in his choral *Song Cycle* (1927), set to texts of Walt Whitman, and in the titles of such choral and/or orchestral works as *An American Portrait* (1929), *Farewell to Pioneers* (1935), *American Creed* (1940), *Railroad Man's*

---

[36] Originating in eighteenth-century England, Shakers were members of a religious society that believed in the dual nature of the Deity, practiced celibacy, community of possessions, pacifism, and equality of the sexes. Shaker worship included prayer dances and marches as well as songs. This tune is given by Edward D. Andrews, *The Gift to be Simple* (New York: Dover, 1940), p. 136.

Ballad (1941), *Freedom's Land* (1941), *"Gettysburg Address" Symphony No. 6* (1944), *Kentucky Spring* (1949), *Cumberland Concerto* (1952), *"Abraham Lincoln" Symphony No. 10* (1965), and others throughout his career.

The American spirit in his earliest compositions was undoubtedly encouraged in the early 1920s by his studies with Arthur Farwell, who became a staunch supporter of his music. The increasing recognition of Harris' music led to a performance in 1926 of his *Andante for Orchestra,* which was conducted by Howard Hanson at the new American Composers' Concerts and Festivals of American Music at the Eastman School of Music in Rochester. This was followed, at the encouragement of Copland, by a sojourn in Paris from 1926 to 1929 to study with Boulanger, who recognized in him an independent and rugged individualist. Through his own independent studies of late-Renaissance and Baroque composers as well as Bach and Beethoven during this time, Harris had begun to acquire a firm knowledge of the traditional European styles and techniques. Nevertheless, in his *Piano Sonata* (1928) of these Paris years, his rural American spirit was strongly evident, as in the theme of the scherzo movement that seems to suggest *Turkey in the Straw.* Following the works of this Paris Period, which had begun with the *Concerto for Piano, String Quartet, and Clarinet* (1927), he moved toward greater technical control and compositional complexity in such abstract polyphonic works as the piano *Trio* (1934).

After his return to the United States in the early 1930s, Harris' reputation was firmly established in works revealing the craftsmanship that he had acquired during his studies with Boulanger. It was at this time that great efforts were being made in the United States to induce public interest in the symphonic and choral literature of the great European masters. This led to the development of numerous professional and community orchestras beginning in the 1930s, and Harris was among the most prolific of composers to look toward this new market. His *Symphony No. 1* (1933), which resulted from Koussevitzky's request for a "great symphony from the west," was premièred in 1934 by the latter and the Boston Symphony. This work was the first of Harris's more than one dozen symphonies, which spanned the entire period of the European "grand tradition" in the United States from the 1930s through 1970s.

In the 1930s, Harris' music came under the increasing influence of folk sources. He had always been inclined toward the diatonic modes, which are essential to the folk sources of his American background, and in the mid 1930s he began to approach modality more systematically. He classified the seven diatonic modes according to the size of the intervals in relation to the modal tonic. At one extreme is the "darkest" mode, Locrian (B–C–D–E–F–G–A–B), which contains all minor intervals from the tonic B, except for the perfect fourth (B–E) and "dark" diminished fifth (B–F), while at the other extreme lies the "lightest" mode, Lydian (F–G–A–B–C–D–E–F), which contains all major intervals from the tonic F, except for the "bright" augmented fourth (F–B) and perfect fifth (F–C). These two modes are intervallic inversions of each other, as are specific pairings of the other modes in corresponding positions of this scheme (C-major/E-Phrygian, G-Mixolydian/A-Aeolian, and D-Dorian/D-Dorian). The modes of the preludes and fugues that form *String Quartet No. 3* (1937) are organized according to this scheme, moving from "light" to "dark" in this piece. He categorized chords according to their degree of intervallic relation to the overtone series similarly.

Many of the characteristics of Harris' style were combined in his *Symphony No. 3* (1937). Although an American feeling permeates this symphonic medium, the work is untitled and is generally more abstract than his other symphonies, so the American quality is perceived more in terms of its general individualism and grand style rather than through any specific use of authentic folk materials. The melodic lines and harmonies reveal a stylistic eclecticism common to American composers. The work is in five continuous movements, each based on a different mood. It opens with a rhythmically fluid, continuously spun-out modal melody, based on a gradual widening of intervals to produce a sense of spaciousness. This mood is supported by the gradual addition of voices in parallel motion, leading eventually to a fuller polyphonic texture, which perhaps suggests the influence of early polyphony. Such parallelism may also suggest an impressionistic style, of which there is evidence in some of his earliest compositions with open fourths and fifths. The lyric theme of the second section is ambiguous tonally and modally, as the melody shifts continually from one modal segment to another to produce long chromatic lines of great metric and rhythmic elasticity. In the third section, pastoral woodwind lines unfold against a polytonal string figuration (No. 21, mm. 6ff), the upper strings outlining a C♯-minor triad, the lower strings an A-major triad, the modal wind solo linearly suggesting a motion from A to C♯. This gradually increases polytonal harmonies and density that lead into the contrasting, rhythmically angular fugue of the fourth section. Earlier themes are brought back eventually in a counterpoint based on syncopations and cross rhythms, and the spun-out melodic style of the opening returns to introduce the final section.

With the increasing influence of folk sources in the late 1930s, Harris began to move away from this type of continuous melody and organic form. In his later works, he established more clearly articulated and contoured phrases in simpler rhythms based on irregular stresses. According to Paul Henry Lang, in his 1957 *Herald Tribune* review of *Symphony No. 3*: "If Mr. Harris had only continued in this vein instead of attempting to naturalize a native-born American, he would have retained the freshness as well as the individuality of his gifts; only good and unselfconscious composition is needed to produce genuine American music."[37]

After 1918, Stravinsky's neoclassicism had become a guiding force for the younger generation of French composers as well as for the American

---

[37] See John Tasker Howard and George Kent Bellows, *A Short History of Music in America* (New York: Thomas Y. Crowell Company, 1957), p. 290.

composers who came to study with Boulanger in the 1920s. Virgil Thomson, however, found a closer affinity than did his American colleagues with the neoclassical aesthetics of the younger French composers of the group known as *Les Six* and with the ironic wit and objectivity manifested in the extremely reduced and simplified mechanistic textures of Erik Satie. During his first sojourn to Paris, in which he studied with Boulanger from 1921 to 1922, Thomson also came into contact with other musical sources, all of which lent themselves to his inclination toward an eclectic, universal approach to composition. Throughout his career, he was to employ both traditional and contemporary techniques (diatonic themes and triadic harmonies as well as polytonal combinations) in traditional art-music or popular forms (passacaglias, chorales, fugues, variations, waltzes, tangos, etc.). He used popular dance rhythms as early as his piano pieces *Two Sentimental Tangos* (1923) and the *Synthetic Waltzes* (1925), his interest in these realistic sources equalling that of the French composers. His neo-Baroque *Sonata da Chiesa* (1926) for clarinet, trumpet, horn, trombone, and viola, which was the first work he composed after his second arrival in Paris in the mid 1920s, reveals an even greater eclecticism and varied approach to sources in his mixture of Chorale, Tango, and Fugue within a single work. Shortly afterwards, in his *Symphony on a Hymn Tune* (1926–1928), he also absorbed vernacular elements from his own American heritage into the traditional symphonic medium, the two hymns *How firm a foundation ye Saints of the Lord* and *Yes, Jesus Loves Me* serving as the basic thematic materials for the larger, highly crafted orchestral form. Hymn tunes had already appeared prominently in one of his many organ works, *Variations on Sunday School Tunes* (1926–1927).

Through Thomson's personal harmonic and rhythmic approach, the opening traditional tune of the *Symphony* is drawn immediately into the contemporary neoclassical idiom. The tune unfolds in four varied statements (to No. 2), each punctuated by a short contrasting interlude that contributes to the distinction and separation of the successive phrases characteristic of neoclassical block construction (Ex. 7–6). At the same time, subtle metric and rhythmic manipulations within each statement contribute further to the dissociation of the tune from its traditional syntactical organization by creating ambiguity in thematic shape and tonal direction. In the first statement of the modal tune, the archaic nonfunctional tonality, produced by the parallel-fifth motion of the two horns in a chant-like free-flowing rhythm, is drawn into a contemporary idiom by means of an ambiguously syncopated and repetitive rhythmic encirclement of the basic D–A harmony. The basic harmonic fifth (D–A) is also weakened by means of metric emphasis on the respective seconds (E and B, at m. 2) and sevenths (C and G, at m. 4) of these parallel D- and A-Mixolydian modes, thereby precluding any sense of harmonic motion. This results in a static phrasal construction characteristic of the dissociated planes and layers found in the works of Poulenc, Stravinsky, and Satie. The first cadential metric change to 3/4 plays a special role in producing still further structural ambiguity by permitting a kind of phrasal elision with the next, otherwise contrasting timbral block based on a held C♯ octave. While the latter is articulated by its placement on the downbeat, the foreshortening

EXAMPLE 7-6. Thomson, *Symphony on a Hymn Tune,* Opening to No. 2, four varied statements of modal tune based on metric changes

of the previous measure by one beat produces the impression that the C♯ occurs on the last beat of a hypothetical 4/4 measure instead. This C♯ interlude seems simply to reiterate, or echo, the syncopated function of C♯ in the first phrase (m. 2, Horn I), thereby serving as an indeterminate, nontonic cadential extension of the tune.

The next statement of the tune one fifth higher increases the structural ambiguity through more radical metric and rhythmic reinterpretations. The original C♯ syncopation (over the barline of mm. 2–3) is moved forward in the phrase (mm. 7–8), so the respective second degrees of the transposed parallel modes also become syncopated. An appoggiatura leap in flute I replaces the stepwise motion of the original C♯ syncopation to expand the thematic range and heighten the tension. This departure from parallel fifths also results in the first real counterpoint of the section, producing a sense of development. All these reinterpretations produce more complex structural ambiguities. Despite the basic 4/4 barring, the meter is in 3/4 implicitly, an allusion to the single metric (3/4) deviation that disrupted the 4/4 meter at the original cadence. The expansion of the earlier metric conflict between the now continuous 3/4 unfolding within the 4/4 barring results in a heightening of the metric tension and transformation of the original thematic form. The next cadential deviation to 5/4 (at No. 1) extends rather than foreshortens the phrase this time, permitting the sense of 3/4 to continue without interruption. The new cadential major-second harmony at the 4/2 meter and the increasingly rapid metric changes together contribute to the absorption of the traditional tune into Thomson's own contemporary idiom, which is clearly imbued with an American popular flavor.

Shortly after Thomson's return to Paris, where he remained from 1925 to 1940, he made the acquaintance of Gertrude Stein, with whom he was to collaborate on some of his most important works. Thomson's metric distortions that had resulted in static, repetitive, and mechanical rhythms in the *Symphony* were further developed under the influence of Stein's texts. The first major work of this collaboration was the opera *Four Saints in Three Acts* (1927–1928; orchestrated 1933), the plans of which were being made while Thomson was setting two other Stein texts, including the song *Preciosilla* (1927) and *Capitals, Capitals* (1927), for four male voices and piano, after having already set the song *La Asado* (1926). In her objective and amusing approach to text, Stein aimed primarily at the dissociation of word from meaning, which she accomplished by seemingly random and absurd word repetitions, rhythmic distortions, and nonsyntactical reorderings, so the sounds themselves became the object of the poetic meaning. Such a "Dadaist" approach had its precedent in the symbolist texts of Mallarmé and other French poets of the late nineteenth century.

Stein's manipulations of simple word repetitions and stutterings are seen in her amusing play on words in the Prologue: "Four Saints two at a time have to have to have to have to. Have to have have to have to." Thomson's own musical style lent itself to the setting of such texts, and he derived his musical syntax according to the following procedure: "With the text on my piano's music rack, I would sing and play, improvising melody to fit the words and harmony for underpinning them with shape."[38] The musical style of his setting in this opera is typical of his highly eclectic and varied use of sources, including tunes set in hymn style, contrasted by free-flowing Anglican chant-like lines, arias, tango and waltz rhythms, etc., in a series of distinct tableaux incorporating varied simple or bitonal harmonic settings. One of the secrets of Thomson's Americanism in this work lies in his derivation of his melodic structures from the rhythm and pacing of American-English speech. The opening of the *Prologue* exemplifies his adaptation of melody to text, the basically 4/4 meter of which is contradicted by the mechanical 3/4 waltz accompaniment. The unexpected metric and rhythmic shifts in relation to the sentence structure, as at the two statements of "well fish. Four Saints," produce a run-on quality in the melodic phrase segments. The result is an ideal musical parallel of Stein's textual style and "sound." Furthermore, while the harmonic structure seems simple enough in its alternations between tonic and dominant chords, the metric displacement between melody and accompaniment produces bichordal coincidences and further displaces the textual rhythm. This work foreshadowed the new musical objectivity that became prevalent in American music in the next decade. It also set a precedent for a series of new American stage works beginning in the 1930s, including George Gershwin's *Porgy and Bess* (1935), Marc Blitzstein's *The Cradle Will Rock* (1937), and the operas of the American-trained Gian-Carlo Menotti, his first in English being *The Old Maid and the Thief* (1939). Since that time, others such as Douglas Moore, Roger Sessions, Samuel Barber, Hugo Weisgall, and Gunther Schuller have contributed significantly to the development of stage works that are highly accessible to the English-speaking audience.

In the early 1930s, Thomson temporarily turned away from the use of identifiably authentic American sources (hymns, etc.) toward more abstract materials in his string chamber music, *Symphony No. 2* (1931; arranged from the *First Piano Sonata*), and other works. In the late 1930s, he turned to composition for American government-sponsored films in which he now drew from American folk and popular sources, including cowboy songs in *The Plow that Broke the Plains* (1936), spirituals and hymn tunes in *The River* (1937), and a mixture of American folk materials as well as such art-music forms as Pastorale, Chorale, Fugue, and Passacaglia in the *Louisiana Story* (1948). His ballet *The Filling Station* (1937) and another opera on a Stein text, *The Mother of Us All* (1947), are also among his many works of this period based on American subjects, the latter work dealing with the women's suffrage movement in nineteenth-century America. Thomson's literary abilities were also evident in his work as music critic for the *New York Herald Tribune* from 1940 to 1954 and in a wealth of other writings.

[38] See Victor Fell Yellin, "The Operas of Virgil Thomson," in Thomson, *American Music Since 1910,* n.28, above, p. 94.

WALTER PISTON, ROGER SESSIONS, AND HOWARD HANSON

Walter Piston (1894–1976) and Roger Sessions (1896–1985) both began their careers as neoclassicists in the 1920s, and both generally remained inclined, though according to different aesthetic approaches, toward the European tradition for their compositional forms and techniques. In contrast to Sessions, however, Piston was drawn to Boulanger's studio from 1924 to 1926, and despite his contact with all of the varied musical sources known in Paris at that time—both modern and traditional—he remained essentially a traditionalist in his use of older forms (especially sonata and symphony) and a neoclassicist in his emotional restraint. After 1960, these inclinations were prevalent even in works based on experiments with twelve-tone sets, the first evidence of which appeared in his *Chromatic Study on the Name of Bach* (1940) for organ. His controlled, meticulous craftsmanship, often in Baroque-like textures, reflects the rigorous training he received from Boulanger in such scholastic musical disciplines as *species counterpoint* (a method founded by Johann Joseph Fux in 1725 for teaching sixteenth-century counterpoint in five progressive categories). His own academic orientation was manifested not only in his general compositional disposition, but in his teachings and publications on harmony and counterpoint as well.[39]

Most of Piston's music is instrumental, and many of these works are rooted in Baroque or Classical forms and techniques. The larger works include eight symphonies (1937–1965), two piano concertos (1959), two violin concertos (1940 and 1959), a viola concerto (1958), and other types of orchestral pieces, which are based specifically on Baroque models. The latter are exemplified by the *Prelude and Fugue* (1934), *Toccata* (1948), and *Concerto for Orchestra* (1933), which is Brandenburg-like in its rhythmic, contrapuntal style and in its use of fugue in the finale. His many chamber works include varied instrumental combinations from four to nine instruments, many of which are also reminiscent of Baroque and Classical forms, such as the *Passacaglia* (1943) for piano, *Partita* (1944) for violin, viola, and organ, the *Suite for Oboe* (1931) with its Baroque dance movements, and *Divertimento* (1946) for nine instruments. The influence of Stravinsky is discerned to some extent in Piston's early neoclassical works, but by the 1930s he revealed an increasing infusion of a broader, more sweeping melodic style into his mechanical neoclassical textures, characterized by incisive syncopated rhythms, as in the Allegro (m. 28) of the first movement of *Symphony No. 1*. Here, we find a typically strong harmonic underpinning based on the traditional triadic intervals, but the strong contrapuntal motion based on constantly shifting modal segments produces pungent harmonic dissonances and draws our

---

[39] See Piston's textbooks on *Principles of Harmonic Analysis* (Boston: E.C. Schirmer Music Co., 1933), *Harmony* (New York: W.W. Norton and Co., Inc., 1941), *Counterpoint* (New York: W.W. Norton and Co., Inc., 1947), and *Orchestration* (New York: W.W. Norton and Co., Inc., 1955).

attention to the motivically generated modal chromaticism. In a contrasting thematic segment (No. 125ff.), a homophonic modal-diatonic theme is supported entirely by fourth chords in parallel motion.

In contrast to Piston, Sessions evolved more radically away from his distinctive neoclassical style of the 1920s, which had been consciously influenced by Stravinsky and Bloch, toward an increasingly dense and expressionistic chromaticism in the 1930s and 1940s. Coming ever closer to Schoenberg, his stylistic evolution was to culminate in an extremely intense twelve-tone serialism in the 1950s.[40] Historically as well, Sessions followed a different course than Piston and the other American composers who studied in Paris during the 1920s. Although he met Boulanger often, he remained entirely independent of her studio, choosing to spend his early European sojourn (from 1925 to 1933) in Florence, Rome, and Berlin, rather than to be swayed by her direction. His travels to other parts of Europe during this time, including France, Austria, and England, added to his awareness of the variety of international styles, leading him to oppose Boulanger's belief that France should guide the development of American music.[41] While he always considered himself an American composer, these travels contributed to his eclectic tendencies, and he was to remain more of a European-American composer than his compatriots. Sessions did play a significant role in American musical developments however—he and Copland inaugurated the Copland-Sessions Concerts (held in New York from 1928 to 1931) to promote the music of both American and European composers—but he opposed the strong nationalist bent of Copland, Harris, and Thomson. As far as Sessions was concerned, "You create music and if it's genuine and spontaneous music written by an American, why then it *is* American music. These things have to grow naturally. For me, nationalism is the wrong approach."[42]

Paradoxically, despite his opposition to a self-conscious Americanism, Sessions' evolution in the 1930s toward the "long line" conception, which Boulanger herself had advocated, contributed to one of the most characteristic, stylistic features of American music during the 1930s and 1940s. This tendency in Sessions' music can be traced from his early *The Black Maskers* (1923) to the *First Symphony* (1927) and *First Piano Sonata* (1928–1930), the last work of which Copland referred to as a "cornerstone" for the development of an American music. The new long-arched linear style was

[40] For a more in-depth discussion of Sessions' chromatic works and his evolution toward twelve-tone serialism, see Chapter 16, below.

[41] See the interview with Vivian Perlis, May 4, 1983, New York City, in Aaron Copland and Vivian Perlis, *Copland, 1900 Through 1942* (New York: St. Martin's/Marek, 1984), p. 150.

[42] See ibid., p. 149. Also see Sessions' views on nationalism in "Music and Nationalism," *Modern Music* 9/1 (November-December 1933): 3–12, "On the American Future," *Modern Music* 17/2 (January-February 1940): 71–75, and in *Reflections on the Musical Life in the United States* (New York: W.W. Norton, 1963), pp. 146–153.

then established firmly in the densely contrapuntal style of the *Violin Concerto* (1935) and the works that followed during this more intense chromatic period.[43]

Howard Hanson (1896–1981), a staunch supporter of American composers in his American Music Festivals at the Eastman School since the 1930s, nevertheless tended, as did Piston and Sessions, more toward the European traditional forms than did the Americanist composers of the Boulanger group, and he also contributed to the long-line conception in his large-scale symphonic and vocal works. Hanson's lyrical neo-Romantic style, however, which was influenced significantly by Sibelius and Grieg, as in his *Symphony No. 1 "Nordic"* (1923), lies somewhere between the objective neoclassical bent of Piston and the more intense chromatic expressionism of Sessions, as evidenced already in his earliest works, such as the *California Forest Play of 1920* (1919) for solo voices, chorus, dancers, and orchestra, *The Lament for Beowulf* (1925) for chorus and orchestra, *Symphony No. 2 "Romantic"* (1930), and the opera *Merry Mount* (1933), after Hawthorne. There is also some degree of eclecticism in Hanson's style, as seen in his use of frequent quotations of chorale tunes and stylistic references to Gregorian Chant in such works as the symphonic poem *Lux aeterna* (1923), as well as impressionistic passages and Stravinskian misaccentuated rhythmic patterns, as in *Symphony No. 2* (the second and fourth movements, respectively). Hanson himself claimed his music was of an American quality. This is perhaps a result of his absorption of varied sources, in creating a characteristically "long-line" style in a tonal idiom often spiced with dissonances that contributed to the building of tension. Among the younger generation of American composers to be influenced by Hanson were Robert Palmer, Robert Ward, William Bergsma, and Peter Mennin. Other American composers as well, such as Vincent Persichetti and William Schuman (a pupil of Harris), were to bring many of these characteristic American developments of the interwar period to full fruition.[44]

SUGGESTED READINGS

CHRISTINA BARNETT.   "Charles Ives: *114 Songs* and Transcendental Philosophy" (D.M.A. treatise, The University of Texas at Austin, 1986).

CAROL BARON.   "Ives on His Own Terms: An Explication, A Theory of Pitch Organization, and a New Critical Edition for the *3-Page Sonata*," (Ph.D. dissertation, The City University of New York, 1986).

GEOFFREY BLOCK.   *Charles Ives: A Bio-Bibliography* (New York and Westport: Greenwood Press, 1988).

PETER BURKHOLDER.   *Charles Ives, The Ideas Behind the Music* (New Haven and London: Yale University Press, 1985).

[43] See Chapter 16, below.
[44] See Chapter 20, below.

NEIL BUTTERWORTH.   *The Music of Aaron Copland* (n.p.: Toccata Press, 1985).

GILBERT CHASE.   *America's Music from the Pilgrims to the Present* (New York: McGraw-Hill Book Company, 1955; 2nd ed., 1966).

AARON COPLAND AND VIVIAN PERLIS.   *Copland, 1900 Through 1942* (New York: St. Martin's/Marek, 1984).

HENRY COWELL.   *New Musical Resources* (New York: Alfred A. Knopf, 1930).

HENRY AND SYDNEY COWELL.   *Charles Ives and His Music* (New York: Oxford University Press, 1955; 2nd edition enlarged and reprinted 1969; unabridged reprint of 2nd edition, New York: Da Capo Press, 1983).

ARNOLD DOBRIN.   *Aaron Copland: His Life and Times* (New York: Thomas Y. Crowell Company, 1967).

LOU HARRISON.   "Ruggles, Ives, Varèse," *Soundings: Ives, Ruggles, Varèse*, ed. Peter Garland (Spring 1974).

H. WILEY HITCHCOCK.   *Ives: A Survey of the Music* (London: Oxford University Press, 1977).

———.   *Music in the United States: A Historical Introduction* (Englewood Cliffs. Prentice-Hall, Inc., 1969, 1974, 1988).

JOHN TASKER HOWARD AND GEORGE KENT BELLOWS.   *A Short History of Music in America* (New York: Thomas Y. Crowell Company, 1957).

CHARLES IVES.   *Essays Before a Sonata and Other Writings*, ed. Howard Boatwright (New York: W.W. Norton and Co., 1961, 1962).

———.   *Memos*, ed. John Kirkpatrick (New York: W.W. Norton and Co., Inc., 1972).

EDWARD M. MAISEL.   *Charles T. Griffes, The Life of an American Composer* (New York: Alfred A. Knopf, 1943).

RITA MEAD.   *Henry Cowell's New Music 1925–1936, The Society, The Music Editions, and the Recordings* (Ph.D. dissertation, The City University of New York, 1978; reprinted in *Studies in Musicology*, No. 40, Ann Arbor: UMI Research Press, 1981).

RÉGIS MICHAUD.   *L'esthétique d'Emerson* (Paris: Libraire Felix Alcan, 1927).

ROGER SESSIONS.   "Music and Nationalism," *Modern Music* 9/1 (November-December 1933): 3–12.

———.   "On the American Future," *Modern Music* 17/2 (January-February 1940): 71–75.

———.   *Reflections on the Musical Life in the United States* (New York: W.W. Norton, 1963), pp. 146–153.

VIRGIL THOMSON.   *American Music Since 1910* (New York: Holt, Rinehart and Winston, 1970, 1971).

LAURENCE WALLACH.   "The New England Education of Charles Ives" (Ph.D dissertation, Columbia University, 1973).

ROBERT E. WEAVER.   "The Piano Works of Charles T. Griffes" (Master's thesis, The University of Texas at Austin, 1956).

VICTOR FELL YELLIN.   "The Operas of Virgil Thomson," in Virgil Thomson, *American Music Since 1910* (New York: Holt, Rinehart and Winston, 1970, 1971).

8 Early national developments in Latin America

In the early twentieth century, Latin American composers also turned to national musical sources as the basis for developing their personal musical languages. Some of these composers were trained either in Europe or the United States, enabling them to draw from Romantic, impressionistic, and neoclassical as well as more modernistic styles as the basis for establishing a contemporary idiom imbued with the color of their own musical folklore. The individual nationalistic inclinations of these Latin American composers varied according to prevailing socio-political and cultural conditions within their own national boundaries. Nevertheless, in all cases, the search for a national identity in the arts was an outgrowth of increasing national awareness stemming from the movement toward national independence. The emergence of distinctive national styles in Latin America became evident only in the late nineteenth century, with a more global movement toward the breakdown of German musical hegemony, which was first challenged by a nationalistic surge in Russia and new styles in France. In the nineteenth century, colonial institutions and the presence of foreign artists in Latin America continued to influence musical developments, and it was only with increasing emphasis on the training of national artists and the new awareness of the possibilities inherent in folk and popular sources that a shift away from the prevalence of European musical traditions was finally possible.

MEXICO: MANUEL M. PONCE, CARLOS CHÁVEZ, AND SILVESTRE REVUELTAS

Several musical forces were evident in Mexico during the nineteenth century, most prominent of which were Italian opera, Mexican opera in an Italian style, and instrumental compositions by Mexican composers strongly rooted in European Romantic traditions (Austrian, French, and others). Juventino Rosas (1868–1894), an Otomi Indian, wrote Straussian waltzes, polkas, mazurkas, and other Romantic types of salon piano music, while other Mexican composers absorbed European elements from their studies abroad, as did the musical pioneers in the United States around the same time. Gustavo E. Campa (1863–1934) visited Paris in 1900 and drew from the stylistic features of Massenet, which can be witnessed in such works as his opera *Le roi poète* (1901); Ricardo Castro (1864–1907) studied piano with Eugen d'Albert in Paris and toured Europe. Aniceto Ortega (1825–1875) was among the earliest to absorb national folk elements into the Italian operatic form in his *Guatimotzin* (premièred in 1871), which is also reminiscent of Beethoven stylistically, whom Ortega had paid homage to in his piano *Invocación á Beethoven*, Op. 2 (premièred in 1867).

Absorption of indigenous Mexican musical elements, especially from

Indian and Mestizo sources, received momentum from the Mexican Revolution after 1910, and the Aztec Renaissance after World War I. Such Mestizo types as the *corrido,* a Mexican narrative ballad, had developed in connection with the Revolution and were employed by composers as an expression of patriotic sentiment. Manuel M. Ponce (1882–1948) was the first major nationalistic composer to investigate and absorb intensively Mestizo folk types (including the category of *son,* or rural peasant music, usually characterized by unequal triple rhythm in six-beat patterns) into Classical and Romantic forms and styles during the Revolutionary period. Around this time, Ponce composed his Romantic/popular song *Estrellita* (1912) and several of his earliest arrangements of folk tunes in the *Canciones Mexicanas* for piano. He had already begun to develop an eclectic international orientation after his first piano concerts in the United States and Europe in 1904, which led to studies in Bologna with Torchi and in Berlin at the Stern Conservatorium. His teaching appointments, first at the *National Conservatorio* upon his return to Mexico in 1906 and then in Havana from 1915 to 1918, were eventually followed by an influential period of study with Paul Dukas during his stay in Paris from 1925 to 1933. While the Romantic influences can be seen in his early salon-type piano pieces, the *Trio romántico* (1911) for piano, violin, and cello, the *Mazurkas, Preludio y fuga sobre un tema de Haendel,* and other traditional European forms, his studies in Paris also resulted in a synthesis of impressionistic techniques and Mexican folk characteristics, evidenced in such works as his *Chapultepec: Tres Bocetos Sinfonicos* (1929, revised 1934). During the 1930s, Indian tunes were also used in his *Canto y Danza de los antiguos Mexicanos* (1933) and other works.

The quiet tremolo chords that open *Chapultepec* are based on a static undulating motion entirely characteristic of French impressionist textures. The individual strings within the ostinato of the first three measures unfold divergent scalar segments linearly—an ambiguous diatonic/whole-tone figure in violin I (G♭–A♭–B♭–C), two alternating diatonic figures in violin II (E♭–F–G♭–A♭ and E♭–F♭–G♭–A♭), and an octatonic segment in the viola (B♭–C–D♭–E♭–F♭)—suggesting a fusion of both traditional and nontraditional modal constructions found in impressionistic and folk-music sources. This polymodal texture, which produces chromatic cross-relations between F♭ and F, and G♭ and G, is characteristic of Ponce's compositional approach and contributes to the contemporary sound of his music.

The alternation of Ponce's musical activities between Europe and Mexico, where he also taught folklore at the Universidad Nacional Autónoma upon his return from Paris to Mexico City in 1933, contributed to his compositional synthesis of divergent art- and folk-music sources. Development of his style in later works resulted from the absorption of these varied elements into a more neoclassical contrapuntal idiom, as in his Spanish-influenced *Concierto del Sur* (1941) for guitar and orchestra and the *Violin Concerto* (1943). In these works, he absorbed folk rhythms into contexts based on chromatic and dissonant elaborations of the modal melodies, which shift constantly by means of chromatic root progressions. The *Concierto del Sur* is exemplary of the fusion of the rhythms and modes of Spanish Flamenco and Mexican folk sources with lyrical Romantic passages and mechanical ostinato patterns typical of the neoclassical style, also manifested in the juxtaposition of distinct phrasal and sectional blocks. At the same time, passages tend toward tonal instability through touches of dissonant polymodality as well as unexpected chromatic shifts from one modal segment to another, all within a tertian harmonic context pervaded by nonfunctional seventh chords. Folk characteristics are suggested by a comparison of the accompanying ostinato patterns (dotted rhythm followed by alternating pairs of short and long notes) and the descending cadential contour and rhythm of a Mexican processional melody[1] with a passage from the second movement of the *Concierto* (Ex. 8–1). In the Ponce excerpt, two ostinati are combined to form a mechanical counterpoint to the folk-like melody. However, the composer transforms these folk-like elements into a contemporary idiom by the seventh-chord harmonizations, the chromatically descending motion of the bass, and the bimodal melodic shift from F major to F Phrygian at the cadence. The tonality of the latter is weakened both by the quintal (though modal) harmony at this point (G♭–D♭–[   ]–E♭–B♭–F) and the following chromatic shifts to unrelated tonal areas. In this way, Ponce had fused international

EXAMPLE 8–1. Ponce, *Concierto del Sur,* second movement, No. 41, mm. 9–11

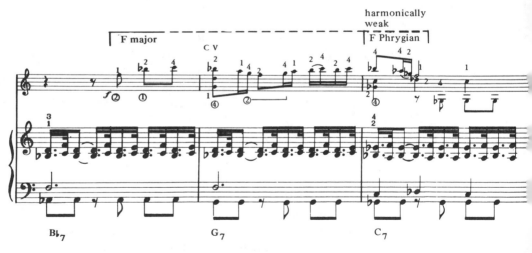

[1] See the processional melody transcribed by E. Thomas Stanford, in "Mexico, II, 3: Folk Music, Indigenous Forms," *The New Grove Dictionary of Music and Musicians,* ed. Stanley Sadie (London: Macmillan Publishers Ltd., 1980), p. 239.

art-music styles with Spanish and Mexican folk-music elements in various works to produce a contemporary national idiom.

In his works of the 1920s through early 1930s, Carlos Chávez (1899–1978) had infused national elements comprehensively (these included most prominently Mexican Aztec music of the preconquest era and also Mestizo traditions) into a highly personal idiom—one that was more modernistic and dissonant than that of Ponce. Chávez's colleague and friend Aaron Copland provides us with a perspective regarding Chávez's special position as a contemporary Mexican composer: "Singlehandedly, he has created a tradition no future Mexican composer can afford to ignore . . . no other composer—not even Béla Bartók or Manuel de Falla—has succeeded so well in using folk material in its pure form while at the same time solving the problem of its complete amalgamation into an art form."[2]

The two extremes of Chávez's musical orientation, one toward national folk sources—albeit from a remote chronological standpoint in that he drew primarily from ancient native Indian traditions—the other toward a contemporary international musical language based on the absorption of folk rhythms into a highly abstract and dissonant idiom, were reflected in his divergent institutional musical activities after the 1920s. He founded several *academias de investigación,* including one for research into folk and popular music and another for developing new musical theories. As Director of the *Conservatorio Nacional* from 1928 to 1934, he promoted interest in a revival of native art. He also associated himself with Copland, Cowell, Varèse, and others in New York from 1926 to 1928 as a member of the *International Composers' Guild* and the *Pan American Association of Composers,* which enabled him to promote contemporary Latin American music beyond its local boundaries. Copland pointed out that Chávez, a thoroughly contemporary composer, was indebted to the United States in the same way that Thomson and Piston were indebted to France.[3] Although Chávez had visited Berlin and other European cities, he ultimately rejected the Germanic ideal, feeling a greater kinship with the composers and musical conditions in the United States. He even composed one of his most famous national works, the *Sinfonía India* (1935–1936), in the United States, and certain critics referred to him as more of a North American, rather than Mexican composer.

Chávez's inclination toward absorption of native elements into his music in the 1920s and 1930s was motivated by the patriotic ideals of the Mexican Revolution between 1910 and 1920 as well as the more concrete political, social, economic, and cultural reforms that developed from the Revolution. With a government commission to write a work on a native theme, he composed his ballet *El fuego nuevo* (1921), based on an Aztec ceremony invoking the gods to ensure the appearance of the sun throughout

[2] Aaron Copland, *Our New Music* (New York: McGraw-Hill, 1941), pp. 206–207.

[3] Ibid., p. 203.

the next century. This was his first work to reject his earlier European Romanticism, although the critic Paul Rosenfeld referred to it as "the very early, still very dainty and Debussian forerunner of *Los Cuatro Soles*."[4] Chávez's interest in Aztec folklore continued in the latter work, *Los cuatro soles* (1925), both ballets of which are scored for voices and orchestra, perhaps reflecting the composer's awareness that instruments and voices were connected inextricably in Aztec musical performance. In his *Xochipili-Macuilxochitl* (1940), subtitled "An Imagined Aztec Music," for four winds and six percussion players, Chávez revealed his knowledge of the ancient Aztec instruments and his ability to capture the melodic, rhythmic, and timbral quality of the folk sources.

Although the essence of the Indian style underlies these primitivistic works, Chávez's general intention was not to make arrangements of the folk tunes, but rather to transform them into an original musical idiom that would reflect the national spirit—*El fuego nuevo* and *Sinfonía India* were two of the few exceptions in which he had made literal use of Indian themes. A basic characteristic that Chávez observed in the Aztec melodies was their pentatonic construction, with a prevalence of the minor third and perfect fifth. The lack of semitones in the pentatonic structure of these melodies precluded the possibility of modulation which, according to Chávez, "was alien to the simple and straightforward spirit of the Indian."[5] Yet, he observed that shifting tonal emphases did occur within the pentatonic scale, so five different melodic modes were evident in what he referred to as *polymodality*. His knowledge of these characteristics inherent in the Aztec melodies permitted him to absorb their essence into his own contemporary national style without literal quotation. While his three *Sonatinas,* for violin and piano, cello and piano, and piano solo (1924), have no Indian melodies, they invoke the Mexican spirit. The first reveals Chávez's early tendency toward sublimated use of folk-music elements in an idiom influenced by the dissonant "ultra-modernist" trend of the time. His use of motivic repetition, ostinati, and layered textures in the modal context of this work also suggests Stravinsky's primitivism. The *Sonatina* was published in Cowell's *New Music Quarterly* (July 1928), after Chávez had already been in New York for several years, as an example of *contrapuntal polytonality*.[6]

[4] Paul Rosenfeld, *By Way of Art* (New York: Coward-McCann, Inc., 1928), pp. 273–283.

[5] See the translated quote from Chávez's lecture on Aztec music, given at the National University of Mexico in October 1928, in Robert Stevenson, *Music in Mexico: A Historical Survey* (New York: Thomas Y. Crowell Company, 1952), p. 7.

[6] See Henry Cowell, "New Terms for New Music," *Modern Music* 5 (May–June 1928): 21–27. For further discussion of the history of this work in connection to Cowell's *New Music* as well as the fusion of folk and contemporary characteristics, see Rita Mead, *Henry Cowell's New Music 1925–1936* (Ann Arbor: UMI Research Press, 1981, 1978), pp. 93–94.

The Stravinskian style was further manifested in Chávez's *Sinfonía India,* another one of the few works to incorporate authentic Indian tunes into an orchestral texture containing a large complement of Indian percussion: Yaqui Drum and Metal Rattle, Water Gourd, Tenabari (a string of Butterfly Cocoons), and so on. The entire work is based on the juxtaposition of large disparate blocks, which are differentiated by the changes of melodic and rhythmic patterns as well as timbre and tempo (as at No. 14, *Vivo*). The local angles and planes are also sharpened by the continual changes of meter as well as the use of displaced accentuation in individual layers within a single meter, a procedure which further contributes to the distinction between simultaneous ostinato patterns (e.g., No. 10, m. 4, between percussion, doubled lower strings/winds, and doubled upper strings/winds). In addition to the permeation of all the motivic-ostinato lines by pentatonic or diatonic modality, the folk-like Indian quality is established by literal references to authentic modal Indian tunes.[7] These include *Cora* (Nos. 9–10), *Yaqui* (Nos. 29–33), and *Sonora* (Nos. 43–44, m. 3) Indian melodies.[8] (The *Cora* are an Indian people living in the states of Jalisco and Nayarit in Western Mexico, the *Yaqui* primarily along the Yaqui River in Sonora, Northwest Mexico.) At the same time, the combination of these diatonic-modal layers results in a percussive, dissonant harmonic setting. While such a setting lends itself to primitivistic folk expression, it absorbs the folk style, creating a modernistic idiom characteristic not only of Stravinsky, but of the contrapuntal dissonance of Cowell, Ruggles, Varèse, and other "ultramodernists" in the United States during the 1920s and 1930s.

Both Indian elements and contemporary harmonic features are absorbed into a large-scale formal construction reminiscent of the symphonic poem, in which the traditional multimovement format of the symphony had been condensed into a continuous one-movement framework based on the outline of the traditional sonata-allegro plan (Ex. 8–2).[9] The unfolding of the mechanistic fabric of this anti-Romantic work, based on a succession of shifting ostinati within the framework of the traditional sonata form, points to a neoclassical conception. The entire work is based on minimal changes of tonality, each confined primarily to a prominent structural point in the sonata form, so that individual sections are static and harmonically nonfunctional internally. Within pentatonic or modal pitch collections, occasional shifts of tonal emphasis do occur, as Chávez had observed in the Indian music itself.[10]

[7] In these cases, the tunes are modal rather than pentatonic, in contrast to Chávez's general pentatonic observations presented in his lecture in Stevenson, *Music in Mexico,* n.5, above, pp. 6–7.

[8] For an outline of these authentic tunes, see Gerard Béhague, *Music in Latin America: An Introduction* (Englewood Cliffs: Prentice-Hall, Inc., 1979), pp. 136–138.

[9] The composer's own outline is given by Roberto García Morillo, in *Carlos Chávez: vida y obra* (Mexico: Fondo de Cultura Económica, 1960), p. 94.

[10] See Chávez's statement in Stevenson, *Music in Mexico,* n.5, above, p. 6.

EXAMPLE 8–2. Chávez, *Sinfonía India,* one-movement framework based on outline of traditional sonata-allegro plan

REHEARSAL NUMBERS	SECTIONS	KEY CENTERS
Beginning	Introduction	B♭ Maj
9	Allegro, Exposition: Main theme and its development	B♭ Maj
14	Bridge	B♭ Maj to E♭ Maj
27	Second theme and its development	E♭ Maj
43	Slow movement (poco lento). Main theme and its development	
59	Allegro, Recapitulation: Main theme and its development	B♭ Maj
64	Bridge	F Maj to B♭ Maj
73	Second theme and its development	B♭ Maj
81	Coda of the Allegro (elements of the Introduction)	B♭ Maj
88	Finale	F Maj

At the opening of the Introduction, two basic sonic planes are articulated by both the rhythmic and modal disposition of the layers. The sustained, oscillating, long notes in the first two measures outline a B♭-pentatonic collection, B♭–C–D–F–G, with some weakening of the tonic by the placement of the fifth and sixth degrees (F–G) in the bass. At the same time, the eighth-note arpeggiations expand the B♭-pentatonic foundation modally by the linear addition of E♭–G to the tonic triad (B♭–D–F), the total pentatonic and modal content of which produces a B♭-major segment, B♭–C–D–E♭–F–G.

The modal addition of E♭ (first in the eighth-note ostinato, then in the trombone entry at m. 3), a note which is outside the B♭-pentatonic content, subsequently acquires *modulatory* or *polymodal* significance (see the tonal scheme of Ex. 8–2).[11] At the next textural block (No. 2), the trumpet enters with a segment (D–F–G) from the B♭-pentatonic scale, its cadential focus on F–G tending to weaken the B♭ tonic. Following the next block (Nos. 4–7), based on a more dense layering of modal segments within the complete

[11] See ibid.

B♭-major collection, we get a return to the opening material (No. 7). However, the earlier trumpet cadence on G–F is now extended to G–F–E♭, the E♭ priority of which is established not only by the doubling of this melodic cadence in the other winds, but also by a rhythmic extension of the original E♭–G eighth-notes in the accompanying ostinato. This combination of layers produces a modal-tonal conflict between the held B♭–C (in oboe and horn I), which is supported by the B♭ triad in the eighths, and held E♭–F–G segment. Together, the sustained layers outline a new pentatonic scale, E♭–F–G–B♭–C, which is the perfect-fourth transposition of the original (B♭–C–D–F–G). The rhythmic, registral, and timbral disposition establishes E♭ as a new local tonic priority, so that within the unchanged modal spectrum of B♭-major (B♭–C–D–E♭–F–G–A–B♭), we get a pentatonic permutation founded on a new tonic note (E♭–F–G–[ ]–B♭–C–[ ]). In a retransitional block (Nos. 8–9), marked by the prominence of the percussion, the held tonic E♭ tends to be weakened by the C–F segments in the bass. Both these notes, common to both the E♭- and B♭-pentatonic collections, prepare us for a return to the original B♭ area (No. 9) at the first appearance of the main theme (*Cora* Indian melody). Although brief, the preceding modal permutation to E♭ represents an adumbration of one of the basic tonal juxtapositions of the work—the bridge (No. 14) takes us from B♭ to E♭ (at No. 27) at the appearance of the second theme (*Yaqui* Indian melody from Sonora). A minimal change in the key signature at this new theme effects the shift from B♭ to E♭ major, the latter key containing the original B♭-pentatonic content (B♭–C–D–F–G).

The authentic folk materials permitted the contemporary Mexican composer to depart from the traditional principles of rhythm and harmony. In the *Cora* melody (Ex. 8–3a), the repetitive rhythmic character and irregular metric shift between 3/2 and 2/2 reveal the rhythmic sources for the folk character of Chávez's surrounding invented material. The motoric rhythmic quality of the theme is enhanced further by the trumpet layers (in parallel fourths), which produce a metric conflict against the melody (4×3 eighths against 3×4 eighths). This cross relation, based on a conflict between duple and triple groupings, is characteristic of these folk sources and may also be observed within the structure of the *Yaqui* melody as well (Ex. 8–3b). Against the latter, percussion also produces a polyphonic conflict between duple and triple groupings.[12]

Notwithstanding the absorption of the Indian essence into his compositions, Chávez was far more than a nationalist composer, as observed in his more abstract modernistic works during his "populist" period. These works include the *Polygons* for piano (1923), the *Symphony of Antigone* (1933), the *Concerto for Four Horns and Orchestra* (1937–1938), and even those works based most prominently on Mexican elements, such as the *Sinfonía India,*

---

[12] As pointed out by Béhague, *Music in Latin America,* n.8, p. 138, certain types of duple-triple conflicts, specifically hemiola, are derived from Mestizo rather than Indian music in Mexico.

EXAMPLE 8–3. Chávez, *Sinfonia India,* No. 9, Cora melody (a), folk rhythm based on irregular metric shift in melody and projection of metric conflict in accompanying layers; No. 27, Yaqui melody (b), also based on cross relation between duple and triple groupings

which "is less a 'nationalist' work than a formal synthesis of indigenous musical elements, thematic and rhythmic," as well as the *Concerto for Piano and Orchestra* (1938–1940) and the *Toccata for Percussion Instruments* (1942).[13] His adherence to traditional formal structures is one of the features of his more international bent. Chávez's pupils, including Daniel Ayala Pérez, Salvador Contreras, José Pablo Moncayo, and Blas Galindo, who became known as "El Grupo de Los Cuatro," absorbed national elements similarly into universal styles and forms.[14] Galindo subsequently studied with Copland at the Tanglewood Music Center and absorbed Mestizo features into a more neoclassical style in his works after 1940. A stylistic perspective of "Los Cuatros" is provided by Copland: "their use of form . . . tends always to be sectionally constructed and in types of melodic material which always tend toward the Mexican popular tune. Their forte is orchestration, learned mostly by performing under Chávez in the Orquesta Sinfónica de México."[15] The Spanish-born composer Rodolfo Halffter (b. 1900) was among the most influential on post–World War II Mexican composers, through his own evolution toward serialism especially.

Another Mexican composer to be influenced strongly by the indigenous sources and his sojourn in the United States was Silvestre Revueltas (1899–1940). After his violin training during and after World War I in both Mexico and the United States, he performed European works with Chávez in Mexico City in the mid-1920s. He alternately held teaching and conducting positions in both countries from 1926 on, and began to compose his earliest orchestral works under the influence of Chávez, who also conducted their premières. The first of his orchestral compositions was the symphonic poem *Cuauhnahuac* (1930), named after the town of Cuernavaca, composed in a chromatic and dissonant modernistic idiom infused by a Stravinskian primitivistic folk-like quality by means of percussive polyrhythmic cross-relations, ostinati, and irregular metric schemes. However, in contrast to Chávez, who primarily drew from the pre-Conquest Indian sources for his chronologically remote "exotic" basis in a predominantly pentatonic/diatonic idiom, the nationalistic quality of Revueltas' personal idiom developed from his absorption of contemporary Mexican folk and popular sources into a dissonant chromaticism not only in the polyphonic web, but also within individual melodic lines. His modern style fuses the popular/folk- and art-music spheres to a point where they often seem indistinguishable.

According to Copland, "Revueltas was the spontaneously inspired

[13] Gilbert Chase, "Music in Latin America," in Virgil Thomson, *American Music Since 1910* (New York: Holt, Rinehart, and Winston, 1970, 1971), p. 114.

[14] Blas Galindo himself has provided an in-depth study of the group in his essay "Compositores de mi Generación," *Nuestra Música* (April 1948): 73–81.

[15] Aaron Copland and Vivian Perlis, *Copland: 1900 Through 1942* (New York: St. Martin's/Marek Press, 1984), p. 324.

type of composer, whose music is colorful, picturesque, and gay. . . . Certain circles in Mexico are anxious to prove that in comparison with the music of Revueltas, with its natural spontaneity, that of Chávez is essentially cold and cerebral. But I see no need to choose here."[16] Folk-like melodies of Revueltas' own inventions unfold in complex and timbrally colorful polyphonic textures also in his next orchestral works: *Esquinas* (1930), *Ventanas* (1931), *Alcancías* (1932), *Colorines* (1932), *Janitzio* (1933), and *Caminos* (1934), but the most striking absorption of the Mexican tunes and their dynamic rhythms into a dissonant idiom is evidenced in the *Homenaje a García Lorca* (1935). In *Sensemayá* (1938), the verses of the Afro-Cuban poet Nicolás Guillén "imitate onomatopoeically the sounds and rhythms of Afro-Cuban cult music."[17] The composer's lively and colorful style, always imbued with the characteristics of Mexican folk melodies and rhythms, can also be observed in a variety of other genres, including chamber music, songs, and film scores. The humorous side of Revueltas' musical personality may be observed in his chamber piece *8 × Radio* (1933) for eight instruments. Basic features of Mestizo melodic structure, rhythm, and parallel polyphony are combined satirically with dissonant polytonal elements in a style that "plays with typical Mexican tunes and thumbs its nose at the purveyors of a more pompous nationalism."[18] This attitude contrasts with his serious settings of Lorca's texts in his seven *Canciones* (1938) for voice and instruments.

BRAZIL: HEITOR VILLA-LOBOS

Although Brazil achieved independence as early as 1822, the concert repertory continued to be dominated during the nineteenth century by European styles, as it had been in Mexico. Political conditions in Brazil in the early part of the nineteenth century stimulated the international cultural scene, which had developed earlier during the colonial era. With the establishment of the Portuguese royal court in Rio de Janeiro in 1808, a number of European composers settled there during the following decades. Through government subsidy under Pedro II, the operas of Bellini, Verdi, and other Italian composers prevailed in the theatres of Rio from the mid-1840s on, Italian opera having been in fashion there since the eighteenth century. European Romantic salon styles were also cultivated. By the late nineteenth century, local composers also began to assimilate German late-Romantic and French impressionist styles at a time when an increasing number of foreign performers were contributing to the international styles of Brazilian concert life. Only after 1847, and the establishment of the *Imperial Academy of Music and National Opera,* was there any significant attempt to develop a national operatic repertory. The first publications of Brazilian works revealing national popular

[16] See Copland, *Our New Music,* n.2, above, pp. 209–210.
[17] See Béhague, *Music in Latin America,* n.8, above, p. 145.
[18] See Chase, "Music in Latin America," n.13, above, p. 114.

features came from the pianist-composer Itiberê da Cunha, his piano piece *A Sertaneja* of which appeared in 1869, but it was only by the late nineteenth and early twentieth centuries that the varied melodic and rhythmic dance features (e.g., tango and maxixe) of Brazilian popular music became pervasive in art-music compositions of a more distinctive national character. According to Vasco Mariz, the establishment of the Brazilian "ethnic type" and the first national compositions had come from three basic influences, "white, black, and red,"—the white from Portuguese, Spanish, French, Italian, German, and Polish immigrants, the black from the slave traffic (to 1850), which contributed to the "Brazilian soul and ethnic type," and the exploitation by missionaries (from the sixteenth century on) of "the Indian's inherent love of music."[19]

The most prominent twentieth-century Brazilian composer to synthesize international styles and popular- and folk-music sources into a decidedly national style based on contemporary art-music techniques was Heitor Villa-Lobos (1887–1959), whose orchestral, chamber, dramatic, choral, solo vocal, solo guitar, and piano works became known internationally only after 1920. His inclination toward a contemporary national style was already evident in his explorations of folk-music sources and his use of them in his *Cânticos Sertenejos* (1910) for small orchestra and his *Suite populaire brásilienne* (1908–1912) for solo guitar. The combination of European and Brazilian musical elements in the latter work foreshadowed his prominent synthesis of these sources in his set of *Bachianas brasileiras* (1930s and 1940s).

As early as 1905, he began to tour several of the Brazilian states, gradually working his way into the Northeastern territory. This fertile area for folk-music investigation contrasted with the Southern area, which was contaminated by the infusion of European sources. On this first trip to the Northeast, he studied the style of popular singers and their folk instruments, cowboy songs, dramatic dances, and other types, all of which were to come to fruition in the development of his own national style. While he never investigated the folk-music sources as systematically as Bartók in Eastern Europe, he collected more than a thousand tunes during his tours of Brazil. After 1907, he also travelled to São Paulo in the Southeast, Mato Grosso and Goiás in the central plateau, and to the Northeast as well as to Acre in the Amazon subsequently, where he came in contact with various Indian tribes. He made his first study of inland Indian music in 1912, though he had already drawn from secondary collections of Indian music when he was in Mato Grosso. By 1912, he had travelled throughout Brazil and even to Barbados in the West Indies, where he apparently derived tunes for his *Danças características africanas* (1915) for piano. Brazilian popular and folk music is influenced most strongly by the African sources.

[19] Vasco Mariz, *Heitor Villa-Lobos: Life and Work of the Brazilian Composer* (Washington, D.C.: Brazilian American Cultural Institute, Inc., 1970; first edition, University of Florida Press, 1963), pp. ix–x.

These tours alternated with periods in Rio, one in 1907 involving a brief attempt at a disciplined musical training at the *National Institute of Music*. However, this was unsuccessful because of his rebellious attitude and interest in developing an original national style. Yet, several works from this period reveal fleeting international influences. One can detect in his four-act opera *Izaht* (1912–1914), a fusion of his one-act operas *Aglaia* and *Eliza,* the orchestrational and motivic influences of Wagner and Puccini, respectively.[20] French cultural influences were also prominent in Brazil from the time of the late nineteenth century, so Villa-Lobos had the opportunity to study Vincent D'Indy's treatise on composition and absorb certain technical aspects of the French composer, evidenced in several of his symphonic and chamber works during World War I. While he also came into brief contact with Debussy's music in the early years, that influence did not manifest itself in his works of that time. None of the international influences were to persist in his compositions, since his own original stylistic interests were directed primarily toward his Brazilian national sources. Toward the end of the war (1917), he came into contact with Darius Milhaud, who was in Brazil as an attaché to the French diplomat Paul Claudel. This relationship led to reciprocal influences, Milhaud becoming acquainted with Brazilian popular music, Villa-Lobos strengthening his knowledge of Debussy's impressionism and the more objective styles of the new generation of French composers to which Milhaud belonged. He himself had been moving in recent works toward the anti-Romantic musical aesthetics of the latter, in a more primitivistic idiom and yet had not up to that point been familiar with the Russian works of Stravinsky. His awareness of the larger international musical scene was to be enriched by his stay in Paris from 1923 to 1930. During this time he also became an intimate friend of a group that included Pablo Picasso, Fernand Léger, Edgard Varèse, Florent Schmitt, and others. During these Paris years, he was also to travel to various European as well as Latin American cities and his works began to receive international acclaim; it was not until performances of his music at the 1939–1940 New York World's Fair, however, that he began to be known in the United States.

While he combined traditional compositional techniques, including contrapuntal and imitative writing as well as Classical genres and forms, with the stylistic features of his national music, his works of this period also tended toward integration of the diverse types of Brazilian popular and folk sources themselves. These national elements had been employed consistently since 1922. The main works of this period are the set of sixteen *Chôros* (1920–1929), scored for varied combinations of voices and/or instruments. Villa-Lobos drew upon the *chorões,* a type of late nineteenth century urban popular instrumental music (best described by the term "serenade"), which served as the basis for his own personal synthesis of the different rhythmic and modal elements of Indian and popular Brazilian music. These pieces of Villa-Lobos

---

[20] Ibid., pp. 9–10.

encompass a wide range of instrumental settings, including the solo guitar of *No. 1* (1920); solo piano of *No. 5;* various ensemble media of *Nos. 2* (duo for flute and clarinet), *3* (male chorus and six winds), *4* (three horns and trombone), and *7* (seven strings and woodwinds), large orchestra of *Nos. 6, 8* (with two pianos), *9, 10* (with chorus), and *12;* two orchestras and band of *No. 13;* chorus, band, and orchestra of *No. 14;* and orchestra and soloists of *No. 11 (Introdução).*

    Chôros No. 10 (1926), based on a large-scale setting for mixed chorus and orchestra, represents a synthesis of the composer's national stylistic development with contemporary techniques. The opening instrumental portion contains instrumental motifs that evoke the rich variety of bird calls and other natural sounds of the Brazilian forests. In the choral-orchestral portion (from No. 6), a chant-like ritualistic momentum is induced by the additive contrapuntal unfolding of the Indian-sounding verbal articulations, to which is added *Rasga o coração* ("Rend my heart"), "a lyrical and sentimental melody in the manner of the urban *modinha* extracted from a popular song."[21] (The urban *modinha* was originally a simple, nostalgic, Portuguese song, introduced in Brazil in the late-nineteenth century.) The Indian-sounding syllables of the choral chant are used onomatopoeically, so the voices acquire an instrumental role simply as another sonic plane within the larger orchestral texture. The ritualistic Indian quality is further enhanced by the percussive Afro-Brazilian dance ostinati as well as a colorful and "exotic" orchestration, all of which suggest Stravinsky's primitivism absorbed into a highly personal, nationally imbued contemporary idiom. The numerous blocks that comprise the two-part cumulative form are themselves made up of differentiated motivic and textural planes, all of which are essential to evoking the primitivistic quality. While each of these local planes and layers is distinguished by its own individual rhythmic pattern, contour, timbre, and intervallic construction to produce a sharply defined kaleidoscopic fabric, pitch and intervallic connections among them contribute to the integration of the structure.

    Against the held *fortissimo* chord of the opening, an exotic melody, which characterizes the song of a rare bird of the Brazilian forests, known as *Azulão da mata,* unfolds in two pairs of varied statements (flutes, then clarinets) as the structural basis of the opening formal block (to letter B).[22] The initial flute statement unfolds above the spare "dissonant" G and B♭ pedals (in horn and clarinet, respectively), whereas the extended consequent of the closing statement in the clarinets (letter A) is set within a more complex, planed, contrapuntal texture, which serves as a focal point in the structural building of the first large sectional block. The opening timbral and rhythmic polarity between harmony and melody is enhanced by differentia-

[21] See Villa-Lobos, *Villa-Lobos—sua obra* (2nd ed., Rio de Janeiro: Museu Villa-Lobos, 1972), p. 204.

[22] See ibid., p. 203.

tion of pitch content, the opening chord revealing the "octatonic-1" source (E♭–E–G–A–B♭, plus one "odd" note, D) of the G and B♭ pedals and establishing one of the fundamental types of pitch-sets of the work.[23] The flute theme also unfolds an octatonic segment, this time from octatonic-0 (D–E♭–E♯–F♯–G♯–B, plus the "odd" cadential note, B♭). Maximal differentiation of pitch content between chord and melody is permitted by the use of two different octatonic collections, so a kind of *polymodal chromaticism* is suggested (i.e., the combined pitch content of both octatonic segments produces most of the twelve tones). The disruptive role of the "odd" D and "odd" B♭ within these two octatonic collections, respectively, foreshadows one of the basic means for producing chromaticism. Such intrusions serve as preparation for progressions either between transpositions of a set or from one type of set (diatonic or octatonic) to another (as will be seen in Ex. 8–4, below).

A contrasting textural plane appears in the strings, piano, and harp against the held G of the horn (mm. 6ff.). This plane is distinguished from the opening octatonic segments not only by its ostinato rhythmic character, but also by its "white-key" diatonic content, which is partitioned into two alternating tertian harmonic constructions, A–C–E–G and E–G–B–D–F. The lack of tonal function of these diatonic chords draws the entire collection into the pitch-set premise, that is, the diatonic collection is defined exclusively in terms of intervallic content. This appearance of the "white-key" collection establishes the first polarity between octatonic and diatonic sets in the work.

Toward the end of the first sectional block (letter A, mm. 2ff.), the consequent phrase of the octatonic theme in the clarinet is absorbed into a more complex, layered texture of symmetrical pitch formations, the combination of which produces a *polymodal chromatic fusion* of the work's two basic types of sets—octatonic and diatonic (Ex. 8–4). While the four-against-three juxtaposition of the two basic rhythmic patterns (sixteenths and sextuplets) contributes to the distinction between these layers, the inversionally related chromatic scales of the sextuplet lines themselves produce yet another level of linear distinction. Similarly,the sixteenth-note lines are distinguished from each other by their contrasting contours and scalar content based on conflicting octatonic segments. Violin I unfolds a series of symmetrical tetrachords (E–D♯–C♯–B♯, G–F♯–E♭–D, etc.), which form octatonic (interval-ratio-1:2) and expanded (interval-ratio-1:3) segments, respectively. It can be demonstrated that the interval-ratio-1:3 tetrachord represents a joining of half steps from two different octatonic scales, the entire tetrachordal succession resulting in an elided series of larger six-note octatonic segments: B♯–C♯–D♯–E/ F♯–G (octatonic 1), D–E♭/E♯–F♯–G♯–A (octatonic 0), F×–G♯–A♯–B/C♯–D

---

[23] The octatonic scale on C (C–D–E♭–F–F♯–G♯–A–B), i.e., according to the interval-2,1,2,1,2,1,2,1 model, will be referred to as "octatonic-0," that on C♯ (C♯–D♯–E–F♯–G–A–B♭–C] "octatonic-1," and the remaining one on D (D–E–F–G–G♯–A♯–B–C♯) "octatonic-2," regardless of ordering or enharmonic spelling within a given scale.

EXAMPLE 8–4. Villa-Lobos, *Chôros No. 10*, ending of first sectional block (letter A, mm. 2ff.), layered texture based on "polymodal" chromatic fusion of two basic types of pitch sets—octatonic and diatonic

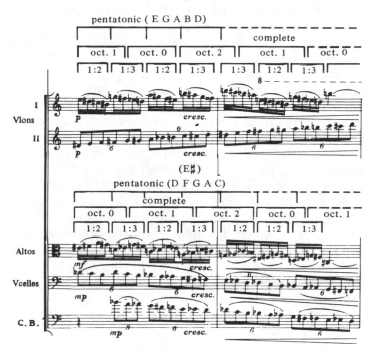

(octatonic 2), A–B♭/B♯–C♯–D♯–E/F♯–G (complete octatonic 1), and a concluding smaller segment, B–D–E♭ (from octatonic 0). This succession of all three octatonic collections produces a linear chromaticism, compounded harmonically by the sixteenth-note lines of the violas and clarinets stated simultaneously. As in the violin-I line, these tetrachordal adjacencies also form larger six-note octatonic segments: A–G♯–F♯–E♯/E♭–D (octatonic 0), G–F♯/F♭–E♭–D♭–C/B♭–A(complete octatonic 1), D–C♯/C♭–B♭–A♭–G (octatonic 2), etc. However, the latter octatonic transpositions are not synchronized with those in violin I, so chromatic harmonies are produced.

Each of the two sixteenth-note successions (in violin I and viola/ clarinet) is based on a fusion of octatonic and pentatonic sets. The initial notes of the successive tetrachords in violin I outline an ascending pentatonic scale (E–G–A–B–D), while the initial notes of the successive tetrachords in viola/ clarinet outline a different descending pentatonic scale (in enharmonic spelling F–D–C–A–G). These two pentatonic scales (E–G–A–B–D and D–F–G–A–C) together produce the entire "white-key" diatonic collection. The brass instruments form a contrasting plane, in which two of the lines unfold diatonic (G–A♭–B♭–C and F♯–G–A–B) and two of the lines octatonic

(E♭–F♯–G and D♭–E♭–F♯–G) segments simultaneously. Thus, this passage fuses contrasting modes systematically (octatonic and diatonic), which had appeared separately in the preceding passages, into a polymodally chromatic context, the fusion of which contributes to the closure of the first large formal block.

Segments of these sets are juxtaposed between the triplets at the cadence of this block (two before B), based on an octatonic-segment G–C–C♯, and the multiple layers at the beginning of the next block (B), based on linear diatonic segments in contrary motion. The descending diatonic form, which emerges as a prominent thematic construction (letter F, m. 2), foreshadows the main thematic chant of the choral section (see No. 6f.). At the same time, the ascending pentatonic segment, A–B–D–E (violins, violas, and horn I, at letter B), anticipated in the pentatonic outline (E–G–A–B–D) of the preceding passage (see Ex. 8–4), emerges as a distinct idea in the next block (unison strings at letter C), the latter of which is set off by a metric return from 3/2 of the preceding block (letter B) to the original 2/2 meter. This trend from octatonic to pentatonic is also reflected in the highest structural levels of the work. The final section (*Largo*) reestablishes the fundamental pentatonic segment (A–B–D–E) in the clarinet, horn I, trumpet, upper piano line, and upper strings, against which the chorus now sustains the complete pentatonic form (A–B–D–E–F♯). Thus, the work moves from the opening octatonic to final pentatonic-diatonic sphere.

Several varied manifestations of the choral theme appear in the first half of the work in both chromatic and diatonic forms (as at letter C, mm. 9ff., strings, and letter G, respectively). A striking manifestation of the chromatic form (letter I, mm. 3–5, clarinet and trumpet) is reminiscent of the quarter-tone "hammock" chants of the Parecis Indians of Mato Grosso.[24] However, its larger minor-third boundary (B–D) acquires a more global compositional significance in terms of the basic diatonic and octatonic sets by its placement within a contrapuntal context of overlapping minor thirds (Ex. 8–5). The contrapuntal alignment of flute and oboe thirds (B♭–D♭ and G–B♭) with the clarinet/trumpet boundary (B–D) implies the presence of a gapped octatonic-2 segment, G–[ ]–B♭–B–D♭–D, which outlines interval-ratios 1:2 and 1:3, while the contrapuntal alignment of bassoon and saxophone thirds (A♭–C♭ and C–E♭) with the same thematic clarinet/trumpet boundary (B–D) implies the presence of an analogously gapped octatonic-0 segment, A♭–[ ]–B–C–D–E♭. Both segments together (G–A♭–[ ]–B♭–B–C–D♭–D–E♭) produce the larger polymodal chromatic content of this passage. Two of these linearly stated thirds are each part of a longer diatonic and/or octatonic line, the flute B♭–D♭ unfolding as part of the segment F–G–A♭–B♭–[ ]–D♭, the oboe G–B♭ as part of F–G–A♭–B♭.

The most extreme polarity of the diatonic and octatonic forms is then manifested in the two contrasting central blocks, the chromatic form in the bass instruments at the beginning of the main part of the work (No. 5f.), the

---

[24] See *Villa-Lobos—sua obra*, n.21, above, p. 204.

EXAMPLE 8–5. Villa-Lobos, *Chôros No. 10*, transformed choral theme in a form reminiscent of quarter-tone "hammock" chant of Parecis Indians, letter I, mm. 3–5, in contrapuntal context of overlapping minor thirds based on diatonic-octatonic interactions

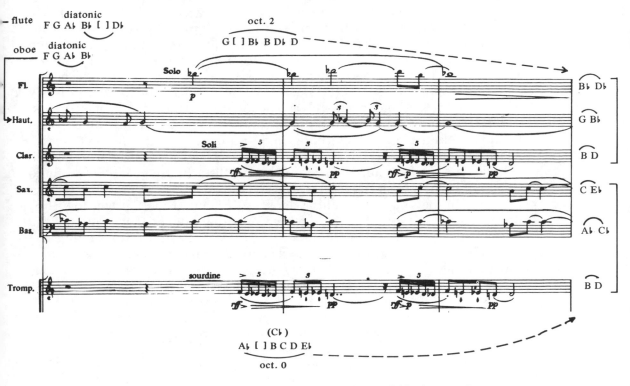

diatonic form at the choral entry (No. 6f). Thus, in a context of layers and blocks based on extreme textural, timbral, rhythmic, and pitch-set polarities, unity is produced by special pitch-set interactions and transformations between octatonic and pentatonic/diatonic forms primarily. These "modal" features contribute to the distinctive Brazilian atmosphere of the work, the varied themes evoking the natural sounds of the forest, the "phonetic atmosphere characteristic of the language of the aborigines," and "a lyrical and sentimental melody in the manner of the urban modinha extracted from a popular song."[25]

The variety of instrumental combinations that make up the set of *Chôros* is also reflected in Villa-Lobos' vast repertoire of solo, chamber, orchestral, and vocal works throughout his career. However, his most original stage of development, as manifested in the intensive fusion of the varied

[25] Ibid.

national elements with contemporary pitch-set techniques, is reflected in the works composed during the period of the *Chôros* in the 1920s. Although it was in the mid-1920s that his original national style began to appeal to the most progressive musical circles in Paris, his intensive turn toward national sources had already been inspired during The Week of Modern Art in São Paulo in 1922, and some of his most original nationalistic works were composed in the early 1920s. The *Trio No. 3* (1921) for oboe, clarinet, and bassoon is remarkable for its rhythmic sophistication and vitality as well as technical demands. In the first movement, two basic rhythmic motives, which produce a complex counterpoint of overlapping angular ostinati, are primarily made up of diatonic, octatonic, and whole-tone tetrachordal tone patches. These are broken up into distinct intervals in the separate instruments and often presented in parallel seconds. In the third movement, allusion to Indian drumming pervades the succession of contrasting block structures, which build to a dynamic climax. The result is a ritualistic Indian quality infused into a complex Stravinskian idiom.

In the same year, Villa-Lobos also produced the *Quatuor* for harp, celesta, flute, saxophone, and women's chorus, a work that combines the popular urban atmosphere of Rio de Janeiro with the impressionist influence of Debussy. Nevertheless, the varied national sources remained most prominent at this time, as in the *Nonetto* (1923) for eight instruments, percussion, and mixed chorus, which is among his earliest works composed in Paris. Suggested by its subtitle "A Rapid Impression of All Brazil," the work combines urban popular dance rhythms (including tango, maxixe, samba, etc.), based on complex syncopations, duple-triple combinations, and other types of cross-rhythms, Indian and Afro-Brazilian chanting, and jungle sounds. Toward the end of this decade in Paris, he composed the *Quintette en forme de Chôros* (1928), for an unusual combination of flute, oboe, clarinet, bassoon, and english horn. This work reveals a combination of an even greater diversity of elements within a highly improvisatory style, the condensed one-movement plan based on a multiplicity of contrasting yet unified sections (including twelve tempo changes). Slow impressionistic blocks are juxtaposed with sections that employ energetic drum rhythms, bird calls, and other sounds of the Brazilian forests. In his seventeen string quartets (composed between 1915 and 1957), we find his widest stylistic range, moving from the most concrete national elements of the early quartets through increasing transformation and sublimation of the folk sources to a more abstract and synthetic style. While the *Sixth, Seventh,* and *Eighth Quartets* (1938, 1941, and 1944) still reveal the lyric and plaintive qualities of the popular Brazilian melodies, the *Seventh* is particularly absorbing for its contrasting polyrhythmic passages in more abstract and complex contrapuntal textures. The *Ninth Quartet* (1945) begins his move away from distinct national influences entirely. Its abstract style reveals the most remarkable variety of rhythmic and timbral interactions which, while having been manifested in varying degrees throughout his preceding works, were to be epitomized in the remaining quartets.

The 1930s and early 1940s mark a definite break from the aesthetics of Villa-Lobos' European years. This distinction is indicated partly by the change of his activities, which corresponds to the general change of political climate of the 1930s not only in Brazil, but internationally as well. Villa-Lobos returned from Paris to Brazil in 1930, at which time he became one of the favored artistic figures of the new nationalistic political leadership. He grew to be concerned with musical education for the masses, developing school and concert programs between 1930 and 1945. This resulted in many children's choruses and other types of didactic works, including harmonizations of Brazilian folk tunes. His change of approach to composition was manifested most prominently in his set of nine *Bachianas brasileiras,* which span this fifteen-year period. In these works, he moved toward a less modernistic style, in which he fused a more Classical-Romantic lyricism and formalism with Brazilian folk music. While his works of the 1920s had revealed influences of his contemporaries, primarily Stravinsky, Debussy, and other French composers, it was J. S. Bach's style that was to serve as a more traditional European model during this period. In this cycle of diversely orchestrated pieces, Bach's style was used as a kind of universal language, or "intermediary between all cultures," and at the same time could serve as a musical source for the juxtaposition of more accessible traditional techniques with the elements of Brazilian music.

ARGENTINA: INDIGENOUS INFLUENCES IN ALBERTO GINASTERA'S EARLY STYLE

As in Mexico and Brazil, the Argentinian musical scene in the nineteenth century was also influenced by Italian, French, and German operas. The salon types, which were quite nationalistic (i.e., relying heavily on folk songs and salon dances), were also influenced by Italians and other Europeans in Argentina. Argentinian composers also drew from international styles during their studies at European conservatories, from the time of the late-nineteenth century especially. While the compositions of such composers as Amancio Alcorta (1805–1862) reflected pre-Romantic salon styles, with only a suggestion of local influences, national sentiment began to emerge prominently in the music of Alberto Williams (1862–1952). Upon returning from Paris, where he studied from 1882 to 1889, Williams began to immerse himself in his native musical traditions in order to capture an authentic Argentinian quality in his music. His contact with folk music during his trip to the rural areas resulted in the first of his nationalistic pieces, *El Rancho Abandonado* (1890) for piano, as well as many other folk-influenced works, which drew from the dance rhythms of such types as the *milonga*. While he tended more toward synthesis of folk and French international sources after 1910, it was primarily through his influence and that of many others that the nationalist tendency was to prevail in the music of Argentinian composers throughout the first half of the twentieth century.

One of the major figures of contemporary Latin American music to absorb both national folk sources and a broad range of European styles and techniques into a personal idiom was the Argentinian composer Alberto Ginastera (1916–1988). The evolution of his music after World War II away from his earlier nationalist orientation foreshadowed the decline of the nationalist movement in Argentina after the 1950s. Several countercurrents coexisted from the time of the late 1930s (for example, the expressionistic serialism of Juan Carlos Paz, who founded the *Agrupación Nueva Música* in 1937), but the nationalist works were more often performed. Ginastera subdivided his stylistic evolution into three periods, beginning his career in the 1930s with an *objective nationalism* (though he rarely quoted the Argentinian folk sources literally), gradually moving by the late 1940s to a more *subjective nationalism* based on a sublimated nonliteral use of the folk elements, and finally an *expressionism* in the early 1960s.[26] He considered the *Pampeana No. 1* (1947) for violin and piano a transitional work toward this more subjective style, while the more sublimated folk references to the music of the *pampas* in his *String Quartet No. 1* (1948), *Pampeana No. 2* (1950), the *Sonata for Piano* (1952), the *Variaciones Concertantes* (1953), and the orchestral *Pameana No. 3* (1954), all of which still employed melodic and rhythmic folk elements, were part of the transformation of his more abstract final period.[27]

In his early works, Ginastera relied partially on the *gauchesco* tradition, as in the piano *Danzas Argentinas* (1937), and the ballet *Estancia* (1941), which presents a vivid picture of Argentinian rural life, the *Cinco canciones populares argentinas* (1943), the Overture to *The Creole Faust* (1943), and other works. In his early ballet *Panambi* (1934–1936), based on Indian legend, he had also revealed an eclecticism in his use of a Stravinskian primitivism in the ritualistic second movement (exclusively for percussion and brass) and a more impressionistic style in other passages. Certain folk rhythms toward the end of this ballet also foreshadowed his use of the *malambo*, a typical dance of the gauchos based on rapid motoric rhythmic patterns in 6/8 meter, as in his piano piece entitled *Malambo* (1940) and in the dynamic "Danza Final (*Malambo*)" section of the ballet *Estancia*. Rhythmic variants of the *malambo*, some of which have been outlined by Gilbert Chase, are absorbed by Ginastera into complex melodic and harmonic textures to produce a highly personal contemporary idiom imbued with strong national flavor.[28]

The folk rhythm of the piano piece *Malambo* acquires an abstract

[26] Through analysis of the music, one must refute the notion of distinct subdivisions of Ginastera's oeuvre, though the composer himself outlined them explicitly in his interview with Pola Suárez Urtubey, *Alberto Ginastera* (Buenos Aires: Ediciones Cultural Argentinas, 1967), pp. 68–69. According to Malena Kuss, Preface to *Alberto Ginastera: A Complete Catalogue* (London: Boosey and Hawkes, Inc., 1986, revised edition), "it is more accurate to view . . . his total oeuvre (1937–1983) as an uninterrupted search for synthesis between the sounds that carry the stamp of his culture and the twentieth-century techniques he learned to master with consummate virtuosity."

[27] See Chapter 20.

[28] See Gilbert Chase, "Alberto Ginastera: Argentinian Composer," *Musical Quarterly* 43/4 (October 1957): 441. For manifestations of these rhythms, see also Béhague, *Music in Latin America*, n.8, above, pp. 216–218.

compositional significance by its deployment as two contrapuntally-aligned ostinati within a rigidly controlled type of Classical rondo form.[29] In Section A, the mechanical shift in the right hand to a new pitch level at the end of each pair of repeated phrases (every eight measures), in contrast to the unchanging pattern of the left hand, produces an additive succession of contrasting periods. These right-hand shifts produce increasing tonal tension between the two hands because of the gradually diverging harmonic levels (compare mm. 1, 9, 17, 25, and 33), which result in an increasingly dissonant polytonality. The slow opening arpeggiation establishes the folk mood from the outset by its allusion to the tuning of the guitar, E–A–D–G/B–E, which establishes E as the basic tonality. The sudden change from the cadential E-minor triad of the arpeggiation to the initial E-major triad of the 6/8 prepares for an ambiguous bimodal conflict either between E-Mixolydian and E-Dorian modes (E–F♯–G–G♯–A–B–C♯–D) or, because of the cadential placement of the D-major triad, D-major and D-Lydian modes (D–E–F♯–G–G♯–A–B–C♯), the E♭–G major third on the weak beat having a chromatic passing function (Ex. 8–6a).

Despite the polarity between the two E or D modes, the two contrapuntal layers of the first pair of phrases together produce consonant (triadic) harmonies. At the second pair of phrases (mm. 9–16), the right-hand shift to a new pitch level, beginning on E and doubled by lower thirds, produces a bitonal conflict between the initial E-major third of the original left-hand ostinato and C–E. More significantly, the original ambiguity regarding the primacy of the initial E-major or cadential D-major triads (see mm. 1–2) is brought into contrapuntal conflict at each local cadence (m. 10, etc.). At the third pair of phrases (mm. 17–24), another right-hand shift to a new pitch level beginning on A and doubled now in triads produces a more prominent bitonal conflict between E-major and D-major triads. These bitonal relations are compounded further as a new triad (F♯ major) appears in conflict with the cadential D-major triad (m. 18, etc.). Polytonal implications are greatly compounded in the fourth pair of phrases (mm. 25–32), this time by the departure of the right hand from the traditional triad to form a series of parallel 0–5–11 (e.g., G–C–F♯) chords (Ex. 8–6b). At this point, the original left-hand ostinato is also compounded to form a succession of inverted 0–5–11 constructions (e.g., F–B–E). This new chord type is significant in that it implies a pairing of two perfect fifths, e.g., C–G/F♯–[ ] and E–B/[ ]–F, so that each hand unfolds two tonal layers simultaneously, both hands together suggesting four altogether. This double-fifth interpretation of 0–5–11 is confirmed in the left hand in the cadential configuration, D–A/G♯–D♯, which is extended to D–A/D♯–G♯–C♯–F♯ cyclically (at m. 32).

The final pairing of phrases at Section A (mm. 33–40) suggests a return to the original pitch levels of the two layers (lowest and highest lines),

---

[29] The rondo form may be outlined as follows: Introduction; A (mm. 1–40); B (mm. 41–48); A (mm. 49–56); B′ (mm. 57–60); A (mm. 61–76); B variant and developmental extension (mm. 77–113); B (mm. 114–121); A (mm. 122–145); Coda (146ff.).

EXAMPLE 8–6. Ginastera, *Malambo:* (a) opening period, ambiguous bimodal conflict either between E-Mixolydian and E-Dorian or D-major and D-Lydian modes, but in basically consonant contrapuntal-harmonic context; (b) fourth period, mm. 25–32, polytonal implications in series of nontriadic, parallel 0–5–11 chords in each hand

Used by kind permission of Ricordi Americana S.A.E.C., Buenos Aires, Argentina.

but in a highly compounded texture in which the lower ostinato continues the inverted 0–5–11 constructions while the upper layer unfolds a series of parallel augmented triads with sevenths (e.g., initial chord, C–E–G♯–B). While the upper E-major triad of this chord represents a reconvergence with the initial E–B of the left hand, the augmented triad (C–E–G♯) suggests a whole-tone alteration of the primary diatonic interval (the perfect fifth). This is confirmed by the linear projection of the whole-tone set in the upper line of the right-hand ostinato, i.e., the original upper modal line (B–C♯–D/G–A–B–C♯–D) of the first pair of phrases is transformed here into the whole-tone scale, B–C♯–D♯/G–A–B–C♯–D♯. The arrival at Section B (m. 41), marked by several new variants of the *malambo* rhythm, reestablishes the diatonic perfect fifth by means of the cyclic-interval extension of the original cadential D-major triad to D–A–E–B–F♯ (in the new left-hand ostinato).[30] The latter is a cyclic extension of the preceding cadence

[30] See Chase's outline of rhythmic variants, in "Alberto Ginastera: Argentinian Composer," n.28, above, p. 455.

(D–A/D♯–G♯–C♯–F♯), so the white-key (D–A) and black-key (G♯) components of the earlier 0-5-11 construction are completed (A–D/D♯–G♯) and the gap between them finally closed by the larger cyclic configuration, D–A–E–B–F♯–C♯–G♯–D♯ (mm. 40–41, left hand). Thus, Ginastera has absorbed Argentinian folk rhythms and modal constructions into an abstract set of polytonal contrapuntal layers within a rigidly constructed art-music form. The result is an integrated, developmental context in an objective, yet personal contemporary idiom, imbued with the essence of the composer's national sources.

SUGGESTED READING

GERARD BÉHAGUE. *Music in Latin America: An Introduction* (Englewood Cliffs: Prentice-Hall, Inc., 1979).

GILBERT CHASE. "Alberto Ginastera: Argentine Composer," *Musical Quarterly* 43/4 (October 1957): 439–460.

————. "Music in Latin America," in Virgil Thomson, *American Music Since 1910* (New York: Holt, Rinehart and Winston, 1970, 1971), pp. 110–117.

HENRY COWELL. "New Terms for New Music," *Modern Music* 5 (May-June 1928): 21–27.

MALENA KUSS. Preface to *Alberto Ginastera: A Complete Catalogue* (London: Boosey and Hawkes, Inc., 1986, revised edition).

VASCO MARIZ. *Heitor Villa-Lobos: Life and Work of the Brazilian Composer* (Washington, DC: Brazilian American Cultural Institute, Inc., 1970; first edition, University of Florida Press, 1963).

ROBERTO GARCÍA MORILLO. *Carlos Chávez: vida y obra* (Mexico: Fondo de Cultura Económica, 1960).

ROBERT STEVENSON. *Music in Mexico: A Historical Survey* (New York: Thomas Y. Crowell Company, 1952).

POLA SUÁREZ URTUBEY. *Alberto Ginastera* (Buenos Aires: Ediciones Cultural Argentinas, 1967).

HEITOR VILLA-LOBOS. *Villa-Lobos—sua obra* (2nd ed., Rio de Janeiro: Museu Villa-Lobos, 1972).

9 The rise of neoclassicism in France: The Cocteau-Satie era and "Les Six"

IMPACT OF POLITICAL DICTATORSHIP, ECONOMIC DEPRESSION, TECHNOLOGY, AND ANTIROMANTICISM ON THE DEVELOPMENT OF NEOCLASSICISM In the interwar period, socio-political, economic, and aesthetic factors had a bearing on the course of musical trends. With the worldwide economic depression and the rise of fascism in the early 1930s, restrictions were placed on the more experimental tendencies that had been developing in the arts since the first decades of the century. Composers of various countries turned toward more accessible musical idioms increasingly, partly because of the censorship of avant-garde music in totalitarian states, and partly because of the desire composers had to reach their musical public, whose cultural activities had been limited by the devastating international economic conditions.

The practical use of recording and broadcasting as well as these political and economic factors led to a schism that developed between the "new music" and the traditional and popular types during the interwar decades. Through the new media, an average listener could select music that was easily understood and appreciated. This contributed to the eclipse of esoteric contemporary styles during the 1930s by more conservative musical idioms. As a result, many composers attempted to combine modern musical features with traditional forms and textures in order to reconcile the divergent tendencies and bring contemporary sonorities to the general public. Composers of different countries borrowed from popular musical idioms, including jazz, and from the art-music of preceding eras.

Pre–World War I reaction against the ultrachromatic emotionalism of German late-Romantic music and the more dissonant and atonal subjectivity of Expressionism contributed to the revival of interest in earlier music. In this connection, the term *Neoclassicism,* first applied to music in the twentieth century by Ferruccio Busoni, has come to represent those styles devoid of personal expression and extra-musical symbolization underlying the aesthetics of the late-Romantic and Expressionist movements. Eighteenth-century Classical ideals were to provide those conceptual and stylistic sources from which could be drawn more objective, purely musical bases. In contradistinction to the exaggerated pathos and ambiguous forms of nineteenth-century Romantic music, a new ethos was found in the intellectual and formalistic Classical tradition of the late eighteenth century. Furthermore, the concept of a simple and clear formalism was to lend itself to the post–World War I need for economy of means not only in the overall formal-thematic structure, but in the reduction of the large Romantic orchestra to a chamber-like, clearly layered skeletal instrumentation.

The establishment of a precise definition for Neoclassicism, beyond its identification with Classical formulation and its assumed antithetical

242

stance to the Romantic aesthetics, has been problematical. Some twentieth-century composers of the Neoclassical tradition have drawn not only from late eighteenth-century Classical forms and tonality, but also from the contrapuntal linear textures and figurations of the Baroque masters and the polyphonic forms and modalities of the Renaissance composers. However, if we rely on the concept of "return" to earlier principles of objectivity and control as well as established formal principles (sonata, suite, symphony, etc.) and procedures (canon, fugue, etc.) for subsuming a body of music under the Neoclassical heading, then most contemporary music would qualify. Such definition could conceivably encompass the traditional forms and contrapuntal textures of composers as varied in style as Stravinsky, Bartók, Schoenberg, Hindemith, Milhaud, Copland, and Sessions, as well as the aesthetics of the objective, intellectually controlled mathematical constructions of the post-Webernists. In order to narrow the concept of Neoclassicism so that it can be applied meaningfully to a body of twentieth-century music, we shall focus on specific aesthetic and stylistic developments of individual composers whose works formed the core of this movement.

DEVELOPMENTS IN PARIS

As France recovered under the Third Republic following French defeat by Prussia in 1871, a new era of intellectual and artistic creativity emerged in Paris. New styles in literature, painting, and music revealed distinctive qualities that characterized French culture profoundly in the late nineteenth and early twentieth centuries. Paris was unique at this time, having become "a vast theater for herself and all the world . . . which gave *La belle époque* its particular flavor."[1] However, the Parisian avant-garde of the era was, and still is, an enigma. It was "neither a place nor a class nor an activity nor a body of work," but rather "a way of life, both dedicated and frivolous."[2] The newest developments of this era in Paris may be understood through an evaluation of diverse groups of the personalities, the members of each group who may be considered to be associated with each other by their common orientation to a particular source of inspiration or some broader aesthetic or stylistic current. One "family group" might consist hypothetically of Renoir, Ravel, and Proust, a later one, Picasso, Stravinsky, and Gertrude Stein, another Debussy, Mallarmé, Cézanne, and Valéry, and finally one consisting of Henri Rousseau, Erik Satie, Alfred Jarry, and Guillaume Apollinaire.[3] It is the last of these groups which, perhaps more than any other, may be considered to represent uniformly all those aspects that characterize the era, and set the stage for what Apollinaire referred to as the "New Spirit."[4]

[1] Roger Shattuck, *The Banquet Years* (New York: Alfred A. Knopf, Inc., 1955; rev. ed. 1968), pp. 5–6.
[2] Ibid., p. 29.
[3] Ibid., p. 30.
[4] Ibid., pp. 31–32.

ERIK SATIE

The basic assumptions that paved the way for a new approach to the aesthetic principles of Classicism after the First World War were already manifested in the personal artistic attitudes and small musical forms of Erik Satie (1866–1925). In the last decades of the nineteenth century, Wagnerism maintained a hypnotic hold on composers in the musical centers of Europe, and Pris was no exception. However, while the Wagnerian fervor remained strong amongst such French composers as Emmanuel Chabrier, the latter's personal approach to dissonance as well as seventh and ninth chords in lighter, more lyrical and often humorous modal contexts foreshadowed a new course for French composers. This musical current, which represents one of several in French artistic life, had provided an independent French alternative to the dramatic Wagnerian idiom. However, it was Satie and Debussy who sensed the need to establish a style different from the charged emotionalism of the German Romantics most clearly. In a lecture, Satie expressed his view:

> I explained to Debussy the necessity for a Frenchman to free himself from the Wagnerian adventure which in no way corresponded to our national aspirations. And I told him I was not anti-Wagner in any way but that we ought to have our own music—if possible, without sauerkraut. Why shouldn't we make use of the methods employed by Claude Monet, Cézanne, Toulouse-Lautrec, etc.?[5]

In Satie's early compositions, we find an approach that provided a viable stylistic antithesis not only to the dense chromaticism of Wagner's *Tristan,* but to the delicate textures of Debussy's impressionism as well. The three *Gnossiennes* (1890) for piano are the first obvious manifestations of Satie's literary wit and humor.[6] The score, composed without barlines, keys, or time signature, includes the ironic instructions, "ouvrez la tete," "de manière à obtenir un creux," "avec étonnement," and "sur la langue," an attitude later revealed in the titles of such piano pieces as *Pièces froides* (Cold Pieces, 1897), *Trois Morceaux en forme de poire* (Three pieces in the form of a pear, 1903), *Véritables préludes flasques (pour un chien)* (truly flabby preludes [for a dog], 1912), *Descriptions automatiques* (Automatic Descriptions, 1913), and *Embryons desséchés* (dried embryos, 1913).

More significantly, however, the musical style of these works pointed the direction away from the impressionistic idiom of Debussy toward the more clearly defined structures and textures of the Neoclassical ideal. Prior to *Gnossiennes,* the three *Sarabandes* (1887) and three *Gymnopédies* (1888) for piano had already demonstrated Satie's originality in both style and musical language. For instance, the first piece of *Gymnopédies* shows the composer's characteristic use of unresolved dissonances in a progression of supertertian harmonies (in this case, seventh chords) that are entirely removed from the

---

[5] Rollo H. Myers, *Erik Satie* (New York: Denis Dobson Ltd., 1948; Dover Publications, Inc., 1968), pp. 32–33.

[6] Ibid., pp. 71–72.

functional voice-leading principles of the major-minor scale system. The static alternation of the opening major-seventh chords, on G and D, eliminates the necessity for logical preparation and resolution of the sevenths, thereby also undermining the traditional distinction between concepts of consonance and dissonance. This harmonic ostinato supports a linear thematic statement, the modality of which further contributes to the dissolution of traditional tonal functions. The result is a sequence of nondirected sonorities that exist simply within a static framework.

Given these modal-harmonic premises of Satie's musical language, which also included parallel progressions of fourths and fifths as well as seventh through thirteenth chords as early as the 1890s, we can find no meaningful distinction from Debussy's impressionistic settings. Rather, it is in the dimensions of texture and rhythm that the two composers are differentiated stylistically. In contrast to Debussy's delicately elaborated figurations as well as vague and irregular rhythmic patterns, which together obscure thematic linearity, Satie's textures are clarified by their reduction to the barest essentials of harmonic and melodic construction. The result is a spareness and mechanical precision that was to become the basis of the objectivity associated with Neoclassical aesthetics. The simple, clear, intact linearity as well as incessant reiteration of symmetrical melodic phrases, persistent rhythmic bass patterns, and pervasive use of modality are the basic traits that were to run throughout the works of all composers—including Milhaud, Stravinsky, Prokofiev, and others—that have been categorized as Neoclassical. It is in the economical features of Satie's style—their role in producing a sense of detachment and objectivity—that the Neoclassical idea may find its most relevant and meaningful application.

During the different periods of Satie's life, his art was influenced by new interests representing a more literal and conscious absorption of older as well as popular styles. In the works of his Rosicrucian period (1890s), modal and other traits of Gregorian chant became evident in his music, while his years in the cafés of Montmartre led to his absorption of popular dance-hall tunes. At the Schola Cantorum (1905–1908), he studied counterpoint and fugue with d'Indy and Roussel, which led to his interest in a more serious style. This became evident in his abundant use of fugues and chorales in the *Aperçus désagréables* and *En habit de cheval,* his own comments revealing an awareness of these elements so basic to the music of Bach. His later *Sonatine bureaucratique* (1917) draws upon material from the piano music of Clementi. Satie's interest in these traditional and popular sources and especially their infusion into a style of simplicity, economy, and objectivity represents a primary factor in the development of Neoclassicism in France after the First World War.

COCTEAU-SATIE ERA

By the First World War, Satie was beginning to be recognized in Paris by important artistic circles as well as music critics. In 1915, the young poet, Jean Cocteau, after hearing Satie and Riccardo Viñes perform the *Trois Morceaux,* requested that Satie and Picasso collaborate with him on the ballet *Parade* (1915–1917), the scenario of which he was commissioned to write for Diag-hilev's Ballets Russes. This revolutionary stage work, which is the first example of *Cubism* in music as well as dance, had a stormy impact on both audience and critics alike at its first performance in 1917, and was to establish Satie's fame. This *ballet réaliste* was intended by Cocteau as a reaction to the refinement and vagueness of impressionism, its performance producing strained relations between Satie and Debussy. The scenario was noted by Cocteau to be "a simple roughly outlined action which combines the attrac-tions of circus and music hall," involving a crowd that is unwittingly drawn to the parade, or sideshow, instead of the main action inside the tent. Picasso's set and costume designs appropriately combined characteristics of his Harle-quin period and angular Cubist style. The Cubistic setting of the Managers in wooden frames was described by Cocteau as "a kind of human scenery, animated pictures by Picasso," in which "the problem was to take a series of natural gestures and to metamorphose them into a dance without depriving them of their realistic force."[7]

Satie's innovative musical setting is drawn into the Cocteau-Picasso conception, based on an intentionally simple and objective approach to reality, as described by Georges Auric in his Preface to the ballet:

> Like that of Picasso, his art does not attempt to seduce us by means of a brilliant and lively evocation . . . all the sadness of the circus is here. . . . Satie's score is planned so as to serve as a musical background to the scenic noises and percussion which occupy the foreground. In this way it is made very humbly subservient to that "reality" which stifles the nightingale's song beneath the noise of tramcars.[8]

Both the instrumentation and general musical style reflect Satie's "anti-romantic," "anti-impressionistic" clarity, simplicity, and objectivity. The sound is intentionally percussive and brassy, elaborated by the scoring of such everyday noise-producing machines as typewriters, airplane propellers, si-rens, and lottery wheels. These effects may have come indirectly from the Italian Futurists, whom Diaghilev was in contact with while in Rome.[9] The musical texture is pervaded by layers of mechanically repeated patterns that proceed in a disconnected and static succession of small block-like sections. This mosaic-like fabric, with its limited and spare instrumental coloration, corresponds to the cubist planes and blocks of the Picasso designs. The clarity of the sections as well as character presentations is heightened by the distinc-tion of musical types, including syncopated jazz passages, popular themes, a

---

[7] Jean Cocteau, *Le Coq et l'Arlequin: notes autour de la musique* (Paris: Éditions de la Sirène, 1918); trans. Rollo H. Myers (n.p.: The Egoist Press, 1921).

[8] Myers, *Erik Satie,* n.5, above, p. 51.

[9] Shattuck, *The Banquet Years,* n.1, above, p. 153.

fast waltz of two Acrobats, and fugal exposition that appears as a prelude to the entry of the first Manager and epilogue to the ballet.

One of the most characteristic and significant of Satie's late works, which may well be considered the epitome of this simplicity, balance, and unassuming objectivity, as well as his strong literary orientation, is his *Socrate, Drame symphonique en trois parties avec voix* (1918), for four sopranos, piano, and chamber orchestra (including cor anglais, horn, trumpet, harp, kettledrum, and strings). Satie's emotionally detached vocal setting of the ancient classical text, based on three *Dialogues* of Plato, seems to serve simply as an unobtrusive vehicle for the rhythms and inflections of the speech. The extraordinary harmonic transparency, linear distinctness, and emotional detachment so clear in Satie's earliest piano pieces were to provide the aesthetic and stylistic foundation for a new generation in France.

LES SIX AND NEOCLASSICISM

The success of *Parade* in 1917 drew a group of young French composers to Satie, whose aesthetic ideals represented the new spirit of French music independent of foreign elements. The original members of this group, referred to by Satie as *Les Nouveaux Jeunes,* included Georges Auric, Louis Durey, Arthur Honegger, and Germaine Tailleferre. After the war, the group was joined by Darius Milhaud and finally Francis Poulenc. A news article by Henri Collet, entitled "Un livre de Rimsky et un livre de Cocteau—les cinq Russes et les six Français," in *Comoedia* (January 16 and 23, 1920), incidentally established the group as "Les Six," of which Milhaud and Poulenc are now considered to be the most representative members.

The principles of Satie and Les Six were set forth in Cocteau's manifesto, *Le Coq et l'Arlequin,* which proposed a French music removed from the colossal Romanticism of Wagner and opposed to the impressionist aesthetics of the "Debussyistes" as well (though never to Debussy himself). In the final analysis, this manifesto expressed opposition to the idea of any school of followers, imitators, or eclectics—the idea of "isms"—and, as Satie himself wrote in one of these Broad-sheets, the preclusion of a "Satisme" also. Instead, it proposed the realistic popular sources of the cafés, French dance halls, jazz, and the familiar forms and techniques of pre–nineteenth–century music.

One of the most striking qualities encountered in the large compositional repertoire of Darius Milhaud (1892–1974) is his ability to combine the diverse techniques and styles of the past and popular sources with a sense of down-to-earth directness, in both works of a monumental seriousness and whimsical, unpretentious humor. Traditional elements of harmonic tertian construction and tonal function are utilized as part of polytonal harmonic constructions and progressions in a free counterpoint that bears the stamp of his individual approach to a contemporary musical language. The elements of this musical language as well as of the various sources from which he drew are permitted clarity yet coherence by means of a highly crafted technique. The latter was the result of his intense training at the Paris Conservatory in counterpoint and fugue as well as in the Classical tradition, but tempered by his natural abilities and a strong sense of that spontaneous and unsuppressed freedom so basic to the new French spirit.

In his incidental music to Paul Claudel's French translations of several ancient Greek plays by Aeschylus, Milhaud began to employ new techniques that were to become hallmarks of his style. He established polytonality as a basic premise of his musical language before the end of World War I, in *Les Choéphores,* Op. 24 (1915). Here, he also moved between rhythmically measured, speech-like choral narrative (supported by pitchless percussion) and singing styles. This technique, which was first evident in *Agamemnon,* Op. 14 (1913–1914), continued to be employed within the polytonal context of *Les euménides,* Op. 41 (1917–1922). The latter gradually joins as many as six different keys simultaneously, eventually reducing or resolving them to the single key of C major. The distinction of simultaneous tonalities is accomplished usually by means of differentiated instrumental timbres in what would otherwise be perceived as a context of nonfunctionally superimposed dissonances. (Such distinction by means of the spatial juxtaposition of timbres also appeared at this time in his ballet *L'Homme et son désir* of 1918.) Thus, in these works, Milhaud joined the contemporary technique of polytonality to a Neoclassical conception, i.e., the return to ancient Classical drama reminiscent of the French Baroque *tragédie lyrique,* in which Lully and Rameau had set French translations of ancient Greek tragedy to music in "measured recitative" style.

After his return from Rio de Janeiro in November 1918, where he had served during the war as secretary to the diplomat and poet Paul Claudel, Milhaud began to draw upon other traditional and popular sources for the development of his Neoclassical aesthetics. In 1919, he intended his fantasia *Le boeuf sur le toit* ("The Ox on the Roof" or "The Nothing-Doing Bar"), the title taken from a Brazilian popular song, to serve as an accompaniment to one of Charlie Chaplin's silent films. The sequence of distinct musical themes of popular character was imbued with the appropriately humorous, light polytonality for such a film, though the music was never to be used in that role. Milhaud's practical attitude towards realistic, popular stimuli that he was in contact with both at home and in Brazil led him to join Brazilian folk and popular melodies and rhythms (including *tangos, maxixes, sambas, rhumbas, street marches,* and a Portuguese *fado*) with French dance-hall music. In 1920, *Le boeuf* became a ballet based on a Cocteau scenario, employing clowns, acrobats, and designs by Raoul Dufy. The absurdity of much of the action gave the music a surrealistic quality; the lively music accompanied the action in slow motion, in an irony of sorts. Milhaud summarizes the scenario in his autobiography.[10]

[10] Darius Milhaud, *Notes Without Music,* trans. Donald Evans, ed. Rollo H. Myers (London: Dennis Dodson Ltd., 1952), p. 87.

The musical materials, which are presented in a seemingly endless series of sections, are actually arranged according to a traditional rondo form reminiscent of the rondo-reprise idea characteristic of the French Baroque. This formal scheme unfolds in a balanced sequence of sectional blocks and mechanically controlled tonalities, the opening block, Section A (mm. 1–16), returning between successive, contrasting pairs of sections. At the same time, certain structural features of the sections provide interrelations among them that suggest the variation principle. A sense of both contrast and unity is produced.

Traditional and popular elements are combined with twentieth-century techniques from the outset. The syncopated, sharply accented, and angular character of the opening Brazilian tune, which unfolds primarily in the violins, is heightened by the contrasting layers of woodwind, brass, and low string timbres that freely double the violins in heterophony. The bright brassy quality is enhanced by distinct rhythmic layers in the percussion and vnII/va syncopations. Another contrasting timbral-rhythmic layer is added as the flutes and clarinets enter against the extended cadence of the second phrase of the tune. This capricious figure serves to articulate this opening formal block. It disrupts the functional triadic context of the C-major theme, which unfolds in two phrases repeated exactly, each harmonized by a simple $I–V_7–I_6–V_7–I$ progression. The capricious figure forms a contrasting layer of fourths, B♭–E♭–A♭/G♯–C♯–F♯ (in enharmonic spelling, A♯–D♯–G♯–C♯–F♯), which is based on the mutually exclusive pentatonic black-key collection. Cadencing on C♯ against the C tonic of the white keys, it anticipates the successive polytonal intrusions into the ensuing sequence of diatonic sections. Increasing polytonality and dissonance in the course of the work provide direction and overall shape in a traditional form based otherwise on a purely mechanical flow of sectional blocks.

The next block, Section B (letter A), is introduced by a seemingly conventional transition to the parallel minor, effected simply by substitution of the major tonic by that of the minor in the alternating dominant and tonic harmonies. This new section is set off sharply from Section A by an explicit change of tempo, mode, and the appearance of a new lyrical theme (oboe and violin). A striking dissonance is introduced in the first measure (m. A1), which, while providing color, also suggests a brief bitonal intrusion. The melodic-note B, which is part of the dominant harmony, forms a dissonance against the tonic triad held simultaneously. The remainder of the tune then simply alternates tonic and dominant-ninth (or seventh) chords in a consonant context.

As in Section A, the theme of Section B is presented in two distinctly Classical (antecedent and consequent) phrases. As in the former (mm. 9ff.), a polytonal element also intrudes into the consequent phrase of the latter (m. A9). This intrusion, as part of a more pervasive counterpoint, now appears from the beginning of the consequent phrase. The flute and clarinet unfold a chromatically ascending series of triads against the descending contour of the theme. While the progression of triads is ambiguous tonally, each triad forms a local bitonal relationship with each note of the tune. The second (G-minor) triad supports the interpretation that the original statement of the melodic-note B (m. A1) is part of a bitonal relation between dominant and tonic chords. In the second statement, however, three rather than two tonal levels are suggested in the conflict between major- and minor-dominant chords against the held tonic triad.

This bitonal intrusion contributes to the distinction between the two phrases of the Section-B theme. It also suggests a kind of variation of the earlier bitonal intrusion in Section A. In both cases, the main conflict is between the notes C and C♯ (compare m. A9 with m. 13), and, in both cases, an interval cycle serves as the linearly-stated intrusion into the original key. In Section A we get a segment of the cycle of fourths, while in Section B the bitonal statement in the winds unfolds the entire cycle of semitones in parallel triads, which results in a more dissonant setting. The implied tritone relationship (C–F♯) between the fourths (B♭–E♭–A♭/G♯–C♯–F♯) and C major in Section A is established explicitly between the C-minor tonic and F♯-minor triad in the first chord of Section B (m. A9).

A sudden shift of key, i.e., without modulatory preparation, and the appearance of a new theme in a more heavily doubled instrumentation and distinct counterpoint begin Section C (m. B). A mechanical alternation of dominant and tonic chords establishes E♭ major, which seems to serve as nothing more than the traditional relative major of the preceding C-minor tonality. The consequent thematic statement (mm. B9ff.) adds the same polytonal figuration that appeared in Section B (mm. A9ff.), but now in a chromatically descending rather than ascending series of triads. This inversional relationship between corresponding phrases of Sections B and C contributes to the architectonic balance between the sectional blocks, and at the same time, produces a sense that one section is a variation of the other.

A significant difference between the two sections is in the relation between the initial F♯-minor triad (clarinet and flute) and main key of each section. In Section C (at m. B9), it forms a minor-third bitonal relationship with the E♭-major key in contrast to its previous tritone relation to the C-minor tonic (m. A9). These polytonal minor-third and tritone relations, which have intruded into the otherwise traditional key relations, foreshadow locally the nontraditional scheme of keys that emerges on the highest architectonic level of the work (Ex. 9–1). This scheme is initiated by what seems to be a traditional progression from C minor to its relative, E♭ major, in section C. The first reprise of Section A (m. B16) picks up and firmly establishes the preceding key of E♭, a function found commonly in the ritornello principle of such Baroque instrumental forms as the concerto grosso.

The traditional scheme of relative keys is drawn into complete cycles of minor thirds, so the concept of cyclic-interval unfolding is evident in the tonal relations of the successive sections (see Ex. 9–1). The next new block, Section D (mm. Cff.), moves to the parallel minor (E♭ minor). This provides a traditional tonal preparation for the motion to the relative key of G♭ major in Section E (m. C17). Again, the next reprise of Section A (m. D) establishes

EXAMPLE 9–1. Milhaud, *Le boeuf sur le toit,* overall tonal scheme outlining interval cycles

Sections:	[A]	B	C	[A]	D	E	[A]	F	G	[A]	trans.
Keys:	C	c	E♭	E♭	e♭	G♭	G♭	g♭	A	A	(A – – G)

Sections:	[A]	H	I	[A]	J	K	[A]	L	M	[A]	trans.
Keys:	G	g	B♭	B♭	b♭	D♭	D♭	d♭	E	E	(E – – D)

Sections:	[A]	N	O	[A]	P	Q	[A]	R	S	[A]	trans.
Keys:	D	d	F	F	f	A♭	A♭	a♭	B	B	(B – – A)

Sections:	[A]	T	U	[A}	coda
Keys:	A	a	C	C	

the latter key. This progression of relative keys continues through Sections F and G (mm. E and F), first in the parallel key of F♯-minor, then the relative of the latter (A major), which is firmly established by its continuation in the next reprise (m. F16). What unfolds is a series of motions between traditional parallel and relative keys. However, the large-scale progression, which unfolds a cycle of minor-thirds, has little to do with Classical schemes. The cyclic significance of the local traditional progressions is confirmed on a higher architectonic level of key relations. After the first cycle of third-related keys (C, E♭, F♯, A) is rounded out by the fourth occurrence of Section A, a transitional theme takes the last key down a whole-step to G major (mm. G13ff.) to begin the cyclic sequence again at a new pitch level. This procedure occurs several times until the original key of C is reached. The result is a large-scale unfolding of all three minor-third (interval-3) cycles, the successions of cyclic groups transposed by perfect-fifths on yet a higher architectonic level (Ex. 9-1). The local traditional tonal relationships and harmonic progressions as well as the large rondo form are all absorbed into a contemporary context of polytonal harmonies and an overall scheme of cyclic-interval key relations.

Milhaud continued to combine popular sources and traditional techniques and forms (symphonies, concertos, etc.) with contemporary ones in a clear Neoclassical style. The orchestral dance suites *Saudades do Brasil* (Souvenirs of Brazil, 1920–1921) infuse popular Brazilian melodies and rhythms with polytonal combinations further. In London in 1920, Milhaud first encountered the jazz of Billy Arnold and his band from New York. Jazz had already been described by Cocteau in *Le Coq et l'Arlequin,* and employed, as interpretations of dance music primarily, by Satie in the *Ragtime du Paquebot* of *Parade,* Auric in the foxtrot *Adieu New York* for orchestra, and Stravinsky in his *Ragtime* for eleven solo instruments including cimbalom.[11] In 1923, Milhaud had his first experience in Harlem with the pure tradition of New Orleans jazz, in which "the singers were accompanied by a flute, a clarinet, two trumpets, a trombone, a complicated percussion section played by one man, a piano, and a string quintet."[12]

The composer was resolved to use jazz for a chamber-music work, and the result was the ballet, *La création du monde,* Op. 81 (The creation of the world, 1923), set to a scenario by Blaise Cendrars, with stage designs and costumes by Fernand Léger. Written about a year before Gershwin's *Rhapsody in Blue,* Milhaud's intention was to use the jazz style to create a Classical feeling. At the same time, this African story of creation based on Negro folklore, with all its stylistic borrowings, is essentially French in its aesthetics. The instrumentation is characteristic of the jazz ensemble of the time, expanded into a large chamber ensemble of woodwinds and brass, piano, percussion, and strings, including the jazz saxophone in place of viola. Set in four movements, the first is a jazz fugue introduced by a slow prelude, this synthesis drawing the neo-Baroque procedures and forms of Bach into the realistic popular style of the contemporary Harlem dance hall. The extensive counterpoint not only in the fugue but also in the prelude, which features the solo saxophone as well as numerous syncopated passages for pairs of winds in parallel thirds or sixths, is also characteristic of the improvisational counterpoint of Dixieland jazz. Most evocative of the jazz idiom is the fugue subject itself, which is based on the major-minor third of the blues style in a pervasively syncopated rhythm. At the same time, increasingly chromatic layers are added continually as countersubjects to the fugue to produce a continually varying fabric reminiscent of Bach's textures. All of these sources are absorbed into the mechanical layers and mosaic-like planes (as manifested in the accompanying ostinato patterns) so typical of Milhaud's French Neoclassicism. Milhaud's musical language is defined further by the successive entries of the fugue subject (contrabass on D, trombone on E, saxophone on A, etc.), which gradually move from a single key to an intentionally cacophonous polytonality.

Throughout the interwar period, Milhaud continued to integrate new styles and techniques into his compositions as his travels to many countries brought him in contact with new sources at various music festivals and

[11] Ibid., p. 102.
[12] Ibid., p. 118.

congresses. While his light, satirical approach continued to manifest itself in such works as the ballet *Le train bleu* (The blue train, 1924) for Diaghilev, he preferred a more serious approach to subject and style.[13] This attitude is found in his *Les malheurs d'Orphée* (The misfortunes of Orpheus, 1925), which was the first of his series of chamber operas based on extreme reduction in form and performing forces, and in his large opera–oratorio *Christophe Colomb* (1928), for forty-five solo voices, nonsinging parts, large chorus, orchestra, and use of film inserts, the work at times suggesting the use of Greek chorus. Seriousness of intention is especially evident in his Jewish *Service sacré* (1947) and Psalm settings. Like Orff and Hindemith, Milhaud also turned during the 1930s to the more accessible styles of music for children and amateurs, including *A propos de bottes* and *Un petit peu de musique* (both 1932) and *Un petit peu d'exercice* (1934), as well as film music set to *Madame Bovary* (1933), *Tartarin de Tarascon* (1934), and *La citadelle du silence* (1937). In homage to his native Aix en Provence, his realistic Neoclassical approach continued to manifest itself in the traditional form of the *Suite Provençale* (1937), in which he employs melodies of the French Baroque composer André Campra and seems to capture the natural angular quality of the Provençal landscape.

Francis Poulenc (1899–1963) also produced light, amusing, as well as serious works, revealing those aesthetic qualities and attitudes so typically French. The simplicity, directness, and objectivity of Poulenc's Neoclassicism pervade all his works, regardless of their subject matter or genre. In general, the music seems to be closer to the ideals of Satie and Cocteau than any other member of the group, as exemplified in his early *Trois Mouvements perpétuels* (1918), which are short, simple, witty pieces for piano underlaid by a sort of Alberti bass or repetitive type of figuration. With this work, Poulenc achieved some early popularity with pianists, though it was not until Diaghilev's performance in 1924 of *Les biches,* a ballet with chorus and orchestra on a seventeenth-century text, that he received widespread recognition. All his piano works are based on traditional forms (sonata, suite, nocturne, impromptu, etc.).

The ideals established by Satie and Cocteau were perhaps manifested most significantly in Poulenc's large repertoire of songs, in which he infused the French song tradition (from Fauré to Ravel) with the elegant, popular style of French café music. The early song cycle, *Cocardes* (1919), set to texts by Cocteau, captures the light, simple quality of the Parisian popular chanson through its graceful, lyrical vocal style and its use of a small, brassy instrumental accompaniment—consisting of cornet, trombone, bass drum, triangle, and violin. The *Banalités* (1940), set to five poems of Apollinaire, represents a later example of his satire. The surrealistic quality of the latter is more evident in his first opera, *Les mamelles de Tirésias* (1944), set to an Apollinaire comedy. Here, Poulenc employs a variety of traditional musical styles and techniques (with satirical references to Puccini, Massenet, and even Debussy,

---

[13] Ibid., p. 89.

as well as the use of lyrical solos, rapid duets, chorales, etc.) for a lively action that could only belong to the theatre of the absurd—it has duels, sex changes, falsetto for singing babies, etc.

The popular flavor of many of Poulenc's piano and vocal works (with their clear textures and forms, distinct, often angular rhythms, and highly lyrical quality) is also evident in some of his chamber music. All the chamber works are in familiar forms, including several *Sonatas* for various instrumental combinations, *Trio* for oboe, bassoon, and piano (1926), and *Sextet* for wind quintet and piano (1932–1939), as well as older forms, including a *Villanelle* for pipe and piano (1934), *Suite française* for winds and percussion (1935), after the French Renaissance composer Claude Gervaise, an *Elégie* for horn and piano (1957), and a *Sarabande* for guitar (1960). The four works from his early chamber-music period (1918–1926)—the three *Sonatas* and the *Trio*—are most characteristic of his musical wit and direct approach. These works are essentially triadic, often seemingly traditional in the local harmonic progressions, but colored by pungent dissonances and the occasional capricious chromaticism, including some bitonality and jazz elements as well (e.g., *Sonata* for clarinet and bassoon, 1922).

The *Sonata* for horn, trumpet, and trombone (1922) recalls the light divertimento style of the eighteenth century. The clear traditional forms of the three movements and the typical use of wind timbres in lightly figured homophonic textures are drawn into Poulenc's French Neoclassical style. This is accomplished partly through the use of themes imbued with the French popular flavor. As Classical as the work may seem, it could have been produced in the twentieth century only, a result of the composer's personal handling of Classical phrase structure and nontraditional use of dissonance. Motion and tension are produced primarily by means of abrupt changes of meter, effected through overlaps, shifts, and reinterpretations of the various mechanical rhythmic figures. The structural significance of these metric, rhythmic manipulations is made all the more evident by sudden tempo changes, which contribute to the distinction between periods, themes, and sectional blocks, and to sharp contrasts in the meticulously worked out types of instrumental figuration and articulations.

The trumpet establishes the spare, mechanical main theme at the opening of Movement I, the two-measure antecedent segment (phrase 1a) based simply on reiterated arpeggiations of the G-major tonic triad.[14] The supporting ostinato unfolds a conventional I–IV–V$_9$ progression, which is balanced by the perfect cadence at the end of the two-measure consequent (phrase 1b). Perfect balance and distinction between these phrase members are achieved further by the contrasting legato and staccato articulations, as well as by the abrupt appearance of rapid harmonic alternations between

---

[14] The sonata-allegro form of the movement is as follows: exposition (mm. 1–39)—theme 1 (m. 1–25), theme 2 (mm. 26–39); development (mm. 39–57); recapitulation (mm. 58–85); coda (mm. 86–89).

dominant and tonic chords in phrase 1b. Classical phrasal contrast is also provided by the delicately pungent dissonances that first appear between the angular solo trumpet line and contrary scalar motions of the accompaniment in the consequent phrase (m. 3, first and sixth eighth notes) and on the I_4^6 downbeat of the cadential measure. The nontraditional quality of what otherwise appears to be purely Classical style is seen in the clock-like precision not only in the skeletal and mechanical figuration, but also in the meticulous articulation markings. While the second period adheres to its traditional role as modulator to the dominant, the tonal motion is supported by a rhythmic technique typified by Stravinsky's Neoclassical works. Phrases 2a and 2b (mm. 5–8) appear to be a modified repetition of the first two, in which rhythmic reinterpretation of the figuration permits some weakening of tonal stability.

Thus far, all this seems traditional enough, the consequent phrase (2b) rounding out the first double-period with a perfect cadence in the dominant. However, instability in the next double-period (mm. 9–17), which now remains entirely in the tonic key, is produced rather exclusively by means of metric and rhythmic reinterpretations of the linear figurations, the structural significance of these metric/rhythmic relations having nothing to do with traditional Classical procedures. The basic trumpet line unfolds two closely related phrases (3a and 3b), again two measures each (Ex. 9–2). This time, an ambiguity is permitted by the first explicit metric changes in the movement (between 3/4 and 4/4). These two distinct (though similar) phrases are elided through the overlapping of two melodically identical internal segments. The pitch structure of the first internal segment (m. 10 through m. 11, beat 2)—consisting of the cadential measure of phrase 3a and the first three notes of phrase 3b—is duplicated exactly by the second internal segment (m. 10, last eighth note, through m. 12, beat 2). Ambiguity results in two ways from the rhythmic reinterpretation in the second segment. On the one hand, it produces a sense of "aimless circling" around this small group of pitches, and on the other, it permits a shift away from a metric emphasis on the tonic-degree G (m. 10) to a metric emphasis on the seventh-degree C (m. 12) of the dominant-ninth harmonic outline of this cadential measure. The two accompanying instruments contribute further to the phrasal complexity of the passage.

The horn supports the trumpet line in strict parallel sixths, but contains one linear deviation (between the major- and minor-sixth degrees, E and E♭). This produces a conflict with the elisional procedure in the trumpet, since it does not contain exact pitch duplication of the corresponding internal segments, and permits some clarity to be maintained in the distinction between the main antecedent-consequent phrase structure. The trombone conflicts with the structure of this period, unfolding a single phrase of three measures against it in a closed progression from V_7 to I. Another level of phrasal elision is produced in this double-period (to m. 17) by further overlapping of internal segments. Phrase 3b (mm. 11–12) functions simultaneously as the antecedent phrase (4a) of another overlapping period. Con-

EXAMPLE 9–2. Poulenc, *Sonata* for horn, trumpet, and trombone, Mov. I, mm. 9–17, metric and rhythmic reinterpretations

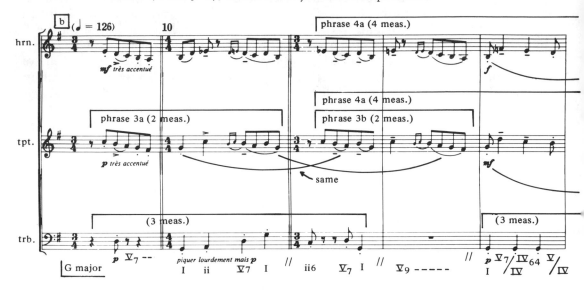

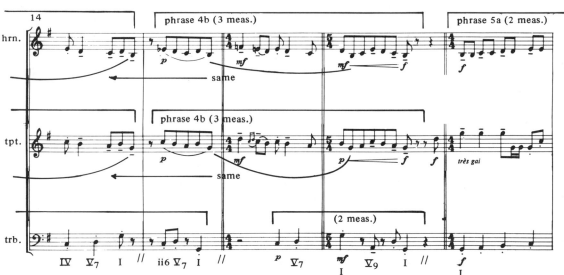

sidered as phrase 4a, it is extended to four measures, where it comes to a perfect authentic cadence. The remaining three-measure consequent (phrase 4b, mm. 15–17), a varied and shortened repeat of 4a, closes the period. The omission of m. 12 from its "expected" point of recurrence in phrase 4b (between mm. 15 and 16) produces a shift of emphasis in the trumpet line from the fourth degree (C) of the key to the fifth degree (D). The tonal strength of the latter, a linear anticipation of the dominant-tonic resolution of the passage, is weakened momentarily by the modal inflection in the horn at this point. This inflection maintains the earlier harmonic function of the D as part of the V_7 of IV (see mm. 13–14). This entire, rhythmically complex double period (mm. 9–17) is closed off as a distinct sectional block by the rhythmic and harmonic function of the trombone. The first pair of three-measure phrases in the trombone (mm. 9–11 and 13–15) had overlapped the phrasal pairings in the other two instruments, so both its cadences appeared nonsynchronized. Its final phrase (mm. 16–17), contracted to two measures, now coincides with the dominant-tonic cadence of the other instruments. The remaining two periods (phrases 5a/5b and 6a/6b) then round out the first-theme group in unambiguously symmetrical pairs of 2 + 2 measures each, the second pair (phrases 6a/6b) returning to the initial thematic idea with the root of the arpeggiated tonic triad again at the barline.

Concern with such mechanically organized architectural constructions is characteristic of French Neoclassical composers in general. The ternary form of the first-theme group—a rounded pattern determined by the groupings of double-periods that moved from symmetrical phrase pairings to irregularly elided ones and back—is reflected further in the structure of the second-theme group (mm. 26–39). The latter, in popular French style, provides an extreme contrast to the style of the first-theme by its lyrical quality, increased dissonance (suggesting polytonality), change of tempo, and sudden shift of key to the flat-sixth degree (E♭ major).

Movement III provides overall balance by returning to the style and character of the opening movement, the specific handling of the rounded construction of this *Rondeau* providing associations with the first two movements. References may be seen on both the local thematic and phrasal levels. The arpeggiation of the opening measure alludes to the main theme of Movement I, but the rhythmic structure of the antecedent phrase (mm. 1–2) is basically that of the second theme of Movement I and main theme of Movement II. The rounded exposition (ABA) is based on disruption and return analogous to the departure (through phrasal elision) and return to the phrase/period symmetry within the first-theme group of Movement I. In Movement III, however, this principle is established rather by contrapuntal divergence from and reconvergence on tertian harmonic construction. The counterpoint in Section A (mm. 1–6) almost exclusively produces pure triadic harmonies, one of two colorful dissonances in phrase 1a and its repeat (mm. 2 and 6, downbeat) resulting simply from the mixture of the melodic-minor seventh degrees, C and C♯. At the same time, the consecutive unfolding of conflicting D modes (major and minor) in phrase 1a foreshadows the more intense contrapuntal conflict of these D modes in the first period of Section B (mm. 7–10). In phrase 1a of this new section, the main D-major line of the trumpet is opposed by the accompanying counterpoint, which contains the flat third and seventh degrees to suggest an ambiguous D-Dorian. Dissonance from this simultaneous modal mixture is heightened by the contrapuntal relations, which do not permit the harmonic alignment of triadic elements; a sense of "wrong" notes is produced through the linear nonalignment of these major and minor modes. The instrumental articulations, which produce a syncopated shift away from the barline, also contribute to the instability of the passage. (At the recapitulation of this passage, mm. 45ff., this rhythmic-metric conflict is resolved through reinterpretation of the instrumental articulations that permit rhythmic-metric coincidence at the barline.) At the return of Section A (mm. 15–20), the exposition is rounded out by the confluence of lines on tertian harmonic construction. The last measure of the movement summarizes these relations as the dissonant nontriadic counterpoint converges on the final tonic chord. Poulenc's whimsical use of dissonance and polymodality as well as rhythmic-metric ambiguities in a strictly organized, mathematical Classical framework results in his own objective approach to the Neoclassical style.

The light, graceful style of Poulenc's small forms represents only one side of his musical personality. In the mid-1930s, he returned to Roman Catholicism at a time when his style was entering a new period of maturity. Among the first significant results were a number of religious choral pieces, including the *Litanies á la vierge noire* (1936), for three-part women's chorus and organ, the a cappella *Mass in G* (1937), and collections of motets. Works on subjects of tragic expression can be represented by his cantata, *Figure humaine* (1943), on poems of Paul Éluard, based on France's suffering during the German occupation, and his opera, *Dialogues des carmélites* (1956), in which the execution of nuns during the French Revolution is examined.

Despite Poulenc's varied moods and approaches, certain consistent stylistic features and traditional source references continued to unify his objective Neoclassical approach. (His choral *Chansons françaises* [1945–1946] suggest the French Renaissance styles of Janequin and Sermisy, his *Organ Concerto* [1938] modelled on Bach.) The *Mass in G,* inspired by the architecture of Romanesque cathedrals, is a model of economy and emotional restraint. The work reveals Neoclassical traits in its formal blocks (based on sudden changes of texture, dynamics, and mode) as well as in its melodic angularity, complex tertian harmonies and pungent dissonances, and frequent metric changes that permit a close adherence to the irregular rhythm of the text. The relative conciseness of the five movements (without Credo), mostly in homophonic textures throughout, provides an ideal vehicle for the sacred text, an approach suggesting the principles of the *Motu Proprio,* a Vatican encyclical of 1903.[15]

An article of Collet's, in *Comoedia,* implies that *Les Six* formed a monolithic group musically. This was fortuitous; the bonds among its members were based largely on friendship rather than similarity of musical temperament. The arbitrariness of this musical association seems most applicable to Arthur Honegger (1892–1955). While Poulenc's aesthetics are most closely

---

[15] See these principles in the discussion of Vaughan Williams' *Mass* in Chap. 6, above.

associated with Cocteau's ideas, and Milhaud's with "Mediterranean lyricism," Honegger's style reveals a kinship with German Romanticism.[16] Milhaud provides evidence of Honegger's strong attraction to the German tradition.[17] During their student years in the counterpoint classes of André Gédalge, which began in 1911, Honegger was immersed constantly in the scores of Strauss and Reger, and Honegger occasionally gave Milhaud a Schoenberg score as a gift. Straussian and other Romantic influences are evident in Honegger's *String Quartet* (1916–1917). His opera on Cocteau's version of Sophocles' *Antigone* (1924–1927), though somewhat austere, is pervaded by a degree of dissonance that sometimes approaches those levels found in the most intense music of the post-Romantic and expressionist composers. The emotionally intense oratorio setting of Claudel's text, *Jeanne d'Arc au bûcher* (1934–1935), infuses Gregorian Chant and folk-like materials with a strong use of nonfunctional dissonance.

Other styles are also evident in Honegger's compositions. Despite his individuality, he borrowed objectively whatever forms and tonal resources suited his intentions. While his individualistic approach was viewed by *Les Six* as antithetical to the general compositional aesthetics of the group, mostly represented by the music of Auric and Poulenc, some of Honegger's works during the postwar period are nevertheless characterized similarly by a less personalized expression as well as a mingling of traditional and nontraditional elements. His jazz-influenced *Concertino* for piano and orchestra (1924), piano music, songs, five symphonies between 1930 and 1951, and many film scores, including *La roue* (1923), *Napoléon* (1927), *Les misérables* (1934), and others, contributed to the accessibility of his music. Honegger's intention in all his works was to provide a depth of musical thought for those with a more genuine musical interest.

His first significant composition for chorus and orchestra was *Le roi David* (1921), which resulted from his efforts to produce a type of composition that was accessible to the general musical masses.[18] Written to be sung by mountaineers at the theatre of Mèziéres, Switzerland, the work is devoid of technical difficulties. Through its successes, it also served to familiarize the general Parisian audiences with a more contemporary musical language than they had previously been able to comprehend.[19] Originally conceived as a score to accompany a drama, but now performed as an oratorio in which the actors are replaced by a narrator, the work joins certain melodic and rhythmic elements of the French with stylistic features of the Wagnerian music drama and more sectionalized form of the Baroque oratorio. The work is in three

[16] See Milhaud, *Notes Without Music,* n.10, above, p. 97.

[17] Milhaud, "To Arnold Schoenberg on His Seventieth Birthday: Personal Recollections," *The Musical Quarterly* 30 (October 1944): 381.

[18] For a detailed historical and analytical study of the choral works, see Herrold E. Headley, "The Choral Works of Arthur Honegger," Ph.D. diss., North Texas State College, 1959, p. 249.

[19] See Milhaud, *Notes Without Music,* n.10, above, p. 162.

parts, each based on a different phase of David's life. In the diverse styles of the numbers, one often finds strong allusions to Bach, as in the third section where the unison choral singing of the psalm is set contrapuntally against the orchestra with its brilliant trumpet sound. The exotic, opening oboe line contributes to the oriental quality of the biblical setting, while shifting diatonic modality throughout the work is often juxtaposed with, or colored by, pungent dissonances, polytonal fanfares, and local whole-tone modal extensions (as in the ascending lines in No. 10, "Le camp de Saül," mm. 9–10).

His more objective aesthetic concerns are manifested in a highly constructivist and mechanical approach to form and texture in many of his compositions. In his triptych of symphonic poems, including *Pacific 231* (1923), *Rugby* (1928), and *Symphonic Movement No. 3* (1932–1933), he reveals an interest in dynamic motion and sports, such concerns of which were common to the futurists as well. In the first of these three pieces, which he referred originally to as *Mouvement Symphonique,* Honegger was after an entirely abstract concept, by which he intended to produce a sense of mathematical acceleration of rhythm, while at the same time slowing the movement conversely. His pervasive use of an ongoing counterpoint "in the manner of J. S. Bach" within the framework of a large and "diversified chorale" contributes to the mechanistic quality of *Pacific*.[20] Despite the Romantic idea suggested by the extra-musical title, the composer's own commentary reveals his intentions of avoiding a programmatic basis: "I have not aimed to imitate the noise of an engine, but rather to express in terms of music a visual impression and physical enjoyment."[21] (This work served as a model for the "machine music" of the Soviet realist group around Alexandr Vasil'yevich Mosolov, 1900–1973.) Honegger's approach is often manifested in a Bachian polyphony resulting in sonorous, often dissonant textures derived from nonfunctional harmonic superimpositions. However, he asserted that because of his precise, unambiguous melodic and rhythmic contours, dissonance will not disturb the listener. The accessibility of the musical language is due to clarity of line, figuration, and texture so typical of even his most grandiose structures, which frequently unfold according to an elusive though innate sense of internal logic and proportion.[22]

Pacific 231 may be viewed as a set of "Chorale" variations, the main theme functioning as a cantus firmus (G♯–C♯–E–G♯/F×–C♯–E–F×/ G♯–C♯–E–G♯/B–A–E–F♯/G, etc.).[23] The overall rhythmic-metric structure and tempo relationships serve as the basis of the developmental form, in which the rhythmic values diminish systematically in consecutive stages from

---

[20] See Arthur Honegger, *Je suis compositeur* (Paris: Éditions du Conquistador, 1951), p. 118; *I Am a Composer,* Eng. trans. Wilson O. Clough and Allan Arthur Willman (New York: St. Martin's Press; Faber & Faber, 1966), p. 101.

[21] See the preface to the miniature score (Paris and New York: Éditions Salabert, 1924).

[22] Honegger, *Je suis compositor,* n.20, above, p. 87; *I Am a Composer,* p. 74.

[23] Willy Tappolet, *Arthur Honegger* (Zürich: Atlantis Verlag AG, 1954), pp. 76–82.

whole-notes to sixteenths. These mathematical calculations are set within a scheme of sudden changes of texture and rhythm in a mechanical series of blocks, which contribute to regularly occurring moments of renewed propulsion. The main theme (No. 2) is prepared subtly by a gradual shortening of note values in the introductory passage. (These diminutions extend over most of the movement, while the tempo slows down conversely. Rhythmic augmentation is induced finally in the last fourteen measures.) The opening passage (mm. 1–11) implies the presence of the cantus firmus (main theme) already, which unfolds from the trills of the contrabass (G♯) in the lowest register through the harmonics of the first violins (C♯–E, then F×, in enharmonic spelling, G, and G♯). These introductory measures (half-note = 60) evoke the impression of a machine straining under pressure. Above the heavy tremolo of the cymbal and the contrabass, the strings trill *sul ponticello* under an unbroken chord of harmonics.

The first theme is then established at the tempo of half-note = 80, powerful and straining in the bassoon, contrabasses, celli, and muted horns. The interruptive, regular pauses signify the "respiration" of the machine, after which the trombones in alternation with the tuba try to bring the cantus firmus into prominence (No. 2). The persistent half-step ascent of the initial motivic seconds and thirds (Ex. 9–3, in which A–B–A–C♯–A♯–C♯ of cello I moves by sequence to B♭–C–B♭–D–B–D, etc.) and the contrapuntally aligned half-step linear motions together anticipate the cantus firmus' main intervals (seconds and thirds). These characteristic intervals are separately defined by trombone I and tuba (at No. 2). This gradual emergence of the cantus firmus enhances the image of the steam engine's increasing force, in which the compression pumps lift and lower their pistons. The animated action presses incessantly forward at No. 3. The fragmented distribution of the components of the cantus firmus is interrupted suddenly by a wedge-shaped texture produced by contrary linear motion, such inversionally related contours of which are common to Honegger's textures. Following a shimmering tremolo figure in the flutes and clarinets (No. 3, m. 8), the horns then introduce a new, more active triplet theme, which contains a leap of a perfect fourth, or fifth (No. 4). This theme seems to grow from the triadic segment of the main theme (G♯–C♯–E–G♯), thereby producing a sense of transformation, or variation.

Theme 2 proceeds through diverse rhythmic transformations that produce an acceleration—quarter notes proceeding to triplets, quarter-triplets to quintuplets, sextuplets, and finally to uniform eighths (eighth = 152; seven measures after No. 5)—the increasing number of notes in the measure culminating eventually in uniform motion. In a more rhythmically firm third theme, which is played by the horns (four measures before No. 6) and then bassoons (at No. 6), the seconds of the cantus firmus are at first only suggested, becoming more prominent. A fugal Episode leads to a close stretto, so that in eight measures the new theme occurs eight times in distribution among all the instruments. Whereas the trombones and tuba suggested the main theme in quarter notes (No. 2) originally, the trumpets intone a segment of the cantus firmus in more active triplets, eighths, and

EXAMPLE 9–3. Honegger, *Pacific 231*, introductory passage, gradual shortening of note values leading to main theme (at No. 2)

septuplets (No. 5), during the course of which the flutes and oboes transform the cantus firmus by expanding it to a more lyrical theme (No. 8, m. 5). The latter is introduced by another sudden change to a characteristic wedge-shaped texture based on contrary motion. In apposition to the lyrical cantus firmus, the strings play a contrapuntally and rhythmically modified form of the latter (No. 8, m. 5).

To this point, the figures were disconnected and angular. A sense of effort is expressed in an increased joining of thematic material, which propels the motion until the racing locomotive reaches its maximum speed. At this moment, the disconnected figures give in to a revolving motion, widening at first over one, then four measures (No. 9). The accelerando arrives at a smooth and effortless motion, in which the locomotive is now propelled by its own inertial rhythm. At the same time, the tempo slows down from a quarter = 152 to a quarter = 144 as a new, fourth theme is introduced. This rotating triplet theme forms the middle point of the movement. The other themes are then joined with it to form a tightly woven polyphonic and polyrhythmic fabric. The rhythm is stretched further as the tempo is retarded to a quarter = 132 (No. 14), where further diminution of note values is implemented conversely. From the entire orchestra, the cantus firmus sounds above all other themes, stretched out in the horns, then trombones, to half and dotted halves. Through condensation of the sound masses and a large crescendo, the high point of the movement is reached. Without transition, the coda is established, and sixteenths are expanded to eighth-triplets, while the tempo is now correspondingly slowed to the quarter = 126 (roughly equivalent to the opening half-note = 60). The sudden change of direction in this new rhythmic block seems to function as a brake. Finally, the fourteen-measure coda, which provides the last clear reference to the cantus firmus (flutes, oboes, trumpets, violins), ends on a powerful unison C♯. The cadential motion from G♯ (and dissonant D) to the C♯ has been foreshadowed throughout in the G♯–C♯ fifth structure of the cantus firmus, thus providing a sense of inevitable resolution to a tonic in an otherwise nonfunctional harmonic context.

Nadia Boulanger points to Honegger's extraordinary capacity for musical assimilation, stating that "Bach, Handel, Wagner, Debussy, Schoenberg, and Stravinsky have all contributed to the formation of his language."[24] One may speculate about the influence of Stravinsky's *Le sacre* on the motoric rhythmic quality of *Pacific 231,* or Honegger's temperamental orientation to Schoenberg rather than Stravinsky,[25] but Honegger himself denied any adherence to polytonality, atonality, or dodecaphony, asserting rather that his contemporary musical material is based on the scale of twelve chromatic tones employed with freedom.[26]

[24] Nadia Boulanger, Lectures on Modern Music: "Modern French music," "Debussy: The *Préludes,*" and "Stravinsky," *The Rice Institute Pamphlet 13* (April 1926), p. 147.

[25] See Marion Bauer, *Twentieth Century Music* (New York and London: G. P. Putnam's Sons, 1933), p. 238.

[26] Honegger, *Je suis compositeur,* n.20, above, p. 97; *I Am a Composer,* p. 83.

SUGGESTED READINGS

NADIA BOULANGER. Lectures on Modern Music: "Modern French music," "Debussy: The Préludes", and "Stravinsky," *The Rice Institute Pamphlet* 13 (April 1926), pp. 113–195.

JEAN COCTEAU. *Le Coq et l'Arlequin: notes autour de la musique* (Paris: Éditions de la Sirène, 1918); trans. Rollo H. Myers (n.p.: The Egoist Press, 1921).

HERROLD E. HEADLEY. "The Choral Works of Arthur Honegger," Ph.D. diss., North Texas State College, 1959.

ARTHUR HONEGGER.   *Je suis compositeur* (Paris: Éditions du Conquistador, 1951); *I Am a Composer,* Eng. trans. Wilson O. Clough and Allan Arthur Willman (New York: St. Martin's Press; Faber and Faber, 1966).

DARIUS MILHAUD.   *Notes Without Music,* trans. Donald Evans, ed. Rollo H. Myers (London: Denis Dobson Ltd., 1952).

ROLLO H. MYERS.   *Erik Satie* (New York: Denis Dobson Ltd., 1948; Dover Publications, Inc., 1968).

ROGER SHATTUCK.   *The Banquet Years* (New York: Alfred A. Knopf, Inc., 1955; rev. ed. 1968).

WILLY TAPPOLET.   *Arthur Honegger* (Zürich: Atlantis Verlag AG, 1954).

10 Stravinsky in Switzerland and Paris (1914–1939): The neoclassical style

TRANSFORMATION OF THE EARLY RUSSIAN STYLE Stravinsky's musical idiom underwent several major changes throughout his career, the first stylistic transformation occurring around the beginning of the First World War. The première performance of his large, brilliantly orchestrated ballet, *The Firebird,* which brought him to Paris in 1910, and his two remaining prewar Russian ballets, *Petrushka* and *Le sacre,* had established his international reputation firmly. However, the extreme political and economic conditions in Europe beginning in 1914 contributed to the new direction that his compositional style and aesthetics were to take during the next several decades.

Stravinsky remained in close proximity to the Parisian musical scene during his prewar visits to Switzerland, which became his home of exile from 1914 to 1920. He continued to employ Russian subjects as the basis of his musical settings nevertheless, as long as it seemed his Swiss home would serve as a temporary refuge only. At this time , the economic pressures of the war and the composer's isolation from his predominantly German music publishers led to financial straits and a narrowed musical milieu for his Russian subjects. This tendency, based on reduction of formal length, thematic material, and instrumental combinations, provided a more austere musical framework within which Stravinsky continued to adhere to the objective quality of the Russian folk sources.[1] This combination of political, economic, and musical factors brought Stravinsky increasingly closer to the more impersonal aesthetic approach that was emerging among his French contemporaries.

Stravinsky's first work belonging to his more concise and objective style is the *Three Pieces* for string quartet (1914). In the first piece, the repeated unequal-beat meter of the Russian dance (3/4 + 2/4 + 2/4) is set off against a constant rhythmic/metric reinterpretation of an incessantly repeated diatonic figure that revolves around a few notes. These irregular rhythms are set in yet more angular and contrasting textural blocks and layers in the second piece, and extreme harmonic staticism is reached in the third. While this style apparently evolved from the idiom of *Le sacre,* a fundamental difference lies in the reduction of the ballet's complex contrapuntal network of modal tone patches to a spare texture of only a few elements. These short pieces were

---

[1] Evidence for the "essentially emotionless quality of folk performance" was provided by the Russian ethnologist, Evgeniia Linyova, in her diaries kept during her fieldwork; see Richard Taruskin, "From Subject to Style: Stravinsky and the Painters," *Confronting Stravinsky,* ed. Jann Pasler (Berkeley and Los Angeles: University of California Press, 1986), p. 31.

included in the first three of the *Four Studies* for orchestra (1914–1918; No. 4 was composed in 1928), while some of its themes also appeared in other works of his Neoclassical period, including *Symphonies of Wind Instruments* (1920), the double fugue of the *Symphony of Psalms* (1930), and *Symphony in C* (1939–1940). The style of *Three Pieces* is developed further in *Pribaoutki* (1914), i.e., "song games" or limericks on Russian popular texts. Its skeletal chamber orchestra, which consists of baritone, flute, oboe, clarinet, bassoon, violin, viola, cello, and bass, provides a concise setting for the blocked and layered textures that appear to be a direct outgrowth of Russian folk music.[2]

The bearing that the Russian folk sources had on Stravinsky's postwar modernist aesthetics is reflected in his increasing adherence to the classical principles of objectivity, equilibrium, and simplicity. Linyova's own references to the "pure, classical strictness of style" in the folk sources supports this connection.[3] A decisive move toward objectivity is seen first in Stravinsky's new metric approach to the text in the *Three Japanese Lyrics* (1912–1913), which laid the groundwork for the more mechanical rhythmic style that came to characterize his Neoclassical works. In his musical setting of the Russian text by the orientalist A. Brandt, Stravinsky departed intentionally from the proper accentuation of the Russian declamation.[4] The drafts of the first song, *Akahito,* show that Stravinsky originally had the correct accentuation, but then distorted the textual meter by shifting the musical stresses.[5] Such transgressions of the language accents are also found not only in the French works of the war years, such as *Renard* and *Les noces,* but subsequently in his English and Latin settings as well.[6] Such accentual shifts also occur in the authentic Russian tunes themselves and in songs from other folk collections. Stravinsky's postwar modernist idiom, based on abstraction and objectivity, seems to have resulted largely from this principle in which sound became dissociated from meaning.[7]

Stravinsky's one-act opera, *Renard* (1916), based on a Russian burlesque tale for voice and chamber orchestra, and the dance cantata, *Les noces* (1914–1917, orchestrated by 1923 for the première by Diaghilev's Ballets Russes), are the last works of his Russian period. *Les noces,* based on Stravinsky's adaptation from Kireievsky's anthology of popular poems, contains

---

[2] Bartók cites this work as typical in "Der Einfluss der Volksmusik auf die heutige Kunstmusik" ("The Influence of Folk Music on the Art Music of Today"), *Melos* (Berlin) 1/17 (October 1920): 384–386; No. 2 (February 1930): 66–67. See also *Béla Bartók Essays,* ed. Benjamin Suchoff (New York: St. Martin's Press, 1976), p. 318.

[3] See Taruskin, "From Subject to Style," n.1, above, pp. 31–32.

[4] "Misaccentuation" is discussed by Taruskin, in "Stravinsky's 'Rejoicing Discovery' and What It Meant: In Defense of His Notorious Text Setting," *Stravinsky Retrospectives,* ed. Ethan Haimo and Paul Johnson (Lincoln and London: University of Nebraska Press, 1987), pp. 162–199; especially p. 169.

[5] Ibid., p. 170, Exs. 5a and 5b.

[6] Ibid., p. 169.

[7] Ibid., p. 174.

the last obvious vestiges of the Russian period and also served stylistically as the immediate precursor of his Neoclassical compositions. While composing his first Neoclassical works—*Histoire du soldat* (1918), *Ragtime* (1918), *Pulcinella* (1919), the *Concertino* (1920), the *Symphonies of Wind Instruments* (1920), and *Mavra* (1922)—orchestration of *Les noces* continued. Between 1917 and 1923, the sketch drafts reveal a gradual reduction from a large instrumental conception of strings, winds, percussion, and keyboard instruments to four pianos and extensive percussion.[8] The final reduction permitted Stravinsky to achieve a greater sonic homogeneity as well as an impersonal, mechanical style appropriate to the anti-Romantic, ritualistic choral-solo alternations of the pagan Russian wedding.[9]

This phase of Stravinsky's development is characterized by a general simplification of the melodic elements and a drastic reduction of the number of elements within a given texture. The responsorial character of the text throughout the four tableaux lends itself to his inclination toward mechanical block juxtaposition.[10] Local blocks are distinguished from one another by means of sharper changes of melodic contour, meter, ostinato rhythmic layers, and vocal and instrumental colors, as well as frequent and sudden occurrences of nonfunctional dissonance used simply as color to offset the Russian modes. Differentiation between the individual blocks is also achieved by the assignment of distinctive types of pitch-sets—specifically pentatonic/diatonic and octatonic pitch-sets.[11] This general aesthetic approach based on both a disconnected series of mosaic constructions and an archaic subject suggests the cubist paintings of Pablo Picasso and Georges Braque. In the early 1920s, the Neoclassical Braque showed his concern for the most classical of ideals by "combining sculptural representations with architectural bases," often treating his human subjects as archaic and hardened objects.[12]

The opening sectional block establishes the basic motivic cell of the entire cantata. The incessant permution of this single, embellished three-note pentatonic figure, E–D–B, around one or two of its pitches asserts a sense of tonal priority in an otherwise nonfunctional harmonic context. At the same time, a sense of motion is achieved by this constant rhythmic and metric

---

[8] These orchestrational sketches can be seen at the Stravinsky Archive in the Paul Sacher Stiftung in Basel.

[9] These aims are expressed by the composer, in Igor Stravinsky and Robert Craft, *Expositions and Developments* (London: Faber and Faber, 1962; rep. Berkeley and Los Angeles: University of California Press, 1981), pp. 117–118.

[10] Tableau I enacts the ceremonial braiding of the bride's hair, Tableau II the blessing of the bridegroom by his mother and father, Tableau III the escorting and blessing of the bride, and Tableau IV the entertainment of the guests by the groom's parents.

[11] For a study of these pitch-set occurrences and their interactions in *Les noces,* see Pieter C. van den Toorn, *The Music of Igor Stravinsky* (New Haven and London: Yale University Press, 1983), pp. 164–176.

[12] See Jacques Damase, *Georges Braque* (New York: Barnes & Noble, 1963), pp. 12–13.

reinterpretation. Against this motif, pns. I and III and the xylophone provide a simple, crisp heterophonic accompaniment. A new block is established (at No. 1) by the tempo change, a more varied rhythmic reinterpretation of the motif, and the abrupt addition of an angular sixteenth-note ostinato in pns. II and IV. The repeated B♭–F of this layer provides the first pungent dissonances against the E and B (as well as grace-note F♯) of the main E–D–B motif. The juxtaposition of this new diatonic element against the original one suggests the first octatonic transformation of the basic diatonic material; the bimodal diatonic combination resulting in an octatonic segment, B♭–B–[ ]–D–E–F, producing a polarity of pitch sets between the blocks. While the work unfolds according to this disconnected mosaic principle, large-scale coherence is created nevertheless by schemes among the blocks within each Tableau. For instance, the responsorial tendency of Tableau I is from high to low voices and back, with more rapid mixing toward the end. Such schemes create increasing mathematical calculation in works found in the Neoclassical through serial periods.

PERMANENT EXILE FROM RUSSIA (1917) AND THE EMERGENCE OF THE NEOCLASSICAL STYLE

Stravinsky's turn away from overtly Russian subjects after *Les noces* coincided with the permanent exile from his homeland after the October revolution of 1917. This crisis, in which Stravinsky's life and work were affected deeply by the loss of his country, language, and music, led him to a new decade of "samplings, experiments, and amalgamations."[13] His first significant Neoclassical work is *Histoire du soldat* (1918), which can be found on a libretto by C.F. Ramuz. The setting is for narrator, three characters (with speaking, dancing, and acting parts), and seven instruments grouped in contrasting families of strings, winds, and percussion. The story was derived from Afanasiev's collection of Russian folk tales, but Stravinsky was now concerned with reaching a more universal audience. While his wartime works had been translated into French, the attitude in this work extended beyond mere linguistic considerations. The story itself was not to be associated with any specific time or location. Furthermore, while certain tunes could still be traced to Russian sources, different national elements are juxtaposed in a unified work intended ultimately as absolute music. These include a stylized Spanish *pasodoble* band in the "Marche Royale," with a trumpet-trombone theme influenced by a popular French song, both an Argentinian tango and Viennese waltz, an American ragtime, Swiss brass band, and Bachian preludes and a Lutheran chorale ("Ein Feste Burg"). This diversity also contributes to the stylistic distinctions between local blocks or larger scenes, the

---

[13] Igor Stravinsky and Robert Craft, *Themes and Episodes* (New York: Alfred A. Knopf, 1966, 2/1967), p. 23.

narrations separating them further into a series of incidental musical settings in the manner of a suite.

The origins of *Histoire* also lie in the financial as well as political and cultural conditions of the period. In coping with the severe economic straits, Stravinsky established a small enough complement of players to create a *théâtre ambulant* (little travelling theater) that could perform on a tour of the Swiss villages, with a simple and accessible story.[14] A direct source for Stravinsky's choice of instruments came from his contact with jazz, which he knew from sheet music only. The American jazz ensemble was based on distinct instrumental categories (strings, woodwinds, brass, and percussion), each of which contained a polarity of treble and bass instruments. His skeletal approach to the instrumentation of *Histoire* (for violin and double bass, clarinet and bassoon, cornet à pistons and trombone, and percussion consisting of two side drums, bass drum, cymbal, tambourine, and triangle) contributes to the distinction of its planes and layers. Around the same time, he also composed *Ragtime,* for eleven instruments, and his *Piano-rag-music,* such popular manifestations coinciding with the new interests of his French Neoclassical contemporaries. The brassy timbres and humorous element of *Histoire* are also characteristic of many Neoclassical works of Les Six.

The principle of polarity, evident in his nonblending instrumental planes and contrasting blocks in an abstract anti-Romantic form, is manifested in the drama itself. This principle, apparent in the antithesis of human and magical spheres in *Firebird* and *Petrushka,* was to become a fundamental feature of Stravinsky's Neoclassicism. A conflict between good and evil is suggested in *Histoire* as the deserter trades his soul (symbolized by his violin) for the temptations of the devil. At the end of the "Devil's March," only the soldier's body remains as the devil, leading the soldier over the frontier, usurps his soul (violin). This is reflected musically by the dissolution of the melody, leaving only the percussive shell.

Polarity between the soul and the devil is also reflected in juxtapositions of specific pitch constructions, the interrelationships of which contribute to the coherence between otherwise separate formal blocks. The opening "Soldier's March" is in several sections (A, B, A', B', A'') determined by alternations between diatonic and chromatic materials.[15] The increasing weariness of the trudging soldier is reflected in the relative proportions of the diatonic (A) and chromatic (B) sections: A diminishes in length and activity by its final occurrence (A''), whereas the climactic B' conversely increases in

---

[14] Stravinsky, *Expositions and Developments,* n.9, above, p. 89.

[15] Section A (m. 1–No. 3, m.4) is built on a diatonic motif; section B (No. 3, m. 5–No. 5) on a form of the motif in the winds compressed chromatically; A' (No. 5–No. 10) on a more active return to the diatonic material rhythmically; B' (No. 10–No. 15) serving as a climax through its more dense and extended setting of the motivic form compressed chromatically; and A'' (No. 15, mm. 1–4) rounding off the March as an abridged occurrence of the diatonic idea.

length, texture, and metric irregularity, the meter ultimately settling down to a regular 2/4 at the final narration, "Longs to find himself at home, counts the weary miles to come. No more weary miles to roam."

The main dramatic polarity is supported by a tension set up between the consonance of the perfect-fifth, which stems from the inherent tuning of the violin (E–A–D–G), and the dissonance of the tritone, the interval of which is associated traditionally with the "devil" in music. The fifths of the violin underlie the large-scale tonal succession as well as the local double-bass ostinato and violin figurations. Corresponding to the "wearying" trend of the March, the overall keys outline the upper to lower fifths of the violin. The tonality of E is asserted at the first cadence (No. 1). This is supported by an ambiguous E-Dorian modal permutation (E–F♯–G–A–B–C♯–D) in the winds (Nos. 1–2), the principal modal tones (E–[   ]–D–G) unfolding simultaneously in the double-bass ostinato to suggest the perfect-fifth tuning of the strings.

In contrast, the opening motivic statement in the brass anticipates the tritone distortion of the fifths, a transformation that plays an important role subsequently in connection with the devil. The contours of the two brass lines, related inversionally, are each encompassed registrally by a tritone—E–A♯ in the cornet à pistons and D♭–G in the trombone—suggesting a tritone alteration of the string fifths (E–A and D–G) (Ex. 10–1). The two juxtaposed diatonic segments in the cornet line (F–G–A and A♯–G♯–F♯–E) together produce systematically a chromatic interlocking of pitch content (E–F–F♯–G–G♯–A–A♯), which foreshadows the compressed form of the theme chromatically in the B sections. The pitch content of the trombone line also fills in its tritone boundary chromatically (E–[   ]–G–A♭–A–B♭–B–C–D♭–[   ]–E).

EXAMPLE 10–1. Stravinsky, *Histoire,* opening, inversionally related contour of brass lines

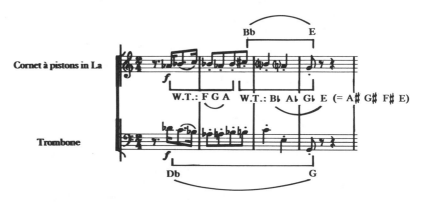

While the highest and lowest strings (E and G) are suggested in the two opening tonal planes (Nos. 1–2), the latter tonality of which is independently implied by the alternating G and D (tonic-dominant) in the bass, the first shift to the other fifths occurs at the third motivic statement (No. 2). Against the bass layer in G, the brass permutes the ambiguous E-Dorian pitch content (E–F♯–G–A–B–C♯–D) to a more distinct A-Mixolydian form (A–B–C♯–D–E–F♯–G). Both diatonic modal permutations contain a single tritone, C♯–G (in enharmonic spelling, D♭–G), one of the suggested tritone alterations of the violin fifth tuning that encompassed the opening trombone motif. Such modal tritone infusions into the unfolding perfect-fifth key scheme play an important role increasingly in the basic dramatic polarity of the work.

Following the first complete foreground articulation of the "violin" fifths (E–A–D–G) at the main cadence of section A, section B (No. 3, m. 5f.) intensifies the diatonic-chromatic polarity in the juxtaposed layers of the strings and brass. A new, arpeggiated diatonic figure (E–G♯–B–E/C♯–A♯–F♯–C♯/B–G♯–E) appears in the brass against the E–[ ]–D–G ostinato. The linear polytonal relation between E-major and F♯-major triads as well as vertical polytonal relation to the ostinato produces several tritones (a single one, E–A♯, embedded linearly, and a pair of tritones, G♯–D and C♯–G, resulting contrapuntally). Each of these tritones (in enharmonic spelling, E–B♭, A♭–D, and D♭–G) suggests an alteration of the violin fifths (E–A, A–D, D–G), readjusted at the cadence in the shift of the arpeggiated motif from brass to violin. This is the first occurrence of the "violin" fifths (E–A–D–G) in that instrument explicitly. In A′ (No. 5f.), contrapuntal juxtapositions of D major (strings) occur against linear statements of D major and A major in the bassoon and brass, respectively. At B′ (No. 10), which is the climax of the March, the key of G is established in strings and percussion against the extended motif of the brass, which is chromatically compressed. The main key of A is established by the A-minor-7th chord at the final cadence of A″.

The soldier stops to rest at the banks of a stream and begins to tune his violin. In the "Music to Scene I," in A-Aeolian, we get many musical references to the violin. In connection with the narrative ("out of tune in every string," and "keep screwing up to pitch"), metric reinterpretations of the G–D–A double-bass ostinato produce barline shifts between modal seventh (G) and tonic (A), followed by shifts between D and G, the last return to G rounding out the first section (to No. 5, m. 5). At its first two cadences (No. 1, m. 4, and No. 2, m. 3), the violin theme also shifts the metric emphasis between tonic and seventh (A and G). It is in this scene that the soldier, returning to his native village, is first accosted by the devil, who is disguised as an old man with a butterfly net. The omission of the modal sixth degree (F) of the incomplete A-Aeolian collection (A–B–C–D–E–[ ]–G) at the opening of this scene (mm. 1–6) precludes the occurrence of the modal tritone (B–F). We may represent the pitch content of the A-Aeolian modal segment conveniently as a six-note segment of the cycle of fifths. C–G–D–A–E–B. As the devil waits in hiding, tritones intrude gradually by means of the cyclic expansion of the latter collection, first by the addition of F, then F♯, etc.

The "Little Concert," with its Gypsy fiddle reference to the *Dies Irae* (at No. 13), the "Three Dances," and "Devil's Dance" are followed by "The Devil's Song," which is framed by "The Little Choral" and "Great Choral." The text of the song, a strophic melodrama, presents the main dramatic and musical polarity of the work in its simplest and most balanced form. The first stanza establishes the basic contrast between the soldier's luck and his worse fate: "Now the luck is on your side, But the Kingdom's not so great and wide; Who tries the frontiers to traverse, Recaught by me, his fate is worse." The second stanza presents the ultimatum in a pair of clauses based on a balance of statements: "So don't attempt to do what's not allowed, or back again to bed you'll go, my Princess proud; and as to that young Prince your plighted spouse, let him beware, lest he my anger should arouse." The concluding couplet shifts entirely to the devil's side: "I'll hand him to my demon hosts, Who'll see that all alive he roasts." This basic polarity is reflected musically in the opposition between the perfect-fifth (C–G) and tritone (C♯–G). Stanza 1 is accompanied by a string ostinato based on the C-major triad. The original trombone theme of the Soldier's March then punctuates the cadence in support of the words, "Recaught by me." This chromatic figure, encompassed by tritone C♯–G, produces a conflict with the triadic perfect-fifth, C–G, the latter weakened further by its absorption into the C-minor-7th harmonic change in the ostinato. The transformation from the string C–G to brass C♯–G is supported further by the cornet's A-dominant-7th arpeggiation that forms the first interlude, a chord that contains the C♯–G tritone prominently. As the ultimatum is presented in Stanza 2, C major moves again into a direct cadential conflict with C♯ at the words, "Lest he my anger should arouse." The final couplet is then based entirely on the original cadential conflict between the strings and trombone. The increased intensity in the second half of the song is also supported by a more continuous narrative, broken by a rest in Stanza 1 (m. 9).

The "Devil's Song" is followed by the "Great Choral," a striking example of Stravinsky's use of "wrong-note" dissonances and strange harmonic cadences in this new style period. This harmonic technique is even more astonishing in the final "Triumphal March of the Devil," where the devil leads the soldier over the frontier. Here we get the most striking clashes of tritones and perfect-fifths. The initial dissonant chord, A–C–E♭–E, which juxtaposes A–E and A–E♭, moves in the third measure to another, D–E–A♭–A, which juxtaposes D–A and D–A♭. These interval conflicts occur prominently as the violin theme gradually gives way to the underlying percussion.

Histoire also paved the way for Stravinsky's imitation and quotation of melodies and styles of earlier composers. Parody techniques permeate most of his works from *Pulcinella* (1919) to *The Rake's Progress* (1951). Baroque concerto grosso instrumentation is suggested in *Pulcinella,* a one-act ballet scored for small orchestra and string quintet concertino as well as soprano, tenor, and bass voices. Omission of clarinets and percussion contributes further to the Baroque sound. Furthermore, parody technique is seen in such Baroque forms and textures as the trio sonata, canzona, and suite, as well as quotation of what Stravinsky assumed to be Pergolesi melodies and bass progressions. Traditional tonal functions are neutralized by accentual and metric reinterpretation, repetition, and addition of foreign harmonies and dissonances, so that the traditional materials are consigned to isolated layers and planes. Baroque sonorities are also prominent in *Symphonies of Wind Instruments* (1920) and other works throughout the period. However, the opera buffa, *Mavra* (1922), with its contrasting episodes, has a wider range of sources based on fusion of Russian Romantic and Italian *bel canto* vocal styles. Melodic, harmonic, and orchestrational techniques of Tchaikovsky have been in evidence since *Pulcinella,* this influence continuing in Stravinsky's subsequent ballets, notably *Le Baiser de la fée* (1928) and *Apollon musagète* (1927–1928).[16]

The *Octet* for winds (1923) marks a significant stage in the development of Stravinsky's Neoclassical style. He now goes beyond mere reference to earlier models, absorbing Baroque and Classical forms thoroughly and creating a new context synthesized with contemporary notions of harmony and voice leading. His stated intention regarding the sonata form was to "build a new music on eighteenth-century classicism using the constructive principles of that classicism."[17] All three movements are pervaded by Baroque and Classical forms and procedures, as well as metric and rhythmic devices revealing the influence of jazz. There is an increased concern for more rigid architectural plans, stark separation of timbres by means of a highly contrapuntal and exclusive use of wind instruments (flute, clarinet, two bassoons, two trumpets, two trombones), terraced dynamics, and sudden tonal shifts, all of which contribute to a distinction of the sectional blocks.[18] The sonata-allegro form of Movement I (entitled "Sinfonia") is preceded by a slow introduction, which suggests a tutti-concertino juxtaposition often

[16] For discussion of this influence, see Claudio Spies, "Influence of Russian Composers on Stravinsky," *Stravinsky Retrospectives,* n.4, above, pp. 76–140. See also Lawrence Morton, "Stravinsky and Tchaikovsky: Le Baiser de la fée," *Stravinsky, a New Appraisal of His Work,* ed. Paul Henry Lang (New York: W. W. Norton & Company, 1963), pp. 47–60.

[17] Igor Stravinsky and Robert Craft, *Conversations with Igor Stravinsky* (London: Faber and Faber, 1959; rep. Berkeley: University of California Press, 1980), p. 21. See also Joseph Straus, "Sonata Form in Stravinsky," *Stravinsky Retrospectives,* ibid., pp. 141–161, in which he analyzes the *Sonata for Two Pianos,* the *Symphony in C,* and the *Octet,* with a view to their relatedness to the past.

[18] For a study of hierarchical, but nonfunctional tonal relations based on the principle of "collectional and noncollectional tones," see Ethan Haimo, "Problems of Hierarchy in Stravinsky's Octet," *Stravinsky Retrospectives,* n.4, above, pp. 36–53.

characteristic of the eighteenth-century Italian sinfonia (overture). Movement II ("Tema con Variazione") is a set of D-minor variations, in which the first variation serves as a reprise typical of the instrumental works of Rameau and Couperin, while the last variation is a "Fugato." The Finale, in the form of a rondo with coda, opens in two-part counterpoint between the two bassoons in the style of the two-part inventions of Bach. These ostinato layers are reinterpreted contrapuntally in relation to each other and in connection to the barline. Layers are then added in the style of Bachian contrapuntal accumulation. The resulting syncopations as well as new thematic material in the B section (No. 61, m. 3) reveal the influence of jazz.

Other instrumental works of the 1920s continue this trend toward the establishment of an abstracted, nonfunctional tonality within the framework of reinterpreted, closed traditional forms and procedures. These include the three-movement *Concerto for Piano and Winds* (1924), with its toccata-like spun-out thematic material, the three-movement *Sonata for Piano* (1924), with its Bachian linear counterpoint (reminiscent of two-part inventions in Movement III) and a more classically defined melodic and harmonic style in Movement II, and the four-movement *Sérénade en La* (1925), which includes titled movements (Hymn, Romanza, Rondoletto, and Cadenza Finale) framed by the tonality of A. To this group of works belong the *Four Etudes* for orchestra (1928–1930) and the *Cappriccio* for piano and orchestra (1929), in which the earlier percussive style is tempered by a more Tchaikovskian lyricism. Also, many new piano works of the 1920s, written for his own concerts, reveal a more limited technical capacity.

TOWARD GREATER AUSTERITY AND OBJECTIVITY

The basic aesthetic trend of Stravinsky's works from the late 1920s through the late 1940s was toward increasing austerity and objectivity as manifested in more mechanical rhythms, sparsity of textures, and a concern for more rigidly mathematical, architectural formal constructions. This trend was first evident in *Oedipus Rex* (1927), an opera-oratorio in two acts (based on the Sophocles play) by Stravinsky and Cocteau. Scored for narrator, male chorus, soloists, and orchestra, a sense of total abstraction is produced by the archaic sound of the Latin language (rather than the original Greek), interpolated vernacular narrations that articulate the formal blocks, use of masks for the characters, sparse action, and contrasting styles ranging from Italian operatic lyricism to recurrent ritualistic rhythmic ostinati.

The *Symphony of Psalms* (1930) is the true precursor of the *Mass* (1948), which is the most austere of his Neoclassical works. Stravinsky has pointed to his more objective and abstract approach to the text of *Psalms:* "Apparently people have lost all capacity to treat the Holy Scriptures otherwise than from the point of view of ethnography, history, and picturesqueness. . . . Music has an entity of its own apart from anything that it may suggest to them. . . . When people have learned to love music for itself . . . their enjoyment will be of a far higher and more potent order."[19] The archaic Latin texts of the three psalms from the *Vulgate* (ancient Latin Bible) contribute to this quality of distance and emotional detachment. Reduction of emotion is supported by Stravinsky's more austere vocal and instrumental scoring: children's voices are preferred in place of sopranos and altos; and the larger orchestral forces of the early ballets are reduced by omission of the clarinets, violins, and violas.[20] The ritualistic quality is enhanced by the addition of harp and two pianos.

The rigid framework of borrowed Baroque and Classical forms, within which a limited number of mechanical ostinati and ornamental figurations unfold, also represents a stylistic restraint imposed by the discipline of the sacred texts. Such impersonal formulas of distant eras are entirely suitable to the austere and solemn mood. Furthermore, the design of each movement serves to enhance the meaning of each set of psalm verses. The text of Movement I (Psalm XXXVIII, Verses 13 and 14; or Psalm 39, Verses 12 and 13 in the King James version), in which man pleads with God to hear his prayer, is set appropriately as an insistent choral chant that unfolds simultaneously against the toccata style of the instrumental configurations. The overall form of the movement, determined by the accumulation of voices in a large binary form, reflects the gradual intensification of the vocal incantation. The second half, which begins at line 2 of Verse 13 (No. 9), is marked by the last abrupt return of the opening E-minor chord, after which the voices begin their accumulation. First, the tenors are overlapped by the sopranos, both voices momentarily dropping out as the altos and basses enter. Then, all the voices widen together in range. In connection to the words of Verse 14, "Remitte mihi, ut refrigerer priusque abeam, et amplius non ero" ("O spare me, that I may recover strength, before I go hence, and be no more"), the sopranos and basses briefly drop out (No. 12, mm. 4–5) only to recover strength as the full complement of voices move toward the final cadence inexorably. The overall cumulative form of the voices is outlined in connection with the verses (Ex. 10–2). The toccata serves, in turn, as a prelude to the double fugue of Movement II, which supports man's testimony to faith (Psalm XXXIX, Verses 2, 3, and 4; Psalm 40, Verses 1, 2, and 3 in the King James version).[21] The text of Movement III (Psalm CL, complete; Psalm 150 in the King James version), based on praise of the Lord, is set in Stravinsky's most impersonal style, the stuttering figurations and rhythmic ostinati preventing any expression of sentimentality.

[19] Igor Stravinsky, *Autobiography* (New York: Simon and Schuster, Inc., 1936; W. W. Norton & Company, Inc. 1962), pp. 162–163.

[20] This appears to be in keeping with the dictates of the 1903 *Motu Proprio* of Pope Pius X based on reaction of the Vatican to earlier Romantic concert settings of the sacred texts.

[21] One of the rhetorical symbolic meanings of "fugue" in the *Affektenlehre* of the eighteenth century, as suggested by Matheson, is "companionship."

EXAMPLE 10–2. Stravinsky, *Symphony of Psalms*, Mov. I, overall cumulative form of voices

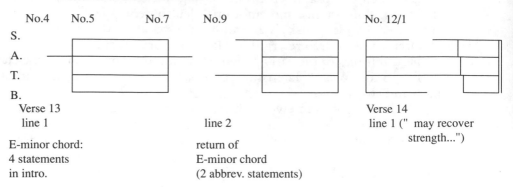

The work is made up of a series of mosaic textural and rhythmic blocks, each of which is a distinct, closed form defined by means of its own internal set of constructive principles. These forms and their relation to the larger scheme of blocks contribute to one of Stravinsky's most mathematical and rigid architectural designs. The four-measure block at the first choral entry (No. 5, mm. 1–4), based on the first polarity between vocal and instrumental planes, is defined by the metric contradiction between these two planes and their relation to the explicit barring (Ex. 10–3). Against the 4/4 barring of the first three measures and 3/4 of the fourth, which gives us 15/4 altogether, the descending octatonic line of broken thirds in the winds unfolds in an implied meter of 4 + 5 + 6/4, also adding up to 15/4. While this expanding arithmetic progression departs from the barline at the beginning of the third measure, it returns to the final barline to close the block. At the same time, the diatonic or ambiguously octatonic dominant-7th (G–B–D–F) of the chorus (excluding altos) unfolds in an implied meter of 3 + 3 + 3 + 3 + 3/4, which again gives us 15/4. This regular pattern, which conflicts with both the octatonic instrumental meter and the explicit barline from which it departs in the first measure, once again converges at the final barline with the instrumental plane to close the block. This polymetric scheme serves a dual function: it contributes to the polarity between vocal and instrumental planes and is the sole formal determinant of this block.

Perhaps more than in any preceding work of Stravinsky's Neoclassical period, principles of Classical balance and proportion in *Psalms* serve a rigidly architectural function that seems to acquire a symbolic religious significance. A dual structural role is served by these principles as the perfect temporal symmetry of each block is absorbed into an expanding, cumulative form. Such fusion of principles is linked to the meaning of the text. The general trend of the three movements from Man, to Man-God connection, to God (i.e., from man's prayer in the toccata of Movement I, through his testimony to faith and God's companionship in the double fugue of Movement II, to final praise and fusion of Man and God in the more defined

EXAMPLE 10–3. Stravinsky, *Symphony of Psalms,* Mov. I, No. 5, mm. 1–4, first choral entry, polymetric contradiction between vocal and instrumental planes

rondo-like, free sonata–allegro formal construction of Movement III) is established at the outset.[22]

---

[22] See Wilfrid Mellers' discussion of the Man-God polarity, in "1930: Symphony of Psalms," *Tempo* 97 (1971): 19–27.

Prayer is introduced by an orchestral introduction, which gradually expands and intensifies around the framework of the first four statements of an E-minor chord. The seeming irregularity of these metric placements is purely illusory, however, since the actual distances between the chordal statements expand proportionally according to a mathematically balanced formula (Ex. 10–4). Between the first two chordal statements, we have a temporal span of exactly six quarter beats, in which the sixteenth-note arpeggiations and quarter rest are partitioned into $3 + 2 + 1/4 (= 6)$. Between the second and third chordal statements, we again have a span of six beats, in which the ascending and descending arpeggiations now produce a $3 + 3/4$ $(= 6)$ partitioning. Thus far, we have twelve beats divided by an intervening chordal statement into two six-beat groupings. Between the third and fourth chordal statements, we have a temporal expansion of the basic six-beat grouping. A six-beat arpeggiation is followed by an ascending E♭-major scale of four beats, this time without an intervening chordal statement, so we get an expanded grouping of $6 + 4/4 (= 10)$. The larger groupings of $12 (6 + 6)$ and $10 (6 + 4)$, which suggest both expansion and contraction ambiguously depending on whether one is comparing the smaller $(6, 6, 6 + 4)$ or larger units $(12, 10)$, are balanced symmetrically by the remaining groups that lead to the alto entry (No. 4). Following the fourth chordal statement (No. 1, m. 6), diatonic (E-Phrygian) arpeggiations unfold for ten beats, this time forming a complete unit in contrast to the preceding $6 + 4/4$ partitioning. This is followed (at No. 2, mm. 6ff.) by a shift to octatonic arpeggiations consisting of twelve uninterrupted beats. (We may consider the alto entry on E, at No. 4, as a substitution for the articulative structural function of the E-minor chordal interjections, the vocal E serving as a final interruption of the proportional introductory scheme.) In effect, while the larger groupings form a closed symmetrical structure of 12, 10, 10, and 12 quarter-note partitions simultaneously, the local distances expand $(6, 6, 6 + 4, 10,$ and $12)$. Thus, we

EXAMPLE 10–4. Stravinksy, *Symphony of Psalms,* Mov. I, proportional formal scheme of instrumental introduction (to No. 4)

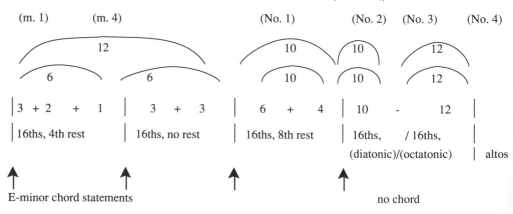

are provided with a balanced yet expanding framework, which contributes to the rigid architectural concept. This framework also initiates the overall cumulative structure, in connection to the relentless prayer.[23]

The dramatic polarity between Man and God appears to be supported by the basic scheme of keys. According to Mellers, Stravinsky adheres to a strict plan, in which "the key of E♭—whose humanistic associations extend from the compassion of Bach and Mozart to the heroism and power of Beethoven—emerges as Man's key, while C, the 'white note' key in the major and E♭'s relative in the minor, becomes God's key. . . . Between the two poles stands a Phrygian E minor as the key of prayer and intercession." The motion from the E-Phrygian prayer key to G major (the dominant of C) at the end of Movement I prepares us for the move to "God's key" in the instrumental fugue that opens Movement II. The shift from E to G has been prepared in the initial E-minor chord already, where the third degree (G) is doubled prominently in the orchestration. The second (choral) fugue in Movement II is in Man's key of E♭, opposed contrapuntally by the continuation of the first fugue. At the opening of Movement I, the three tonal areas are represented by the E-minor chord and dominant-7ths of E♭ and C. The three areas (C, E♭, and E) are joined in the E♭-major and C-major harmonies of the chorus and instruments at the opening of Movement III, and absorbed into the C–minor/C–major superstructure in the final measures.

We may extend Mellers' idea of musico-dramatic polarity to a larger set of interactions between diatonic and octatonic spheres, which are usually separated between vocal and instrumental planes, respectively. Diatonic (nonsymmetrical) partitions of the octatonic scale are basic to this polarity and to the general pitch-set interactions of the work.[24] Although Stravinsky became opposed to the folk-music orientation after he composed *Les noces,* his exploitation of traditional modal (diatonic) properties in the diatonic-octatonic context of the *Symphony* is related closely to procedures (the use of invariant segments as a means of progression between divergent pitch-sets) in the music of many other posttonal composers. The upper winds at No. 5f. of the first movement unfold a descending octatonic scale (A♭–G–F–E–D–C♯–B–B♭) in alternating minor thirds in juxtaposition to the pleading chorus on the static dominant-7th chord of C (see Ex. 10–3, above). The opening of the movement (mm. 1–4) anticipates the pitch content of this octatonic set with the three basic diatonic tertian constructions: E-minor triad (E–G–B), B♭-dominant-7th (B♭–D–F–A♭), and a first-inversion G-dominant-7th (B–D–F–G). These chords, which are dissociated from any traditional voice-leading concept of harmonic progression, function merely

[23] For analyses of other works that also reveal Stravinksy's increasing concern for proportional ratios on all formal levels, see Jonathan Kramer, "Discontinuity and Proportion in the Music of Stravinsky," *Confronting Stravinsky,* n.1, above, pp. 174–194.

[24] See Elliott Antokoletz, *The Music of Béla Bartók: A Study of Tonality and Progression in Twentieth-Century Music* (Berkeley and Los Angeles: University of California Press, 1984), pp. 319–320.

as local diatonic cellular patches within a larger succession of planes. (The suggested tonics, E♭ and C, of the two respective dominant-7th chords have relevance only as background-level tonal centers.) The total pitch-content of these three diatonic constructions foreshadows that of the octatonic scale exclusively (Ex. 10–5).[25] The three tertian chords together give us seven of the eight octatonic tones, A♭–G–F–E–D–[ ]–B–B♭. This hypothesis is supported by the local unfolding (at No. 5, m. 3, in the bassoons) of both dominant-7ths, G–F–D–B and B♭–A♭–F–D. The strings and chorus, based on the former (G–B–D–F), support the entire passage.

Another diatonic-octatonic link occurs in the introductory passage leading to the alto entry at No. 4. At No. 2, mm. 1–5, the piano unfolds the E-Phrygian mode; the initial two notes of the mode (E–F) then form the basis of the alto chant (Nos. 4–5). The alto E–F shifts (at No. 5f.) to a new semitone, G–A♭ (see Ex. 10–3, above), to give us a four-note symmetrical segment (E–F–G–A♭) of the octatonic scale of the winds. The octatonic reinterpretation of the original Phrygian dyad, E–F, is anticipated at No. 2, mm. 5–6, by the chromatic shift in the pianos from the Phrygian-dyad G–A to the octatonic G–A♭. At No. 9, the octatonic material returns to the E-Phrygian mode, after which the two sets (diatonic and octatonic) alternate throughout the remainder of the movement. Thus, the opening movement establishes special invariant relationships between the separate collectional planes in preparation for their subsequent fusion.

According to Mellers, there is no implication of harmonic movement or modulation in Movement II until No. 4. He states that "since God contains all human experience but doesn't 'progress'—'in my beginning is my end'—

EXAMPLE 10–5. Stravinsky, *Symphony of Psalms,* Mov. I, partitioning of octatonic scale (No. 5) into three diatonic chords (opening)

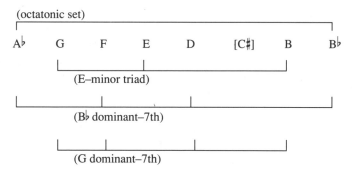

[25] The permutation of the octatonic scale in its 1,2,1,2,1,2,1 interval sequence permits the octatonic partitioning into these diatonic 0–4–7 and 0–4–7–10 constructions, thereby supporting van den Toorn's "Model-A" form of the octatonic scale in the Neoclassical works; see van den Toorn, *The Music of Igor Stravinsky,* n.11, above, pp. 50–51.

his theme doesn't 'progress' either."[26] Nevertheless, the textural buildup of the double fugue and its uniform motion in a slow 4/8, in contrast to the changing meters of Movement I, contribute to the relentless and inevitable sense expressed by the text: "I waited patiently for the Lord . . . [who] set my feet upon a rock, and established my goings. And he hath put a new song in my mouth, even praise unto our God. . . ." (This buildup is reminiscent of Bach's textural approach in many of his sacred choral works.) The polarity between Man and God intensifies in the overlapping of the two distinct fugue subjects in the contrasting instrumental and vocal planes (at No. 5), one subject in God's key (C), the other in Man's (E♭).[27]

This musical paradox between harmonic staticism and textural/ rhythmic intensification is reflected in the structure of the local thematic blocks themselves. The God subject, derived from the alternating thirds in Movement I (at No. 5 and No. 7f.), transforms the latter ostinato by means of octave displacement. This results in the more static, angular character of the encircling melodic line, which precludes any sense of traditional voice-leading functions. Each block is isolated from the others by its own internal means of closure, produced by rhythmic departures and returns to the barline (Ex. 10–6). The main segment of the subject (mm. 1–3 plus the first six-teenth) is based exclusively on intervals 3/9, C–E♭ and B–D, the first at the barline initially, the second at the weak part of the measure. By the rhythmic extension of D and B (m. 2), the metric positions of these two intervals 3/9

EXAMPLE 10–6. Stravinksy, *Symphony of Psalms,* Mov. II, opening fugue subject, rhythmic departures and returns to barline

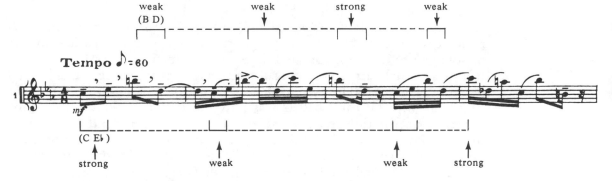

© Copyright 1931 by Edition Russe de Musique; copyright renewed. Copyright and Renewal assigned to Boosey & Hawkes, Inc. Revised edition © Copyright 1948 by Boosey & Hawkes, Inc.; Copyright Renewed. Reprinted by permission.

[26] See Mellers, "1930: Symphony of Psalms," n.22, above, p. 21.
[27] See ibid. for a more detailed discussion of the overall tonal scheme of all the movements.

are reversed (m. 3). Conversely, shortening of the note values brings C back to the barline (m. 4) to close off this portion of the theme.

Despite the tonal staticism of the subject, a sense of continuity results from special pitch-set relations between blocks. The two intervals 3/9 (C–E♭ and B–D), which suggest C minor, may be interpreted more relevantly as a symmetrical octatonic segment, B–C–D–E♭. At m. 4, notes 2–5 of the free part of the subject induce a sudden shift, i.e., without modulatory preparation, to another octatonic segment, A–B♭–C–D♭. This serves as a disconnected anticipation of the answer at the traditional (perfect-fifth) transposition (No. 1), based on another tetrachordal segment of the new octatonic set. The latter tetrachord (F♯–G–A–B♭) expands that of the free part (A–B♭–C–D♭) to suggest the larger octatonic segment, F♯–G–A–B♭–C–D♭. After several alternations between subject (at the tonic) and answer (at the dominant), which together imply two of the three octatonic collections, we get a complete statement of the remaining octatonic collection, E–F–G–A♭–B♭–C♭–D♭–D (at No. 4, m. 2, fl.gr.II), within the more rhythmically active and chromatically mixed episodic material. This octatonic transposition was the primary one of Movement I (No. 3 through No. 5, m. 4), where it was associated with the altos' key of intercession (E-octatonic). Thus, diatonic-octatonic pitch-set interactions are basic to the delineation of the mathematically and architecturally organized blocks and layers, while serving as the primary means of articulating the musico-dramatic polarity of the entire work.

All the forms and procedures that had been developing in Stravinsky's works from the time of World War I became standardized thoroughly in many of the works of the 1930s and 1940s. Classical formal models are absorbed into his own framework in contexts largely divorced from the tonal and harmonic principles basic to the generation of the traditional structural models. The *Violin Concerto in D* (1931), with its external traditional references to the toccata, aria, and capriccio, as well as the concerto principle of solo and tutti alternations within each movement, moves farther away from traditional harmonic (vertical) concepts in many passages than in any previous work. Stravinsky's tendency toward strong linear counterpoint beginning with his early ballets was now manifested in the most extreme example of separation and dissociation of layered textures and block structures.[28] However, we find a diversity of polyphonic and homophonic approaches that span the styles of many eras within the framework of the traditional structural models—in *Perséphone* (1933), a melodrama in three scenes with dance and narrative text-setting of a poem by André Gide (based on the *Homeric Hymn to Demeter*), *Concerto for Two Solo Pianos,* without orchestra (1935), *Jeu de cartes,* a ballet in three deals (1936), *Concerto in E♭,* "Dumbarton Oaks," in three movements for chamber orchestra (inspired by

---

[28] See Lynne Rogers, "Stravinsky's Alternative Approach to Counterpoint," Ph.D. dissertation, Princeton University, 1989.

Bach's *Brandenburg Concerti*) (1937–1938), *Symphony in C* (1940), of which the first two movements were written in Europe, the last two after his move to the United States, *Symphony in Three Movements* (1942–1945), *Ebony Concerto* (1946), written for Woody Herman and his band, *Concerto in D* (1946), in the style of a concerto grosso for strings, the ballet *Orpheus* (1948), inspired by Monteverdi, and other smaller works of the period. The *Mass,* for boys' and men's voices, winds, and brass (1948), and the number opera *The Rake's Progress* (1951) are culminating points for Stravinsky's Neoclassicism, the former in terms of its austerity and architectural balance, the latter in terms of its absorption and juxtaposition of the many traditional styles and forms appearing in his works beginning in 1918.

SUGGESTED READINGS

ETHAN HAIMO AND PAUL JOHNSON.   ed., *Stravinsky Retrospectives* (Lincoln and London: University of Nebraska Press, 1987), including: Ethan Haimo, "Problems of Hierarchy in Stravinsky's Octet," pp. 36–53; Paul Johnson, "Cross-Collectional Techniques of Structure in Stravinsky's Centric Music," pp. 55–75; Claudio Spies, "Influence of Russian Composers on Stravinsky," pp. 76–140; Joseph Straus, "Sonata Form in Stravinsky," pp. 141–161; Richard Taruskin, "Stravinsky's 'Rejoicing Discovery' and What It Meant: In Defense of His Notorious Text Setting," pp. 162–199.

WILFRID MELLERS.   "1930: Symphony of Psalms," *Tempo* 97 (1971): 19–27.

LAWRENCE MORTON.   "Stravinsky and Tchaikovsky: Le Baiser de la fée," *Stravinsky, a New Appraisal of His Work,* ed. Paul Henry Lang (New York: W. W. Norton & Company, 1963), pp. 47–60.

JANN PASLER.   ed., *Confronting Stravinsky, Man, Musician, and Modernist* (Berkeley and Los Angeles: University of California Press, 1986), including: Jonathan Kramer. "Discontinuity and Proportion in the Music of Stravinsky," pp. 174–194; Richard Taruskin. "From Subject to Style: Stravinsky and the Painters," pp. 16–38.

LYNNE ROGERS.   "Stravinsky's Alternative Approach to Counterpoint," Ph.D. dissertation, Princeton University, 1989.

IGOR STRAVINSKY.   *Autobiography* (New York: Simon and Schuster, Inc., 1936; W. W. Norton & Company, Inc., 1962).

———AND ROBERT CRAFT.   *Conversations with Igor Stravinsky* (London: Faber and Faber, 1959; rep. Berkeley and Los Angeles: University of California Press, 1980).

———.   *Dialogues* (Berkeley and Los Angeles: University of California Press, 1983).

———.   *Expositions and Developments* (London: Faber and Faber, 1962; rep. Berkeley and Los Angeles: University of California Press, 1981).

———.   *Memories and Commentaries* (Berkeley and Los Angeles: University of California Press, 1981).

———.   *Themes and Episodes* (New York: Alfred A. Knopf, 1966, 2/1967).

PIETER C. VAN DEN TOORN.   *The Music of Igor Stravinsky* (New Haven and London: Yale University Press, 1983), pp. 178–371 (on the Neoclassical works).

Neotonality and *Gebrauchsmusik* in Germany

SOCIO-CULTURAL CONDITIONS IN GERMANY AFTER WORLD WAR I

Despite Germany's political instability, mass unemployment, and ravaging inflation after World War I, governmental sources provided support for the reestablishment and development of cultural institutions throughout Germany. Opera and concert halls as well as new schools in all the arts began to flourish, with Berlin as a major international center. In connection to the strong postwar proletarian movement, German composers began to reveal, as did composers in France, an interest in creating more accessible musical idioms that would draw the composer and general public closer together. This attitude was already evident in the early 1920s in the artistic festivals held in various German cities.

During this period, conflicting conservative and progressive tendencies ran concurrently in both the political and artistic spheres. In music, a more conservative post-Romantic expression was continued in Germany by Richard Strauss most notably, who had retreated from the ultrachromaticism and extreme emotional intensity of *Elektra* in *Der Rosenkavalier* (1909–1910) and *Ariadne auf Naxos* (1911–1912). At the same time, many German artists and writers, in reaction to the intense emotional aesthetics and psychological attitudes of the Expressionists, established a movement known as the *neue Sachlichkeit,* or "New Objectivity," which advocated a return to simplicity, austerity, and a directness of expression devoid of the superfluous elaborations that had been acquired in the arts throughout the preceding eras. One of the most dynamic proponents of the *neue Sachlichkeit* was the German painter and caricaturist George Grosz, who opposed the Expressionists and also satirized bourgeois society through his drawings based on proletarian themes.

In 1919, these new aesthetic interests emerged with the founding of the *Bauhaus* in Weimar, a school of design and architecture where instruction in the pure arts was joined with the study of crafts. Walter Gropius, one of the leaders of modern *functional architecture,* served as the school's first Director, the artistic faculty of the school including Paul Klee, Lyonel Feininger, Vasily Kandinsky, László Moholy-Nagy, and Marcel Lajos Breuer. The curriculum, which emphasized practical craftsmanship and an understanding of the problems of mechanical mass production, was to have wide international artistic and aesthetic consequences well into our own era.

By the late 1920s, Paul Hindemith (1895–1963), Carl Orff (1895–1982), Ernst Pepping (1901–1981), Kurt Weill (1900–1950), and others were to espouse the artistic principles of the *neue Sachlichkeit,* as they directed their music towards a mass audience. All the principles of a popular, accessible Neoclassical style are perhaps most concisely represented in the works of

284

Orff. In Munich in 1924, he became familiar with the Dalcroze method of eurhythmics and turned to a study of the relationship between music and bodily movement, with an interest in the application of these studies toward educational goals. This was formulated eventually in his graded studies in five basic collections entitled *Music for Children* (1950–1954), based on accessible materials in the form of folk songs and dance tunes as well as group improvisation. Orff's musical methods for school use were already known by the early 1930s, but school activities were soon curtailed with the rise of Hitler. His first popular success came in 1937, with his *Carmina Burana,* based on medieval Latin lyrics. Here, we find a fusion of all of Orff's stylistic principles in an accessible theatre music based on techniques that appear to be influenced most directly by the French Neoclassicists, Stravinsky especially. This choral-orchestral work, with its extensive use of percussion and colorful instrumentation, is set within a series of formal block juxtapositions based on static ostinato patterns, choral chanting, and simple triadic harmonic contexts based on nonfunctional tonality. This style, seen in Stravinsky's *Les noces* and *Oedipus Rex,* was to have considerable influence inside and outside Germany during the interwar period. Orff's compositions through the post–World War II period continued along the stylistic lines established in *Carmina.* These include *Der Mond* (1939), *Catulli carmina* (1943), *Die Kluge* (1943), *Die Bernauerin* (1947), and *Antigone* (1949). In 1948, he also began to adapt his ideas for radio broadcasting of children's programs. The style of Orff and the French Neoclassicists was to continue in Germany in the popular but somewhat more complex and developmental theatre works of Werner Egk (1901–1983).

HINDEMITH: EXPRESSIONISTIC CHROMATICISM TO *GEBRAUCHSMUSIK*

The term *Gebrauchsmusik* ("music for use" by school children or other amateurs, or "functional music" for social occasions) emerged in the mid-1920s, although Hindemith himself preferred *Sing-und-Spielmusik* for his works composed for amateurs. Hindemith's own stylistic development may be traced from his early experimental attitude beginning in 1918 to the more objective and accessible aesthetics of the late 1920s. His works from the early 1930s on also began to reveal his political and social concerns, and he moved toward a neotonal style in traditional forms and genres as well. Much later, he moved to a dissonant harmonic idiom and became reconciled with the twelve-tone system to some degree.

Hindemith's first important works following World War I tended toward an intensely contrapuntal, almost expressionistic chromaticism that was similar to Schoenberg's; a style that appears to have its reference in the Romantic idiom of Brahms and Reger. The various *Sonatas* for string instruments which comprise Op. 11 and Op. 25 (1917 to 1922), four *String Quartets* (1919–1923), several one-act dramatic works (1919–1922), the intense tragic opera *Cardillac* (1926), the song cycles *Die junge Magd* (1922) and *Das Marien-*

leben (first version, 1922–1923), and the seven *Kammermusik* (1922–1927), mostly comprised of chamber concertos for various instrumental combinations, are pervaded by pungent harmonic dissonance and melodic angularity as well as constantly shifting and ambiguous tonality. The expressionistic elements of these works are intermingled with influences of Stravinsky and Milhaud in *Kammermusik No. 1* as well as in the witty *Suite '1922'* for piano (1922), also imbued with jazz and popular music. Certain movements of the *Third Quartet* reveal the influence of Bartók, while others are reminiscent of the Baroque.

The *Kleine Kammermusik,* Op. 24/2 (1922), a "Quintet for Wind Instruments" (flute/piccolo, oboe, clarinet in B♭, horn in F, and bassoon) in five movements, is striking for its fusing of characteristics from the chromatic Expressionistic period with that of the more objective, impersonal Neoclassical period of the 1930s. The intense chromatic counterpoint is joined with a lucid thematic, instrumental fabric within a formalized and balanced structural framework. His choice of clearly differentiated wind timbres, as opposed to the sensual blending of string instruments, contributes further to the Classical distinction of figurations, motifs, contrapuntal layers, and general formal shape. These features and the occasional witticisms, which hark back to the eighteenth-century divertimento style, suggest some kinship to the Neoclassical aesthetics of Hindemith's French contemporaries as well. Hindemith's dedication of the work to the Wind Chamber Music Society of Frankfurt foreshadows his move toward *Gebrauchsmusik* in that it is written for a special organization or purpose.

Each movement is devoted to distinctive, spun-out motifs or figures, which lend themselves to contrapuntal fluidity, development, and transformation, as well as Classical structural formulization. Movement I (marked "Playful, moderately fast") is balanced on all structural levels. On the highest architectural level, areas thematically defined contribute to the articulation of the overall ABA-Coda plan.[1] On lower levels, antecedent and consequent phrases and periods are built from paired members symmetrically, contrasting in contour and tonality. Phrase 1 (mm. 1–2) is comprised of two contrasting motifs (a and b), the first a repeated figure and the second an arpeggiation, while the larger phrase segments (1a and 1b) are contrasted by their descending and ascending contours (Ex. 11–1). Rapid multitonal shifts contribute to the symmetry of these phrase segments. Each measure of the clarinet theme suggests two distinct diatonic tonalities, the succession of which results in a multitonal chromatic scheme: phrase 1a moves from a D-major to G♭-major triadic outline, phrase 1b from F-major to an ambiguous E-minor or G-major. While the whole-tone harmonies (C–E–D, B–E♭–A, B♭–D–A♭, A–C♯–E♭, etc.) provide sonic unity within this multitonal scheme, the

---

[1] Movement I form: A (mm. 1–23)—theme a_1 (mm. 1–17), theme a_2 or transition (mm. 18–23); B (mm. 24–48)—theme b_1 (mm. 24–31), theme b_2 (mm. 32–36), theme b_1 (mm. 37–46), theme b_2 (mm. 47–48); A (mm. 48–63); Coda (mm. 64–end), based on alternations of themes a and b.

EXAMPLE 11–1. Hindemith, *Quintet for Wind Instruments,* Op. 24/2, Mov. I, opening two pairs of phrases, multitonal chromatic scheme

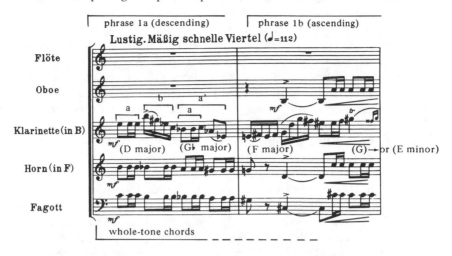

bass is partitioned into two contrasting figurations, which support the phrase-1a and -1b contours, respectively. The chromatic bass descent is interrupted by a static C♯ that leaps an octave in the opposite direction. These two measures are contrasted further by the added oboe layer, which reinforces the cadence of phrase 1b. Thus, within the first phrase, balance and contrast are established by the collaboration of numerous factors that suggest both traditional and contemporary techniques.

While the second pair of phrase segments (mm. 3–4 and 5–6) seems to balance the first pair, it expands the latter proportionally by doubling the length of 1a and 1b. Phrase 2a is based on a sequential expansion of motifs a and a′ exclusively, while phrase 2b expands motif b by bringing its earlier ascending and descending forms into proximity to produce the registral peak of the theme. The cadence of this first period (mm. 5–6), articulated by the contrapuntal joining of motifs a and b, is part of a larger phrasal closure, its descending contour balancing the ascending one of phrase 1b (m. 2).

Proportional expansion and structural balance are demonstrated in more complex ways in the second period as part of a larger building process (mm. 7–17). Phrases 1a and 1b of the theme (now in the oboe) are a literal repeat of the first two measures. However, the accompanying ostinato figurations, derived from motifs a and b, are added as a mechanical basis for the more active counterpoint, the anticipation of these motivic forms at the preceding cadence tending to elide both periods to form a larger coherent structural unit. Phrase 2 (mm. 9–12) again doubles the length of phrase 1 (mm. 7–8) by modifying phrase 1b through repetition and sequential expansion. A fuller texture unfolds over an extended form of the original chromatic bass descent (mm. 13–17), which together with the broadly arched lines, contribute to a greater sense of continuity than do the additive block structures of *Les Six* and Stravinsky. The soaring linear contours reach a textural and registral peak at m. 14 and then diminish to the cadence of this period (m. 17) analogous to the smaller peak at the first cadence (mm. 5–6).

The interplay of instrumental timbres also contributes to the overall shape. An arch-like thematic-instrumental pattern has thus far unfolded in a sequence of rising timbres. The clarinet has the first thematic statement (mm. 1–6), the oboe the second (mm. 7–12), and the flute the third (mm. 13–16), with a rounding out of the arch by a return to the clarinet (mm. 16–17). Each timbre is permitted maximal distinction at its thematic entry by means of its absence or unobtrusive accompanimental status in the preceding passages; for example, the oboe appears only as a brief accompanimental segment prior to m. 7, while the flute does not appear until m. 13.

The closing period (mm. 18–22) rounds out the arch shape of Section A by returning to the two-plus-four-measure phrases of the opening, extending the original sequence of phrase 1b downward as well as omitting the wide cadential flourish of m. 5. This thematic statement completes a long-range tonal projection of the first whole-tone chord (C–D–E) of the movement: clarinet entry on D (period 1, m. 1), oboe entry on E (period 2, m. 7), and flute entry on C (period 3, m. 18). This whole-tone projection is then supported locally in the descending cadential passage of the flute and oboe (Ex. 11–2). Here, the whole-tone form of motif a (from the clarinet in m. 3) is isolated and presented sequentially in minor-third transpositions in the flute, so segments of both complete whole-tone scales (F♯–E–D/C–B♭–A♭ and D♯–C♯–B/A–G–F) are unfolded alternately. A mutation occurs in the sequence (at m. 22), thereby permitting cadential reiterations of the basic C–D–E segment in the flute. The oboe motif (F♯–E–D) extends the whole-tone content of this basic form, so both instruments together give us a larger whole-tone tetrachordal segment, C–D–E–F♯.

Wider structural relations are anticipated in this closing passage. The accompanying oboe figure (mm. 20–21) supports the whole-tone segments

EXAMPLE 11–2. Hindemith, *Quintet for Wind Instruments*, Op. 24/2, Mov. I, mm. 20–23, flute and oboe, alternate unfolding of complementary whole-tone segments

by articulating each long note of the flute harmonically at the minor-seventh below (or whole-step above). At the same time, the minor-third succession of these vertical whole-tone dyads, E–D/C♯–B/B♭–A♭/G–F, implies a complete octatonic collection. At the corresponding point in the return phase of the symmetrical ABA form (m. 48), Section A is reintroduced by an octatonic scale (F♯–G♯–A–B–C–D–E♭–[ ]). While this octatonic transposition on F♯ differs from the earlier one in the flute and oboe (at mm. 20ff.), it was already suggested there in the chords of the lower winds, C–F♯–E♭ and F♯–G–E (i.e., octatonic segment C–[ ]–E♭–E–F♯–G–[ ]–[ ]). The sustained octatonic F♯ in the bassoon (m. 48), the tritone transposition of the opening bassoon C (m. 1), foreshadows Hindemith's characteristic use of tritone recapitulations in his later works. This long-range tonal relation of the tritone, an important property of both the octatonic and whole-tone collections, is reflected on all levels of the closing period (mm. 20ff.): in the registral boundary of the entire passage (between bassoon and flute), in the bassoon ostinato itself, and in the combined flute and oboe cadential whole-tone tetrachord (C–D–E–F♯).

Several elements link the closing period with the contrasting middle section (mm. 24–48). While the sharply defined rhythm of motif a moves to the lower winds as an ostinato accompaniment, the more lyrical form of the motif in the oboe is transformed into the flowing triplet theme in the same instrument. Phrase structure and thematic contour are now more mechanically balanced than in the preceding section. Phrase 1a (mm. 24–25) begins with ascending triplets and ends with an ascending dotted rhythm, while phrase 1b (mm. 26–27) inverts the contour of these corresponding figures. At the same time, the developmental process is prevalent. While each of these two phrases is supported by two 4/4 statements of the motif-a ostinato, a change of the explicit meter from 4/4 to 3/4 in the second measure produces a metric reinterpretation between theme and accompaniment. While the structure of the theme corresponds to this irregular metric change, the regular ostinato is "thrown off" from the barline. The metric realignment of theme and accompaniment becomes particularly apparent at the phrasal repeat, or second period (mm. 28–31). The same metric change occurs again in the second measure, so the ostinato becomes yet more removed from the barline. The contrast of the two theme-b statements is heightened further by the fuller texture, in which the flute doubles the oboe in thirds and the horn adds a sustained D. Overall structural balance and development are fulfilled in the remaining sections of the movement.

The large five-movement plan outlines an arch-form on the highest level. The central slow movement (marked "placid and simple"), with its own internally rounded form of ABA with coda, is flanked by two scherzo-like movements that outline more intricately balanced formal structures, while Movement V mirrors Movement I in its "Very lively" character, ternary ABA-Coda outline as well as in its close thematic associations. Movement II ("Waltz"), which reinforces the light mood of Movement I in rhythm and also the use of piccolo in place of flute, unfolds a series of phrasal pairings in a large symmetrical scheme of AA′BCBA-Coda. This movement, which is a kind of variant of Movement I in terms of motifs, structure, and concluding reference to "Slow" and "Again playful," contributes to the integration of the overall work.

Movement IV warrants special attention in terms of its motivic association to Movement I, and in its mechanically precise and balanced structure, which appears to have its basis in the Baroque ritornello principle. In this scherzo-like movement, we find the most extreme examples of polarity on various levels. Contrast between the repeated-note rhythm of motif a and the wide-ranging arpeggiated contour of motif b is the most essential factor in the distinction between the six ritornello and five solo sections (Rit–A–Rit–B–Rit–C–Rit–D–Rit–E–Rit). Structural proportions and timbral relations contribute more specifically to the perfect symmetrical balance of the movement. The number of measures in each of the ritornello sections forms an overall scheme of 2 + 2 + 1 + 2 + 2 (with codetta in the last two measures). At the same time, the relation of solo sections, while not revealing a similar scheme in the number of measures, does suggest this balance in the figurations. Solo sections A, C, and E are based on duple figurations (sixteenths, then eighths), while corresponding sections B and D in the arch-form are based on triplet figurations. The irregularity in the pattern, produced by augmentation of the sixteenths to eighths in section E (marked "largamente"), appears to correspond simply with the similar slowing down before the return to tempo at the end of each of the preceding movements.

As in the preceding movements, contour and timbre again have structural significance, but here they are more distinctly and mechanically employed. The contours of the solo instruments in corresponding sections of the arch-form contribute to the symmetrical structure. In A the flute ascends and descends, in C the clarinet inverts the latter contour, and in E the horn returns to that of the flute, while in B and D the bassoon and oboe have equally nebulous shapes. Perhaps most strikingly mechanical is the symmetrical organization of the timbres themselves: R1 omits the highest instrument (flute) and R2 the lowest (bassoon), while R3 omits the middle timbre (clarinet); R4 then omits the middle instrument (oboe) between the two upper ones, while R5 omits the middle timbre (horn) between the two lower ones; R6 includes all the instruments, while the codetta suggests a rounding out of the movement by returning to the instrumentation of R1. These successive timbral omissions permit a link to the solo sections, each solo played by the instrument that was omitted in the preceding ritornello. Thus, this *Quintet,* while containing many characteristics of the chromatic, almost expressionistic period to which it belongs, also foreshadows the more objective, highly constructivist techniques of Hindemith's Neoclassical works.

In a lecture given to choral conductors in Berlin in October 1928, Hindemith began to reveal consequential changes in his attitude toward the composer, the performer, and the audience, all of whom he felt should have a closer understanding of the others. These attitudinal changes stemmed from his increasing concern regarding the social significance of art, and his own broad activities as composer, conductor, and performer of many instruments also reflect his socio-musical philosophy. This new attitude had developed in opposition to music based on an individualistic approach geared especially to the elite. Instead, Hindemith became concerned with composition as a craft, in which melodic, harmonic, and contrapuntal materials were clear, simple, and without technical difficulties. These concerns were part of Hindemith's interest in returning to pre-nineteenth-century assumptions, in which the Romantic idea of the "genius composing for posterity and an ideal audience" was unknown. His earlier inclination towards smaller and more distinct chamber-music textures during his chromatic and expressionistic period continued in works now belonging to the new style, which he referred to as *Sing-und-Spielmusik.* The most significant feature of these works was the focus on musical practicality and accessibility to amateurs. His first works of this type in the late 1920s include: *Spielmusik* (1927), for 2 flutes, 2 oboes, and string orchestra; *Zwei Lieder für Singkreise* (1927), for 3 voices; *Schulwerk für Instrumental-Zusammenspiel* (1927), in groups of 9 pieces for 2 violins, 8 canons for 2 violins and violin/viola, 8 pieces for string quartet and double bass, and 5 pieces for string orchestra; and *Sing-und-Spielmusiken für Liebhaber und Musikfreunde* (1928–1929), for various combinations of voices and/or instruments in several volumes.

In combination with these new musical aesthetics and techniques, Hindemith and several other German composers also turned toward socially and politically relevant operatic music subjects designed for the masses, an approach which found support in the German Socialist movement. This conception was evident especially in a new category of works known as *Zeitopern,* that made its first appearance with Ernst Krenek's *Jonny spielt auf* (Jonny Strikes Up the Band; 1925–1926). Krenek stated that he "returned to the tonal idiom, the cantilena of Puccini, seasoning the whole with the condiments of jazz," the opera also including fox trot, tango, and other such popular elements in a lively and sharply dissonant idiom. The libretto, written by the composer, tells the tale of a lawless black American jazz musician in Europe, who plays the saxophone, steals a violin, and makes his way to fame in a bizarre series of scenes, the finale of which places Jonny on a large revolving globe of the world with violin in hand. While the opera brought Krenek success, scandal resulted at the Leipzig première in 1927 and first Munich performance in 1929, where members of the audience equipped themselves with rotten eggs as they were "warned that the work heralded the conquering of the world by the black race through music."[2] Krenek continued to use this style in several one-act operas having similar social relevance, including the tragic *Der Diktator* (1926), based on Mussolini, the fairy tale opera *Das geheime Königreich* (1926–1927), and *Schwergewicht, oder Die Ehre der Nation* (1926–1927), which mocks the idolizing of sports champions. While Krenek's style began to change in the 1930s as he moved into the twelve-tone system, his new works continued in the spirit of political and social protest, which led to censorship by the Nazis.

COLLABORATORS OF BERTOLT BRECHT: SOCIAL PROTEST IN MUSIC

The basic stylistic workings of Krenek's Zeitopern and an inclination toward social protest in the arts were taken up in the late 1920s by Kurt Weill (1900–1950), Hanns Eisler (1898–1962), and Hindemith, all of whom turned to the expressionistic social satires of the German dramatist and poet, Bertolt Brecht (1898–1956). The Weill-Brecht combination, though lasting only three years, was the most prolific of these collaborations and was also the most successful in stirring up public reaction. The early Songspiel, *Mahagonny,* commissioned by Hindemith's new organization, *Deutsche Kammermusik Baden-Baden,* and performed on the same program with Hindemith's *Hin und Zurück* at the Baden-Baden Festival in 1927, represented a violent attack on the exploitation and decay of capitalism. The first major landmark in the Weill-Brecht collaboration was the subsequent operatic result, *Aufstieg und Fall der Stadt Mahagonny* (Rise and Fall of the City of Mahagonny, 1927–1929), which caused a scandal at its first performance in Leipzig in 1930. This public reaction shortly after the onset of the economic depression foreshadowed efforts to ostracize Weill's works from the state-subsidized theatres. In 1928, the Weill-Brecht collaboration resulted in *Die Dreigroschenoper* (Three Penny Opera). The international success of this anti Romantic Zeitoper brought a new song style to the stage, joined with the realistic sounds of the contemporary jazz band that paved the way for a new relationship with the audiences. A new aesthetic concept was firmly established, in which "both the music and the words dug into the anarchy implicit in contemporary world-art to birth a mode of music drama suitable for sociopolitical statement, hardnosed and simple so the workers can get it the first time."[3] Subsequently, in his opera for school children, *Der Jasager* (1930),

---

[2] Ethan Mordden, *Opera in the Twentieth Century: Sacred, Profane, Godot* (New York: Oxford University Press, 1978), p. 144.

[3] Ibid., p. 145.

Weill moved into a more rigidly Neoclassical framework and style, in which some allusion to the early Baroque as well as late eighteenth century begins to appear.

Eisler also contributed to these new socio-musical attitudes by turning against certain modern musical tendencies embodied primarily in the aesthetic and stylistic principles of his teacher, Arnold Schoenberg. After becoming a member of the German Communist Party in 1926, Eisler began to concern himself with the means by which the artist may serve society and, through his articles, choral works, and marching songs, received strong support from Marxist groups throughout Europe. During his years of exile after the advent of Hitler, he devoted a number of works to the overthrow of fascism, eventually becoming an advocate of folk-like music, especially when he later became one of the leading composers of East Germany. Eisler began his friendship with Brecht in 1930, and one of the first results of their artistic collaboration was the *Lehrstück* (didactic work) *Die Massnahme,* in nine numbers for tenor, three speakers, male chorus, chorus, and small brass and percussion orchestra. Stylistically, this oratorio reflects the new interest in reaching the general audience, the text set in a diatonically clear and simple vocal and instrumental framework. Although written for Hindemith's Festival for New Music in Berlin (1930), it was not performed there because of its strong political implications.

These were the musical and social circumstances in which Hindemith's new practical approach to composition emerged. In 1927, Hindemith was appointed Professor of Composition at the Hochschule für Musik in Berlin at the request of Franz Schreker, Hindemith's turn to teaching having contributed directly to the development of the *Gebrauchsmusik* concept. After composing *Neues vom Tage* (1929), a Zeitoper based on a bizarre subject in the jazzy style of Krenek's *Jonny,* he collaborated with Brecht on his didactic *Lehrstück* (1929), which was intended for performance by amateur musicians exclusively. In 1931 he expressed his aims in the preface of his musical play for children, *Wir bauen eine Stadt* (Let's Build a City). These works were to be landmarks in the development of his new approach, in which he was to join the aesthetic, stylistic, and technical principles of Neoclassicism with the musical and social interests embodied in the concept of *Gebrauchsmusik.* What followed during the next several decades was a series of solo and chamber pieces for almost every instrument or combination of instruments, concerti, symphonic works, song cycles, operas, and ballets. All these genres reveal Hindemith's concern for simplification of style, as manifested in his tendency toward clarification of form, thematic structure, counterpoint, instrumental texture, and the development of a new system for establishing tonal priority and harmonic progression. Several best-known works of this period include *Mathis der Maler,* an opera in seven scenes (also arranged as a three-movement symphonic suite) (1934–1935), *Der Schwanendreher,* a concerto for viola and small orchestra inspired by folk songs (1935), *Trauermusik,* an occasional work for viola, violin, cello, and strings, mourning the death of King George V (1936), *Ludus Tonalis* (subtitled "Studies in Counterpoint, Tonal Organization, and Piano Playing"), consisting of twelve fugues and interludes for piano in all the keys (1942), *Symphonic Metamorphoses on Themes of Carl Maria von Weber* (1943), the revised version of the song cycle *Das Marienleben,* for soprano and piano (1936–1948), *Symphony,* in B♭, for concert band (1951), the opera *Die Harmonie der Welt* (1956–1957), on the life of the seventeenth-century astronomer and mathematician, Johannes Kepler, and the many sonatas for various instruments.

HINDEMITH'S NEW THEORETICAL AND COMPOSITIONAL CODIFICATIONS

In the late 1930s, Hindemith began to codify his technical goals in several studies.[4] In keeping with his ideals of clarity, coherence, objectivity, and accessibility, Hindemith devised a hierarchical system of pitch relations that was intended to provide a structural basis analogous to that of traditional tonality in order to remedy what he considered to be confusion and whim in modern music.[5] The new tonal principles, including the harmonic means by which degrees of consonance and dissonance are established within the context of his contemporary musical sonorities, may be described as a system of *extended tonality*. According to this concept, the hierarchical relations of the twelve chromatic tones in his tonal and chordal classifications were to be derived from the degrees of relatedness between the partials and the fundamental tone of the overtone series.[6] As a result, the ranking of the successive partials, showing their gradually decreasing relation to the principal tone, provides an alternative to the distinction between the traditional functions of consonance and dissonance. In traditional tonal music, these functions were determined by the structure and content of the supporting triadic harmony as well as by the given diatonic framework. Hindemith's hierarchical ranking of tonal degrees as well as intervals and their harmonic inversions are outlined in two series (Ex. 11–3).[7]

Series 1, derived from the overtone series, shows the diminishing degree of relatedness between consecutive partials and the principal tone. This scheme serves as the basis for the relationship between tones and chords, for chordal succession, and for the overall tonal organization of a work. It also provides the secondary materials of the system, in which the fundamental unit of musical construction is the interval. The phenomenon of *combination tones,* involuntarily produced when two or more tones are sounded simulta-

---

[4] The first systematic formulation of Hindemith's tonal theory was his *Unterweisung im Tonsatz, i: Theoretischer Teil* (Mainz, 1937, rev. 2/1940); in Eng., *The Craft of Musical Composition, Book I, Theoretical Part,* trans. Arthur Mendel (New York: Associated Music Publishers, Inc., 1942, rev. 2/1948).

[5] Ibid., Hindemith, *The Craft,* p. 2.

[6] The overtone series also served the formulations of several other twentieth-century theorists, notably Henry Cowell, who devised a "rhythm-harmony" system in which interval ratios from the overtone series are translated into rhythmic patterns.

[7] See Hindemith, *The Craft,* n.4, above, pp. 53ff. and 87ff.

EXAMPLE 11–3. Hindemith, *The Craft of Musical Composition,* pp. 53ff. and 87ff., hierarchical ranking of tonal degrees, intervals and their harmonic inversions in two series

Series 1: hierarchy of tonal degrees in relationship to the fundamental, C

C G F A E E♭ A♭ D B♭ D♭ B F♯

Series 2: hierarchy of intervals and their harmonic inversions

C | G C | E C | E♭ C | D C | D♭ C | F♯
| | | | | | | | | | | | |
C | C G | C E | C E♭ | C D | C D♭ | C

neously, is discussed by Hindemith as a determinant in the hierarchical ordering of intervals: "Starting with the octave, as the clearest, unclouded interval, and passing through the fifth (slightly clouded), each interval in succession carries a greater burden than its predecessors; that is to say, the purity and harmonic clarity of the intervals diminish step by step."[8]

This phenomenon is important for understanding the degrees of "strength, hardness, and density" both in the diminishing relation of the intervals to the octave as we move from left to right in Series 2, and between an interval and its harmonic inversion. The priority of one interval over the other in each pair related inversionally depends on the determination of an *interval root,* i.e., the tone of an interval that is reinforced through doubling by the *combination tone.* According to Hindemith, "Harmonic force is strongest in the intervals at the beginning of the series, and diminishes towards the end, while melodic force is distributed in just the opposite order."[9]

The interval, in turn, serves as the basis of chord construction. From the hierarchy of intervals outlined in Series 2, Hindemith derived a chart made up of all possible chords.[10] The triad, which Hindemith assumed to be the simplest, most stable, and delightful phenomenon in music because of its derivation from the first six tones of the overtone series, serves as the point of departure in his hierarchical scheme. Six chordal subgroups are subsumed under two main Groups (A and B). Chords in subgroups I, III, and V of Group A are without tritone and are therefore more stable than chords in subgroups II, IV, and VI of Group B, which include tritone. The six subgroups are then ranked more specifically according to their component intervals and the position of their roots. The first four subgroups move from the most stable to least stable, or dissonant combinations, while the fifth and

---

[8] Ibid., p. 65.

[9] Ibid., p. 88. See p. 87 for this distribution of harmonic and melodic characteristics of the intervals.

[10] Ibid., pp. 100–106, and last fold-out page.

sixth subgroups consist of chords that have several superimposed intervals of the same size and are therefore ambiguous or uncertain. While Hindemith has attempted to apply these principles to the music of other composers, his formulations have generally not found support outside of their application to his own works.

These systematic neotonal formulations of the late 1930s were already evident in *Mathis der Maler,* which may be considered Hindemith's first major political statement to be set within a Neoclassical formal framework. In reaction to the oppressive cultural atmosphere of pre–World War II Germany, Hindemith found the need to turn to musical representation of political and social issues and to explore the role of the artist in society. In November 1934, the Nazi Kulturgemeinde banned most performances of his music because of his openly anti-Nazi views. While the symphonic version of *Mathis* was performed several months earlier in Berlin, the operatic version had to wait four years for its première in Zürich.

Hindemith's own moral concerns and sense of social responsibility as an artist are reflected in his choice of subject for the opera, which centers around the career of the painter Mathias Grünewald during the time of the Reformation and the Peasants' War in Germany. While at work on a fresco at St. Anthony's monastery, Mathis begins to question his mission as artist and becomes convinced that he should take part in the peasants' struggle for freedom. After joining the revolution and turning against his employer, the Cardinal Archbishop of Mainz, Mathis becomes disillusioned by the terroristic behavior of the peasants toward the local nobility. Beset with uncertainty about himself as a man of political action and ideals, he is convinced by the Cardinal that he has been untrue to himself in denying his artistic gifts, and that it is in his studio where he could best serve the cause of the peasants. The three panels of Mathias' *Isenheim* alterpiece, now at the Colmar Museum in Alsace, served as inspiration for the opera and appear as the titles of the symphonic suite's three movements: *Angelic Concert, Entombment,* and *The Temptation of St. Anthony.*

A study of Movement I, inspired by the scene of the Virgin and Child, with angel playing the viola da gamba, reveals the means by which specific details of the new tonality and the more classically oriented style serve to capture the joyful mood and heavenly splendor of its historical subject. While the large orchestral context, soaring melodic contours, and chromatically shifting diatonic segments suggest the melodic and contrapuntal styles of Brahms and Reger as opposed to the reduced textures and mechanically shaped ostinato patterns of the French Neoclassicists, the clear formal planes and figural layers as well as distinct instrumental families point to Hindemith's own approach to the Neoclassical aesthetics. Furthermore, tonal ambiguity on the local level of the long and continuous phrases, a characteristic which harks back to Hindemith's more expressionistic and chromatic works, is now subordinated to a framework of tonally demarcated cadential points within the classical form. Nonfunctional relations of the unambiguous background-level tonalities foreshadow the new tonal principles of Hindemith's subsequent theoretical formulations. The new tonal system permits chromatic tones to be perceived not as elements foreign to a given tonality or diatonic mode, but rather as elements in a hierarchy of relative distances. This concept and the succession of spun-out yet clearly contrasting themes contribute both to the establishment of a rigid Classical formal framework as well as a highly developmental, ongoing process. In a context devoid of traditional tonal functions, rhythmic structure plays an equally important role in producing a sense of directed motion and overall shape.

The movement opens with an introductory section in a ternary (ABA) arch-form.[11] The three sections of the introduction are entirely closed off from one another by their distinct thematic materials, instrumental timbres, rhythmic-metric structures, and keys separated by a tritone (G and D♭). At the same time, the local tonal, harmonic, and rhythmic procedures produce a directed motion that is released only at the appearance of the main G-major theme at the opening of the sonata-allegro exposition. The fundamental tone of the work, established at the outset as an unharmonized G octave in the sustaining winds, is colored by three vertical statements of the G-major tonic triad in the contrasting string timbre. The radiant quality of this most consonant of harmonic constructions (the triad) in Hindemith's chordal system is enhanced further by the predominance of the triadic fifth and octave in the orchestration of these chords. While the three chordal statements round out Section A (mm. 1–8) by their metric departure from and return to the barline, a higher-level tension is produced in the winds. Against the G-major triad, the rising thematic wind segments establish the minor third (B♭) and minor sixth (E♭) as they unfold the G-Aeolian mode. In correspondence to the hierarchical relationships of Hindemith's chordal subgroup I(1) and I(2), this linear progression produces increasingly unstable chords above the sustained G: the major triad is followed in m. 3 by G-minor (G–B♭–[   ]) and first-inversion E♭-major (G–B♭–E♭) triads. This increasing instability is supported by the gradual departure of the linear thematic resolutions from the barline: E♭–D is at the barline (mm. 3–4), B♭–A resolves before the barline (m. 5), and the third thematic phrase begins and ends still farther from the barline (mm. 6 and 7). While the final chord brings us back to the strong beat, the harmony has moved to the less stable cadential fourth chords, G–D–A–E–B and A–E–B–F♯, which belong to the indeterminate type in subgroup V of Hindemith's chord chart. At the same time, the rising linear contour reaches its peak.

An anacrustic trombone theme demarcates the barline to usher in Section B. This medieval cantus firmus, under the inscription "Es sungen drei Engel," appears three times in counterpoint above the weaving lines of the strings, the second statement of the tune of which is expanded timbrally to two pairs of winds, the third statement to all the winds. These three occurrences are basic to the structure of the introduction as they suggest a

---

[11] An objective approach in the construction of the work is perhaps suggested by the pervasive use of the number three for the number of movements, sections, motifs, and harmonic patterns, etc., which may have a symbolic reference in the three Isenheim panels.

numerical analogy to the three chordal statements of Section A and to the overall ternary form. The trombone statement, on the unison D♭, establishes the distant tritone relation of the original key of G, thereby contributing to the tonal polarity of the sectional blocks. This central section also contains its own tonal hierarchy as the entry pitches of the three thematic statements unfold a series of major-third transpositions, on D♭, F, and A. The third thematic entry (at No. 2) is part of a fuller harmonic context, in which the anacrusis is built on the less stable quartal harmony, G–D–A–E–B, the downbeat on a bright-sounding D-major triad, which serves as a local resolution of the chordal tension. The original G tonality is alluded to at the cadence of Section B (No. 2, mm. 7–8), where it serves as the suggested root of the same unstable quartal harmony (G–D–A–E–B); this tonality is supported by the bass motion in vc (D to B), implying a V–I_6 progression in G major.

The return of Section A, which reverses both the instrumentation and the order of entry of the original theme and chord, increases the tension of the entire introduction further. Brought back at the tritone transposition (D♭), the three chords depart from but do not return to the barline. Reestablishment of the downbeat occurs only at the cadential chord of the thematic material in the strings, while tension is maintained in the construction of the two cadential quartal harmonies, D♭–A♭–E♭–B♭–F and E♭–B♭–F–C–G. The combined content of these two chords (D♭–A♭–E♭–B♭–F–C–G) is encompassed by the basic tritone polarity, G–D♭.

The large-scale sonata-allegro plan of the movement contains structural references to the introduction. At the center of the development section (Nos. 16ff.), the medieval theme from the center of the introduction returns in three statements on the same tonalities, in increasingly fuller contrapuntal textures: trombones on D♭ (upbeat to No. 16), the horns on F (upbeat to No. 16, m. 12), and the trumpets on A (downbeat of No. 17). The thematic materials of the exposition and recapitulation seem to refer to the linear, chordal ideas of the corresponding outer sections of the introduction. Theme 1, with its winding contour and accented appoggiaturas over the sustained G tonic and fifth, suggests a transformation of the opening linear material of the introduction. This hypothesis is supported by the successive statements of this main theme (at No. 3, m. 5ff.), which are punctuated by three statements diminished rhythmically of the original three-chord pattern. This juxtaposition of the linear thematic idea and three groups of punctuating chords recurs throughout the movement.

A more detailed study of the musical language and tonal scheme reveals a combination of Hindemith's earlier chromatically ambiguous tonal approach and his later more distinct neotonal formulations.[12] The opening

---

[12] For Hindemith's own diagrammatic representation of the Prelude of *Mathis,* according to melodic analysis, based on degree-progression and step-progression, and harmonic analysis, based on two-voice framework, harmonic fluctuation, degree-progression, and tonality, see *The Craft,* n.4, above, pp. 220–223. The following analysis of Movement I is presented independently from that of the composer.

segment of theme 1 and pedal establish the main key of G major. However, as in the earlier *Quintet,* Op. 24, No. 2, tonal ambiguity results immediately from the rapidly shifting modal-diatonic segments that form the spun-out thematic line (Ex. 11–4). The first accent, on F, which produces tension by departing from the barline, linearly induces a G-Mixolydian inflection. From the first thematic cadence (m. 4), a linear shift to A minor is suggested. However, the cadential-note A is part of a less stable quartal harmony, G–D–A–E–B, still based on the fundamental tone, G. The consequent phrase, while returning to the barline accentually and to G in the thematic line, remains relatively unstable due to fluctuations between the major and minor modal forms on G and the momentary establishment of the C-Lydian mode at the cadence of the first period (No. 3). In the second, extended period, new accentual departures and tonal shifts lead to a transposed thematic statement, which now begins before the barline, in a fuller texture, and on F♯. This initiating tone, in contrast to the first statement on G, appears in a reharmonized context, so that it functions as the fifth degree of B. The successive thematic statements return to the barline in the fullest statement of the second period (at No. 4, m. 4). Here, the initiating tone, A, appears as the fifth of the D-Lydian mode. While tonality and modality within each spun-out phrase tend toward an ambiguous multitonal scheme, tonality is clearly asserted at cadential points.

Thus far, three distinct and closely related tonal areas, G, B, and D, have been articulated within the first-theme group, the triadic outline suggesting the first six partials of the overtone series. The tonalities in the remainder of the exposition move through increasingly distant areas more or

EXAMPLE 11–4. Hindemith, *Mathis der Maler,* Mov. I, exposition, opening segment of theme 1, tonal ambiguity from rapidly shifting modal-diatonic segments

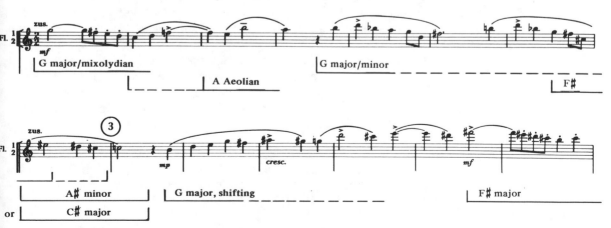

less according to Hindemith's theoretical formulations. The transition (No. 5, m. 10) begins in E major, a major sixth from the G fundamental. After a brief return to G (at No. 6, m. 2), the final cadence on a harmonic inversion of the minor tonic triad of E moves to theme 2 (No. 7). The latter is initiated in D♯-Dorian, a minor sixth from the fundamental G. The final statement of theme 2 (No. 9, mm. 4ff.) appears over an F♯ pedal, suggesting a harmonic reemphasis on the major-seventh degree away from the fundamental G. The tonic, G, returns at the opening of the closing theme (No. 10), once again moving to the third above (B) at the end of the exposition to establish a closely related tonal relationship on a higher level of the sonata form. The development section, which begins with a series of fugatos characteristic of the Neoclassical style, finally arrives at the tritone, D♭, in the medieval trombone theme at the midpoint of the development (No. 16). This most distant key also begins the recapitulation (No. 18), moving back to the tonic in the last part of the movement gradually.

The key scheme as well as the intervallic structure of the linear thematic materials in the revised version of *Das Marienleben* reflect the composer's new tonal formulations more systematically. In the preface of the song cycle, Hindemith presents his mystical interpretations of the relationships in his Series 1.[13] As the vocal lines are simplified in this version by the softening of the dissonant melodic intervals and the relationships between voice and piano, the tonal scheme of the consecutive songs closely follows the Series. The relations stemming from the fundamental tonality of E (Series 1: E–B–A–C♯–G♯–G–C–F♯–D–A♯–F–D♯) correspond to the gradual distancing from the central idea of Christ in the poetic associations: Christ—E; Mary—B; Celestial beings (angels)—A; The inevitable (fixed and unalterable)—C♯; Anything that lies outside of our power of conception—G♯; Idyllic—G; Infinity and the Eternal—C; Acknowledgment of the smallness one feels in the face of the exalted—F♯; Trust and Confidence—D; Everything in the domain of human feelings that at first opposes itself to the believing acceptance of all the wondrous happenings—A♯; Everything that moves us by its mistakenness or short sightedness to regret and pity—F; The greatest purity—D♯.

Thus, Hindemith's move toward greater stylistic and technical accessibility as part of his musical philosophy regarding the relationship between the composer and the community as well as the means by which his own theories and compositional craft could serve his higher artistic ideals are best summarized by his own comments:

> I tried to show at least one method by which the composer, in
> addition to the mere technical practice of his craft, could be the helper
> and even the spiritual leader in a search for a more salubrious musical
> world: it should be his main objective to lift the consumer to a higher

---

[13] Hindemith, *Das Marienleben, Introductory Remarks for the New Version* (New York: Associated Music Publishers, Inc., 1954).

level by convincing him of the harm a constant yearning for entertainment produces; and as a means to this end the writing of suitable music for the amateur was recommended . . . it will be the form in which the desire for replacing external brilliancy with genuine musical values finds its clearest expression . . . the emphasis on moral aspects will now become recognizable also in his works written for the concertizing professional, and now he will talk with a different spirit to the general audience, which, in its basic benevolence, will be ready to accept his leadership towards better goals.[14]

SUGGESTED READINGS

PAUL HINDEMITH. *A Composer's World, Horizons and Limitations* (Cambridge: Harvard University Press, 1952).

———. *Unterweisung im Tonsatz, i: Theoretischer Teil* (Mainz, 1937, rev. 2/1940); in Eng., *The Craft of Musical Composition, Book I, Theoretical Part,* trans. Arthur Mendel (New York: Associated Music Publishers, Inc., 1942, rev. 2/1948).

ETHAN MORDDEN. *Opera in the Twentieth Century: Sacred, Profane, Godot* (New York: Oxford University Press, 1978), pp. 139–148 passim (includes discussions of *Zeitoper*).

DAVID NEUMAYER. *The Music of Paul Hindemith* (New Haven: Yale University Press, 1986).

HANS TISCHLER. "Hindemith's *Ludus Tonalis* and Bach's *Well-Tempered Clavier*—A Comparison," *Music Review* 21 (February 1960): 217–227.

---

[14] Hindemith, *A Composer's World, Horizons and Limitations* (Cambridge: Harvard University Press, 1952), pp. 218–219.

12 The music of Soviet composers

The break in 1917 from certain musical attitudes that prevailed in Tsarist Russia was linked directly to the radical political and social changes that were ushered in by the Bolshevik Revolution. One of the major factors in determining the course of the new Soviet music was the rigorous effort by the revolutionary government under Lenin to establish an official social program in which the arts would play a significant role in the education of the culturally oppressed masses. This interest in identifying music with the people was not a new one to Russia, the "Mighty Five" having already turned in the late-nineteenth century toward folk music as a fundamental source for their own artistic creativity and as a manifestation of the essence of the Russian people. However, the unfavorable political conditions for the preventing of free artistic expression under Tsar Nicholas II were protested in an open letter signed in 1905 by well-known Moscow musicians, including Rachmaninov, Chaliapin, Taneyev, Gretchaninov, and Glière, after the "Blood Sunday" massacre outside the Tsar's Winter Palace in St. Petersburg: "Only free art is vital, only free creativity is joyful. . . . We are not free artists but, like all Russian citizens, the disfranchised victims of today's abnormal social conditions. In our opinion, there is only one solution: Russia must at last embark on a road of basic reforms."[1]

This protest was endorsed subsequently by Rimsky-Korsakov, whose involvement resulted in his dismissal from the Petersburg Conservatory. With the 1917 Revolution, composers felt that these reforms could be realized fully. Lenin was to assert the right for the artist to "create freely" and "independently of everything," but urged that as Communists, "we must not stand with folded hands and let chaos develop as it pleases. We must systematically guide this process and form its result."[2] Lenin's ideal, as embodied in this statement, differed from the Western bourgeois concept of freedom, which he identified as both anarchistic and individualistic. His qualified assertion of the artist's right to creative freedom is essential to understanding Soviet musical developments in the immediate postrevolutionary period (1920s) and in the more restrictive era from the 1930s to the death of Stalin in 1953. Although the Revolution resulted in a break from the varied, individualistic musical ideals of the prerevolutionary period, the new

---

[1] V. Yastrebtsev, *N.A. Rimsky-Korsakov, Vospominania*, L, Vol. 2 (1959–60), pp. 327–328; English translation from Boris Schwartz, *Music and Musical Life in Soviet Russia* (enlarged edition, 1917–1981; Bloomington: Indiana University Press, 1972, 1983), p. 4.

[2] Lenin, *O Kulture i Iskusstve* [About Culture and Art] (Moscow, 1957), pp. 519–520; English translations from James Bakst, *A History of Russian-Soviet Music* (Westport, Connecticut: Dodd, Mead and Company, 1966), p. 275.

generation of Soviet composers, which most significantly included Sergey Prokofiev (1891–1953), Dmitry Shostakovich (1906–1975), Dmitry Kabalevsky (1904–1987), and Aram Khachaturian (1903–1978), were still able to enjoy a degree of freedom during the 1920s as they attempted to cojoin the modernistic idiom with the new Soviet principles.

Diverse Russian musical styles of both a traditional and modernistic bent, with origins in both national and international sources, had characterized Russian music throughout the early part of the century and also had some bearing on the subsequent development of Soviet musical styles. Several early twentieth-century Russian composers represent distinctive positions in the development of these antithetical tendencies. Scriabin, who had died two years before the Revolution, transformed his early Romantic style into a modernistic atonal idiom, whereas Rachmaninov, who left Russia shortly after the Revolution in 1917, remained faithful to the Romantic tradition of the Western-oriented Russians of the nineteenth century. Scriabin, like Rachmaninov, had extensive contact with the Western European musical world through his concert tours beginning in the 1890s, perhaps one of the factors that contributed to his remoteness from the Russian folk sources. Any general Russian influences that might be discerned in Scriabin's music were overshadowed strongly by the international influences of nineteenth-century Romantic composers—Chopin, Liszt, and Wagner especially. In contrast to either the Romantic style of Rachmaninov or the atonally transformed Romanticism of Scriabin, the modernistic idiom of Stravinsky was rooted deeply in his absorption of Russian folk sources, his interest in Russian subjects continuing unabated until the outbreak of the Revolution despite his residence in Switzerland in 1914 as a temporary self-exile from his homeland.[3] With the realization that he would never return to Russia after the Revolution, he turned, after the completion of *Les Noces* (1917), to more universal types of subjects and abandoned his Russian modal forms for a Neoclassically oriented C-scale idiom as he became "acculturated" into the Parisian musical scene.[4] After 1917, Diaghilev and the Russian Ballet also remained in Paris, their musical activities having been international since the first decade of the century.

Like the Russian musicians Koussevitzky and Tcherepnin, Prokofiev also preferred to detach himself from the new Russian political and cultural

[3] According to Richard Taruskin, "From Subject to Style: Stravinsky and the Painters," in *Confronting Stravinsky: Man, Musician, and Modernist,* ed. Jann Pasler (Berkeley and Los Angeles: University of California Press, 1986), pp. 16–17, Stravinsky was "the only Russian composer fully to realize the implications" of the late nineteenth-century Russian "neonationalist" trend, which foreshadowed his transformation of Russian folk sources and their synthesis with elements of Western European art-music.

[4] For discussion of this transformation of the Russian modal "D-scale" source into the primarily "C-scale" idiom of Stravinsky's Neoclassical works, see Pieter C. van den Toorn, *The Music of Igor Stravinsky* (New Haven: Yale University Press, 1983), pp. 48–52.

environment, leaving Russia in 1918 for a time. During his participation in the international musical arena between 1918 and 1933, he developed a personal modernistic style that had been evident in his prewar compositions. However, despite his early innovative approach, which was to remain essentially unchanged throughout his life, Prokofiev had also absorbed pre-revolutionary stylistic and technical features into his modernistic idiom. Both stylistic aspects were fused in what was to become prototypic of the musical principles that emerged under the new Soviet government in the 1920s. A comparison of the changing historical roles of Stravinsky and Prokofiev in the national Russian school of the 1910s and 1920s reveals an inextricable connection of the two composers to the Revolutionary situation. Their positions were ironically reversed with respect to the nationalist and non-nationalist ideologies in the post–World War I period, which accords with Stravinsky's permanent exile and Prokofiev's subsequent return to his home-land.[5] This reversal, in which Stravinsky moved toward an international attitude, Prokofiev toward a national one, is indicative of the effect that the Revolution had on the musical ideologies of Russian composers both at home and abroad from 1917 on. While Stravinsky and Prokofiev have both been categorized as "modernists," early critical views had regarded Stravinsky as a modernist who was "bound to the past" paradoxically, as opposed to the consistent view of Prokofiev as progressive and an innovator.[6]

Under the new Soviet system, Prokofiev moved toward nationalism, but his nontraditionalist stance also fit in with the Revolutionary mood of the 1920s. Ironically, at Prokofiev's earlier meeting with Stravinsky and Diaghilev, the latter two had advocated a modernist position devoid of sentimentalism, pathos, and internationalism, which, according to Prokofiev himself, was to have a bearing on his own change of attitude.[7]

REVOLUTION TO EARLY 1930s: ERA OF EXPERIMENTATION

International political and economic conditions in the 1920s and 1930s had a direct bearing on the course of artistic development. Two general tendencies prevailed internationally during the interwar period. The decade following World War I tended toward political and economic instability and change, the most extreme circumstances leading to fascism and nazism in Italy and Germany and worldwide economic depression in the 1930s. These conditions

---

[5] An evaluation of early critical Russian opinions regarding the positions of the two Russian composers is documented by Malcolm Hamrick Brown, in "Stravinsky and Prokofiev: Sizing Up the Competition," *Confronting Stravinsky: Man, Musician, and Modernist,* see n.3, above, pp. 39ff.

[6] Ibid., p. 43.

[7] See Prokofiev to Myaskovsky, April 10, 1915, in *S.S. Prokofiev i N. Ya. Miaskovsky: Perepiska* [Prokofiev to Myaskovksy: Correspondence], comp. and ed. M. G. Koslova and N. R. Yatsenko (Moscow: Vsehsoyuznoi Izdatel-'stvo "Sovietskii Kompozitor," 1977), p. 133.

were accompanied by experimentation and change in all areas of society during the 1920s as the major political powers made intensive efforts toward technological development and industrialization. In contrast, the 1930s were marked by attempts to stabilize conditions both politically and economically during a period of increasing international tensions. Conditions in the Soviet Union during these decades corresponded with these international trends. The first decade was characterized by continual economic experimentation in the efforts to move toward a communist ideal. During the first several years (1918–1921) after the Revolution, Soviet Russia was devastated by civil war, foreign intervention, changes in its geographic boundaries, and the establishment of a "quarantine belt" to separate Communist Russia from the rest of Europe. Political disagreement within the Communist Party and the failure of the experiment of War Communism toward radical socialization led Lenin to introduce the New Economic Policy (NEP) in 1921, a temporary program of "strategic retreat" that reintroduced small-scale free enterprise to improve the severe economic conditions. During the period of the NEP, Lenin made economic concessions to the public, while at the same time curtailing extreme leftist sentiment and factionalism within the Party. While Lenin further implemented Party control through a purge of its membership between 1921 and 1922, the nonpolitical sphere was not yet to come under the total control of official dictates.

It was under these more relaxed ideological circumstances of the NEP that the attitude toward the arts also reverted to that prior to the Revolution, leading to a period of an intellectual experimentalism and freedom unknown either under the previous War Communism or since the 1930s. During this period, a multiplicity of artistic views was permitted in Soviet society, as evidenced by the appearance of two opposing musical organizations in 1923. The *Association for Contemporary Music* (ACM), which adhered to the more liberal attitude toward modernistic currents in Western Europe and the idea of creative freedom and experimentation, was directly opposed by the *Russian Association of Proletarian Musicians* (RAPM). The latter followed the intellectuals of the earlier Proletkult, which advocated a radical break from tradition and Western ideals, and supported the direct participation of the masses in the development of the new proletarian culture. Based on the idea that Western artistic approaches could be conditioned to serve the proletarian state, a belief which led to Russia's significant position in the advancement of international modern artistic developments, Lenin opposed the extremist viewpoint of Proletkult. His speech on October 2, 1920, on "proletarian culture," led to the curtailment of the group.[8]

By the mid-1920s, economic conditions and the need for the most intensive effort toward industrialization under Stalin's leadership brought

---

[8] Vladimir Lenin, "The Tasks of the Youth Leagues," trans. in V. Lenin, *New Economic Policy* (New York, 1937), p. 471, as cited in Schwarz, *Music and Musical Life in Soviet Russia,* n.1, above, p. 21.

two contrasting views to a head within the Communist Party, one advocating a continuation of the gradual move into socialism, the other advocating a radical break from the existing policies under NEP in order to move directly into an economy planned centrally and to effect a substantial increase in industrial and agricultural production. The more aggressive approach was adopted, and the State Planning Commission, known as *Gosplan* (established in 1921), was assigned the task of drawing up the first five-year plan in 1927. Along with its inception in 1928, the Communist Party under Stalin's undisputed leadership imposed complete control on all aspects of Soviet society. Thus, intellectual and artistic activities were also brought completely into line with Marxist ideology and the strict dictates of the Party. As part of that ideology, traditional and Western bourgeois attitudes were suppressed entirely as the primary concern for artists was now directed toward serving socialist ideals and Party doctrine. In music, both the ACM and RAPM were dissolved in 1930 and 1932, respectively. With the establishment of the *Union of Soviet Composers* and the *Resolution of 1932*, the role of music in Soviet society became far removed from that of Western Europe or Soviet artistic developments during the 1920s. Abstract artistic creativity and experimentalism were no longer permitted (i.e., in the form of art for art's sake), but had to be realistic (accessible), have an educational function, and relate to social issues according to a doctrine known as *Socialist Realism*. The extra-musical associations essential to the realization of this doctrine provide a partial explanation for the common use of opera and ballet by many Soviet composers.

PROKOFIEV: FROM THE PREREVOLUTIONARY WORKS TO THE EARLY 1930s

One of the most striking aspects of Prokofiev's music is his variety of styles and moods (yet within a consistent and integrated personal musical language), which characterize not only his separate works, but also the individual passages within them. The distinctness and suddenness with which these characteristics manifest themselves within individual compositions are heightened by his planed and layered (often ostinato-based) textures that had been in evidence since his early compositions. This particular formal/textural trait shows an affinity to both the Russian and Neoclassical styles of Stravinsky. At the same time, different aspects of Prokofiev's style appear to be rooted in several divergent international sources, both traditional and contemporary, all of which were transformed by his imagination into a personal modernistic idiom characterized by wit, expressiveness, rhythmic excitement, and a harmonic boldness based on unconventional uses of seventh and ninth chords and the pervasive use of nonfunctional dissonance.

The varied aspects of Prokofiev's style point, in part, to sources in nineteenth-century Russian musical traditions, including early Russian musical influences of Glinka and the more excessive lyricism and often bottom-heavy orchestrations of Tchaikovsky, as well as the modal coloring of the Russian nationalists. For instance, Prokofiev's early opera *The Gambler*

(1915–1916), after Dostoyevsky, belongs to the operatic tradition assumed by Mussorgsky. The national quality of Prokofiev's music also derives from an infusion of Russian folk-music inflections, his intimate contact with peasant songs originating in his agrarian family background. Furthermore, the toccata-like quality of his piano compositions suggests a contemporary source in Stravinsky's mechanistic and motoric rhythms, though Prokofiev himself referred to the influence of the *Toccata in C,* Op. 7, of Schumann. Nevertheless, his tendency toward primitivism in several of his pre–World War I piano compositions as well as in the ancient Slavic subjects and paganistic style of the ballet *Ala i Lolli,* which Diaghilev commissioned in 1914, and the resulting *Scythian Suite,* Op. 20 (1915), are full of Stravinskian rhythmic and harmonic elements owing much to *Le sacre.*[9] It was on a trip to London at this time that Prokofiev met Diaghilev and attended performances of several of Stravinsky's stage works. The Russian style of Prokofiev was continued in 1915 in *Chout* (The Buffoon), another ballet based on a folk tale and commissioned by Diaghilev.

Prokofiev's harmonic style also evolved from the principles of the chromaticized diatonicism of various nineteenth-century Romantics, about whom, for instance, "Prokofiev used to speak of the kindred nature of Schubert's music. He had in mind Schubert's favorite device of 'explosive' tonal digressions."[10] However, the tonal irony of Prokofiev's harmonic idiom, which results from unexpected multitonal shifts, reveals more extensively the influence of late nineteenth-century developments, especially those of Mahler. Thus, the numerous stylistic sources of Prokofiev's musical development were largely acquired during his early years.

To what extent Prokofiev's early studies with Rimsky-Korsakov, Lyadov, and Tcherepnin at the Petrograd Conservatory from 1904 to 1914 were to have on the course of his stylistic development is difficult to determine. These teachers were knowledgeable in both Russian musical sources as well as the styles of the non-Russian Romantic composers, but the modernistic attitude of Tcherepnin, who showed a stylistic affinity with Debussy and Scriabin, had a significant bearing on Prokofiev's own inclination toward experimentation. It was through his association with Myaskovsky, however, that Prokofiev became familiar with the newest musical developments in St. Petersburg, where he acquired an intimate knowledge of the most recent works of Scriabin as well as the music of Debussy and others. Prokofiev's own "ultramodernistic" approach to composition was also recognized at his 1908 public piano debut, the most striking piece on the program being his

[9] According to Glenn Watkins, *Soundings: Music in the Twentieth Century* (New York and London: Schirmer Books, 1988), p. 412, the scenario of Prokofiev's ballet, stemming from Gorodetsky's research into Russian mythology, is also indebted to Rimsky-Korsakov's *Snow Maiden.*

[10] V. Berkov, *"Kizucheniya Sovremyonoi Garmonii"* [Study of Contemporary Harmony] *Sovetskaya Muzyka* 4 (1962): p. 42, cited in Bakst, *A History of Russian-Soviet Music,* n.2, above, p. 300.

Suggestion diabolique. It was during the next several years (1908–1913) that Prokofiev produced his first mature, highly original piano compositions, including the *First Piano Concerto* (1911).

During the war, yet another source entered into Prokofiev's compositions. In the *First Symphony in D Major* (1916–1917), entitled *"Classical" Symphony*, the established features of his technique and style were absorbed into a more clearly defined neoclassical structure modelled consciously on the Classical forms and aesthetics of Haydn. This work established those features that were to remain essential for the remainder of his career. At the same time, Prokofiev was completing his *First Violin Concerto*, Op. 19 (1915–1917), also in D major, a work of extraordinary variety in its contrasting passages of extreme lyricism, primitivistic motoric rhythms, highly refined, brilliantly orchestrated figurations in rapid scherzando style, sharply contrasting changes of melodic figuration, poignantly dissonant and unstable diatonic harmonies based on harmonic (tonal) block shifts moving through numerous and unrelated tonal areas, and unconventional metric accentuations of sevenths, ninths, and nonchordal tones. Many of the rapid ostinati, as in the second movement (Scherzo), are similar to those in the *Classical Symphony*. These and the works of the next several years, between 1918 (when he left Russia for the United States) and 1923 (when he settled in Paris), reached the peak of his stylistic variety. The composer's summary in his autobiography establishes four basic features common to these and his remaining compositions: *Neoclassical, modern* (experimental and innovative), *toccata* (motoric), and *lyric*.

The *Violin Concerto* is exemplary of Prokofiev's approach to transformational or variational relations between local layers of the contrasting thematic areas, an aspect of his ability to unify within a diversity of figurations and moods. The main theme of the first movement, a lyrically spun-out and open-ended melody above a quiet tremolando figure, implies the presence of several linearly unfolding contour configurations, each of which contains potential for development. Several of these configurations, or motifs, also projected into the multilayered counterpoint of the accompaniment, are later transformed into the structure and accompanying layered counterpoint of the second theme (No. 7). As shown in Ex. 12–1, the clarinet joins two of the thematic figures of the solo violin linearly, the first, E–F♯–G–G♯–A (mm. 6–8), a slightly chromaticized version of the ascending violin figure, E–F♯–G–A–B (mm. 8–9), which was already suggested in the cadential descent of the violin (mm. 5–6), the second, A–C♯–F♯ (m. 8), an intervallically mutated form of the violin's E–F♯–C♯ (mm. 6–7). Both these motivic ideas are projected into the solo and bass lines of the second theme, the ascending, embellished structure of the solo line, E–F–F♯–G–A–A♭ (No. 7, mm. 1–3), implying the presence of both the chromaticized and diatonic forms in the first theme (in enharmonic spelling, E–F♯–G–G♯–A and E–F♯–G–A–[　]). (This rising E-chromatic structure of the second theme is projected as a complete chromatic scale in the main theme of the Scherzo movement.) The accompanying ostinato bass motif of the second theme,

EXAMPLE 12–1. Prokofiev, *First Violin Concerto,* Op. 19, Mov. I, main theme, mm. 3–8, linear joining in clarinet of two thematic figures of the solo violin

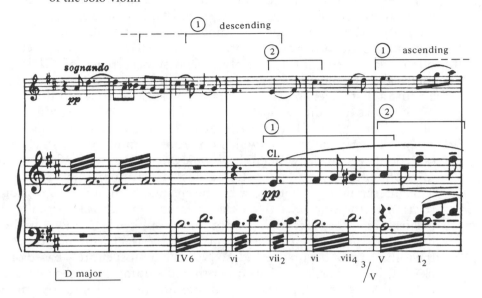

E–G–C, suggests the other, more disjunct segment of the first theme. The remaining accompanimental layers of the second theme also suggest transformations of two other figures from the opening thematic material. The contour of the opening thematic neighbor-note figure, A–Bb–A–G–F♯ (m. 4), is retrograded as a whole-tone motif in the violin, G–A–B–C♯–B (at No. 1), the same whole-tone tetrachord having appeared already in the descending cadential figure of the violin as C♯–B–A–G (m. 5). The motivic form in the parallel thirds of the clarinets (at No. 1), anticipated in the eighth-note figure, D–E–F♯–G–F♯ (mm. 8–9), is also projected as one of the ostinato layers, C–D–Eb–D, in the counterpoint against the second theme. Finally, the remaining undulating half-note figure in parallel thirds against the second theme (e.g., upper line, B–A–B–A to A–Ab) appears to be derived from the disposition of the upper notes of the opening tremolando, D–C♯–D–C♯ to B–Bb (mm. 6–12). Thus, pervasive structural connections are established between the diverse figures of the opening lyrical theme and the contrasting motoric and jocular second theme.

Despite the underlying diatonicism of both melodic and tertian harmonic construction, the musical language of the *Concerto* has little to do with traditional tonal functions and harmonic progression. Prokofiev's musical syntax is based rather on an unconventional metric/rhythmic deployment of principal harmonic tones, appoggiaturas, and dissonances. Part of the modernism of his musical language seems to lie in a kind of Stravinskian reversal in the traditional relation between the metric-rhythmic and melodic-harmonic spheres. The opening tremolando on the tonic triad asserts the key of D major, but the structure of the theme, based on a major-minor mixture in the alteration of the sixth degree (B to B♭), emphasizes the seventh degree (C♯) of the key metrically. This note occurs not as the third degree of the dominant, but rather as part of a melodic-harmonic duality between two other triadic structures. Linearly, the first occurrence of C♯ is part of a metrically prominent F♯-minor triad, while vertically it forms a dissonance against a first-inversion G-major triad, or IV$_6$, the root and third (G and B) occurring as melodic passing tones (see Ex. 12–1). At the second occurrence of the C♯ (m. 7), this duality is heightened by the vertical projection of the F♯.

This triadic duality, which is part of the multiplicity so characteristic of Prokofiev's music, weakens harmonic direction and transfers our attention to the nonfunctional "coloristic" aspect of harmonic-melodic dissonance. This interpretation is borne out by the ensuing harmonic progression and its relation to the solo line. After the opening tonic chord, virtually the only occurrence of the tonic triad (except for the implied I$_2$ harmony in the second half of m. 8) until the recapitulation (No. 21), the harmonic progression for the remainder of the first period (to No. 1) is almost entirely based on seventh chords, inversions, and triads other than the dominant and tonic (except for the local V–I$_2$ at m. 8). The harmonic nonfunctionality of the overall progression is determined further by the longer descending D-melodic-minor bass line, of which the exclusively whole-tone portion following the initial D (B–A–G–C♯–A–C♯–A–G–F; in scalar form, C♯–B–A–G–F) serves as a projection of the diatonic whole-tone figure of the theme (m. 5 and No. 1). The whole-tone character of the bass line contributes to the static and uniform tonal quality of the passage and sets off the first (solo) statement of the theme from the second (orchestral) statement, the latter of which is also articulated by the abrupt shift to the unrelated key of C major (No. 1, m. 9). This harmonic block shift is an adumbration of the larger tonal block shift to C major at the second theme (No. 7).

Disparity of tonal elements is also suggested within the first thematic announcement, a technique which contributes to the local distinction of melodic and harmonic spheres and also serves to anticipate (in a non-traditional way) the sudden modulation to C major in the second thematic announcement. In the second period (No. 1, mm. 1–4), the single altered element (F) results in the larger dominant-seventh of C (G–B–D–F) as combined with the basic dominant-ninth harmony (A–C♯–E–G–B) of D; the latter dominant is also essential to the solo line (A–C♯–[   ]–G–B). This modal mixture, produced by the cross-relation between the major and minor thirds (F and F♯) of the basic key, therefore plays both a coloristic dissonant function as well as a modulatory one by means of anticipation through interpolation. The cross-relation of F and F♯ is reiterated as a local detail in both solo and accompaniment at the cadential point of modulation (No. 1, m. 8), where the dominant-ninth of C now moves to that key. Another unrelated tonal block shift at the next statement of the theme (No. 2, m. 4, oboe) takes us to D♭ major immediately. One more abrupt change, now within this remote D♭-major statement (No. 3), induces a return to the original key by an enharmonic reinterpretation of D♭ as C♯ in the solo line. Here, the original thematic material (from mm. 9ff.) is also recapitulated. However, the recurring, suggested shift to C major in the figurally varied solo line (No. 4) is now supported by an F-major chord, while the oboe unfolds a sequence of thematic segments initiated in A minor. Thus, this variation of the opening, which rounds out the first-theme group, is based on still more divergent melodic and harmonic levels.

The tonal separation of the second announcement of the main theme (No. 1, m. 9) from the first announcement is also articulated by the sudden change of figuration, from dotted-quarters, quarters, and eighths primarily to the smaller figural subdivisions of the meter into 2 × 3 eighths in the solo line. This change establishes the basic formal-textural premise of block juxtaposition for the rest of the movement. The next several blocks, which lead to the second theme, are articulated by further arithmetic subdivisions of the beat. The Stravinskian structural principle of surface-level disconnection in both tonality and figuration is therefore also essential to Prokofiev's modernistic idiom.

The Scherzo exemplifies further Prokofiev's approach to diverse elements. In addition to the more foreground-level harmonic block shifts (from E through E♭ and D to C♯) underlying the two identical opening statements of the whimsical E-chromatic idea, the polarity of timbres is also striking. A brittle quality of the solo violin is enhanced by the predominance of winds in the orchestration. The traditional ABA Scherzo form is clearly demarcated, so both local and large-scale structural clarity is also provided. The third movement, which returns to the lyrical quality of the opening movement to round out an outline of *Andantino, Vivacissimo, Moderato* (i.e., the converse of the traditional fast-slow-fast format), synthesizes thematic elements from the first two movements. The initial theme of this movement, for instance, joins the rhythm of the chromatic Scherzo idea with the arpeggiated motivic contour of the ostinato bass accompaniment of the second theme of the first movement, which was derived in turn from the disjunct segment within the opening lyrical theme.

The *Violin Concerto* was first performed after Prokofiev's arrival in Paris in 1923, during which period his works began to reveal a more avant-garde style after initial criticisms of the *Concerto*. At the same time, certain works were to reveal a more direct expression of the spirit of the Revolution. Although Prokofiev was away from Russia during the early postrevolutionary years, he did maintain contact with his homeland through correspondences with Myaskovsky and others. During his sojourn to the United States between 1918 and 1922, he had completed the comic opera *The Love for Three Oranges* (1919) for the Chicago Opera Association, a work begun in Russia in 1917, while composing several other works during his excitement over the success of the February Revolution. He was to serve that summer as a member of the *Council of Workers in the Arts,* which supported the more radical and experimental artistic attitudes.

Some of his most original, dynamic works to be completed in Paris in the 1920s were his *Piano Concertos Nos. 3–5,* the *Symphonies Nos. 2–4, No. 3* of which was derived from his highly dramatic opera *The Fiery Angel* (1919–1923, rev. 1926–1927) based on a story of the contemporary Russian writer Valery Bryusov, and the two contrasting (percussive and lyrical) one-act ballets *Le Pas d'acier* (The Steel Step) (1925–1926) and *L'Enfant prodigue* (The Prodigal Son) (1928–1929), both works of which grew out of his renewed relation with Diaghilev and the Ballets Russes. *Le Pas d'acier* reveals Prokofiev's sympathy with the ideals of the Revolution in both subject and style expressly. In view of his close contact with the music of *Les Six,* especially Honegger's *Pacific 231* (1924), as well as his interest in the industrialization under the new Soviet government, it is not surprising to find Prokofiev employing a constructivist and percussive machine-like style as the basis for depicting the production of steel in the Soviet factories. Diaghilev's commission for the subject of this ballet came after the official acknowledgment of the new Soviet government by Western nations. Prokofiev's international tours during the 1920s and early 1930s brought him several times after 1927 to the Soviet Union, where he was recognized as a revolutionary composer. He was to return to his homeland finally in 1933, where, despite opposition to his modernistic approach by the RAPM in the late 1920s, he was to establish himself as one of the leading Soviet composers. Brown points out that "as a direct consequence of [Prokofiev's] resettling, he escaped Stravinsky's shadow completely. Stravinsky's name was anathema in the Soviet Union during the Stalinist period," while Prokofiev "enjoyed a prestige . . . such as he had never known in the West."[11]

SHOSTAKOVICH: SOVIET WORKS OF THE 1920s

Whereas Prokofiev's experimental idiom was a product of prerevolutionary Russia and the international influences with which he was in direct contact in the 1910s and 1920s, the musical attitudes and approaches of his younger Soviet contemporaries were a more direct outgrowth of postrevolutionary Soviet political and artistic conditions. Nevertheless, of these younger Soviet composers, Dmitry Shostakovich had also combined a modernistic idiom derived from traditional and contemporary sources with Soviet ideology in the mid-1920s, from which time his music also began to reveal a strong political basis. Solomon Volkov points out that "despite the conservatory tradition, the 1920s were a time when 'left' art predominated in the new Russia's cultural life. There were many reasons for this, and one of the

[11] See Brown, "Stravinsky and Prokofiev: Sizing Up the Competition," n. 5, above, p. 49.

primary ones was the readiness of the avant-garde to cooperate with Soviet power."[12] Outside influences had a significant bearing on the development of Shostakovich's early modernistic style, although, unlike Prokofiev, Shostakovich had remained in the Soviet Union throughout his career. During the period of the NEP, contemporary Western musical styles were received in Russian cities with great enthusiasm—weekly premières were given in the mid-1920s in Leningrad. Included were the modernistic works of Krenek, *Les Six,* and the "foreign" Russian composers Stravinsky and Prokofiev, as well as performances by Bartók and Hindemith of their own works, all of whom drew the interest of Shostakovich.[13]

Shostakovich's style of this early period reflected influences similar to Prokofiev's, ranging from the late nineteenth-century Russian Romantic idiom of Tchaikovsky to the quite different musical tradition of the Rimsky-Korsakov school that prevailed at the Petersburg conservatory. Here, Shostakovich studied with Rimsky's son-in-law, Maximilian Steinberg, and was in contact with the more modernistic idiom of Prokofiev as well as the more dissonant avant-garde tendencies prevailing in Western Europe at the time. These varied sources were already manifested in his *First Symphony* in F minor (1924–1925), which Shostakovich composed for his graduation from the Petrograd Conservatory. This symphony, which was "striking, temperamental, and masterfully orchestrated, and at the same time traditional and accessible," was to have an immediate success and a broad international audience.[14] While the lyrical, emotional quality hints at that in his later symphonies, the structure of this symphony reveals an affinity to the blocked (or distinctly delineated sectional) structures and layered counterpoint of Prokofiev, based on contrasting variational, thematic manifestations rather than cumulative or developmental form. As part of this more "Neoclassical" structural approach, in which the four movements are each based on clearly defined traditional (sonata and ternary) forms, the contrasting themes are often characterized by distinctive and angular contours that evoke different moods (march, waltz, etc.). The whimsical scherzo is similar to Prokofiev's, and this foreshadows his own later development of this type of movement. Despite its descriptive sectional character, the symphony contains climactic emotional tension in an integrated context based on the cyclical use of themes and their transformations.

In his next works, Shostakovich indulged in a more experimental style, still in accordance with the prevailingly free artistic attitudes of Soviet cultural policies prior to the First Five-Year Plan of 1928. Greater abstraction

---

[12] *Testimony: The Memoirs of Dmitri Shostakovich as related to and edited by Solomon Volkov,* trans. Antonina W. Bouis (New York: Harper and Row, Inc., 1979; Limelight Editions, 1989), p. xxiv. The book's general authenticity, however, is disputed by Laurel Fay, "Shostakovich versus Volkov: Whose Testimony?" *Russian Review* 39 (1980): 484–493.

[13] Ibid.

[14] Ibid., p. xxiii–xxiv.

and dissonance emerged in his *First Piano Sonata* (1926), and these were manifested further in his opera *Nos* (The Nose) (1928), a social satire based on a story of Gogol. This opera typified his stage works of the next several years, its witticism and irony also infusing the modernistic idiom of the ballets *Zolotoy vek* (The Golden Age) (1927–1930) and *The Bolt* (1931), both of which satirize bourgeois values, and *Svetlïy ruchey* (The Limpid Stream) (1934), involving the activities of artists on a collective farm. In these and other satirical works of these years, such as the film score *Novïy vavilon* (New Babylon) (1928–1929), sharp rhythms and orchestral brilliance predominate over lyricism. Shostakovich had already begun to express revolutionary Soviet themes within a more abstract modernistic idiom, based on angular rhythms and a dissonant chromaticism, in his *Second Symphony* for chorus and orchestra (1927), dedicated "To October," a similar political orientation of which underlies the *Third Symphony* for chorus and orchestra (1929), dedicated to "The First of May," and others of his fifteen symphonies as well.

SOCIALIST REALISM FROM THE EARLY 1930s TO EARLY 1950s: PROKOFIEV, SHOSTAKOVICH, KABALEVSKY, KHACHATURIAN

With the establishment of the Union of Soviet Composers in 1932, musical policies came entirely under the administrative control of the government. Already, since 1929, the earlier experimentalism in education shifted to the industrial training of the peasantry as Lunacharsky was replaced by Bubnov as Commissar of Education. These changes were accompanied by the Central Committee's official and extreme implementation of Marxist ideology into all aspects of intellectual life. Party rules were now set for composers, who turned their attention to the social content of their music and its appeal to the masses by means of establishing connections with Russian musical tradition, especially that of Tchaikovsky and the Russian nationalists, and the folk resources within the various republics of the Soviet Union. This new centralized policy resulted in the first radical shift away from the creative attitudes and aesthetics of the earlier postrevolutionary period. There was also a sharp divergence of artistic developments away from those of Western Europe, of which the more experimental music was prevented from receiving public performance. With the Second Five-Year Plan came the purges of 1933, which solidified Stalin's leadership during a period of extreme political, social, and economic tensions, and the most extreme restrictions upon the activities of Soviet artists.

The new aesthetic principle of Socialist Realism was presented officially in the Resolution of 1932 and further defined by Andrei Zhdanov at the meeting of artists at the First All-Union Congress of Soviet Writers in 1934. One of the main Soviet sources describes Socialist Realism as "a doctrine of artistic creation founded on the truthful, historically valid representation of reality in its revolutionary development," further stating that "Socialist Realism combines a feeling for contemporary reality with a leap of the imagination into the future."[15] The vagueness of this and other formulations did not lend themselves to a systematic approach by artists, and this opened the way to official charges against composers in the cultural purges of 1936 and 1948, in which Zhdanov was to play a significant role. The following statement provides a less vague definition of this principle, revealing the opposition by the Composers' Union to *modernism*:

> The main attention of the Soviet composer must be directed towards the victorious progressive principles of reality, towards all that is heroic, bright, and beautiful. This distinguishes the spiritual world of Soviet man and must be embodied in musical images full of beauty and strength. Socialist Realism demands an implacable struggle against folk-negating modernistic directions that are typical of the decay of contemporary bourgeois art, against subservience and servility towards modern bourgeois culture.[16]

Music had to be "refined, harmonious, and melodious,"[17] in simplified contexts devoid of *Formalism* (that is, the separation or abstraction of the formal framework from the organic interconnections of the musical content), that came to be associated with modernism and was antithetical to the ideals of Socialist Realism.[18] Boris Asaf'yev, one of the key figures in the development of Soviet musicology and founder of the theory of *intonazia* [intonation], which deals with the varied associative functions of musical form to life experiences, stated that he was "indebted to [Stasov] for his persistence and a stubborn belief in the invincible strength of an idea, if only it be organically vital" [*Materialy,* p. 7].[19]

With his gradual readjustment to Soviet life between 1933 and 1935, Prokofiev made efforts to adapt his compositional approach to the new artistic policies. He attempted to make the works reflect Soviet life as well, and during this time began to participate in the newly formed Composers' Union. The compositions of this era reveal decisive changes toward simplicity and have a prevailingly lyrical Romantic quality, often of a soaring,

---

[15] *Entsiklopedicheskii Muzykal' Nyi Slovar* [Encyclopedic Musical Dictionary], ed. B. Steinpress and I. Yampolski, 2nd ed. (Moscow, 1966), p. 486, cited by Malcolm H. Brown, in "The Soviet Russian Concepts of 'Intonazia' and 'Musical Imagery,'" *Musical Quarterly* 60/4 (October 1974): 557.

[16] From "Statutes of Composers' Union," quoted in "Sotsialisticheskii Realism," *Entsiklopedicheskii Muzykal'Nyi Slovar,* ibid., as cited in Schwartz, *Music and Musical Life in Soviet Russia,* n.1, above, p. 114.

[17] See *Testimony: The Memoirs of Dmitri Shostakovich,* n.12, above, p. 146.

[18] One of the Soviet definitions of Formalism in art is "the expression of bourgeois ideology that is hostile to the Soviet people;" see ibid., p. 83.

[19] See Gordon D. McQuere, "Boris Asafiev and *Musical Form as a Process,*" in *Russian Theoretical Thought in Music,* ed. Gordon D. McQuere (Ann Arbor: UMI Research Press, 1983), p. 218.

national, epic character—many of his works were composed for theatre and film texts based on fervent nationalistic subjects. Typical of his patriotic tendency are the *Cantata for the 20th Anniversary of the October Revolution* (1936–1937), on texts of Marx, Lenin, and Stalin, for two choruses and varied instrumental bands; the music for Eisenstein's film *Alexander Nevsky* (1938), based on the epic Russian struggle against the Medieval Teutonic Knights, the film score of which became the basis for the cantata of the same title (1939); the opera *Semyon Kotko* (1939), a modern folk drama dealing with the civil war in the Ukraine; and, after the outbreak of World War II, a preoccupation with his epic opera *War and Peace* (1941–1943, rev. 1946–1952), after Tolstoy, in which he equated the subject of Russia's defense against the Napoleonic invasion in 1812 with the present Soviet struggle.

While living in the Ural mountains, he was also in touch with folk-music sources more closely, which were manifested in various works during and after the war. These include the comic opera *Khan Buzai* (1942, unfinished), based on Kazakh folk tales, the *String Quartet No. 2 in F Major,* Op. 92 (1941), which incorporates authentic Kabardinian and Balkarian folk tunes, the last three symphonies (1944–1952), and the ballet *The Tale of the Stone Flower* (1948–1953). The epic quality and powerful imagery so essential to the principles of Socialist Realism also pervade the instrumental works (i.e., without texts)—as in the monumental *Symphony No. 5 in Bb Major* (1944) and the *Piano Sonatas Nos. 6–8* (1940, 1942, and 1944), *No. 7* especially. In many works written for children during the 1930s, such as the *Three Children's Songs* (1936) and the popular *Peter and the Wolf* (1936), for narrator and orchestra, Prokofiev revealed a fusion of his earlier whimsical style with a new simplicity and tonal clarity in contexts having practical or contemporary social significance. The latter stylistic fusion had already been evident in his satirical film suite *Lieutenant Kijé* (1934).

Due to increased artistic regimentation in the 1930s, Prokofiev's Soviet works began to reveal some reconciliation between his earlier experimental approach (based on bold and unrelated harmonic and tonal shifts in an underlying diatonic style colored by dissonances, sevenths, and chromatic alterations) and more distinct Classical formal schemes incorporating lyrical and often folk-like melodies, clear textures based frequently on simple ostinato harmonic figurations, and greater tonal clarity through more decisive cadential resolutions. These new contexts also adhered increasingly to heroic and socially realistic features. Despite these efforts toward a more Neoclassical style, however, his music, along with that of Shostakovich and others, was attacked in 1936 by *Pravda* as decadent. He responded to this charge by reaffirming his conformity to the principles of Socialist Realism and Party cultural policy. The difference between his earlier and later symphonies is the direct influence of Soviet artistic policy on his aesthetic and stylistic development. His tendency toward greater structural clarity, simplification, and integration of the thematic content became completely evident in the *Fifth Symphony,* which was composed after fourteen years away from the symphonic form. Whereas the *Fourth Symphony* (1930), which was composed prior to his return to the Soviet Union, lacked the epic quality and organic formal integration found in the later symphony, the structure of the *Fifth Symphony* benefitted from his experience with the intervening works. These include such lyrical instrumental masterpieces as the *Sonata No. 1 for Violin and Piano* (1938–1946), in F minor, *Violin Concerto No. 2* (1935), in G minor, and the *Sixth* and *Seventh Piano Sonatas.*

Composed toward the end of World War II, the *Fifth Symphony* was intended as "a hymn to free and happy Man, to his mighty power, his pure and noble spirit," hence the more dramatic, emotional, and epic quality of the work.[20] The musical fabric is wrought from the varied, fluid type of configurations found in his earlier works (e.g., *First Violin Concerto*), but we now find a greater structural control over the diverse materials. Except for the tempo *(Andante)* of the opening sonata movement, each of the four movements outlines a traditional scheme, the second *(Allegro marcato)* a scherzo, the third *(Adagio)* a ternary form with coda, and the fourth *(Allegro giocoso)* a full sonata-allegro plan. The tonal schemes of the thematic groups within each movement also suggest traditional relations, but the more local tonalities are established primarily by nonfunctional harmonic progressions, except for occasional cadential dominant–tonic assertions. As in the *First Violin Concerto,* the constant chromatic tonal shifts (often by half-step) are basic to the character of the spun-out lyrical themes, and these chromatic shifts contribute to the process of thematic variation. In contrast with the earlier *Concerto,* however, the kaleidoscopic thematic blocks and layers of the symphony are constructed more distinctly according to Classical phrasal and periodic as well as large-scale structural principles.

The opening thematic idea (1a) of the first movement contains most of the basic rhythmic figures and contours of the other themes both in this, and the other movements.[21] For instance, the cadential figure (F–B♭–D) of the first phrasal segment (Ex. 12–2a) is projected into the little "arch-shaped" figures (A–F–B, B–D♭–G♯, and F–A–C) of the contrasting, more motoric closing theme (Ex. 12–2b), the latter of which is projected as one of the subsidiary thematic ideas of the finale (No. 81, violin I; Ex. 12–2c). This "arch-shaped" figure, which contributes to the long-range thematic associations, is also basic to the articulation of local tonal mutations within the second announcement of theme 1a (No. 1). Such mutations, often found in Prokofiev's diatonic melodies, produce phrasal diversification and thematic variation between otherwise identical or related ideas. The initial eight-

---

[20] Prokofiev, *Autobiography, Articles, Reminiscences,* compiled, edited, and notes by S. Shlifshstein, trans. R. Prokofieva (Moscow: Foreign Languages Publishing House, 1956), p. 134.

[21] In Classical sonata form: Exposition (mm. 1–No. 10)—themes 1a (m. 1), 1b (No. 3), 2a (No. 6), 2b (No. 7, m.10), closing (No. 9); Development (Nos. 10–17)—sections 1 (No. 10), 2 (No. 11, m. 2), 3 (No. 12, m. 12), 4 (No. 14), 5 (No. 16); Recapitulation (Nos. 17–23)—themes 1a (No. 17), 1b (No. 18, m. 8), 2a (No. 21), 2b (No. 21, m. 10), closing (No. 22, m. 6); Coda (No. 23).

EXAMPLE 12–2. Prokofiev, *Fifth Symphony,* motivic figures: Mov. I
(a) theme 1a, (b) closing theme, No. 9; Finale (c) subsidiary thematic
idea, No. 81

measure statement of the theme, which is comprised of several distinct
diatonic phrasal members, remains within the B♭-major scale, the tonality of
which is asserted harmonically by the two held statements of the tonic fifth,
B♭–F. The otherwise contrasting four-measure phrasal extension (mm.
8–11), which introduces some embellishing chromatic details, suggests a
structural parallel with the first period by asserting two harmonic statements
of the dominant fifth, F–C, analogously. A more local harmonic detail
contributes to this implied periodic parallel in support of the Classical structure further. The leading-note E in the opening period (mm. 3 and 5, celli) is
reiterated in the second period (m. 11), but now leads to F as the root of the
rather than fifth of the tonic chord.

Thus far, the structural and tonal relations are related closely to those
of traditional Classical forms. These seemingly traditional functional relations are absorbed into a nontraditional procedure in the second announcement of the theme (No. 1), which is mutated tonally, i.e., as part of an
unexpected tonal block shift within the initial linear segment. While the latter
is the same as the opening melody, which suggests a restatement in B♭, the
original leading-note E is reinterpreted harmonically as the fifth degree of A.
At the same time, the thematic G♯–E mutation of the theme suggests a linear
alteration to F minor, producing a momentary tonal divergence of layers. It is
the unexpected linear thematic shift precisely at the triadic "arch-shaped"
figure (E–A–C♯), now beginning with E instead of the original F (see m. 2),
that establishes the new tonality of A major, i.e., a half-step below the
primary key. This second thematic announcement is disrupted by another
tonal block shift, this time to D♭ major (No. 1, m. 6). The new tonal mutation
is also articulated by the basic "arch-shaped" figure, which is then isolated as

a more foreground event (No. 2 and No. 2, mm. 3ff.) as the theme becomes fragmented increasingly in the extended consequent period leading to theme 1b. The latter theme takes us back, without preparation, from D♭ to B♭ major, after which more diversified antiphonal and contrapuntal textures shift to new local tonal areas similarly. Thus, within the opening Classical phrase and period structure of the two announcements of theme 1a, we get sudden nontraditional tonal disconnections that ultimately function simply as local eddies within the basic area of B♭ major. These locally disconnected harmonic/tonal blocks are held together by certain interrelated harmonic details and by one of the special figural properties of the theme.

Theme 1b reveals similarities to theme 1a in general contour and local details, as in the corresponding penultimate figures based on the expanded "arch-shaped" segment in both subsidiary thematic ideas (Ex. 12–3). Theme 1b also contains characteristics that distinguish it from theme 1a and contribute to the articulation of the formal block construction, planing, and layering so characteristic of Prokofiev's diverse textures. This thematic idea is placed in sharp juxtaposition to the preceding passage by its sudden change of orchestration to heavy unison bass doubling (low woodwinds, brass, and strings)—also typical of Prokofiev's music. Each distinct instrumental block coincides with a figural change to articulate the two contrasting antecedent and consequent phrase members of 2 + 4 measures, respectively. The last two measures of the consequent are overlapped contrapuntally by a two-measure return of theme 1a (low brass), which serves as a bridge to the second statement of theme 1b, now in the contrasting key of E♭ major. These balanced Classical juxtapositions of two- and/or four-measure phrase segments are continued in the E♭-major (second-period) statement of this theme, which is contrapuntally and antiphonally juxtaposed with theme 1a (entering at No. 4, upper winds and violin I) and further disrupted by other tonal block shifts (to B major, etc.). This technique of phrasal planing and disconnection

EXAMPLE 12–3. Prokofiev, *Fifth Symphony,* contour and figural similarities between (a) theme 1a, opening, and (b) theme 1b, No. 3, tonal segmentation in thematic structure

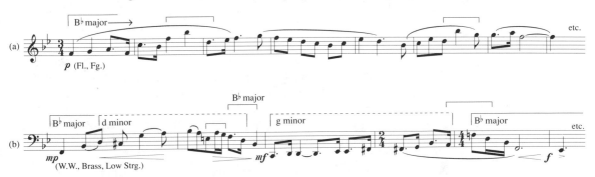

within the theme-1b area is also reflected locally in the foreground structure of the theme itself, which is segmented tonally (see Ex. 12–3b). Again, transformations of the "arch-shaped" figure articulate these tonal mutations. Thus, as part of a coherent developmental process within the otherwise diversified materials of the larger first theme-group, constructed Classically, Prokofiev establishes deep-level connections by means of thematic variation or transformation, the sense of development produced by the increasing sharpness of tonal disconnection and block juxtaposition.

Classical structural balance is articulated further by distinctly contrasting figural and tonal members of the more lyrical second theme-group (No. 6f.): theme 2a is divided into two tonal halves, F major (dominant of the basic tonality) and E major, while theme 2b (No. 8) is stabilized tonally by an F-pedal throughout. Within this balanced framework, the seemingly traditional diatonic portions of the local thematic members are harmonized entirely by nontraditional means, in which static nonfunctional chords again move abruptly from one tonal area to another. The F-major tonality of the antecedent phrase of theme 2a is established exclusively by the disposition of the diatonic melodic line and the descending, nonfunctional diatonic bass line, A–G–F–E–D–C. Above the local bass tones are unfolded F- and E-ninth chords, in root and inverted positions, the larger arpeggiated flow outlining larger thirteenth chords (Ex. 12–4). While the local chord progression is static tonally, the alternation of F and E roots, either in or above the bass, prepares (in a disconnected anticipatory manner similar to that shown earlier in the *First Violin Concerto*) for the sudden shift to E major at the change of key signature in the consequent phrase. The latter tonality is established exclusively by the diatonic thematic line, whereas the bass line, in contrast to the descending form of the antecedent, now ascends chromatically from B through A a seventh above (No. 7). At this point, the second period, a variation of the initial thematic announcement, returns abruptly to F major to repeat the two bass progressions. While the contrasting character of both melody and bass in the two phrases of the first period produces structural separation and a degree of block disconnection, the continuous harmonic arpeggiations contribute to cohesion of the entire passage. Thus, the second theme-group reveals Prokofiev's ability during his mature Soviet period to reconcile the distinct phrasal and sectional framework of the traditional Classical form with his "modernistic" harmonic and melodic language, based on diverse local blocks, planes, and layers, in an entirely accessible "lyric, epic, and expressive" idiom. The sense of unity within diversity in the five parts of the development section, based on juxtapositions of all the thematic ideas of the exposition, is permitted by the close structural and figural relations of these themes. The scherzo movement, in D minor, has all the characteristic wit and brilliance of this type of movement in Prokofiev's works throughout his career and is representative of the fusion of Classical form and local content.

Despite Prokofiev's move toward greater integration of form and content, he and the other major Soviet composers came under severe attack at the 1948 Congress headed by Zhdanov, and this led to a lightening of his style

EXAMPLE 12–4. Prokofiev, *Fifth Symphony,* theme 2a, Nos. 6–7, phrasal and tonal structure

new era of political control over the philosophical, aesthetic, and stylistic and an attempt at still greater accessibility in subsequent works. The shift in Soviet cultural policies after 1934 (as part of Stalin's more general shift of Party policies away from the revolutionary stance toward more traditional plans) was to bring the first extreme restrictions on artistic creativity and a

attitudes of Soviet composers. The first major event to induce Shostakovich's decisive withdrawal from his earlier experiments with modernistic trends came in 1936. During the many early Soviet and international performances between 1934 and 1936 of his second opera *Lady Macbeth of the Mtsensk District* (1930–1932), which had been retitled *Katerina Izmaylova,* this more accessible work was proudly acclaimed as a model of Soviet art. However, on January 28, 1936, following Stalin's personal displeasure at a performance, *Pravda* attacked the subject of the opera for its obscenity and for its popularity among bourgeois audiences abroad: "Is it not because the opera is so confused and so entirely free of political bias [!] that it is praised by bourgeois critics? Is it not perhaps because it titillates the depraved tastes of bourgeois audiences with its witching, clamorous, neurasthenic music?"[22]

This censorship, which ended what would have been a great operatic career, was to set the official tone for other composers as well. Consequently, Shostakovich's newly completed *Fourth Symphony* (1935–1936) was banned along with the opera, and it did not receive its première until 1961, due supposedly to the composer's own criticism of the work. As "A Soviet artist's reply to just criticism," Shostakovich then composed his *Fifth Symphony* (1937), its success with both public and official critics reestablishing his position as one of the leading Soviet composers. This symphony marked a radical break from his approach in the *Fourth,* though both symphonies owe much to Mahler in their grandiose structural designs, fantasia-like kaleidoscopic unfolding of numerous themes, Romantic contradictions, and epic struggles. It was the *Fifth* that paved the way for the more personal style of many of his remaining works. Similar to Prokofiev's development during this time, Shostakovich also moved toward large-scale integration of diverse thematic ideas in this symphony as the basis of a highly developmental and climactic style. Although the *Fifth Symphony* has no explicit extramusical subtitle, as do *Symphonies Nos. 2* "Dedication to October," *3* "On the First of May," *6* originally planned as a choral setting of Mayakovsky's "Ode to Lenin," *7* "Leningrad," *11* "The Year 1905," *12* "To the Memory of Lenin" ("The Year 1917"), *13* "Babiy Yar" (Evtushenko), and *14* on texts of Apollinaire, Küchelbecker, Lorca, and Rilke, many of which include choral settings, Shostakovich did suggest an extramusical association for the otherwise purely orchestral context of the *Fifth,* stating that "the theme of my composition is the formation of personality. It is precisely man with all of his experiences whom I saw in the center of the conception of this composition, which from beginning to end is lyrical in its cast. The finale of the symphony resolves the tense, tragic moments of the first parts in an optimistic, cheerful vein."[23] This provided a more apparent than real programmatic imagery,

[22] See the larger quote in Richard Taruskin, "The Opera and the Dictator," *The New Republic* (March 20, 1989): 40.

[23] Boris Asafiev, *Izbranniye Trudi* [Selected Works], Vol. 5 (Moscow: Edition of the Academy of Science USSR, 1957), pp. 83–84, as cited in Bakst, *A History of Russian-Soviet Music,* n.2, above, p. 315.

which seems to have contributed to the composer's official redemption as a Soviet composer.

The intense Romantic quality and dramatic buildup of the *Fifth Symphony* is achieved despite the tendency of both texture and form toward extreme Classical clarity. The reconciliation of these aesthetic and stylistic features point to one of the most remarkable accomplishments of the work. Classical clarity is largely due to the extreme distinction of the many themes (though there are many subtle connections among them) and the adherence to the Classical principles of contrast and balance between their antecedent and consequent phrase members. These characteristics permit textural transparency in both the overlapping of a theme with itself in canon, as well as the juxtaposition of the different themes against each other in changing contrapuntal interpretations. Despite unexpected local chromatic-tonal shifts or mutations within several of the otherwise diatonic themes, similar to both Prokofiev and Mahler, the greater degree of motivic and rhythmic uniformity within Shostakovich's themes also contributes to textural and formal clarity and lends itself to a less complex style in relation to his preceding symphonies. Tonal uniformity within larger thematic areas also contributes to structural clarity.

As in Prokofiev's *Fifth Symphony* and many of Shostakovich's own works, this symphony begins with a slow *(Moderato)* movement based on the traditional sonata plan.[24] Each of the remaining three movements is also based on a traditional formal scheme, the second *(Allegretto)* a scherzo in large ternary form with central trio, the third *(Largo)* a fully developed sonata plan, and the fourth *(Allegro non troppo)* a sonata with rondo elements based on a more repetitive succession of thematic figurations, the character of the movement established by its well-known march theme. Within these traditional forms, the interplay of many distinct ideas serves to articulate the local Classical phrase constructions as well as contribute to the Romantic buildup of emotional tension. Like Prokofiev, this dramatic accumulation is achieved by means of the interaction of separate blocks, planes, and layers, rather than by the generation of material from a single motif. The opening thematic idea (1a) establishes an incisive, lean texture by means of angular leaps and sharp dotted rhythms in two contrasting phrasal members. A variety of figures is permitted within the short span of four measures by the use of the canon, i.e., the canonic procedure permits two different consequent figures (violins vs. celli) to unfold simultaneously from the same dotted antecedent idea. The result is an immediate buildup of tension and conflict, which pervades the rest of the movement. This sense of dramatic urgency is induced further by another rapid change of figure, based on a canonic extension of the initial

---

[24] Exposition (mm. 1–No. 17)—themes 1a (m. 1), 1b (No. 1), 1c (No. 3), 1d (No. 5, m. 2), 2a (No. 8, m. 6), 2b (No. 13, m. 3), 2a return (No. 15); Development (Nos. 17–38, m. 3)—sections 1 (No. 17), 2 (No. 19), 3 (No. 20, m. 4), 4 (No. 22), 5 (No. 24), 6 (No. 26), 7 (No. 27), 8 (No. 29), 9 (No. 32), 10 (No. 36); Recapitulation (No. 38, m. 3–44)—themes 1a (No. 38, m. 3), 2a (No. 39), 1d (No. 41), 2b (No. 42); Coda (No. 44)—themes 1a and 1d (No. 44).

dotted motif as an ostinato (mm. 4ff.). A contrasting lyrical theme (1b) in violin I, which forms yet another contrapuntal layer in juxtaposition to the original dotted figure, appears to disrupt the "expected" double-period structure of theme 1a. While this new thematic idea adds to the textural diversity, it also belongs to a deep-level structural relation that maintains the Classical double-period construction. The consequent phrase of this theme (No. 1, mm. 3–6) is based primarily on the consequent figure of theme 1a (m. 3), so the dotted ostinato accompaniment underlying the theme-1b antecedent and this consequent figure (in violin I) together suggest a variation of the opening theme-1a period.

Tension in these opening phrases is also produced by modal mutations in the thematic line within the otherwise stable D-harmonic-minor frame. The implied harmony (in m. 1) following the initial D is the dominant-ninth (Ex. 12–5). However, the chromatic shift from C♯ to C initiates a series of linear polymodal inflections—i.e., notes C, D♯ (implied enharmonic spelling of E♭), and F♯ suggest D-melodic-minor, D-Phrygian, and D-major inflections, respectively—resulting in a contrapuntal divergence and harmonic dissonance that momentarily obscure the basic D-minor tonality. The beginning of the ostinato (m. 4) abruptly reconfirms the latter by the A–D (5–1) reiterations. These chromatic alterations, which imply a mosaic of D modes, result in a higher-level scalar unity; except for the first note, D, the pitch content in the lower canonic statement of the first period (to m. 4, beat 3) forms a complete octatonic collection, B♭–C–C♯–D♯–E–F♯–G–A, exclusively. This entire thematic statement thus forms a unified entity in which there is no real tonal divergence, only polymodal inflections that have local octatonic significance. This octatonic scalar structure heightens the distinction between the two consequent phrases of the canon stated simultaneously (m. 3), as the upper line unfolds a D-minor scalar segment (D–C–B♭–A–G–A) against the lower octatonic line. The long-range significance of each of these divergent modal formations (melodic-minor, Phrygian, and octatonic) is their projection into the following passages to produce a larger structural integration of otherwise contrasting thematic figures and phrases.

Such coloristic modal elements intrude into the D-minor spectrum at the antecedent phrase of theme 1b, which forms a D-Phrygian segment, D–E♭–F–G–A. The latter is altered and expanded octatonically in the consequent phrase (at its segment E♭–G–D♭–C–B♭) by the shift in the accompaniment to the original octatonic collection, B♭–C–D♭–E♭–F♭ (Ex. 12–5), so both together form the larger octatonic segment B♭–C–D♭–E♭–F♭–[   ]–G–[   ]. Through further melodic alterations, we arrive at a new and complete octatonic scale (B–C–D–E♭–F–G♭–A♭–A–B–C) at the end of the theme-1b consequent (No. 1, m. 6–No. 2, m. 2). "Modulation" has thereby occurred simply by linear chromatic inflections and alterations rather than by functional harmonic means. However, the higher-level tonal unity of D, implied in all of this, is realized at the second announcement of theme 1a a whole-step lower (No. 2, m. 1). This thematic transposition, which begins with the minor-sixth leap of C–A♭, grows directly from the

EXAMPLE 12–5. Shostakovich, *Fifth Symphony*, Mov. I, opening, themes 1a and 1b, polymodal inflections and contrapuntal divergence in Classical phrase and period structure

EXAMPLE 12–5 CON'T.

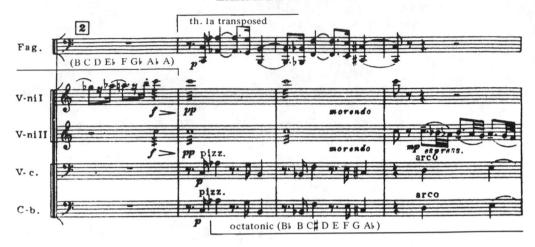

preceding cadential octatonic transposition (B–C–D–E♭–F–G♭–A♭–A–B–C); the thematic C–A♭ belongs to this octatonic scale. The significance of the new pitch level of the thematic restatement is revealed in its third measure (No. 2, m. 4), where the theme is mutated a half-step up (from C♯ to D) rather than the original half-step down (from D♯ to D). At this point, all the notes except the initial C are octatonic, which now includes the tonic note, D, the only one excluded from the opening octatonic collection. While these passages are based on octatonic shifts, the tonality of D is established firmly as a diatonic and octatonic element. This reveals an integration of materials that are otherwise planed and layered distinctly, and set in a Classical structural framework of contrasting phrasal, periodic, and thematic members. The imagery of conflict, struggle, and resolution are prepared in the opening materials.

The first theme-group continues to overlap new with old thematic figurations. Theme 1c (No. 3) and the overlapping of theme 1d with a return of 1a (at No. 6) suggest the variation principle of the first two periods similarly (themes 1a and 1b). Shostakovich's approach to structure and development is similar in this way to that of Prokofiev's during this period. However, while Prokofiev's local tonal mutations induced shifts to distant tonalities within the first theme-group, Shostakovich's chromatic alterations tend to remain within the basic area until the final statement of theme 1a (No. 8, mm. 2–3), where a decisive tonal mutation prepares us for the shift to E♭ minor in the second theme-group (No. 8, m. 6). This shift accompanies a change to a contrasting lyrical thematic style. From this point on, the tonalities become increasingly unstable, theme 2b (No. 13, m. 3) shifting to F♯ minor and back to a more dissonant E♭ tonality (at No. 16) before moving into the development section (No. 17). The latter then juxtaposes all the thematic materials in ten distinct parts in planed and layered counterpoint in increasingly complex textures.

The contrasting moods and characterizations of the two middle movements contribute to the notion of an overall program. The uproarious scherzo has no less than four distinct, though figurally related themes (No. 49, m. 1, No. 53, and No. 54, m. 1), while the more coquettish trio contains two (Nos. 57 and 61). The motoric first idea, which is played *fortissimo* in the lower strings, reminds one of the "magical," often grotesque moods of certain scherzos of Mahler, with their unexpected tonal twists, turns, and colorful instrumental elaborations. In contrast, the slow movement provides a uniformly tragic mood, in which the entire movement seems to grow from the expressive opening F♯-minor melody, despite the many thematic and textural changes that occur throughout. A spun-out type of Baroque counterpoint contributes to this singularity of mood in an increasing variety of chromatic tonal shifts marked by a continuum of expressive, dissonant appoggiaturas. These contrasting moods of the central movements lead to the Mahlerian fantasia-like quality of the finale, the interaction of the dynamic sectional blocks building toward a climactic and triumphant brassy ending after the return of the march-like theme that began the movement.

The German invasion of the Soviet Union in 1941 found Shostakovich in Leningrad, where he had been teaching at the Conservatory after his redemption by Soviet authorities in 1937. Living conditions in Leningrad were extreme during the German blockade of the city for the first two years of the war, during which time hundreds of thousands of people died of starvation and cold. Yet, during the siege of Leningrad, heroic deeds and the will to survive against the fascist oppressors carried over into the struggling cultural life. Extraordinary efforts were made by artistic institutions, performers, and composers in Leningrad and Moscow to continue their activities in the face of such devastation. Musical performances proved to be "of the essence" in the spiritual revitalization of the people, as thousands attended concerts under the most extreme conditions. It was in this context that Shostakovich produced his first war-time symphony, the *Seventh*, or *"Leningrad"* (1941), its immediate success due more to its ideological significance and response to the surrounding circumstances than to the music itself. The composition of the work was linked directly with the defense of Shostakovich's beloved city and the salvation of Soviet culture, science, and art. Official Soviet statements pointed to its depictions of heroism and humanitarian ideals and its expression of the emotional and spiritual power of the Soviet people in their struggle. The symphonic proportions were expanded beyond those of the earlier works, absorbing his relatively simpler, more accessible tonal planes and repetitive rhythmic and harmonic blocks into large dramatic juxtapositions. The breadth of the music moves from the initial representation of the common people in their everyday existence through heroic transformation during the siege to the final victory of humanity over barbarism. The invading Nazis are depicted by repetitions of a march theme in the middle of the first movement.

It was during and shortly after these war years that Shostakovich produced some of his best and most varied musical expressions, including the tragic *Eighth Symphony* (1943), the more carefree *Ninth Symphony* (1945), composed to celebrate the end of the war, the *Piano Trio* (1944), and the *First Violin Concerto* (1947–1948). While artistic involvement in the war effort evoked a strong unity of sentiment toward the socially significant *Seventh Symphony,* the end of the war once again brought a stricter official stance toward cultural policies. Criticisms of "Formalism" were renewed against Shostakovich's less programmatic works, and the official opposition to the stern mood of the *Eighth Symphony* and the unexpected irreverence of the *Ninth* led to new demands for a more positive, socially realistic attitude. This included a demand for a more accessible musical language devoid of modernistic excesses of dissonance and a renewed interest in the use of the folk idioms that had served as an inspiration during the war. In 1948, the Party Resolution under Zhdanov castigated Shostakovich and his colleagues for their insufficient use of national themes and for their tendency toward more abstract "Formalistic" construction, which led to Shostakovich's dismissal from his teaching posts at the Leningrad and Moscow Conservatories. He then turned to more realistic programmatic works such as the oratorio *The Song About Forests* (1949), *Ten Poems* (1951) for a cappella mixed chorus, based on turn-of-the-century revolutionary texts, and a cantata *The Sun Shines on Our Mother Land* (1952), for children's chorus, mixed chorus, and orchestra. Despite the new restrictions on his works of these final Stalin years, Shostakovich managed to maintain some of his earlier personal artistic inclinations in several of his nonprogrammatic instrumental works, including the *Fourth* and *Fifth String Quartets* (1949 and 1951) and the *Tenth Symphony* (1953). The symphony brought him back to public favor in the more relaxed political atmosphere after Stalin's death again, at which time the definition of "Socialist Realism" became less stringent. Later, in Shostakovich's *Fourteenth Symphony* (1970) and certain chamber works, there is even some local infusion of twelve-tone principles into his primarily tonal contexts.

Khachaturian, Kabalevsky, and other Soviet composers were also affected by the Resolution of 1948. While Kabalevsky was always a politically conscious composer who had consistently espoused Soviet cultural policies—as in his lyric and epic national style, rooted in both instrumental and dramatic Russian traditions, and in his devotion to technical simplification and musical education for children—the 1948 Resolution led him toward a greater lyricism and clarity. At the same time, other composers turned their attention away from instrumental formalism to more socially realistic vocal composition in accessible styles imbued with national elements and based on Soviet political ideology. Khachaturian was attacked for his supposedly formalistic approach in *Symphony No. 3,* "Simfoniya-poema" (1947), written for the thirtieth anniversary of the Revolution. Criticism of what was in reality a less experimental idiom seems to have been due more to his personal connections with the Composers' Union rather than any real inclination toward a modernistic musical language or abstract formalistic approach. Nevertheless, as a result of these attacks, Khachaturian apologized for having lapsed into a more abstract instrumental idiom removed from his Armenian folk sources and from socially realistic subjects. In part, he attempted to reconcile this situation by increasing his number of film scores, one of which was later arranged as the orchestral *Funeral Ode in Memory of Lenin* (1949), another *The Battle of Stalingrad,* in two series (1949). He had already composed several film scores after the mid-1930s, including *Pepo* (1935), *Zangezur* (1938), *The Garden* (1938), *Salavat Yulayev* (1939), *Prisoner No. 217* (1945), and *The Russian Question* (1948). His vocal-music production did not match that of his instrumental music—he composed some choral works and songs, but no operas—the reasons of which were reflected in his 1948 proposal to improve musical conditions according to Soviet demands: "There ought to be an experimental opera theatre. . . . You can't decide, sitting at the piano, whether an opera is good or bad. Theatres are extremely slow in deciding on new productions. Hence our preference for symphonic music."[25] Nevertheless, many cantatas and oratorios by Soviet composers during these final Stalin years were composed under the renewed restrictions of 1948.

Since his student years at the Moscow Conservatory under the tutelage of Myaskovsky between 1929 and 1934, Khachaturian had established a style that accorded to the general principles of Socialist Realism, fusing his native Armenian national folk elements with a brilliant and lyrical instrumental medium that grew out of the Romantic symphonic tradition of Glinka and the Russian nationalists. His deep roots in the music of the people were discussed by the composer himself: "I grew up in an atmosphere rich in folk music: popular festivities, rites, joyous and sad events in the life of the people always accompanied by music, the vivid tunes of Armenian, Azerbaijan and Georgian songs and dances."[26] These folk influences, which came primarily from the improvisatory melodic styles of the Caucasian Ashugs and Khanendes and the *mugams* (modal scales) of the Sazandars, were based on his absorption of the essence of the folk sources rather than their literal use.[27] The fusion of Russian folk- and art-music sources was evident already in his *Symphony No. 1* (1935), dedicated to the fifteenth anniversary of the Soviet Armenian Republic, and the popular ballet *Gayane* (1942), with its exotic, colorful, and brilliantly motoric "Sabre Dance," as well as the *Concertos* for piano (1936), violin (1940), and violoncello (1946).

The *Violin Concerto,* which won Khachaturian the Stalin Prize in 1941, uses an ornamental, spun-out rhapsodic type of melody. The slow movement is based on numerous chromatic embellishments and expressive appoggiaturas in the Ashug recitative style, the "turn" ornaments of which also remind one of folk-instrument performances of Eastern Europe. These form part of an integrated melodic and harmonic network of constantly

[25] Alexander Werth, *Musical Uproar in Moscow* (London: Turnstile Press, 1949), p. 60.

[26] Aram Khachaturian, "My Idea of the Folk Element in Music," *Sovetskaya Muzyka* 5 (1952), as cited by Grigory Shneerson, *Aram Khachaturian* (Moscow: Foreign Language Publishing House, 1959), pp. 10–11.

[27] Georgi Khubov, *Arama Khachaturian, Sovetski Kompozitor* (Moscow, 1962), pp. 9–22. See also Bakst, *A History of Russian-Soviet Music,* n.2, pp. 337–339.

changing modes. The long, open-ended melodic phrases are generated by a succession of changing diatonic and gypsy-like (often octatonic) modal segments. Furthermore, frequent chromatic chordal shifts invoke a Romantic quality that is saturated with the exotic modal coloring of the Armenian folk sources, the synthesis of which produces a style that can only belong to the twentieth century. At the same time, the predominantly tertian harmonies contribute to the accessibility of the style. The Gypsy-like rondo dance theme of the finale initiates an endless array of changing textural planes and instrumental figurations, against which conflicting orchestral ostinati often produce hemiolic and cross-metric patterns. The infusion of national folk-music sources into the Russian art-music tradition in Khachaturian's nonexperimental, pictorial, and accessible musical idiom was essential in establishing his position as a socially realistic Soviet composer, despite the official criticisms leveled against his music.

SUGGESTED READINGS

JAMES BAKST.   *A History of Russian-Soviet Music* (Westport, CT: Dodd, Mead and Company, 1966).

MALCOLM H. BROWN.   "The Soviet Russian Concepts of 'Intonazia' and 'Musical Imagery,'" *Musical Quarterly* 60/4 (October, 1974): 557–567.

LAUREL FAY.   "Shostakovich versus Volkov: Whose Testimony?" *Russian Review* 39 (1980): 484–493.

GORDON D. McQUERE.   ed., *Russian Theoretical Thought in Music* (Ann Arbor: UMI Research Press, 1983).

ISRAEL V. NESTYEV.   *Sergei Prokofiev: His Musical Life,* Eng. trans. by Rose Prokofieva (New York: Alfred A. Knopf, 1946).

JANN PASLER.   ed., *Confronting Stravinsky, Man, Musician, and Modernist* (Berkeley and Los Angeles: University of California Press, 1986), including: Malcolm Hamrick Brown, "Stravinsky and Prokofiev: Sizing Up the Competition," pp. 39–50; Richard Taruskin, "From Subject to Style: Stravinsky and the Painters," pp. 16–38.

SERGEY PROKOFIEV.   *Autobiography, Articles, Reminiscences,* compiled, edited, and notes by S. Shlifshstein, Eng. trans. R. Prokofieva (Moscow: Foreign Languages Publishing House, 1956).

GRIGORY SHNEERSON.   *Aram Khachaturian* (Moscow: Foreign Languages Publishing House, 1959).

BORIS SCHWARZ.   *Music and Musical Life in Soviet Russia* (enlarged edition, 1917–1981; Bloomington: Indiana University Press, 1972, 1983).

RICHARD TARUSKIN.   "The Opera and the Dictator," *The New Republic* (March 20, 1989): 34–40.

SOLOMON VOLKOV.   ed., *Testimony: The Memoirs of Dmitri Shostakovich as related to and edited by Solomon Volkov,* Eng. trans. Antonina W. Bouis (New York: Harper and Row, Inc., 1979; Limelight Editions, 1989).

ALEXANDER WERTH.   *Musical Uproar in Moscow* (London: Turnstile Press, 1949).

13 Color, noise, and new sonorities

KLANGFARBENMELODIEN   In 1909, soon after Schoenberg had produced his first consistently atonal pieces, he also began to conceive of a type of music in which tone color, or timbre, would replace pitch as a primary structural determinant. In his *Harmonielehre* (1911), Schoenberg recognized three characteristics of musical sound (*Klang*): pitch, color, and volume.[1] Until then, musical sound had been measured in only one of those dimensions, namely pitch. He theorized that a musical sound was primarily determined by the second dimension—tone color (*Klangfarbe*)—and suggested the term *Klangfarbenmelodien* to describe a "melodic" pattern produced exclusively by changes in the timbre, duration, and dynamics of a single pitch or chord. Schoenberg anticipated the importance that the systematic organization of tone color was to have in the course of contemporary musical developments:

> Now, if it is possible to create patterns out of tone colors that are differentiated according to pitch, patterns we call "melodies," progressions, whose coherence (*Zusammenhang*) evokes an effect analogous to thought processes, then it must also be possible to make such progressions out of the tone colors of the other dimension, out of that which we call simply "tone color." . . . That has the appearance of a futuristic fantasy and is probably just that. But it is one which, I firmly believe, will be realized.[2]

The *Klangfarben* principle underlies the third piece of the *Five Pieces for Orchestra,* Op. 16 (1909). A single five-part chord, C–G♯–B–E–A, serves as the point of departure (and return) for gradual changes to other chords. At first, only timbral changes occur within the basic chord: the two flutes, clarinet, and bassoon are replaced by cor anglais, bassoon II, horn, and trumpet, while the solo viola maintains the lowest note. Other chords evolve gradually by means of consecutive, stepwise changes of the individual pitches themselves. Schoenberg states in the score that "the chords must change so gently that no emphasis can be perceived at the instrumental entries, and so that the change is made apparent only through the new colour." The static, shimmering quality of the texture seems to evoke the mood of its title, "Summer Morning by a Lake [Colors]," which Schoenberg added at the request of his publisher.

[1] Originally published in Vienna by Universal Edition in 1911; see *Schoenberg: Theory of Harmony,* trans. Roy E. Carter (Berkeley and Los Angeles: University of California Press, 1978; based on the Third Edition, 1922), p. 421.

[2] Ibid., pp. 421–422.

Webern soon followed his teacher with shorter, more extreme examples of the *Klangfarben* technique. His inclination toward control of the structure through the organization of the various parameters was to persist throughout his career and foreshadowed developments toward total serialization by many composers of the post–World War II generation. In the third of his *Five Pieces,* Op. 10, for orchestra (1911–1913), the ternary structure and local texture are articulated almost exclusively by the timbral changes, combinations, and interrelations within the otherwise totally static linear and harmonic context. While the scoring is fairly large, the specific instrumental choices contribute to the distinction of timbral groupings. Section A (mm. 1–4) partitions the texture between violin and horn solos, which contrast with the colorful ostinati of the celesta, mandolin, guitar, and harp, and with the less distinctly pitched, hardly audible glockenspiel, herd bells, and the sectionally punctuating bass drum and harmonium. These figures are reorchestrated at the return of Section A. Most striking is the appearance of the muted trombone, which takes up the original solo idea, the muted cello on a held harmonic, and the snare drum in support of the cadential punctuation of the bass drum. The more active two-bar middle section, in changing meters, contrasts with Section A and its varied return. Here, a kaleidoscope of delicate solo figures produces a pointillistic texture, the contrasting timbres enhanced further by the addition of solo clarinet and muted cello pizzicato (marked "vibrato"). The latter, doubled by guitar, is answered by the quasi-imitative, more lyrical muted viola. A chamber-like texture results from the handling of the instruments, each having its own figuration in an irregular, almost speech-like rhythm.

The distinct timbral layers, which produce contrast within each of the larger sectional blocks, form part of an integrated, symmetrical harmonic fabric. Although each timbral group forms a clearly defined collection of cyclic intervals, each has a special connection to the intervallic structure of the moving solo lines and to each other. The mandolin and guitar together unfold the interval-5/7 segment, D–A–E. In contrast, the harp, with its enharmonic alternations (C♯/D♭–G♯/A♭), and the celesta (B♭) suggest a gapped interval-5/7 segment together, D♭–A♭–[   ]–B♭. While these two harmonic segments (D–A–E and D♭–A♭–[   ]–B♭) represent polarized areas within the cycle of fifths, each is extended cyclically by the violin and horn solos. The violin, in a strained but uniform "G–Saite" timbre, unfolds a symmetrical four-note configuration based on two interval-6 cycles, F–B/F♯–C. This collection can also be analyzed into two other interval couples, including a pair of interval 1/11s (F–F♯ and B–C) and interval 5/7s (B–F♯ and F–C), the two intervals of each pair separated by a tritone. In the last pairing, B–F♯ is a cyclic extension of D–A–E in the mandolin and guitar, giving us a larger 5/7 segment, D–A–E–B–F♯, while F–C is a cyclic extension of D♭–A♭–[   ]–B♭ in the harp and celesta, giving us a larger 5/7 segment, D♭–A♭–[   ]–B♭–F–C. (The gap in the cyclic segment D♭–A♭–[   ]–B♭ is filled in immediately by the E♭ entry of the solo horn to complete the 5/7 segment D♭–A♭–E♭–B♭.) The violin tetrachord thus serves as a link between the polarized cyclic segments: D–A–E–B–F♯/D♭–A♭–[   ]–B♭–F–C–[   ].

A relationship also exists betweeen the violin and horn segments. The horn unfolds an incomplete interval-3 transposition (D–E♭–A♭–[　]) of the violin tetrachord (F–F♯–B–C). While both linear statements unfold seven of the eight notes of an octatonic collection together (D–E♭–F–F♯–A♭–[　]–B–C), they also point to a cellular basis for Section A; i.e., if we reinterpret the timbral combinations within the accompanying harmony, we find that the gapped form of the horn statement (D–E♭–A♭–[　]) is reflected in two inverted transpositions in the guitar/celesta (E–A–B♭–[　]) and harp/mandolin (G♯–C♯–D–[　]). The symmetrical cell of the solo violin implies the presence of both inversionally related forms simultaneously, F–F♯–B and F♯–B–C, so this solo statement serves on many levels as a link for the entire fabric.

The new timbres of the two-bar middle section together unfold all twelve tones, the irregular pitch content of each segment encompassed by the three-note form of the cell (Ex. 13–1). The clarinet collection C♯–D–F–F♯–G is encompassed by both C♯–D–G and C♯–F♯–G. The cello/guitar-triplets/viola collection B–C–E♭–E–F, a transposition of the clarinet collection, is encompassed by both B–C–F and B–E–F. The mandolin/harp sixteenth-note dyad, B♭–B, and the notes stated simultaneously in the other instruments, D–E♭–E–F, together outline an expanded form (B♭–B–D–E♭–E–F) of the clarinet or string transpositions to give us a boundary of the complete four-note form, B♭–B–E–F. The viola B–E♭–E–F is encompassed by B–E–F. Finally, the simultaneity in the guitar and harp, A♭–A–C–D, is encompassed by A♭–A–D. Thus, the differentiation of the various cellular transpositions as well as cyclic segments within the larger, static harmonic context of the overall piece is dependent almost entirely upon the instrumental colors.

Throughout the first half of the century, other composers also showed interest in musical organization based on expanded color possibilities. Some of the most extreme examples of the *Klangfarben* principle occur in Elliott Carter's *Eight Etudes and a Fantasy* (1950), for flute, oboe, clarinet, and bassoon, conceived by Carter as a series of exercises that he worked out in his orchestration class at Columbia University in 1949. He concerned himself with a particular compositional problem in each piece, which led him to new possibilities beyond the primacy of pitch relations for achieving new levels of structural coherence, instrumental interaction, and expanded means of expression.[3] The result is a heightened sense of spatial relations, induced by the exploitation of the heterogeneous timbral potential of the wind instruments in contradistinction to the timbral homogeneity that would have occurred from the use of string instruments. The use of winds has permitted a clearer perception of the contrapuntal combinations and variety of spacings and doublings in the simultaneities, as in Etude I. These spatial distinctions are enhanced further in Etude V by the unusual registral positions of the respective instruments. Special technical devices, which include (in Etude VI) the

---

[3] For a synopsis of each piece, see David Schiff, *The Music of Elliott Carter* (London: Eulenberg Books, 1983), pp. 142–148.

EXAMPLE 13–1. Webern, *Five Pieces,* Op. 10, No. 3, for orchestra, mm. 5–6

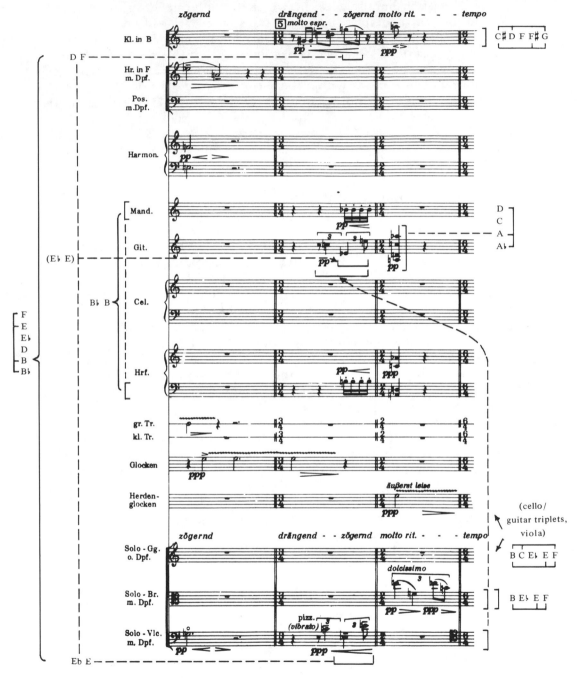

use of flutter-tonguing and trills and (in Etude VIII) shifting instrumental combinations within a continuous texture of rapid scale passages articulated by short, widely spaced single notes, point to the expansion of color possibilities for the individual instruments at a new level of performance virtuosity. Etudes III and VII are exemplars of the *Klangfarben* concept. Both are based exclusively on timbral, durational, dynamic, and articulative changes either in a single chord, D-major triad (Etude III), similar to Schoenberg's unfolding of the five-part chord in Op. 16, No. 3, or in a single pitch-class, G (Etude VII).

The more radical reduction of pitch content to a single pitch-class in Etude VII underlies a more complex formal structure than in Etude III; while the dynamic scheme of III determines a simple overall arch shape, the composite interactions of the various parameters in VII generate a more intricate ternary plan. Each of the four instruments outlines its own dynamic and rhythmic/attack pattern linearly (mm. 1–5). While the four patterns approximate each other in their increasing and decreasing dynamic arch shapes, the different durational values of their individual components produce compositely the irregular rhythmic structure of what may be considered the "theme" (Ex. 13–2). If we label each of the four linear patterns (flute, a; oboe, b; clarinet, c; and bassoon, d), then a reorchestrated recapitulation with slight modifications in the durations is evident (beginning with the flute upbeat to m. 18 through m. 21). The flute retains its original dynamic pattern (a), but its first and last durations are each shortened by a quarter beat. The original oboe pattern (b) reappears exactly the same in the bassoon except for the deletion of its final *mf* note. The clarinet retains its original dynamic pattern (c), but its initial lengthy crescendo is shortened by four beats so that it now begins after rather than before the flute, and its final held *p* note is deleted. The original bassoon pattern (d) reappears exactly the same in the oboe except for the

EXAMPLE 13–2. Carter, Etude VII of *Eight Etudes and a Fantasy*, for woodwind quartet, opening, four linear dynamic and durational patterns

deletion of its final decrescendo indication. The original codetta (mm. 6–8), which continues the "theme's" final decrescendo phase, is extended at its modified recapitulation by several beats (mm. 22–25). This is extended by a lengthy coda, based on the decrescendo phase. The overall arch-form is rounded out by a single note held in the clarinet, suggesting a retrograde of the opening played by the clarinet alone.

The central portion of the piece (mm. 8–17), which may be designated as either Section B or Development, unfolds its own internal arch-form to support the overall arch of the piece, and is derived from the initial crescendo fragment of the "theme." In the first half of this section, the crescendo figure (now *pp*–to–*mf* rather than *p*–to–*ff* of the "theme") is presented as the subject of several regular canons. The first canon (mm. 8–9), which begins in the clarinet, has four entries a beat apart. The composite rhythm produced by the four entries is therefore "regular" in contrast to the irregular composite rhythm of the opening "theme," this difference serving as the main distinction between the middle and outer sections. Two more regular canons follow. The second canon (second half of m. 9 through m. 11), which begins in the bassoon two beats after the last entry in the clarinet, extends the number to six entries one beat apart. The third canon (second half of m. 11 through m. 12), beginning in the flute three beats after the last entry in the oboe, returns to four entries one beat apart.

While these three canons are regular, the distances between them expand from two to three beats. This rhythmic augmentation anticipates the second half of Section B (mm. 12–17), where two more canons, the first now based on the crescendo figure *pp*–to–*f,* the second on *p*–to–*f* (in anticipation of the recapitulation), contain irregular entries. The entries of the first irregular canon (mm. 12–14), beginning in the bassoon, proceed at successively augmented durations of 1, 2, and 4 beat delays. The entries of the final, irregular canon (mm. 15–17), again beginning in the bassoon, now proceed at successively diminishing durations for the most part (3, 2, 2, 1, 2 beat delays). The end of this return phase in the central arch prepares for the recapitulation (at the upbeat to m. 18), which begins in the flute one beat after the last canonic entry in the bassoon, thereby completing the irregularly diminishing pattern (3, 2, 2, 1, 2, 1) of the final canon.

The Etudes are preparatory for the Fantasy, which combines all etudes in a kind of free associative context that develops around a fugue.[4] While Carter suggests that the set may be played in whole or in part for "Incomplete Concert Performance," none of the etudes is intended as isolated entities, but rather to be heard in one of several possible groupings.[5] Thus, the *Klangfarben* concept of Etudes III and VII, either of which must be performed in a group of at least four or five etudes and not as the initiating piece, was not exploited for its own sake, but rather for its relation to other techniques in the set.

---

[4] Ibid., pp. 147–148.
[5] See the preface to the score (Associated Music Publishers, Inc., 1955, 1959).

HARMONY AS COLOR OR TEXTURE: TONE CLUSTERS AND PERCUSSION IN NOTATED MUSIC

In many works throughout the early part of the century, harmony began to be exploited not so much as combinations of pitch-classes or intervals, but rather as simultaneities or densities based on either homogeneous or hetero-geneous timbral combinations. Expansion of the timbral palette to new kinds of sonorities devoid of discernible pitches led to the dissolution of traditional linear voice-leading concepts. Instead, a new concern for the vertical dimension paved the way for the liberation of *"musical space"* from the hierarchy of chordal components, the vertical ordering and spacing of which were previously determined by the traditional tonal principles of triadic construction and function.

At first, many composers began to exploit nontertian and polytonal chord constructions in their attempts to create new harmonic contexts. Ives experimented with polytonality as early as his *First String Quartet* (1896) and *Fugue in 4 Keys* on the hymn tune "The Shining Shore" (flute, cornet, and strings; 1897). He also employed fourth chords in his song *The Cage* (1906), of which the culminating eleven-note chord is organized registrally according to the two whole-tone cyclic partitions. Fourth chords and unresolved dissonances also occur in Schoenberg's *Kammersymphonie No. 1* (1906). Stravinsky began to exploit cyclic-interval chords and bitonal combinations in his early ballets, of which the bitonal chord C–E–G/F♯–A♯–C♯ in *Petrushka* (1910) and the combined E♭-dominant-seventh chord and F♭-major triad (E♭–F♭–G–A♭–B♭–C♭–D♭) in the "Danses des Adolescentes" of *Le sacre* (1912) are among the most well-known examples. Prokofiev, Bartók, the French Neoclassicists, and others also employed polytonal scale and chord combinations throughout their careers. Nevertheless, pitch or interval relations remained the primary consideration in these otherwise innovative approaches to harmonic construction.

In contrast, certain composers began to exploit large conglomerations of small intervals with the intention of neutralizing the separate pitch elements. These sonorities, because of their appearance on the page, resulted in what Henry Cowell termed *tone-clusters*. While the French impressionists employed delicate clusters of several notes each, such as the three-note groupings (G–A–B♭ and G–A–B) that sprinkle the score of Debussy's *On dine,* from *Préludes II* (1913), other composers exploited more extreme possibilities of density and percussive sonority. In many of his piano pieces, Cowell produced clusters with the fists, flat of the hand, or both forearms, his interest in natural sounds and noises having been encouraged early on by his parents' educational philosophy of total artistic freedom. In his *The Tides of Manaunaun* (1912?; published in 1922), he employed white- and black-key clusters for the programmatic depiction of waves produced by the Irish god, and in his *advertisement* (1914), *Tiger* (1928?), *Piano Concerto* (1929), and *Some More Music* for orchestra (1916), we find wide-ranging diatonic and semitonal clusters as well. In the 1920s, Cowell expanded his piano techniques to strumming, plucking, and producing harmonics in *Aeolian Harp* (1923), and glissando slides on the piano strings in *The Banshee* (1925). Ives exploited dissonant clusters similarly, which were foreshadowed by his "piano-drumming," or practicing of drum rhythms on the piano.[6] In *Tone Roads No. 3* (1915), small clusters of four or five notes alternate up and down the keyboard, and, in Movement II of the *Second Piano Sonata "Concord, Mass., 1840–60"* (1910–1915), a bar is used to depress large clusters of alternating white- and black-key collections.

As part of the new interest in expanded sonic possibilities, composers in the early part of the century began to exploit percussion instruments for their structural as well as sonic capabilities. Percussion became increasingly prominent in two general types of composition, the first still organized primarily by pitch relations, and the second by color and noise. Examples of the structural use of percussion instruments in primarily "pitch-organized" music may be observed in compositions of varying styles and aesthetics. The Viennese composers exploited pitched percussion instruments as part of their colorful *Klangfarben* contexts, as in the third of Webern's *Five Orchestral Pieces*, Op. 10, where the more percussive sounds of the bass and snare drums serve to articulate the overall ternary structure. Berg also exploited percussion prominently as an articulating structural factor in his *Three Orchestral Pieces*, Op. 6 (1914).

Equally striking are the sonic and structural uses of percussion in the blocked, layered textures of the Neoclassicists. Milhaud exploited percussion instruments extensively in his ballet *L'Homme et son désir* (1918), which includes fifteen percussionists, and in his *Concerto* for percussion and small orchestra (1929–1930). Stravinsky exploited percussion more significantly as one of several planes, distinct timbrally, in *Histoire du Soldat* (1918). While he used percussion instruments in many of his Russian works (as in *Les noces*), his careful placement of each percussion instrument as well as the other instruments on stage in *Histoire* reveals the composer's interest in spatial relations based on maximal pitch and timbral differentiation.[7]

A remarkable use of percussion in a *Klangfarben* context is found in the first five measures of Movement III of Bartók's *Music for Strings, Percussion, and Celesta* (1936). A single double-tritone cell (F♯–B–C–F) is partitioned into two timbral extremes in these measures. The high xylophone F is reiterated by a distinctive, geometrically expanding and contracting rhythmic pattern (1, 1, 2, 3, 5, 8, 5, 3, 2, 1, 1) based on the numbers of the Fibonacci series, while the low timpani F♯–B–C unfolds in short, repeated glissandi. This passage recurs at prominent structural points throughout the first twenty measures as a ritornello figure, serving to articulate the proportional formal scheme of the section. The symmetrical formal organization of Section 1 is perceived through the alternations of two timbral groups for the most part—xylophone and timpani vs. strings and sustained timpani. The

[6] Charles Ives, *Memos,* ed. John Kirkpatrick (New York: W. W. Norton & Company, 1972), pp. 42–43.

[7] Stravinsky, *Expositions and Developments* (London: Faber and Faber, 1962; Berkeley and Los Angeles: University of California Press, 1981), pp. 91–92.

percussion group serves a primary structural role in the overall expanding and contracting number of instruments in the symmetrical timbral scheme of the six sections of the movement (Ex. 13–3).[8] This scheme is also supported by dynamic and metronomic relations.

An early example of pitch-organized music written entirely for percussion ensemble is Cowell's *Ostinato Pianissimo* (1934). His interest in new

EXAMPLE 13–3. Bartók, *Music for Strings, Percussion, and Celesta,* Mov. III, symmetrically organized timbral scheme of the six sections

I. large-scale symmetry in use of various instrumental timbres in the six sections of the movement

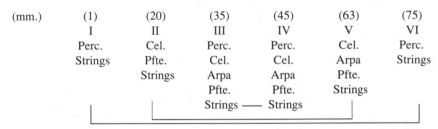

(mm.)	(1)	(20)	(35)	(45)	(63)	(75)
	I	II	III	IV	V	VI
	Perc.	Cel.	Perc.	Perc.	Cel.	Perc.
	Strings	Pfte.	Cel.	Cel.	Arpa	Strings
		Strings	Arpa	Arpa	Pfte.	
			Pfte.	Pfte.	Strings	
			Strings —— Strings			

II. more specific example of timbrally related symmetry occurs in Section I of the movement, in the expanding and contracting number of parts sounding (excluding doubling of lines).

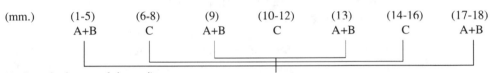

(mm.)	(1-5)	(6-8)	(9)	(10-12)	(13)	(14-16)	(17-18)
	A+B	C	A+B	C	A+B	C	A+B

(A+B=xylophone and timpani)
(C=string melody, low string pedal, timpani)

III. dynamics also form a symmetrical structure for the movement; measure nos. correspond to six sections, fortissimo at peak.

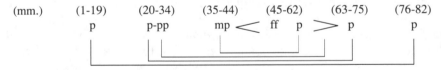

(mm.)	(1-19)	(20-34)	(35-44)	(45-62)	(63-75)	(76-82)
	p	p-pp	mp < ff p > p			p

IV. metronomic relationships

(mm.)	(1)	(6)	(20)	(35)	(45)	(55)	(63)	(65)	(75)	(76)	(79-86)
	♩=66	♩=40	♩=56	♩=66	♩=88-90	♩=104	♩=76	♩=65	♩=50	♩=42	♩=66

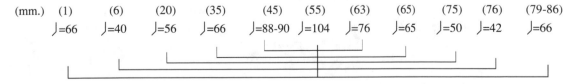

[8] See Judith Shepherd Maxwell, "An Investigation of Axis-Based Symmetrical Structures in Two Compositions of Bartók" (diss., University of Oklahoma, 1975), pp. 88–89, 101–103, and 110–112.

sonorities was expanding in several directions in the 1920s. In addition to his early contact with non-Western and Latin American percussion ensembles in San Francisco, he studied a broader sphere of world musics in Berlin in the early 1930s with Erich von Hornbostel, Sambamoorthy of Madras, and Raden Mas Jodjhana of Java. These sources asserted a strong influence on the orchestration and style of this and his later percussion music. The scoring of *Ostinato Pianissimo,* for two string pianos (plucked piano strings), eight rice bowls, two wood blocks, güiro (a Latin American notched gourd scraped by a stick), tambourine, two bongos, three drums, three gongs, and xylophone, provides a wide gamut of color resources that permits maximal linear distinction within a complex of overlapping melodic ostinato patterns. Timbral distinction is heightened by the differentiation between pitched and indeterminate instruments. Within the pitched group, a reiterated three-note diatonic pattern in one of the string pianos occurs in counterpoint to a reiterated chromatic segment in the other string piano as well as to the more rapid chromatic sixteenths in the xylophone. The last is distinguished further by its own irregular accents into three, five, seven, and nine groupings toward the middle of the work. The static quality of the overall pitch relations, due to the limited pitch configurations of the individual layers, makes this an example of the *Klangfarben* principle. A sense of motion is achieved by means of contrapuntal reinterpretations, the rhythmic ostinati forming a composite set of shifting cross accents together in an increasingly complex continuum of unequal-beat patterns.

John Cage (b. 1912) was one of the strongest followers of Cowell's approach to Eastern-influenced percussion music. Having studied both non-Western folk idioms and new compositional techniques with Cowell in 1933, he turned in the late 1930s and 1940s to composition for percussion instruments almost exclusively. He also began to extend the gamut of piano sounds in his first piece for prepared piano, *Bacchanale* (1938), following Cowell's early experiments. By means of inserting objects in the strings, Cage intended to approximate the sounds of an Eastern Asian percussion ensemble. He wrote pieces based on unusual combinations of percussion instruments. In his *First Construction (in Metal)* (1939), six percussionists play orchestral bells, thunder sheets, piano, sleigh bells, oxen bells, brake drums, cowbells, Japanese temple gongs, Turkish cymbals, anvils, water gongs, and tam tams. The colorful percussive textures include pitches of differing degrees of clarity and complexity (i.e., indeterminacy), limiting the possibilities of organizing the total structure according to pitch relations. Instead, proportional and rhythmic schemes acquire a primacy in the organization and interrelationship of the various structural levels, the proportional pattern 4, 3, 2, 3, 4 underlying the subdivisions of the first sixteen measures as well as the overall sixteen-part form.

NOISE AND PERCUSSION IN NONNOTATED MUSIC

More radical approaches to musical organization based primarily on noise and timbre also began to develop prior to World War I. The aesthetic sources of these musical developments had their roots in Italy during the first decade of the century, where a general reaction against established political, social, and cultural institutions was based on the motivation to sever ties with past traditions. Writers, artists, and musicians began to search for new aesthetic bases and new technical media that would reflect, instead, the dynamic character of contemporary society and extol the age of the machine, motion, war, and violence.

The Italian Futurist movement was launched when the poet, dramatist, and critic Filippo Tommaso Marinetti (1876–1942), an anarchist and early supporter of fascism, published his "Manifeste de Futurisme," in the Paris periodical *Le Figaro* (February 20, 1909). His Futurist ideas were adapted by such Italian writers as Aldo Palazzeschi, Corrado Govoni, and Ardengo Soffici. Primarily through the work of the Futurist painters Umberto Boccioni (also a sculptor), Carlo Carrà, Gino Severini, and Giacomo Balla, who published their own manifestos in 1910, this movement flourished between 1909 and 1915, the nihilistic aims of which foreshadowed the basic tenets of the Dadaist and Surrealist movements. The Futurist painters adhered to certain principles of the cubists, but they were more concerned with simultaneity of action rather than of form as they focused on speeding cars, trains, and other objects of dynamic motion. Balla's "Dynamism of a Dog on a Leash" is a prominent example of how movement is achieved in painting by means of repeating the lines of an object.

Between 1910 and 1912, Francesco Balilla Pratella (1880–1955) produced the first Futurist manifestos in music, including his *Manifesto dei musicisti futuristi* (Manifesto of the Futurist musicians), *Manifesto tecnico della musica futurista* (Technical manifesto of Futurist music), and *La distruzione della quadratura* (The destruction of the Quadratura). Inspired by a war poem of Marinetti, in which weapon sounds were simulated by the use of vowel and consonant syllables, Pratella, and more significantly the Futurist painter and composer Luigi Russolo (1885–1947), began to replace pitch with noise as the basis of their new musical vocabulary. In 1913, Russolo presented his theories in a more radical musical manifesto, *L'arte dei rumori* (The art of noises).

With the help of Ugo Piatti (1888–1953), Russolo created special machines known as *intonarumori* (noise intoners), the first of which was the *scoppiatore* (exploder). These formed the basis of his Futurist orchestra, which he organized into six categories of noises produced mechanically in his *L'arte dei rumori*. These included: (1) rumbles, roars, explosions, crashes, splashes, booms; (2) whistles, hisses, snorts; (3) whispers, murmurs, mumbles, grumbles, gurgles; (4) screeches, creaks, rustles, buzzes, crackles, scrapes; (5) noises obtained by percussion on metal, wood, skin, stone, terra cotta, etc.; and (6) voices of animals and men: shouts, screams, groans, shrieks, howls, laughs, wheezes, sobs. The first performance of these "intonarumori" took place in Milan in 1914, and included Russolo's *Il risveglio di una Città* (The awakening of a city), *Si pranza sulla terrazza del Kursaal* (Luncheon on the Kursaal Terrace), and *Convegno d'automobili e d'aeroplani* (Meeting of automobiles and airplanes). He used the more intricate keyboard-controlled *russolofono*, or *rumorarmonio*, in Paris in 1929.

Although other Italian composers, including Franco Casavola and Nuccio Fiorda, joined the movement in the 1920s, Italian Futurist productions in music were less successful and enduring than those in the plastic arts. Nevertheless, the Futurist composers were significant historically in influencing percussion and nonnotated composition in the interwar and post–World War II periods. Several concerts of machine-produced noise were presented in Paris in 1921, which, while provoking public reaction, attracted the interest of composers such as Ravel, Milhaud, Honegger, Stravinsky, and Varèse. Milhaud had already combined mixed speech-choruses and a large percussion section to produce music of pure noise in certain sections of his *Les Choëphores* (1915). At Cocteau's suggestion, Satie intended originally to use "noises such as sirens, typewriters, aeroplanes and dynamos" in the cubistic textures of his ballet *Parade* (1917), but finally included only the sirens and typewriters in addition to the large number of percussion instruments. More radical experiments in the use of noise-producing devices occurred in various countries in the 1920s and 1930s. George Antheil (1900–1959), an American composer in Paris, began collaborating with Fernand Léger and the filmmaker Dudley Murphy in 1924 on one of the first abstract films to be accompanied by Antheil's *Ballet mécanique* (1923–1925), and scored for sixteen player pianos. Because of synchronization problems with the film, the music was first performed by an ensemble of eight pianos, one player piano, and a large percussion group to which were added two airplane propellers and siren. His earlier *"Airplane" Sonata* (1922) was anticipated by Fedele Azari's use of airplane motors in his "Aerial Theater" (1918) in collaboration with Russolo.[9]

The French composer Edgard Varèse (1883–1965) exploited the structural possibilities of timbre more fully in both notated and nonnotated contexts. As early as 1907 in Berlin, Varèse had become familiar with the new ideas of Busoni.[10] In the interest of developing future music according to scientific principles, Busoni included a discussion of the potential of the dynamophone, a huge electric instrument invented by Thaddeus Cahill in

[9] For further discussions of music based on percussion and noise, see: Henry Cowell, *New Musical Resources* (New York: Alfred A. Knopf, 1931, reprinted 1969); H. H. Stuckenschmidt, *Twentieth Century Music,* trans. Richard Deveson (New York: McGraw-Hill Book Company, 1969), pp. 64–70; Rodney J. Payton, "The Music of Futurism: Concerts and Polemics," *Musical Quarterly 62* (1976): 25–45; Caroline Tisdall and Angelo Bozzollo, *Futurism* (New York: Oxford University Press; London: Thames and Hudson Ltd., 1977); Richard James, *Expansion of Sound Resources in France, 1913–1940, and Its Relationship to Electronic Music* (Ph.D. dissertation, University of Michigan, 1981); Chap. 3, "The Italian Futurists," Chap. 4, "Percussion and Noise in Music of French Provenance"; Glenn Watkins, *Soundings: Music in the Twentieth Century* (New York: Schirmer Books, A Division of Macmillan, Inc., 1988), pp. 242–252.

[10] Ferruccio Busoni, *Entwurf einer neuen Ästhetik der Tonkunst* [Sketch of a new aesthetic of music] (Trieste: C. Schmidl & Company, 1907); Eng. trans. (1911), reprinted in *Three Classics in the Aesthetic of Music* (New York: Dover, 1962).

1906, which could produce infinite pitch gradations and dynamics as well as new timbres through combinations of tones generated electrically. Prior to World War I, Varèse was already familiar with the work of the Italian Futurists, with whom he had a common interest in looking toward both the sounds of modern urban society and technology as a source for developing a music of the future. Within a year after Varèse's arrival in New York from Paris in 1915, he was advocating, with the aid of machines, the expansion of musical sounds in the direction of frequency range, timbral differentiation, and noise. However, from the beginning, Varèse opposed the basic philosophical attitudes of the Futurists and attacked them for their inability to transform the basic sound materials of everyday life into more abstract, integrated formal structures, declaiming: "The Futurists believed in reproducing sounds literally; I believe in the metamorphosis of sounds into music. . . . I was not interested in tearing down, but in finding new means. . . . Unlike the Dadaists I was not an iconoclast."[11]

The significance of Varèse's contributions to the new musical aesthetics lies primarily in his ability to establish a new relationship between timbral content and dynamic form. The possibilities of incorporating extremely divergent timbral and rhythmic layers and planes into an integrated continuum were already evident in his works of the 1920s. Varèse's conception of a spatial music based on the interaction of static sound masses divorced from both linear thematic construction and chordal harmony was first manifested in *Amériques* (1921) and especially *Hyperprism* (1922–1923), for winds and extensive percussion, including sirens and noise instruments. Varèse had discussed his ideas with Massimo Zanotti-Bianco, who provided the first published account of these two works. According to Zanotti-Bianco:

> If we project an imaginary sound-mass into space, we find that it
> appears as constantly changing volumes and combinations of planes,
> that these are animated by the rhythm, and that the substance of which
> they are composed is the sonority. . . . These two works . . . are
> both examples of, what I should call, *sound-geometry,* the objectivization
> of music. . . . [Varèse's] musical body is divided into two parts: the
> sound-mass molded as though in space (the orchestra without the
> percussions); and its stimulus, its movement, its dynamics (the
> percussions).[12]

These principles were continued in Varèse's remaining works of the 1920s, including *Offrandes* (1921), for soprano and chamber orchestra, *Octan-*

---

[11] Ann Florence Parks, "Freedom, Form, and Process in Varèse" (Ph.D. dissertation, Cornell University, January 1974), p. 55; see also Chou Wen-Chung, "Varèse: A Sketch of the Man and His Music," *Musical Quarterly* 52/2 (April 1966): 156.

[12] Massimo Zanotti-Bianco, "Edgard Varèse and the Geometry of Sound," *The Arts* 7 (January 1925): 35–36.

dre (1923), for eight instruments, and *Integrales* (1924), for eleven wind instruments and percussion, as well as *Arcana* (1927), for large orchestra.

Varèse's new conception of *"organized sound"* came to full fruition in *Ionisation* (1931), which exemplifies a dynamic continuum based on the interaction of static, spatial sound masses comprised almost entirely of nonpitched percussion instruments. Scored for thirteen percussionists, its sound medium anticipated the more complex and divergent mixtures of pitched sonorities, nonnotated percussion, noise, and taped materials produced electronically that he was to use after World War II in *Déserts* (1954) and *Poème électronique* (1958). Unity in *Ionisation* is determined by the overlapping and interrelation of two basic concepts of construction: *sectional form* and *dynamic form*. Varèse rejected the notion of traditional sectional forms in his music generally, but a newspaper account of his lecture on *Ionisation* in 1937 attributes to the composer the idea that "the score is in the form of a first movement of a sonata."[13] The sectional (sonata) form is articulated for the most part by means of recurrent rhythmic-thematic elements, the traditional tonal functions replaced by timbral "modulations." The dynamic form is generated primarily by the juxtaposition, overlap, and exchange of contrasting categories of timbres in a nonlinear developmental process.

An outline of timbral categories is essential to the analysis of the formal process of the work. The extensive percussion may be subsumed under seven general categories: (1) *Metal*—triangle, anvils, cowbells, hand cymbals, crash cymbal, suspended cymbal, gong, tam-tams, and rim shot (on tarole, snare drum, parade drum, and tenor drum); (2) *Membrane*—bongos, snare drum without snare (Player 8), tenor drums, and bass drums; (3) *Snare*—tarole, snare drum with snare (Player 9), and parade drum; (4) *Wood*— claves, wood blocks, and slapstick; (5) *Rattle-Scratcher (Multiple Bounce)*—sleigh bells, castanets, tambourine, maracas, and güiros; (6) Air-Friction *(Varying Intensity)*—sirens and string drum; and (7) *Keyboard Mallet (Tone Cluster)*—glockenspiel with resonators, chimes, and piano.[14] These categories may serve also to delineate a nontraditional sectional concept of form based on a series of independent textural blocks, a concept lying somewhere between those of the traditional sectional (sonata) plan and dynamic process. Chou outlines nine such texturally determined sections: Section 1

---

[13] "Modern Percussion Masterpiece Illustrates Composer's Lecture," *Santa Fe, New Mexican* (September 9, 1937): 3. For a thematic outline suggesting the sonata plan, see Nicolas Slonimsky, "Analysis," in the published score of *Ionisation* (New York: Colfranc Music Publishing Corporation, 1966, 1967), p. 7. See also Parks, "Freedom, Form, and Process in Varèse," n.11, above, pp. 357–361, for a detailed, viable alternative to Slonimsky's formal interpretation.

[14] See Chou Wen-Chung, "*Ionisation:* The Function of Timbre in Its Formal and Temporal Organization," *The New Worlds of Edgard Varèse: A Symposium,* ed. Sherman Van Solkema (New York: Institute for Studies in American Music, Department of Music, School of Performing Arts, Brooklyn College of the City University of New York, 1979), pp. 28–29.

(mm. 1–8), *Texture I;* Section 2 (mm. 9–12), *Texture II;* Section 3 (mm. 13–20), *Texture III;* Section 4 (mm. 21–37), *Linear Elaborations;* Section 5 (mm. 38–50), *Verticalization of Textures;* Section 6 (mm. 51–55), *Return of Texture I;* Section 7 (mm. 56–65), *Linear Elaborations;* Section 8 (mm. 66–74), *Culmination of Elaborations;* and Section 9 (mm. 75–91), *Conclusion.*[15] The following discussion is intended to integrate certain features of these formal concepts, which function on several independent but overlapping levels, into a viable musical entity.

One of the main focal points of the work is an all-metal crash (No. 11, m. 6, fermata), which serves as a prominent convergent point between the quasi-traditional sectional (sonata) scheme and the ongoing process based on the continuous interaction of timbral planes. This vertical metal sonority demarcates the end of the large middle section before the recapitulation of Subject 1 (No. 12, upbeat to m. 5, tambour militaire, or parade drum) and the final shift from nonmetal to metal sounds. Prior to the middle section (No. 9f.), these two timbral groups had remained separated maximally. Except for the strong metal and siren sounds in the eight-measure introduction and its partial restatement at No. 2, nonmetal sounds prevail until some mixing begins at the sonic outburst (No. 7) that leads to Subject 2 (No. 8). The gradually-intruding metal sounds—cowbells (cencerro) and cymbals—remain subordinate to the more active nonmetal quintuplets that characterize Subject 2 until a shift to anvils, cymbals, gongs, tam-tams, and triangle changes the timbral balance after this thematic block (No. 9). At this point, the sirens reenter and maintain support of the following mixed timbres, the metal sounds becoming increasingly prominent until the all-metal crash near the ending of the middle section.

The modified recapitulation (No. 12, upbeat to m. 5), which appears to serve a traditional function in the sectional form, has a more significant hierarchical function in the overall dynamic form. The timbral layers and planes that are presented successively in the opening thematic and episodic passages become aligned vertically in the recapitulation, so a sense of structural condensation is produced. Chou states that "the rhythmic excitement of the piece derives not from a conventional use of rhythm but from the 'contrapuntal' and 'chordal' expansion of such rhythmic cells or their derivatives in conjunction with juxtaposition and alteration of timbres identified with these rhythmic ideas."[16]

Within the overall developmental process are subsidiary focal points of (verticalized) timbral and rhythmic unison. The first prominent one occurs, prior to the main peak at the all-metal crash, at the sonorous outburst of rhythmically aligned, mixed timbral groups toward the end of the free episodic development (No. 7), which begins with a free interaction of varied figures (at No. 6). From the partial return of Subject 1 (No. 4) to this

[15] Ibid., pp. 30–34.
[16] Ibid., p. 30.

verticalized sonority (No. 7), the subject is elaborated contrapuntally by the castanets, claves, tambourine, and rim shots, which produce a gradual timbral modulation in preparation for the large sonic outburst compositely. The final prominent simultaneity initiates the coda (No. 13), where the pitched instruments, including glockenspiel with resonator, chimes, and piano, enter for the first time in static tone clusters in support of the same metal and siren sounds that began the work. This simultaneity, analogous to the main all-metal crash just before the recapitulation, also serves as a culminating point for the more active and mixed timbral textures of the recapitulation.

On the more local level, each of the parameters--contrapuntal and vertical textures, timbres, themes, and rhythms—may be isolated and studied as independent structural determinants.[17] Subject 1 (No. 1, mm. 1–4), in sharp contrast to the opening block and its varied return, forms a relatively unified textural block. The individual timbral layers produce local spatial distinctions. Each layer acquires a life of its own subsequently, as it is developed independently in other passages (see No. 5, mm. 3–4, where the countersubject is divorced from the subject, and occurs instead in counterpoint with variations of itself). Differentiation of the layers around the subject is determined by both the individual rhythmic patterns as well as the timbral contrasts within the primarily nonmetal context (Ex. 13–4), the individual linear components providing the seeds for subsequent separation, development, and recombination.

EXAMPLE 13–4. Varèse, *Ionization,* subject and countersubject, mm. 8ff.

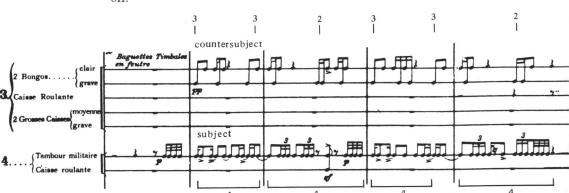

[17] Jay T. Williams, "Elements of Form in the Music of Edgard Varèse (Master's thesis, Indiana University, 1966), pp. 53, 68, 85, 100, 110, and 116.

INVENTION OF NEW INSTRUMENTS

A striking, though shortlived, innovation was an impractical two-hundred-ton electrical instrument known as the *telharmonium* (or *dynamophone*), invented by Thaddeus Cahill around 1900.[18] First exhibited in New York in 1906, this electromechanical keyboard instrument expanded the possibilities of tone and overtone combinations and the additive production of timbres by means of electric tone generators, paving the way for the manually operated electrical instruments of the interwar period and the electronic synthesizer after World War II. In 1907, Busoni discussed the potential for achieving "an infinite gradation of the octave," and how it would serve as a "useful tool of the art of the future."[19]

It was only after World War I that other electronic instruments were developed for wider practical application. In 1920, the Russian scientist Lev Theremin invented the instrument named after him, giving concerts during the 1920s in Europe and the United States with this and other of his inventions. The *theremin* consists of one generator with changing pitch, controlled by the distance of the player's hands from two antennas projecting from a small box. Experiments were carried out by Jörg Mager in the 1920s with the *sphärophone* (electronic organ) and the larger *partiturophone* subsequently, but it was in 1922 that Maurice Martenot invented the most widely used manually operated electronic instrument of the interwar period. The *ondes martenot,* which made its first public appearance in 1928, is a monophonic electronic instrument with keyboard and other manual controls that include a sliding ribbon producing glissandi and heard through two loudspeakers. This instrument was employed prominently by Messiaen, in the *Turangalîla Symphony* (1948), a vast score of varied instrumental colors. One of several individual uses of the instrument, in which it contributes to the distinction of timbres and thematic/figural materials, can be seen in the sixth movement, "Jardin du sommeil d'amour" (e.g., at No. 7ff.). The basic C♯–dominant-seventh chordal structure of the theme is played by the strings and ondes martenot, around which the piano, flute, clarinet, and percussion add embellishments in what appear to be contrasting nontonal elaborations and individualized rhythmic patterns. The ondes martenot was also used by Arthur Honegger and André Jolivet. Another electronic instrument called the *trautonium,* which was developed at the Berlin Hochschule für Musik by Friedrich Trautwein and first performed in 1930, was used until the mid-1950s. This instrument, like the theremin, could only produce one pitch at a time. However, pitch could be articulated exactly and dynamic level controlled by pressing a wire against a metal bar. Several composers wrote for the trautonium, among them Strauss and Hindemith, whose unpublished *Konzertstück* for trautonium and string orchestra was performed in Munich in 1931. The trautonium has also been

[18] This was discussed by R. S. Baker, in "New Music for an Old World," *McClure's Magazine* 27 (July 1906): 291–301.

[19] See Busoni, *Entwurf,* n.10, above.

used in films frequently. Since 1926, Hindemith wrote many pieces for mechanical pianos and organs for radio and films and, together with Ernst Toch, experimented with gramophone records at the Bauhaus in Weimar in the mid-1920s. Their techniques, which included altering the sound of the recordings by scratching them and playing them backwards, foreshadowed those of the musique concrète and electronic tape movements after World War II.

In addition to these electronic instruments, other types of instruments were created in the pre–World War II period as the basis for expanding the timbral spectrum and permitting the use of unusual tunings. Among the most original was the American composer Harry Partch (1901–1976), who developed new instruments in connection to his experiments with traditional tuning systems and the more radical microtonal subdivisions of the octave, including his 43-note scale based on interval ratios derived from just intonation.[20] In addition to the use of the human voice, his instruments were often either Eastern Asian or African, or of his own original invention. Some of his works prior to 1950, which join vocal with original instrumental forces, are *By the Rivers of Babylon (Psalm cxxxvii)* (1931), the stage work *Barstow, Eight Hitchhiker Inscriptions from a Highway Railing at Barstow, California* (1941), *Dark Brother, The Letter, San Francisco,* and *US Highball* (1943), and *Two Settings from "Finnegan's Wake"* (1944).

[20] Harry Partch, *Genesis of a Music* (Madison: University of Wisconsin Press, 1949; rev. New York: Da Capo Press, 1974), pp. 133–134.

SUGGESTED READINGS

R. S. BAKER.   in "New Music for an Old World," *McClure's Magazine* 27 (July 1906): 291–301.

FERRUCCIO BUSONI.   *Entwurf einer neuen Ästhetik der Tonkunst* [Sketch of a new aesthetic of music] (Trieste: C. Schmidl & Company, 1907); Eng. trans. (1911), reprinted in *Three Classics in the Aesthetic of Music* (New York: Dover, 1962).

CHOU WEN-CHUNG.   "*Ionisation:* The Function of Timbre in Its Formal and Temporal Organization," *The New Worlds of Edgard Varèse: A Symposium,* ed. Sherman Van Solkema (New York: Institute for Studies in American Music, Department of Music, School of Performing Arts, Brooklyn College of the City University of New York, 1979), pp. 27–74.

———.   "Varèse: A Sketch of the Man and His Music," *Musical Quarterly* 52/2 (April 1966), 151–170.

HENRY COWELL.   *New Musical Resources* (New York: Alfred A. Knopf, 1931; reprinted 1969).

CHARLES IVES.   *Memos,* ed. John Kirkpatrick (New York: W. W. Norton & Company, 1972), pp. 42–43 (on Ives' "piano-drumming").

RICHARD JAMES.   *Expansion of Sound Resources in France, 1913–1940, and Its Relationship to Electronic Music* (Ph.D. dissertation, University of Michigan, 1981): Chap. 3, "The Italian Futurists;" Chap. 4, "Percussion and Noise in Music of French Provenance."

JUDITH SHEPHERD MAXWELL.   "An Investigation of Axis-Based Symmetrical Structures in Two Compositions of Bartók" (D.M.Ed. thesis, University of Oklahoma, 1975), pp. 88–89, 101–103, and 110–112 (on structural relations of timbre, dynamics, tempo, etc., in *Music for Strings, Percussion, and Celesta*).

ANN FLORENCE PARKS.   "Freedom, Form, and Process in Varèse" (Ph.D. dissertation, Cornell University, January 1974).

HARRY PARTCH.   *Genesis of a Music* (Madison: University of Wisconson Press, 1949; rev. New York: Da Capo Press, 1974).

RODNEY J. PAYTON.   "The Music of Futurism: Concerts and Polemics," *Musical Quarterly* 62/1 (1976): 25–45.

DAVID SCHIFF.   *The Music of Elliott Carter* (London: Eulenberg Books, 1983), pp. 142–148 (on *Eight Etudes and a Fantasy*).

ARNOLD SCHOENBERG.   *Harmonielehre* (Vienna: Universal Edition, 1911); *Theory of Harmony*, Eng. trans. by Roy E. Carter (Berkeley and Los Angeles: University of California Press, 1978), pp. 421–422 (on *Klangfarbe*).

CAROLINE TISDALL AND ANGELO BOZZOLLO.   *Futurism* (New York: Oxford University Press; London: Thames and Hudson Ltd., 1977).

MASSIMO ZANOTTI-BIANCO.   "Edgard Varèse and the Geometry of Sound," *The Arts* 7 (January 1925): 35–36.

14 Early developments of the twelve-tone system beyond Schoenberg, Berg, and Webern

DISSEMINATION OF THE TWELVE-TONE IDIOM Prior to the late 1940s, few composers outside the Schoenberg circle embraced the principles of twelve-tone composition, the influence of Schoenberg remaining limited to his students for the most part. Two prominent outside figures to take up these principles during this period were the Viennese and Italian composers Ernst Krenek and Luigi Dallapiccola. The isolation of Schoenberg's teachings was due largely to economic and political factors, which prevented the dissemination of twelve-tone principles in the interwar period. Worldwide economic depression since about 1930 was in part responsible for the prevention of audience contact with new musical idioms. Furthermore, political censorship in Germany and Russia curtailed the spread of twelve-tone composition. In Germany, such music was considered to represent "Jewish Bolshevism," and in Russia, "bourgeois decadence." The result was the suppression of Schoenberg's teachings and compositions. Instead, neotonality and neoclassical styles came to dominate the international musical scene of the 1930s and early 1940s. These two musical extremes—*Neoclassicism* and atonal *Expressionism*—were already in evidence by the mid-1920s. The polarization of these musical developments can be attributed in part to the longstanding political hostilities that burst forth in the First World War, since composers from one country often avoided composing in the styles of composers from enemy nations vehemently. Furthermore, opportunities to hear performances of foreign works had disappeared during the war. These political tensions were to increase to new levels in the decade prior to World War II. Thus, many factors contributed to the isolation of Schoenberg's teachings in the interwar period.

Certain early attempts were made to remove the barriers that kept international composers isolated from one another. The first major step was taken in 1922, when Viennese musicians initiated the idea of the International Society for Contemporary Music (ISCM).[1] The composer and writer Rudolph Réti and the writer Paul Stefan were active in its formation. Among composers, Egon Wellesz and Paul Pisk (pupils of Schoenberg) decided in private meetings to get together with composers from other countries after the First World War and establish personal contacts, with the purpose of making the music of these different countries known. However, Germany's ban on its section of the ISCM in 1933 and later on those of its occupied countries, as well as the bans by the other axis powers, Italy and Japan, inhibited whatever possibilities the ISCM may have been able to provide for

---

[1] Elliott Antokoletz, "A Survivor of the Vienna Schoenberg Circle: An Interview with Paul A. Pisk," *Tempo* 154 (September 1985): 19.

the spread of serial composition. Although these yearly international concerts did not lead to significant dissemination of the twelve-tone idiom, they did provide opportunities for first performances of works like Berg's *Violin Concerto* (Barcelona, 1936) and Webern's *Das Augenlicht,* Op. 26 (London, 1938), as well as Schoenberg's music. It was only at the international summer course established in 1946 at Darmstadt, Germany, that serial music was to be adopted extensively.

FOREIGN PUPILS OF SCHOENBERG AND WEBERN

Schoenberg's twelve-tone serial principles were disseminated by several of his foreign students, though to a limited extent only, preceding World War II. The Greek composer and violinist Nikolaos Skalkottas (1904–1949) studied with Schoenberg from 1927 to 1931, having had several of his works performed publicly in Berlin by Schoenberg's pupils. While his style remained objective and was based on neoclassical forms throughout his career, he began to employ twelve-tone serial techniques as early as his *First Piano Concerto* and second and third movements of the *Octet* A/K30. These were his only twelve-tone works composed during this time of study with Schoenberg, but his *15 Little Variations for Piano* (1927) had already been set completely in the atonal idiom. Most of his large-scale works between 1935 and 1945 were in the twelve-tone system entirely. While his textures are as dense contrapuntally as those of Schoenberg, Skalkottas, unlike his teacher, was to use many rows in his twelve-tone compositions, as in his first *Symphonic Suite,* sketched as early as 1928. Like Berg, he often employed cellular permutation within the rows.

The Norwegian composer Fartein Valen (1887–1952) had already used twelve-tone themes prior to his contact with Schoenberg's music in the 1920s. Such themes were a part of his earlier dissonant contrapuntal style, which grew out of his knowledge of the polyphony of Palestrina and Bach originally. He continued to develop his twelve-tone writing until 1943. However, few of his works were ever performed, the conservative trend of the Norwegian public in the 1930s contributing to the isolation of his music.

The Spanish-British composer Roberto Gerhard (1896–1970) and the Viennese composer, musicologist, and teacher Egon Wellesz (1885–1974) both disseminated Schoenberg's teachings in England. While Wellesz had begun studying with Schoenberg in 1904, Gerhard came to Vienna to study with Schoenberg from 1923 to 1928. Gerhard employed serial technique in the form of recurring intervallic constructions as early as his *Wind Quintet* (1928, performed in Barcelona in 1930), but did not employ a series again regularly until 1948. In his large-scale transitional work, the *Violin Concerto* (1942–1943), he used a twelve-tone series as the melodic and harmonic basis of certain sections, while other sections employed tonal as well as atonal harmonies. Another Austrian composer and teacher to settle in England (since 1938) was Leopold Spinner (1906–1980). At the recommendation of Alban Berg, he studied in Vienna with Paul Pisk originally (from 1926 to

1930), then Webern (from 1935 to 1938), turning to twelve-tone composition only after his studies with the latter.[2] One of the first English composers to use twelve-tone serial techniques was Humphrey Searle (1915–1982), who studied with Webern in the late 1930s while in Vienna. Webern's influence first became obvious in the spare texture of his *Night Music,* Op. 2 (1943), which, written for Webern's sixtieth birthday, already borders on the use of twelve-tone technique. His first thoroughly twelve-tone work is the *Intermezzo,* Op. 8, for eleven instruments (1946).

The French musicologist, teacher, composer, and conductor of Polish origin, René Leibowitz (1913–1972), studied with Schoenberg and Webern in Vienna and Berlin from 1930 to 1933, and adhered strictly to their serial principles. While his music has become isolated increasingly in postwar France, his work in terms of performance, teaching, and writing has been among the most significant in promoting the music of the Schoenberg School, especially between 1945 and 1947, at a time when their music was largely unacknowledged by composition teachers. In the late 1940s, his efforts as founder of the International Festival of Chamber Music, as teacher, and as author—his writing on twelve-tone music has been studied by serial composers from all countries—served to introduce the Viennese works into Paris for the first time.[3] He was also among the first to teach Schoenberg's principles at Darmstadt in 1946.

The composer and bassoonist Adolph Weiss (1891–1971) was the first American to study with Schoenberg (1925–1926), turning to twelve-tone serial composition shortly afterwards. Also from the United States was Ross Lee Finney (b. 1906), who studied with Berg in 1931–1932. However, his interest in serial techniques became more evident later, in his *String Quartet No. 6* (1950), based on three twelve-tone series, and the *Fantasy in Two Movements* (1958), after which he began to experiment with serialization of other parameters as well.

VIENNA: KRENEK'S EXTENSIONS OF TWELVE-TONE SERIALISM

One of the earliest composers to bridge the gap between the Neoclassical aesthetic of the Parisians and the atonality of the Vienna Schoenberg Circle was Ernst Krenek (b. Vienna, 1900), who was also one of the first outside of this circle to adopt twelve-tone serial principles. In his earliest years, he was inclined toward atonality, but turned away from it between 1925 and 1929. At this time, he led certain young composers in opposition to Schoenberg's complex atonality, which he believed was derived from the "overheated

---

[2] Ibid., pp. 18–19. Spinner's book, *A Short Introduction to the Technique of Twelve-Tone Composition* (London and New York: Boosey & Hawkes, 1960), is an important guide to twelve-tone procedures.

[3] See his book, *Schoenberg et son école* (Paris, 1947); Eng. trans. Dika Newlin (New York: Philosophical Library, 1949; rep. 1975), and his *Introduction à la musique de douze sons* (Paris: L'Arche, 1949).

emotional atmosphere" of Viennese expressionism.[4] Also finding German neoclassicism humorless and unappealing, he became fascinated with the frivolity and impertinence of Parisian neoclassicism between 1925 and 1929. It was during this time that he received recognition with the opera *Jonny Spielt Auf* (1927), in which he returned to tonality and a lyrical style, and was also influenced by jazz.

After many performances of *Jonny* in various European cities, Krenek settled in Vienna in 1928, where he first came into contact with Berg and Webern. These close acquaintances led him to reconsider and alter his previous, negative attitude toward the musical language and aesthetics of the Schoenberg school. In 1930 he met Karl Kraus, who had the first decisive influence on him in his turn to the twelve-tone principles of the Viennese. It was in his setting of a collection of Kraus' poems that he first used the twelve different pitch classes as the basis of motivic segments, though he still remained within the tonal orbit. Then, between 1930 and 1933, he composed his opera *Karl V,* which was his first work based entirely on twelve-tone technique. He now turned to a detailed study of the scores of Schoenberg, Berg, and Webern as he composed the opera.

This work, commissioned for the Vienna Staatsoper, was composed during a period of pessimism due to the advent of Nazism. His choice of a religious subject, based on Charles V, Emperor of the Holy Roman Empire, served as a personal expression as influenced by the surrounding political realities. Because of this, the work was banned from performance in 1934 and the composer had to wait until 1938 to have his première in Prague, after he was referred to as a "Kulturbolschewist" in Germany. Thus, we find in the work an early example of political protest, which was set within a musical idiom that was to come under German censorship.

After his initiation into the twelve-tone system with *Karl V,* he continued to alternate between tonal and twelve-tone composition. Krenek emigrated to the United States in 1937 where, in the 1940s, he moved toward a more strict handling of the twelve-tone idiom. His special serial developments led him gradually to total control of all parameters of the music.[5] This tendency toward total control began in the early 1940s with his own "rotational" method of manipulating note segments, which evolved into a more complex, strictly controlled serialism of the 1950s. He had not originally planned, nor had he been aware of, the implications of this technique in the 1940s with regard to the serialization of musical parameters other than pitch (durations, dynamics, register, density, and timbre). In his *Twelve Variations* for piano (1936) and *Sixth String Quartet* (1937) he had begun to expand twelve-tone procedure in a new direction "by programming the distribution

[4] Will Ogdon, "A Master Composer and a Foremost Musician of Our Time," in Ernst Krenek, *Horizons Circled: Reflections on My Music* (Berkeley and Los Angeles: University of California Press, 1974), pp. 12–13.

[5] For his definition of "Serialism," see Ernst Krenek, "Circling My Horizon," in *Horizons Circled* (see n.4, above), pp. 75–76.

of the forty-eight basic shapes of the twelve-tone row over the total area of the composition." However, he had not yet realized at that time that the principle of "rotation" was to become one of his most important tools once he moved into serial composition. In his *Symphonic Piece for String Orchestra,* Op. 86 (written in 1939), he began to exploit the possibilities of deriving motivic elements from the basic series by means of several systematic procedures. Through combinations of all the derived materials, various themes were constructed.[6] Such permutational methods for deriving secondary sets from the basic one had already been employed in Berg's *Lyric Suite* (as shown in Chapter 3).

In order to relax the rigidity of the twelve-tone technique, Krenek began to exploit the principle of "rotation," or "a special form of permutation" more systematically.[7] In his choral work, *Lamentatio Jeremiae Prophetae,* Op. 93 (1941–1942), he attempted to integrate certain principles of twelve-tone technique with those of the old church or Greek modes. Analogous to the principle of rotating the diatonic scale to get the seven different traditional modal forms (Dorian, Phrygian, Lydian, etc.), he divided the twelve-tone row into two scalar six-note groups, F–G–A–Bb–Db–Eb / B–C–D–E–F#–G#, each of which was then rotated by putting the first note at the end of the hexachord, e.g., [ ]–G–A–Bb–Db–Eb–[F] and [ ]–C–D–E–F#–G#–[B]. Through five such consecutive rotational operations for each hexachord, six permuted forms were established. All six forms in each hexachordal group naturally contained the same six notes, so another set of patterns was then derived by transposing the five new forms in each group to the original pitch level of that group. By this transpositional process, all twelve tones were eventually included within each of the two hexachordal groups (Ex. 14–1). The *Lamentatio* (Ex. 14–2) is an early example of Krenek's motivic (modified)

EXAMPLE 14–1. Krenek, scheme of hexachordal rotation and transposition

Original six-tone groups												Transposed six-tone groups											
F	G	A	Bb	Db	Eb	/ B	C	D	E	F#	G#	// F	G	A	Bb	Db	Eb	/ B	C	D	E	F#	G
G	A	Bb	Db	Eb	F	/ C	D	E	F#	G#	B	// F	G	Ab	Cb	Db	Eb	/ B	C#	D#	F	G	A
A	Bb	Db	Eb	F	G	/ D	E	F#	G#	B	C	// F	F#	A	B	C#	D#	/ B	C#	D#	E#	G#	A
Bb	Db	Eb	F	G	A	/ E	F#	G#	B	C	D	// F	Ab	Bb	C	D	E	/ B	C#	D#	F#	G	A
Db	Eb	F	G	A	Bb	/ F#	G#	B	C	D	E	// F	G	A	B	C#	D	/ B	C#	E	F	G	A
Eb	F	G	A	Bb	Db	/ G#	B	C	D	E	F#	// F	G	A	B	C	Eb	/ B	D	Eb	F	G	A

---

[6] Krenek, "New Developments of the Twelve-Tone Technique," *Music Review* 4 (1943): 87–89.

[7] Krenek, "Circling My Horizon," n. 5, above, p. 81.

manipulations of two rotated-transposed hexachords, F–A♭–B♭–C–D–E and B–C–D–E–F♯–G♯, derived from the rotational diagram of "chromatic" hexachords (see under "Transposed six-tone groups" in Ex. 14–1).[8]

Krenek described the principle of rotation as "a procedure in which the elements of a given series systematically and progressively change their relative positions according to a plan which is serially conceived." In the 1950s, Krenek arrived at stricter and more complex rotational procedures, as in his orchestral composition, *Kette, Kreis, und Spiegel* (1956–1957), in which the derivative row forms are systematically distributed throughout. From the original order of the notes, he built a secondary row according to a symmetrical scheme of pairings (Ex. 14–3). This was followed by a second step that reverses the two notes in successive pairings. These two steps were then repeated continually until the retrograde was achieved. Krenek referred to this as "progressive retrogression."[9] Many other systematic permutations were devised by Krenek in the 1950s. Such successions of permutations determined the exact place in time for each event (including durations, dy-

EXAMPLE 14–2. Krenek, *Lamentatio Jeremiae Prophetae,* Op. 93, from Krenek, "New Developments of the Twelve-Tone Technique," *Music Review* (1943), Ex. 26, Canon a 3, motivic manipulation of two rotated-transposed hexachords, F–A♭–B♭–C–D–E and B–C–D–E–F♯–G♯, derived from the given rotational diagram of "chromatic" hexachords (see under "Transposed six-tone groups" in the diagram)

[8] See Krenek, "New Developments," n.6, above, 87–89.
[9] See Krenek, "Circling My Horizon," n.5, above, p. 83.

EXAMPLE 14–3. Krenek's rotational procedures in *Kette, Kreis und Spiegel* for orchestra

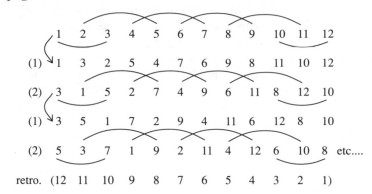

namics, rests, etc.), leading to the total serialization of all parameters. In his *Fibonacci Mobile* for string quartet and piano four hands, Op. 187 (1964), numbers of the Fibonacci series, 2, 3, 5, 8, 13, 21, 34 (each number of which is the sum of the two preceding numbers) determine the durations of the basic elements. Through a variety of choices allowed the performers, these elements may appear in differing, simultaneous combinations. Krenek stated that "the effect should remind one of the aspects of a spatial mobile that, by turning about, shows its elements in constantly changing perspectives."[10]

TWELVE-TONE INFUSION INTO BASICALLY TONAL STRUCTURES

Although the political and economic problems during the 1930s and 1940s resulted in the suppression of musical innovation in concert life and music publishing, certain composers from various countries began to infuse twelve-tone serial principles into their modal or tonal structures. The French-Swiss composer Frank Martin (1890–1974) moved in this direction in his *First Piano Concerto* (1933–1934), the *Rhapsodie* for five strings (1935), the less dissonant *String Trio* (1936), and the *Symphony* (1937), which includes jazz instruments. While Martin infused Schoenberg's serial techniques into a modal-tonal idiom, his focus is harmonic rather than contrapuntal, and from the outset, his freer use of twelve-tone principles bore little resemblance to that of Schoenberg. In the 1940s, he fused serial techniques and Baroque-style features in his *Petite symphonie concertante* (1945), for harp, harpsichord, piano, and two string orchestras.[11] Another Swiss composer, Rolf Liebermann (b. Zurich, 1910), also used twelve-tone techniques freely, often in tonal or bitonal

---

[10] Ibid., p. 91.
[11] Paul Griffiths, *Modern Music: The Avant-garde Since 1945* (New York: George Braziller, Inc., 1981), p. 15.

structures, having studied twelve-tone composition in Switzerland with Wladimir Vogel (b. Moscow, 1896–1984) in Ascona in the late 1930s. Vogel's early style shows influences of Scriabin and, in the 1920s, expressionism as well. Though he never studied with Schoenberg, he soon came to apply the latter's twelve-tone serial techniques in some of his compositions, the first of which was his *Violin Concerto* (1937).

An individual approach to twelve-tone serial composition is that of the German composer and teacher Wolfgang Fortner (b. Leipzig, 1907), whose style also appears to have developed from several different technical and stylistic sources. Prior to his move toward the twelve-tone idiom in 1945, he had developed a contrapuntal style based on extended tonal relations, which reveal his interest in the chromatic counterpoint of both Bach and Reger. Eventually, a more distinctive neoclassical formalism was combined with a kind of modally chromatic counterpoint, revealing his debt to Hindemith and Stravinsky. By 1945, he began to infuse twelve-tone serial writing into his modal counterpoint, an approach based on the derivation of a mode from the twelve notes. Within the basically unordered pitch relations of the mode, serialized cellular segments are inserted at various transpositional levels. His *Symphony* of 1947 is one of his first important works to reveal this infusion of twelve-tone serialism into his contrapuntal neoclassical style. Since then, his music has tended gradually toward greater intellectual control, the serial principle pervading all parameters. However, Fortner has maintained a degree of freedom for the sake of his own individual artistic expression. His teachings of twelve-tone composition at the International Summer Course at Darmstadt during the first years after its inception in 1946 have also had an influence on younger composers, one of the most notable being his German student Hans Werner Henze.

The first British composer to employ twelve-tone serialism was Elizabeth Lutyens (1906–1983), who moved from an early Romantic style to an intense expressionism independent of Schoenberg's or Webern's teachings. Her chromatic contrapuntal style led eventually to an individual approach to serialism in the *Chamber Concerto No. 1* (1939). After several stylistic detours during the war, she arrived at a fully developed twelve-tone technique in *O saisons, o chateaux!* (1946). The Hungarian British composer and teacher Mátyás Seiber (1905–1960) and the theorist Hans Keller also made early contributions to the development of serial principles in England, Seiber's mature style of the 1930s revealing the synthesis of various musical sources, including the influences of both Schoenberg and Bartók.

DALLAPICCOLA: PROTEST MUSIC AND THE TWELVE-TONE SYSTEM

Luigi Dallapiccola (1904–1975), one of the first and most significant non-Germanic composers to employ twelve-tone techniques, moved into the system during the same years that his music began to acquire a tone of political protest. His use of twelve-tone techniques in music that was reflective of the social and political mood of the 1930s and 1940s was to result in a highly personal and expressive style. Dallapiccola first came into contact with the music of the Viennese composers in 1924, when he heard a performance of Schoenberg's *Pierrot Lunaire*. However, it was not until the mid-1930s, after becoming aware of the music of Berg and Webern, that he began to adopt the techniques and aesthetic principles of the Viennese composers. He became acquainted personally with Berg in 1934, but only met Webern in 1942, when passing through Austria.

In certain works of the early 1930s, Dallapiccola began to juxtapose chromatic and diatonic materials, but his first significant stylistic changes were evident in his last pair of *Cori di Michelangelo Buonarroti il giovane:* the "Il coro degli Zitti" and "Il coro dei Lanzi briachi," for chorus and orchestra (1935–1936). The first of these two "Coro," though still mixing diatonic and chromatic elements, demonstrates an awareness of Schoenberg's music in an occasional, but prominent employment of twelve-tone rows. His *Tre laudi* (1936–1937) reveal a further tendency toward use of chromatic contrapuntal textures, the vocal line beginning with a twelve-tone phrase followed by its retrograde. Even traditional elements, such as the joyful diatonic material of the second *laude,* are based on a nontriadic dissonant counterpoint. In these pieces, there is already a kind of Webernian usage of serialized cellular pitch formations.

The first disruption of Dallapiccola's peaceful world came with Mussolini's Ethiopian campaign and the Spanish Civil War. This led to more than a casual connection between the new musical idiom and his political concerns in the late 1930s, as in the *Canti di prigionia* (Songs of Captivity), for chorus and percussion orchestra (1938–1941). After some wartime experiments with twelve-tone formations in his settings of Ungaretti's translations from the Greek (for voice and instruments), he turned to a complex expressionistic style in his twelve-tone opera, *Il prigioniero* (1944–1948), as the basis for presenting his political sentiments. Here, the influences of the Viennese composers are entirely evident in the stylistic and technical milieu, but the twelve-tone principles are employed in a highly personal idiom. As in Berg's *Lulu,* Dallapiccola's symbolic, pictorial, and subjective approach is manifested in a context in which the twelve-tone rows are employed as "Leitmotiv," but these rows also serve as the source for the systematic derivation of all the motivic (or cellular) substructures associated with the drama. As with Berg's use of successive 0167 tetrachords that form the "Erdgeist" fourths in the opening row of *Lulu,* or the successive triads that outline the row of his *Violin Concerto,* Dallapiccola also bases his derived substructures frequently on uniform intervallic schemes, which sometimes unfold in strict canonic textures. He also infuses his twelve-tone serial constructions with numerological significance in connection to his ideas of political and religious freedom. The associations between his political concerns and his musical techniques and expression are confirmed by his own words: "Not in my wildest imagination did I think that such music would one day be described, in a quite appropriate manner, as 'protest music,' in the same way as 'La mort d'un tyran' by Milhaud (1932), 'Thyl Claes' by Vogel (1938) and 'Ode to Napoleon Buonaparte' and 'A Survivor from Warsaw' by Schoenberg (1942 and 1947 respectively)."[12]

Although the subject as well as the musical idiom of the opera grew out of the era in which it was written directly, the source of its bitter message can be traced back to the early years of the century.[13] The composer was born ten years before the outbreak of World War I on the peninsula of Istria, inhabited by Italians and Slavs and dominated by the Austro-Hungarian Empire. Italy had been seething with revolution during the nineteenth century and the desire for Italian independence continued throughout the composer's earliest years. His father's Irredentist involvement against Austria led to the deportation of the family to Graz, Austria, toward the end of World War I, after which they returned to Italy in November 1918. One of his most impressionable memories of 1919 was his exposure to Victor Hugo's poem *La Rose de l'infante,* in which he identified the Infanta's father, Philip II (son of the Holy Roman Emperor, Charles V, and King of Spain during the Spanish Inquisition), with the tyranny of the fallen Austrian Hapsburgs. During the 1930s, however, he was to identify Philip with a more terrible tyranny. After Mussolini made his infamous radio announcement, on September 1, 1938, to initiate Italy's anti-Semitic campaign, the composer felt the need to turn to a musical protest against the totalitarian state. The first result was his *Canti di prigionia,* in which he employed the ancient Church chant "Dies irae, dies illa" like a cantus firmus. In his visit to Paris in 1939, Dallapiccola acquired the writings of Count l'Isle-Adam, from which the composer's wife suggested the story "La torture par l'espérance" (Torture by hope) as a dramatic basis for musical treatment. The cruel story revived Dallapiccola's thoughts of Philip II, and together with the l'Isle-Adam story, the Spanish Inquisition during the reign of Philip was to serve as the basis of the libretto for *Il Prigioniero.*

The musical setting of the opera, with all its leanings toward the expressionistic twelve-tone style of the Viennese composers, also reveals the Italian opera tradition: the vocal line fuses traditional Italian lyricism with Webern's twelve-tone vocal style. The orchestral writing, while reminiscent of the accompanying function of the orchestra in traditional Italian opera, is as brilliant and colorful as the varied instrumental combinations found in Berg's *Wozzeck.* As in the latter, the large orchestration ranges from full sonorities to carefully chosen solo instruments, often giving the impression of a chamber ensemble. In connection to the symbolic and pictorial extramusical dramatic elements, Dallapiccola includes the organ and a group of brass and bells (campana) behind the scene, the latter in connection to the "great bell of

[12] See Luigi Dallapiccola, "Notes on My 'Prigioniero,'" for the recording by The National Symphony Orchestra, Washington, D.C., conducted by Antal Dorati, with The University of Maryland Chorus, Director: Paul Traver (New York: Decca Record Co., Ltd., 1975).

[13] See ibid., and "The genesis of the *Canti di prigionia* and *Il Prigioniero,*" *Musical Quarterly* 39/3 (July 1953): 355–372.

Ghent" that signals revolution. Great sonorities are produced further in the two large choral interludes, the second of which represents the "crushing voice of the Inquisition."[14]

The four large scenes of the opera are unified by transpositions and transformations of three twelve-tone rows, representing prayer, hope, and freedom. The "Prayer" row (D–G–Ab–E–F–B–Bb–Eb–Db–Gb–A–C) opens the Prolog, where it dominates the vocal line of the prisoner's mother, who waits to see her son with a premonition that this will be the last time. After the somewhat hidden statement of the "Freedom" row in the prisoner's opening recitative of Scene 1, we get the first occurrence of the "Hope" row (F♯–G–G♯–A–F–B–Bb–E–C–Db–Eb–D, mm. 201–203) in connection to the dramatic meaning: the prisoner tells his mother of his renewed hope because of the jailer's friendly word, "Fratello" (my brother). A more distinct statement of an incomplete form of the "Freedom" row follows (A–B–D–F–G–Bb–C–Eb–[Gb–Ab–Db–Fb]). While both rows appear in the ensuing passages of this scene, it is the "Hope" row that is developed primarily in strict imitation between prime and inverted forms as the basis of the dialogue. The "Prayer" row closes the scene as the mother exits. The opening of Scene 2 is pervaded by statements of the "Hope" row in anticipation of a visit by the jailer, who continues to torture him with false hope. Only then (mm. 292ff., brass and jailer's vocal line) do we get a flourishing of the complete "Freedom" row, the ascending melodic contour of which blossoms forth in strict imitation in the winds. The prisoner comes to realize only at the end that hope is the worst torture. In Scene 3, he is permitted to escape through the maze of passages in the Saragossa prison, where first the torturer, then priests pretend not to notice him as they pass by. He hears the bell of Ghent and (in Scene 4) finds himself in a garden. His praises of God are juxtaposed with choral chants behind the scene that twice quote the "Prayer of Mary Stuart," from the *Canti di prigionia*. The final horrible realization comes when the prisoner is confronted by the jailer, who now appears as the Grand Inquisitor. The opera ends with the question: "Freedom?"

The three basic twelve-tone rows appear to be the source of all the main musical motifs or thematic cells of the opera, so a highly systematic and integrated network of pitch relations is formed in connection to the dramatic symbology. First, let us observe the two most important motifs.[15] From the opening three dissonant chords, which together supply all twelve tones and "immediately give an idea of the degree of tragic tension," the upper notes (G–A–F) form the motif representing "Roelandt," the great bell of Ghent that signals freedom (Ex. 14–4a). The jailers word, "Fratello" (Scene 2, m. 287), is set to the more central motif of the opera, F–E–C♯, which consists of a minor second and minor third (Ex. 14–4b). The presence of the "Fratello" motif is also implied in the opening three chords: three of the four

---

[14] See "Notes on My 'Prigioniero,' " n.12, above.
[15] Ibid.

EXAMPLE 14–4. Dallapiccola, *Il Prigioniero:* (a) opening chords; (b) Scene 2, m. 287

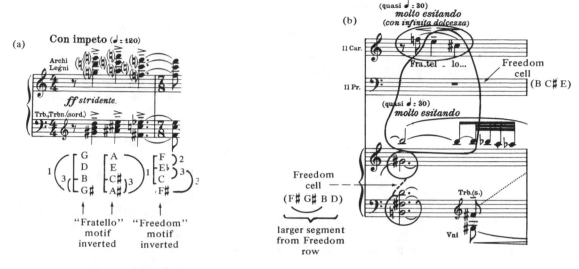

pitch-classes in each of the first two chords (B–G♯–G–[   ] and C♯–A♯–A–[   ]) suggest inverted forms of the motif. Three of the four pitch-classes of the third chord (F–E♭–C–[   ]), however, suggest a prime form expanded intervallically.

The dramatic significance of this relationship between the expanded intervallic form of the "Fratello" motif in the third chord and the basic form in the first two chords becomes apparent in a study of the structure of the three basic twelve-tone rows and their association to the drama. In the first two rows, "Prayer" and "Hope" (Ex. 14–5), certain three-note adjacencies outline the intervals of either prime or inverted forms of the motif. In the "Freedom" row, unlike the first two, there are no minor-second adjacencies, so no suggestion of the unaltered form of the "Fratello" motif is permitted. Instead, whole-steps and minor thirds give us expanded statements in overlapping succession. Thus, the relationship of the three rows, in which the minor second of the embedded "Fratello" motif in the first two rows is expanded to a whole step in the third to represent freedom, appears to be a projection of the same relationship in the opening three dissonant chords.

The latter relationship also appears to be significant within the structure of the "Prayer" row itself (Ex. 14–6). The basic intervallic structure of the "Fratello" motif, which is implied twice within the first half of this row, is replaced in the second half by a predominance of whole steps and minor thirds. The latter intervallic adjacencies foreshadow the structure of the "Freedom" row. This relationship is supported at a prominent dramatic

EXAMPLE 14–5. Dallapiccola, *Il Prigioniero,* three rows and derivative motivic cells

prayer row (Prolog, mm. 9-12, voice)

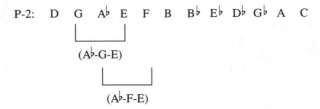

hope row (Scene 2, mm. 275-277, solo cello)

freedom row (Scene 2, mm. 292ff., voices and winds)

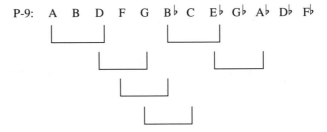

EXAMPLE 14–6. Dallapiccola, *Il Prigioniero,* Prolog. mm. 9–12, voice

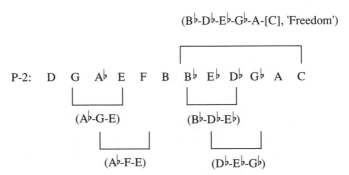

point in Scene 2, in which the original form of the "Fratello" motif, F–E–C♯ (at m. 287), is expanded to F♯–E–C♯ (mm. 428–429) as part of the "Freedom" row: "They are like swans of purest white, flying on for liberty!" Thus, in all these contexts, the basic form of the "Fratello" motif (intervals 1 and 3) is expanded to intervals 2 and 3 to become a segment of the "Freedom" row.

In addition to these motivic links between the twelve-tone rows and the drama, a more complex set of pitch relations within and between rows contributes to musical uniformity and relentless dramatic intensity. Dallapiccola directs our attention to a special property of the opening dissonant chords, stating that "the total chromatic is obtained by means of tritones."[16] Each of the three chords contains one tritone. The first tritone (D–G♯), together with a third note (G) from the same chord, is projected as the first three-note cell of the "Prayer" row (D–G–A♭). Notes 4–7 of this row then give us two overlapping transpositions of the same construction (B–E–F and F–B♭–B), which together outline a larger symmetrical double-tritone tetrachord (E–F–B–B♭). This symmetrical construction serves the same axial functions within the "Prayer" and "Hope" rows of this work as it did in the basic rows of the first movement of Berg's *Lyric Suite,* where its two axial dyads (either at sum 9, F–E/B♭–B, or sum 3, E–B/F–B♭, i.e., based on C = 0, C♯ = 1, etc.) formed part of a larger succession of dyads related symmetrically at one or the other of these two sums.[17] The axial functions of this double-tritone tetrachord in the opera are manifested most clearly in the "Hope" row, the tetrachord of which is placed at the center of the row as part of a succession of three tetrachords related symmetrically (Ex. 14–7a). The second statement of the row is P–3, the tetrachordal dyads reinterpreted as E–F and B♭–B to form tetrachordal axes of sum 9 (Ex. 14–7b).[18]

These consistent symmetrical relations within the "Hope" row link it to the "Prayer" row, which opens the Prolog and also closes Scene 1 (mm. 265–267). The "Prayer" row (P–2) implies, with one special deviation, the same sum-3 tetrachordal symmetries as basic P–6 of the "Hope" row. The one deviation from perfect symmetry is the displacement of D♭ from its hypothetical position as note 4 to its actual position as note 9 (Ex. 14–8). One may take the liberty to speculate on this single deviation based on Dallapiccola's own suggestion, according to his pupil, Luciano Berio, that the "12-tone method must not be so tyrannical as to exclude a priori both expression and humanity."[19] The D♭ disruption of the otherwise perfect tetrachordal

---

[16] Ibid.

[17] See discussion of the *Lyric Suite* in Chapter 3.

[18] The double-tritone tetrachord of the row foreshadows the bell of Ghent (mm. 306–308), the series of tritones descending semitonally, E♭–A/D–A♭/D♭–G, which signify the bell, implying the presence of two overlapping forms of the tetrachord (D–E♭–A♭–A and G–A♭–D♭–D).

[19] Joshua Berrett, program notes to the recording of Berio's *Nones* by the London Symphony Orchestra, conducted by the composer.

EXAMPLE 14–7. Dallapiccola, *Il Prigioniero:* (a) Scene 2, mm. 275ff., cello, tetrachordal axes each of sum 3 (= 15 − 12); (b) Scene 2, mm. 277–281, voice, symmetrically related tetrachords of "Hope" row at sum 9

(a) Hope row at P-6 (opening of Scene 2, mm. 275ff., cello). According to the registral ordering of tetrachordal components, each tetrachordal axis is explicitly at sum 3 (= 15, according to mod. 12; i.e., 15 - 12 = 3):

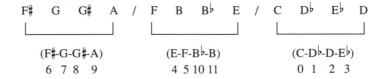

(F♯-G-G♯-A)   (E-F-B♭-B)   (C-D♭-D-E♭)
  6 7 8 9   4 5 10 11   0 1 2 3

(b) Hope row at P-3 (mm. 277-281, voice). According to the registral position of tetrachordal components, each tetrachordal axis is at sum 9 (= 21, according to mod. 12; i.e., 21 - 12 = 9):

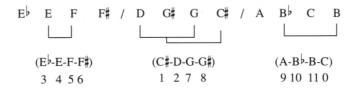

(E♭-E-F-F♯)   (C♯-D-G-G♯)   (A-B♭-B-C)
  3 4 5 6   1 2 7 8   9 10 11 0

symmetry of the row may be explained in two ways: (1) it seems to suggest a kind of "dissonance," which is appropriate to the immediate dramatic context of the mother's forebodings; and (2) it seems to serve as a means of permitting certain adjacencies to occur within the row. In terms of the latter,

EXAMPLE 14–8. Dallapiccola, *Il Prigioniero,* symmetrical relations and derivative motivic cells of "Prayer" row

"Prayer" row with implied sum-3 tetrachords. According to the registral position of tetrachordal components, each tetrachordal axis is at sum 3 (= 15, according to mod. 12; i.e., 15 - 12 = 3).

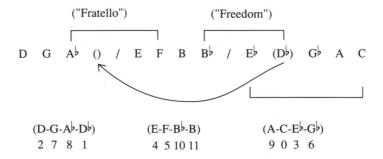

(D-G-A♭-D♭)   (E-F-B♭-B)   (A-C-E♭-G♭)
  2 7 8 1   4 5 10 11   9 0 3 6

its removal from its hypothetical position as note 4 permits an occurrence of the inverted "Fratello" motif, Ab–F–E. Furthermore, its placement between Eb and Gb provides two overlapping occurrences of the expanded "Fratello" motif (i.e., "Freedom" motif), Bb–Db–Eb and Db–Eb–Gb, these inversionally related forms of which pervade the "Freedom" row. In contrast to the "Prayer" and "Hope" rows, however, the "Freedom" row is not confined to a single axis of symmetry. Its departure from the strict inversional, symmetrical relations as well as the semitonal constructions of the first two rows appears to be in keeping with the trend of the drama.

Analogous to traditional tonal functions that demarcate recapitulations in classical forms, specific axial relations between row statements serve to define or round out sections within scenes of this opera. The first seventeen measures of Scene 2 are based exclusively on successive and overlapping statements of the "Hope" row. (This section of the scene ends at the prisoner's incomplete final statement of the "Hope" row, mm. 290–292, which only unfolds through the sixth note of I-2. This note, A, also serves as the first note of the "Freedom" row, which is continued in the jailer's statement, "Spera fratello.") Axial functions of the "Hope" row, together with two interpolated statements of the "Fratello" motif (mm. 281 and 287), which subdivide mm. 275–292 into equal proportions, are the basic form determinants of this opening section of the scene. As the prisoner speaks of being alone, "Solo. Son solo un'altra volta," the solo cello unfolds the first statement of the row, P–6, followed by the first vocal statement, P–3. Both transpositions are linked by means of the symmetrical relationship (sums 3/9) between their double-tritone tetrachordal constructions (E–F–Bb–B and C#–D–G–G#), which are placed at the center of each row transposition, respectively (Ex. 14–9).

EXAMPLE 14–9. Dallapiccola, *Il Prigioniero,* symmetrical relations between transpositions of the "Hope" row

"Hope" Row (Scene 2, mm. 275-280, cello and voice):

P-6:   F#   G   G#   A   /   F   B   Bb   E   /   C   Db   Eb   D

(F#-G-G#-A)   (E-F-Bb-B)   (C-Db-D-Eb)
6 7 8 9   4 5 10 11   0 1 2 3
sum 3   sums 3/9   sum 3

P-3:   Eb   E   F   F#   /   D   G#   G   C#   /   A   Bb   C   B

(Eb-E-F-F#)   (C#-D-G-G#)   (A-Bb-B-C)
3 4 5 6   1 2 7 8   9 10 11 0
sum 9   sum 9/3   sum 9

While these two symmetrically related row transpositions open the section, the first occurrence of the "Fratello" motif (m. 281) is followed directly by a vocal statement of the inverted row form I–0, C–B–Bb–A/C#–G–G#–D/F#–F–D#–E (Ex. 14–10). The latter reestablishes sums 9/3 with the same central double-tritone tetrachord of P–3 (G–G#–C#–D). Directly after the second occurrence of the "Fratello" motif, we have a return of initial P–6 of sums 3/9 (mm. 288–290, orchestra). The section ends (mm. 291–292, flute) with yet another transposition (P–9) within which we find the same double-tritone tetrachord of sums 3/9, so the different row forms at basic structural points are linked by their common axes of symmetry. The intermediary row forms unfold all the other odd sums, thereby providing a sense of systematic departure from, and return to, the basic axes of sums 9/3. The increasing contrapuntal juxtaposition of these "dissonant" row axes against the basic sums 3/9 (for instance, see Ex. 14–10) supports the increasing dramatic intensity produced by the jailer's appearance.

The two interpolations of the "Fratello" motif serve several structural and dramatic functions simultaneously. The format, based on two interpolations of a given element within a specifically defined section, reflects a basic structural principle of the work. For instance, the three dissonant chords at

EXAMPLE 14–10. Dallapiccola, *Il Prigioniero*, Scene 2, mm. 282–284

Used by permission of Edizioni Suvini Zerboni S. p. A.

the opening of the Prolog return twice within the first section (to the Ballata, m. 64) to interrupt the mother's "Prayer" row, and, as another, the two great choral interludes subdivide the large-scale form. In terms of the musico-dramatic relationships, the harmonizations of the two "Fratello" interpolations in Scene 2 anticipate the "Freedom" row. The explicit statement by the jailer (m. 287) is accompanied by a half-diminished-seventh chord, G♯–B–D–F♯, which can also be interpreted as the first four notes of the "Freedom" row transposed: F♯–G♯–B–D (suggested more prominently in the following chord, F♯–G♯–B). Together with the F of the voice, the harmonic segment F♯–B–D–F–[ ] also implies the presence of an intervallic inversion of the initial chord structure of the work (G♯–B–D–G), which provides another long-range association with the opening section. Thus, Dallapiccola's systematic, integrated use of serial techniques in connection to dramatic symbolization reveals the ingenuity found in the twelve-tone serial compositions of Berg.

THE NEW POSTWAR APPROACHES TO TWELVE-TONE COMPOSITION

Certain other international composers also tended toward twelve-tone serial techniques prior to World War II, those removed from the aesthetics, styles, and techniques of the Schoenberg School serving a more significant role in the postwar era.[20] Some of the most prominent anticipations of the diverse and individual postwar twelve-tone developments came from both American and European composers, the Europeans emigrating to the United States as early as the late 1930s. The earliest individual experiments in the United States were made by such American composers as George Perle, Aaron Copland, Milton Babbitt, and later, Roger Sessions.

[20] These twelve-tone composers are discussed in the following chapters.

SUGGESTED READINGS

ELLIOTT ANTOKOLETZ.   "A Survivor of the Vienna Schoenberg Circle: An Interview with Paul A. Pisk," *Tempo* 154 (September 1985): 15–21 passim.

LUIGI DALLAPICCOLA.   "Notes on My 'Prigioniero,'" for the recording by The National Symphony Orchestra, Washington, D.C., conducted by Antal Dorati, with The University of Maryland Chorus, Director: Paul Traver (New York: Decca Record Co., Ltd., 1975).

———.   "The Genesis of the *Canti di prigionia* and *Il Prigioniero*," *Musical Quarterly* 39/3 (July 1953): 355–372.

PAUL GRIFFITHS.   *Modern Music: The Avant-garde Since 1945* (New York: George Braziller, Inc., 1981).

RENÉ LEIBOWITZ.   *Introduction à la musique de douze sons* (Paris: L'Arche, 1949).

————. *Schoenberg et son école* (Paris, 1947); Eng. trans. Dika Newlin (New York: Philosophical Library, 1949; rep. 1975).

ERNST KRENEK.   "Circling My Horizon," in *Horizons Circled: Reflections on My Music* (Berkeley and Los Angeles: University of California Press, 1974), pp. 17–97.

————. "New Developments of the Twelve-Tone Technique," *Music Review* 4 (1943): 81–97.

WILL OGDON.   "A Master Composer and a Foremost Musician of Our Time," in Ernst Krenek, *Horizons Circled: Reflections on My Music* (Berkeley and Los Angeles: University of California Press, 1974), pp. 1–16.

15 Total serialization in Europe

DARMSTADT AND "WEBERNISM" The end of World War II brought significant changes in political and social attitudes toward contemporary music. During the interwar period, Neoclassical styles had prevailed in certain non-Germanic countries, especially France and the United States, while avant-garde idioms were both restricted by international economic conditions and banned from publication and performance in Germany and Italy, being branded products of "cultural Bolshevism." The atonal and twelve-tone serial compositions of the Vienna Schoenberg circle, virtually unknown in Germany after the advent of Hitler, were made accessible in the 1930s and 1940s through exclusive performances at the *International Society for Contemporary Music* (ISCM) held in other areas of Europe.

With the end of the Nazi regime in 1945, a new musical era began with the reemergence and international proliferation of twelve-tone composition. By the early 1950s, composers of varying aesthetics, styles, and techniques turned for the first time to these principles pioneered by Schoenberg and his pupils. The momentum for this revival came from the need for many composers to break from those musical idioms associated with a period of artistic and personal repression. Public demonstrations by a number of young French composers led by Pierre Boulez against a performance of Stravinsky's Neoclassical compositions in Paris in 1945 were symptomatic of a more fundamental dichotomy stemming from the earlier part of the century between the aesthetic and stylistic principles of Neoclassicism and those manifested in atonal and twelve-tone serial procedures. Although the aesthetics, forms, and techniques of both idioms had occasionally found common ground within single compositions in the 1920s (as in Schoenberg's *Suite* for piano, Op. 25, or Berg's opera *Wozzeck, Chamber Concerto,* and *Lyric Suite*), the younger rebels of the post–World War II generation were intent on totally breaking with what they considered to be too traditional and reactionary.

Revitalized interest in avant-garde composition was facilitated in 1946 when Wolfgang Steinecke founded the *Internationale Ferienkurse für Neue Musik* (International Summer Courses for New Music) at Darmstadt, Germany. This postwar center for the study and performance of avant-garde music, which emphasized the music of the Vienna Schoenberg circle, was soon to crystalize into a large-scale revival and development of twelve-tone composition. In 1948, René Leibowitz, a former pupil of Webern, came to Darmstadt to teach the twelve-tone serial methods of Schoenberg rather than the more radical ones of Webern.[1] Schoenberg was revered in the early years

---

[1] See Reginald Smith Brindle, *The New Music: The Avante-garde Since 1945* (Oxford and New York: Oxford University Press, 1975), p. 8.

of the Darmstadt School, as witnessed by the successful performance of his *A Survivor from Warsaw* in 1950, conducted by Hermann Scherchen. The Hebrew rendition of the Jewish prayer, sung by the German choir, produced a profound emotional experience for all those in attendance.[2] The influence of Schoenberg was evident in the works of the young composers who studied with Wolfgang Fortner and Josef Rufer at Darmstadt at this time, many of whom also went to Paris to work with Olivier Messiaen. One of Fortner's pupils at Darmstadt from the first session in 1946 was Hans Werner Henze, the performances of his first two symphonies and cantata *Apollo et Hyacinthus* at Darmstadt between 1946 and 1950 revealing the expressionistic use of the dissonant and angular twelve-tone melodies stemming from Schoenberg's approach to serialism, an influence also found in the works of Bernd Alois Zimmermann.[3]

A shift in interest from Schoenberg's more traditional twelve-tone approach to the principles of Webern was imminent at Darmstadt. Messiaen came there in 1949 as one of the first postwar teachers of twelve-tone technique. He was to serve as a leader in the tendency toward the use of totally predetermined material and the systematic extension of the serial principle to nonpitch parameters (duration, dynamics, articulation, register, timbre, and texture). Although Messiaen apparently drew from Webern's late experiments, which paved the way for such predetermined, ultrarational serial concepts, he exploited them in an idiom that had little to do with the styles and aesthetics of the Viennese composers.[4]

The first work in Europe based on the new aesthetic and technical approach was Messiaen's *Mode de valeurs et d'intensités* (from his *Quatre études de rythme* for piano), composed at Darmstadt in 1949. His earlier concerns with serial rhythmic procedures, which were derived in part from his study of Indian talas,[5] were now transformed into an abstract and systematized set of relationships in what he has since admitted to be an experiment.[6] The entire fabric is narrowed down to its barest components, so each individual detail plays a basic role in the structure. Two premises of the piece were to serve as a model for the younger composers: the strength of the serial principle in generating large-scale structural coherence; and the dissociation of each sound event from traditional concepts of linear and harmonic functions, leading ultimately to the isolation of each sound event in a static spatial context.

Messiaen's approach to the serial principle is entirely different from that of Schoenberg. The one parameter of *Modes de valeurs* that is not serial-

---

[2] See Brigitte Schiffer, "Darmstadt, Citadel of the Avantgarde." *The World of Music* 11/3 (1969), pp. 32–44.

[3] Paul Griffiths, *Modern Music: The Avant Garde Since 1945* (London: J. M. Dent & Sons Ltd.; New York: George Braziller, 1981), pp. 46–47.

[4] See Brindle, *The New Music,* n.1, above, p. 8.

[5] Olivier Messiaen, *Technique de mon langage musical* (Paris: Alphonse Leduc et Cie, Éditions Musicales, 1944); trans. John Satterfield (Paris: Alphonse Leduc, 1956).

[6] Roger Nichols, *Messiaen* (London: Oxford University Press, 1975), p. 48.

ized within the actual compositional context is that of pitch. Instead, Messiaen lays out three abstract twelve-tone "divisions" in the preface of the work (Ex. 15–1), the notes in each of these three "divisions" of the "mode" freely ordered throughout the composition. Each of these ordered "divisions" simply serves precompositionally as the basis for the association of its twelve pitches with a particular succession of durations, intensities (dynamics), and articulations. Each pitch is also fixed registrally within each of the three "divisions" throughout the composition. Through this joining of various parameters in each individual sonority, a fixed and autonomous character is established for each note in each of the three "divisions." The durations of the elements in Division I increase arithmetically by the value of a thirty-second note to produce a rhythmic series of twelve different values. In Division II, the durations increase by the value of a sixteenth note, the twelve values producing six new durations, while in Division III they increase by the value of an eighth note to produce six more values, the total number of durations coming to twenty four. Similarly, each pitch is assigned one of twelve articulations (the twelfth has no articulation sign) and one of seven dynamics within each "division." The result of these associations of the different parameters with that of pitch is a texture based on the juxtaposition of maximally distinct points. This mosaic or "pointillistic" approach thus contributes to the isolation of each individual sound event.

These serialized procedures preclude any sense of tonal direction. Instead, a different kind of motion is produced in two fundamental ways. The first outlines a process in which the descending linear contour of each of the precompositionally determined twelve-tone "divisions" gradually disap-

EXAMPLE 15–1. Messiaen, *Modes de valeurs et d'intensités,* preface, three twelve-tone "Divisions"

pears by means of the continually changing linear note orderings. The second is based on changing spatial relations among the elements of the three "divisions" as achieved by means of contrapuntal interactions, in which the lines are freely and constantly reinterpreted in relation to each other. This multidimensional principle may be expressed through an analogy of the spatial arts. We may imagine a three-dimensional object such as a mobile, which comprises a variety of fixed smaller units, turning in space. The identity of each element remains unchanged, but each appears in a different perspective in relation to the other elements. This dimensional effect, based on changing perspectives, is achieved for the most part by the contrasting dynamic assignments of the different notes, the various fixed parameters for each event contributing to the identity of that event.

In 1950, the French music critic Antoine Goléa came to teach at Darmstadt, bringing with him the gramophone recording of *Mode de valeurs* from Paris that was to cause a sensation among the younger composers. In 1950, Scherchen had brought the twelve-tone Italian composers Luigi Nono and Bruno Maderna to Darmstadt, and in 1951 they joined with Karel Goeyvaerts and Karlheinz Stockhausen to establish the new trend set by the Messiaen work. The following year, Pierre Boulez, who studied with Messiaen in the early 1940s and had also been influenced by the preserial compositions of Schoenberg, now produced his famous written protest, "Schoenberg is Dead," at Darmstadt.[7] This reflected the general consensus among the younger generation opposing Schoenberg's use of traditional forms, textures, melody, and accompaniment as the framework for his twelve-tone procedures. While *Mode de valeurs* was not serialized contextually in terms of pitch, it led to the break with Schoenberg and the establishment of a "post-Webernist" concept at Darmstadt based on the total serialization of structure and content. What appealed to these composers was the potential for a totally systematic approach to serialism suggested by Webern's intellectualized, concise handling of formal and textural details, which revealed the possibilities for eliminating the traditional distinctions between melody and harmony.

The first major public event in "post-Webernist" developments was a concert of several revolutionary works given at Darmstadt in 1952. Stockhausen's *Kreuzspiel* ("Cross-play," 1951), which caused a great stir at this public debut of the composer, was one of the first "pointillistic" works to be influenced by Messiaen's *Mode de valeurs* and Goeyvaerts' *Sonata for two pianos*. Scored for oboe, bass clarinet, piano, and percussion, *Kreuzspiel* is based on "the idea of an intersection (crossing) of temporal and spatial phenomena . . . in three stages," in which the positions of the various

---

[7] Pierre Boulez, "Schönberg est mort." *Score* 6 (1952): 18–22; enlarged version, reprinted in *Relevés d'apprenti* [Notes of an Apprenticeship] (Paris: Alfred A. Knopf, 1966); pp. 268–276; trans. Herbert Weinstock (New York: Alfred A. Knopf, 1968), pp. 265–272.

parameters (pitch–class, register, duration, dynamic level, and timbre) undergo a systematic process of interaction and reinterpretation.[8] In the first stage, two six–note groups are polarized in the extreme registers of the piano. Then, after the notes have been "equally distributed over the entire range of sound," the registral positions of these groupings are reversed by a formal retrograde of the entire process. At the outset of the work, several distinct rhythmic (durational) series occur in assocation with the separate instrumental timbres. The rhythmic series in the piano is articulated by the successive dynamics assigned to the changing pitches of the piano's hexachordal twelve-note series, partitioned registrally. The succession of durations (measured in triplets and based on the "interval of entry") outlines the pattern 11–5–6–9–2–12–1–10–4–7–8–3. Against this, the contrasting tumba and tom-tom layers produce a compounded serialized rhythmic network: the juxtaposition of two registral levels (supported by two contrasting dynamics, *pp* and *ppp*) in the even triplets of the tumbas articulates the durational sequence 2–3–4–5–6–12–1–7–8–9–10–11, while the attacks and their distinguishing dynamics in the two groups of tom-toms (also measured in triplets) compositely unfold the durational series 2–8–7–4–11–1–12–3–9–6–5–10.[9]

On the same program was Bruno Maderna's *Musica su due Dimensioni* ("Music in two dimensions"), which was the first work to combine live aleatoric and taped electronic sounds, Luigi Nono's highly organized yet colorful and expressive vocal setting of the first Lorca Epitaph, *España en el Corazon* ("Spain in the heart"), and Boulez's totally serialized *Trois structures pour deux pianos* ("Three structures for two pianos," 1951–1952), performed by Yvonne Loriod and the composer.[10] In *Structures,* Boulez turned to total serialization as a means of freeing the musical context from notions of melody, harmony, and counterpoint, since the serial principle dissolves any sense of mode and tonality traditionally associated with them. This work, which goes beyond Messiaen's *Mode de valeurs* in its ultrarational approach to the serial principle, was to achieve wider attention than its model. Boulez's own claims that within such a context he attempted paradoxically to produce a sense of absurdity and disorder points to the dichotomous development among the Darmstadt composers in the 1950s toward both total control and randomness in aleatoric composition: "I had taken the experience to absurd lengths . . . this sort of absurdity, of chaos . . . was completely intentional and has probably been one of my most fundamental experiments as a com-

[8] See "Stockhausen's notes on the works," in Karl H. Wörner, *Stockhausen: Life and Work,* ed. and trans. Bill Hopkins (London: Faber and Faber, 1973; Berkeley: University of California Press, 1976), p. 30.

[9] For an outline of the "cross-over" process throughout the section, in which the registrally shifting components of the piano hexachords are reinterpreted timbrally, see the layout of the first six of the twelve statements of the pitch series in Griffiths, *Modern Music,* n.3, p. 53, Ex. 12.

[10] See Schiffer, "Darmstadt," n.2, above, p. 35.

poser. At that point disorder is equivalent to an excess of order and an excess of order reverts to disorder. The general theme of this piece is really the ambiguity of a surfeit of order being equivalent to disorder."[11]

TOTAL SERIALIZATION OF ALL PARAMETERS

Boulez borrowed material from *Mode de valeurs* as the basis for relinquishing all responsibility "to find out how far automatism in musical relationships would go, with individual invention appearing only in some really very simple forms of disposition—in the matter of densities for example."[12] *Structures I* is based on extremes in each of the serialized parameters of dynamics, register, rhythmic complexity, texture, and rate of linear note changes, for which a parallel is made between this "organization of delirium" in *Structures* and the "automatic" technique of the actor-poet Antonin Artaud, associated with the Surrealist movement.[13] According to Stockhausen, Boulez's "technique serves him as a basis for the formation of an unalterable personal style. His objective is the work of art, mine is rather its workings."[14] While Stockhausen's forms are generated by the content, Boulez's approach still permitted personal taste in determining the large-scale form, his intellectual concerns geared to maintaining complete control of the formal framework.

Boulez's *Structures* was central in the development of total serialization. However, only the first part of Book I *(Structures Ia)* actually adheres strictly to serial procedures. The pitch-class series is joined with series of rhythms, articulations, and intensities, but the actual registral position of a given pitch is free and the four series remain independent of each other so they can interact freely in the composer's working out of the structure.[15] Boulez pays homage to his teacher by basing his twelve-note series on Division I of *Mode de valeurs* (E♭–D–A–A♭–G–F♯/E–C♯–C–B♭–F–B).[16]

In the first complete section (marked "Trés Modéré," mm. 1–7) of the fourteen sections and subsections of the piece, the "Original" form of the series (E♭–D–A–A♭–G–F♯–E–C♯–C–B♭–F–B) unfolds in piano I, its "Inversion" (E♭–E–A–B♭–B–C–D–F–F♯–G♯–C♯–G) in piano II (Ex. 15–2). As

---

[11] Pierre Boulez, *Par volonté par hasard: entretiens avec Célestin Deliège* (Paris: Les Éditions du Seuil, 1975; English trans. by Robert Wangermée as *Conversations with Célestin Deliège* (London: Ernst Eulenberg, Ltd., 1976), pp. 56–57.

[12] Ibid., p. 55.

[13] Peter F. Stacey, *Boulez and the Modern Concept* (Aldershot, England: Scolar Press, 1987), p. 22. Boulez himself points to such connections with Artaud, in "Propositions," *Relevés d'apprenti,* n.7, above, p. 74.

[14] See Wörner, *Stockhausen,* n.8, above, p. 229.

[15] See Charles Rosen, "The Piano Music," *Pierre Boulez: A Symposium,* ed. William Glock (London: Ernst Eulenberg, Ltd., 1986), p. 93.

[16] See the analysis of *Structures* by György Ligeti, "Pierre Boulez," *Die Reihe* 4 (Vienna: Universal Edition A.G., 1958); Eng. ed. (Pennsylvania: Theodore Presser Co., 1960), pp. 36–62, which is discussed again by Brindle, *The New Music.* n.1, above, pp. 26–33. Some of the basic points of this analysis are presented below.

EXAMPLE 15–2. Boulez, *Structure Ia* for two pianos, first section, mm. 1–7, "Original" and "Inversion" of the row

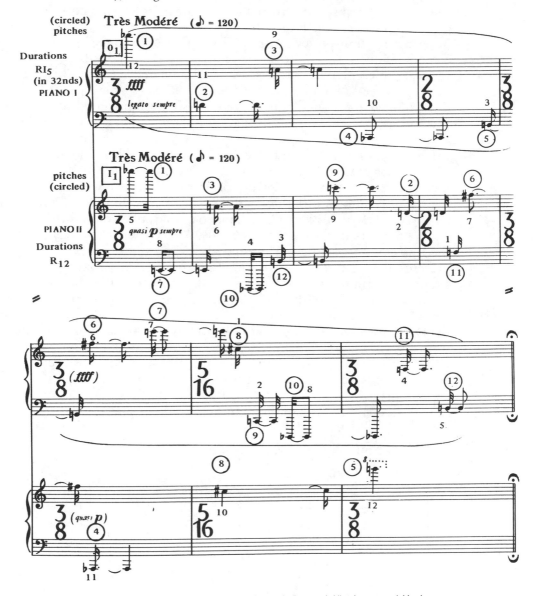

shown in Ex. 15–3a and 3b, the two basic set-forms each generate Boulez's "O" and "I" matrices, respectively. The initial pitch-class of each of the successive O transpositions in the O matrix is determined by the ordinal numbers 1–12 within basic O–1, the same procedure for the consecutive ordering of I transpositions in the I matrix is derived analogously from the ordinal numbers 1–7–3–10–12–9–2–11–6–4–8–5 within basic I–1. The numerical representations for pitches of the inverted set-forms are based ultimately on the same numerical-pitch associations in the basic O-1 ordering (for example, the second note, E, of I is assigned number 7 because that is its ordinal number in O). The Retrogrades of the O and I forms (reading from left to right and top to bottom, respectively) are obtained conventionally by the reversal of these O and I set-form readings. All forty-eight set-forms (twelve each of O, I, R, and RI) are used once in the piece (twenty-four forms for each piano), their special order of occurrence in the work determined by their transpositional ordering in the two matrices. In each of the two large parts (A and B) of *Structure Ia,* each piano unfolds twelve set-forms. In Part A, piano I presents all of the O forms (O–1, O–7, O–3, O–10, etc.) according to the transpositional ordering outlined by I-1 in the I matrix, while piano II presents all of the I forms (I–1, I–2, I–3, I–4, etc.) according to the transpositional ordering outlined by O-1 in the O matrix. For instance, the next section ("Modéré, presque vif," mm. 8ff.) unfolds linear statements of four set-forms simultaneously: O–7 and O–3 in piano I (following the opening O–1) against I–2 and I–3 in piano II (following the opening I–1). In Part B (mm. 65ff.), piano I presents, in contrapuntal alignments, all the RI forms (RI–5, RI–8, RI–4, RI–6, etc.) according to the transpositional ordering outlined by RI–1 in the I matrix, while piano II presents, in contrapuntal alignments, all the R forms (R–12, R–11, R–10, R–9, etc.) according to the transpositional ordering outlined by R–1 in the R matrix.

EXAMPLE 15–3. Boulez, *Structure Ia,* "O" and "I" matrices

(a)   'O' matrix

1	2	3	4	5	6	7	8	9	10	11	12
2	8	4	5	6	11	1	9	12	3	7	10
3	4	1	2	8	9	10	5	6	7	12	11
4	5	2	8	9	12	3	6	11	1	10	7
5	6	8	9	12	10	4	11	7	2	3	1
6	11	9	12	10	3	5	7	1	8	4	2
7	1	10	3	4	5	11	2	8	12	6	9
8	9	5	6	11	7	2	12	10	4	1	3
9	12	6	11	7	1	8	10	3	5	2	4
10	3	7	1	2	8	12	4	5	11	9	6
11	7	12	10	3	4	6	1	2	9	5	8
12	10	11	7	1	2	9	3	4	6	8	5

(b)   'I' matrix

1	7	3	10	12	9	2	11	6	4	8	5
7	11	10	12	9	8	1	6	5	3	2	4
3	10	1	7	11	6	4	12	9	2	5	8
10	12	7	11	6	5	3	9	8	1	4	2
12	9	11	6	5	4	10	8	2	7	3	1
9	8	6	5	4	3	12	2	1	11	10	7
2	1	4	3	10	12	8	7	11	5	9	6
11	6	12	9	8	2	7	5	4	10	1	3
6	5	9	8	2	1	11	4	3	12	7	10
4	3	2	1	7	11	5	10	12	8	6	9
8	2	5	4	3	10	9	1	7	6	12	11
5	4	8	2	1	7	6	3	10	9	11	12

The ordinal pitch numbers within a given set-form also indicate durational values calculated in thirty-second notes. The opening pitch series (O–1) in piano I is assigned the durational values (12–11–9–10–3–6–7–1–2–8–4–5) associated with the ordinal pitch numbers of RI–5 (B–F–C–Bb–A–F#–E–Eb–D–C#–Ab–G), the opening pitch series (I-1) in piano II assigned the durational values (5–8–6–4–3–9–2–1–7–11–10–12) associated to the ordinal pitch numbers of R–12 (G–C#–F#–Ab–A–C–D–Eb–E–F–Bb–B). In the second section (mm. 8ff.), pitch series O–7 and O–3 of piano I are assigned the durational series RI–8 (11–12–6–7–1–9–10–3–4–5–2–8) and RI–4 (9–6–8–12–10–5–11–7–1–2–3–4), respectively, while pitch series I–2 and I–3 of piano II are assigned the durational series R–11 (8–5–9–2–1–6–4–3–10–12–7–11) and R–10 (6–9–11–5–4–12–8–2–1–7–3–10), respectively. Like the transpositional ordering of the successive pitch series, the ordering of the forty-eight durational series in the composition is determined by their ordering in the two matrices. In Part A (mm. 1–64), piano I presents all the durational RI forms (RI–5, RI–8, RI–4, RI–6, etc.) according to the transpositional ordering outlined by RI–1 in the I matrix, while piano II presents all the durational R forms (R–12, R–11, R–10, R–9, etc.) according to the transpositional ordering outlined by R–1 in the O matrix. In Part B (mm. 65ff.), piano I presents, in contrapuntal alignments, all the durational I forms (I–12, I–11, I–10, I–9, etc.) according to the transpositional ordering outlined by R–1 in the O matrix, while piano II presents, in contrapuntal alignments, all the durational O forms (O–5, O–8, O–4, O–6, etc.) according to the transpositional ordering outlined by RI–1 in the I matrix.

Dynamics are also serialized throughout. Twelve different dynamic values from softest to loudest (*pppp* to *ffff*) are assigned systematically to numbers from 1 through 12 (see the abstract diagram in Ex. 15–4a). Then, each of the twenty-four pitch series that unfold in piano I is assigned one of these dynamic levels, the compositional ordering of their dynamic values derived from two diagonal numerical patterns in the O matrix. The first pattern of twelve dynamics is determined by reading from top right to bottom left, 12–7–7–11–11–5–5–11–11–7–7–12, so the initial series of twelve dynamics in piano I (Part A, to m. 64) is *ffff, mf, mf, fff, fff,* quasi *p*, quasi *p, fff, fff, mf, mf, ffff*. The second pattern of twelve dynamics is derived from the O matrix by reading from central bottom to central left (or central right to

EXAMPLE 15–4. Boulez, *Structure Ia*: (a) diagram of twelve dynamic levels; (b) diagram of ten different attacks

(a)	1	2	3	4	5	6	7	8	9	10	11	12
	pppp	*ppp*	*pp*	*p*	quasi *p*	*mp*	*mf*	quasi *f*	*f*	*ff*	*fff*	*ffff*

	1	2	3	[]	5	6	7	8	9	[]	11	12
(b)	>	>	.		normal	⌢	|	sfz	>		—	⌒

central top) and the reverse, 2–3–1–6–9–7–7–9–6–1–3–2, so the remaining series of twelve dynamics in piano I (in Part B) is *ppp, pp, pppp, mp, f, mf, mf, f, mp, pppp, pp, ppp*. An analogous procedure is derived from the I matrix to derive the dynamic series for the twenty-four set-forms of piano II. The dynamic patterns that are formulated for the two pianos are designed to produce maximal contrast between the two instruments.

Attacks are serialized according to a procedure that is similar to that for deriving dynamics. Ten different articulations are assigned to an abstract number series (Ex. 15–4b). Then, the compositional ordering of these attacks, one assigned to each pitch series, is determined by deriving diagonal numerical patterns from the O and I matrices, which are directly opposite to those that determined the dynamics.[17] Thus, the attack patterns for piano I are 1–8–1–8–12–3–11–12–3–11–5–5, 6–6–2–2–6–6, and 9–1–5–5–1–9 in the O matrix. Those for piano II are 1–11–1–11–5–3–8–5–3–8–12–12, 9–9–7–7–9–9, and 6–1–12–12–1–6 in the I matrix.[18]

According to Boulez, *Structure I* was composed on the model of a Klee painting, in which the painting is reduced to construction on horizontal and oblique lines.[19] A further statement on the aesthetic value of the work is provided by Ligeti:

> The "beauty" of a piece like this lies in quite new qualities. Webern's interval-objects . . . still contained a trace of the (discreetly) "expressive." . . . All this has vanished . . . from Boulez' *Structures;* they expose to view something that in Webern already formed the nucleus: beauty in the erection of pure structures. . . . Thus, composition ceases to be essentially "art- work;" to compose now takes on an additional character of research into the newly-discovered relationships of material. This attitude may strike people as negative, "inartistic"—but there is no other way for the composer of today, if he wants to get any further.[20]

Stemming from his experience with total serialization, Boulez summarized the evolution of serial techniques in a series of lectures at Darmstadt in 1963, in which he dealt specifically with those works that he composed after 1957: *Third Piano Sonata, Poésie pour pouvoir, Doubles, Structures II,* and *Pli selon pli.*[21]

---

[17] Numbers 4 and 10 are missing from these particular diagonal patterns in the matrices, hence the ten-number series for the attacks.

[18] For further discussion of other serialized parameters in *Structures Ia,* including the overall form, tempi, octave register, rests, and meter, see Brindle, *The New Music,* n.1, above, pp. 31–33.

[19] See Boulez, *Conversations,* n.11, above, p. 55.

[20] See Ligeti, "Pierre Boulez," n.16, above, p. 62.

[21] These lectures were published as *Musikdenken heute* (= Darmstädter Beiträge zur neuen musik, v) (1963); Eng. trans. as *Boulez on Music Today* (London: Faber and Faber, 1971).

Following this 1952 landmark concert of pointillistic and serial music, a new period in the tendency toward the application of the serial principle to every aspect of the composition began, according to Steinecke, in 1953 with a concert of Boulez's *Polyphonie X* (1951), Stockhausen's *Kontra-punkte* (1952–1953), and Nono's *Due espressioni per orchestra* (1953). Each of these three works contrasts with the other two in its individual aesthetic approach to the serial principle. *Polyphonie X* has greater linear continuity than the pointillistic textures of *Kontra-punkte,* but because of its ultrarational serial approach to timbres, dynamics, and durations (based on transformations of rhythmic cells rather than on the durational serial principle of *Structures Ia*), its performance had presented problems for the eighteen human soloists (eleven winds and seven strings), and led to its withdrawal. As an antithesis to Boulez's conception, Nono's *Due espressioni* reveals a primary concern for intense musical expression over strict adherence to serial principles. This attitude prevails throughout Nono's works, especially in the vocal music where the texts demand greater freedom for the sake of their expression. His *Il canto sospeso,* for soprano, mezzo, tenor, chorus and orchestra (1955–1956), based on texts taken from letters of condemned anti-fascists, reconciles a highly expressive approach with pointillistic serial techniques.

BEYOND POINTILLISM

Stockhausen's *Kontra-punkte* was first performed at the 1953 Cologne Festival of New Music prior to the Darmstadt concert and represents his first published work. Written for ten instruments in six timbral groups, which include three pairs of winds (flute/bassoon, clarinet/bass clarinet, trumpet/trombone) and three string groups (piano, harp, violin/cello, which are struck, plucked, and bowed, respectively), the work is pioneering in its concern for higher structural levels of serialization.[22] It was here and also in his *Klavierstücke I* (also composed in 1952–1953) that he originally developed his notion of "groups," i.e., formal units that combined several tonal points through the intersection of their various parameters. The serialized relation of these groups to each other produces a level of control a stage higher than that of the individual isolated events employed in *Mode de valeurs* or *Structures.* Each group may be defined by the number of its notes and their durations, and each group may be identified by the common dynamic level and registral position of its individual components. A durational series can then be used to establish proportional relationships between the groups themselves. Furthermore, certain properties of a given group can be retained while others may undergo transformation. Thus, groups may be both quantitatively and qualitatively differentiated as they are subjected to a higher structural level of organization. According to Stockhausen, "What, in a true sense are counterpointed in this work are the dimensions of the sound, also known as

---

[22] See Wörner, *Stockhausen,* n.8, above, pp. 91–93.

'parameters;' this happens in a prescribed four-dimensional space: lengths (durations), heights (frequencies), volume (loudnesses), and forms of vibration (timbres)."[23]

The composer's primary interest appears to be the process rather than the object or goal of that process, within which a sense of transformation is produced in an athematic, yet highly integrated, context. The overall construction of the work is determined by the mapping of "regions" that serve as "time-space" frames within which individual details unfold, the succession of these frames stemming from, and resolving into, the single note or point. The basic criteria for these general regions (micro and macro) can be categorized according to the concepts of "time-space" and "time flow."[24] In the first category, the microregion is defined by "fundamental phases of the tempered scale within the compass of the piano" and the macroregion by "the approximately tempered scale of durations from (quaver = 120) semiquaver to dotted long," and "six *intensities* from *ppp–f(sfz)*, with transitions." In the second category, the microregion is defined by "six different sound-rhythms; Flute-Bassoon, Clarinet-Bass Clarinet, Trumpet-Trombone, Piano, Harp, Violin-Cello," the macroregion by "3/8–pulsation in seven different tempi (quaver 120, 126, 136, 152, 168, 184, 200)."

The abstract ordering of these accelerating tempi is projected compositionally into the macrolevel regions, but with one exception. The slowest tempo (120) is omitted from its initial position and is used instead as a sort of rondo element in alternation with the other tempi. This deviation from the accelerating pattern permits maximal speed distinction between adjacent regions and at the same time produces a more complex, regularly ordered pattern. Changing associations between the various parameters and pitch also contribute to a sense of unity and diversity on the micro level. The opening five measures of the first region unfold all twelve notes (C♯–F♯ –G–E♭–A–E–D–B–C–[C]–F–B♭–A♭–[G♯]), the first six of which are assigned the six different intensities (*ppp, pp, p, mp, mf, f [sfz]*) that are then employed throughout the work in constant reinterpretations. Local alternations occur between *pp* and the other five graded (though contextually unordered) dynamic levels analogous to the macrolevel alternation of the basic tempo (120) with each of the other tempi in the systematically accelerating scheme. Finally, a sense of transformation within the otherwise unified context of the initial region (mm. 1–24) is produced by a gradual registral migration of the pitch-classes from low to high.

A hidden unity also exists in the initial ordering of the twelve notes, which otherwise seem to have no serial significance in subsequent passages. Although maximal differentiation of the notes is achieved by means of their pointillistic distribution among the contrasting instrumental timbres and by

[23] Karlheinz Stockhausen, "Orientierung 1952/53," *Texte* vol. 1 (Cologne: M. DuMont Schauberg, 1963), p. 37.

[24] These categories are outlined by Dieter Schnebel, in "Karlheinz Stockhausen," *Die Reihe* 4 (Wien: Universal Edition A.G., 1958; Eng. ed. Pennsylvania: Theodore Presser Co., 1960), p. 122.

their contrasting dynamics, there are frequent recurrences of certain intervallic (cellular) combinations that are prominent in the initial unfolding of the twelve-notes (Ex. 15–5). For instance, the cadential flourish (at mm. 23–24) is permeated by unordered statements of cell 0–1–6: F–G♭–B and C♯–D–G (flute); C–F–F♯ and E–F–B♭ (clarinet). The next region opens (mm. 25ff.) with G–A♭–D♭ (trumpet, bassoon, and piano), B–C–E♯ (trumpet, cello-harp, harp), and C–E♯–F♯–[G♭–] (harp). The entire formal process is closed off at the end of the work by a held chord based on the simultaneous statement of the opening two 0–1–6 trichords, C♯–F♯–G and D♯–A–E (in enharmonic spelling, E♭–A–E), plus a spatial boundary of B and B♭. The latter two points are basic in delimiting the extreme registral and dynamic as well as durational spectra, and are set within the fastest tempo (200). While the temporal and spatial placements of B and B♭– have no relation to their positions in the original twelve-note unfolding, the specific registral placement of each of these two notes in relation to the two held trichords is optimal for extending their cellular properties to larger cellular constructions that are prominent in the original twelve-note statement. The high B extends the upper trichord by a fourth to G–C♯–F♯–B, thereby overlapping the intervallic content of the 0–1–6 cell (G–C♯–F♯) with the interval-5 cell (C♯–F♯–B), while the low B♭ extends the lower trichord to a four-note symmetry, D♯–A–E–B♭, which implies the presence of two inversionally-related forms of the 0–1-6 cell (D♯–E–A and E–A–B♭). Thus, this closing region represents the final transformation of the original space-time (vertical-horizontal) disposition of the opening pitch material. In the overall process, the initially wide timbral distribution of these individual points changes through stages of reinterpretation within the larger homogeneous groups of fluctuating densities and timbres to their ultimate condensation in the unambiguous uni-dimensional color of the piano. Although the work is not serialized in the traditional sense, there is a hidden, higher-level organization that produces "a clear sense of never departing from an unique and extremely unified construction. Not the same figures in a changing light [but rather] different figures in the same, all-penetrating light."[25]

EXAMPLE 15–5. Stockhausen, *Kontra-punkte,* opening twelve notes, recurrent intervallic (cellular) combinations

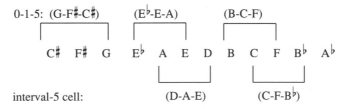

[25] See Stockhausen, "Orientierung," n.23, above, p. 37.

Many composers throughout the early to mid-1950s continued to exploit predetermined schemes in varying degrees of serialization according to the notions of a totally controlled music that stemmed from the work of Messiaen, Boulez, and Stockhausen. In his *Composition in Four Movements* (1955) for piano, Franco Donatoni uses serialized rhythms reminiscent of those discussed earlier by Messiaen, based on variations of rhythmic cells by means of proportional diminution and retrograde (Ex. 15–6a). Four rhythmic cells (1234) also appear in eight permutations, in which a primary ordering and its retrograde (4321) are each rotated systematically (Ex. 15–6b).

The Italian composer Luciano Berio first came into contact with the post-Webernists in 1954 when he met Maderna, Stockhausen, and Pousseur in Basel and attended the Darmstadt summer courses through 1959. His previous studies with Dallapiccola at Tanglewood in 1951 and his initial contact with the early taped electronic compositions of Otto Luening and Vladimir Ussachevsky at Columbia University in 1952 had introduced him to the new media, aesthetics, and techniques that were already becoming established in the music of the European avant-garde. Berio became one of the most prolific craftsmen in his adaptation of the principles of integral serialism, but his humanistic and creative sense took priority over his concern for absolute and objective mathematical control. His own attitudes and approach to composition reflected those of Dallapiccola, whose belief it was that expression and humanity were not to be sacrificed for the rigidity of the twelve-tone method: "Today, for the first time we have the curiosity of composers whom even our fathers would not have hesitated to call 'antimusical.' It is disconcerting to see how the possibility of writing music without being personally involved . . . has already become part of the 'history' of music."[26]

EXAMPLE 15–6. Donatoni, *Composition in Four Movements* for piano: (a) four basic rhythmic cells; and (b) permutations of primary and retrograde forms

(a) 1   2   3   4

(b) 1234 4321

2341 3214

3412 2143

4123 1432

[26] Luciano Berio, "Aspetti di artigianato formale," *Incontri musicali,* no. 1 (Milan, 1956): 55.

FUSION OF LYRICISM AND PERSONAL EXPRESSION WITH THE PRINCIPLE OF TOTAL SERIALISM

Berio was able to reconcile the more traditional serial principles of his teacher with those of total control pioneered by Messiaen and the new generation at Darmstadt. His serial works written during the Darmstadt years also reveal a synthesis of broader philosophical, aesthetic, and stylistic trends that establish his individuality and connections to his colleagues. Nothing could seem more opposing than the lyrical bel canto tradition of the Italian temperament, as differentiated from the complex, predetermined serial constructions of both the German composers at Darmstadt, and the Italian composers. A precedent had already been set by Dallapiccola in his opera *Il prigioniero,* in which the twelve-note series conception served as basis for the lyrical melodic line so characteristic of Italian opera from the time of the seventeenth century. It was Berio who bridged the gap between the expressive Italian style and the principles of total serialism and pointillism.

The poetic, expressive, and lyrical, as well as the complex and controlled, were already evident in Berio's orchestral piece *Nones* (1954), one of his first works composed during his early Darmstadt years. In this work, post–Webernist techniques were employed as the basis for expressing a human idea. Berio's original intention was to set W. H. Auden's poem of the same title as the basis for an oratorio, but abandoned the idea of a vocal setting for a purely instrumental one. The title refers to the Ninth Canonical Hour (3 P.M.), the mood of Auden's social protest transformed by Berio into an abstract musical construction: ". . . it is barely three, midafternoon, yet the blood of our sacrifice is already dry on the grass; . . . The shops will reopen at four, the empty blue bus in the empty pink square fill up and drive off: we have time to misrepresent. . . ."

In contrast to the static quality that characterizes the pointillistic textures of Messiaen's *Mode de valeurs* and Boulez's *Structures I,* the emotive quality of *Nones* is a partial result of the cumulative developmental form that builds to, and away from, a central point. This process, which unfolds within a sectionalized framework of five variations based on a "theme," or rather a composite set of serialized relationships, is generated by durational reinterpretations of the individual serialized events resulting in an overall motion between two polarized spatial conditions: a combined peak of registral saturation and temporal activity at the formal center; a registral depletion of the chromatic continuum culminating in empty octaves toward the end. This polarity is reflected in each of the five variations.[27]

The underlying element of the work is a thirteen-note row (Ex. 15–7), its abstract symmetrical construction giving it a balanced and static quality. The row is generated by four intervallically equivalent three-note cells, the intervallic and temporal ordering of the first two permutations (B–D–B♭ and G–E–E♭) of which are retrograded and inverted literally by the

---

[27] Piero Santi, "Luciano Berio," *Die Reihe* 4, p. 99.

EXAMPLE 15–7. Berio, *Nones,* symmetrical 13-note row generated by four intervallically equivalent three-note cells

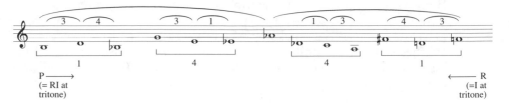

last two permutations (F–D–F♯ and A–C–D♭). The dual axis of symmetry of these two inversionally-related and retrograded hexachords is the repeated D–D and the A♭–[A♭] placed centrally. Since axis-note D is duplicated explicitly, the octave plays a significant role in the course of the composition and serves as a basic element in the polarity of the two spatial conditions (chromatic saturation and the depleted octave).

The systematic contextual manipulations of the cellular intervals and other serialized parameters—these include seven durational values (from two quarters to a sixteenth) with controlled silences, seven dynamic values (from *ppp* to *sffz*), and five types of articulation—produce changes of spatial and temporal activity that are translated into degrees of tension and relaxation so basic to the expressive mood. Both unity and ambiguity result from the major and minor thirds that are basic to the cell and the sixths that connect the two pairs of cell statements. This uniform intervallic chain of thirds and sixths tends to obscure the row as a distinct entity and, at the same time, contributes to overall formal continuity. Serial ambiguity is reinforced by the pointillistic timbral distribution of the notes as well. While the set-forms that unfold in the first twelve measures are relatively distinct and unambiguous, the perception of the series as a unified entity comes into question at the outset. The first six notes are articulated distinctly by means of extreme dynamic and registral differentiation and no more than a few notes at a time are assigned to any single instrumental timbre (the harp plays the first two pitches, the trombone and lower strings the third pitch, and so on). Individual pitches are taken up by different instruments of contrasting durations and articulations, which suggests some use of *Klangfarbenmelodie,* so the varied colors occupy much of the listener's attention. With increasing registral density and temporal activity, it is the thirds and sixths that maintain their sonic priority in a process that produces a sense of relative freedom within the serial conception. In his works of the next several years, we find a still greater freedom, yet coherence, in the handling of serial permutations within the larger structure and design, as in the *String Quartet* (1956), where deviations from the plan of pitches, durations, and registers prescribed serially, and other parameters frequently occur according to his artistic intuition. In *Allelujah I* and *II* (1955–1957), for six and five antiphonal instrumental groups, respectively, the technical procedures of

Nones are still in evidence, but with added acoustical and dimensional concerns within strictly controlled rhythmic procedures.

SUGGESTED READINGS

PIERRE BOULEZ. *Musikdenken heute* (= *Darmstädter Beiträge zur neuen musik, v*) (1963); Eng. trans. as *Boulez on Music Today* (London: Faber and Faber, 1971).

————. *Par volonté et par hasard: entretiens avec Célestin Deliège* (Paris: Les Éditions du Seuil, 1975; English trans. by Robert Wangermáe as *Conversations with Célestin Deliège* (London: Ernst Eulenberg, Ltd., 1976).

————. "Schönberg est mort," *Score* 6 (1952): 18–22; enlarged version, reprinted in *Relevés d'apprenti* [Notes of an Apprenticeship] (Paris: Alfred A. Knopf, 1966); Eng. trans. Herbert Weinstock (New York: Alfred A. Knopf, 1968), pp. 265–272.

REGINALD SMITH BRINDLE. *The New Music: The Avante-garde Since 1945* (Oxford and New York: Oxford University Press, 1975).

DIE REIHE 4 (Vienna: Universal Edition A. G., 1958); Eng. ed. (Pennsylvania: Theodore Presser Co., 1960), including: György Ligeti, "Pierre Boulez," (in German) pp. 38–63; Piero Santi, "Luciano Berio," (in German) pp. 98–102; Dieter Schnebel, "Karlheinz Stockhausen," (in German) pp. 119–133.

PAUL GRIFFITHS. *Modern Music: The Avant Garde Since 1945* (London: J. M. Dent & Sons Ltd.; New York: George Braziller, 1981), pp. 45–65 (on Darmstadt/Paris).

ROBERT SHERLAW JOHNSON. *Messiaen* (Berkeley and Los Angeles: University of California Press, 1975).

OLIVIER MESSIAEN. *Technique de mon langage musical* (Paris: Alphonse Leduc et Cie, Éditions Musicales, 1944); Eng. trans. John Satterfield (Paris: Alphonse Leduc, 1956).

ROGER NICHOLS. *Messiaen* (London: Oxford University Press, 1975).

CHARLES ROSEN. "The Piano Music," *Pierre Boulez: A Symposium,* ed. William Glock (London: Ernst Eulenberg, Ltd., 1986), pp. 85–97.

BRIGITTE SCHIFFER. "Darmstadt, Citadel of the Avantgarde," *The World of Music* 11/3 (1969), pp. 32–44.

PETER F. STACEY. *Boulez and the Modern Concept* (Aldershot, England: Scolar Press, 1987).

KARL H. WÖRNER. *Stockhausen: Life and Work,* ed. and trans. Bill Hopkins (London: Faber and Faber, 1973; Berkeley: University of California Press, 1976).

16 Varied approaches to the twelve-tone principle and rhythmic formulization in the United States

Severe political and economic conditions as well as artistic oppression during the 1930s led many European composers to emigrate to the United States prior to World War II. The most prominent of these was Schoenberg, who settled in the United States in 1933. He was followed by Krenek in 1937, then Bartók, Stravinsky, and Hindemith in 1939, all of whom (except Bartók) developed some form of twelve-tone serial composition further after World War II. While the younger generation of Europeans turned most prominently to the principles of Webern after the initial revival of Schoenberg's teachings by Leibowitz, Fortner, and Rufer at Darmstadt in 1946, members of the Vienna Schoenberg circle have all been influential to varying degrees in the United States since the early 1950s. However, except for the strong Webernist influence on Stravinsky's serial works, especially those of the twelve-tone system employed since 1958, it has been Schoenberg's aesthetics and techniques that have served as the most vital force for the earliest generation of postwar twelve-tone composers in the United States.

The most influential of Schoenbergians on the younger generation of American composers have been Milton Babbitt and Roger Sessions, both of whom have had a following through their teachings at Princeton and elsewhere since the 1950s. At the same time, while Elliott Carter's atonal compositions from the early 1950s on also developed in part from the Viennese influence, George Perle had already been evolving a methodological approach that was very different from his contemporaries since the late 1930s. Although related in special ways to the basic principles of Schoenberg and Berg, Perle's musical language represents the first move toward an integrated system of "tonality" within a kind of twelve-tone idiom.[1] Thus, the American musical scene of the postwar period, which has been strongly influenced by the Schoenberg circle, reveals a multiplicity of styles and approaches in the evolution of twelve-tone or atonal composition.

As in Darmstadt, one of the tendencies in the United States was to move beyond the traditional premises of twelve-tone serialism, which had served earlier as the primary basis for pitch relations. Part of the interest in the revival of the twelve-tone principle was to gain a new level of control over the various musical parameters in order to achieve total integration of the large-scale structure and design. The basic premise was that serialism could be raised from its status simply as a procedure or a methodology to that of a system. In the interest of total serialization, certain composers employed the twelve-tone procedures of Schoenberg as a point of departure for dissolving

---

[1] See the following chapter on "Twelve-Tone Tonality."

any sense of tonal priority as well as traditional structural implications. This development was manifested primarily in the early postwar years in the compositions and theoretical writings of Milton Babbitt.

BABBITT AS THEORIST AND "SCHOENBERGITE"

Babbitt's compositional intentions can be traced in different ways to each of the three Viennese composers. However, he had always felt more inclined toward Schoenberg's rather than Webern's music, not technically but as an "ideal of music."[2] As he had stated, both Webern and Schoenberg were essential to his own musical thinking, in which their approaches converged separately "at a certain point where they became eminently related without becoming intimately related." Aspects of these two composers were to be manifested on entirely different contextual levels in Babbitt's compositions. From Schoenberg came the idea of integrating the musical fabric through the motivic concept, from Webern the tendency to integrate the total structure through the control and interrelation of all the parameters. At the same time, he felt that Berg was the "real composer, [whose] structures . . . have things so recondite that they sometimes make you wonder, again, not can you hear them, but rather, can you conceptualize them?"

Most fundamental, however, were Schoenberg's assumptions regarding the twelve-tone aggregate, which was to serve as the main source for Babbitt's move toward a new concept of a musical totality. The notion of an "aggregate" in Schoenberg's music is founded upon the precept that the four set-forms (prime, inversion, and their respective retrogrades) "together constituted for Schoenberg an *area*—an area which maintained hexachord collections. There are thus twelve distinct areas, each containing four sets."[3] These relations among the four set-forms (P, I, R, and RI) will be explored below as connected to the "combinatoriality" of Babbitt's music.

Coming from mathematics, Babbitt had at his disposal such nonmusical terminology as the above, which could serve to clarify the basic concepts of Schoenbergian twelve-tone theory. Many of these mathematical terms have become standard reference in our twentieth-century musical vocabulary.[4] One of these terms is *"set,"* which Babbitt introduced to Schoenberg in response to the latter's own misgivings about the translation of the word *"Reihe"* (or "row"), which suggested an ordered thematic or motivic concept that progressed from left to right.[5] While Babbitt preferred the term *"series,"* it was his use of the term *"set"* that was finally adopted by both Schoenberg

---

[2] See Milton Babbitt, *Words About Music,* ed. Stephen Dembski and Joseph N. Straus (Madison: The University of Wisconsin Press, 1987), p. 24.

[3] See ibid., pp. 52–53.

[4] One of Babbitt's most significant pioneering essays to define and discuss these terminological concepts is his "Set Structure as a Compositional Determinant," *Journal of Music Theory* 5 (1961): 72–94.

[5] See Babbitt, *Words About Music,* n.2, above, pp. 11–12.

and himself because of its neutrality in regard to the order principle. Babbitt developed the concept of the Schoenbergian set further, not primarily as a source for the serial order principle itself, but rather as a kind of motivic generator. However, this does not mean that the set is equivalent to a theme or motif defined contextually, but rather that, in accordance with Schoenberg's idea of "composing with the tones of a motive," certain criteria of the set are basic to generating a larger twelve-tone context. In Babbitt's words, "the constraints of twelve-tone writing (to the extent that a piece can be called twelve tone at all) are nothing more than a principle of formation of the most characteristic, the most physical materials—the twelve pitch classes of the usual chromatic scale—and certain principles of transformation which are interval preserving."[6]

It is precisely this "motivic" notion of the set that distinguishes Babbitt's music from that of Boulez and the other "Webernists" at Darmstadt, although Babbitt also extended the serial concept to nonpitch parameters. Babbitt was not interested in the set as a basis for pointillistic isolation of the individual sound events as were the "Webernists," but rather in the various ways that the set might assert itself (in the "motivic" sense) as a structural determinant. The surface intervallic (serial) ordering of the set is subsidiary to its deeper-level structural functions; surface orderings are exploited primarily for the purpose of distinguishing different transformations (P, I, R, and RI) of the twelve-tone aggregate contextually in order to establish the premise for continuity.

Babbitt's interest in deep-level structural relations led him to the total control of all the parameters, in which the serial principle served as the all-encompassing premise that coordinated pitch with the rhythmic, dynamic, timbral, registral, and articulative dimensions in such a way as to produce a highly organized approach to the large-scale formal plan. According to the pitch-set premise, one of the fundamental ways in which he was to generate the twelve-tone aggregate and distinguish its transformations (P, I, R, and RI) and their transpositions was by generalizing the Schoenbergian hexachordal concept of the set. As the basis for the strict association of the set-forms in both ordering and content, and the creation of an equal (democratic) relationship among the twelve tones in the contrapuntal and successive unfolding of the twelve-tone aggregate, Babbitt expanded Schoenberg's concept of hexachordal combinatoriality. A set is combinatorial if it can be joined contrapuntally to one or another of the other forty-seven set-forms so the corresponding, aligned hexachords produce no pitch duplications--give us all twelve tones. As a rule, Schoenberg only used the basic set (for example, P–0 or R–0) and its inversion at the lower fifth (I–5 or RI–5), a relation which Babbitt termed *"semi-combinatoriality."*[7] He expanded the combinatorial possibilities by constructing the set in such a way that at least one transposition of

[6] Ibid., p. 170.
[7] See Chap. 3.

each of its four transformations (P, I, R, RI) could be joined to a transposition of each of its four transformations, a minimal requirement for what he called *"all-combinatoriality."* (See Ex. 16–1a,[8] where each of the four set-forms in one column may be joined combinatorially to any one of the four set-forms in the other column, producing all twelve tones in the contrapuntal alignment of their mutually exclusive hexachordal components.)[9] While the hexachordal pitch content remains unchanged under transformation and/or transposition of the set, we get a permutation in the internal ordering of each hexachord.

EXAMPLE 16–1. Babbitt, first of *Three Compositions for Piano:* (a) all-combinatorial set-forms; and (b) inversionally related hexachords and their self-inversional properties as the basis of the combinatorial set

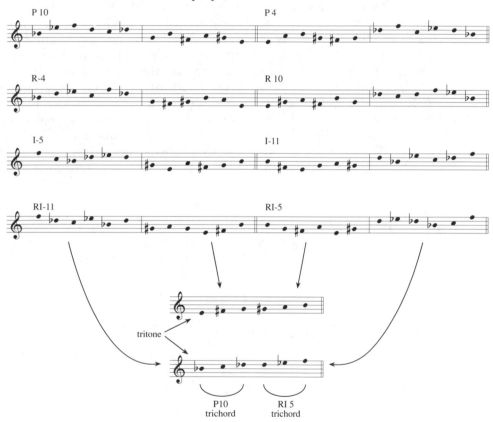

[8] George Perle, *Serial Composition and Atonality* (rev. 6th ed., Berkeley and Los Angeles: University of California Press, 1991), p. 100.

[9] For a definition of "all-combinatoriality," including the "six all-combinatorial hexachords" and their levels of transpositional function ("first-order," "second-order," "third-order," and "sixth-order"), see Babbit, *Words About Music,* n.2, above, p. 193.

The concept of total serialization and the generation of material from the all–combinatorial set was first realized in Babbitt's *Three Compositions for Piano* (1947), *Composition for Four Instruments,* flute, clarinet, violin, and cello, and *Composition for Twelve Instruments,* wind quintet, trumpet, harp, celesta, string trio, and double bass (both written in 1948). The first of the *Three Compositions,* while not yet entirely extending serial control to all the parameters, represents a landmark in this post-Schoenbergian development, predating the ultrarationality of Messiaen's *Mode de valeurs* by two years. A study of the properties of the set in Babbitt's piano piece reveals certain basic principles by which the combinatorial relation can occur. The tritone of each pitch in a hexachord (Ex. 16–1b) is contained only in the other hexachord, the separation of the two hexachords by this interval thereby permitting the combinatorial relation to occur between them. Of more general significance, however, is the symmetrical disposition of the pitch classes in each hexachord, as shown expressly in the unordered form of each of the two hexachords (Ex. 16–1b).[10] This permits the hexachords to be both related to each other inversionally and to be self-inversional, the latter also permitting equivalent intervallic ordering between the R/RI forms of each hexachord and the P/I forms. (Combinatorial sets are often based only on the inversional relation between complementary hexachords, i.e., without the self-inversional property of each hexachord, as in Schoenberg's *Piano Piece,* Op. 33a; Ex. 16–2.)[11] Thus, inversional equivalence of the hexachords in their unordered form permits the combinatorial relation to occur between set-forms at certain transpositional levels.

EXAMPLE 16–2. Schoenberg, Piano Piece, Op. 33a, inversional relation between complementary hexachords (without self-inversional property) of the combinatorial set

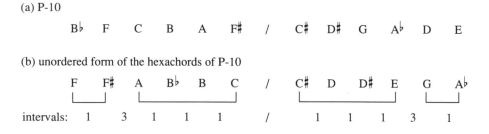

(a) P-10

B♭ F C B A F♯ / C♯ D♯ G A♭ D E

(b) unordered form of the hexachords of P-10

F F♯ A B♭ B C / C♯ D D♯ E G A♭

intervals: 1 3 1 1 1 / 1 1 1 3 1

[10] We continue to assign the following numbers to pitch-classes—C = 0, C♯ = 1, D = 2, E♭ = 3, etc.—as the basis for indicating T-nos.

[11] Conversely, according to Babbitt, in *Words About Music,* n.2, above, pp. 14–15, Schoenberg never completed his early oratorio *Die Jacobsleiter* (1915) because the hexachords of the set were not related to each other inversionally, but self-inversionally only. Thus, it lacked the main criterion that became so basic to Schoenberg's twelve-tone combinatorial works.

The contrapuntal as well as temporal pairings of the combinatorially related set-forms in Babbitt's piano piece permit permutations of the twelve-tone aggregate to circulate continually on both the linear and harmonic levels. Schoenberg's term "developing variation" is applicable to this procedure in what appears to be an athematic context. Except for special passages in the piece, the two set-forms of each contrapuntal pairing throughout are derived from alternate columns (see Ex. 16–1a). At the same time, consecutive linear statements of the twelve-tone aggregate are also produced by the combinatorial relation of hexachords. Because of the linear adjacency relation of hexachords, a given set-form must be followed by another from the same column. The resulting linear twelve-tone aggregate is referred to as a *secondary set* (Ex. 16–3).[12]

Serialized rhythmic and contrapuntal reinterpretations of the paired set-forms also generate an overall serialized form (Ex. 16–4).[13] Each of the six sections is articulated by a particular contrapuntal and rhythmic disposition of the paired set-forms. In Section I (mm. 1–8), the barline serves as a referential point for the distinct alignment of the hexachords of set-forms related combinatorially: P–0/P–6, RI–1/R–0, etc. Section II (mm. 9–18) is differentiated from Section I in part by the change of contrapuntal pattern (see Ex. 16–4), now based on alternations of single and paired set statements. While Sections V and VI mirror the patterns of Sections I and II, a radical change of pattern occurs in Section III (mm. 19–28) and the beginning of the return phase of the formal mirror, Section IV (mm. 29–38). In these two central sections, the hexachords are staggered in canonic inversion, so the second hexachord of

EXAMPLE 16–3. Babbitt, first of *Three Compositions for Piano,* Section I, secondary sets

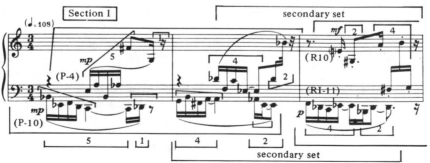

[12] Perle analyzes this and other serial relations of the piece in *Serial Composition and Atonality,* n.8, above, pp. 99–102, 128–129, and 132–134.
[13] Ibid., pp. 128–129.

EXAMPLE 16–4. Babbitt, first of *Three Compositions for Piano,* overall formal scheme of paired set-forms

|A| alignment of corresponding hexachords:

Section I (mm. 1-8)
P-4 | R-10 | RI-5 | I-11
P-10 | RI-11 | I-5 | R-4

Section II (mm. 9-18)
    | R-10 | I-11 | I-11 | R-10 | RI-5 | | P-4 | P-4 | RI-5
P-10 | RI-11 | RI-11 | | I-5 | P-10 | R-4 | I-5 | R-4 | //

|B| alignment of noncorresponding hexachords:

Section III (mm. 19-28)
  I-11   R-10 | R-10 |
P-4 | RI-5 | P-4 | I-11 | |P-4| | P-4   RI-5   //retrograde
                        |R-10| RI-5 RI-5 | I-11 | R-10   I-11 //canon begins

Section IV (mm. 29-38)
RI-11 | P-10| RI-11 | I-5 | I-5 | P-10 |
    I-5   R-4 | R-4 | RI-11 | R-4 | I-5 | R-4 //
                                    | P-10 | P-10 | RI-11

|A| alignment of corresponding hexachords:

Section V (mm. 39-48)
    | P-4 | RI-5 | P-4 | R-10 | RI-5 | | I-11 | I-11 | R-10 //
I-5 | R-4 | R-4 | | I-5 | P-10 | RI-11 | RI-11 | P-10 |

Section VI (mm. 49-56)
P-10 | RI-11 | I-5 | R-4
RI-5 | I-11 | P-4 | R-10

one set–form is aligned with the first hexachord of another set–form. In order to maintain the combinatorial relation between the aligned noncorresponding hexachords, the set-forms must now be derived from the same column (see Ex. 16–1a), e.g., P–4/I–11, RI–5/R–10, etc. This contrapuntal and combinatorial reinterpretation in the central portion of the piece contributes to the articulation of the large ABA form. Also, as part of the large formal mirror, the set-forms in the first three sections are retrograded in the last three sections (see arrow in Ex. 16–4) in terms of both order of occurrence and transformation of the set.

Rhythmic serialization also contributes to the integration of the large-scale structure by defining each of the four set-forms as well as the group of set-forms within each of the six sections. In Section I, a common rhythmic pattern is established linearly in each of the first two statements of the set

(P–10 and P–4), in which each local group of sixteenths is punctuated by a longer note or a rest, producing the pattern 5–1–4–2. The rhythmic pattern for all statements of the retrograde form of the pitch-set is, correspondingly, the rhythmic retrograde 2–4–1–5. The inversion of the basic rhythmic set (5–1–4–2) is derived arbitrarily (by a process analogous to the derivation of a pitch-set inversion)[14] by subtracting each number from a common modulus, in this case 6, to give us the complementary numbers of the inversion, 1–5–2–4. This is precisely the pattern identified throughout with all statements of the pitch-set inversion, the pattern 4–2–5–1 corresponding to statements of the retrograde-inversion. The contextual means of articulating these four rhythmic forms (P = 5–1–4–2; I = 1–5–2–4; R = 2–4–1–5; and RI = 4–2–5–1), however, changes in each section, permitting the composer to produce a sense of development freely in the shaping of an otherwise mechanical and controlled approach to structure. Whereas both set-forms aligned contrapuntally in Section I are based on the same articulative pattern, the different articulations for each set-form in a pair aligned contrapuntally in Section II result in a more complex texture. One of the rhythmic dispositions of the set is determined by slurs and accents in evenly unfolding sixteenths, the other on chords of which the durational values are calculated in sixteenths. The registral ordering of components that form the more dense three-note harmonic textures of certain sections is determined serially by the ordinal positions of those components within the set (Ex. 16–5). Furthermore, as with the rhythmic set-forms, dynamics are also serialized by means of specific identifications with the four pitch-set transformations. All set-forms are assigned a particular dynamic level (P = *mp*, R = *mf*, I = *f*, and RI = *p*), except in Section VI, where each is downgraded by two dynamic levels in support of a return to the slower tempo of the opening.

EXAMPLE 16–5. Babbitt, first of *Three Compositions for Piano*, Section V, e.g., mm. 44–45, rhythmic and registral serialization in more dense trichordal harmonic textures

[14] See ibid., p. 3.

All the pieces of the *Three Compositions* are related serially by what Babbitt has referred to as *derived sets*. While the basis of segmentation in the first piece is the hexachord, harmonic reiterations of smaller trichordal segments are also in evidence (see Ex. 16–5). From the first trichordal fragment of RI–11 of the first piece, a succession of trichordal segments derived serially is generated at the beginning of the second piece (right hand) by means of inversion, retrograde-inversion, and retrograde (Ex. 16–6).[15] In the course of the piece, each trichord of the original set generates other derived sets as well.

Rational control over the various nonpitch dimensions by means of their association with the serialized pitch-set properties was extended by Babbitt in his next compositions. In his *Composition for Twelve Instruments* (1948; rev. 1954), he predated Messiaen in the serialization of durations. Babbitt had already determined series of twelve durational values according to the order numbers of the basic pitch-set. Given P–0, C–C♯–E–A–F–G♯–D♯–A♯–D–B–F♯–G, the durational values, as calculated in sixteenths and sometimes realized in the form of rests, outline the durational series [12]–1–4–9–5–8–3–10–2–[11]–6–7. Where durations are derived from a transposed form of the pitch-set, rhythmic augmentation as well as an occasional mutation will result; compare P–0, above, with P–2, D–D♯–F♯–B–G–A♯–F–C–E–C♯–G♯–A (in numerical designation, [2]–3–6–11–7–10–5–12–4–[1]–8–9). Babbitt's durational sets may also appear arbitrarily dissociated from the forms of the pitch-set from which they are derived (Ex. 16–7). Griffiths states that "Babbitt was not long to remain content with rhythmic manipulations which were at loggerheads with pitch structures and which . . . also proved self-obscuring: there is, for instance, no way for the ear to disentangle two simultaneous or overlapping statements of different forms of the duration set, and the concept of a 'duration interval' is also somewhat problematic."[16]

EXAMPLE 16–6. Babbitt, first and second of *Three Compositions for Piano*, derived set from initial trichord of original RI–11

(a) first piece:

RI-11:   F D♭ C   E♭ B♭ D A♭ A G E F♯ B

(b) second piece, opening: ↕

Derived set: F D♭ C / B♭ D E♭ / A G♯ E / F♯ G B

P-5   I-10   RI-4   R-11

[15] Paul Griffiths, *Modern Music: The Avant Garde Since 1945* (New York: George Braziller, 1981), pp. 40–41.
[16] Ibid., p. 42.

EXAMPLE 16–7. Babbit, *Composition for Twelve Instruments,* No. 7, independent assignment of the durational set derived from pitch-class numbers of basic P–0 (C–C♯–E–A–F–G♯–D♯–A♯–D–B–F♯–G)

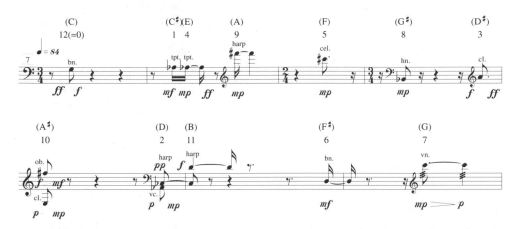

Babbitt continued to employ combinatoriality, derivative sets, and durational sets, and attempted further control over the totality of parameters to integrate the large-scale structure. These were often infused with more popular and lyrical elements, as in his song cycle, *Du,* for soprano and piano (1951), performed at the ISCM Festival in 1953. The first song of the cycle is combinatorial and based on an *all-interval set* (i.e., based on one occurrence of every interval contained within an octave). The vocal lyricism of *Du* was developed further in *Philomel,* composed for soprano and four-track tape (1964).[17] His *All Set,* for a jazz ensemble of alto and tenor saxophones, trumpet, trombone, double bass, drums, vibraphone, and piano (1957), combines total serialism with the improvisatory jazz style of the 1940s. In the *Sextets* for violin and piano (1966), the serial principle is extended to the use of twelve different dynamic levels—*ppppp, pppp, ppp, pp, p, mp, mf, f, ff, fff, ffff, fffff.* Some scholars have been "concerned with the relevance to perception of the twelve-tone arrays employed in the composition of Babbitt's music and routinely invoked in the analysis of it,"[18] while others have gone beyond this

[17] Babbitt's turn to the use of the electronic synthesizer in the mid-1950s will be discussed more appropriately in Chapter 18.

[18] Joseph Dubiel, " 'Thick Array/Of Depth Immeasurable': Some Questions About the Music of Milton Babbitt," a paper presented at the Fourth Michigan Conference on Music Theory, at the University of Michigan, Ann Arbor, March 29, 1985.

concentration on questions of pitch and pitch-class to the dynamic surface as well:

> Even assuming that the performers are capable of realizing and the listener of apprehending such an extended, precise, and refined scale of dynamic values, can a given dynamic value be judged independently of mode of attack, timbre, texture, register, and its relation to adjacent dynamic values? . . . the explicit and absolute differentiation of twelve different dynamic levels which this music . . . requires, is based on an untenable analogy with pitch-class differentiation—most obviously untenable because, unlike the latter, it is beyond the range of "auditory construal," but for other obvious reasons as well. The pitch scale, for example, is cyclical: the interval between pitch-numbers 11 and 0 is the same as that between 0 and 1; the dynamic scale is not cyclical: the interval between *fffff* and *ppppp* is not the same as that between *ppppp* and *pppp*.[19]

CONTRASTING POSTWAR AESTHETIC APPROACHES TO SERIAL COMPOSITION: ORGANIC DEVELOPMENT (SESSIONS) VS. BLOCK CONSTRUCTION (STRAVINSKY AND COPLAND)

Through his teachings, Babbitt has served as a link between the Viennese composers and more recent serial approaches of the younger generation of Americans, those coming from Princeton University especially. Some of these are James K. Randall (b. 1929), Peter Westergaard (b. 1931), Henry Weinberg (b. 1931), Donald Martino (b. 1931), and Benjamin Boretz (b. 1934). Like Babbitt, these composers also studied with Roger Sessions, but Babbitt's own studies with Sessions predate the latter's turn to twelve-tone composition in the early 1950s. Since then, Sessions has been among the most influential teachers in the dissemination of twelve-tone composition.

Two contrasting aesthetic approaches to serial composition emerged in the 1950s, one stemming from the expressionistic milieu characterized by an intense cumulative approach to texture and form, the other stemming from the more objective and mechanical block structures and layers of neo-classicism. These two diverging tendencies are exemplified in the forms and textures of Sessions and Stravinsky. Sessions first turned to twelve-tone serial composition in his *Sonata* for solo violin (1953), but the potential for this development had already been suggested in his works since the 1920s. The diatonic counterpoint of his *Black Maskers* (1923), *First Symphony* (1927), and *First Piano Sonata* (1930) reveals a kinship with the neoclassical styles of Stravinsky and his teacher Ernest Bloch. However, certain elements in the

[19] George Perle, "Pitches or Pitch-Classes?" a paper given at the University of California at Berkeley, Spring 1989. This paper appears as "Lecture 4" in Perle's book, *The Listening Composer* (Berkeley and Los Angeles: University of California Press, 1990), pp. 93–121.

Symphony portended his evolution toward a more expressionistic idiom based on continuous, dense, and chromatic contrapuntal lines that generate his integrated and developmental forms, as in the *Violin Concerto* (1935), *String Quartet in E Minor* (1936), *Second Symphony* (1945), and opera *Trial of Lucullus* (1947). While certain features of Sessions' new chromaticism may be associated with Schoenberg's expressionistic counterpoint, they are essentially different. Sessions' spun-out lines tend toward greater homogeneity and length through the persistent unfolding of uniform figuration and intervallic structure. Sessions' continuous linear counterpoint served as a major influence in the development of a so-called "American style" during this period and foreshadowed the ingredients of his own twelve-tone language.

Although general interest in Schoenberg's twelve-tone serial principles became widespread in the United States after World War II, and although Sessions had already been familiar with Schoenberg's music prior to the war, the twelve-tone approach was not a part of Sessions' own conscious compositional plans: he had never felt inclined toward it as a compositional principle.[20] In 1953, the violinist Robert Gross, who had premièred the *Violin Concerto* a number of years earlier, requested a solo violin work from Sessions, who was at first reluctant to compose in this genre and to use the twelve-tone principle. However, according to Sessions, "my first use of [twelve-tone technique] was, at the beginning, quite involuntary. I had at various times . . . carried out quite small-scale exercises with the technique, but I still envisaged it as not applicable to my own musical ideas. It was therefore a surprise to me when I found the composition of the Sonata flowing easily and without constraint in its terms."[21] This statement reveals how naturally his increasing chromaticism was transformed into the system without "in any way changing its essential nature." This evolution also has ramifications with regard to the disappearance of any neoclassical formal vestiges from his music. According to an entirely different aesthetic approach from that of Schoenberg, Babbitt, or the Darmstadt composers, Sessions establishes an extraordinary degree of interrelatedness between serial content and structure.

In the first of the four movements of the *Sonata,* certain pitch-set, rhythmic, textural, and contour relations are established between the structure of the basic twelve-tone theme and the overall arch-form. The opening thematic statement (mm. 1–4) reflects locally this arch in two phases—one ascending, the other descending (Ex. 16–8). The ascending phase is characterized by expanding intervals in the first seven notes of P–7 (G–G♯– C♯–A–F–E♭–E), a progression supported by expanding durations, a crescendo, and *poco rit.* The second phase, set off from the first by a rest and

---

[20] "Schoenberg in the United States (1944, revised 1972)," *Roger Sessions on Music: Collected Essays,* ed. Edward T. Cone (Princeton, New Jersey: Princeton University Press, 1979), p. 360.
[21] Ibid.

EXAMPLE 16–8. Sessions, *Sonata* for solo violin, opening, thematic archshape in two phases—ascending and descending based on P–7 and I–0, followed by P–7 and R–7

shorter sixteenth-note values, reverses the direction in a slower, more fragmented and irregular descent initiated by the last five notes of P–7 (B–F♯–C–D–B♭). The completion of the descent is achieved gradually by means of two sequential extensions, which now outline the inverted set-form at the lower fifth, I–0 (C–B–F♯–B♭–D/E–E♭–A♭–C♯–G–F–A). The rhythmic grouping (5 and 7 notes) of the latter set-form is the reverse of the rhythmic grouping of P–0 (7 and 5 notes), producing an overall symmetrical pattern of note groupings (7, 5, 5, 7) in support of the thematic arch.

Sessions calculates carefully not only this rhythmic distribution of the fragments of P–7 and I–0, but also the contextual placement of these two set-forms within the thematic arch, i.e., the inversion, though not synchronized with the beginning of the descent, correlates by means of its inherent internal construction with the inversional contour of the theme. The choice of these two set-forms themselves also appears to be calculated. The hexachordal-combinatorial relation between P–7 and I–0, a principle also found in other works of Sessions, permits consistent reiterations of identifiable hexachordal collections in the linear thematic succession. The reversed order of the hexachords of P–7 (G–G♯–C♯–A–F–E♭/E–B–F♯–C–D–B♭) in I–0 (C–B–F♯–B♭–D–E/E♭–A♭–C♯–G–F–A) produces a symmetrical hexachordal pattern (1, 2, 2, 1), which also contributes to the thematic shape and closure.[22]

The next pair of phrases initiates an expanded ascending phase of a new arch shape. This passage begins (end of m. 4 to m. 10) with a linear joining of P–7 with its retrograde related combinatorially (R–7), the linear succession of set-forms resulting again in the symmetrical hexachordal pattern 1, 2, 2, 1. However, both set-forms are now part of a single, longer ascending phase, its rhythmic character and shape reflecting the more fragmented sequences of the original descending phase. This reinterpretion of contour relations between ascending and descending phases produces a sense of continuity and structural integration. The longer ascent, in a more dense

---

[22] As mentioned above, these hexachords are disposed in rhythmic groups of 7, 5, 5, 7 notes.

texture of double-stops, unfolds to a higher peak (mm. 18–23). The latter is followed by a corresponding irregular descent, pervaded by references to the contour of the sequential figure of the original descent (see mm. 2–4) to end this more expanded arch (at m. 29).

Expressionistic intensity is renewed at a higher level in the following passage (mm. 29–54), where a succession of generally ascending figurations establishes the main tendency of this passage and leads into the second of three large sections of the movement (mm. 54ff.). A modified return of the theme begins the most agitated ascending motions, the serial modifications of this thematic statement contributing to the sense of expansion. Beginning one fifth higher than the original statement, the thematic intervals now unfold from a whole-step to a major seventh, the intervallic mutations resulting from a shift between the series and the thematic rhythm (Ex. 16–9). The first three notes (D–E–C) actually form the last three notes of P–9 (A–B♭–E♭–B–G–F–F♯–C♯–G♯/D–E–C), the first portion of this set-form overlapping the ending of the preceding section. This nonsynchronization produces an elision between these otherwise distinct sections and permits the theme to begin with expanded intervals. At the same time, the ascending and descending phases of this thematic statement are synchronized with the two hexachords of either P-6 or R-6 (F♯–G–C–A♭–E–D/E♭–B♭–F–B–C♯–A). The permutation and retrogressive ordering of the internal hexachordal content, 6–5–[3]–[4]–2–1/12–11–10–9–8–7, permits maximal intervallic reference to the opening, i.e., reversal of ordinal positions 3 and 4 results in ascending minor sixths (as in the original theme), while the intervallic mutations contribute to the expressive intentions and formal shaping.

A reversal of direction in the overall arch-form is anticipated toward the end of the middle section (mm. 78ff.) by the descending motions, the final section (mm. 85ff.) of which is then characterized by wide-ranging descents (e.g., at mm. 91ff., 96ff., 107ff., and 123ff.). This section is encompassed by P–7 (mm. 85–88) and R–7 (mm. 123–end), both of which were basic in rounding out certain local arch shapes within the first section (e.g., mm. 25–26 had unfolded the two unordered hexachords of R–7, while mm.

EXAMPLE 16–9. Sessions, *Sonata* for solo violin, Section II, mm. 54ff., intervallic mutation of main theme (at perfect-fifth transposition) resulting from shift between series and thematic rhythm

27–29 reversed these hexachords in an ordered statement of P–7). The thematic roles of P–7 and R–7 are reversed more complexly in the final passage. The penultimate P–7 ascent (mm. 119–121) is based on the fragmented irregular character of the original descent, while the final R–7 descent suggests the more regular expansion of the opening phase conversely, but played in reverse. The contour of this final R–7 statement mixes certain features from both the original ascending and descending phases of the theme. The contour fusion and reversal of this R–7 statement is confirmed by both the systematic contraction of intervals (a reversal of the opening systematic expansion) and several registral deviations, which produce the angular contour of the sequential figures of the descending phase (mm. 2–4).

In his *Idyll of Theocritus,* for soprano and orchestra (1954), *Piano Concerto* (1956), *Fourth Symphony* and *String Quintet* (1958), the opera *Montezuma* (1941–1963), and in his more recent *Third Piano Sonata* (1965), *Symphony No. 8* (1968), and cantata *When Lilacs Last in the Dooryard Bloom'd,* for solo voices, chorus, and orchestra (1970), his serial approach continued to reveal a flexibility that permitted him to realize his personal expressive goals. His technical evolution toward an increasingly systematic chromaticism, which has always been a logical consequence of his aesthetic approach, has provided an alternative to the techniques of the "total serialists" for the integration of the various structural levels: "Serialism is neither the arbitrary nor the rigid set of prescriptions that it is often supposed to be . . . [but] is rather the result of many converging trends of musical development."[23] Sessions has pointed to the strong polyphonic orientation among latter-day serial composers, who are "more concerned with problems of texture and organization than with harmony in the hitherto accepted meaning of the term."[24]

Under the influence of Sessions, many other American composers have also been drawn to this developmental approach to serialized polyphonic textures, but the 1950s also gave rise to a contrasting aesthetic approach to serial composition in the United States. Soon after the death of Schoenberg in 1951, Stravinsky began to turn from the diatonic-octatonic tonal assumptions of his Neoclassical period toward experiments with serialism, at first in a nontwelve-tone idiom. Stravinsky began to have more than a casual contact with the serial idiom of the Viennese composers, the aesthetics of Webern drawing his interest especially. Despite Stravinsky's technical change, his new works continued to manifest his stylistic and aesthetic traits so typical since his early Russian and Neoclassical periods. In contrast to the developmental expressionistic forms of Sessions, Stravinsky's static block structures in mechanically layered textures continued to produce the detached anti-Romantic quality that he had proclaimed so explicitly for his own music throughout his life. In more fundamental ways, too, Stravinsky was to hold

---

[23] Roger Sessions, "Problems and Issues Facing the Composer Today," *Roger Sessions on Music,* n.20, above, p. 81.
[24] Ibid., p. 80.

on to certain technical elements that had become so engrained in his musical language, that at this critical moment of change (the second in his career) one finds a synthesis as much as a departure from his previous technical approach. His own observations provide insight into the evolutionary nature of this change. He had pointed to a certain serial attitude in his Russian works composed as early as 1910: "if an interesting construction exists in *The Firebird,* it will be found in the treatment of intervals. . . . When some poor Ph.D. candidate is obliged to sift my early works for their 'serial tendencies,' this sort of thing will, I suppose, rate as an *Ur*-example."[25] In a 1952 interview, his attitude toward the serial issue tended conversely to be somewhat conservative, yet enthusiastic: "Serialism? Personally I find quite enough to do with seven notes of the scale. Nevertheless, the serial composers are the only ones with a discipline that I respect. Whatever else serial music may be, it is certainly pure music. Only, the serialists are prisoners of the figure twelve, while I feel greater freedom with the figure seven."[26]

In support of the latter comments, Stravinsky's continuation of the familiar elements of his musical language can be traced to his pervasive use of diatonic and octatonic collections, even in the apparently more chromatic serial contexts of the 1950s.[27] In his serial compositions prior to *Threni,* for soloists, chorus, and orchestra (1957–1958), he was not yet a "prisoner of the figure twelve," turning at first to nontwelve-tone serial writing in the *Cantata,* for solo voices, female choir, and chamber ensemble (1951–1952). The tenor part of Riccrcar II of this work unfolds all four transformations of an eleven-note set serially at two different transpositional levels. Certain basic features of Stravinsky's earlier styles are seen in the strong diatonic character of the series as well as its narrow range and mechanical ostinato-like encir-clings so characteristic of both the Russian and Neoclassical motivic layers. Stravinsky's new serialism was to endow the contrapuntal techniques of his Neoclassical period with a greater discipline than ever before, a concern enhanced further by his more pervasive use of strict canonic procedures in the *Cantata* and most of his works since then.[28] As he moved toward twelve-tone

[25] Igor Stravinsky and Robert Craft, *Expositions and Developments* (Berkeley and Los Angeles: University of California Press, 1962), pp. 132–133.

[26] "Recontre avec Stravinsky," *Preuves* (May 1952). Also see this quote in Eric Walter White, *Stravinsky* (Berkeley and Los Angeles: University of California Press, 1966), pp. 133–134.

[27] The carry-over of Stravinsky's octatonicism from his Neoclassical period into his serial works and the connection with certain octatonic implications of Webern's twelve-tone constructions are discussed by Pieter C. van den Toorn, *The Music of Igor Stravinsky* (New Haven: Yale University Press, 1983), p. 381. Van den Toorn's premises are supported by Henri Pousseur's study, "Stravinsky by Way of Webern: The Consistency of a Syntax," *Perspectives of New Music* 10 (1972): 13–15; and 11 (1972): 112–145.

[28] See Glenn Watkins, "The Canon and Stravinsky's Late Style," *Confronting Stravinsky: Man, Musician, and Modernist,* ed. Jann Pasler (Berkeley and Los Angeles: University of California Press, 1986), p. 244.

serialization, partly in the *Canticum Sacrum* (1955) and the ballet *Agon* (1953–1957) and entirely in *Threni* (1958), the canonic writing was to acquire an increasingly distinctive Renaissance quality. Thus, the evolutionary rather than radical nature of Stravinsky's move into his new style period is revealed by this fusion of traditional contrapuntal techniques with the serial principle, about which he asserted that "the rules and restrictions of serial writing differ little from the rigidity of the great contrapuntal schools of old."[29]

The shift in Stravinsky's earlier style from the brilliantly orchestrated Russian ballets toward the miniaturized forms and skeletal instrumental structures of the *Three Pieces for String Quartet* and *Pribaoutki* (1914), which foreshadowed *Histoire* and other early Neoclassical works, can be seen similarly in the early serial works of the 1950s. The chamber quality of the *Cantata* was continued in the partially serialized *Septet* (1952–1953), for clarinet, horn, bassoon, piano, violin, viola, and violoncello, of which the three movements (*Sonata Allegro, Passacaglia, Gigue*) also suggest his continuing Neoclassical interests.[30] Infusion of the nontwelve-tone serial principle into a strongly diatonic contrapuntal context based on older English verse (as in the *Cantata*) was developed further in the *Three Songs From William Shakespeare* (1953), entitled "Musick to heare," "Full Fadom Five," and "When Dasies Pied," for a reduced and transparent chamber group consisting of mezzo-soprano, flute, clarinet, and viola.

The most strictly serial of these early nontwelve-tone works is *In Memoriam Dylan Thomas* (1954), in which we find a perfect fusion of the archaic counterpoint reminiscent of certain late Renaissance instrumental canzonas—this is exemplified in the Venetian "polychoral motet style" of Giovanni Gabrieli's *Sonata Pian'e Forte* (1597),[31] with its formal block juxtapositions of antiphonal trombone choirs and repeated notes in characteristic canzona rhythms—and the rigidly proportional, architectural concerns that had already appeared in Stravinsky's austere, religious *Symphony of Psalms* (1930) and *Mass* (1948). *In Memoriam* has a mournful, requiem-like quality, a fitting monument to the memory of the poet, who died just before he and Stravinsky could fulfill their plans to collaborate on an opera. Stravinsky then chose the appropriate poetic verses, "Do not go gentle into that good night,"

[29] Igor Stravinsky and Robert Craft, *Conversations with Stravinsky* (London: Faber and Faber, 1959; Berkeley and Los Angeles: University of California Press, 1980), p. 25.

[30] However, Robert Craft, in "A Personal Preface," *The Score* 20 (June 1957): 7, has also suggested the influence of Schoenberg's *Suite*, Op. 29, on Stravinsky's use of the gigue.

[31] This connection with the early Venetian style stems from Gabrieli's pupil, Heinrich Schütz, more directly. While composing *In Memoriam Dylan Thomas*, Stravinsky had learned that Schütz's *Fili Mi Absalon*, with its four trombones, was to be performed on the same program of Monday Evening Concerts at Los Angeles, hence the use of trombones in the Stravinsky work. See Robert Craft, "A Concert for St. Mark" *The Score* 18 (December 1956): 35.

which Thomas had written in memory of his own father, as the basis for a canonic setting for tenor and string quartet. The song setting is flanked by an instrumental Prelude and Postlude in the form of five Dirge-Canons and five Ritornelli, which are set antiphonally between a quartet of trombones and string quartet.

Stravinsky's use of mechanically alternating polyphonic block structures is in keeping with his own Neoclassical approach to form. However, the increased discipline of the serial approach is basic to all levels of the architecture and also points to a heightened preoccupation with numerical symbology. The number five is fundamental to the structure of the series, the metric and rhythmic scheme, and overall formal divisions within the prelude and postlude, while the song is based on six couplets.[32] The basic five-note set, employed in all four of its aspects (P, I, R, and RI) and at special transpositional levels, implies the presence of residual diatonic elements reminiscent of his earlier Neoclassical thinking. However, these are now absorbed into a serialized chromatic context and transformed into symmetrical and cyclic-interval constructions, which serve as the basis of a new means of progression, the total integration of the formal blocks, and the establishment of connections between the linear counterpoint and primary structural harmonic points.

The derivation of a whole-tone (diatonic) segment, C–D–E, from the linear symmetrical structure of the basic five-note series, E–E♭–C–C♯–D (in abstract symmetrical scale ordering, E–E♭–D–C♯–C), has significant compositional implications for the concepts of the interval cycle and of pitch-class symmetry based on an "axis."[33] Dirge-Canon I is initiated by P–4 (E–E♭–C–C♯–D), both its linear contour and metric disposition of which establish the priority of the whole-tone trichordal substructure, C–D–E, as well as the D axis. Each 5/4 measure is divided into two metrical units of 3 + 2/4, E, C, and D appearing on the consecutive strong (first and fourth) beats of the first two measures, the two remaining notes (C♯ and E♭) of the other whole-tone cycle appearing on the weak beats.[34] Initial P–4 encircles

---

[32] One may suggest an association between these two numbers and the name "Dylan Thomas," which consists of five and six letters, respectively. In any case, these are the same numerical relations found previously in the keys, grouping of instruments, and the form of each of the five movements of his *Mass,* in which the central Credo has six sections.

[33] See George Perle, *Serial Composition and Atonality,* n.8, above, pp. 54–59 passim. Perle's discussion points to the possibility of a more comprehensive analysis revealing the unfolding of both whole-tone cycles. See also Glen Scott Preston, "Serial Procedures in Two Works of Stravinsky: *In Memoriam Dylan Thomas* and *Three Songs From William Shakespeare*" (M.M. thesis, The University of Texas at Austin, 1980).

[34] This partitioning of the five chromatic tones into three and two whole-tone cyclic segments in correspondence to the 3 + 2/4 meter has a large-scale formal analogue in the distribution of the five Dirge-Canons into three and two occurrences between Prelude and Postlude, respectively, the five Ritornelli divided conversely into two and three occurrences.

and ends on its axis of symmetry, D, which also serves as the basis for a linear elision with I–2, D–E♭–G♭–F–F♭ (in abstract symmetrical scale ordering, D–E♭–F♭–F–G♭). Together, P–4 and I–2 expand the major-third boundary (C–E) of P–4 to a tritone (C–G♭). Furthermore, the primary whole-tone segment (D–F♭–G♭) of I–2 belongs to the same whole-tone cycle as that of P–4, the basic trichords (C–D–E and D–F♭–G♭) of both set-forms together implying a cyclic expansion to C–D–E–G♭ (Ex. 16–10). Against the first canonic answer in trombone IV, which is based on the same linear P–4/I–2 combination, trombone III enters with R–0 (B♭–A–A♭–C♭–C), the primary whole-tone trichord (A♭–B♭–C) now implying a completion of the whole-tone-0 cycle (C–D–E–G♭–A♭–B♭–C). Of the remaining set-forms in this Dirge-Canon, the structure of only two of them, P–1 (D♭–C–A–B♭–C♭) in trombone II (m. 4, beat 2f.) and RI–11 (D♭–D–E♭–C–C♭) in trombone III (m. 4, beat 4f.), gives trichordal priority to the whole-tone-1 cycle. However, the combined trichords (A–C♭–D♭ and C♭–D♭–E♭) of these two set-forms produce only part of this secondary whole-tone cycle.

The priority of the basic C–D–E trichord is confirmed by its projection into the deep-level structure. The D axis of this trichord is established as the entry pitch of each of the five Ritornello occurrences (strings in the Prelude, trombones in the Postlude), the complete trichord projected vertically as the cadential chord. The importance of the whole-tone-0 cycle is also established in the relation of the four set-forms of the Ritornello: the three lower strings, which unfold P–4, R–4, and RI–0, respectively, all contain the same pitch-class content (i.e., C–C♯–D–E♭–E of basic P–4). At the same time, vnI unfolds the original I–2 form, thereby expanding the

EXAMPLE 16–10. Stravinsky, *In Memoriam Dylan Thomas,* Dirge-Canon I, whole-tone substructures of the five-note set-forms

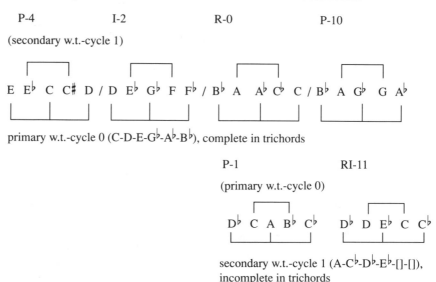

P-4   I-2   R-0   P-10

(secondary w.t.-cycle 1)

E E♭ C C♯ D / D E♭ G♭ F F♭ / B♭ A A♭ C♭ C / B♭ A G♭ G A♭

primary w.t.-cycle 0 (C-D-E-G♭-A♭-B♭), complete in trichords

P-1   RI-11

(primary w.t.-cycle 0)

D♭ C A B♭ C♭   D♭ D E♭ C C♭

secondary w.t.-cycle 1 (A-C♭-D♭-E♭-[]-[]),
incomplete in trichords

major-third boundary filled chromatically (C–E) of the three lower instruments to a tritone boundary (C–F♯); this is the same procedure that had occurred in the single line of the opening trombone-II statement, which elided P–4 and I–2. The basic trichord is also projected as the entry pitches (E, D, and C, respectively) of the first three Dirge Canons (trombones at mm. 1, 9, and 17 of the Prelude) and the entry pitches (C and D, respectively) of the last two Dirge-Canons (strings at mm. 4 and 11 of the Postlude). These entries (E, D, C, C, D) together suggest a whole-tone reflection of the local chromatic contour of the P–4 theme (E–E♭–C–C♯–D).

In Dirge-Canon II, a new set of implied whole-tone trichordal substructures this time gives priority to the whole-tone-1 cycle, the whole-tone-0 cycle remaining incomplete conversely, so a balance is produced between the two whole-tone cycles in the first two Dirge-Canons. In Dirge-Canon III, the whole-tone trichordal substructures in the linear set-forms for the first time imply both complete whole-tone cycles simultaneously, a balance which contributes to the rounding out of the Prelude. As part of this balance between the two whole-tone cycles, a long-range complementary relation between the entry and closing pitches of this Dirge-Canon serves as preparation for a shift from the even (unison) D–D axis of the whole-tone-0 spectrum to an odd (semitonal) axis, C♯–D, of both whole-tone spectra in the Ritornello of the Song. The entry pitches of this last Dirge-Canon, C–B♭–E–E♯, which initiate R–2, RI–8, RI–2, and RI–3, respectively, outline an asymmetrical formation together. The closing pitches, E–D♯–B–E, which also outline an asymmetrical formation, form a more background-level complementary relation with the entry pitches: B♭–C–E–F and B–D♯–E–E together imply the presence of a symmetrical collection, B♭–B–C–D♯–E–F, the axis of symmetry (C♯–D) of which is established at the opening of the Song.

The contrast of odd and even axes between the outer instrumental sections and the Song, and the move into a balanced contrapuntal alignment of set-forms related inversionally in the new Ritornello of the Song (Ex. 16–11), contributes to the architectural character of the work. Violin I and cello unfold P–4 and I–11, respectively, while violin II and viola unfold P–1 and I–2, respectively. Both inversional pairings—P–4/I–11 (combined symmetrical content, B–C–D♭–D–E♭–F♭) and P–1/I–2 (combined symmetrical content, A–B♭–C♭–C–D♭–D–E♭–F♭–F–G♭)—are based on the same axis of symmetry (D♭–D) of sum 3 (= 15), as expressed in each pair of P/I transposition numbers. This choice of set-forms implies the presence of whole-tone trichordal substructures that provide equal representation of both whole-tone cycles: P–4 (C–D–F♭) and I–2 (D–F♭–G♭) together imply the larger original whole-tone-0 segment (in enharmonic spelling, C–D–E–F♯), while P–1 (A–C♭–D♭) and I–11 (B–D♭–E♭) together imply the larger whole-tone-1 segment (in enharmonic spelling, A–B–C♯–D♯).

This boundary-tritone property, which is referable to the tritone boundary (C–F♯) of the combined set-forms of the Ritornello in the Prelude (and Postlude), is essential to the relations of the combined set-forms in the

EXAMPLE 16–11. Stravinsky, *In Memoriam Dylan Thomas,* Ritornello of Song, pairs of inversionally related set-forms

Couplets of the Song. For instance, the incipit of Couplet 1 ("Do not go gentle into that good night") is based on a three-note elision of I–10 (B♭–C♭–D–D♭–C) and R–4 (D–D♭–C–E♭–F♭), the combined collection encompassed by tritone B♭–F♭. The axis of symmetry of this vocal statement is D♭, one of the two components of the basic axis, D♭–D. The axis of the second phrase ("Old age should burn and rave at close of day"), which unfolds RI–0 (D–E♭–E–D♭–C), establishes the other main axial component, D, so both phrases together linearly confirm the D♭–D axis of the Ritornello. The accompanying instrumental phrases unfold RI–8, B♭–C♭–C–A–A♭ successively (cello/vnI, end of m. 3f.), and P–9, A–A♭–F–G♭–G (viola, at No. 1), their combined axes (B♭ and G) establishing sum 5 (D–D♯). Thus, both vocal and instrumental axes together (D♭–D/D–D♯) suggest a more background-level reference to the original D–D axis of the Prelude Ritornello.

These strictly serialized mathematical relations among the set-forms contribute to the rigid proportions of the overall architecture of the Song. The sectional form is determined by alternations between six Couplets and Ritornello. While Couplets 2–5 are rounded out by Refrain A ("Do not go gentle into that good night") or Refrain B alternately ("Rage, rage against the dying of the light"), Couplets 1 and 6 each contain both refrains. Within this mechanically symmetrical form, linear contour and word painting contribute to the intensity and poetic expression. Stravinsky was aware of Webern's vocal as well as instrumental style, and this is reflected in his special handling of the vocal line. As in Webern's *Cantata,* Op. 29, No. 1, or the first of the *Drei Lieder,* Op. 25, the tenor solo of *In Memoriam* moves from relatively conjunct, narrow-ranged phrases to increasingly wider intervals.

Stravinsky's serial works also reveal connections between the cellular row structure of certain Webern works as well as his own earlier octatonic writing. For instance, the five-note series of *In Memoriam* seems to be a parody of the row of Webern's *Variations,* Op. 30.[35] Webern's twelve-tone row is made up of a succession of 0–1–3–4 tetrachords in symmetrical relationships, established by serialized cellular transformations (for example, retrograde inversion of the cell) within the row. This minor-major-third grouping, like that of 0–1–4/0–3–4 found in other Webern works, is basic to the serial mechanism of both *In Memoriam* and *Agon.* The first four adjacencies (4–3–0–1) of the five-note series (E–E♭–C–C♯–D) of *In Memoriam* form a direct link with van den Toorn's octatonic "Model A" partitioning of the Neoclassical period. Other examples of such linkage (comprehending other octatonic partitionings as well) may also be drawn from the twelve-tone serial works, including *Epitaphium* (1959), *Anthem "The Dove Descending Breaks the Air"* (1962), etc. However, the serial rather than octatonic meaning is more relevant, since the 0–1–3–4 gap is closed off in the continuation of the series, as in the 0–1–4–3–2 structure of *In Memoriam.*

A basic feature of Stravinsky's evolution from the sensuality of the early ballets to the more cerebral approach in his late works is the serial-rotation principle.[36] Stravinsky's primary concern was to generate the vertical material, or chord combinations, resulting from a matrix derived from hexachordal rotation and transposition to a single pitch level, as in the sacred ballad *Abraham and Isaac* (1962–1963).[37] The rotational principle is also essential in the derivation of inversional relations based on a pitch-class center or axis, a role assigned to pitch-class E♭ in the *Movements,* for piano and orchestra (1958–1959) and F in the *Requiem Canticles* (1965–1966). By comparing the first 6 × 6 array of the set (S) with the 6 × 6 array of the inversion (I) of *Movements* (Ex. 16–12), a special relationship can be observed between them.[38] Commencement at successive elements of the first S hexachord (0, 1, 7, 5, 6, 11) followed by transposition of each rotation to a single pitch level, projects the hexachordal inversion diagonally (0, 11, 5, 7, 6, 1) within the S array. The latter forms the first linear hexachord of I. What becomes apparent in a comparison of the S and I arrays is an "inversion, retrogression duality" between pairs of pitch-class equivalent S and I verticals placed symmetrically,

---

[35] See van den Toorn, *The Music of Igor Stravinsky,* n.27, above, p. 381.

[36] Principles of hexachordal rotation in Stravinsky's serial works have been discussed in detail by Claudio Spies, e.g., "Some Notes on Stravinsky's Requiem Settings," *Perspectives on Schoenberg and Stravinsky,* rev. ed. Benjamin Boretz and Edward T. Cone (New York: W. W. Norton and Company, Inc., 1972), pp. 233–249, and by Milton Babbitt, "Order, Symmetry, and Centricity in Late Stravinsky," *Confronting Stravinsky: Man, Musician, and Modernist,* ed. Jann Pasler (Berkeley and Los Angeles: University of California Press, 1986), pp. 247–261.

[37] See Krenek's rotational scheme in Ex. 14–1.

[38] See Babbitt, n.36, above, Table 14.1.

EXAMPLE 16–12. Stravinksy, *Movements for Piano and Orchestra*, rotational 6 × 6 (hexachordal) arrays of the set (S) and inversion (I), symmetrically inversional relations defining a pitch-class center or axis of symmetry

```
                    ( = 6  5  4)
                      2  3  4
                      ↓  ↓  ↓

        Eᵇ = 0        H₁              H₂
       ┌──────┬─────────────────┬─────────────────┬────┐
  t=0  │  0  1  7  5  6  11 │ 9  8  10  3  4  2 │  0
  11   │  0  6  4  5  10 11 │ 9  11  4  5  3  10 │  1
   5   │  0  10 11 4  5  6  │ 9  2  3  1  8  7  │  11
S  7   │  0  1  6  7  8  2  │ 9  10 8  3  2  4  │  6
   6   │  0  5  6  7  1  11 │ 9  7  2  1  3  8  │  5
   1   │  0  1  2  8  6  7  │ 9  4  3  5  10 11 │  7
   0   │  0—11—5—7—6—1      │ 3  4  2  9  8  10 │  0
   1   │  0  6  8  7  2  1  │ 3  1  8  7  9  2  │  11
   7   │  0  2  1  8  7  6  │ 3  10 9  11 4  5  │  1
I  5   │  0  11 6  5  4  10 │ 3  2  4  9  10 8  │  6
   6   │  0  7  6  5  11 1  │ 3  5  10 11 9  4  │  7
   11  │  0  11 10 4  6  5  │ 3  8  9  7  2  1  │  5

                      ↑  ↑  ↑
                      4  5  6
                    ( =4  3  2)
```

i.e., compare the content of vertical-hexachord 2 of S (1, 6, 10, 1, 5, 1) with that of vertical-hexachord 6 of I (1, 1, 6, 10, 1, 5), vertical-hexachord 3 of S (7, 4, 11, 6, 6, 2) with vertical-hexachord 5 of I (6, 2, 7, 4, 11, 6), or vertical-hexachord 4 of each. The axis for all the verticals related symmetrically is the initial pitch-class of the hexachords. Thus, the tonal primacy of Stravinsky's first two style periods appears to be significant in his serial period as well. We may also observe certain diatonic properties (including triads, leading-tones, and 2–1 descents) within the serial contexts, which further suggests a fusion of tonal and serial principles.[39]

Aaron Copland began to infuse the planed and layered textures of his earlier Neoclassical style with twelve-tone serial principles in the early 1950s, thereby allowing his typically angular constructions a stricter framework of pitch relations. Although Copland's initial adoption of the twelve-tone method in his *Piano Quartet* (1950) represents an abrupt change from the technical approach of his popular film scores of the 1930s and 1940s as well as

[39] Charles Wuorinen and Jeffrey Kresky, "On the Significance of Stravinsky's Last Works," *Confronting Stravinsky: Man, Musician, and Modernist*, n.36, above, pp. 262–270.

his orchestral suites, *Billy the Kid* (1938), *Rodeo* (1942), and *Appalachian Spring* (1943–1944), his interest in serialism had already surfaced as early as 1930 in his *Piano Variations*. Despite Copland's lack of sympathy, as an American composer, with the "German music" of Schoenberg, Berg, and Webern during the interwar period of international tension and the tendency toward political isolationism, the concentrated use of the four-note motif that generates the chromatic context of the *Variations* is reminiscent of Webern's pointillistic and angular approach to the row, although Copland himself suggested the influence of Schoenberg.[40]

Copland lectured on serialism at the New School as early as 1928 and, as he pointed out subsequently, serial technique had provided him with a fresh view of his music, "somewhat like looking at a picture from a different angle so that you see things you might not have noticed otherwise."[41] Thus, despite a reversion to his earlier interest in promoting the American style during the more conservative era of the 1930s and early 1940s, the clear tonality of his folk-like American idiom was enriched by his increased use of dissonance in a more fragmented and angular melodic language (including octave displacements, with emphases on sevenths and ninths). This style was influenced more prominently, however, by Stravinsky and the French Neoclassicists with whom he had always felt a greater kinship. The fusion of features from both tendencies (serial and Neoclassical) was to come to full fruition in the personal style of many of his postwar compositions.

Copland's development of twelve-tone technique in the 1950s was less consistent than that of Stravinsky, whose serialism evolved more systematically from a nontwelve-tone serial idiom toward an increasing strictness and complexity that culminated in his twelve-tone rotational procedures. Following his *Piano Quartet* of 1950, Copland showed increasing flexibility and technical control of the new idiom in his *Piano Fantasy* (1952–1957). The ten-note series (E♭–B♭–F–D♭–B–F♯–A–G–D–C) generates a context that still maintains a sense of tonality, in which a sort of "E major" is articulated by the special cadential deployment of the two remaining chromatic tones (E and G♯). Stylistically, the *Fantasy* is a continuation of the earlier *Variations,* but the sparse and wide-ranging intervals are now drawn into a more controlled context based on a greater adherence to the serial-order principle (compare Ex. 16–13, a and b). The partitioning of the row into cells, each of which is articulated by sudden metric and dynamic changes as well as contrasting degrees of harmonic density (as at m. 14), points to an important correlation between the *Variations* and *Fantasy*. This correlation reveals a common approach to the textural disposition of the motivic material that underscores Copland's own stylistic continuity. According to the composer, "younger men, like Pierre Boulez, effectively demonstrated that the twelve-

---

[40] Aaron Copland and Vivian Perlis, *Copland, 1900 through 1942* (New York: St. Martin's/Marke, 1984), p. 182.
[41] Ibid.

EXAMPLE 16–13. Copland, (a) *Piano Variations,* opening, four-note set; (b) *Piano Fantasy,* opening, ten-note series, move toward serialization of motivic and cellular structures

Piano Variations © 1932 by Aaron Copland; Copyright renewed. Reprinted by permission of Aaron Copland, Copyright owner, and Boosey & Hawkes, Inc., sole licensee.
Piano Fantasy © 1957 by Aaron Copland; Copyright renewed. Reprinted by permission of Aaron Copland, Copyright owner, and Boosey & Hawkes, Inc., sole licensee.

tone method could be retained without the German esthetic, and, by 1950, I was involved. I was interested in the simple outlines of the theory and in adapting them to my own purposes."[42]

Copland continued to develop along his prewar stylistic lines not only in the sporadically occurring nontwelve-tone works of this period (including the diatonic *Old American Songs,* which appeared in the 1950s shortly after the *Piano Quartet,* and the *Nonet,* 1960), but also in the more developed serial contexts of his orchestral *Connotations* (1962) and *Inscape* (1967). The bright sound of triads, open fifths, sixths, and especially tenths, which had been so characteristic of his *Appalachian Spring,* are still in evidence in these more abstract serial contexts. Copland had stated that even in the *Connotations* "the dodecaphonic method supplies the building blocks, but it does not create the edifice. The composer must do that."[43]

INDIVIDUAL PHILOSOPHICAL AND AESTHETIC ASSUMPTIONS UNDERLYING ATONAL AND TWELVE-TONE CONCEPTIONS: WOLPE AND CARTER

Individualized and diversified approaches to twelve-tone composition were also developed by other American composers in the postwar years. The twelve-tone principle has been employed occasionally by Samuel Barber, Ross Lee Finney, Walter Piston, Gunther Schuller, Wallingford Riegger, George Rochberg, and Charles Wuorinen, the last two of whom began as fervent serialists. Wuorinen has worked with some of the highly controlled twelve-tone principles of his teacher, Milton Babbitt, though in his own personally expressive and contrapuntally dense idiom.

A special attitude toward the twelve-tone continuum has been manifested in the works of the Berlin-born composer Stefan Wolpe (1902–1972), who has developed a concept of integration of the various musical parameters according to premises that essentially differ from the strict order principle of Schoenberg or the more contrived contexts of the integral serialists.[44] Prior to his emigration in 1933 from Berlin to Vienna, then Palestine, and finally the United States in 1938, Wolpe had already been exposed to a variety of aesthetics and styles as well as political conditions, the influences of which were to converge in compositions that found their most natural expression in the atonal idiom. While his early involvement in the Socialist cause led to his composition of accessible tonal songs based on political and populist themes, he was also influenced by Scriabin, Satie, and Busoni since 1917, and he himself became the music director for the Berlin Dadaists. One of the most

---

[42] Notes to Columbia Record MS 7431.

[43] See Copland and Perlis, *Copland,* n.40, above, p. 209.

[44] Stefan Wolpe, "Thinking Twice," in *Contemporary Composers on Contemporary Music,* ed. Elliott Schwartz and Barney Childs (New York: Holt, Rinehart, and Winston, 1967), p. 277.

significant sources for his later visual and spatial approach to the twelve-tone chromatic continuum, based on a complex interaction of the musical parameters that matured after his arrival in New York, was his early association with a large group of visual artists, among them Klee and Feininger. Musically, Varèse's concern for form, as the result of process rather than form as a "mold to be filled," is particularly relevant to Wolpe's aesthetic concerns.[45] At the same time, the ideas of the Viennese atonalists were germinal in his early musical thought not only for their development of atonality, but also for their pioneering work in the equally radical inception of the *Klangfarben* principle.

Wolpe's concern was to integrate the multidimensional levels within the chromatic continuum as the basis for generating the large-scale form and, at the same time, to produce a constellation of textural changes resulting in constant reinterpretations of the colors of the individual elements. While he was producing a large number of solo and chamber pieces in his more complex late style of the 1950s, among them the *Enactments for Three Pianos* (1950–1953), the *Symphony* (1955–1956), many chamber pieces (1950s and 1960s), and the piano pieces *Form* (1959) and *Form IV: Broken Sequences* (1969), he was also expounding upon his philosophical, aesthetic, and technical ideas in a series of essays, central to which are his concepts of "chromatic circulation," "registral saturation," and "maximum and minimum chroma."[46] According to Wolpe, the rate of chromatic circulation is influenced by the rate of structural change: "Every pitch constellation smaller than the all-chromatic circuit is either a delay in completing the whole, or is an autonomous fragment which can exist outside of the total circuit. It may be first unhinged as a part of the total circuit . . . the modified speed of the all-chromatic circuit points to a concept of modulatory circulation, to an increase or decrease of pitch quantities."[47]

An extension of the temporal concept of chromatic circulation is the spatial or registral concept of chromatic saturation, in which registral position is no longer tied to the idea of pitch-class equivalence, so that registral changes play a fundamental role in "disconnecting, disturbing—thereby differentiating—the exclusive continuum of the all-chromatic circuit."[48] As part of this transformational process within the chromatic continuum, Wolpe also exploits textural interactions based on relative degrees of density, in which "the most densified mass of a most diversified all-intervallic sound ['maximum chroma'] corresponds to the shrivel of a shredded tone ['minimum chroma']."[49] Depending on context, one "chroma" may serve as the

[45] Edgard Varèse, "The Liberation of Sound," *Perspectives of New Music* 5/1 (1966): 16.

[46] See Jacquelin Mae Helin, "The Ever-Restored and Ever-Advancing Moment: Stefan Wolpe's Compositional Philosophy and Aesthetic As Seen in *Form* for Piano" (D.M.A. treatise, The University of Texas at Austin, 1982).

[47] See Wolpe, "Thinking Twice," n.44, above, p. 287.

[48] Ibid., pp. 278–279.

[49] Ibid., p. 286.

norm, the other the extreme, a principle leading to the equivalence of opposites.

In *Form,* the changing role of individual intervals and tones in the process of chromatic saturation is implemented through the use of the twelve-tone hexachordal-trope principle, according to which the hexachordal pitch content rather than ordering is maintained. Interactions between these unordered hexachordal subcollections, which include further partitionings into smaller trichordal segments, result in the systematic interchange, fusion, separation, and ultimate transformation of the individual elements.[50] The work opens with a hexachord stated linearly (in abstract scalar ordering, E–F–[ ]–G–A♭–A–B♭), based on maximal chromatic filling of its registral boundary, tritone E–B♭ (Ex. 16–14a). The hexachord is subdivided further into two intervallically equivalent (0–3–5) trichords, F–A♭–B♭ and E–G–A. The entire hexachord is immediately reinterpreted rhythmically, texturally, registrally, and dynamically in the second phrase (m. 2). Whereas the repetition of the hexachordal pitch content itself delays the completion of the all-chromatic circuit, the specific reinterpretations produce a situation that is conducive to the developmental process. The expansion of the registral boundary (tritone E–B♭) to three and a half octaves provides a larger frame in preparation for fuller registral saturation. The content of the first trichordal segment is kept intact (F–A♭–B♭), but the closer temporal proximity of the two tritone components (E–B♭) produces some trichordal mixture while establishing further the priority of this original registral boundary. The second simultaneity maintains the content of the second trichord conversely (E–G–A), but the repetition of F–A♭ in that simultaneity produces further trichordal mixing, so we get five of the six hexachordal components together. The repetition of the A♭ in this chord also brings the original temporal boundary (E–A♭) into closer proximity. Thus, within the context of the first hexachord, Wolpe has moved rapidly from "minimum" to "maximum chroma," in which the rate of chromatic circulation is connected inextricably to the rate of structural transformation: in this case, fusion of the trichordal substructures.

The first disruptive element outside the content of hexachord I is F♯ (m. 4), which ushers in complementary hexachord II (Ex. 16–14b). This disruptive element (F♯) is precisely the pitch-class that was missing from the otherwise perfect chromatic continuum of hexachord I (E–F–[ ]–G–A♭–A–B♭), so it represents a significant step toward chromatic saturation on a higher architectonic level. Hexachord II, completed at the return of the original tempo (m. 6), is also based on maximal chromatic filling, B–C–C♯–D–E♭–[ ]–[ ]–F♯, the single note, F♯, serving again as a disruptive element, in this case appearing conversely outside of the chromatically saturated boundary (B–E♭) of its own hexachord. The minor-third

---

[50] See Helin, "The Ever-Restored," n.46, above, Chap. II.

EXAMPLE 16–14. Wolpe, *Form* for piano: (a) opening, maximal chromatic filling of hexachord I based on two intervallically equivalent trichords; (b) mm. 4ff., intrusion of hexachord II

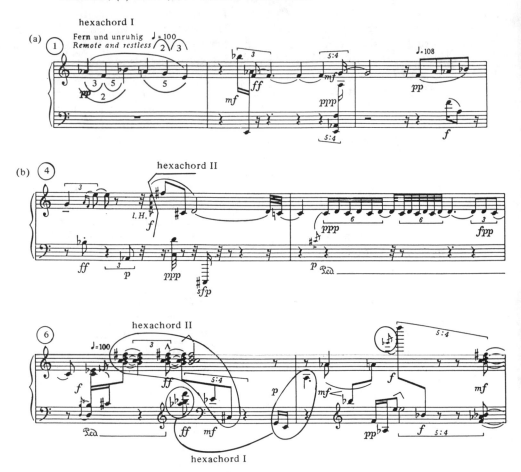

gap (E♭–F♯) of this hexachord has larger structural significance, both notes serving as the temporal boundary of this initial hexachord-II statement (middle of m. 4 to m. 6, second articulation). While F♯ forms the upper registral boundary of this hexachord, the initial lower boundary within the first trichord (C–D–F♯) is its tritone, C, analogous to the establishment of a tritone boundary as a primary element of hexachord I.

Also of structural significance is the simultaneous linear and vertical projection of the C–D from this initial trichord as whole-step and minor-seventh, respectively (mm. 4–5). In both cases, this interval-class appears in proximity with C♯ of the second trichord. While this "axis" interval (C–D) and the C♯ together unfold a chromatically saturated segment linearly, the vertical disposition based on octave displacement of these components (m. 4) points to a new registral span in preparation for more dense, complex chromatic saturation on a higher architectonic level.[51]

The entire process is based on rates of change of the individual parameters, including register, density, hexachordal and trichordal interactions and transformations, tempo, and chromatic saturation. All these together, which contribute to the fulfillment of the possibilities for unfolding and reinterpretation within the chromatic continuum, are essential to the notion of "form" in this work. Ultimately, the overall shape of the work, in terms of the highest rate of hexachordal mixture, greatest density, most extreme and rapid dynamic changes, as well as strictest registral invariance of pitch-class, appears to be an arch, the peak occurring almost at the exact midpoint (mm. 27–29). Thus, Wolpe has achieved a highly individual approach to the twelve-tone idiom, in which the nontraditional formal concept grows out of a free (nonserialized) handling of diverse yet integrated materials in a continuous developmental process.

Elliott Carter (b. 1908) also began to move toward a personal approach to both the spatial and temporal dimensions in his postwar works. In the nonserialized atonal contexts of this period, Carter evolved toward increasingly complex, integrated structures based on the continuous interaction of opposing forces. These new expressive intentions mark a radical change from his aesthetics of the interwar period, in which the political conditions in Europe had led temporarily to his negative attitude toward German expressionism. During that time, he cultivated a simpler diatonicism in a more accessible and moderate Neoclassical style as a pupil of Nadia Boulanger, revealing the influences of Stravinsky, Copland, and Hindemith especially, as well as certain early Baroque English composers. By the late 1940s, he realized that the traditional schemes and mechanical objectivism of Neoclassicism no longer accorded with his renewed desire for a more intense expression. However, it took several years before these personal intentions were to clarify themselves: "I still view with considerable perplexity the renewal of many of the so-called experiments of the earlier avant-garde style. . . . In any case, around 1945, as the Populist period was nearing its end. . . . I felt I had exhausted my interest in that style and started a thorough-going reassessment of musical materials."[52]

Carter's aesthetic, stylistic, and technical formulations of the 1950s were already foreshadowed in the last works of his Neoclassical period—the *Piano Sonata* (1945), *Emblems* (1947), and the *Wind Quintet* and *Cello Sonata* (1948). The agitated, dynamic quality of divergent contrapuntal lines, in the last two works especially, were to become a hallmark of his next style period.

---

[51] See Wolpe, "Thinking Twice," n.44, above, pp. 282–283.

[52] Elliott Carter, "Music and the Time Screen, *Current Thought in Musicology*, ed. John W. Grubbs (Austin: University of Texas Press, 1976), p. 67.

Many of Carter's new concerns stemmed from the musical thought of the early avant-garde composers. He had personal contact with Ives and his music and Schoenberg's first twelve-tone works in the 1920s, and he attended premières of the works of Varèse, Ruggles, and others. His early interests also extended to modernist literature and painting, which included the German expressionists. Furthermore, he was introduced to non-Western sources, with a particular interest in Indian *talas,* the changing "tempi" of Balinese gamelans, and Watusi music. In different ways, all these sources were to have a bearing on Carter's later formulations, in which he explored new possibilities for achieving large-scale structural organization of complex pitch and metric/rhythmic factors in an original and expressive idiom.

Carter's exposure to these sources led him to consider basic aspects of musical time from an original point of view. Prior to World War II, he was concerned with more conventional notions of "physical" time, based on a mechanistic approach, though he was skeptical of the methodology of Cowell and others, who "applied numerical patterns from the tuning of the musical scales."[53] It was only after 1944 that Carter began to explore concepts of time as set forth in several important theoretical writings, the most basic notions including *psychological time* (measured according to a relative or subjective view of life) and *mathematically measured time* (measured independently of temporal experience).[54] He also attempted to link, by way of analogy, concepts of time and space, in which "time is the canvas on which you consider music to be presented, just as the spatial canvas of painting furnishes the surface on which a painting is presented," hence the title of his essay "Music and the Time Screen." In the *Cello Sonata,* Carter began the simultaneous exploitation of these two concepts of time (mathematical and psychological), which resulted in the rhythmic divergence between cello and piano. In conjunction with this concept, Carter also began using "metric modulation," which permits rhythmically independent—thus spatially defined—contrapuntal lines to change tempo according to a common pulse.[55]

Carter's concept of a spatial music, based on increasingly complex contrapuntal textures, began to take shape in the early 1950s. In his intensification of the means of expression, he also began to exploit other parameters as the basis for heightening the distinction among the separate dimensions. He explored new mathematical means of pitch organization to draw together his contrapuntal divergencies into a coherent whole.[56] The *Eight Etudes and a Fantasy for Woodwind Quartet* (1950) reveals a focus on tone colors in specific

[53] Ibid., p. 66.

[54] These include Charles Koechlin, "Le Temps et la musique," *LaRevue musicale* (January 1926), pp. 45–62; and Suzanne Langer, *Feeling and Form* (New York: Scribner Library, 1953), p. 114.

[55] This principle is discussed below.

[56] For discussion of the various parameters and their relation to the concepts of musical time and space, see David Schiff, *The Music of Elliott Carter* (London: Eulenberg Books, 1983), especially Chapters 2 and 3.

combinations, juxtapositions, and variations as the basis of formal articulation.[57] Each etude defines a particular aspect in terms of articulation, dynamics, doublings, intervals, etc. Carter's reputation was established with his *First String Quartet* (1950–1951), in which he synthesized his new techniques further within the free-sounding yet calculated framework. Complex polymetric relations unfold as part of an atonal context generated from an all-interval (0–1–4–6) tetrachordal set. His exploitation of single interval structures and metric units (as in the *Allegro scorrevole* movement, based on a stream of sixteenth notes in various fragments) as well as contrasting characters (as in the *Adagio,* with its high muted strings against the loud recitative of the lower strings) was part of his tendency toward "reduction of the musical ideas to their simplest terms." He continued this tendency toward expressively free but calculated contexts in his traditionally scored *Sonata* for flute, oboe, cello, and harpsichord (1952), *Variations* for orchestra (1954–1955), based on a form suited ideally to the exploitation of thematic, harmonic, textural, and stylistic reinterpretations, the *Second String Quartet* (1959), *Double Concerto* (1961), *Piano Concerto* (1964–1965), *Concerto for Orchestra* (1969), *Third String Quartet* (1971), *Brass Quintet* (1974), and the simpler and clearer *A Mirror on which to Dwell,* for soprano and mixed instrumental ensemble (1975).

Carter's "Canaries," from *Eight Pieces* for four timpani (1950–1966), exemplifies the fusion of both psychological and mathematical time.[58] In this reduced instrumental setting, based on a single set of four notes, E–B–C♯–F, a sense of rubato is built into a scheme of complex polyrhythmic patterns mathematically, in which the principle of *metric modulation* serves to integrate the entire form through frequent but smooth changes of pulse speed from one tempo to another. Thus, expressive control is shifted from performer to composer, an assumption similar to that of the "total serialists."

Two elements are basic to gleaning an understanding of these new metric/rhythmic functions: (1) the conductor beat, or pulse, and (2) the individual unit. Smooth modulation is produced by the establishment of a common speed for the basic units of two adjacent passages (i.e., in which there is no heard difference between the units themselves), while changing the speed of the conductor beat according to exact ratios. The opening 6/8 meter is established at a metronomic speed of "dotted-quarter = 90," the conductor beat subdividing the measure into two parts, or 2×3 eighth-note groupings. Replacement of the three-unit (eighth-note) grouping by four dotted-sixteenths prepares us for modulation to the next passage (m. 11). Within the opening passsage (m. 3), the effect of this replacement is an acceleration of the unit only, while the pulse speed ("90") remains unchanged. The cadential indication of "dotted-sixteenth = eighth" (m. 10)

---

[57] See Chap. 13 regarding the *Klangfarben* principle in certain etudes.

[58] The 6/8-dotted rhythm of the piece suggests a Baroque Gigue, hence the title; it is assumed that this form came from the Canary Islands.

now suggests that, at the following return to the original eighth-note grouping, the eighth-note unit will be equivalent to the shorter duration of the dotted-sixteenth. The ratio between the dotted-sixteenth and eighth is (according to the common denominator of thirty-second notes) 3:4, and this is reflected in the same ratio between the original metronomic indication ("90") and the new one ("120"). The faster conductor beat has also been prepared smoothly by the regular three-note misaccentuations of the cadential four-note groupings (mm. 9–10), this metrically dissonant pattern of which is then aligned with the barline to establish the proportionally faster tempo (m. 11).

Another modulation takes us from "dotted-quarter = 120" to another, still faster pulse. This is prepared by the conductor-beat mixture of three and two eighth-note units at the 5/8, which results (at m. 18) in a proportional reduction of the pulse to two-thirds of its value, i.e., 120 (dotted-quarter pulse) is two-thirds of 180 (quarter pulse). Within the latter pulse, the pairs of eighth-note units are replaced by triplets. At the following indication ("quarter = dotted-quarter = 180"), the eighth-note unit returns, but at a reduction to two-thirds of its preceding value and is now equivalent to the triplet. At the 3/4, the equivalence of these units results in a faster conductor beat of "quarter = 270," so the common speed of the units (at mm. 19–21) serves as modulator. At this point ("quarter = 270"), the first metric-formal cycle is completed. While the new conductor beat (270) is three times as fast as the original one, a simple reinterpretation of the conductor beat as the unit reveals that we are actually back in the original tempo. This reinterpretation is expressed by the following metronomic indication: "dotted-half = dotted-quarter = 90." Thus, the overall sense of acceleration is integrated by means of relations calculated mathematically between pulse and unit. Furthermore, Carter's detailed performance directions (indicated by C, N, R, DS, NS), which determine the different timbres that are produced by striking the drum at the "Center," "Rim," etc., together with the rhythmic distribution of the four pitches, support the "metric modulations" in the unfolding of the large-scale structural design.

These interrelations of the parameters, which are basic to the perception of the spatial and temporal organization, are developed further in the *Second String Quartet*. Carter has expressed his aim at achieving a heightened sense of both the spatial and temporal dimensions in this otherwise conventional performance medium. He suggested that the performers sit farther apart than usual to separate them from one another in space as well as in character, and that "each of the four instruments has a repertory of musical characters of its own, while contributing to the total effect in many different capacities, sometimes following, sometimes opposing the leader, usually according to its own capabilities—that is, according to the repertory of expression, continuity, interval, and rhythmic patterns assigned to it."[59] The

---

[59] Carter, "Music and the Time Screen," n. 52, above, p. 74.

two violins play in contrasting styles, the first most often virtuoso and bravura in the greatest variety of characters, the second adhering to its regular rhythms. The two lower strings are of a similar contrast—the viola in an expressive style, the cello in a stricter one.

The four continuous movements suggest a spontaneous set of improvisations, an impression created by the assignment to each instrument not only of contrasting styles, but also rhythms, intervals, and motifs, which are developed separately by means of fragmentation and transformation.[60] The Introduction (mm. 1–34), which presents the raw motivic and intervallic materials of the work, has its own local shape that approximates an arch in three sections (mm. 1–10, 11–28, and 29–34). These divisions are articulated by changing tempi, which are made cohesive by proportional relations (metric modulations) between them. These changes of tempo coincide with reassignments of the intervallic structures in each instrument. In the first section, the perfect fourth is the primary interval in the cello, the minor-third in violin I, the major-third in violin II, and the tritone in the viola. At the same time, each of these intervals is compounded linearly to form larger symmetrical or cyclic-interval sets (Ex. 16–15). The opening cello statement outlines two perfect-fourth cyclic segments, A–E–B/B♭–E♭, which contain secondary intervallic connections between them, i.e., B♭–E♭ and E–A also imply the presence of pairs of tritones and minor seconds, while B♭–E♭ and B–E are separated by the minor-second; a reordered transposition, B♭–F–C/B–E, follows in the same instrument (at mm. 5–6). Conversely, the viola unfolds pairs of tritones, B–F/G♭–C (mm. 4–7) and D–A♭/E♭–A (mm. 7–8), which also imply the presence of perfect-fourth and minor-second interval couples. Violin II unfolds three of the four major-third cycles (C–E–A♭, B–D♯–G, and [　]–D–F♯).

Furthermore, analogously to the common pulse that holds together the divergent linear rhythms, common larger intervallic sets hold together the independent linear intervallic structures. The minor-thirds of violin I are in special relation to the cyclic structures of the two lower instruments, especially the viola; the thirds of violin I produce a six-note segment of the octatonic scale, D–E–F–G–A♭–B♭, while the two pairs of tritones in the viola (mm. 4–8) together unfold another, complete octatonic collection, C–D–E♭–F–G♭–A♭–A–B.

In the second section (mm. 11–29), each instrument adds a new interval to its original one: violin I adds the perfect fifth to its minor third to unfold a larger octatonic segment, E♭–E–G♭–[　]–A–B♭–C–D♭ (m. 15 to middle of m. 16); violin II adds the major sixth and major seventh to its

---

[60] For an "interval division graph" illustrating the intervallic separations, additions, and rates of interchange among the instruments throughout the four movements, see Eugene William Schweitzer, "Generation in String Quartets of Carter, Sessions, Kirchner, and Schuller: A Concept of Forward Thrust and Its Relationship to the Structure in Aurally Complex Styles" (Ph.D. dissertation, University of Rochester, Eastman School of Music, 1965), p. 24.

EXAMPLE 16–15. Carter, *Second String Quartet,* opening, spatial texture based on linearly independent intervallic construction

original major third (mm. 17ff.); the viola adds the minor seventh to its tritone to unfold a complete octatonic collection, D–E–F–G–G♯–A♯–B–C♯ (mm. 17–22); and the cello adds the minor sixth to its perfect fourth. In the third section (mm. 29ff.), the intervals of each compounded line are mixed more intensively within the same instrumental lines, respectively. This occurs in a more static harmonically-oriented context, which contributes to the formal closure of the Introduction and prepares for the following release of tension at the opening of Movement I. Thus, while the four virtuoso instruments remain distinct from one another in an atonal idiom, they are often accountable to a common larger intervallic set (for instance, the octatonic scale) as well as a common pulse.

MORE RECENT USES OF INTERVAL SETS AND FUSION WITH TRADITIONAL ELEMENTS: WUORINEN, ROREM, KORTE, AND WELCHER

Many composers in the United States have continued to employ, in a mixture of styles and aesthetics, various twelve-tone and/or atonal methods stemming from the early post–World War II era. Musical institutions of higher learning as well as the recording industry in the United States and many other countries have created an expanded audience and new conditions for the performance of twelve-tone and other types of composition. The most recent developments in serial composition in the United States alone are too numerous to discuss in-depth here, but a few stemming from the early 1960s may be summarized.

Charles Wuorinen (b. 1938) evolved the twelve-tone approach of his *Third Symphony* (1959) toward an increasingly strict and more generalized use of serial principles in his *Piano Concerto* (1966), in which durations and structural proportions are projected from the intervallic ratios of the basic twelve-tone set. He extended the principle of "integral serialism" further in his one-act opera *The Politics of Harmony* (1968) to the register and length of vowel sounds, while in the late 1960s, Ned Rorem (b. 1923) began to infuse a variety of serialized elements into his expanded concepts of modality and tonality as well. Karl Korte (b. 1928), a former pupil of Copland, Luening, Mennin, Persichetti, Bergsma, and Petrassi, has on occasion joined the non-twelve-tone serial principle to a more popular jazz style. In his one-movement *Trio for Piano, Violin, and Cello* (1979), two four-note, serialized, all-interval sets (from the octatonic scale) serve as the basis for integration of the melodic and harmonic levels. The expansion and contraction of the intervals in these sets recall the same principle used by Sessions in his *Sonata* for solo violin. Korte's sets are similarly angular and disjunct, covering extreme ranges in all the instruments. While Korte's chord constructions, progressions, and rhythms have some reference to jazz sources, an expressionistic, rhapsodic, virtuosic style predominates from the outset, in cadenza-like passages initiated by the piano.

A variety of styles and techniques characterize the works of Dan Welcher (b. 1948), ranging from the light, colorfully orchestrated tonal (or polytonal) style of his nostalgic two-act opera *Della's Gift* (1986), on a libretto of Paul Woodruff after O'Henry's *Gift of the Magi,* to the intense, expressionistic quality that characterizes such twelve-tone chamber works as his *Partita* for horn, violin, and piano (1980) and *String Quartet No. 1* (1987).

Welcher's *Flute Concerto* (1973) was his first work to combine a freely chromatic, extended tonal style (in Mov. I) with a completely serialized approach in the variations (Mov. II), where a twelve-tone series is set in a context of nonfunctional triadic block harmony. In his works thereafter, he combined various styles and techniques. The orchestral work *Dervishes* (1976) is in a strictly serial twelve-tone idiom, while the *Dance Variations* (1979) juxtaposes a twelve-tone series against a pentatonic structure, the latter of which is used to harmonize the row in the sixth variation. Both the twelve-tone series and pentatonic structure are integrated at the end. In *Merlin* (1980), leitmotifs unfold in a freely chromatic, nontraditional tonal idiom, whereas in the poems of *Vox Femina* (1984), the composer reveals his ability to integrate a multiplicity of styles within a single work. This is exemplified in his synthesis of wide-ranging materials from Medieval Troubadour song and Renaissance elements of Cabezón and Victoria to more contemporary features that include Shostakovich, jazz, and the introduction of a twelve-note theme in the second poem.

In the *String Quartet,* Welcher's characteristically transparent textures and dynamic rhythms are absorbed into a serialized, yet free-sounding twelve-tone idiom based on the exploitation of triadic and other types of cellular structures that partition the larger twelve-tone set. The basic set, D–G–B♭–A♭–C♭–E♭–E–C–F♯–A–F–D♭, is one of several sources for the pitch relations of the work. It first appears in its clearest form toward the middle of Mov. I (m. 98), in contrapuntal alignment to both its transposition and two transposed inversions. The set is segmented into four three-note cells (Ex. 16–16), including two minor triads (G–B♭–D and A♭–C♭–E♭) one half-step apart in the first hexachord and two nonequivalent whole-tone segments (C–E–F♯ and D♭–F–A) one half-step apart in the second, so we find once again a fusion of traditional and nontraditional pitch constructions. The relation of the initial triadic pairing in the set to the opening theme is shown in Ex. 16–16.

Special relations between the two trichords within each hexachord are basic to the transformation of the set at prominent structural points of the quartet. Five of the six notes in each of the two trichordal pairings form an

EXAMPLE 16–16. Welcher, *String Quartet No. 1,* relation of initial triadic pairing in the twelve-tone set to opening theme

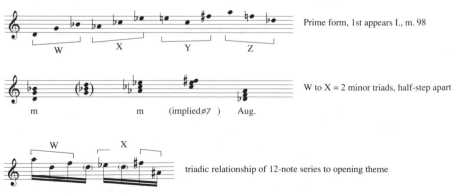

incomplete octatonic segment—we can show arbitrarily the combined content of the first pairing in a descending scalar order, B♭–A♭–G–[ ]–[ ]–D–[ ]–C♭ (plus one nonoctatonic note, E♭), the second pairing in an ascending scalar order, [ ]–C–D♭–[ ]–E–F♯–[ ]–A (plus one nonoctatonic note, F). Near the end of the last movement (mm. 187ff.), both these octatonic collections appear in their mutually exclusive, complete forms in the inversionally related scales of the cello (B♭–A♭–G–F–E–D–D♭–C♭) and violin I (B♭–C–D♭–E♭–E–F♯–G–A), so the single "dissonant" (nonoctatonic) element in each hexachord disappears locally at this point. The cellular structure of the set is significant in the overall formal design. The set itself is based on a progressive intervallic expansion from the minor and major thirds of the triads to the major thirds of the last trichord. The initial two triadic components are emphasized in vnI at the opening of Mov. I by the absence of the second hexachord of the series, while the augmented triad expanded intervallically is unfolded in the long dotted rhythms (C–E–G♯) at the climax of Mov. IV (mm. 191–194, vnI) and in the final stretto, based on F♯–B♭–D (mm. 201ff.). This expansion is anticipated (mm. 179–180) by the transformation of the two minor triads to major triads (on C and B), a relation established previously in the inverted form of the series. The large-scale projection of these cellular substructures of the set also occurs on more local levels of the quartet, as in the long accelerando (mm. 172ff.) toward the end of Mov. I, where both the augmented triad and its adjacent whole-tone trichord are structurally prominent (see also mm. 199ff. and 231ff.).

A special link among certain serialized pitch relations, durational values, and metric patterns is found in an abstract number series, 5–4–3–4–5–6. The first four-note segment of the opening motivic statement (A–D–F–D), which outlines the initial triadic cell of the set, closes the movement in a metric progression based on this number series (5/8, 4/8, 3/8, 4/8, 5/8, 6/8), the same metric progression of which initiates the movement in quarter-note units. The accompanying chromatic figure, E♭–E–F–E–E♭–D (lower strings of this final passage), an inversion of the basic six-note thematic figure that pervades the next movement, is derived directly from this number series. The figure appears first at its basic transpositional level (F–E–D♯–E–F–F♯) near the beginning of Mov. I (mm. 26ff.). Given C = 0, C♯ = 1, etc., the pitch-class numbers of the latter are 5–4–3–4–5–6, this pattern also serving as the source for the assigned durational values calculated in eighth notes (Ex. 16–17). A transposition, C–B–B♭–B–C–C♯ (mm. 79ff.), initiates a developmental section following a cadence articulated by one of several exact metric returns of the number series in the movement directly. The six-note pitch series returns to its original transpositional level in the coda of Mov. I (mm. 290–295, cello), suggesting an analogy to the recapitulation of "key" in traditional classical forms. Thus, in his own personal approach to twelve-tone composition, Welcher extended the serial concept to durational and metric parameters freely as a means of integrating the overall structure and, at the same time, absorbed traditional tertian sonorities into an exclusively twelve-tone context.

EXAMPLE 16–17. Welcher, *String Quartet No. 1,* Mov. I, mm. 26ff., number series as basis for pitch-class numbers of a subsidiary six-note set and its durational values in eighth notes

©1987 Theodore Presser Company. Used by permission.

SUGGESTED READINGS

MILTON BABBITT. *Words About Music,* ed. Stephen Dembski and Joseph N. Straus (Madison: University of Wisconsin Press, 1987).

———. "Set Structure as a Compositional Determinant," *Journal of Music Theory* 5 (1961): 72–94.

ELLIOTT CARTER. "Music and the Time Screen," *Current Thought in Musicology,* ed. John W. Grubbs (Austin: The University of Texas Press, 1976), pp. 63–88.

EDWARD T. CONE. ed., "Schoenberg in the United States" (1944, revised 1972), *Roger Sessions on Music: Collected Essays* (Princeton, New Jersey: Princeton University Press, 1979), pp. 353–369.

AARON COPLAND AND VIVIAN PERLIS. *Copland, 1900 through 1942* (New York: St. Martin's/ Marek, 1984).

JOSEPH DUBIEL. " 'Thick Array/Of Depth Immeasurable': Some Questions About the Music of Milton Babbitt," a paper presented at the Fourth Michigan Conference on Music Theory, at the University of Michigan, Ann Arbor, March 29, 1985.

PAUL GRIFFITHS. *Modern Music: The Avant Garde Since 1945* (New York: George Braziller, 1981), pp. 37–44.

JACQUELIN MAE HELIN. "'The Ever-Restored and Ever-Advancing Moment': Stefan Wolpe's Compositional Philosophy and Aesthetic As Seen in *Form* for Piano" (D.M.A. treatise, The University of Texas at Austin, 1982).

CHARLES KOECHLIN. "Le Temps et la musique," *La Revue musicale* (January 1926), pp. 45–62.

JANN PASLER. ed., *Confronting Stravinsky: Man, Musician, and Modernist* (Berkeley and Los Angeles: University of California Press, 1986), including: Milton Babbitt, "Order, Symmetry, and Centricity in Late Stravinsky," pp. 247–261; Glenn Watkins, "The Canon and Stravinsky's Late Style," pp. 217–246; Charles Wuorinen and Jeffrey Kresky, "On the Significance of Stravinsky's Last Works," pp. 262–270.

GEORGE PERLE. "Pitches or Pitch-Classes?" a paper given at the University of California at Berkeley, Spring 1989. This paper appears as "Lecture 4" in Perle's book, *The Listening Composer* (Berkeley and Los Angeles: University of California Press, 1990), pp. 93–121.

———. *Serial Composition and Atonality* (rev. 6th ed., Berkeley and Los Angeles: University of California Press, 1991, see discussion of Babbitt, Krenek, Perle, and late Stravinsky.

HENRI POUSSEUR. "Stravinsky by Way of Webern: The Consistency of a Syntax," *Perspectives of New Music* 10 (1972): 13–15; and 11 (1972): 112–145.

GLEN SCOTT PRESTON. "Serial Procedures in Two Works of Stravinsky: *In Memoriam Dylan Thomas and Three Songs From William Shakespeare*" (M. M. thesis, The University of Texas at Austin, 1980).

DAVID SCHIFF. *The Music of Elliott Carter* (London: Eulenberg Books, 1983).

EUGENE WILLIAM SCHWEITZER. "Generation in String Quartets of Carter, Sessions, Kirchner, and Schuller: A Concept of Forward Thrust and Its Relationship to Structure in Aurally Complex Styles," Ph.D thesis, University of Rochester, Eastman School of Music, 1965.

ROGER SESSIONS. "Problems and Issues Facing the Composer Today," *Roger Sessions on Music: Collected Essays* (Princeton, New Jersey: Princeton University Press, 1979), pp. 71–87.

CLAUDIO SPIES. "Some Notes on Stravinsky's Requiem Settings," *Perspectives on Schoenberg and Stravinsky,* rev. ed. Benjamin Boretz and Edward T. Cone (New York: W. W. Norton and Company, Inc., 1972), pp. 233–249.

PIETER C. VAN DEN TOORN. *The Music of Igor Stravinsky* (New Haven: Yale University Press, 1983), pp. 372–455 (on Stravinsky's serial period).

EDGARD VARÈSE, "The Liberation of Sound," *Perspectives of New Music* 5/1 (1966): 11–19.

STEFAN WOLPE. "Thinking Twice," in *Contemporary Composers on Contemporary Music,* ed. Elliott Schwartz and Barney Childs (New York: Holt, Rinehart and Winston, 1967), pp. 274–307.

17 Twelve-tone tonality

TOWARD A NEW CONCEPT OF TONALITY The American composer George Perle (b. 1915) has been developing a consistent theory of postdiatonic music since 1939, the significance of which lies in the growth toward a new kind of tonal system and a new means of progression. Perle felt that, during the early stages of development, his new harmonic principles had served sufficiently in the organization of his small-scale compositional structures, but it was only in 1960, with the *Fifth String Quartet* and *Three Movements for Orchestra,* that he made his first major breakthrough in the application of the system toward large-scale harmonic and tonal integration. While Perle's theoretical formulations have certain historical connections to the twelve-tone music of the Viennese composers, his formulations also have fundamental connections to the nonserial compositions of Debussy, Scriabin, Stravinsky, Bartók, and Varèse.

As part of an evolution stemming from these early twentieth-century sources, especially the music of Berg and Bartók, Perle has arrived at a generalized system, as natural and as comprehensive as that of traditional tonality, which permits the utilization of the totality of relations inherent in the chromatic continuum. Through the joining of two concepts—the interval cycle and inversional symmetry—he has defined a new concept of musical space, in which coherence in progression and a sense of tonality are realized to a degree unknown since the major-minor scale system. Perle's music, which has an affinity to that of the earlier major figures of this century, has evolved to a new stage of synthesis and development in both the recognition of the shared elements of their disparate styles, and in the realization of the possibilities suggested by their pioneering musical languages.

EVOLUTION OF THE TONE ROW

In 1937, through his initial encounter with the use of a twelve-tone theme in the score of Berg's *Lyric Suite,* Perle first became aware of the new path for twentieth-century music established by Schoenberg. It was in Berg's score that Perle saw how a twelve-tone theme could be exploited as a source for new harmonic and rhythmic possibilities. While the principles of Perle's musical language have very much to do with the deepest implications of Schoenberg's system, what he did was to find another way to define the set, one that permits it to function on a deep level in the same way that the scale does in tonal music. Perle began in 1939 with a fundamental critique of the twelve-tone system.[1] He found an inherent contradiction in the

---

[1] See Perle's letter to the editor in the *Boston Review* (March 16, 1987).

Schoenbergian concept of a tone row that, according to Schoenberg in his 1941 essay, "Composition with Twelve Tones (I)," "functions in the manner of a motive" and must therefore "be invented anew for every piece," while serving simultaneously as a background structure that "is invented to substitute for some of the unifying and formative advantages of scale and tonality."[2] In Perle's very first article, he provided an alternative to the function of the twelve-tone set as an ostinato motif, i.e, as a thematic entity that is consistently repeated on the surface level of the composition.[3] Since the role of the special twelve-tone set in Perle's own music is analogous to the precompositional assumptions of the major and minor scales in traditional tonal music, he was to refer to this language as "twelve-tone tonality."[4]

FIRST MANIFESTATIONS OF THE INTERVAL CYCLE AND INVERSIONAL SYMMETRY

The concepts that underlie Perle's special twelve-tone set may be introduced by a brief history of the interval cycle—a series based on a single recurrent interval—and symmetrical pitch formations. Such structures began to appear as local textural or structural devices in the nineteenth century. The dictates of traditional tertian harmony had severely limited the possibilities for symmetrical vertical construction, which only included the diminished-seventh, French-sixth, and dominant-ninth chords. However, Romantic composers often employed symmetrical or cyclic-interval constructions as the basis of triadic root progression. Motion by way of the intervals of the whole-tone or octatonic scales as well as minor- or major-third cycles had appeared extensively in the works of Schubert, Glinka, Berlioz, Liszt, Chopin, Mussorgsky, and others.

At the turn of the century, speculative as well as practical theorists had begun serious explorations of symmetrical pitch construction as the basis for expanding compositional techniques.[5] Among the most notable were the German theorists Bernard Ziehn, Georg Capellen, and Hermann Schroeder, all of whom were concerned specifically with procedures of symmetrical inversion. Ziehn's own concepts developed from his studies of contrapuntal practices stemming from the Renaissance, and he arrived at the concept of an "axis of symmetry" as "tonal center" from these studies of strict contrapuntal

---

[2] Leonard Stein, ed., *Style and Idea, Selected Writings of Arnold Schoenberg,* trans. Leo Black (London: Faber and Faber, 1975), p. 219.

[3] George Perle, "Evolution of the Tone-Row: The Twelve-Tone Modal System," *Music Review* 2/4 (November 1941): 273–287.

[4] Title of his early article, "Twelve-Tone Tonality," *Monthly Musical Record* 73 (1943): 175–179, and second book, *Twelve-Tone Tonality* (Berkeley and Los Angeles: University of California Press, 1977).

[5] A history of these theories of pitch symmetry is discussed by David Bernstein, in "Symmetry and Symmetrical Inversion in Turn-of-the-Century Theory and Practice," paper given at a national meeting of the American Musicological Society (Baltimore, November 3, 1988).

inversion in earlier music. Busoni's *Fantasia Contrapuntistica* (1910) reveals Ziehn's influence, both men having met in the United States in that year. Radical expansion of these principles came in the late 1930s, when Perle began to evolve his theory of "twelve-tone tonality" based on the concepts of the interval cycle and inversional symmetry. About twenty years later, Howard Hanson made one of the earliest significant post–World–War–II attempts to outline a compendium of possibilities for symmetrical arrangement based on twenty of the six-tone scales with their complementary inversions,[6] though Hanson's intention was to produce a compendium of harmonic-melodic material rather than to develop a "method" or a "system."[7] The cyclic-interval projection of the twelve-tone continuum, i.e., as a series of fifths, is basic to his discussions of equal temperament, analysis of intervals, the theory of "Involution" (inversion), and key modulation. Part of his theory deals with "complementary sonorities," in which he explores hexachords that are either related transpositionally or inversionally as well as those that do not form either of these relationships, but contain the same intervallic content.[8] Perle had also identified the . . . symmetrical properties of hexachords and all other pitch-class collections in the Appendix of his first book (beginning with the 2nd edition, rev. and enl., 1968).[9] Thus, Hanson's theories have fundamental connections to the principles of Perle's system of "twelve-tone tonality."

In many early twentieth-century compositions, the tendency toward equalization of the twelve tones led to more pervasive usage of symmetrical formations as the primary means of integrating the large-scale structure. As early as 1910, Berg appears to have been the first to employ symmetrical inversion as the basis for modulating from one axis of symmetry to another. In his *String Quartet,* Op. 3, the exposition of Movement II ends (mm. 68–71) with a symmetrical "French-sixth" type of construction that interlocks two tritones. As shown in Ex. 17–1, permutation C–D–F♯–A♭ establishes an implied axis of E–E, while permutation D–F♯–A♭–C produces a modulation from the original axis to a new one (G–G). The latter axis begins the development section (m. 72). The two axes are shown to be part of two inversionally symmetrical arrays, one intersecting at axis E–E (or B♭–B♭), the other at axis G–G (or C♯–C♯). A single symmetrical tetrachord serves then, as a common pivot between these two different axes a minor third apart.

Bartók also employed the interval cycles and strict inversional symmetry in certain early works, but in his *Fourth String Quartet* (1928) he exploited the possibilities of modulation based on symmetrical chords more

[6] Howard Hanson, *Harmonic Materials of Modern Music; Resources of the Tempered Scale* (New York: Appleton-Century-Crofts, 1960), "Symmetrical Twelve-Tone Forms," pp. 373–376.

[7] Ibid., p. xi.

[8] Ibid., e.g., chapter on "The Complementary Hexad," pp. 249ff.

[9] See George Perle, *Serial Composition and Atonality* (Berkeley and Los Angeles: University of California Press, 1962; rev. 6th ed., 1991).

EXAMPLE 17–1. Berg. *String Quartet,* Op. 3, Mov. II, end of exposition, mm. 68–71, and beginning of development, symmetrical modulation by common (symmetrical) "French-6th" chord

French-6th
(at axis E-E)

French-6th
(at axis G-G)

E	F	F♯	G	A♭	A	B♭ ‖	G	A♭	A	B♭	B	C	C♯
E	E♭	D	C♯	C	B	B♭ ‖	G	F♯	F	E	E♭	D	C♯

fully. In Ex. 17–2, modulation is also based on the use of a double-tritone tetrachord as a means of pivoting between two axes of symmetry a minor third apart.[10] Bartók employs two mutually exclusive transpositions of this tetrachord a minor third apart (G♯–C♯–D–G and B–E–F–B♭). In Ex. 17–2a, one of these transpositions (G♯–C♯–D–G) is shown to progress to a permutation of the other (B♭–B–E–F) symmetrically around the common axis of C♯–D (or G–G♯). In Ex. 17–2b, both tetrachords are rotated so that they again progress from one to the other, but around a new common axis of E–F (or B♭–B). In Ex. 17–2c and 17–2d, both of these transpositions are shown to belong to two different pairs of inversionally related semitonal cycles simultaneously that intersect at C♯–D and G–G♯ or E–F and B♭–B. The two axes of these symmetrically related tetrachords are expressed by sums 3 and 9.[11]

As employed by Berg and Bartók, these symmetrical relations represent only part of a larger system that is beyond their development. Expansion of these principles is shown in Ex. 17–3, in which any pitch collection, whether symmetrical or nonsymmetrical, represents the intersection of numerous symmetrical arrays. We can show that any nonsymmetrical tetrachord, e.g., C–D♭–E–A♭ (Ex. 17–3a), can be analyzed into three dyadic pairings, each of which contains two nonequivalent dyads. This differs from the dyadic relations in the literally symmetrical tetrachords of Berg and Bartók, where the two dyads in each pairing are equivalent. The nonequivalent dyads C–D♭/E–A♭ represent two different dyadic arrays of sums 1/0, C–E/D♭–A♭ of sums 4/9 and C–A♭/D♭–E of sums 8/5. The sums in each of the three pairings, while nonequivalent, give us the total symmetrical content of sum 1 (= 13) together. As was shown in cell Z (Ex. 17–2), transposition of this nonsymmetrical tetrachord by the minor third (or tritone) produces no

---

[10] See also Ex. 5–9, and corresponding discussion of Cell Z.
[11] We continue to assign 0 to pitch-class C, 1 to C♯, 2 to D, 3 to E♭, etc.

EXAMPLE 17–2. Bartók, *Fourth String Quartet*, Mov. I, two equivalent double-tritone tetrachords

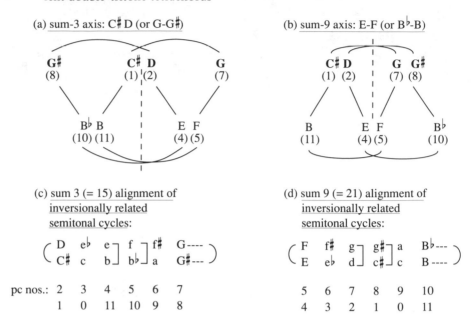

(a) sum-3 axis: C♯ D (or G-G♯)

(b) sum-9 axis: E-F (or B♭-B)

(c) sum 3 (= 15) alignment of inversionally related semitonal cycles:

(d) sum 9 (= 21) alignment of inversionally related semitonal cycles:

pc nos.:

2	3	4	5	6	7
1	0	11	10	9	8

5	6	7	8	9	10
4	3	2	1	0	11

change of the total tetrachordal sum content, since we are adding 3 (or 6) to each note and 4 × 3 (or 4 × 6) = 0 change. For instance, the minor-third transposition (T–3), E♭–E–G–B, can be partitioned into the dyadic pairings E♭–E/G–B of sums 7/6, E♭–G/E–B of sums 10/3, and E♭–B/E–G of sums 2/11. Thus, the total tetrachordal sum of 13 (= 1) is common to both transpositions.

The common total sum content permits modulation exclusively by symmetrical means between these minor-third transpositions of the tetrachord. In other words, as shown in Ex. 17–3b, we can move within the same set of dyadic arrays by maintaining each local sum in the progression. Dyads C–D♭ and E–A♭ can move symmetrically to the two new dyads B♭–E♭ and F–G, respectively, to produce a new tetrachordal collection (B♭–E♭–F–G). By interpreting the latter tetrachord in terms of its interval-couple B♭–F/E♭–G (of sums 3/10), we can move symmetrically from dyad B♭–F to a new dyad B–E. If we retain dyad E♭–G, we have arrived at the minor-third transposition (E♭–E–G–B) of the original collection (C–D♭–E–A♭).

Perle showed how his special twelve-tone set, based on the interval cycle and the strictly symmetrical projection of a single interval, can serve as the source for deriving all possible arrays of such symmetrically related chords. Most of Perle's compositions between 1939 and 1969 and all of them since are based on the *nonserial* compositional unfolding of such arrays—that is to say, there is no foreground notion in his music of a consistently re-

EXAMPLE 17–3. Nonsymmetrical tetrachord C–D♭–E–A♭ (T–0) and its minor-third transposition E♭–E–G–B, based on intersection of numerous symmetrical dyadic arrays

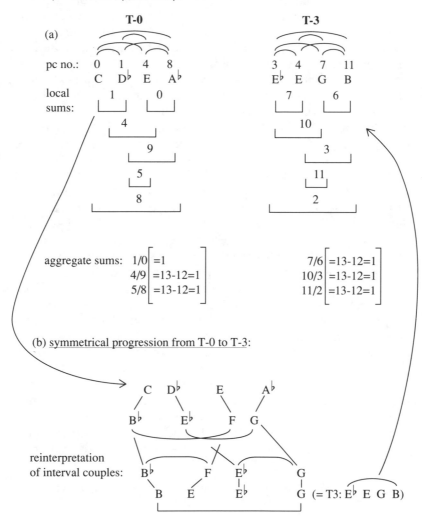

iterated, twelve-tone theme ordered serially from which such chord progressions are derived. Instead, Perle's nonserial compositional approach to the twelve tones is associated more closely with the principles of Bartók's music, something Perle had become fully aware of only in the early 1950s when he subjected several of Bartók's works to careful analysis.[12]

[12] See George Perle, "Symmetrical Formations in the String Quartets of Béla Bartók," *Music Review* 16 (November 1955): 300–312.

THE CYCLIC SET

What is this special twelve-tone set that presents a strictly symmetrical projection of a single interval? How can a twelve-tone series be the basis of nonserial composition? And how does the special twelve-tone set take us beyond the essentially primitive notion of an ostinato twelve-tone motifc? In his first, though unfinished, string quartet, in which Perle had originally intended to follow the principles of Schoenberg's twelve-tone system, he was aware of the fixed relations of each note to its two neighbors in any given form of the series, and that these adjacency relations of the specific pitches would change only under transposition or inversion of the set-form. While Perle's understanding of these relations accorded with the Schoenbergian conception of the series, his interpretation deviated in a fundamental respect (Ex. 17–4). In his pairing of the basic series (B–C–D–F–A–Ab–G–F♯–D♯–E–Bb–C♯–[B]) with the inversion (B–Bb–Ab–F–C♯–D–D♯–E–G–F♯–C–A–[B]), he observed that C, for instance, had B and D as neighbors in the prime form of the series and F♯ and A in the inverted form. Given these two forms, he decided that C could freely move to, or be combined with, any of its four neighboring notes.[13] The idea that each pitch-class represents a point of intersection between different set-forms is foreign to the Schoenbergian conception of the row as a coherent thematic entity. Perle's interpretation of the row simply as a set of local adjacency relationships then led him to another new assumption: that while such neighbor-note relations in the Schoenbergian twelve-tone row can have no logical ordering, they will appear complete and systematic if the twelve-tone set is presented in the form of a succession of equivalent intervals, i.e., a cycle based either on the perfect fifth (interval 7) or the semitone (interval 1), which are the only two intervals that will each generate a single cyclic partition of all twelve tones.

Example 17–5a presents an abstract alignment of two pairs of statements related inversionally of the cycle of fifths that share the same axis notes (C–C, G–G, D–D, etc.). The axes of the two pairings are represented by sums 0, 5, 9, 2. Any two "neighbor-note" dyads that are adjacent to the

EXAMPLE 17–4. Perle's unfinished quartet, alignment of the basic twelve-tone series and its inversion

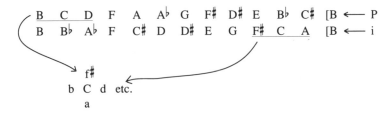

[13] Dennis Miller, "Perle on Perle," *Music Associates of America* (New Jersey: League-ISCM, Boston Publication Series, 1987): 8–9.

EXAMPLE 17–5. (a) array of two pairs of inversionally complementary perfect-fifth cycles; (b) cyclic (neighbor) chords of primary
interval-couple 7,7 (pair of perfect fifths) and secondary interval-couple
3,3 (pair of minor thirds)

(a) sums:

	0	5	0	5	0	5	0	5	0	5	0	5	0	5
c	C	f	G	b♭	D	e♭	A	a♭	E	d♭	B	[g♭	G♭	b
a	C	d	G	g	D	c	A	f	E	b♭	B	e♭	G♭	a♭

sums: 9 2 9 2 9 2 9 2 9 2 9 2 9 2

(b)

$$7\left(\begin{matrix}c\\a\end{matrix}\right]3 \quad \left(\begin{matrix}f\\d\end{matrix}\right] \quad \left(\begin{matrix}b♭\\g\end{matrix}\right] \quad \left(\begin{matrix}e♭\\c\end{matrix}\right] \quad \left(\begin{matrix}a♭\\f\end{matrix}\right] \quad \left(\begin{matrix}d♭\\b♭\end{matrix}\right] \quad \left(\begin{matrix}g♭\\e♭\end{matrix}\right]$$

$$7\left(\begin{matrix}f\\d\end{matrix}\right]3 \quad \left(\begin{matrix}b♭\\g\end{matrix}\right] \quad \left(\begin{matrix}e♭\\c\end{matrix}\right] \quad \left(\begin{matrix}a♭\\f\end{matrix}\right] \quad \left(\begin{matrix}d♭\\b♭\end{matrix}\right] \quad \left(\begin{matrix}g♭\\e♭\end{matrix}\right] \quad \left(\begin{matrix}b\\a♭\end{matrix}\right]$$

axis
notes: C   G   D   A   E   B   G♭

same axis–note in these two cyclic sets form a "minor-seventh" cyclic tetrachord. If we choose axis-note C–C, then the two perfect-fifth neighbor-note
dyads d–a and f–c together form the cyclic chord d–f–a–c (Ex. 17–5b), of
which the primary interval couple is based on the perfect fifth, or intervals
7, 7. The cyclic set was to provide Perle with a new criterion for harmonic
construction, or simultaneity, as one of its most significant consequences. It
eliminated the necessity of the motivic function of the tone-row because "the
cyclic set, unlike the general twelve-tone set, is implied in its entirety by any
one of its three-note segments, since each segment comprises all the criteria
that define the set—the alternate sums formed by adjacent pitch classes and
the cyclic interval expressed in the difference between these sums."[14] All
twelve forms of the cyclic set (Ex. 17–6)—the six primes and the six inversions—form a closed system through the cognate relation, just as the
circle of fifths forms a closed system for the scales of the major-minor
system.[15]

THE EARLY WORKS OF GEORGE PERLE

Following his *Pantomime, Interlude,* and *Fugue* for piano (1937), which
brought his neoclassical phase of tonality to a close, Perle turned to his first
work to be composed in what he referred to originally as the "twelve-tone
modal system"—the three little piano pieces, entitled *Modal Suite* for piano,
which was composed in 1940. It was not until 1960, however, in the *Three
Movements for Orchestra* and the *Fifth String Quartet,* that he made his first
breakthrough in the evolution of the system. No significant changes had

[14] See Perle, *Twelve-Tone Tonality,* n.4, above, p. 34.
[15] The cognate relation is expressed in the common sums of the p and i forms
within and between the adjacent arrays.

EXAMPLE 17–6. All twelve forms of the cyclic set in the interval-7,7 system

```
sums    0   7   0   7
p0,p7:  c   c   g   f   d   b♭  a   e♭  e   a♭  b   d♭  [g♭ g♭  d♭
i0,i5:  c   c   f   g   b♭  d   e♭  a   a♭  e   d♭  b   [g♭ g♭  b
        0   5   0   5

        2   9   2   9
p2,p9:  g   g   d   c   a   f   e   b♭  b   e♭  g♭  a♭  [d♭ d♭  a♭
i2,i7:  g   g   c   d   f   a   b♭  e   e♭  b   a♭  g♭  [d♭ d♭  g♭
        2   7   2   7

        4   11  4   11
p4,p11: d   d   a   g   e   c   b   f   g♭  b♭  d♭  e♭  [a♭ a♭  e♭
i4,i9:  d   d   g   a   c   e   f   b   b♭  g♭  e♭  d♭  [a♭ a♭  d♭
        4   9   4   9

        6   1   6   1
p6,p1:  a   a   e   d   b   g   g♭  c   d♭  f   a♭  b♭  [e♭ e♭  b♭
i6,i11: a   a   d   e   g   b   c   g♭  f   d♭  b♭  a♭  [e♭ e♭  a♭
        6   11  6   11

        8   3   8   3
p8,p3:  e   e   b   a   g♭  d   d♭  g   a♭  c   e♭  f   [b♭ b♭  f
i8,i1:  e   e   a   b   d   g♭  g   d♭  c   a♭  f   e♭  [b♭ b♭  e♭
        8   1   8   1

        10  5   10  5
p10,p5: b   b   g♭  e   d♭  a   a♭  d   e♭  g   b♭  c   [f  f   c
i10,i3: b   b   e   g♭  a   d♭  d   a♭  g   e♭  c   b♭  [f  f   b♭
        10  3   10  3
```

transpired in the first twenty years or so since his original discovery of the cyclic series. Nor did careful scrutiny of Schoenberg's twelve-tone system provide any new insights, but only brought out the limitations of the latter in comparison to the possibilities inherent in the "twelve-tone modal system." His special affinity with Bartók and Berg, however, helped Perle maintain his confidence regarding the validity of the system throughout the early decades of its development.

The development of very different aspects of "twelve-tone tonality" in each of the three movements of the *Fifth Quartet* reveals the flexibility permitted by the system. Every complete vertical sonority is comprised of a minor-seventh chord plus an axis note. This produces a variety of sonorities going beyond the minor-seventh chord. The latter appears either in its complete four-note form or is represented by any of its three-note segments and usually has some other pitch added to it throughout the work. Since the minor-seventh chord interlocks two perfect fifths, the primary interval couple for the piece is 7, 7. Because of its interlocking fifths, we may anticipate that the minor-seventh chord will function as a cyclic or neighbor-note chord, and the additional pitch will function as the axis note. When the axis note duplicates one of the cyclic notes, a "tonic" chord is produced.

Although the tertian intervallic construction of the minor-seventh chord invokes what seems to be an almost romantic harmonic fabric, it has nothing to do with traditional tonal functions. Nevertheless, the interactions of the cyclic chords and axis notes are basic to generating what appears to be a traditional sonata plan for Movement I.

From the initial chord of the movement (Ex. 17–8a, score), which consists of three notes of a minor-seventh chord (g#–b–d#–[ ]) and an axis tone (G), we can determine the main array as well as the "key" of the movement (Ex. 17–7a).[16] Based on these two pairs of inversionally comple-

EXAMPLE 17–7. Arrays of Perle's *Fifth String Quartet,* Mov. I

(a) key 4,4; mode 3,3

```
            6    1    6    1
p6,p1:  a    a    e    d    b    g    f#   c    c#   f    g#   a#  (d#   d#   a#
i3,i10: b    b    e    f#   a    c#   d    g#   g    d#   c    a#  (f    f    a#
           10    3   10    3
```

(b) key 0,0; mode 3,3

```
           10    5   10    5
p10,p5: f    f    c    a#   g    d#   d    g#   a    c#   e    f#  (b    b    f#
i7,i2:  g    g    c    d    f    a    a#   e    d#   b    g#   f#  (c#   c#   f#
            2    7    2    7
```

(c) key 8,8; mode 3,3

```
            2    9    2    9
p2,p9:  c#   c#   g#   f#   d#   b    a#   e    f    a    c    d   (g    g    d
i11,i6: d#   d#   g#   a#   c#   f    f#   c    b    g    e    d   (a    a    d
            6   11    6   11
```

(d) key 10,10; mode 9,9

```
            0    7    0    7
p0,p7:  c    c    g    f    d    bb   a    eb   e    ab   b    db  (gb   gb   db
i3,i10: b    b    e    f#   a    c#   d    g#   g    d#   c    a#  (f    f    a#
           10    3   10    3
```

(e) key 6,6: mode 9,9

```
           10    5   10    5
p10,p5: f    f    c    a#   g    d#   d    g#   a    c#   e    f#  (b    b    f#
i1,i8:  e    e    a    b    d    f#   g    c#   c    g#   f    d#  (a#   a#   d#
            8    1    8    1
```

(f) key 0,0; mode 3,3 (minor-third transposition of Ex. b)

```
            4   11    4   11
p4,p11: d    d    a    g    e    c    b    f    f#   bb   c#   eb  (g#   g#   c#
i1,i8:  e    e    a    b    d    f#   g    c#   c    g#   f    d#  (a#   a#   d#
            8    1    8    1
```

[16] In "Evolution of the Tone Row," n.3, above, p. 282 n.9, Perle states that "the term 'key' is here divorced of all connotations dependent upon tonality and refers only to the transfer of a series of tone-relationships to a new degree in pitch."

EXAMPLE 17–8. Perle, *Fifth String Quartet:* (a) Mov. I, opening, part of first-theme group; (b) diagrammatic analysis of chords of (a)

EXAMPLE 17–8. Continued

EXAMPLE 17–8. Continued

(b)   SUM ARRAY of p6, p1/i3, i10

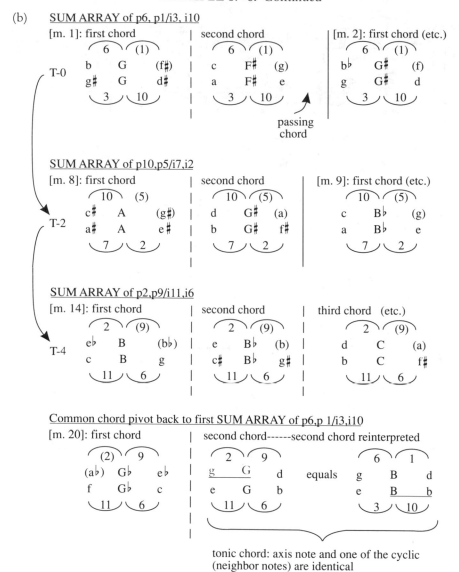

tonic chord: axis note and one of the cyclic
(neighbor notes) are identical

mentary perfect-fifth cycles, we can identify interlocking set-forms of this array as sums p6, p1/i3, i10.[17] The G axis in i3, i10 has g#–d# of the minor-seventh chord as its neighbor notes, and in p6, p1 it has b–f# of the minor-seventh chord as its neighbor notes (see Ex. 17–8b, m. 1). The second chord also consists of three notes of a minor-seventh chord (a–c–e–[ ]) and

---

[17] In this example (17–7a), the two numbers of "key 4, 4" refer to the sum (or axis) of the two aligned sums in each p/i pairing: Sums 10 + 6 = 16 (or 4), Sums 1 + 3 = 4. "Mode 3, 3" refers to the difference (or interval) between the two sums in each pairing: 1 (or 13) − 10 = 3, 6 − 3 = 3.

an axis note (F♯). Axis-note F♯ in i3, i10 has a–e as its neighbor notes, and in p6, p1 it has c–g as its neighbor notes. The opening partial minor-seventh chord returns on the last beat of m. 1, where it functions simply as a passing chord to the downbeat of m. 2. All the chords in this initial statement of theme 1 (mm. 1–7) can be found similarly in the same array (p6, p1/i3, i10). Repeat of the theme a whole-step higher (at mm. 8–13) establishes a new array of p10, p5/i7, i2 (Ex. 17–7b). A second, slightly modified repeat of the theme another whole-step higher (at mm. 14–20), which introduces further appoggiatura-chord elaborations in the metrically expanded measures, establishes a third array of p2, p9/i11, i6 (Ex. 17–7c). The cadential chord (m. 20), which forms a complete minor-seventh chordal construction (e–g–b–d), prepares for modulation back to the first array. If we interpret the chord according to axis-note G (see Ex. 17–8b), then it belongs to array p2, p9/i11, i6 of the preceding passage. However, if we reinterpret the chord according to axis-note B (see Ex. 17–8b, same measure), then it serves as a common pivot between the latter array and the original one of p6, p1/i3, i10.

The next passage (mm. 21ff.) begins with a series of partial minor-seventh chords without axis notes. Each of these chords belongs simultaneously to all three of the arrays that have unfolded thus far (Ex. 17–7a, b, and c). At the entry of violin I on axis-note G (end of m. 22), we get a return to the first chord of the piece (G–[g♯]–b–[d♯]–f♯), which belongs to the initial p6, p1/i3, i10 array. The latter then serves as the "key" for a modified or subsidiary statement within the first-theme group, which we may refer to as theme 1b (mm. 25ff.). Thus, the quartet reveals a pervasive concern for the minor-seventh chord as a basic unifying harmonic construction, perhaps analogously to the use of the triad in the traditional major-minor scale system. The minor-seventh chord is only one of many types of cyclic chords that may serve a cellular function in the generation of a coherent harmonic/melodic fabric and a sense of tonal centricity.

MORE RECENT WORKS OF PERLE

The next, more radical expansion of the system came in the summer of 1969, while Perle was at the MacDowell Colony. Paul Lansky, a former pupil, suggested another possibility of pairing set-forms of the cyclic series.[18] Perle had derived his "twelve-tone modes" by pairing *inversionally related* set-forms of the cyclic series. However, by pairing *transpositionally related* set-forms (i.e., either two prime set-forms, or two inverted set-forms), other equally consistent collections of cyclic chords could be derived. From these developments, all the basic formulations of the dyadic arrays of "twelve-tone tonality" were established finally in the *Seventh Quartet* (1973). What followed were the *Songs of Praise and Lamentation* (1974) and the *Six Etudes* for piano (1976), the new formulations of all three of these mature works leading in 1977 to his second book, *Twelve-Tone Tonality*.

In No. 5 ("Beauty—be not caused—it is") of *Thirteen Dickinson Songs* (Ex. 17–9), composed during the following year (1977–1978), we can ob-

[18] See "Perle on Perle," n.13, above, pp. 18–19.

EXAMPLE 17–9. Perle, *Thirteen Dickinson Songs,* Vol. II, No. 5 ("Beauty—be not caused—it is"), mm. 15–21

serve some of the means by which Perle expanded the compositional possibilities of symmetrical modulation. A segment of the first vocal phrase and surrounding accompaniment of the song (at mm. 17–21) can be analyzed consistently and unequivocally into axis-dyad chords (Ex. 17–10a). If we compare the chord on the first quarter note with the chord on the second quarter note, we see that two notes (E–F♯) of the first chord move up one semitone (to F–G) and four notes (f–e–a♭–b♭) of the first chord move down one semitone (to e–e♭–g–a).

While the chords are not symmetrical in and of themselves, each dyad of a chord (E–F♯, etc.) may be continued as a pair of parallel 1/11 cycles (Ex. 17–10b). We have three possible interval couples (1, 2; 3, 6; 5, 4) for the cyclic notes (Ex. 17–10c). Suppose we assume that the interval-system is 1, 2, then the actual array will be one of the two in Ex. 17–11 (this is the point at which the sums enter). As long as the same axis-interval (E–F♯) is transposed to get the second chord, the array can be any of the ones implied in Ex. 17–11. If that same difference between the two axis notes is preserved (Ex. 17–12), the above series of twelve chords (Ex. 17–11) can represent any of the arrays in Ex. 17–12 (those permutations in the 1, 2 interval-system are underlined; this

EXAMPLE 17–10. Perle, *Thirteen Dickinson Songs,* Vol. II: (a) No. 5, two chords in m. 17; (b) cyclic implications of chords in (a), (c) interval couples 1,2; 3,6; 5,4 for the cyclic notes

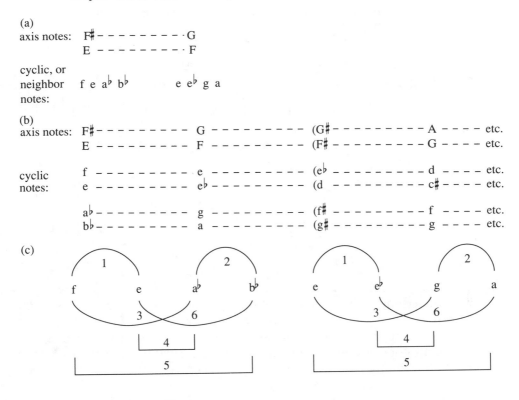

(a)
axis notes: F♯ – – – – – – – – ·G
             E – – – – – – – – ·F

cyclic, or
neighbor   f e a♭ b♭   e e♭ g a
notes:

(b)
axis notes: F♯ – – – – – – – – G – – – – – – – – (G♯ – – – – – – – – A – – – – etc.
             E – – – – – – – – F – – – – – – – – (F♯ – – – – – – – – G – – – – etc.

cyclic   f – – – – – – – – e – – – – – – – – (e♭ – – – – – – – – d – – – – etc.
notes: e – – – – – – – – e♭ – – – – – – – – (d – – – – – – – – c♯ – – – – etc.

          a♭ – – – – – – – – g – – – – – – – – (f♯ – – – – – – – – f – – – – etc.
          b♭ – – – – – – – – a – – – – – – – – (g♯ – – – – – – – – g – – – – etc.

(c)

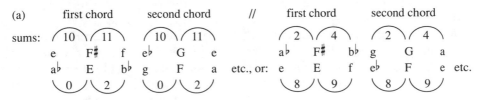

EXAMPLE 17–11. Perle, *Thirteen Dickinson Songs,* Vol. II, No. 5, symmetrical properties of the two chords in m. 17

(a)   first chord   second chord   //   first chord   second chord
sums: 10   11   10   11   2   4   2   4
         e   F♯   f   e♭   G   e   a♭   F♯   b♭   g   G   a
         a♭   E   b♭   g   F   a   etc., or: e   E   f   e♭   F   e   etc.
         0   2   0   2   8   9   8   9

(b): arrays for the two chords, in interval-system 1,2.

          10 11 10 11
p10,p11: f f f♯ e g e♭ a♭ d a d♭ b♭ c (b b c etc.

p0,i2:   c c d b♭ e a♭ (f♯ f♯ a♭ etc.
        0 2 0 2

or:

        2 4 2 4
p2,i4:   c♯ c♯ d♯ b f a g g a / d c e b♭ f♯ a♭ a♭ f♯

p8,p9:   e e f e♭ f♯ d g c♯ a♭ c a b (b♭ b♭ b
        8 9 8 9

EXAMPLE 17–12. Perle, *Thirteen Dickinson Songs*, Vol. II, No. 5, symmetrical relation (common sums) between the two chords, in either of two arrays

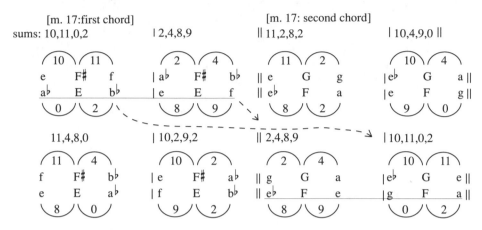

also shows the symmetrical relations, i.e., common sums, between these two collections). The sum 2, 4, 8, 9 interpretation of the chords in Ex. 17–12 is also basic to the chords in the preceding measures (Ex. 17–13).

In the next two measures (mm. 18–19), we find repeated statements of another pair of chords related symmetrically (Ex. 17–14). Here we have half as many possible interpretations because of the repeated axis note. If we look at the second chord of m. 17 again, we find that it can be reinterpreted as one of these three arrays (Ex. 17–15). We now realize that we have modulated by reinterpreting the set segments (Ex. 17–15). Example 17–16 gives the entire progression of the passage from mm. 17 to 21. The chord across the barline of mm. 20–21 is reinterpreted and progresses into a new array (Ex. 17–17). Ex. 17–18 shows the sets forming the three arrays.

In his compositions of the last several years, Perle has been further expanding the principles inherent in the system of "twelve-tone tonality" and has been exploiting them with increasing mastery. He shows increased facility in his handling of a new concept of "consonance" and "dissonance," in which the sum (or symmetrical) content that defines a given chordal construction serves, analogously to the tertian construction of the traditional triad, as the referential consonant factor to which notes foreign to it are

EXAMPLE 17–13. Perle, *Thirteen Dickinson Songs*, Vol. II, No. 5, symmetrically related chords in mm. 15–16

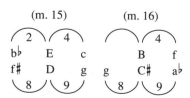

EXAMPLE 17–14. Perle, *Thirteen Dickinson Songs, Vol. II, No.* 5, new pair of symmetrically related chords (mm. 18–19); (a) axis notes, cyclic (or neighbor notes); (b) three interpretations of the two new symmetrically related chords (mm. 18–19)

(a)
axis notes:
```
C – – – – – – – – – A
C – – – – – – – – – A
```

cyclic, or
neighbor   e g♯ b♭ d♭   g b c♯ e
notes:

(b)

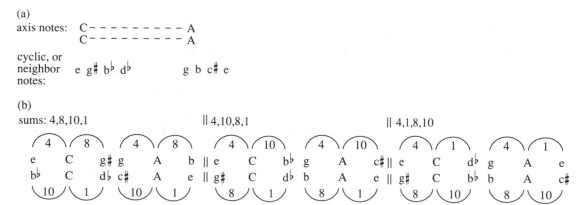

EXAMPLE 17–15. Perle, *Thirteen Dickinson Songs*, Vol. II, No. 5, reinterpretation of the second chord of m. 17 (see Ex. 17–12) as one of the three arrays of Ex. 17–14b

(m. 17, second chord) reinterpreted as

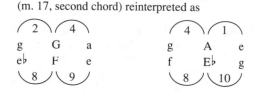

EXAMPLE 17–16. Perle, *Thirteen Dickinson Songs,* Vol. II, No. 5, entire progression of the passage (mm. 17–21)

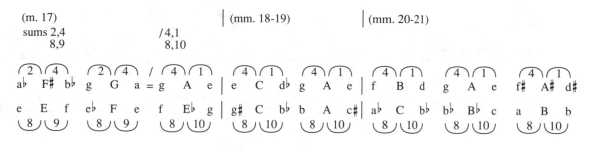

EXAMPLE 17–17. Perle, *Thirteen Dickinson Songs,* Vol. II, No. 5, chord held across the barline of mm. 20–21, reinterpreted and progressing into a new array

443

EXAMPLE 17–18. Perle, *Thirteen Dickinson Songs,* Vol. II, No. 5, the three cyclic arrays from which the progression in Exx. 17–16 and 17–17 is derived

sums: 2,4:   c♯ c♯ d♯ b f a g g a / d c e b♭ f♯ a♭ a♭ f♯
8,9:   e e f e♭ f♯ d g c♯ a♭ c a b (b♭ b♭ b

sums: 1,4   b d d b f a♭ a♭ f b d / c c♯ e♭ b♭ f♯ g a e c c♯
8,10   a b b a c♯ g e♭ f f e♭ / b♭ b♭ c a♭ d f♯ e e f♯

sums 1,9   c c♯ g♯ f e a c c♯ / b d g f♯ e♭ b♭ b d
8,10   a b b a c♯ g e♭ f f e♭ / b♭ b♭ c a♭ d f♯ e e f♯

ultimately accountable. Such foreign elements, which are disruptive and therefore "dissonant" within this new set of syntactical rules, may be employed as suspensions, passing notes, and other types of dissonances.

The *Quartet* is Perle's first in this genre to be written within the framework of a single movement. The sense of structural integration grows from the network of motivic relations that generate the rich contrapuntal fabric of four equal instruments. One can always discern sectional changes that are defined partly by an awareness of articulative possibilities on the string instruments, varying from separate to slurred staccatos to carefully phrased and contoured legato passages. The instrumental sonorities are ex-

EXAMPLE 17–19. Perle, *Eighth String Quartet* ("Windows of Order"), opening, metric relations and symmetrical progression

EXAMPLE 17–19. Continued

ploited in their most flattering registers, resulting in full but transparent counterpoint.

Sectionalization may also be discerned by directed textures, in which stretti often move to an increasing focus on harmonic alignments. Such focal points are supported by the structural use of dynamics and calculated changes of meter and tempo. The opening phrasal arch (Ex. 17–19), an ascending rhythmic motif in stretto and crescendo followed by a descent of instruments aligned harmonically in subito *pianissimo,* establishes what seems to be the prototypic shape for many of the phrases throughout the work. The second phrase ascends and descends slightly more irregularly and agitatedly, but still in delicate and crisp rhythmic fragments. Within the larger context of changing tempi and contrasting dynamic levels, the arch-shape acquires increasing structural significance in the development of the expressive whole. Rhythm and tempo also contribute to the integration of the structure. Everything falls into four tempi related proportionately, of which there is a common factor of 17 for the different metronomic numbers (51, 68, 102, 136, and 153). By exploiting the appropriate durational values in any one of these tempi, you can imply any of the other tempi. For instance, in the move from Tempo I to Tempo II in the second phrase, one-third of a quarter-note becomes the equivalent of a sixteenth-note in the new tempo. That one-third of a quarter-note is expressed in the head-motif in m. 1, a figure which recurs throughout the work, and the same value recurs at the entrance of violin I at the beginning of the second phrase.

In terms of pitch relations, Perle has handled them more freely in this piece than he ever has before in a "twelve-tone-tonal" work. In the head-motif, for example (first three eighth-note values of m. 1), the first note (G♯) returns at the octave (A♭), of which there is only one instance in the chord. The latter is based on the following array: sums 5, 11—g♯–A–d (d–A–a♭), and sums 1, 2—b♭–E♭–b. On the downbeat of m. 3, the axis dyad becomes G♯–G♯, which is striking in view of the octave doubling in the opening figure. Unison axes have a special place in the structural hierarchy, because no matter how the neighbor notes are interpreted, we still get the same four tonic sums. These are reinterpreted so that the opening array (5, 11/1, 2) becomes 5, 1/11, 2; that is, a–G♯–e♭ (5, 11)/f–G♯–f♯ (1, 2), becomes a–G♯–f (5, 1)/e♭–G♯–f♯ (11, 2).

Next, we should note what happens in the viola. Against one of the basic sums, 11 (as represented by the sustained A and D of the cello and violin II), the viola (together with the sustained F♯ of violin I) unfolds, successively, sums 5, 1 (b♭–G–f♯), 4, 1 (a–G–f♯), 3, 1 (a♭–G–f♯), and 2, 1 (g–G–f♯). The last again shows how one note can stand for two, as a result of a certain progression. This is not the result of an ordinary passing-note procedure, but rather of a series of "modulations" that is analogous to going through secondary dominants in a tonal piece. b♭–G–f♯ can be reinterpreted as 4, 1 (b♭–F♯–g); a–G–f♯ as 3, 1 (a–F♯–g); a♭–G–f♯ as 2, 1 (a♭–F♯–g).[19]

In m. 6, a new interpretation of the last array, 2, 1/11, 2, restores the original array, 2, 1/11, 5; f♯–A♭–f is retained, g–E–b♭ becomes e–G–b♭. At the last chord of this measure (F♯–B–C–A–E–B♭), the neighbor notes are a,

---

[19] A simple rule applies here. For any three-note segment, one of the notes can always move by the interval given by the other two notes. Thus, the composer could have reinterpreted the 5, 1 segment, b♭–G–f♯, as 5, 4 (g–B♭–f♯) and continued to b♭–G–a, without having to think about "modulating." Given the segment b♭–G–f♯, the composer can sustain the minor third (b♭–G), while F♯ moves through A, C, E♭, F♯. Perle carries this procedure much further in the first movement of his *Sinfonietta* (1987).

b♭/c, f♯, for axis-notes E and B, giving us sums 1, 2 (a–E–b♭)/11, 5 (c–B–f♯). In the next measure, the neighbor-note chord moves up by successive semi-tones, without concern for the axis notes, i.e., only the cyclic intervals are represented here. The semitonal ascent brings us to C♯–D/E–A♯ (end of first beat). The implied axis notes for this chord would be either C–G or C–C♯ (there is always an option of a tritone where the neighbor notes are a tritone). The cello follows this neighbor-note chord with the two axis notes, C–C♯, which is followed immediately by a final semitonal ascent of the neighbor-note chord and a corresponding semitonal descent of the axis notes. In m. 8, we get a return to the unison axis interval, and again reinterpret the array as 5, 1/11, 2 (e.g., last chord, a♭–[F]–c/e–[G]–g). Thus, in his *Eighth Quartet* and other recent works, Perle has moved toward greater sophistication in the relation of the various parameters and in the development of a new kind of tonality.

SUGGESTED READINGS

ELLIOTT ANTOKOLETZ. *The Music of Béla Bartók: A Study of Tonality and Progression in Twentieth-Century Music* (Berkeley and Los Angeles: University of California Press, 1984).

DAVID BERNSTEIN. "Symmetry and Symmetrical Inversion in Turn-of-the-Century Theory and Practice," paper given at a national meeting of the American Musicological Society (Baltimore, November 3, 1988).

HOWARD HANSON. *Harmonic Materials of Modern Music; Resources of the Tempered Scale* (New York: Appleton-Century-Crofts, 1960), "Symmetrical Twelve-Tone Forms," pp. 373–376.

DENNIS MILLER. "Perle on Perle," *Music Associates of America* (New Jersey: League-ISCM, Boston Publication Series, 1987).

GEORGE PERLE. "Evolution of the Tone-Row: The Twelve-Tone Modal System," *Music Review* 2/4 (November 1941): 273–287.

———. "Letter to the Editor," *Boston Review* (March 16, 1987).

———. *Serial Composition and Atonality* (Berkeley and Los Angeles: University of California Press, 1962; rev. 6th ed. 1991).

———. "Symmetrical Formations in the String Quartets of Béla Bartók," *Music Review* 16 (November 1955): 300–312.

———. *The Listening Composer* (Berkeley and Los Angeles: University of California Press, 1990).

———. *Twelve-Tone Tonality* (Berkeley and Los Angeles: University of California Press, 1977).

18 Musique concrète and electronic music

By the early 1950s, two general tendencies had become preeminent. The first was based on the need for mathematical control of the various parameters in totally serialized contexts, the other motivated by an interest in new possibilities for radical expansion of timbre. Despite technological advancements in electronic instruments operated manually beginning in the 1920s and continued interest in music organized by noise since the pre–World War I experiments of the Italian futurists, both tendencies had remained unfulfilled for the most part until after World War II. A crucial factor that permitted great strides in these areas of mathematical control and timbral expansion after 1950 was the invention of magnetic tape.

PARIS: MUSIQUE CONCRÈTE WITHOUT TAPE

Just prior to the use of tape, early postwar timbral experiments in Paris had already laid the groundwork for developing new possibilities in the generation of musical sound. In 1948, Pierre Schaeffer, a composer and electronic engineer at the French National Radio, began to consider the use of natural sounds as the basis for musical composition, an interest which had developed from his research into musical acoustics since 1942 as head of the *Studio d'Essai* (entitled *Club d'Essai* in 1946). Schaeffer's research has some historical precedent in the early experiments of the Italian futurists, who sought to create a musical idiom based on noises produced both naturally and mechanically. However, Schaeffer had the gramophone at his disposal, so available sounds could be transformed by means of mechanical manipulation of the recordings, such use of gramophones having been anticipated by the acoustical experiments of Hindemith and Toch in Berlin in the 1920s. Schaeffer's first important product after his earliest experiments with the attack and decay of recorded bell tones was his *Étude aux chemins de fer* (1948), in which he made disc recordings of six steam engines straining and accelerating rhythmically over the rails. Together with *Étude aux tourniquets* and *Étude aux casseroles, Étude aux chemins* was broadcast as part of a "concert de bruits" in October 1948. While the possibilities of playing the recorded sounds backwards and changing their speed permitted some alteration of the natural sounds, resynthesis of the original materials by means of available techniques could neither completely disguise their original identity nor integrate them into a unified musical medium.[1]

---

[1] See Peter Manning, *Electronic and Computer Music* (Oxford: Clarendon Press, 1987), pp. 19–42, for a more detailed discussion of these *musique concrète* developments.

Schaeffer's use of several gramophones in canon and speed changes of the recorded material led to new possibilities as well as partial solutions of the ongoing problems in the creation of a new sound medium. For instance, the use of speed change led to radical modifications in pitch, duration, and in other aspects as well. However, it was not until tape recording came into practical use in the early 1950s that each sound element in a recorded group could be modified individually and more drastically. Meanwhile, in collaboration with his colleague Pierre Henry, Schaeffer produced his first major nontape work, *Symphonie pour un homme seul* (1949), which was originally conceived as a *Symphonie de bruits.* The work formed a central part of the first public performance of *musique concrète* at the École Normale de Musique in March of 1950, which provided an opportunity for the composer to observe an acoustical situation with an elaborate setting of gramophones and loud-speakers. Techniques employed in the *Symphonie* superseded the earlier manipulations of gramophone recordings by a more systematic use of available resources based on both human and mechanical sounds, including pitched sounds and noise in both categories. In final form, the eleven sections of the work were based on the mixing of two sound groups: (1) *Human sounds*—different types of breathing, vocal fragments, shouting, humming, whistled tunes; and (2) *Nonhuman sounds*—footsteps, knocking on doors, percussion, prepared piano, and orchestral instruments.[2]

In 1951, Schaeffer and Henry began to collaborate on the large *musique concrète* opera *Orphée,* the scoring of which produced formidable problems, so two different types of scores—*la partition opératoire,* notating the technical procedures, and *la partition d'effet,* indicating the musical structure and development—were prepared.[3] It premièred in Paris, was first revised and enlarged for the more successful performance at Donaueschingen in 1953, and revised finally as *Le voile d'Orphée* (1966). Its collage technique is based on the juxtaposition of explosive sonorities of noise against Gluck-like recitatives and arias for two female voices with harpsichord and contrasting passages for solo violin. Some solutions to Schaeffer's problems in the area of graphic communication and perception were aided by the work of the scientist André Moles.

In the early 1950s, controversy between German and French composers at Darmstadt over Schaeffer's aesthetic approach led him to a defense of his principles and to a reaction against those of electronic music. He lectured at Darmstadt in 1951 on his own experiments after a special studio, which was attended by Boulez, Scherchen, and Stockhausen, was set up for him by the Paris Broadcasting System. In 1952, he outlined a history of his early *musique concrète* developments and formulated the principles of *concrète*

---

[2] Schaeffer's use of the prepared piano, based on alteration of the piano sounds by insertion of extraneous objects between the strings, was influenced by John Cage, whom he met in the same year.

[3] See Peter Manning, *Electronic and Computer Music,* n.1, above, p. 29.

composition systematically, defining and describing the use of sound objects that included both human and nonhuman pitched sounds and noises and the use of the prepared piano.[4] By the late 1950s, the aesthetics of both *musique concrète* and electronic music, often joined in single compositions, had found increasing mutual acceptance among composers in both areas. Significant among them were the German electronic composers and members of the "*Groupe de Recherche de Musique Concrète*" (renamed "*Groupe de Recherches Musicales*" in 1958), the latter composers of whom were connected intimately with Schaeffer's studio. Prominent members or associates of the *Groupe,* who represented wide-ranging approaches from pure *concrète* and indeterminacy to mathematical calculation in electronic and computerized idioms, were François Bayle (director of the *Groupe* since 1966), Pierre Henry, Luc Ferrari, François-Bernard Mache, Ivo Malec, Iannis Xenakis (Greek architect and composer Luciano Berio, Michel Philippot, André Boucourechliev (Bulgarian-French composer), Varèse, and others. Even Bayle, one of the staunchest advocates of *musique concrète,* began to incorporate electronically produced elements into his works after 1963. These more general developments within the *musique concrète* movement led to the adoption of the term *expèriences musicales* in place of Schaeffer's designation, which was originally narrower.[5]

PARIS: MUSIQUE CONCRÈTE WITH TAPE

Radical developments in *musique concrète* composition were permitted by the use of the tape recorder in the early 1950s. Schaeffer introduced the term *musique concrète* to designate this new musical concept, in which natural sounds are recorded directly on tape, in contrast to the use of the abstract notational signs of the score for tones produced by instruments. Various kinds of recorded natural sounds and noises from vocal and instrumental sources to wind, motor, and other machine-produced noises could now be modified and transformed by manipulations of the magnetic tape, including speed change resulting in frequency and durational modulations, retrograde of tape, greater control and extension of dynamic range, ostinato patterns produced by the use of tape loops, multiple tapes employed in overlap, isolation of the core of a given sound or noise by elimination of its attack and/or decay, use of echo chambers, and other techniques. The earliest *concrète* works to use such tape techniques were Henry's *Concerto des ambiguités* and Schaeffer's and Henry's *Bidule en ut* (1950). Many other works after 1950 were to be based on the synthesis of both *concrète* and electronically generated

---

[4] See Pierre Schaeffer, *A la recherche d'une musique concrète* (Paris: Éditions du Seuil, 1952). His theories were more extensively developed in his *Traité des objets musicaux* (Paris: Éditions du Seuil, 1966).

[5] H. H. Stuckenschmidt, *Twentieth-Century Music,* translated from the German by Richard Deveson (New York and Toronto: McGraw-Hill Book Company, 1969), p. 182.

sounds and may, therefore, be subsumed under the heading of electronic music.

FIRST POSTWAR ELECTRONIC DEVELOPMENTS IN EUROPE: COLOGNE

Few works have adhered strictly to either purely *concrète* or electronic principles from even the early 1950s, such compositions having been referred to more accurately as *tape recorder music*. The basic difference between the techniques of *musique concrète* and electronic music is the source of the sounds themselves. The purely electronic idiom, in which musical sounds are generated exclusively from electronic devices and recorded on magnetic tape, had its inception at the Studio for Electronic Music of the West German Radio in Cologne in 1951. The two main figures associated with this studio were its founder Dr. Herbert Eimert, a composer, musicologist, and critic who explored the aesthetics of electronic music and its technical similarities with *musique concrète*, and the ultraserialist Karlheinz Stockhausen, who became the director of the studio in 1963. While their earliest electronic experiments owed much to the serial principles of Webern, Eimert had already discussed systematically the aesthetics and techniques of twelve-note composition in the 1920s, further developing them in his *Lehrbuch der Zwölftontechnik* (1950) and his *Grundlagen der musikalischen Reihentechnic* (1963). These studies influenced Stockhausen and others in dealing with the possibilities inherent in the serial principle. Among Eimert's earliest important electronic experiments were his *Four Pieces* (1952–1953), in which electronically synthesized tones were recorded on tape.

In these early years, pure electronic sounds, or *sine tones* (i.e., tones without overtones), which are produced by an alternating electric current, or sine-wave oscillator, were the primordial elements of the new medium. The production, manipulation, and synthesis of these elements by means of electronic generators and the use of the magnetic tape have resulted in radical expansion and transformation of our musical sound world and may be seen as a fulfillment of Busoni's pre–World War I prophetic assertions regarding the need for an entirely scientific music. The new electronic technology has led to almost unlimited possibilities for the exploitation of the frequencies available within the range of the human ear and also expanded spectra of durations, timbres, and dynamics. From the outset, Eimert linked the serial concept to all levels of the process of electronic composition and to the aesthetic basis of the music:

> everything, to the last element of the single note, is subjected to serial permutation. . . . Examination of the material invariably leads one to serially ordered composition; no choice exists but the ordering of sinus-tones within a note. . . . A note may be said to "exist" where elements of time, pitch, and intensity meet; this fundamental process repeats itself at every level of the serial network which organizes the other partials related to it . . . electronic music is not "another"

music, but is serial music. . . . Today the physical magnification of a sound is known, quite apart from any musical, expressionist psychology, as exact scientific data.[6]

Although there are basic procedural connections between electronic and *concrète* techniques discussed by Eimert—including the superposition of sound, multiple tapes in canon, cutting, splicing, and reassembling of the tape, speed change, retrograde, ostinato produced by tape loop, durational values determined by tape length, dynamic change, multiple loudspeakers, etc.—his attitude has suggested a fundamental philosophical difference from the assumptions of *musique concrète,* the latter by its very connections with the world of natural sounds lying closer to human sources. In contrast, pure electronic serialism paved the way for use of the computer by the late 1950s and a greater removal from the human performer/interpreter. From the beginning, the electronic composer was able to generate the raw materials directly from the electronic sources and then to work directly with the tape.

The first complete electronic composition to be based entirely on pure (sine-wave) tones was Stockhausen's totally serialized *Elektronische Studie I* (summer of 1953), and the first such score to be published was his *Elektronische Studie II* (Universal Edition, 1954), both works produced at the West German Radio in Cologne. While the sine-wave generator served as the exclusive sound source for both pieces, the electronic sounds of *Studie II* were based on the separation of "white noise" into "coloured noise," rather than on the addition of sine-wave frequencies to "stationary sounds and note-mixtures."[7] Thus, the noise spectrum was introduced systematically into electronic composition.

The first step in the composition of *Studie II* was a tape recording of the raw materials comprising 193 tone mixtures, of which the individual frequencies were derived serially (mathematically).[8] Selection was then made from this "scale" of mixtures and recorded according to a notational, or graphic scheme (Ex. 18–1).[9] The degree of noise that was introduced into the composition was determined both by the use of harmonically unrelated partials of the overtone series and the density, or closeness in the adjacency of these superimposed sine-wave oscillations. Control of the ratios between the sine waves thereby permitted graded sound transformations along the continuum between notes and noise. In contrast to *Studie I,* the use of a reverberation chamber in *Studie II* contributed to the systematic introduction of noise into the composition by creating greater density through the distortion of the superimposed sine tones.

[6] Herbert Eimert, "What is Electronic Music?" *Die Reihe* 1 (1955; English trans. 1958): 8–9.

[7] See "Stockhausen's Notes on the Works," in Karl H. Wörner, *Stockhausen: Life and Work,* rev. and trans. Bill Hopkins (London: Faber and Faber, 1973), p. 33.

[8] See the preface to the score, p. IV, *Tabelle A.*

[9] For the realization of the piece, see the preface (see n.8 above).

EXAMPLE 18–1. Stockhausen, *Studie II*, graphic score notation, opening

Other parameters are also indicated in the three layers of the score. The volume envelopes, measured in decibels, are indicated at the bottom of the score in correspondence with each note mixture in the frequency/timbre section at the top. The duration of a note-mixture is indicated by tape length, measured in centimeters, in correspondence to the length of the pitch and volume lines. The piece opens with several successive and overlapping note-mixtures, the first with a range of five frequencies (690 to 2500 Hz) forming mixture number 67.[10]

By the mid-1950s, Stockhausen made further advances in the generation of electronic sounds and the exploitation of expanded timbral possibilities.[11] In *Gesang der Jünglinge* (1955–1956), he went beyond *Studie II* by filtering "white noise" more completely into different noise bands and continuing the filtration process until the single note reemerged. Through further superimposition of the noise bands, he was able to arrive at possibilities still more expanded for timbral invention. Another development in this work was the use of electrical impulse generators, in which the sequences of impulses were filtered to produce a still greater variety of sound mixtures. The increased importance of musical space in *Gesang* was manifested both in the juxtaposition of extreme sounds along the continuum between pitch and noise and their dimensional projection by means of five loudspeaker groups. The distribution of these groups around the listener was calculated to heighten spatial perception—i.e., by the use of the loudspeakers in a wide variety of combinations and in varying degrees of spatial movement.

The sound source is derived from a single untransformed boy's voice reading from the *Book of Daniel,* the sung sounds of which are combined with ones produced electronically including "vowel-type sounds, consonant noises" and "a scale of the intermediary forms of tone-mixtures."[12] Special means are employed for the interaction between the electronic and vocal spheres. Words such as "Blitze" (lightning) and "Scharen" (host) are divided into their syllabic components as well as into smaller consonant and vowel articulations, between which electronic sounds of varying lengths are interpolated, the longer interpolations disrupting the word meanings more than the shorter ones (Ex. 18–2).[13] Synthetic words may also be produced by the rearrangement of the word components themselves. More direct connections between vocal and electronic sources are created by the interchangeability of their functions; sine tones were used to represent vowels, noise bands for consonants, and electronic impulses for certain speech sounds produced by

---

[10] Ibid.

[11] See Wörner, *Stockhausen,* n.7, above, p. 127.

[12] See Stockhausen's commentary to the *Deutsche Gramophon Gesellschaft* recording (DGG 138 811).

[13] David Ernst, *The Evolution of Electronic Music* (New York: Schirmer Books, 1977), p. 89.

EXAMPLE 18–2. Stockhausen, *Gesang der Jünglinge,* rearrangement of word components and division by interpolated electronic sounds

Blitze ⟶ Blit___ ze ⟶ Blit___(electronic sounds)___ze

Scharen ⟶ Sc ___ ha ___ ren ⟶ Screnha
                                    haScren
                                    renScha
                                    renhaSc

Sc___(electronic sounds)___ha___(electronic sounds)___ren

Blitze = Lightning
Scharen = Hosts

the stoppage and sudden release of the breath for consonants such as "k," "p," and "t."[14] As summarized by Stockhausen, "Sung noises are individual 'organic' members of the more comprehensive 'synthetic' sound family. At certain points in the composition, the sung sounds become comprehensible words; at various degrees of comprehensibility of the word. Whenever speech momentarily emerges from the sound-symbols in the music, it is to praise God (Daniel 3, 'Song of the Men in the Fiery Furnace'). This work is the first to use the direction of the sounds and their movement in space as aspects of form." Thus, *Gesang* represents a historical landmark in the tendency toward the fusion of natural (in this case, live vocal) sounds and ones generated electronically, their juxtapositions, interactions, and electronic manipulations resulting in the dissolution of the traditional distinctions between pitch and noise, electronic and vocal sounds, sound and silence, vertical and linear projection, and other differences between aspects that had been so essential to the definition and perception of traditional structural organization.

Stockhausen's sound technology and aesthetics, stemming from his enriched experience with *Gesang der Jünglinge,* were expanded radically in other electronic works beginning in the late 1950s, from *Kontakte* (1959/1960), based on "contacts" between mobile sound forms in space and, in the second version, between the electronic and instrumental sounds, through *Mantra* (1970), for two pianists, taped shortwave sounds, two ring modulators, two oscillators, wood-blocks, antique symbols, and sound projection controlled manually, and other such works since the early 1970s. In all these works, Stockhausen explores the relation of known sounds with what he referred to as the "unknown world of electronic sounds," like "finding an apple, perhaps even an ashtray, on a distant star."[15]

---

[14] Ibid., p. 90.
[15] See Wörner, *Stockhausen,* n.7, above, p. 67.

Within two years of Stockhausen's *Gesang der Jünglinge,* the Austro-Hungarian composer György Ligeti also realized his *Glissandi* (1957) and *Artikulation* (1958) at the Cologne studio. In *Artikulation,* based on tape manipulations of sounds generated electronically and recorded on four-track tape, Ligeti exploited special techniques that initiated his own use of an invented "language." Many of Ligeti's techniques, including the invention of synthetic words produced by the rearrangement of the word components themselves and the use of additive electronic synthesis, were similar to those used by Stockhausen. In the complex form of this electronic work, Ligeti was to exploit the results of his research in phonetics, in which he attempted to establish correlations between speech and musical sound.[16] The gamut of forty-two basic sounds included sine tones, harmonic combinations formed above and subharmonic combinations formed below a fundamental pitch, and the use of noise. They were then grouped according to degree of sonic-relatedness and subjected to stages of splicing and electronic manipulation to form words and, ultimately, "languages." The musical structure is based on a process moving from abstract conversation to reorganization of the sonic details. The entire procedure is outlined in Ex. 18–3.[17] Thus, by the mid-1950s in Cologne, both *concrète* and electronic sources and techniques were integral to the field of electronic music.

ELECTRONIC STUDIO IN MILAN

While Stockhausen was expanding his electronic and natural sound spectra in the mid-1950s and Hermann Scherchen was experimenting with electronic filtration in his new studio at Gravesano in 1957, developments were also taking place at the *Studio di Fonologia Musicale* at the Italian Radio (RAI) in Milan, which was initiated in June 1955 by Luciano Berio (director until 1959) and Bruno Maderna. This studio, which drew the interest of such diverse international figures as Pousseur and Cage, also sparked activity in the public

EXAMPLE 18–3. György Ligeti, *Artikulation,* stages of tape splicing and electronic transformation as basis of an organic process

SOUNDS ──→	TEXTS ──→	WORDS ──→	LANGUAGES ──→	SENTENCES ──→	"ARTIKULATION"
sine tones; harmonic and subharmonic spectra; noise spectra; impulses; glissando forms.	ten categories derived from SOUNDS.	tape and electronic modifications of TEXTS.	tape and electronic modifications of WORDS.	splicing together of LANGUAGES.	tape and electronic modifications of SENTENCES.

[16] A somewhat more detailed discussion is provided by Ernst, *The Evolution of Electronic Music,* n.13, above, pp. 38–41.

[17] Ibid., p. 40.

performance of electronic music in a series of concerts directed by Berio and Maderna under the title *Incontri musicali,* which included, among others, Scherchen, Boulez, and Cage as the participants.[18] With the inception of the Milan studio came a series of works which, influenced by the Cologne studio, were concerned primarily with the development of timbral synthesis based on additive construction from simple elements. Motivated by a reaction to the distinction between *musique concrète* and "electronic music," a distinction coming partly from earlier "retarded-futuristic pioneerism," the Milan composers concerned themselves with "the approach itself in its purest conception," based on the social as well as musical significance of the compositional process.[19] What mattered was not the means of sound production and manipulation, but rather the improvisational expressivity, gesture, and perception of the sonorities and textures resulting from the interplay of synthesized sine tones, filtered noise, and live sounds.

Maderna appears to have been the first to have combined taped electronic music with solo live performance as early as 1952 in his *Musica su due dimensioni I* for flute, cymbals, and tape. Problems were to arise in such attempts to synchronize live sounds with the recorded electronic material, but Maderna's work foreshadowed the reconciliation between the polarized attitudes of the French and German composers over the issue of *concrète* and electronic principles. Interest in the fusion of natural and synthetically produced sounds for the development of a colorful, sonorous, and expressive new idiom was manifested in all of the products of the Milan studio, which included Berio's *Mutazioni* (1955), *Perspectives* (1957), *Thema—Ommaggio a Joyce* (1958), *Différences* (1958–1960), *Momenti* (1960), and *Visage* (1961); Maderna's *Notturno* (1956) and *Continuo* (1958); Nono's *Omaggio a Emilio Vedova* (1960); Boucourechliev's *Etude I* (1956) and *Text I* (1958); Pousseur's *Scambi* (1957); and Cage's *Fontana Mix* (1958–1959). Many of these works are characterized by a less severe, more ornate and lyrical style than the more rigid, serialized electronic conceptions of many Darmstadt products.

In his *Thema—Ommaggio a Joyce,* Berio expanded his expressive and sonic intentions further by use of an electronic elaboration of sound material derived from a portion of the spoken text, in several languages, of James Joyce's *Ulysses.* The complete text is presented in unaltered form, after which the timbre of the text is altered by means of electronic filtration of certain overtones. Other tape manipulations also contribute to the transformation of the original text sounds into new ones, thereby divorcing the sounds from meaning gradually as a means of creating his own expressive idiom in homage to Joyce.[20] Berio investigated the possibilities of using electronically

---

[18] A magazine of the same title, published between 1956 and 1960, was also initiated by this studio.

[19] Luciano Berio, "The Studio di Fonologia musicale," *Score* 15: (March 1956): 83.

[20] See Ernst, *The Evolution of Electronic Music,* n.13, above, pp. 4–5.

elaborated words more fully for both their expressive and sonic capabilities in *Questo vuol dire che,* for voices, instruments, and tape (1969).

As the most advanced electronic technical facility in Europe in the mid-1950s, the Milan studio was significant not only in contributing to the breakdown of the distinction between natural and synthesized electronic sounds by means of manipulations, transformations, and juxtapositions of diverse sound sources, but also in serving as a kind of intermediary among the relatively separate, isolated studios such as those in Cologne and Paris. However, the Milan studio was only part of the proliferation of electronic studios that were becoming involved increasingly in a larger international context of aesthetic and technical cross-fertilization.[21]

ELECTRONIC MUSIC IN PARIS, BRUSSELS, AND THE NETHERLANDS

Edgard Varèse began, in the 1940s, to explore the possibilities of juxtaposing taped sounds with live instrumental performance after his work with percussion and sirens, as in *Ionization* (1931), a landmark in his experiments with sounds as objects in spatial music. As early as 1933, while he was in Paris, Varèse was interested in developing a center for electric-instrument research, which did not come to fruition. He already had some experience with electronic instruments operated manually, having replaced the siren by the ondes martenot for the French première of *Amériques* in 1929 and having used two theremin parts in *Ecuatorial* (1932–1934). Only when he was given an Ampex tape recorder in 1953 could he begin to employ those techniques that would fulfill his interest in the radical transformation of sound.[22]

In 1954, about four years after his initial instrumental sketch of *Déserts,* Varèse visited Schaeffer's studio in Paris, where he worked on the tape part for the first version of the work. It was then presented as the first live stereo broadcast by the French Radio. *Déserts* is scored for two basic sound groups, the first consisting of instruments (winds, piano, and percussion), the changing relations of the juxtaposed sound masses which are intended to produce a sense of spatial movement and association with the human realm, the second consisting of two-channel stereo tape of electronically organized sound suggesting distance and nonhuman elements. For Varèse, the title implied not only the physical deserts of the earth and outer space, but also the deserts at the depths of the human mind, "that remote *inner* space no telescope can reach, where man is alone, a world of mystery and essential loneliness."

[21] Some of these studios included, in addition to those in Cologne, Paris, and Milan, the Columbia-Princeton Electronic Music Center in New York (1951), the Electronic Music Studio at the Japanese Radio in Tokyo (1953), Philips Research Laboratories in Eindhoven (1956), Studio für Elektronische Musik in Siemens and Munich (1957), Studio Eksperymentalne of the Polish Radio in Warsaw (1957), Studio de Musique Electronique in Brussels, and San Francisco Tape Music Center (1959, moved to Oakland in 1966).

[22] See Edgard Varèse, "The Liberation of Sound," *Perspectives of New Music* 5/1 (1966): 18.

The musical conception is removed from traditional sources entirely. The form of the work is determined contextually by the systematic juxtapositions of the two opposing sound masses—live instrumental and electronic. The taped organized sound (OS) is interpolated at three points (end of m. 82, middle of m. 224, and end of m. 263), so the two basic sonic planes alternate, but without ever overlapping, at ever-shorter distances and diminishing textures in an unbroken continuum.

The formal concept, based on these calculated temporal and textural relations between the alternating blocks, is a continuation of the assumptions manifested in the interactions of metal and wood sounds in *Ionization.* However, *Déserts* differs from the latter both in its use of the taped sound source and in its exploitation of the principle of nonrepetition, which produces an atonal and athematic work.[23] Varèse stated that "although the intervals between the pitches determine the constantly changing and contrasted volumes and planes, they are not based on any fixed set of intervals such as a scale, a series, or any existing principle of musical measurement."[24] Here, the timbral shapes and the disposition of the individual sound events, related integrally, appear to be the sole basis of structural development. Thus, the tape medium, as a new source of timbral differentiation, serves an important role in the articulation of the formal process. At the same time, the electronic tape figures prominently in Varèse's underlying philosophy of the work, in which man is isolated within a hostile environment. Other composers have also exploited the electronic medium as an expression of the modern conflict between man and machine.

Iannis Xenakis was also drawn to the Paris studio in the 1950s, his *Diamorphoses* (1957; revised 1968) foreshadowing the expanded timbral resources and electronic manipulations of Varèse's *Poème Électronique* (1958). Xenakis used tape transposition, reversal, and filtering to modify the *concrète* sources derived from jets, earthquakes, colliding railroad cars, and bells, the latter of which were modified into glissandi electronically. The same processes were used to transform the natural sound sources in his *Concret P-H* (1958), performed at the pavilion of the Philips Radio Corporation at the 1958 Brussels World Fair. His own participation in the designing of the pavilion with the French architect Le Corbusier reveals his architectural and mathematical inclinations so basic to the aesthetic principles underlying the organization of his musical sound masses.[25]

In *Poème Électronique* (1958), Varèse went still further in expanding,

[23] Arnold Whittall, "Varèse and Organic Athematicism," *Music Review* 28/4 (November 1967): 311.

[24] Edgard Varèse, "Electronic Music," Lecture presented at "A Sunday Afternoon of Contemporary Music, New York, November 9, 1958" (Reprint from Wolcott & Associates, Public Relations Counsel, New York). A copy is in the New York Public Library Clipping File on Varèse.

[25] Xenakis also wrote a significant essay in connection with this event, entitled "Le Corbusier's 'Elektronisches Gedicht' und der Philips Pavillion," *Gravesaner Blätter* 9 (1957): 43.

transforming, and juxtaposing electronic and *concrète* elements as a means of liberating sound from the tempered scale and mechanical (instrumental) sources. The work was also performed at the Philips pavilion in 1958 after it was realized at the Philips studio at Eindhoven on three-channel tape. The pavilion resembled a three-peaked circus tent externally, while simulating "the shape of a cow's stomach" internally. Along the architectural curves were placed over 400 loudspeakers grouped in what he called sound routes, the sonic arcs of which were accompanied by lighting and slide projections, though no special synchronization of these multimedia sources was intended. Mixed and transposed sine waves were produced by the electronic oscillator and generated as combined with electronically treated natural sounds (including feet and finger tapping, voices, etc.), the most recognizable of which are the female voice, male chorus, gong, bell, organ, piano, and percussion, some remaining in their original form, others modified electronically.[26] Filters, loops, and reverberation units, which comprise two of the three channels, were used for mixing, separating, and transforming the contrasting sound components. An elaborate network was set up (Ex. 18–4), in which the 3-track taped sounds were distributed by way of amplifiers and telephone relays through the loudspeakers, a 15-track control tape regulating the sound paths and the multiple visual sources.[27]

The cumulative form of the work is determined primarily by the

EXAMPLE 18–4. Varèse, *Poème Électronique,* control tape regulating sound paths and multiple visual sources

[26] Despite the natural sources, Varèse rejected the term *musique concrète* as incompatible with his own compositional assumptions.

[27] See Ernst, *The Evolution of Electronic Music,* n.13, above, p. 42.

temporal rate of sonic interaction, resulting in varying degrees of spatial density as well. Varèse stated that "one of the most valuable possibilities that electronics has added to musical composition . . . is that of metric simultaneity. My music being based on unrelated sound masses, I have long felt the need and anticipated the effect of having them move simultaneously at different speeds."[28] At the same time, recurrent motivic fragments contribute to what may be perceived as a two-part form, in which each part is initiated similarly by a gong and cadenced by a siren. However, the basic formal conception is that of contrast and accumulation rather than recapitulation and is determined for the most part by the direction of the sound movement, in which the vocal and organ passages are reserved for the latter half of the work. Although a program was not intended, Varèse suggested an expression of "tragedy—and inquisition," which is evident in the vocal excerpts especially. This mood is further supported by the accumulation of tension resulting from the rate of interaction and length of the sonic events. This cumulative process culminates in the gradual shortening of an organ passage to two chords, leading to an intensification in the final upward surge of the siren.[29] Thus, radical expansion of timbral and metric/rhythmic spectra by means of electronic generation and manipulation permitted Varèse a greater freedom in the realization of spatial form according to his own personal expressive conception.

As early as 1952, Henk Badings was already working with tape pieces for the Nederlandsche Radi Unie at Hilversum, though the electronic facilities were more primitive than those in Cologne. The first result was his radio opera *Orestes* (1954), which employed electronic sound generators, filters, and tape techniques, including dramatic changes of tape speed for a male chorus and instrumental sections. Other manipulations resulted in the expansion of possibilities in pitch, rhythm, and timbre. A more important development took place at the Philips branch at Eindhoven in 1957, where Badings was able to advance his electronic techniques prior to Varèse's work on *Poème Électronique* at this studio. In his *Genese* (1958), Badings employed five oscillators as the basis for the purely electronic sources, but his approach was somewhat conventional in the formal organization of the sound sources. From the early 1960s, Badings moved toward greater mixing of electronic and instrumental sources.

TAPE-RECORDER MUSIC, SYNTHESIZERS, AND COMPUTERS IN THE UNITED STATES

In the late 1950s, Vladimir Ussachevsky and Otto Luening at Columbia University, in collaboration with Milton Babbitt and Roger Sessions at

---

[28] "Autobiographical Remarks (dedicated to the memory of Ferruccio Busoni), from a Talk given at Princeton, September 4, 1959," in the New York Public Library Clipping File on Varèse, pp. 8–9.

[29] Anne Florence Parks, "Freedom, Form, and Process in Varèse (Ph.d. dissertation, Cornell University, 1974), p. 394.

Princeton, established the *Columbia-Princeton Electronic Music Center*. In contrast with the first realizations at the Paris and Cologne studios, the tendency in New York was toward combination of taped pure electronic and *musique concrète* sounds from the beginning, so the musical results were to be termed *tape-recorder* music more appropriately. Prior to his awareness of the pioneering *concrète* and electronic experiments developed separately at the Paris and Cologne studios, Ussachevsky had already embarked in 1951 on the first major tape experiments in the United States and, in collaboration with Luening beginning in 1952, combined both live and electronic sources involving the transformation of natural sounds (especially instrumental) rather than electronic synthesis. These efforts were preceded by some experiments with tape that were begun in 1948 in New York by Louis and Bebe Barron. From 1951 to 1953, John Cage drew together several composers, including Earle Brown, Morton Feldman, David Tudor, and Christian Wolff, at the Barron studio for further development of what was to be referred to as *Music for Magnetic Tape*. This group was more radical in its interest in producing new sounds, often tending toward aleatoric results unlike Ussachevsky and Luening, who remained closer to the traditional sound sources and the preservation of their musical ordering on tape.[30]

Ussachevsky's first set of taped *concrète* pieces, produced between 1951 and 1952, were *Transposition, Experiment, Reverberation, Composition,* and *Underwater Valse,* derived entirely from the sounds of the piano. These titles indicate the tape techniques used in the transformation and musical organization of the original sounds, including speed changes for pitch and duration modification, repetition by use of echo devices, etc., techniques of which were developed further in his *Sonic Contours* (1952) derived from piano and vocal sources. In *Incantation* (1952), by both Ussachevsky and Luening, the recorded sound sources were expanded for the first time to flute, clarinet, voice, bell, and gong. The first public concert of their tape music occurred on October 28, 1952, at the home of Henry Cowell at Woodstock, New York, a concert attended by Luciano Berio. Included on the program were Ussachevsky's *Sonic Contours* and Luenings *Invention in 12 Notes, Low Speed,* and *Fantasy in Space*. In subsequent compositions, they began to add prepared tape to the recorded instrumental materials.

Through a grant from the Rockefeller Foundation in the mid-1950s, both composers were able to investigate various international studios, including those in Paris, Cologne, and Milan as well as Canada and the United States. While progress in the United States lagged behind that in Europe generally, they had observed a significant development at the University of Illinois, where Lejaren Hiller and Leonard Isaacson were exploring possible musical applications of the computer prior to the commercial availability of electronic synthesizers. Hiller and Isaacson programmed a table of numbers,

---

[30] For a more detailed history of the developments of these two independent early groups in New York, see Manning, *Electronic and Computer Music,* n.1, pp. 86–88.

which were then applied to pitch, duration, and orchestration to produce the first important work programmed digitally, the *Illiac Suite for String Quartet* (1955–1956), named after the computer.[31] The function of the computer in this early example was to generate the data for an otherwise traditional score, the sounds of which were generated by the string quartet rather than an electronic source. Nevertheless, the computer, which no longer necessitated tape splicing and other manipulations associated with electronic techniques, served to remove the compositional process further from human sources. Similar approaches followed in Paris, England, and the Netherlands. However, the first true computer music, in which the computer itself was to serve as the sound source by means of digital-to-analog conversion (DAC), was permitted first by research at the Bell Telephone Laboratories in Murray Hill, New Jersey, in 1957.[32] These techniques were developed further in 1964 by Hubert Howe and Godfrey Winham at Princeton University, John Chowning at Stanford University, and at the more recently developed studio in Stockholm and elsewhere. In 1969, Hiller and Cage used computer-generated and electronically processed sounds in *HPSCHD* for one to seven harpsichords and one to fifty-one computer-generated tapes. Some of the most recent developments are based on *hybrid systems,* in which computers are used to control synthesizers.[33] Others contributing to the development of the Illinois studio were the European Herbert Brün, whose interest in phonetics appears to have stemmed from his earlier work at the Cologne studio, and Kenneth Louis Gaburo, who showed similar synthetic speech influences of Berio.[34]

Based on the recommendation of Ussachevsky and Luening in the mid-1950s for financial support to develop electronic music in the United States, in the universities most beneficially, the Radio Corporation of America (RCA) developed an electronic sound synthesizer, and this led to its acquisition as the basis of the newly formed Columbia-Princeton Electronic Music Center in 1958. The synthesizer can generate, modify, and order sound by purely electronic means. One of its main advantages was that, after Robert Moog developed the principle of voltage control in 1964, all aspects of the sounds generated electronically—frequency, envelope (growth and decay characteristics), amplitude, timbre, reverberation, modulation, etc.—could be controlled independently by automatic devices and manipulated by control dials, keyboards, and other such means. These developments eliminated the need for tape cutting and splicing—i.e., any tape reassemblage based on

[31] For a description of the work and its compositional procedures, see Lejaren Hiller and Leonard Isaacson, *Experimental Music: Composition with an Electronic Computer* (New York: McGraw-Hill Book Company, 1959).

[32] See Ernst, *The Evolution of Electronic Music,* n.13, above, p. 59, for a technical discussion of this process.

[33] Ibid., p. 60.

[34] See Manning, *Electronic and Computer Music,* n.1, pp. 181–182.

hand techniques, an advantage the synthesizer had in common with the computer.

Among the first to work with the new facilities at the Columbia-Princeton studio were the Argentinian Mario Davidovsky (present director of the Columbia studio) and Turkish Bülent Arel. Electronic pieces of both composers were performed at the first concerts of the Center, given on May 9 and 10, 1961, at the McMillin Theater at Columbia University, along with those of Ussachevsky, Luening, Babbitt, and Halim El-Dabh. In his works after *Electronic Study No. 1* (1960), Davidovsky has shown a continuing inclination towards combining recorded electronic sounds with live instruments, among his most important products of which are his set of *Synchronisms, No. 1* (1962) for flute and tape, *No. 2* (1964) for flute, clarinet, violin, cello, and tape, *No. 3* (1964) for cello and tape, *No. 4* (1966) for chorus and tape, *No. 5* (1969) for percussion and tape, *No. 6* (1970) for piano and tape, *No. 7* (1974) for orchestra and tape, and *No. 8* (1974) for wind quintet and tape. The first three are characterized primarily by juxtaposition of the contrasting live and electronic materials, while the last three tend toward free mixture and fusion of these sonic sources. In these works, Davidovsky exploits all possible electronic techniques to produce an extraordinary range of sonic possibilities and textural combinations, so that true instrumental virtuosity is required for producing sonic and timbral flexibility in the interactions of the live and electronic resources.

Synchronism No. 1 is exemplary of such wide contrasts of articulations, dynamics, and registers both within the sonic range and technique of the flute and within the gamut of the electronic sounds, which range from some pitched elements to noise. Both textural spheres always remain distinct and transparent even in the sectional overlapping of the two spectra, because of the sonic and rhythmic divergency between them. The main difficulty in the compositional process and in the performance of the work was to synchronize both rhythm and pitch. Vertical control of the timing between flute and tape is maintained in the overlapping shorter sections, while in the longer overlapping ones, a degree of vertical flexibility is introduced to accommodate the inevitable time discrepancies that result between the live performer and the constant speed of the tape recorder.[35] The rate of figural and textural activity and of interaction (relative lengths of sections) between the flute and tape as well as the changing degrees of density appear to be the basic structural determinants, the form tending to peak at the fourth of the five taped sections in combination with the longest and freest flute passage (Ex. 18–5). While the work is athematic, each section appears to be organized internally by a specific motivic gesture and its variants, which are defined by contour, timbre, and rhythmic direction.

As a mathematician and composer, Babbitt's interest in working with the electronic equipment at the Center since the late 1950s has been motivated

---

[35] Davidovsky, program note to the Nonesuch recording H–71289 (stereo).

EXAMPLE 18–5. Davidovsky, *Synchronism No. 1,* for flute and tape, formal peak at electronic Section 4, with longest and freest flute passage

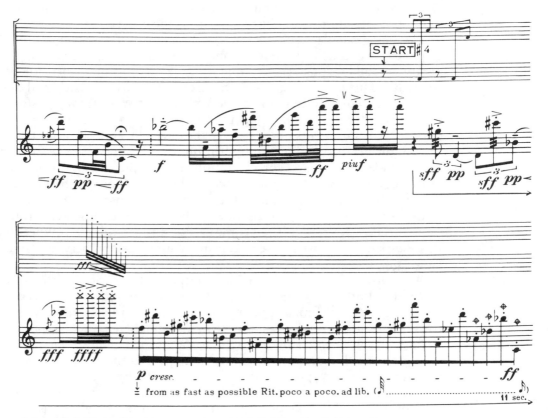

primarily by his inclination toward serialized control of all aspects of the musical structure. He was to work extensively with the special Mark II RCA Synthesizer, the most advanced electronic instrument of the period, after it was given to the Center in the late 1950s by its builders Herbert Belar and Harry Olsen. With this electronic instrument, Babbitt's ongoing concerns with formal and temporal organization, based on rate of timbral and textural change, were now able to be realized more precisely. *Composition for Synthesizer* (1961) and the more complex *Ensembles for Synthesizer* (1962–1964), both for four-track tape, represent two of his earliest pieces synthesized entirely, and in which the new synthesizer facilitated the difficult task of reproducing instrumental (piano and woodwind) timbres electronically and controlling them in more complex textures.

Babbitt also combined live soprano and tape in several works, including *Vision and Prayer* (1961), text by Dylan Thomas, *Philomel* (1963–1964), poem by Hollander on the *Metamorphoses* of Ovid, and *Phenomena* (1974).

These works reveal varying degrees of distinction and integration of the vocal and electronic materials. In *Vision,* there is no attempt to integrate the intact text and conventional timbral character of the voice with the instrumental-like electronic sounds. Babbitt's concern is focused rather on the possibilities of producing calculated correspondences, in terms of duration, tempo, length of phrases, stanzaic organization, and large-scale form, between the musical parameters and formalized, arithmetically expanding and contracting syllabic structure of the poetic text. However, a tendency toward vocal and electronic integration is manifested in *Philomel,* where certain timbral transformations of the recorded vocal sounds, as permitted by the synthesizer, are necessary due to the requirements of the text. In the Greek legend, the gods take pity on the tongueless maiden by turning her into a nightingale. While the live vocal part includes singing and sprechstimme in recitative and aria styles, recorded vocal segments as well as the synthesized sounds (ranging from the distinct pitches of simulated instrumental sonorities to percussive sounds and filtered noise) are modified by means of reverberation and other electronic techniques. The resources of the synthesizer and the flexible live vocal styles in this work are essential in the transformational flow between music and language.

Others who have also made important use of the facilities at the Columbia-Princeton Center in widely varying and individual ways since the 1960s were Ilhan Mimaroglu, who was concerned primarily with the electronic generation of *concrète* rather than instrumental sounds, Andrés Lewin-Richter, Jacob Druckman, and Charles Wuorinen, whose *Time's Encomium* (1969) reveals, like Babbitt's works, an interest in the electronic synthesis of varied instrumental (piano, harpsichord, and organ) timbres and the achievement of control over complex temporal and rhythmic relations by means of the synthesizer. The proportional structural relations on all levels of the work are derived from the equal-tempered intervallic ratios of the basic twelve-note set, a basic characteristic of the RCA synthesizer. Here, "everything depends on the absolute, not the seeming, length of events and sections. Being electronic, *Time's Encomium* has no inflective dimension."[36] Thus, since the early 1960s, the RCA synthesizer has provided expanded possibilities for the realization of complex structural relations, increased serial control over the various parameters, and more complex structural interrelations of timbre and sonic events.

In addition to the developments at the Columbia-Princeton Center and at the University of Illinois, many other studios have emerged throughout the United States. Gordon Mumma and Robert Ashley established a private *Cooperative Studio for Electronic Music* in Ann Arbor, Michigan, as early as 1958. The private studio at the San Francisco Tape Music Center (SFTMC) was established in 1959 under the direction of Ramon Sender and Morton Subotnik, the facilities of which were moved to Oakland

[36] See Charles Wuorinen, note to the Nonesuch recording H—71225 (stereo).

in 1966. At Stony Point, New York, the collaboration of John Cage and David Tudor in the 1960s was significant particularly in the development of live electronic music, their work influencing that of the Sonic Arts Union established by Mumma and others in 1966. In the last two decades, studios have been proliferating at various universities and colleges.

While many electronic composers have continued to work along the aesthetic and technical lines established at the Columbia-Princeton and Illinois studios originally, others have developed individual approaches to the composition of electronic and computer music. A variety of aesthetics, styles, and techniques is evident among the seven winners of the 1974 International Electronic Music Competition, held by the League of Composers-International Society for Contemporary Music, U.S. Section.[37] For instance, Menachem Zur's *Chants, for Magnetic Tape* (1974) is based on a fusion of Gregorian-chant style and serial principles, while Paul Lansky's *Mild und leise* (1973/1974) uses the IBM 360/91 computer to compose and synthesize motivic material from Wagner's *Tristan*. Joel Gressel's *Points in Time,* a title derived from a cliché used at the United States Senate Watergate Hearings, is based on principles of time similar to those used by Wuorinen in his *Time's Encomium.* Overlapping and consecutive rhythmic blocks are determined by the mathematical ratios of the equal-tempered twelve-tone scale, producing rhythmically accelerating or decelerating patterns "approximating the sound pattern made by a freely bouncing ping-pong ball." At certain points these patterns converge and, together with changing timbral combinations, serve to organize the large-scale structure. Furthermore, according to the composer, "Pitches are derived from a set (F–F♯–C–B–A–D♯–E–G–G♯–D–C♯–A♮), the properties of which eventuate in tritone-related structures and long-term associations of pitch-class tetrachords (e.g., F–F♯–C–B), trichords (D♯–E–G), and dyads." Thus, mathematical calculation, the contrapuntal and temporal accuracy of which relies on the use of the computer, is basic to the integration of the various parameters and structural levels of the composition.

Continued interest in either the electronic simulation of instrumental sounds or the combination of live instruments with tape is demonstrated in Donald Erb's preoccupation beginning in the 1960s with experiments exploring the sonic and interactive possibilities of live instruments and tape, as in his *Fission* (1968), for saxophone, piano, tape, dancers, and lighting, *In No Strange Land* (1968), for trombone, string bass, and tape, and *Souvenir* (1970), for instruments, tape, and lighting. Morton Subotnik, founder and director of the San Francisco Tape Music Center from 1961 to 1966, often employs serial procedures, which are realized with the Buchla Synthesizer. In such mixed-media works as his *Laminations* (1970), for instrumental ensemble and tape, the interplay of corresponding sonorities is achieved by means of special

[37] These works, with commentary by the composers, are recorded on Columbia-Odyssey Y 34139.

instrumental (e.g., flutter tonguing and muting) and electronic (e.g., modulating and filtering) techniques.

Three of the composers who have worked with the modern electronic facilities at the University of Texas at Austin in the 1970s and 1980s are Karl Korte, Barton McLean, and Russell Pinkston. Korte, in his *Remembrances* (1971), written for the flutist Samuel Baron, exploits the wide range of timbral and expressive possibilities of the alto flute, flute, and piccolo, respectively, in the three sections of the piece, in combination with taped electronic sounds. Tempered pitches generated electronically form the basis of the underlying twelve-tone series, the intervallic subsets often producing a sense of tonal priority. From the beginning, synthesized bell-like sounds produced by ring modulation interact with the flute's more sustained line to produce a wide spectrum of sonic possibilities. These sonorities then interact with the improvisatory alto flute line, which elides with the ending of the series, the initially slow repeated notes of the solo developing into narrow-ranged glissandi, microtonal inflections, and embellishing flutter-tongue techniques as part of the gradual expansion of instrumental color. Increasingly rapid gestures in both flute and tape, based on the continual addition of new timbres in the latter, result in more complex contrapuntal and rhythmic interactions between the two spheres. While flute and tape generally remain distinct, they are linked by common serialized intervallic structures, of which tritones and larger octatonic segments are often prominent.

Barton McLean has performed extensively throughout the United States and Europe in collaboration with Priscilla McLean as part of a husband-wife electroacoustic duo called *The McLean Mix*. Their music retains classical structures and stylistic elements, but expands them by means of extended *musique concrète* techniques and performance virtuosity. Among their most recent works, the evocative set of five pieces *In Wilderness Is the Preservation of the World* often uses performance-gestural modes rather than specific pitch content. The work includes material for soprano, chorus, amplified bicycle wheel, digital electronics, percussion and woodwind instruments, audience singing, and various animal, bird, and other sounds of the wilderness on tape. Much use is made of other media, including multiple slide projections, lighting effects, and special light-performance patterns, which form intricate designs behind a screen while slides are projected on the front. The first composition in which Priscilla McLean exploits wilderness sounds directly is *Beneath the Horizon I* (1978) for tuba quartet and taped whale ensemble, based on *controlled improvisation*.

Barton McLean's *Dimensions I* (1977), for violin and tape, the first piece of his set of *Dimensions* based on various types of relations between instrument and tape part, bears certain external similarities to Davidowsky's *Synchronisms*. Similarly, McLean has permitted total vertical freedom between the improvisatory violin part and more mechanical tape, except at the beginnings and endings of passages or sections, where these spheres, which are polarized stylistically, are synchronized by special cues. In Ex. 18–6, "the violin part, enclosed in solid boxes, is coordinated to the two tape channels, enclosed in dotted lines, by means of arrows." Most striking in the generation

EXAMPLE 18-6. Barton McLean, *Dimensions I*, performance score, Section 5, coordination of violin part and two tape channels

of the overall structure is the changing degree of distinction and integration of violin and tape. One of the means by which McLean achieves sonic integration is through the addition of recorded violin sounds into the synthesized material.

McLean conceived of the work as a conflict between the human being and the modern machine. Throughout most of the work, this attitude is manifested in the expressive styles of the performer, which vary from lyrical disposition to savage virtuosity, and the relentless and overwhelming power of the taped mechanical material. Increasing excitement in the cumulative form is based on a move from stylistic distinction to stylistic integration, as the human soloist struggles increasingly with the electronic machine. At the end, the violin drops out as the synthesizer melody takes over and finally winds down. The formal shape of this conflict is reflected on local structural levels of the work. A succession of related gestures is established by the performer from the outset. A three-page violin cadenza, which moves from improvisatory calm to frenzied excitement before the tape enters, is made up of a series of rhythmically free phrases in an unbarred score. Each phrase, which reflects the overall form, outlines an asymmetrical arch that peaks toward its cadence, and each phrase is longer and more agitated than the previous one. At the end of the cadenza, the violin plays behind the bridge to produce a sonic transition to the more mechanical sonorities of the synthesized tape, the mechanical rhythmic fragments of which are also anticipated by the violin. After the central slow section, based on extreme differentiation between violin and soft electronic sounds, the cadenza returns. This time, however, the tape continues with an ever-widening spectrum of synthesized timbres, which eventually take over in the struggle.

Despite the distinction between sonic and stylistic spheres, the entire work is integrated by means of common intervallic sets. Interval 5/7 (perfect fourths/fifths) and tritones are the primary intervallic sources, their combinations resulting in larger cyclic-interval collections forming nonserialized sets. The first explicit manifestation of such an intervallic combination (0–1–6–7 tetrachord, F#–G–C–C#) occurs as the first four notes (F#–C/G–C#) of a lyrical phrase (Ex. 18–7, line 3), one of the gaps (G–C#) of which is filled in chromatically by a cyclic-interval-1 tetrachord, A–A#–B–C. The opening gesture begins with a three-note (0–1–[ ]–7) segment, A–B♭–E♭–[ ], the "white-key" component (A) of which is extended by an unordered 5/7 segment, C–G–D–[A]–E–B. Similarly unordered cyclic-interval extensions of the 0–1–6–7 set are basic to the variation process of the next two phrases. The second phrase unfolds two unordered interval-1/11 (minor-second/ major-seventh) segments, G–G♭–A♭ and D♭–C–D, each of which is also based on a chromatic filling in that gives us G♭–G–A♭ and C–D♭–D. The latter three-note segment is the tritone transposition of the first, so the presence of two 0–1–6–7 tetrachords (C–D♭–G♭–G and D♭–D–G–A♭) is implied in the combined segments. An interval expansion of the 0–1–6–7 tetrachord occurs in the third phrase: two interval-5/7 segments (G–C–F and C#–F#–B) a tritone apart imply the presence of C–C#–F#–G and B–C–F–F#. Constant registral reinterpretations and permutations of the 0–1–6–7

EXAMPLE 18-7. Barton McLean, *Dimensions I*, opening, arch-shaped phrases of violin cadenza, structural occurrences of unordered transpositions of 0–1–6–7 tetrachord, with cyclic-interval fillings and extensions

set appear as cadential punctuations, as in the soaring figures toward the center of the cadenza. As part of the cumulative process, 0–1–6–7 transpositions are combined to form larger octatonic collections. In the descending portions of the most rapid scale passages (marked "AFAP"), octatonic segment G–F–E–D–C♯ is completed by C♯–B–A♯–G♯–G to give us G–F–E–D–C♯–B–A♯–G♯–G, which implies the presence of two 0–1–6–7 tetrachords, D–C♯–G♯–G and F–E–B–A♯. In the taped sections (see Ex. 18–6), 0–1–6–7 transpositions appear in tritone and interval-5/7 partitions, as at the opening of Section 5, tape a: for instance, G♯–D♯/A–D (upper staff) is followed by [ ]–D♯–G♯–A and [ ]–F♯–B–C, which form a larger octatonic segment together, D–D♯–[ ]–F♯–G♯–A–B–C. Thus, divergent instrumental and electronically processed sonorities are absorbed into an integrated context by means of common intervallic sets, rhythmic configurations, and intermediary recorded violin timbres.

To some extent, Pinkston also follows the tradition of the early Columbia-Princeton products, especially those of his former teacher, Davidovsky. In certain respects, Pinkston's *Quartet* for four horns with tape (1978) owes much to Davidowsky, in the tight interlocking of electronic and acoustic sounds, and the basic concept of using the electronic medium to "extend" and expand the timbral capabilities of the acoustic instruments. This concern is suggested in part by the composer's indication: "Speakers should be placed on each side of the performers—at an equal distance and preferably close enough to provide a feeling of ensemble between horns and tape while still allowing sufficient space for good stereo." However, in his attempt to create a quasi-concerto for horns and electronic orchestra in this piece, in which he wanted a massive, weighty sound from the horns and a truly symphonic texture from the tape, the piece is antithetical in every respect to the ascetic, chamber-music-like style in most of Davidowsky's *Synchronisms*. Pinkston conceived the form as being essentially symmetrical after the slow introduction (i.e., Introduction, A, B, A′, Coda), the A′ section of which is a nonliteral retrograde of the A section. As in the overall process of McLean's *Dimension I,* where the lyrical violin style is transformed into the more savage and mechanical style of the tape, the horns and tape in the *Quartet* switch roles during the A′ section. Another unifying feature of the piece, in addition to the interlocking of electronic and acoustic sounds, is the extensive use of octatonic segments.

DIRECTIONS FOR FUTURE ELECTRONIC RESEARCH AND COMPOSITION

With advances in electronic and computer technology, the possibilities for both control and freedom as well as expansion of the musical sound world seems almost unlimited: from simulation of existing instrumental and vocal sounds through an infinite number of stages of transformation into varied types of invented musical sounds within the entire range of human perception. Such technological possibilities have not yet been exhausted as the basis of musical composition, nor does it seem likely that they ever will be. While some composers have not been inclined toward the electronic sound medium, others have continued to experiment with it at studios throughout the world. Significant activity in electronic music research is currently taking place in both private and public educational institutions. Among them are the international research centers at Utrecht, Stanford, MIT, and IRCAM (*Institut de Recherche et Coordination Acoustique/Musique*), directed by Boulez in Paris. The direction the contemporary composer must take when confronted with the new possibilities of both sonic production and musical order is perhaps one of the most pressing aesthetic issues.

SUGGESTED READINGS

LUCIANO BERIO.   *"The Studio di Fonologia Musicale," The Score* 15 (March 1956): 83.

HERBERT EIMERT.   "What is Electronic Music?" *Die Reihe* 1 (Vienna: Universal Edition A. G., 1955; Eng. ed., Bryn Mawr, PA: Theodore Presser, 1958): 1–10.

DAVID ERNST.   *The Evolution of Electronic Music* (New York: Schirmer Books, 1977).

LEJAREN HILLER AND LEONARD ISAACSON.   *Experimental Music: Composition with an Electronic Computer* (New York: McGraw-Hill Book Company, 1959).

PETER MANNING.   *Electronic and Computer Music* (Oxford: Clarendon Press, 1987).

ANNE FLORENCE PARKS.   "Freedom, Form, and Process in Varèse" (Ph.D. dissertation, Cornell University, 1974).

PIERRE SCHAEFFER.   *A la recherche d'une musique concrète* (Paris: Éditions du Seuil, 1952).

———.   *Traité des objets musicaux* (Paris: Éditions du Seuil, 1966).

EDGARD VARÈSE.   "Autobiographical Remarks (dedicated to the memory of Ferruccio Busoni), from a Talk given at Princeton, September 4, 1959," in the *New York Public Library Clipping File on Varèse,* pp. 8–9.

———.   "Electronic Music," Lecture presented at "A Sunday Afternoon of Contemporary Music, New York, November 9, 1958" (Reprint from Wolcott & Associates, Public Relations Counsel, New York). A copy is in the New York Public Library Clipping File on Varèse.

———.   "The Liberation of Sound," *Perspectives of New Music* 5/1 (1966): 11–19.

ARNOLD WHITTALL.   "Varèse and Organic Athematicism," *Music Review* 28/4 (November 1967): 311–315.

KARL H. WÖRNER.   *Stockhausen: Life and Work,* rev. and trans. Bill Hopkins (London: Faber and Faber, 1973).

IANNIS XENAKIS.   "Le Corbusier's 'Elektronisches Gedicht' und der Philips Pavillion," *Gravesaner Blätter* 9 (1957): 43.

19 Chance, improvisation, open form, and minimalism

Two opposing compositional tendencies, which stem from the early twentieth century, had reached their most intensive stage of polarization in the 1950s. With the move toward integral serialism, which was founded upon the precepts of total composer control over all aspects of the musical edifice, a reaction also led many of the same composers to consider the possibility of relinquishing rational control over both the generation and organization of the musical events. The historical factors that led to this schism are manifold. There has always been some degree of rhythmic, harmonic, and formal freedom for both the composer and the performer throughout earlier centuries, as manifested in the use of rubato or *ad libitum* indications, fermatas and grand pauses, improvisation in cadenza-like passages, realization of figured bass, and even the elimination of the barline resulting in metric freedom, as in keyboard fantasias of C. P. E. Bach.

Since the early twentieth century, attempts to free the performer from the exactness dictated by conventional notation were manifested in connection with various aspects of performance in otherwise fixed compositions. The use of tone clusters and the elimination of the barline in works of Ives and Cowell resulted in both harmonic and rhythmic indeterminacy, while the use of *sprechstimme* permitted a degree of pitch and harmonic indeterminacy in works of Schoenberg and others. More radical possibilities in terms of composer control over structural unification were implied already in the early futurist experiments with collages of noise drawn from nontempered natural and mechanical sources. However, it was only after World War II, with the emergence of a more clearly defined philosophical basis, that a decisive shift occurred from fixed composition to spontaneous performance (or realization). Thus, several distinctions may be observed in the approach to aleatoric (or chance) composition. These include the elimination of rational composer control over content and/or form in producing a composition that is nevertheless fixed as far as the performer is concerned, use of special indications and notation (either conventional or newly invented) leading to a shift toward performer determination in the generation and ordering of events, and the elimination of both composer and performer control leading to randomness and indeterminacy.

PIONEERS OF CHANCE OPERATIONS IN THE UNITED STATES: IVES, COWELL, AND CAGE

The first decisive steps toward full realization of chance operations were taken by the American composer John Cage (b. 1912), who came to his first entirely aleatoric compositions in the early 1950s through a series of evolutionary stages in his technical and philosophical development. Among his first compositions to be conceived in terms of chance operations was his *Music of Changes* for piano (1951). This tendency was foreshadowed in his earliest works, in which he continued along certain lines of both Ives and Cowell. The latter two experimented with percussive sonorities and nontempered pitches, but it was Ives who had first thought in terms of introducing an element of choice or chance, as indicated in his score commentaries and in the notation itself. Occasional use of unrealizable notation led the performer to introduce his own improvisations. Ives' *Hallowe'en* (1906), for string quartet and piano with drum *ad libitum,* permits either three or four repeats of the piece in an indeterminate tempo to be played "as fast as possible without disabling any player or instrument." In *Scherzo: Over the Pavements,* for winds, percussion, and piano, a cadenza is provided "to play or not to play." Cowell also began to introduce the possibility of choice and indeterminacy in the 1930s. His *String Quartet No. 3 "Mosaic"* (1934) is comprised of fragments to be organized by the performers, and also includes certain flexible notations resulting in chance and complete improvisation.

As early as the 1930s and 1940s, Cage began to experiment with diverse approaches to composition, including a tendency toward both pitch serialization and mathematical rhythmic formulation, extensive use of percussion instruments, and the invention of new sonorities for piano, which led to the breakdown in the distinction between pitched and nonpitched elements. He also began to use electrically produced sounds and manipulations of phonograph recordings in such works as *Imaginary Landscape No. 3* (1942). In his *Bacchanale* (1938), for prepared piano, in which he modified conventional piano sounds by inserting metal, rubber, wood, and other types of objects between the piano strings, he was able to simulate a kind of percussive texture reminiscent of the Eastern-Asian gamelan orchestra, an idiom that Cowell had already imitated in his *Ostinato Pianissimo* (1934) for percussion ensemble. This early non-Western orientation was to serve Cage's interest not only in the expansion of the sonic spectrum, but also as one of the most significant sources in his later philosophical formulations leading to chance operations and improvisation.

Cage's most radical departure from traditional Western influences began in 1949, when he turned to Indian philosophy and music and to Zen Buddhism, studies sparked in part by his own doubts and questions regarding the meaning and purpose of music. An Indian student of Cage informed him that, according to her Indian teacher, music served to open the soul to the Divine spirit. Indian musical sources, based on improvisation around scalar and rhythmic formulas (*ragas* and *talas*), was one of the factors contributing to Cage's move toward indeterminacy. His move away from musical rationality came more specifically from the concepts inherent in Zen Buddhist philosophy, based on the mystical and antirational in which one does not look for universal purposes:

Every being is the Buddha just as, for the anarchist, every being is a ruler. Now, my music liberates because I give people the chance to change their minds in the way I've changed mine. I don't want to police them.[1]

We need first of all a music in which not only are sounds just sounds but in which people are just people, not subject, that is, to laws established by any one of them, even if he is "the composer" or the "conductor."

The situation relates to individuals differently, because attention isn't focused in one direction. Freedom of movement is basic to both this art and this society.[2]

The idea that one "is to choose flexibility when one can, as opposed to 'fixity,'" led Cage to devise various means not only by which the composer could relinquish control (either partially or totally) over the creation and organization of musical events, but also to provide for varying degrees of indeterminacy for the performer as well.[3] One of the basic techniques came as early as 1950 from his study of the *I Ching* (ancient Chinese *Classic of Changes*), a book originally used for divination and claimed by followers throughout history to be a means of understanding and controlling future events. For Cage, the use of the *I Ching* sticks, analogous to rolling dice, provided an objective means for realization of the various musical parameters: pitch, duration, dynamics, mode of articulation, etc. In his *Music of Changes* for piano, special connections are established between chance procedures and mathematical proportions that define relations between durations and the hierarchy of structural levels. As indicated by the composer, "the rhythmic structure . . . is expressed in changing tempi (indicated by large numbers) (beats per minute) [69, 176, 100, etc.]."[4] While intricate mathematical patterns are reminiscent of the proportional and rhythmic subdivisions employed in his *First Construction in Metal* (1939), the use of the *I Ching* sticks and the tossing of coins determined the charts, which were then reinterpreted into traditional notation. Some freedom is also allowed in performance by "the notation of durations . . . in space" (Ex. 19–1).

Similar chance operations for achieving freedom of content in both composition and performance followed in *Music for Piano 1* (1952). Imperfections on the original music paper served as an objective basis for determining the pitches, which were written arbitrarily in whole notes. Durations, pedals, and the manner of producing the piano tones (pizzicato, striking, scratching,

[1] Michael John White, "King of the Avant-Garde," *Observer (London)* (September 26, 1982); also see Richard Kostelanetz, *Conversing with Cage* (New York: Limelight Editions, 1988), p. 257.

[2] Kostelanetz, ibid.

[3] Ibid., p. 268.

[4] For more detailed information on these proportional relations, see Cage's preface to the score.

EXAMPLE 19–1. John Cage, *Music of Changes* for piano, opening, notation of durations in space

and muting the strings, etc.) are left to the performer freely, while tempi are free within a controlled framework of seven seconds per system. In *Music for Piano 2* (1953), dynamics and tempi are also free, while the modes of tone production are set compositionally. In *Music for Piano 4–19* (1953), another aspect of chance was introduced for further removing composition from predictability and fixity in performance: "The 16 pages may be played as separate pieces or continuously as one piece, or.[sic]" In *Music for Piano 21–52* (1955) and *53–84* (1956), more radical possibilities were provided for spontaneity and variety in performance. In the former set, in which coin tossing is used, pieces from each of two groupings (*21–36* and *37–52*) may be played simultaneously or individually and with freedom in tempi, durations, and dynamics, while in the latter set varying numbers of pianists may perform the pieces in whole or in part.

In other works of the early 1950s, Cage exploited the possibilities for achieving freedom in content through unpredictability in performance by use of either graphic or conventional notation, as in the *Two Pastorales* (1951–1952) and *Music for Carillon, No. 1* (1952). His increasing concern for freedom of form also became·evident in the 1950s. In the *Concert for Piano and Orchestra* (1957–1958), the orchestral score was eliminated, so greater indeterminacy could be achieved by the use of the instrumental parts alone. The work, based on a sixty-three page piano part consisting of eighty-four graphically distinct stylistic groupings, permits the soloist and the thirteen players to realize all, some, or none of the notes in any ordering. The graphic notation of one piano aggregate may be singled out, where "the four meandering lines represent frequency, duration, amplitude, and overtone structure in any correspondence" (Ex. 19–2).[5] Based on Cage's instructions for realizing the *Concert,* the performers are free to produce an infinite number of versions, including one that could result in total silence.

The shift of responsibility from the composer to the performer and the establishment of maximal freedom in sound production and formal disposition is a corollary to the shift from conventional notation to an indeterminate graphic representation. Such methods based on minimal notation or no notation at all were already foreshadowed by Cage's use of groups of radios.

EXAMPLE 19–2. John Cage, *Concert for Piano and Orchestra,* p. 57, graphic notation of a piano aggregate, with four meandering lines representing frequency, duration, amplitude, and overtone structure in any correspondence

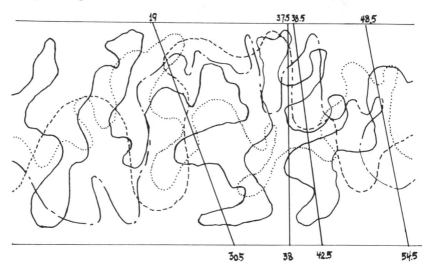

[5] Paul Griffiths, *Cage* (London: Oxford University Press, 1981), pp. 33–35.

In *Imaginary Landscape No. 4* (1951), for twelve radios, and other works for groups of radios turned on and off by stopwatches, we find one of Cage's most radical steps toward achieving total randomness-- neither the composer nor the performers have control over the sounds that are being broadcast at a particular moment. However, it is in *4' 33"* (1952), for any instrument or combination of instruments in a score indicating three sections, each followed by the word "TACET," that Cage's philosophy is manifested most prominently. The basic assumptions regarding artistic meaning, in which the will or ego of the composer is removed from the creative musical process, were largely a result of Cage's interest in Zen Buddhism. Morphological musical structure in this work as a purposeful, goal-oriented concept is thereby relinquished, so that one is immersed in sound in and of itself. Structural perception, is then, in the domain of the listener, or spectator. In reality, there are always sounds in the world, so that in the traditional concert setting, which serves simply as a frame for the performer to remain silent, we are made aware of the possibility of tuning in to the natural sounds around us:[6]

Cage continued along these more radical lines, abandoning control over both the compositional process and performance by the elimination of explicit notation. The *Aria* for solo voice (1958), which could be combined in performance with segments of the *Concert for Piano and Orchestra* or his *Fontana Mix* for tape (1958), is based on unusual orderings of words in which the musical style is only suggested. His interest in gesture and theatre was already evident in his *Water Music* (1952), in which the pianist pours water from pots, blows whistles under water, and plays a radio. Such activities were developed further in his *Theatre Piece* (1960), for one to eight performers, and in his *o' o"* (1962), in which Cage himself performed the work in a concert hall by slicing vegetables, mixing them in an electric blender, and drinking the juice as the basis for producing the "musical" sounds. Thus, Cage's activities tended toward the complete breakdown in conventional notions of art, and in what he considered to be artificial distinctions between art and life itself, so the spectator could be as involved in the creative process as the composer and performer.

ALEATORIC COMPOSERS OF THE "NEW YORK SCHOOL"

Several composers who became associated with Cage in New York in the early 1950s, including Christian Wolff, Morton Feldman, Earle Brown, and David Tudor, were also interested in the dissociation of sound from personal expression and artistic taste: "sound come into its own . . . indifferent in motive, originating in no psychology nor in dramatic intentions, nor in literary or pictorial purposes . . . but . . . nothing, in the end, is denied."[7]

---

[6] John Cage, *Silence* (Middletown, Connecticut: Wesleyan University Press, 1961), pp. 3 and 8.

[7] Christian Wolff, as quoted by Cage, in *Silence,* ibid., p. 68.

According to Cage, Wolff was the first to eliminate the "glue" of musical continuity.[8] However, in contrast to Cage's initial compositional intentions, these composers were concerned primarily from the outset not so much with indeterminacy in the compositional process (as could be achieved by the use of the *I Ching* sticks or groups of radios), but rather with the establishment of conditions leading to spontaneity in performance by means of graphic notation. The intention was to set the spatial and temporal framework within which any number of possibilities could be realized spontaneously. Sound and silence were only aspects of a larger set of gestures and visualizations in a music of "action." The mobiles of Alexander Calder and the "action" paintings of Jackson Pollock, for example, also served as influences on Brown's use of graphic musical possibilities for allowing numerous changes in spatial perception from one performance to the next and for achieving spontaneity.

Feldman was interested in the work of the abstract expressionist painters in New York particularly, whose influence led him to the invention of new notational means for achieving partially unplanned results in performance. He began to experiment with graphic notation in the early 1950s in several works for various combinations of conventional instruments. The two series of pieces entitled *Projection* (1950–1951) and *Intersection* (1951–1953) were the first of Feldman's works in which graphic notation provided only a general framework for each of the parameters, so that performance flexibility was permitted within a given range of possibilities. In *Intersection I* for orchestra (Ex. 19–3), as in the other pieces of these two sets, boxes are

EXAMPLE 19–3. Morton Feldman, *Intersection I* for orchestra, boxes used in place of notes, with pitches only relatively determined by their placement within one of three registral areas

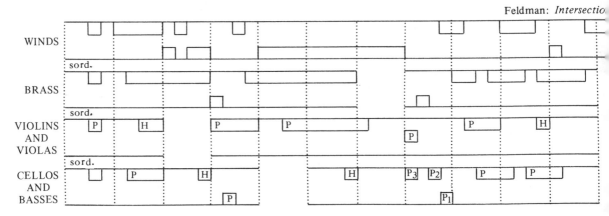

© 1962 by C.F. Peters Corporation. Reprinted by permission of the publisher.

[8] Ibid., p. 71.

used in place of notes, so pitches are determined only relatively by their placement within one of three registral areas (high, middle, and low). This allows for any tone to be sounded within a given range that is delimited flexibly by the performer. The performer may enter at any point within a given time frame, the individual durations determined "by the amount of space taken up by the square or rectangle, each box [delimited by vertical dotted lines] being potentially 4 icti. The single ictus or pulse is at the tempo 72 or thereabouts." In certain cases, a numeral may also be assigned to a segment to indicate how many events are to occur within a given time frame. The performers may also choose the dynamics freely, which must then be maintained at the same level for the remainder of a given time frame. Despite the general flexibility and indeterminacy in connection with certain parameters, the composer's personal style is clear and consistent. The composer's primary interest in timbral color is revealed, for instance, in the indication that "a minimum of vibrato should be used throughout by all instruments."

By 1953, Feldman moved from graphic back to more conventional notation, but the restrictions induced by the latter tended to conflict with his general musical aims for achieving freedom and spontaneity in performance. In his works of the late 1950s and 1960s, he refined his various notational procedures in an attempt to fulfill his aesthetic goals. In his *Last Pieces* for piano (1963), he reconciled his use of traditional notation with his interest in achieving partial spontaneity in performance. This was accomplished by controlling the tempi and representing exact pitches by rhythmically undetermined note values. In his *Piece* for four pianos (1957), a single part served as the basis for independent realization by the group of performers to produce a freely polyphonic or heterophonic texture. Such sound generation from one source simultaneously permits a sense of both relatedness and dissociation among the separate parts. In his set of pieces entitled *Durations* (1960–1962), all aspects of the notation, except for the durations themselves, are controlled. Somewhat more indeterminate in realization is *The Swallows of Salangan* (1961) for wordless chorus and instruments. In the 1970s, Feldman reestablished his use of conventional notation in composer controlled works.

Brown also turned in the early 1950s to new notational methods for achieving degrees of indeterminacy in performance. In his series of pieces entitled *Folio* (1952–1953), for undetermined instrumentation, he began to use what he referred to as *time notation,* based on different notehead lengths to indicate relative durations, while the exact pitches are defined. In his *Twenty-Five Pages* (1953) for piano, he first developed his principles for achieving mobility according to the concept of *open form,* which allows the performer the choice of reordering the pages of composed material and to read the score upside down. Indeterminacy in performance is introduced further by the use of *time notation,* the spontaneous assignment of bass or treble clefs to the two staves, and the flexible determination of the time span for each system. By way of analogy to sculpture and painting, his graphic notation, which he first used in his *November 1952 (Synergy)* and *December 1952,* served as a kind of spatial representation for the performer to "set all this in motion."[9] The "score" of the latter, which is the first entirely graphic work (i.e., in which any hint of traditional notation is abandoned), has itself been used as an example of visual art. The horizontal and vertical lines and rectangles, which provide indeterminate indications for extremely flexible possibilities in the performance realization of the various parameters, suggest a graphic source in the mechanically abstract canvases of Pieter Mondrian.[10] In the Preface to the score, Brown indicates that "the composition may be performed in any direction from any point in the defined space for any length of time and may be performed from any of the four rotational positions in any sequence."

Brown's move toward greater formal mobility and spontaneity in performance (as derived from the visual artistic assumptions of Calder and Pollock, respectively) led to his first orchestral works in open form. In *Available Forms I* (1961), for eighteen instruments, and *Available Forms II* (1961–1962), for large orchestra and two conductors, Brown evolved his open-form concept based on an original approach to the relation between controlled and improvised elements fully. In these works, the local events themselves are fixed while the structural framework is not. This is a reversal of Feldman's partially unplanned techniques, in which a given range of possibilities for each of the parameters serves as a structural delimitation within which the local events could be improvised freely. Through the choices of the individual performers, Brown's local events, which are determined and fixed, can be improvised into "available forms." In the first of these two works, each of the large sections is subdivided into five smaller ones, which can be performed in any order and combination according to the decisions of the conductor. This procedure was expanded in the second piece, in which two conductors make independent choices. These are nevertheless part of an interaction based on an awareness of the spontaneous decisions of the other conductor. Several sections of the latter score are shown in Ex. 19–4.

EXAMPLE 19–4. (facing page) Earle Brown, *Available Forms II,* for large orchestra and two conductors, excerpt from Orchestra I score, open form based on free ordering and combination of subsections according to independent choices of two conductors. (Copyright © 1962 (Renewed) Associated Music Publishers, Inc. International copyright secured. All rights reserved. Reprinted by permission.)

GROUPS DEVOTED TO A MUSIC OF RANDOM SOUNDS AND ACTIONS

Out of the experiments of Cage and the New York School, which resulted in a new perspective regarding the relation of the composer, performer, and spectator to each other and to the creation of the musical happening, came

---

[9] See Earle Brown, in the foreward to *Folio and Four Systems* (1952).

[10] For a comparison of Brown's graphic score with Mondrian's *Composition with Lines,* see Brian Simms, *Music of Twentieth Century* (New York: Schirmer Books, 1986), pp. 366–367.

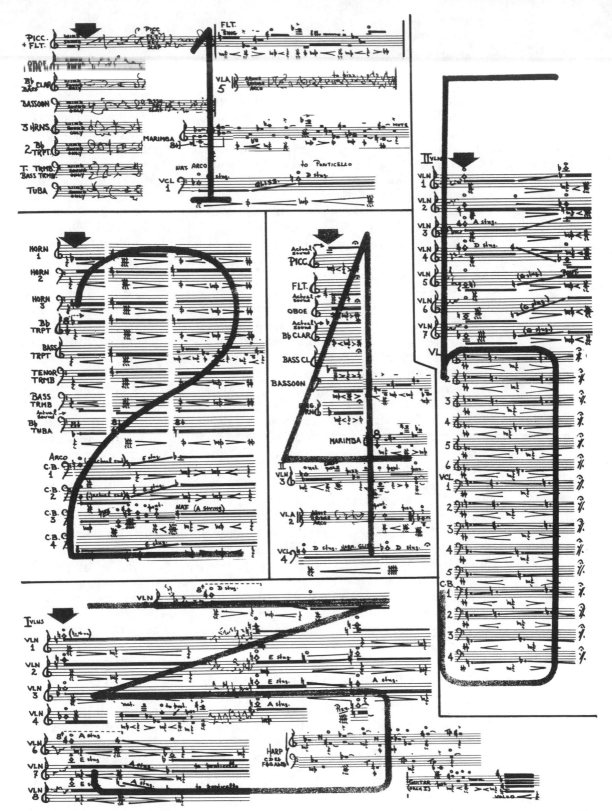

several groups concerned with the concept of an all-inclusive art. In the late 1950s and 1960s, several groups of aleatoric composers experimented with the possibilities inherent in the breakdown of the distinctions between isolated musical sounds and real life events. Motivation for this development came from the theatrical and gestural implications contained in such works as Cage's *Water Music* and *0' 0"* and in the graphic scores that were based on the principle of mobile or open form. All these sources permitted extreme freedom of choice for the performer in an unbounded process having little to do with any structural notions delimited traditionally. These expanded concepts were embodied prominently in the philosophy and aesthetics of the *Fluxus group* (situated at several international locations and in New York), *ONCE* (at Ann Arbor, Michigan), and others that emerged in various parts of the United States during the 1960s.

La Monte Young and George Brecht, both of whom became members of the *Fluxus group,* were interested in the extension of aleatoric performance techniques into the areas of theatre, gesture, and particularly mixed-media. Cage gave lectures, concerts, and classes in experimental music in the summer of 1958 at Darmstadt, where he was to have a significant influence on American, European, and other composers. Young's contact with the music of Cage at Darmstadt in 1959, while studying with Stockhausen, led him away from his previous twelve-tone orientation toward a diversified and "intentionally purposeless" musical theatricality. His interest in a music of action, in which he had often only included textual indications for the realization of his intentions, was first revealed significantly in his *Poem for Chairs, Tables, Benches, etc.* (1960) and *Compositions 1960.* In *No. 2* of the latter, the performer is instructed to build a fire, in *No. 5* to let a butterfly loose and end the composition when it flies out of the door, and in *No. 7* to hold a perfect fifth "for a long time." In *Compositions 1961 Nos. 1–29,* the performer is instructed to "draw a straight line and follow it." In one of his works, he has also provided instructions whereby the performer should "prepare any piece and play it." Many of the above compositions were included in *An Anthology* (1963), edited by both Young and Brecht, based on "chance operations, concept art, meaningless work, natural disasters, indeterminacy, antiart, plans of action, improvisation, stories, diagrams, poetry, essays, dance constructions, compositions, mathematics, music." These categories reveal Young's interest in the fusion of various aleatoric practices, which are reminiscent of both Cage's interests in Zen Buddhism, Indian improvisation, and the nihilistic assumptions in the antiart of the early twentieth-century Dadaist movement. In 1962, Young had founded the *Theatre of Eternal Music,* the conception of which appears to have been anticipated in his works of the late 1950s and early 1960s. At this time, he began to employ transparent textures that consisted of a minimal number of held notes of indeterminate length (as in *Compositions 1960 No. 5*), an approach that was to become the basis of the "Minimalist" movement. His composition entitled *The Tortoise, his Dreams and Journeys,* which he has continued to compose since 1964, exemplifies his concept of "eternal" time that underlies his open-ended compositional process.

Two of the main composers of the *ONCE* group, Robert Ashley and Gordon Mumma, made significant attempts to revitalize the live musical situation by producing a type of music that would maximize both performer and audience participation. Creation of the musical experience, based on gesture and activity among the performers and spectators, was thus intended to be as removed as possible from the traditional role of the composer. Ashley and Mumma also extended their work into the visual arts and the theatre, collaborating with artists and architects in the establishment of the ONCE Festival (1961–1968). In Ashley's *Public Opinion Descends Upon the Demonstrators* (1961), audience sounds and activities determine the composer's choice in the presentation of prerecorded taped sounds. As the work develops, there is an increasing interaction between the audience and the tape operator (performer). The significance of live audience and performer interaction, in which gesture and activity are primary, is also evident in Mumma's scores that provide instructions for the physical movement and gestures of the performers, as in his *Gestures II* for two pianos (1962). Thus, the implementation of action in the music of the *Fluxus* and *ONCE* groups reveal the belief in Cage's own idea that everything in life is music.[11]

DARMSTADT: TOWARD INDETERMINACY

In 1954, Cage and Tudor presented aleatoric concerts throughout Europe, a tour that served to introduce aleatoric operations into the European avant-garde community. However, because of their strong commitment to the principles of integral serialism and total composer control, the younger generation of European composers came to absorb aleatoric techniques only gradually and cautiously. Nevertheless, the seeds for change had been ripening since the mid-1950s. The complexities stemming from the preoccupation with mathematical abstraction in the predetermined post-Webernian contexts of Boulez's *Structures I* and *Second Piano Sonata* and Stockhausen's *Kreuzspiel, Klavierstücke I,* and *Kontra-punkte* were to present formidable demands on the listener's perception as well as on the live performer. Music that was totally controlled in every detail and based on the narrowing of focus to single isolated events resulted in athematic, nondevelopmental linear surfaces. Total control of all the parameters often produced the opposite effect: total randomness. By the mid-1950s, strict adherence to the principles of integral serialism began to loosen and the ultrarational pointillistic style was combined with techniques intended to produce degrees of unpredictability. Rigid structuralism and extreme complexity were replaced by a sense of spontaneity and improvisation, simplicity, and a more subjective or emotive basis.

In their more flexible works of the 1950s, European composers tended to be consistent as to which parameters were to be controlled and which might introduce elements of indeterminacy. Because these composers were emerging from a strong tradition based on the principle of organized

[11] See Cage, *Silence,* n.6, above, p. 95.

sound, they seemed least inclined to relinquish control over fixed pitch. For many of these composers, indeterminate sounds could result in a nonmusical product only, a prospect foreign to those "brought up in the ultraprecision of integral serialism."[12] Instead, the first steps toward indeterminacy among the Darmstadt composers were manifested in the spontaneous and flexible ordering of composed sections, tempi, and durations.

In 1957, Boulez's lecture on "Alea" signaled the final dissolution of the extreme serial restrictions of the early 1950s. In contrast to Cage, however, chance was to be introduced without the abandonment of composer responsibility. The interest was in the accommodation of, rather than the submission to, chance. As early as *Le Marteau sans maître* ("The Masterless Hammer," 1952–1954; revised 1957), Boulez's interest in "organized delirium" was evident in the setting of certain portions of René Char's surrealistic text and in his expansion of serial techniques, which created paradoxically a flexibility that permitted the joining of the rational to the irrational. One aspect of this flexibility is manifested in the possibility of variable structural perceptions on the part of the listener within the framework of an otherwise fixed form. While little freedom is permitted in performance, except for occasional indications of free tempo, each movement may be perceived ambiguously either as part of one large integrated cycle of movements or as part of three smaller interlocking cycles consisting of "l'Artisanat furieux" (Movs. 1, 3, and 7), "Bourreaux de solitude" (Movs. 2, 4, 6, and 8), and "Bel édifice et les pressentiments" (Mov. 5 and its "double," Mov. 9), the latter cycle of which is central to the work.[13] Boulez's increasing need for flexibilty, as portended in this work, is expressed in his own self-critical statement:

> Some of the concerts at Darmstadt in 1953/54 were of quite lunatic sterility and academicism, and above all became totally uninteresting. . . . [*Le Marteau*] is much easier to understand, and more attractive than the first book of *Structures* or *Polyphonie*. . . . There is in fact a very clear and very strict element of control [but] there is also room for what I call *local indiscipline*. . . .[14]

Between 1955 and 1957, in his *Piano Sonata No. 3*, *Structures II* for two pianos, and *Pli selon pli* for soprano and orchestra, Boulez established his notion of *guided chance*, in which indeterminacy occurs under rigidly con-

---

[12] Reginald Smith Brindle, *The New Music* (London: Oxford University Press, 1975), pp. 66–67.

[13] Degrees of clarity and ambiguity among these three cycles of movements are discussed by Dominique Jameux, "Analytical Remarks on the Three Cycles of *Le Marteau sans Maître*," in *From Pierrot to Marteau* (Los Angeles: Arnold Schoenberg Institute, 1987), pp. 22–24.

[14] Pierre Boulez, *Par volonté et par hasard: entretiens avec Célestin Deliège* (Paris: Les Éditions du Seuil, 1976; Eng. trans. by Robert Wangermée as *Conversations with Célestin Deliège* (London: Ernst Eulenberg, Ltd., 1976), p. 66.

trolled conditions. In the *Sonata,* his approach to the five movements, or *formants* (*antiphonie, trope, constellation* and its double, *constellation-miroir, strophe,* and *séquence*), reveals a structural mobility in performance similar to, but more controlled than, that in the music of Earle Brown. The degree of flexibility in what the composer has referred to as a "work in progress" varies at different levels of organization. The overall order of the five movements, which permit the creation of additionally distinct but related *developants,* may be permuted in eight ways, except for the position of *constellation,* which must remain as the central movement.[15] Degrees of determinacy and flexibility can occur within each of the movements. In *antiphonie,* only the form is variable, while the tempo and style of its sections are fixed. In accordance with its title, this piece consists of two antiphonal groups (A and B) of two and three fragments written on two separate pages, and there are four possibilities of organization to choose from (Ex. 19–5).[16] According to the composer, if each of these four possibilities were written out completely, we would see that "each of the original fragments written on the right-hand page is doubled on the left-hand page by the same fragment varied." Thus, the performer is free to give us various alternations of the two antiphonal elements according to one of the four schemes provided.

Trope consists of two simple and two complex subsections (A. *texte* and B. *parenthèse,* C. *commentaire* and D. *glose,* respectively), which can be played in various orderings and with elaborative segments interpolated freely (i.e., troped). At the same time, the formal mobility of this movement, which results from the performer's option of introducing segmental interpolations into the four subsections as well as permuting these subsections to produce an open, or circular form, is a projection of the permutational possibilities inherent in the four pitch cells that outline the basic twelve-tone series and its variant set-forms. Example 19–6 outlines the cellular properties of the set and provides an illustration of a sectional interpolation between the third and fourth cells in the opening statement of the series of *parenthèse.*[17] Thus, the structure is controlled but flexible.

Fixed and variable aspects are based on more complex interrelations in *constellation* and its retrograde, *constellation-miroir.* The title itself is derived from the manner in which groups of notes are distributed on long unfolding sheets. The movement is modelled on Mallarmé's poem *Un Coup de Dés,* in which word sounds are transformed by means of reorganization and segmentation, thereby producing a sense of indeterminacy through dissociation or ambiguity of meaning. Similarly, Boulez permitted dissociation and trans-

---

[15] See Pierre Boulez "Sonata, que me veux-tu?" trans. D. Noakes and P. Jacobs, *Perspectives of New Music* 1/2 (1963): 32–44, for a detailed plan of the work and its possibilities of development.

[16] Ibid., p. 39.

[17] See ibid., pp. 38–40. See also Paul Griffiths, *Boulez* (London: Oxford University Press, 1978), pp. 39–41, for a more specific discussion of the relation between the aleatoric form and the properties of the series.

EXAMPLE 19–5. Pierre Boulez, *Piano Sonata No 3, antiphonie,* variable form consisting of two antiphonal groups (A and B) of two and three fragments on two separate pages, including four possible choices of organization

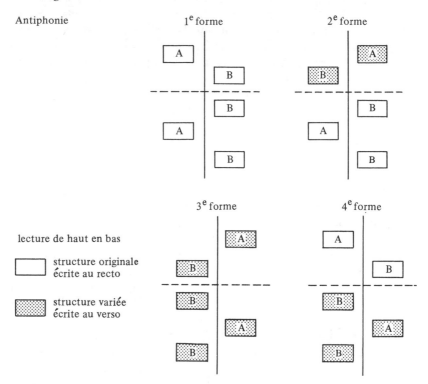

formation of pitch and intervallic components by removing them from their "serial matrix" by means of structural flexibility in performance.[18] While the overall mobility of the musical structure results from certain choices permitted within a scheme of fifty-eight segments printed on nine pages, two general paths are indicated, one in red for chordal textures (*blocs*), the other in green for pointillistic ones (*points*), in which local signs indicate the path that the performer can follow. Other rules are provided for determining the tempi. In addition to fixed tempo indications in certain sections, there are conditional indications at the beginning or ending of each line, which are dependent upon the performer's choice of progression from one segment to

[18] See Anne Trenkamp, "The Concept of 'Alea' in Boulez's Constellation-Miroir," *Music and Letters* 57/1 (January 1976): 4–5.

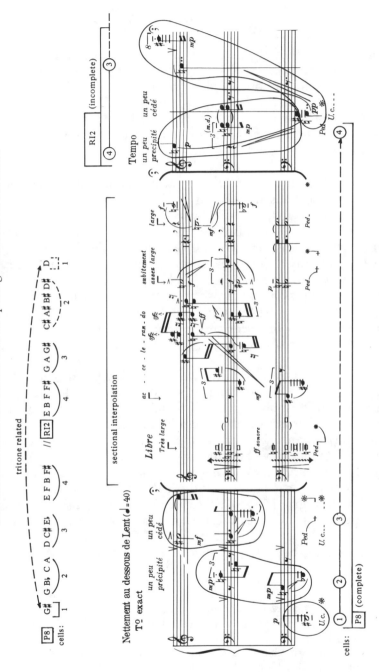

EXAMPLE 19–6. Pierre Boulez, *Piano Sonata No. 3, trope (B. parenthèse)*, cellular properties of twelve-tone series and sectional interpolation between third and fourth cells at opening statement of the series

the next. There is also a range of variables in other parameters such as timbre and register, etc. While *strophe* is somewhat strophic in construction, in which the lines are chosen by rules of guided chance, *Séquence* is based on more variable possibilities for the succession of the sections as determined by the use of transparent paper placed randomly over the music sheet. Thus, the degree of flexibility throughout the *Sonata* varies according to the particular structural direction, in which the performer is given limited choices within a mobile scheme of composed segmental groups. Boulez himself compared such works to the street-map of a town: "You don't change the map, you perceive the town as it is, but there are different ways of going through it . . . when you visit it you choose your own direction and your own route; but it is obvious that to get to know the town you need an accurate map and knowledge of the traffic regulations."[19]

Aleatoric principles were also established with the Darmstadt première of Stockhausen's *Zeitmasze* (1955–1956) and the *Klavierstück IX* (1954, completed in 1961), in which "variable" and "fixed" are joined in contexts of "order" and "relative disorder" within a process of "open form."[20] In *Zeitmasze,* time measurements are determined flexibly within the dictates of several prescribed time measurements and by the technical capacities of the five woodwind players (e.g., duration of a prescribed group within a single breath, or to play as fast as possible, etc.). The form is a continuum connecting two extremes of "playing synchronously" and "playing in isolation—and turmoil—in different and mutually independent time-strata," between which "is a series of degrees of reciprocal dependence and individual freedom."[21]

Klavierstück XI (1956), which was first performed at Darmstadt in the summer of 1957, is Stockhausen's first completed aleatoric piece of his *Klavierstücke.* In its mobile or open form, nineteen note-groups are printed in conventional notation in an irregular distribution on a single sheet of paper, with performance instructions given on the reverse side. The performer begins by randomly choosing any group at any tempo, dynamic level, and mode of attack. At the end of that fragment, one of six tempi, dynamic levels, and modes of articulation is indicated to determine how the next randomly chosen note-group is to be realized. Other indications regarding octave transpositions, etc., are observed upon a second playing of any of the nineteen groups. Once a group has been played for the third time, the piece is over. Thus, some groups may be repeated while others may be omitted in a given

[19] See Boulez, *Conversations,* n.14, above, p. 82.

[20] Brigitte Schiffer, "Darmstadt, Citadel of the Avantgarde," *The World of Music* 11/3 (1969), p. 37.

[21] See Stockhausen's comments in Karl H. Wörner, *Stockhausen, Life and Work,* ed. and trans. Bill Hopkins (London: Faber and Faber, 1973; original version 1963; Berkeley and Los Angeles: University of California Press, 1976), p. 37.

performance, so every performance is indeterminate (variable) in terms of the choice and ordering of the composed sections and in the assignment of tempi, dynamics, and articulations within specified ranges. Stockhausen continued to experiment with open form in *Zyklus* (1959), the title indicating a circular formal procedure in which the beginning, ending, and direction are undetermined.

Expanded possibilities in the relation between improvisation and control were introduced to European composers by Ravi Shankar in his performances of Indian music at Darmstadt and other European cities in the mid-1950s. However, the first appearances of both John Cage and the Argentinian-born composer Mauricio Kagel at Darmstadt in 1958 were to have the most significant influence on aleatoric developments in Europe. Kagel's ideas of "instrumental" theatre and absurdity, like Cage's chance-music concerts, contributed to the increasing emphasis on gesture, theatre, and language, which tended toward further complication of existing musical conditions. As early as 1950, in his choral *Palimsestos,* and more significantly in his *Anagrama* (1955–1958), for solo voices, speaking chorus, and instruments, Kagel had experimented already with the possibilities of word dissociation, in which the sounds were more important than their meaning. In the latter work, he also began to reveal an interest in theatrical musical performance. This was developed further in *Sonant* (1960), for guitar, harp, double bass, and drums, the exclusively verbal score of which is indicative of his aleatoric approach. The performers are permitted flexibility of action within a minimally fixed framework, that is, durational and dynamic restrictions are given at the left of the score as a control for the less determinate musical realization of the verbal instructions, which the performers may read aloud.[22] Although Kagel did not associate his compositional activities with Dadaism, or antiart, his interest in mobility between musical and dramatic media, his exploration of new sound possibilities, and the exploitation of both controlled and flexible structures, as in the *Sexteto de cuerdas,* which was performed at Darmstadt in 1958, were to contribute to the general trend toward a breakdown in the distinction between musical and nonmusical spheres.

OTHER EUROPEAN COMPOSERS OF ALEATORIC MUSIC

The multiplicity of conceptual and technical possibilities at Darmstadt resulted in the need for a complete reevaluation by European composers not only of the notion of limited freedom for the performer, but also of the composer's role in the use of guided chance. In 1960, Boulez attempted to clarify the current state of the art in six lectures, entitled "Penser la musique

[22] For further description of this and some of the following works, see Erhard Karkoschka, *Notation in New Music, A Critical Guide to Interpretation and Realization,* trans. Ruth Koenig (New York: Praeger Publishers, 1972), Part Three.

aujourd'hui," and these concerns for the direction of music were expressed by others at conferences and lectures at Darmstadt in subsequent years.[23] Boulez and other European aleatoric composers never accepted chance procedures as the exclusive basis for composition. Rather, they continued to experiment with graphic and conventional notational systems in order to achieve degrees of flexibility in both the compositional process and performance. Henri Pousseur, Luciano Berio, György Ligeti, Witold Lutosławsky, and Krzysztof Penderecki, while occasionally employing serial procedures, exploited the possibilities of fixed and variable elements in highly individual styles.

A continuing interest in mobile form, based either on fixed or variable details, and in the transitional possibilities between musical sounds and spoken language is evident in the works of Pousseur beginning in the 1950s. In two of his piano pieces, *Mobile* (performed at Darmstadt in 1958) and *Caractères* (1961), which include a mixture of conventional and unconventional notational signs to indicate degrees of flexibility in the realization of details, the composer developed special techniques to insure indeterminacy and mobility in the ordering of events. In *Caractères,* sheets with cut-out windows are placed over sheets with printed notes. The notes are then played as they appear in the windows, and in accordance with marginal indications for dynamics and meter. Within the mobile form of his "fantaisie variable genre opéra" *Votre Faust* (1960–1967), for voices, five actors, twelve instruments, and tape, Pousseur used the speaking voice as a basic sound source and incorporated noises according to the dictates of the drama.

The fusion and interchangeability of musical sounds with words and syllables in partially indeterminate graphic contexts became widespread by the late 1950s. Berio had become acquainted with the new experiments in action and theatre music at Darmstadt and had by that time also moved away from the principles of integral serialism toward greater formal mobility and indeterminacy in performance. The latter interest became evident in his use of proportional notation in *Sequenza I* (1958), for solo flute, and in *Tempi Concertanti* (1958–1959), for flute, violin, two pianos, and four groups, in which the spatial distance between the notes indicates their relative, unmeasured temporal distances. Flexibility also results from the composer's instruction that a particular figure "can be read starting from any point whatsoever and going left to right or vice-versa. The pattern may be repeated several times—always as fast as possible and within the limits of proportionally indicated duration."

Certain sections of Berio's *Circles* (1962), for voice, harp, and two percussion, are characterized by such flexibility and graphic indeterminacy as well as by a smooth transition between sung and spoken sounds. This is produced by means of special manipulations and transformations of words and syllables. The musical arrangement of three poems by E.E. Cummings

---

[23] Published as *Penser la musique aujourd'hui* (Paris: Gonthier, 1963); Eng. trans. as *Boulez on Music Today* (London: Faber and Faber, 1971).

outlines a chiasmal form (A B C B' A'), in which the third poem serves as the central musical focus, after which the first two poems return in reversed ordering and with internal variation. The intention was to create fluidity between the vocal and instrumental sounds, so that towards the center of the work the singer and certain instrumentalists reverse both their musical and physical roles. The singer begins to produce fragmented instrument-like sounds and noises, followed by her movement closer to the instruments, where she begins to play the chimes and the percussionists utter syllabic fragments. The transformed instrumental-vocal style of the singer is maintained to the end of the work. The graphic notation (e.g., see p. 24 of the score) reveals some degree of indeterminacy in both pitch and rhythm. The following comment provides insight into the composer's flexible approach to both vocal and instrumental realizations in many of his compositions: "The coupling of vivid, directly comprehensible musical gestures and partly baffling verbal fragments is entirely characteristic of Berio. It reverses the situation all too frequently found in contemporary music of a linear, coherent text that holds together a rather loose agglomeration of musical ideas."[24]

Both instrumental composition and composition produced by the manipulation of words and syllables in which fixed and variable elements are integrated into the musical process, were also exploited by the Hungarian composer György Ligeti. From 1956 on, he was in close contact with the European avant-garde and in the late 1950s lectured regularly at Darmstadt. In his *Apparitions* (1958–1959) and *Atmosphères* (1961) for orchestra, and in the organ piece *Volumina* (1961–1962), Ligeti moved toward a sense of flexibility in pitch and rhythm as he evolved his technique based on interwoven chromatic masses resulting in the obscuration of the individual sound components. While the composer's instructions are often detailed, the graphic score of such works as *Volumina* (Ex. 19–7) fosters a sense of indeterminacy in the area of extreme chromatic density and its rhythmic disposition, for which he only indicates the durational extremes of a given page. Around the same time, Ligeti's expanding interest in the musical possibilities of phonetics was revealed in the score of *Aventures* (1962), for three solo voices and seven instruments, in which his detailed graphic notation includes numerous symbols to indicate the diversity of flexible spoken and instrumental sounds and the general activities within an intricate polyphonic texture. As indicated by the composer (e.g., see p. 7 of the score), the soprano, alto, and bass singers add hand-produced sounds to their extremely rapid contrapuntal syllabic reiterations, while the flute and horn players gesticulate without musical tone production and the percussionist is instructed to create noises by shuffling the pages of a book. Thus, notwithstanding the composer's explicit compositional intentions, degrees of sonic flexibility result inevitably from the realization of the exactly notated and the graphically represented materials.

[24] David Osmond-Smith, *Playing on Words, a Guide to Luciano Berio's Sinfonia* (London: Royal Musical Association, 1985), p. 90.

EXAMPLE 19–7. György Ligeti, *Volumina,* for organ, graphic score, p. 11, permitting sense of indeterminacy in extreme chromatic density and rhythmic disposition

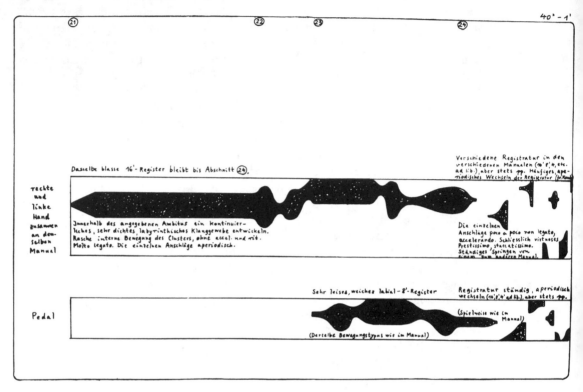

While Ligeti was opposed to the aesthetics of John Cage and the notion of the "happening," as expressed in his satire on Cage in his *Trois bagatelles* and the "musical provocation" *Die Zukunft der Musik* (1961), for lecturer and audience, the Polish composer Witold Lutosławski (b. 1913) turned to aleatoric operations in the early 1960s after being influenced by a hearing of Cage's *Concert for Piano and Orchestra.*[25] This change of compositional attitude was one of several that his style had undergone since the late 1930s. His earliest works had revealed a concern for integrated formal construction based on a nonfunctional diatonic tonal-harmonic system within an Eastern European folkloristic idiom similar to that of Bartók. During the next two decades, he moved toward a more integrated tonality infused by a kind of twelve-tone serialism. The first radical change in his controlled approach to form and other compositional aspects, however, came in 1961

[25] Steven Stucky, *Lutosławski and His Music* (Cambridge: Oxford University Press, 1981), p. 84.

with his *Jeux vénitiens* ("Venetian Games"), for chamber orchestra, in which he implemented the notion of open form. A degree of variability in the ordering and synchronization of material is manifested at certain points, where the "abundance of potentialities concealed within the individual psyche of each performer" is included in the compositional process, but without any abandonment of the composer's "claim to authorship." Fixed and variable were joined in what Lutoslawski called "aleatoric counterpoint," based on the principles of guided chance, or controlled freedom.

Within differentiated sections of this work, the pitches are precisely notated, while indeterminate rhythmic notation permits a degree of free and independent polyphonic unfolding between the separate instrumental groups within certain guidelines controlled by the conductor. The conductor gives entry cues to the brass and woodwinds at one-second intervals, after which each group continues without the conductor, but observes the conductor cues for the entries of the other groups. The large letters indicate points of synchronization, so local rhythmic and contrapuntal indeterminacy is actually controlled on a higher architectonic level. Open form and other aleatoric features were only suggested in several of his works during the next two decades, as observed in the dialectical formal process of his *Symphony No. 2* (1966–1967), in which the sections "Hesitant" and "Direct" indicate transformation from chaos to order.

In the early 1960s, the Polish composer Krzysztof Penderecki (b. 1933) also tended toward some indeterminacy in pitch and sonority in an original approach to pitch combinations, which generally resulted in chromatic densities or clusters. His interest in a variety of dramatic subjects in varied vocal and instrumental scorings, often characterized by the juxtaposition of contrasting sonorities ranging from conventional musical sounds to speech and noise, were already evident since his first important works of the late 1950s. Such range of sonic materials has been exploited by the composer primarily for the purpose of a heightened expression of his underlying social or political statement, as in the choral and orchestral *St. Luke Passion* (1963–1965) and *Dies irae* (1967), the latter based on the extermination at Auschwitz. More specifically, Penderecki's interest in expanded sonic possibilities and flexibility, which he achieved by means of special performance techniques that often result in semitone or quarter-tone clusters, may be observed in several works of the early 1960s. In *Anaklasis* (1960), for strings and percussion, the use of tremolo glissandi, harmonics, col legno, sul ponticello, and extreme registers results in colorful and often indistinct note clusters. In *Threnody to the Victims of Hiroshima* (1960), for fifty-two strings, timbral combinations and transformations occur in contexts defined by exact and indeterminate graphic notation, the latter consisting of such signs as blackened pyramids for playing "as high as possible" and other indications for use of the bow behind the bridge, etc. In the *Stabat Mater* (1962), cluster-like vocal writing is a result of indistinct sonic utterances in the three choruses, whereas in *Fluorescences* (1961), for full orchestra, graphic notation distinguishes different types of clusters. In Ex. 19–8, thick black lines indicate chromatic clusters, whereas combinations of thin parallel lines indicate whole-tone clusters, the delimiting pitch content

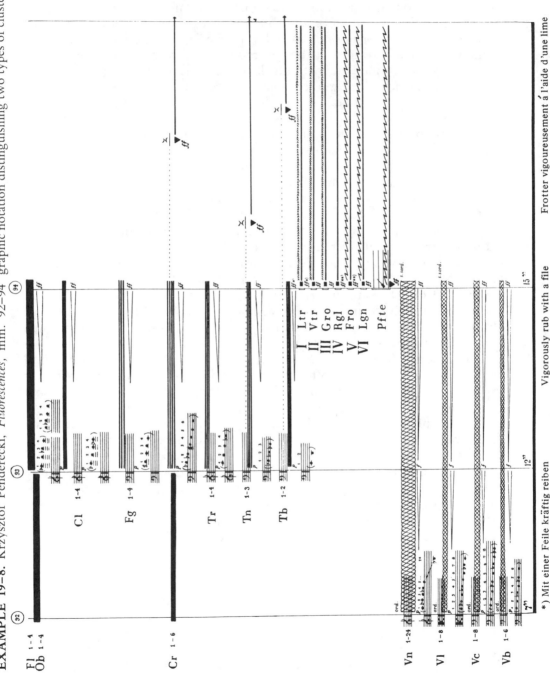

EXAMPLE 19–8. Krzysztof Penderecki, *Fluorescences*, mm. 92–94 graphic notation distinguishing two types of clusters

for each cluster of which is given directly underneath. Pitch indeterminacy is yet more evident in the percussion instruments, which the players are instructed to "vigorously rub with a file" or "saw a piece of wood (iron) with a hand-saw." In each of the indeterminate string glissandi, only the ranges are defined by the given sets of interwoven lines.

Other European composers have also employed graphic notation to realize contexts based on degrees of flexibility and indeterminacy. However, few have ventured toward the extremes of freedom established by John Cage. Nevertheless, some have attempted a greater abandonment of composer control for a more flexible formal conception, and an improvisatory one, due to Eastern influence. At Darmstadt in 1967, Stockhausen expanded his interpretation of the traditional notion of "concert," and also aimed at a more active involvement of the listener in the compositional process.[26] In a joint composition, entitled *Music für ein Haus,* by fourteen international composers, the traditional notion of form was replaced entirely by that of "process," and notation by the more direct use of instructions for the performers. Schiffer informs us further that "contemplation was practised and trances evoked. World outlook, philosophy and mysticism were brought into the picture, for in the meantime Stockhausen had succumbed to the attraction of Indian doctrines. He went the way of the Beatles, Yoga made its appearance at Darmstadt."[27]

MINIMAL OR "SYSTEMATIC" MUSIC SINCE THE EARLY 1960s: LA MONTE YOUNG, TERRY RILEY, STEVE REICH, AND PHILIP GLASS

Minimal or "repetitive" music, which has been developing in the United States since the mid-1960s, has served as a prominent factor in blurring the distinction between art- and popular-music spheres. This movement, which has been reaching an increasingly wider and more diversified audience, has also had a certain influence on similar developments in Europe since the 1970s. While there are essential aesthetic and stylistic differences between European and American composers of *minimal music,* we may nevertheless observe European connections with American "repetitive" techniques in the music of the British composers Cornelius Cardew and Michael Nyman, the Hollander Louis Andriessen, the French Urban Sax group, and others. Among the first to compose *minimal music* in the United States was La Monte Young, who evolved gradually from a serial approach in the late 1950s to techniques based on repetition in 1962 following his association with the *Fluxus* group between 1959 and 1961. This transition from a serial to minimal context was first manifested prominently in his *Octet for Brass* (1957), in which he introduced extremely long, sustained notes into a serial context. According to Wim Mertens, certain aspects of Webern's music contributed to

---

[26] See Schiffer, "Darmstadt," n.20, above, p. 44.
[27] Ibid.

Young's evolution, "especially the duality between [Webern's] structural variation and the static sound that results from it. In Webern there is a tendency to produce continuous variations by using notes in the same octave position throughout a piece, whatever their position in the row. However, the listener perceives this process more as a stasis, as if the same information is being repeated over and over again."[28]

Minimalist techniques may also be traced back to divergent late nineteenth- and early twentieth-century sources, which range from the early works of Satie, for example, the three piano pieces of *Gymnopedie* (1886–1888), with their simple, spare, and minimally changing mechanistic textures based on incessant alternations or repetitions of seventh chords, etc., to Schoenberg's first *Klangfarben* music, *Five Pieces for Orchestra,* Op. 16, No. 3 (1909), based on a gradual "process" of pitch changes stemming from a single five-note chord. The basic assumptions of the latter, in which "process" is perceived primarily through changes of certain parameters (e.g., timbre) while other parameters change minimally and tend to remain static (e.g., pitch), were to be manifested in various ways in the music of the *minimalists.* The American composer and performer Terry Riley (b. 1935), who also came to be associated with the *Fluxus group* of artists in 1959, collaborated with Young in exploiting the possibilities of sustaining sounds for extended periods (as exemplified in Riley's *All-Night-Concerts*), both composers linking this technique to gesture, improvisation, and the dance.

Riley's *In C* (1964), for any number of melodic instruments, is a prototype of minimalist "process" technique based on limited and static pitch content in a gradually changing continuum. In basic ways, this work foreshadowed his study and performance of Indian music since 1970, his *A Rainbow in Curved Air* (1970) reflecting the new influence of the modal melodic formulas and rhythmic patterns of Indian music. The affinity of certain Western composers with Eastern Asian improvisation was already evident in Cowell's gamelan-like percussion piece, *Ostinato Pianissimo* (1934), in which repetitive motivic patterns of limited pitch content had interacted in a continuum of layers based on a steady pulse, but with complex cross accents. During his work at the ORTF recording studios in Europe between 1962 to 1964, Riley had already acquired an interest in extended repetition of short phrases, tape loops producing ostinato patterns, and the layered accumulation of recorded sound, all unfolding within the framework of a regular pulse. In his *In C,* the rhythm is essential to a context based exclusively on a C-major chord throughout. While a single pulse is maintained, each performer plays through a sequence of fifty-three motifs, repeating each one an unspecified number of times. This results in changing overlappings and juxtapositions of each motif with itself and other motifs in a gradually developing continuum based on multiple canons and polyrhythmic combinations. Despite the complexity of

[28] Wim Mertens, *American Minimal Music: La Monte Young, Terry Riley, Steve Reich, and Philip Glass,* trans J. Hautekiet (London: Kahn & Averill, 1983), p. 20.

In C, the possibilities of improvisation are limited. The composer has determined that the form "has to be simple enough to lead the improvisational ensemble of the musicians through good channels."[29] Nevertheless, it is primarily in his use of improvisation that Riley differs from the other three minimalists.

Exotic influences in addition to certain assumptions of Schoenberg's Op. 16, No. 3, are also manifested in the aesthetics of Steve Reich (b. 1936), whose writings on music and innovative techniques of composition carried the notion of "process" to its fullest development.[30] His interest in African drumming, which he studied at the University of Ghana in 1970 (prior to which he had studied Western drumming and had also developed an interest in jazz), contributed further to his minimalist or "systematic" approach. This is evident in his *Phase Patterns* (1970), for four electric organs, which is based on changes in one aspect only. According to Reich, the piece entails "literally drumming on the keyboard: your left hand stays in one position and your right hand stays in one position and you alternate them in what's called a paradiddle pattern, which produces a very interesting musical texture because it sets up melodic things you could never arrive at if you just followed your melodic prejudices and your musical background."[31] In *Drumming* (1970–1971), for eight small tuned drums, three maracas, three glockenspiels, voices, and piccolo, the rhythmic element reflects his African studies clearly, and combines many techniques characteristic of his more mature works, including "phasing-shifting" (gradual shifting between two or more identical repeating figures), the augmentation process, etc.[32]

His *Music for 18 Musicians* (1974–1976), based on an expanded timbral spectrum, introduces a new dimension into Reich's conception of "process." While the basic premises of *minimalism* (i.e., gradual change within a context of static pitch materials, use of a repetitious melodic pattern, and regular pulse) are still in evidence, more complex interactions of the various parameters (especially timbric and harmonic) are now permitted. The work opens and closes with a cycle of eleven chords, within each of which the players present pulsing notes.[33] Each new chord is introduced gradually, after which there is a return to the initial pulsing chord. The latter is then sustained for about five minutes by two pianos and two marimbas as a kind of cantus firmus, above which sections are constructed in the form of arches or as "musical processes." As part of the formal "process," the changing harmonic rhythm introduces accentual reinterpretations into the recurring melodic

---

[29] Ibid., p. 42.

[30] Steve Reich, "Music as a Gradual Process" (1968), in *Writings about Music,* ed. K. Koenig (Halifax University of Nova Scotia Press, 1974), pp. 9–11.

[31] Steve Reich, "An Interview with Michael Nyman," *The Musical Times* 112 (1971): 230.

[32] See Mertens, *American Minimal Music,* n.28, above, pp. 56–57.

[33] Notes by the composer to the ECM Recording, 1978. See also ibid., p. 62.

pattern. Reich's interest in an expanded and diversified palette continued in his *Music for a Large Ensemble* and the *Octet* (1979).

Repetition in the minimalist musical contexts of Philip Glass (b. 1937) is based primarily on additive construction, a principle which finds its direct sources in Indian music. In the mid-1960s, after having worked with Ravi Shankar in Paris, Glass toured Central Asia and India, and his works from that time on reveal a decisive reorientation toward non-Western traditions. He established the Philip Glass Ensemble in New York in 1967, and in his following ensemble pieces he was to draw the minimalist techniques of repetition into a more popular, often loud rock-like idiom. From the influence of Indian rhythms, he was to develop one of his characteristic techniques of rhythmic extension and contraction, which he combined with a simple diatonic, pervasively tonal surface. His first opera, *Einstein on the Beach* (1975), which exemplifies this new popular style, was one of a trilogy of what Glass has referred to as "portrait" operas—the other two are *Satyagraha* (1980) and *Akhnaten* (1984)—that drew his minimalism into a theatre idiom inspired by his contact with the new European theatre of Brecht and Beckett. However, it was already in the mid-1960s in Paris that Glass' "music work and theatre music became closely intertwined."[34]

In his first *minimalist* works, such as *Strung Out* (1967) for amplified violin, the additive principle is only one of several rhythmic procedures derived from Indian music. In this work, large units are comprised of smaller rhythmic cells that are unrelated to them structurally. According to Glass, "these larger units are integrated in a cyclical process. Other cycles with different rhythms are added afterwards like in a wheel-work: everything works simultaneously in a continuous transformation."[35] While there are basic aesthetic connections to the approaches of the other minimalists, it is in these rhythmic features—cyclic occurrences, repetition, and progressive lengthening of cellular units by the gradual addition of new notes—that Glass' personal style is distinguished. Glass' additive principles were developed further in 1969 in his *Two Pages, Music in Fifths,* and many other ensemble pieces after that time.

SUGGESTED READINGS

PIERRE BOULEZ. *Par volonté et par hasard: entretiens avec Célestin Deliège* (Paris: Les Éditions du Seuil, 1975; Eng. trans. by Robert Wangermée as *Conversations with Célestin Deliège* (London: Ernst Eulenberg, Ltd., 1976).

———. *Penser la musique aujourd'hui* (Paris: Gonthier, 1963); Eng. trans. as *Boulez on Music Today* (London: Faber and Faber, 1971).

[34] Philip Glass, *Music by Philip Glass,* ed. Robert T. Jones (New York: Harper & Row, Publishers, Inc., 1987), p. 4.

[35] See Mertens, *American Minimal Music,* n.2, above, p. 68.

————. "Sonata, que me veux-tu?" trans. D. Noakes and P. Jacobs, *Perspectives of New Music* 1/2 (1963): 32–44.

REGINALD SMITH BRINDLE. *The New Music* (London: Oxford University Press, 1975), pp. 60–98 (on indeterminacy, chance, aleatory, and improvisation).

JOHN CAGE. *Silence* (Middletown, Connecticut: Wesleyan University Press, 1961).

PHILIP GLASS. *Music by Philip Glass,* ed. Robert T. Jones (New York: Harper & Row, Publishers, Inc., 1987).

PAUL GRIFFITHS. *Boulez* (London: Oxford University Press, 1978).

————. *Cage* (London: Oxford University Press, 1981).

————. *György Ligeti* (London: Robson Books Ltd., 1983).

DOMINIQUE JAMEUX. "Analytical Remarks on the Three Cycles of *Le Marteau sans Maître,*" in *From Pierrot to Marteau* (Los Angeles: Arnold Schoenberg Institute, 1987), pp. 22–24.

ERHARD KARKOSCHKA. *Notation in New Music, A Critical Guide to Interpretation and Realization,* trans. Ruth Koenig (New York: Praeger Publishers, 1972), Part Three.

RICHARD KOSTELANETZ. *Conversing with Cage* (New York: Limelight Editions, 1988).

WIM MERTENS. *American Minimal Music: La Monte Young, Terry Riley, Steve Reich, and Philip Glass,* trans. J. Hautekiet (London: Kahn & Averill, 1983).

DAVID OSMOND-SMITH. *Playing on Words, a Guide to Luciano Berio's Sinfonia* (London: Royal Musical Association, 1985).

STEVE REICH. "An Interview with Michael Nyman," *The Musical Times* 112 (1971): 229–

————. "Music As a Gradual Process" (1968), in *Writings about Music,* ed. K. Koenig (Halifax: University of Nova Scotia Press, 1974), pp. 9–11.

BRIGITTE SCHIFFER. "Darmstadt, Citadel of the Avantgarde," *The World of Music* 11/3 (1969):32–44.

STEVEN STUCKY. *Lutosławski and His Music* (Cambridge: Oxford University Press, 1981).

ANNE TRENKAMP. "The Concept of 'Alea' in Boulez's 'Constellation-Miroir,' " *Music and Letters* 57/1 (January 1976): 1–10.

KARL H. WÖRNER. *Stockhausen, Life and Work,* ed. and trans. Bill Hopkins (London: Faber and Faber, 1973; original version 1963; Berkeley and Los Angeles: University of California Press, 1976).

20

Continuation and development of national characteristics and other earlier trends in Europe and the Americas

The history of music of the last several decades can be distinguished sharply from the first modernistic wave that shaped the course of music throughout the first half of the present century. Since World War II, philosophical and political attitudes as well as aesthetic and technical approaches have been modified radically by composers of contrasting national backgrounds—each composer or group of composers seems to be speaking a unique and often isolated "musical language." Thus, while there are interconnections among the various musical approaches, an overwhelming sense of multiplicity and disconnection characterizes the present situation, an uncertain one regarding the future course of musical developments.

Extreme technical divergence is evident between electronic and live musical media, integral serialism and aleatoric music, neoclassical construction and flexible aleatoric forms, and organization by noise rather than pitched sounds. Supranational and national trends have also continued to be juxtaposed. This new pluralistic musical era, which is characterized for the most part by isolation of compositional approaches, is reflected further in the many notational systems that have been invented not only for groups of works, but for the individual compositions themselves.

The dissociation of many post–World War II composers from their immediate past is deeply rooted in sociological and technological as well as musical factors. The revival and transformation of serialism at Darmstadt and elsewhere, due to the reaction against the more traditional aesthetics, forms, and techniques of neoclassicism that had prevailed during the interwar period in part, came with the end of fascist censorship of the avant-garde in 1945. Furthermore, the introduction of magnetic tape and new electronic and computer resources also contributed to greater possibilities for mathematical control beyond the existing capabilities of the human performer and to the expansion and invention of new timbres and means of structural organization.

GENERAL TRENDS IN VARIOUS COUNTRIES

We may discern in our rapidly changing and diversified era a continuation of certain early twentieth-century aesthetic and technical tendencies, though as isolated evolutionary threads within otherwise varied eclectic contexts. Vaughan Williams' fusion of both English Renaissance and folk-music sources with Classical-Romantic and impressionistic techniques of the Central European tradition as the basis of his distinctly English modal-tonal idiom had paved the way not only for his own continuing musical development after World War II, but also for that of such younger English composers as Benjamin Britten and Michael Tippett. The use of English sources in Britten's postwar style, however, contrasts with the more pervasive use of native elements in the works of Vaughan Williams, Bartók, Kodály, the Russian Stravinsky, Spanish composers, and other early twentieth-century nationalists. Britten's English influences are only identifiable as part of a larger eclectic contemporary style generally, despite his espousal of traditional English art- and folk-music idioms since World War II. His modal-tonal idiom is based equally on the confluence of Central European contemporary techniques and styles that led to his use of more complex interactions of traditional (diatonic) and nontraditional (octatonic and whole-tone etc.) types of pitch formations. His works since the mid-1950s also include some infusion of twelve-tone technique. Tippett's early English style, as manifested in the irregular meters and polyphonic influences of the English madrigalists in his basically modal-triadic idiom, is also diffused by a more general absorption of contemporary influences, including those of Sibelius, Stravinsky, Bartók, Hindemith, and jazz. His later, more dissonant contemporary approach within traditional genres reveals jazz elements in juxtaposition with quotes from Beethoven, Wagner, and Mussorgsky, as in his *Songs for Dov* (1969–1970), or with elements of Beethoven's *Ninth Symphony*, as in his *Third Symphony* (1970–1972). The Beethoven influence may also be observed in his later *Triple Concerto* (1979). Other English composers such as Humphrey Searle followed the Schoenbergian tradition, while Walton continued along the Romantic lines of Elgar.

Postwar Eastern European composers also drew from many early twentieth-century traditions for their personal styles, in which folk sources served as one of several stylistic threads. In Eastern Europe after the war, Witold Lutosławski continued to employ Polish folk tunes, as in the *Melodie ludowe* ("Folk Melodies," 1945) for piano. Under the pressures of the new Stalinist era to establish a national idiom in Poland since 1948, he turned away from certain "formalistic" tendencies and continued to produce folk-influenced pieces, such as the *Mala suita* ("Little suite," 1951) and *Bukoliki* ("Bucolics," 1952) for piano. After Stalin's death, however, he was to absorb these sources, under the influence of Bartók, and create a more complex set of traditional (formal) as well as nontraditional (pitch-related) elements in his *Concerto for Orchestra* (1951–1954), his personal tonal approach of which was manifested further in his *Muzyka zalobna* ("Funeral music," 1958), dedicated to Bartók. Lutosławski's stylistic development of the next two decades encompassed both Neoclassical and avante-garde tendencies. For instance, the *Preludes and Fugue* for thirteen strings (1972) absorbed the traditional Bachian idiom into the creation of a personal style that included quarter tones. The Polish composer Krzysztof Penderecki did not turn to his native folk sources as Lutosławski did, but began to absorb traditional elements in 1964 in the creation of his own personal idiom, in which his experimental approach to timbre and form is often presented in an expressive style conveying an urgent political message, as in the *Threnody to the Victims of Hiroshima* (1960) and in the invocation of Auschwitz in his *Dies irae* (1967). However, his references to tradition were manifested in his move toward more clearly defined forms by the early 1960s and in his allusion to Bach in his *St. Luke Passion* (1963–1965) as well as Gregorian-chant style in his *Stabat Mater* (1962) and *Utrenia* (1970–1971). We also find a return to traditional genres in his *String Quartets* (1960, 1968) and the *Partita* (1971) for harpsichord and chamber orchestra, though without significant reference to traditional tonal elements. In the Soviet Union, Edison Denisov (b. 1929) fused Russian folk sources, which he acquired from his folk-music investigations in Siberia and elsewhere, into the twelve-tone idiom of *Plachi* ("Laments," 1966) for soprano, piano, and three percussion, in a style reminiscent of Stravinsky's Russian works. On the other hand, Andrey Volkonsky (b. 1933) moved from an idiom influenced by the styles of both Schoenberg and Webern toward the flexible aleatoric forms of the postwar Central European avant-garde, while Valentin Silvestrov (b. 1937) moved from the dramatic lyricism of Shostakovich toward atonality and twelve-tone serialism, arriving at works based on a complex mixture of both contemporary and traditional elements, though he remained typically lyrical.

After World War II, Spanish composers espoused the more modern Central European traditions without the prominent references to Spanish folk-music sources that had characterized the works of Albéniz, Granados, and Falla. Joaquín Rodrigo has come closest to the Spanish national flavor of Falla within his basically Neoclassical approach, beginning primarily with his *Concierto de Aranjuez* (1940). However, he has captured only the general essence of Spanish music, i.e., without any significant absorption of folk sources, and employed traditional Spanish art-music styles only superficially in an idiom infused with early twentieth-century French features, those reminiscent of Dukas especially. Cristóbal Halffter (b. 1930) infused the Spanish idiom with the styles of Stravinsky and Bartók more prominently, as in his *Dos movimientos* (1956) for timpani and string orchestra, and he absorbed the chromatic and serial tendencies of the Vienna Schoenberg circle and the Darmstadt composers decidedly, infusing them in his later Spanish works.

Several composers in the United States have continued, in the post–World War II era, to develop the general aesthetic and stylistic principles of the first generation of Boulanger students, thereby representing a thread within the multiplicity of trends that have characterized music of this country during the past half century. Among the diversity of postwar American composers, including William Schuman, Vincent Persichetti, Vittorio Giannini, Peter Mennen, William Bergsma, Lukas Foss, George Crumb, Gunther Schuller, Leonard Bernstein, Elie Siegmeister, Samuel Barber, and such foreign-born composers as Gian-Carlo Menotti, Hugo Weisgall, and Robert Starer, some have clearly drawn from early twentieth-century American trends. Schuman is perhaps most representative of those that have attempted consciously to perpetuate and develop further inherently American features in their music. Siegmeister also adhered to a distinctly American style colored by jazz and folk music, while Bernstein absorbed these elements into a more popular idiom. The "third stream" compositions of Schuller (e.g., the *Woodwind Quintet* of 1958) and those of other contemporary American composers represent a confluence of more general earlier tendencies, including jazz, *Klangfarben,* and twelve-tone serialism.

Although some Latin American composers have continued to combine elements from their heritages with contemporary influences, the tendency amongst the younger generation from the 1950s on has been toward more varied cosmopolitan styles, combining both traditional (Neoclassical) and the most modernistic approaches. This tendency has been evident in the postwar works of the Mexican composers Carlos Chávez and Rodolfo Halffter, Argentinians Alberto Ginastera and Juan-Carlo Paz, Brazilian Cláudio Santoro and composers of the São Paulo Música Nova Group (Gilberto Mendes, Rogério Duprat, and Willy Corrêa de Oliveira, Colombians Fabio González-Zuleta and Luis Antonio Escobar), and those living in Europe and the United States, including the Argentinian-German composer Mauricio Kagel, Cuban Aurelio de la Vega, Argentinian Luis Jorge González, Chilean Juan Orrego-Salas, and others. Chilean and Peruvian composers who have remained at home have continued in more traditional idioms without infusing them with modernistic postwar techniques. Representative composers of diverse national backgrounds who have continued to develop earlier twentieth-century tendencies, both cosmopolitan and national, are chosen for the following discussions. Certain works of each of these composers represent a confluence of early twentieth-century techniques that include the use of either distinctive or sublimated national elements.

ENGLAND: BENJAMIN BRITTEN

After his sojourn to the United States between 1939 and 1942, during which time he espoused American culture and folklore, Benjamin Britten (1913–1976) was to reestablish his connections to his English heritage. His return home during the war was motivated in part by E. M. Forster's article on the Suffolk poet George Crabbe (1754–1832), whose poetry was to serve later as the basis for the libretto of Britten's opera *Peter Grimes* (1945). Wartime conditions contributed to the rekindling of Britten's interest in British culture, his new patriotism first manifested during his return voyage to England in 1942 in several works based on English literary and musical sources. One of these works was the *Hymn to St. Cecilia,* for a cappella chorus, on the text of W. H. Auden, with whom Britten had already collaborated earlier in his large symphonic song-cycle *Our Hunting Fathers* (1936), for high voice and orchestra, and the *Ballad of Heroes* (1939), for high voice, chorus, and orchestra. The latter was composed in the same year that Britten had followed Auden to the United States. Another work composed on the return trip was the *Ceremony of Carols,* for boys' chorus and harp, its literary and stylistic source in English medieval carols pointing more directly to his national musical tradition. In 1943, through a commission from the Church of England, he composed the festival cantata *Rejoice in the Lamb,* for boys' voices, on the text of the eighteenth-century English poet Christopher Smart, its musical style revealing roots in the English tradition of Purcell. This is reflected in its brilliant sonorities, the dotted rhythm of the Hallelujah and other declamatory features found in Purcell's verse anthems, and some reference to the Baroque ritornello principle. Britten's interest in Purcell-like dotted rhythms is also evident in the canon "Fair and fair and twice so fair" from his *Spring Symphony* (1949), for solo voices, boys' voices, mixed chorus, and orchestra, on the texts of various poets. In his preface to *Peter Grimes,* he asserted his desire to "restore to the musical setting of the English language a brilliance, freedom, and vitality that have been curiously rare since the death of Purcell." His homage to Purcell and other early English composers is also seen in his realizations of Gay's *The Beggar's Opera* and Purcell's *Dido and Aeneas, The Fairy Queen,* several sets of songs, and other works. The *Serenade* (1943), for tenor, horn, and strings, is another example of his revived interest in his English heritage during the war, the conglomerate of texts encompassing English poets from the fifteenth through twentieth centuries. The impact of the English language on the inflections of Britten's musical language is one of the factors that has contributed to the "English" quality of his music.

Also reflective of Britten's new nationalism and his change of style toward greater simplicity and clarity was his adoption of British folk song. However, it was only one of the many features that contributed to the more general English feeling of his music. Many of his folk-song settings, while faithful to the original folk melodies, are always based on a personal enhancement of the tunes in a variety of textural and harmonic approaches. *The Ash Grove* contains a polymodal contrapuntal relation between the stable diatonic modality of the vocal line (in F major) and the shifting modal tonalities (B♭-Aeolian, etc.) of the accompaniment (Ex. 20–1), the colorful dissonant

EXAMPLE 20–1. Benjamin Britten, *The Ash Grove,* folk-song setting, polymodal contrapuntal relation between diatonic modality of vocal line (F major) and shifting modal tonalities (B♭-Aeolian, etc.) of accompaniment

clashes seeming to reflect the poetic mood, "Still trembles the moonbeam on streamlet and fountain." The simultaneous modal-tonal polarity between voice and accompaniment is characteristic of many of Britten's works. While other folk-song arrangements, such as *Men of Goodwill* (based on "God rest ye merry, gentlemen"), also reveal a faithfulness to the original tune, other settings are based on more complex absorptions and transformations of the folk-song materials. Peter Evans provides insight into Britten's free approach to the folk sources in the *Suite on English Folk Tunes,* Op. 90 (1966–1975), for chamber orchestra, Britten's generation of composers finding "uncongenial the consciously cultivated folk influences so evident in the work of many of their English forerunners."[1]

Britten had drawn from a variety of English literary and musical sources, but his special position as one of the most original of English composers can be seen in his more general ability to integrate many influences from beyond his own national boundaries. In addition to English verse, he also set Italian (*Seven Sonnets of Michelangelo,* 1940), German (*Sechs Hölderlin-Fragmente,* 1958), and French (*Les Illuminations,* 1939, after Rimbaud) texts in musical contexts combining his own national modal features and traditional harmonic (triadic) elements with contemporary stylistic and technical principles; he acquired an intimate knowledge of the music of Bartók, Schoenberg, Berg, and others through his studies with Frank Bridge. His *Variations on a Theme of Frank Bridge* (1937), for string orchestra, reveals his debt to the Viennese tradition from Mahler to the Schoenberg circle distinctly. Donald Mitchell asserts that often "the style a composer parodies is a style which holds for him the greatest possible attraction and by which he has been and will be influenced."[2] In parts of the cycle of five songs *On This Island* (1937), for high voice and piano on poems of Auden, we also find the influence of Stravinsky's *Apollon Musagète.*[3] The influence of Stravinsky continued to be evident in the polarized textural and formal planes of many of his later works (e.g., the *War Requiem*). While Britten often incorporated these materials into simple traditional formal outlines, he was to absorb his varied sources, both national and cosmopolitan, into a unified and intense Romantic idiom. He expanded the Romantic aesthetics of his late nineteenth- and early twentieth-century English forebears to accommodate the expression of his personal convictions regarding the most urgent contemporary political, social, religious, and moral issues of our time.

Britten composed in all genres—opera, incidental music, choral and solo vocal music with piano or orchestra, solo chamber music, string quartets

---

[1] Peter Evans, *The Music of Benjamin Britten* (Minneapolis: University of Minnesota Press, 1979), p. 338.

[2] Donald Mitchell, "The Musical Atmosphere," in *Benjamin Britten: A Commentary on His Works from a Group of Specialists,* ed. Donald Mitchell and Hans Keller (Salisbury Square, London: Rockliff Publishing Corporation Limited, 1952), p. 11.

[3] For a comparison of specific passages of the Britten and Stravinsky works, see Evans, *The Music of Benjamin Britten,* n.1, above, pp. 73–74, and Mitchell, "The Vocal Music," in ibid., p. 64.

and other small combinations, and orchestral pieces, including a *Sinfonietta* (1932), *Simple Symphony* (1933–1934), *Piano Concerto* (1938), *Violin Concerto* (1939), etc.—but his philosophical and stylistic evolution may best be traced in his vocal works from the 1930s to the *War Requiem* (1961). *A Boy Was Born* (1933), for a cappella chorus, reveals his early ability to join various sources, among them old German and English Carol tunes and texts, into a coherent yet formally distinct set of variations. This traditional formal scheme serves as an ideal framework for the juxtaposition of contrasting sonorities and textures so characteristic of his approach. Most striking is the contrast between the fifth variation, with its layered contrapuntal rhythmic style and dissonant treatment reminiscent of the French medieval motet, and the final variation, with its static harmonic context based on changing colors that suggests the *Klangfarben* technique of Schoenberg.[4] Britten's lifelong religious sense is already apparent in this work, but his commitment to more general moral and social issues first became evident in the mid-1930s. During this time, his philosophical views developed in connection to his increasing political concerns and his collaboration with Auden, which resulted in his first landmark work, *Our Hunting Fathers* (1936). Despite the influence of Stravinsky's angular style in "Rats away," or the Romantic influence of Mahler in the final "Funeral March," we are provided a view of the era from an original and personal standpoint. The music underscores Auden's textual commentary protesting the senseless slaughter of animals for sport, thereby revealing both Auden's and Britten's general concern for life. In his diary, Britten referred to this work while expressing his increasing political concerns during the Spanish Civil War.[5]

Britten's political and moral views expressed in both his diary and his music revealed the stance he was to take during World War II as a conscientious objector. As a pacifist during the increasing international tensions of the prewar period, he collaborated with Paul Rotha on a documentary "Peace Film" in 1936. In his *Ballad of Heroes* (1939), for solo, chorus, and orchestra, which was dedicated to those of the British Battalion of the International Brigade who died in the Spanish Civil War, we find a more direct and bitter musical setting of the Auden and Swingler text. It was composed under the worsening political situation just before Britten left England for the United States. This work is significant for its confluence of the philosophical and stylistic tendencies that characterize much of his remaining repertoire. In addition to its political associations and Mahlerian musical allusions, which are manifested in the musical characterizations and titles of the movements—"Funeral March," "Scherzo (Dance of Death)," "Recitative and Choral," and "Epilogue (Funeral March),"—we already find the personal dramatic style of his postwar solo vocal and choral works.

---

[4] Mitchell, ibid., p. 89.

[5] Britten's statement is quoted in Donald Mitchell, *Britten and Auden in the Thirties: The Year 1936* (London and Boston: Faber and Faber, 1981), p. 46.

All of the features of Britten's musical language, in which he absorbed traditional triadic structures into bitonal or polytonal combinations in contexts based on the interaction of modes and other types of nontraditional pitch-sets, were to be synthesized in the *War Requiem.* The musico-dramatic relations of the *Requiem* reveal his combined experiences gained from working with opera, choral media, and instrumental genres after World War II. In his series of operas, including *Peter Grimes,* which, after 1945, established his reputation as the most important English operatic composer since Purcell, *The Rape of Lucretia* (1946), *Albert Herring* (1947), *Let's Make an Opera* (1948), *Billy Budd* (1951), *Gloriana* (1953), *The Turn of the Screw* (1954), *Noye's Fludde* (1957), and *Midsummer Night's Dream* (1960), we find many of the musico-dramatic effects that were to be combined in the *War Requiem.* The dark dramatic mood in the final passages of *Peter Grimes* is underlaid musically by a dissonant bitonal relation between the colorful C-major orchestral arpeggiations and the A-major tonality of the voices. Equally striking is the argument between Ellen and Peter in Act II, Scene I, which occurs against the choral background of the Credo sung by the congregation during a church service. This religious aura in a context of extreme dramatic and musical tension, induced by the polarization of distinct textural, timbral, and tonal levels, foreshadows Britten's aesthetic and technical approach in the *War Requiem.* These and other passages of *Peter Grimes* reveal dramatic and musical similarities to Berg's *Wozzeck.* During this postwar period of operatic composition, Britten continued to reveal his religious faith in many sacred choral works following those composed during his return voyage to England in 1942. These include *A Shepherd's Carol* (1944), after Auden, *Festival Te Deum* (1944), *St. Nicolas* (1948), *Hymn to St. Peter* (1955), *Antiphon* (1956), *Missa brevis* (1959), *Jubilate Deo* (1961), and others following the *War Requiem.* He also set sacred texts in the solo vocal medium.

Britten's philosophical, political, national, and religious convictions are joined in the *War Requiem,* in which he exploits the resources of both the vocal and symphonic media to produce one of his most powerful and original dramatic expressions. In this work, traditional forms and procedures (fugue, chaconne, ritornello, etc.) serve as the framework for nontraditional pitch-set relations, which include the modal, octatonic, and whole-tone interactions characteristic of the Bartók and Stravinsky idioms. These are often fused with traditional, though nonfunctional triadic harmonies. The work was commissioned for the Festival to celebrate the Consecration of St. Michael's Cathedral, Coventry, which was destroyed in World War II. Interpolation of the antiwar poems of Wilfred Owen, an English poet and hero killed in France at the end of World War I, into the setting of the Missa pro Defunctis represents the most direct manifestation of Britten's religious and political convictions as a conscientious objector during World War II. The polarity inherent in the juxtaposition of the sacred Latin text and English poetic commentary associated with the world of war, suffering, and death is reflected musically in both the large-scale and local formal schemes and in the interaction of melodic and harmonic details.

Britten's characteristic use of contrasting textural and timbral blocks and layers is basic to the realization of his philosophical statement. The brilliant scoring of the sacred Latin text, for soprano solo and full chorus with large orchestra, contrasts with that of the English poems, sung by the tenor and baritone soloists (two soldiers who have died in combat) with chamber orchestra. Between these polarized extremes is the objective, distant, and archaic sound of the boys' chorus with organ. The polarity inherent in these textual and musical planes is intensified gradually in the larger formal plan, the most extreme point of divergence occurring between the sixth poem, "So Abram rose" (baritone and tenor solos), based on one of the most bitter and pessimistic statements, and the *Sanctus* (soprano solo and bells, followed by chorus), which represents sublime purity. The *Hostias* (boys' voices) serves as the intercessory between these extremes: "make them, O Lord, to pass from death unto life."

The main musical principles of polarity and conflict are established in the Introit, where they reflect the meaning of the text: "Requiem aeternam dona eis Domine: et lux perpetua luceat eis" ("Rest eternal grant unto them, O Lord: and let light eternal shine upon them"). Two contrasting concepts are suggested in these words—*death* in "rest eternal" and *life* in "light eternal." The somber quality of the opening "Requiem aeternam" is established by the quiet antiphonal choral declamation on two notes, F♯ and C. This tritone, which forms a local polarity within the choral block itself, is juxtaposed against several larger orchestral planes and layers that unfold similarly in a dark register. While the tolling bells form a timbral layer that simply colors the choral chant by doubling its tritone, the opposing orchestral block is made up of several modal and sustained layers contrasting internally, none of which contains the basic choral/bell tritone. Above the A pedal (tuba, timpani, and piano), which is axial to the choral tritone and together with it produces a larger cyclic-interval-3 segment, F♯–A–C, two modal blocks are discerned between the rising angular theme of the upper winds/strings and rising scale of the lower winds. These two orchestral planes are closely related in pitch content, but one alteration (pitch-class A in the thirty-second-note embellishing figure of the upper winds/strings) distinguishes the D-harmonic-minor theme (D–E–F–G–A–B♭–C♯–D, with G♯ as a lower-neighbor) from the E-octatonic scale (E–F–G–G♯–A♯–B–C♯–D) of the lower winds. The musico-dramatic significance of these three contrasting choral and orchestral pitch collections lies primarily in the dissonant role of the basic choral tritone (F♯–C) in relation to the D-harmonic-minor and E-octatonic modes. Tritone F♯–C does not belong to these modal collections (Ex. 20–2), but rather forms a chromatic relationship with them. It forms a complementary symmetrical relation with the E-octatonic scale. Thus, while the sustained A (axis of F♯–A–C) is drawn into the orchestral plane as an element of the D-harmonic-minor theme, the C–F♯ tritone remains the only dissonant, or noncommon element.

In the move toward "et lux perpetua" ("light"), this divergent relation between the choral tritone and the orchestral modes is resolved to reflect

EXAMPLE 20–2. Benjamin Britten, *War Requiem,* opening, dissonant relation of three contrasting choral and orchestral pitch collections: cyclic-interval-3 segment (F♯–A–C), D-harmonic-minor theme, and E-octatonic mode (E–F–G–A♭–B♭–B–C♯–D)

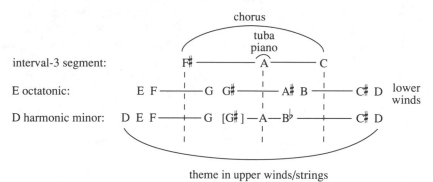

the translucence of the text. At the second (ritornello) orchestral statement (m. 6 to No. 1), the original E-octatonic scale is replaced in the lower winds by ascending parallel five-note segments of the two whole-tone scales a minor third apart, B–C♯–D♯–F–G and D–E–F♯–A♭–B♭ (Ex. 20–3). The first whole-tone scale is completed by the original axial A (tuba, timpani, and piano) to give us [A]–B–C♯–D♯–F–G, the other by the C of the choral tritone to give us [C]–D–E–F♯–A♭–B♭. The other tritone component (F♯) is already contained in the latter scale. Thus, all three components of the sustained primary cyclic-interval-3 segment, F♯–A–C, have become consonant elements within the orchestral plane as they map into, or generate systematically, the two whole-tone cycles, respectively. The result is a more transparent and consonant relation between the otherwise divergent choral

EXAMPLE 20–3. Benjamin Britten, *War Requiem,* mm. 6–9, new modal layers (whole-tone scales) in lower wind plane against mixed modal segments of theme in upper winds/strings

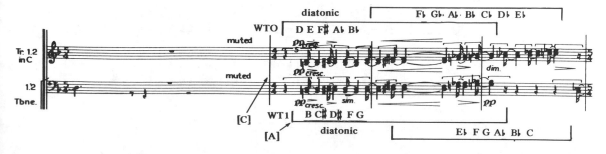

and orchestral blocks, a transformation of the musical texture which anticipates "light."

This new consonant role of tritone F♯–C in the whole-tone passage is established further toward the end of the next orchestral statement (No. 1, mm. 7–8) in anticipation of "et lux perpetua." The ascending octatonic quintuplet figure, A–B♭–C–D♭–E♭ (Ex. 20–4), is transformed in the cadential crescendo figure of the next measure into a diatonic segment, C–D♭–E♭–F–G♭, so the basic tritone (in enharmonic spelling, C–G♭) is interpreted as both octatonic and diatonic. The basic frame of this winding octatonic-diatonic passage in the most radiant register of the upper winds and strings is the interval-3 cycle, A–C–E♭–G♭, a completion of the original F♯–A–C symmetry. The significance of this frame is confirmed at "et lux perpetua," where the choral stretto on F♯ and C is accompanied only by the sustained A. Thus, in the progression toward "light," the choral tritone has moved from its position as a dissonant element to a consonant one, as it maps into—becomes part of—whole-tone, octatonic, and diatonic pitch-sets systematically.

The *Te decet hymnus* (Nos. 3–7), for boys' choir, organ, and strings, represents an intercessory stage, as the text refers to prayer and the promise of deliverance: "Thou who hearest the prayer, unto Thee shall all flesh come."

EXAMPLE 20–4. Benjamin Britten, *War Requiem*, No. 1, mm. 7–8, octatonic quintuplet figure (A–B♭–C–D♭–E♭) transformed into diatonic segment (C–D♭–E♭–F–G♭), giving basic tritone (C–G♭) both octatonic and diatonic interpretations as part of common cyclic-interval-3 frame (A–C–E♭–G♭)

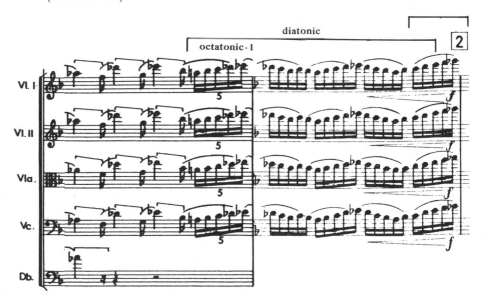

In a contrasting mood of detachment in a style reminiscent of plainchant, we get a more perfect intersection of the C–F♯ tritone with the three types of pitch-sets—whole-tone, octatonic, and diatonic—within a formal structure controlled rigidly. The first four-measure phrase, divided into "white- and black-key" diatonic segments, is bounded temporally by C and F♯, both of which belong to these two diatonic spheres, respectively, and are supported by string pedals on these two notes. The antecedent phrase is balanced by a four-measure consequent to complete the first musico-textual section (A). While the tritone polarity is basic to the linear phrase structure of the entire section, a special conflict emerges with the very first chord—F-major triad, a conflict which has long-range significance in connection to the dramatic resolution at the cadence of the entire work following the words "Requiescant in pace. Amen" ("May they rest in peace. Amen"). The initiating F-major chord of the *Te decet* suggests a transformation of the original cyclic-interval-3 collection, F♯–A–C, framed by the tritone polarity. The F-major triad anticipates the resolution of the tritone (F♯–C) polarity to the perfect-fifth F–C. However, since the *Te decet* represents an intermediary stage, both conflicting intervals are presented explicitly on the separate melodic and harmonic levels.

Thus far, the C–F♯ tritone components have been identified melodically with the two diatonic ("white- and black-key") spheres. In counterpoint with the vocal line, the organ unfolds a triadic progression built on a chaconne bass, the initial bass segment under the first phrase of which forms a symmetrical structure encompassed by the basic tritone (C–D–E♭–E–F♯). This chromatic symmetry implies an interlocking of components of the other two types of pitch-sets: octatonic (C–D–E♭–[ ]–F♯ or C–[ ]–E♭–E–F♯), of which the tritone transposition (C–E♭–F♯) of the original cyclic-interval-3 construction (F♯–A–C) serves as the axial superstructure; and whole-tone (C–D–[ ]–E–F♯). While this fusion of pitch-sets is implied at this point, the remaining phrases of the *Te decet* move toward increasingly explicit partitions of these particular pitch-set segments in correspondence with the direction of the text: "exaudi orationem meam, ad te omnis caro veniet" ("Thou who hearest the prayer, unto Thee shall all flesh come").

The chaconne organ bass (beginning with the F♯ at No. 3, m. 4, to the third note, E♭, of the chaconne repeat at No. 4, m. 3) establishes a complete octatonic collection (in scalar ordering, C–D–E♭–F–F♯–G♯–A–B) against the diatonic vocal phrases. Tritone C–F♯ belongs to this octatonic collection as well as to the diatonic vocal phrases. Following the expanded five-measure antecedent and consequent phrases of Section B (No. 4f.), the diatonic phrases of which are again related inversionally and bounded temporally by the basic tritone, we get a shift for the first time in the vocal line (Section C, Nos. 5–6) to the octatonic segments implied in the recurrent primary chaconne-bass figure (C–D–E♭–E–F♯). The antecedent phrase completes the implied C–[ ]–E♭–E–F♯ of the latter to give us C–D♭–E♭–E–F♯, while the inverted consequent completes the implied C–D–E♭–[ ]–F♯ to give us C–D–E♭–F–F♯ (in enharmonic spelling and inversion, F♯–E♯–D♯–D–C).

The vocal line of Section D (No. 6, mm. 1–4), which is now contracted to two-measure antecedent and consequent phrases, unfolds the tritone transposition and inversion (C–B♭–A♭–G♭) of the whole-tone tetrachord (C–D–E–F♯) implied in the primary chaconne-bass figure. Thus, tritone C–F♯ is common to all three of the basic types of sets and serves as their structural frame.

A dynamic fugue at the words "quam olim Abrahae promisisti, et semini ejus" ("which, of old, Thou didst promise unto Abraham and his seed") leads to the peak of divergence between the bitter text of the sixth poem and the sublime purity of the *Sanctus*. The dramatic role and musical disposition of this fugue is similar to the hunting fugue in Bartók's *Cantata Profana*. Both fugues foreshadow a transcendent moment, in both cases the voices moving toward increasingly close stretto and a final homophonic convergence. Bartók's fugue leads to a magical transformation of nine sons into stags resulting in their ultimate freedom, while Britten's refers to the promise given to Abraham and his sons for deliverance "in lucem sanctam" ("into the holy light"). However, man instead of the lamb is sacrificed (crucified).

As a reflection of the transcendent purity of the *Sanctus,* the basic pitch-sets of the work are transformed musically into their primordial and most lucid state, i.e., in the form of the interval cycles, which are commonly generated from the basic tritone cycle, F♯–C. The pitched percussion instruments provide a glowing background based on the single note, F♯, against which the soprano unfolds two whole-tone segments (E–F♯ and G♯–F♯) on "Sanctus." The combined whole-tone content (E–F♯–F♯–G♯) of this pair of phrase segments establishes F♯ as an axis of symmetry. A longer consequent phrase balances the first two declamatory statements with a more complex unfolding of both whole-tone cycles. The brilliant soprano line, still accompanied by the orchestral F♯, unfolds a series of arpeggiated (diatonic) triads within an F♯-octave boundary (Ex. 20–5a). The upper notes of these triads unfold a whole-tone tetrachord, F♯–E–D–C, which is extended to the complete primary whole-tone cycle by the cadential whole-tone segment, B♭–A♭–F♯, to give us F♯–E–D–C–B♭–A♭–F♯. At the same time, the lower triadic notes unfold a whole-tone segment, B–[   ]–G–F, which is complemented by the succession of middle triadic notes to outline the complete secondary whole-tone cycle, D♯–C♯–B–A–G–F.

The entire initial passage is repeated with special modifications and cyclic expansions (Nos. 84–85). The background note, F♯, of the percussion is replaced by its tritone, C, and each of the whole-tone segments of the original phrasal pair is expanded to four- (A♯–B♯–C×–F♯) and five- (A♯–B♯–C×–F♯–G♯) note segments, respectively, of the primary whole-tone cycle. Both of these expanded phrases are now bounded temporally by the basic tritone, C–F♯ (i.e., enharmonically spelled as B♯–F♯). Analogously to the consequent phrase of the initial period, we again get a longer arpeggiated soprano line, but this time based on an ascending contour bounded temporally by both notes (B♯–F♯, i.e., C–F♯) of the basic tritone. While the

EXAMPLE 20–5. Benjamin Britten, *War Requiem,* "Sanctus," (a) mm. 5–6, soprano, series of triads (diatonic) linearly unfolding two whole-tone scales in upper (F♯–E–D–C–B♭–A♭–F♯) and lower (B–[A]–G–F) triadic notes, respectively; (b) No. 84, mm. 5–6, more complex linear interaction of whole-tone and cyclic-interval-3 segments in lower and upper notes, respectively

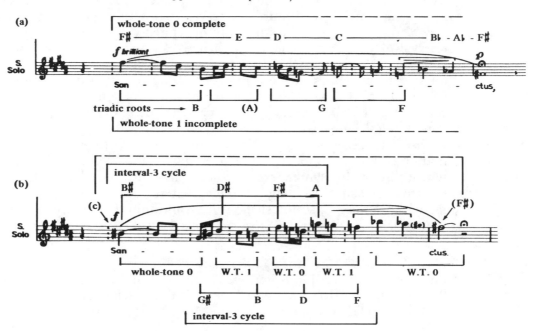

cadential figure (B♭–A♭–F♯) is the same as that of the earlier consequent phrase, a more complex cyclic-interval interaction characterizes the entire line (Ex. 20–5b). The original triadic arpeggiations are replaced by whole-tone trichords (B♯–A♯–G♯, D♯–C♯–B, F♯–E–D, A–G–F), which alternately unfold both complete whole-tone cycles. The succession of the upper trichordal boundary notes outlines an interval-3 cycle, B♯–D♯–F♯–A, the lower ones, G♯–B–D–F, another, both interval-3 cycles together implying the presence of an octatonic collection, B♯–D–D♯–F–F♯–G♯–A–B.

In the final passage of this first large section, "Pleni sunt coeli et terra gloria tua" ("Heaven and earth are full of Thy glory"), we get a more systematic generation of the interval cycles from F♯ and C. The eight-part chorus builds by means of stretto and crescendo, the accumulation of voices and instruments within a symmetrical cyclic-interval context reflecting the text. The first six entries of this stretto, F♯–G♯–B–C♯–E–F♯, systematically alternate the two preceding cyclic-intervals, 2 and 3 (see Ex. 20–5b), within the octave frame of the basic F♯. The resulting pentatonic scale, which alternates interval-2 dyads from both whole-tone cycles, also implies the presence of two intercalated segments of the interval-5 cycle, F♯–B–E and

G#–C#–F# (see Ex. 20–6). The C then begins the same alternating pattern of intervals 2 and 3 within the basic C-octave frame. The basic cyclic-interval-3 segment, F#–A–C (Ex. 20–6), so essential near the very opening of the *Requiem,* serves as a trichordal axis for the unfolding of the two larger cyclic-interval-5 (pentatonic) segments in this stretto. Thus, the earlier pervasive interactions among diatonic, octatonic, and whole-tone sets are reduced in the *Sanctus* to their primordial intervallic structures, cyclic-intervals 5, 3, and 2, respectively, all of which are generated exclusively from the basic interval-6 cycle, F#–C. The stretto then gives way (at No. 87) to a Bach-like fanfare in D major, in which the basses replace the original soprano whole-tone segments (E–F# and G#–F#), on "Sanctus," with diatonic segments (A–B–D and B–C#–D). This abrupt change from symmetrical to diatonic contexts at "Hosanna in excelsis" is characteristic of the principle of polarity underlying the work.

The *War Requiem,* which is a continuation of the great English choral tradition, fuses traditional forms, procedures, and harmonic constructions with those pitch-set premises exploited earlier by Bartók and Stravinsky. Britten's personal handling of these materials in "polymodally" chromaticized contexts also foreshadowed his infusion, temporarily, of twelve-tone serial principles in the *Songs and Proverbs of William Blake* (1965).

UNITED STATES: WILLIAM SCHUMAN; GEORGE CRUMB

One of the prominent American composers to have grown out of the "Americanist" movement of the 1930s is William Schuman (b. 1910), a pupil of Roy Harris at the Juilliard School of Music from 1936 to 1938. As president

EXAMPLE 20–6. Benjamin Britten, *War Requiem,* "Sanctus," Nos. 85–86, pentatonic stretto entries, first from F# to F#, then C to C, alternating whole-tone dyads implying two intercalated segments of the interval-5 cycle, with basic cyclic-interval-3 segment (F#–A–C) linking both halves of stretto

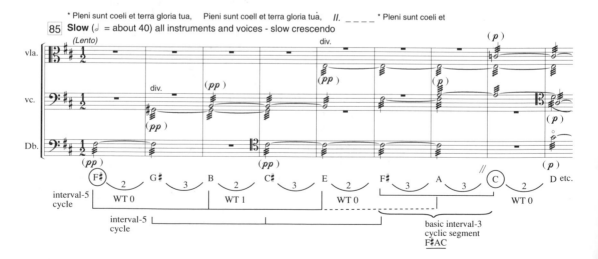

of the Juilliard School since 1945 and Lincoln Center since 1962, Schuman helped to promote many American composers and their works—he brought to the Juilliard faculty William Bergsma and Peter Mennin—just as Harris helped to promote Schuman's music by bringing his works to the attention of Copland and Koussevitzky. The influence of Harris is evident in Schuman's contributions to the "grand" American symphonic tradition, which had been established in the 1930s by Harris, Copland, Piston, Hanson, and Sessions as an offshoot of the European symphonic tradition. The long spun-out lines that characterize Schuman's symphonic medium also reveal the legacy of Harris. Schuman's *American Festival Overture* (1939), the opera *The Mighty Casey* (1951–1953), *New England Triptych* (1956), and other works combine identifiable American traits with traditional procedures, including fugue, passacaglia, and other Baroque-like techniques. However, these are part of a contemporary idiom often based on polytonal-triadic and other types of dissonant chromatic combinations.

In his varied repertoire of orchestral compositions, ballets (including *Undertow,* 1945, and *Night Journey,* 1947, both written for Martha Graham), concertos, chamber, and vocal music, his ten symphonies are among his most representative works. The *American Festival Overture,* which is among his earliest works, suggests a general American mood in its fresh dynamic quality, but is more specifically American in its use of sounds stemming from the composer's youth in New York City, as discussed in his notes to the first performance: "The first three notes of this piece will be recognized by some listeners as the 'call to play' of boyhood days. In New York City it is yelled on the syllables 'Wee-Awk-Eee' to get the gang together for a festive occasion of some sort. . . . From this it should not be inferred that the Overture is program music. . . . The development of this bit of 'folk material,' then, is along purely musical lines."[6]

The general American feeling of Schuman's music is also manifested in several works for band, including *Newsreel (in Five Shots)* (1941) and *George Washington Bridge* (1950), such compositions reflecting the increase of school marching and football bands in the United States. Similarly, the proliferation of symphonic writing by Schuman and other Americans came partly as a response to the growing number of symphony orchestras in this country. While Schuman's works evoke an American mood, national elements are only part of a synthesis based on a combination of historical and contemporary international musical resources. Outside of the obvious American references in the extramusical aspects of his works, as in the titles of his *American Overture, The Mighty Casey, George Washington Bridge,* and *New England Triptych,* Schuman's intrinsic musical Americanism is identifiable not by any

---

[6] As quoted by Edward Downes, *Guide to Symphonic Music* (New York: The Philharmonic-Symphony Society of New York, Inc., 1976 and 1981), p. 820; first published as *The New York Philharmonic Guide to the Symphony* (New York: Walker Publishing Company, Inc., 1976).

significant use of authentic regional musical elements, but in the general qualities stemming from the Harris tradition based on a sense of spaciousness, freshness, melodic fluidity, and a directness often manifested in powerful antiphonal instrumental choirs set in angular and dynamic rhythms. Metrically displaced accents also suggest a source in American jazz, which was a part of his early musical experience. In his early works, Schuman had already ventured beyond the technical means employed by Harris in his continuation of the American symphonic tradition, moving toward a more varied palette, in which increasingly chromatic and dissonant, often polytonal harmonies are set within clear traditional forms. His formalistic control over his expansive and often lyrical content also points to his roots in the Classical-Romantic tradition.

Schuman's mastery of traditional forms and procedures in a modern—often triadic and tonal, but nonfunctional—musical language is already evident in his *Symphony No. 3* (1941). The overall form does not adhere to the traditional symphonic plan, its two large parts based instead on Baroque types: Part I is divided into *Passacaglia* and *Fugue,* Part II into *Chorale* and *Toccata.* The *Passacaglia,* a set of variations traditionally, establishes the formal procedure for the initial section. Rhythmic accumulation by means of increasing subdivisions of the beat, which characterizes variations traditionally, lends itself to the development and expansion reminiscent of the American symphonic idiom of Harris. The linearity of much of Schuman's writing, like that of Harris, is evident in the long, spun-out passacaglia theme, the Baroque reference of which is also supported by the fugal accumulation of polyphonic layers around the theme.

These Baroque features, infused with stylistic elements established by Harris, are absorbed into Schuman's personal idiom by means of additional contemporary techniques. The binary phrase construction of traditional passacaglia themes is reflected in Schuman's theme, but the latter deviates from the traditional symmetrical structure of 4 + 4 measures by the diminution of the second thematic half to three measures. This deviation tends to shift the emphasis from the balanced phrasal pairing to an irregular, rhythmically directed thematic motion characteristic of Schuman's style. This traditional thematic type is also drawn into Schuman's contemporary idiom by the infusion of a nonfunctional modal chromaticism into a somewhat tonal style. The theme is comprised of a succession of tonally ambiguous modal-diatonic segments (Ex. 20–7), the first (E–E–C–B) perhaps suggesting modes on A, E, or B. However, the addition of the next note, F♯, which gives us E–E–C–B–F♯, points more specifically to either an implied E-Aeolian (E–F♯–G–A–B–C–D–E) or B-Phrygian (B–C–D–E–F♯–G–A–B) collection. These modal implications are dissolved immediately through the addition of another perfect fourth followed by a perfect fifth, the segment B–F♯–C♯–G♯ suggesting a new modal tonic, F♯. While this tonal area is supported by the following implied leading-tone, E♯, a replacement of the latter pitch by E produces another chromatic disruption, after which the first phrase then moves to its modified repetition in the second half of the theme.

EXAMPLE 20–7. William Schuman, *Symphony No. 3,* "Passacaglia," opening, spun-out passacaglia theme, succession of tonally ambiguous modal–diatonic segments

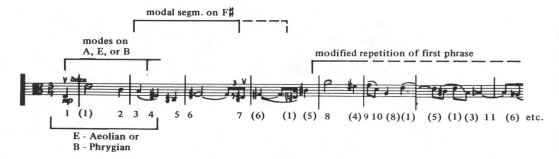

While similar modal-diatonic shifts are implied in this half as well, the linear adjacencies or overlappings of these segments add up to a theme containing all twelve tones with only minimal recurrence of several pitch-classes (G♯, E, A, and C♯). Due to the reiterative thematic principle in the use of canon and passacaglia (variation), a twelve-tone serial conception is imminent.

These procedures and techniques foreshadow Schuman's more intensive fusion of an angular linear chromaticism and traditional diatonic (harmonic and melodic) structures with more dissonant polytonal harmonies, as in *Symphony Nos. 6–9* (1947, 1960, 1963, and 1968). In these more complex symphonies, he was to join Baroque forms and procedures as well as jazz influences (final scherzo of *Symphony No. 7*) with more Classical outlines (the four middle movements of the six that comprise *Symphony No. 6* suggest the traditional four-movement symphonic plan with scherzo, while rondo, scherzo, or variation movements occur in the otherwise nontraditional schemes of the other symphonies).[7] In *Symphony No. 3*, the repetitions of the opening passacaglia theme are presented in the form of seven fugal entries (mm. 1–50), each new statement appearing against the continuing contrapuntal line of the preceding thematic statement. While unity among the contrapuntal lines is produced by their free contour association with the theme, each line unfolds its own succession of changing diatonic-modal segments independently. These contribute to the increasing chromaticism that results from the accumulation of layers. This chromaticism is heightened by the entries of the theme in ascending half-step transpositions, which replace the traditional perfect-fifth relation of successive entries: the initial entry on E is followed by F, then F♯, and so on through the tritone, B♭. The

[7] The forms of the symphonies are summarized by Preston Stedman, *The Symphony* (Englewood Cliffs, NJ: Prentice-Hall, Inc., 1979), pp. 354–366.

simultaneously unfolding lines are held together vertically by traditional tertian harmonies, so the latter are absorbed into a nontraditional linear modal chromaticism.

The variational (sectional) scheme of both the *Passacaglia* and *Fugue* permits maximal distinction in structural, figural, and timbral organization. At the same time, the use of variation permits structural unity based on motivic-thematic relations among the sections and the contrapuntal lines themselves. The variation format also lends itself to textural building in contrasting stages in support of the broadening lyrical lines, these characteristics underlying the expansive developmental "American" quality of Schuman's style. A sudden increase of rhythmic activity from the accompanying eighth-note figuration of the thematic section to the triplet figuration of Variation I (mm. 51–73) contributes to the articulation and differentiation of these larger formal blocks. An increased sense of motion is also introduced not only by the smaller triplet subdivisions, but by the sharper antiphonal juxtapositions of homophonic triadic blocks (especially mm. 63–73) within the latter part of the variation. While textural accumulation in the opening thematic section occurred by means of the additive fugal procedure, this section builds by the use of sharper and faster textural rhythm.

Block interaction is intensified in the remaining variations by means of more simultaneous occurrences of divergent planes, often unified homophonically. In Variation II (mm. 75–86), the preceding triplet figuration is absorbed into the theme itself, against which the preceding antiphonal dotted figure unfolds simultaneously as the basis for a more continuous accompaniment. The sharpness of these two textural planes is heightened further by the first prominent polytonal combinations of the work, the lower strings and winds reiterating a C-major triad against an A-major triad in the upper strings (mm. 74–76), the triplet theme shifting from a C-major segment to a partial B-major/minor (B–F♯) triad (m. 76). As the theme fuses certain components from these triads linearly (mm. 77ff.), the accompanying block shifts to a C-major/E♭-major triadic combination. Thus, formal shape and direction in the *Passacaglia* are determined primarily by the interrelations of the contrasting planes and layers, the harmonic combinations (triadic or polytonal) contributing primarily to the structural functions of the various textures rather than to any traditional concept of tonal organization.

The *Fugue* reveals the same structural and technical principles as the *Passacaglia*. The fugue subject also consists of shifting modal (often triadic) segments, which outline a longer chromatic line together based on minimal pitch-class repetition, so we again have a fusion of traditional and nontraditional elements. The fugue exposition also presents the subject in successive half-step transpositions rather than the traditional perfect-fifth entries, the series of seven entries (mm. 146, 150, 157, 165, 172, 180, and 187) beginning at the tritone, B♭, and continuing through the tonic E to complete the entire chromatic cycle. This scheme of transpositions contributes to the textural intensification, in which increasing polytonal intrusions (often as simultaneous linear modal patches) also play an obvious textural rather than tonal role by contributing to an accumulation of dissonances. The variational procedures of the *Passacaglia* and *Fugue* are exploited further in the *Chorale* and *Toccata,* the diversity of textural planes and layers of these sections continuing to be unified by means of thematic transformation or the projection of common elements (motivic, intervallic, rhythmic, and structural) throughout. Thus, polytonal and textural juxtapositions and the pervasive use of jazz-derived dynamic rhythms, in a context joining traditional and nontraditional features, are basic to the fresh and brilliant sound associated with the American symphonic idiom.

Schuman's inclination toward a more explicit Americana is evident in his *New England Triptych* (1956), based on three pieces by the American composer William Billings (1746–1800). The overt American quality of this work, as manifested primarily in the titles of the three pieces drawn from Billings' own texts—"Be Glad Then, America," "When Jesus Wept," and "Chester"—and in Schuman's more general feelings of identification with the earlier American composer, is described by Schuman: "The works of this dynamic composer capture the spirit of sinewy ruggedness, deep religiosity and patriotic fervor that we associate with the Revolutionary period. . . . [My] pieces do not constitute a 'fantasy' on themes of Billings, nor 'variations' on his themes, but rather a fusion of styles and musical language."[8]

The timpani solo that opens the first piece, "Be Glad Then, America," establishes certain stylized melodic and rhythmic characteristics that evoke a feeling of the popular American musical heritage. The melodic contour is defined by a simple, folk-like D-pentatonic segment, D–F–C, repeated in constantly varied repetitions based on a syncopated march-like rhythm. While this suggests the Stravinskian ostinato technique based on constant rhythmic reinterpretations of narrow-ranged modal layers, the addition of an octave-D pedal in the low clarinets and double bass also immediately establishes the open quality found in the American symphonic works of Harris and Copland. A feeling of the spacious landscape of New England is evoked by Schuman's accumulation of long melodic lines of "sinewy ruggedness," the widening modal compass of the individual string layers unfolding in an additive texture over the D pedal, first in open parallel thirds (mm. 21ff.), then in a mixture of triads in a general parallel contour. A sense of expansion and development is also induced by constant local shifts of linear modal segments, resulting in simultaneous as well as successive increases in polymodal chromaticism. While the local linear pentatonic-diatonic segments maintain some reference to the American popular sphere, the latter is drawn into a contemporary idiom by these polymodal techniques. In both its specific features and general quality, this introductory section foreshadows the "Hallelujah" that closes the piece.

The joyous mood is established by the trombones and trumpets at the beginning of the main section (*Allegro Vivo*) which, as described by the composer, is "a free and varied setting of the words 'Be Glad Then, America,

---

[8] See Schuman's program notes in the preface to the score (Bryn Mawr: Merion Music, Inc., 1957).

Shout and Rejoice.' " Large antiphonal blocks in dotted rhythm then lead to a new timpani solo, in which the syncopated rhythms now incorporate the sharp dotted rhythm in a more angular melodic contour than had character-ized the very opening timpani solo. As the composer points out, this "leads to a middle fugal section stemming from the words 'And Ye Shall Be Satisfied.' The music gains momentum and combined themes lead to a climax. There follows a free adaptation of the 'Hallelujah' music with which Billings con-cludes his original choral piece and a final reference to the 'Shout and Rejoice' music." Thus, the sharply contrasting formal and textural juxtapositions of blocks and layers, based on sudden rhythmic, timbral, and polymodal con-trasts, and their fusion with traditional features (including an underlying diatonicism, the use of fugue, jazz- and popular-influenced rhythms, and the traditional American influence of Billings), represent a continuation of the American symphonic tradition established especially by Copland and Harris.

The absorption of traditional American elements into Schuman's personal contemporary idiom is manifested further in the two pieces. In "When Jesus Wept," the composer informs us that "the setting of the [Billings] text is in the form of a round," in which "Billings' music is used in its original form, as well as in new settings with contrapuntal embellishments and melodic extensions." In "Chester," the composer also reveals that "this music, composed as a church hymn, was adopted subsequently by the Con-tinental Army as a marching song and enjoyed great popularity. The or-chestral piece derives from the spirit both of the hymn and the marching song."

The American composer George Crumb (b. 1929) has drawn from early twentieth-century sources in ways that differ entirely from the "Ameri-canist" inclinations of Schuman. Although Crumb was trained in the United States, primarily as a pupil of Ross Lee Finney, his idiom has been influenced most prominently by Mahler, Debussy, and Bartók, as well as other interna-tional figures who have pioneered some of the earliest experiments in sono-rity and media. Crumb's music cannot be placed conveniently within any single stylistic or technical category, but represents instead a confluence of various musical interests. The two volumes of *Makrokosmos* for piano (1972–1973), for instance, are based on certain conscious external associations to Bartók's *Mikrokosmos* and Debussy's *24 Préludes,* although, as the composer himself has stated, the "spiritual impulse" of his music points to the "darker side" of Chopin instead—there are quoted fragments of Chopin's *Fantaisie-Impromptu* in *Dream Images (Love-Death Music)*— and the "childlike fantasy" of early Schumann.[9] In addition to the use of tonal elements in many of his works, direct quotations are used as part of "an urge to fuse various unrelated stylistic elements,"[10] as in *Ancient Voices of Children* (1970), where a quote

[9] Composer's program note for the recording of *Makrokosmos,* Volume I, on Nonesuch H–71293.

[10] Composer's program note for the recording of *Ancient Voices of Children I* on Nonesuch H–71255.

from the Notebook of Anna Magdalena Bach is juxtaposed with stylistic elements as divergent as the sounds and moods of Flamenco and Mahler, or in *Black Angels,* where he quotes Schubert's *String Quartet in D Minor (Death and the Maiden)* at the opening of Section 6 in juxtaposition with other stylistic elements. In *Night Music I* (1963), which is scored for soprano, piano, celesta, and two percussion, *Four Nocturnes (Night Music II)* (1964) for violin and piano, and *Star Child* (1977) for soprano, children's chorus, and orchestra, we also find direct sonic and mood references to Debussy's and Bartók's "Night Music" (e.g., the Adagio of the second movement of Bartók's *Piano Concerto No. 2*).

Crumb's varied idiom is also based on more radical experiments in timbre and sonority. The three books of *Makrokosmos* include muted tones, harmonics of various partials, various types of pizzicato, the use of a light metal chain that vibrates through contact with the strings, the scraping of the bass strings with metal plectrum, and so on. *Ancient Voices of Children* includes a vocalization on purely phonetic sounds sung into an amplified piano as well as vocal interjections and whispers by the instrumentalists, use of a musical saw by the mandolinist, alteration of piano pitch by contact of a chisel to the strings, retuning of certain mandolin strings by a quarter-tone, percussion instruments (including Japanese temple bells, Tibetan prayer stones, etc.) evoking Eastern Asian religious ritual, and other such timbral effects. Thus, these works include both traditional and nontraditional approaches to vocal and instrumental techniques, the latter often found in the music of Berio, Boulez, Cage, and others, the possibilities of which had been foreshadowed in experiments that may be traced back to the Italian futurists, Cowell, and Ives.

Crumb's exploitation of instrumental/vocal timbres and his experiments with a variety of sonic possibilities, as well as some use of indeterminacy in one or another of the musical parameters, often serve as a means of realizing his highly symbolic, intense personal expression. His musical philosophy and aesthetics are reflected most significantly in his close spiritual affinity to the poetry of Federico García Lorca, evidenced in his many settings of the Spanish poet's texts. The composer's varied timbral resources and use of quotations or imitations of divergent styles are all absorbed into his symbolic and dramatic idiom in an extended cycle of colorfully orchestrated vocal works that have resulted from his intense preoccupation with Lorca's poetry. These settings include: *Night Music I* (1963), for soprano, keyboard, and percussion; four books of *Madrigals* (1965–1969), for soprano and different combinations of instruments; *Songs, Drones, and Refrains of Death* (1968) for baritone, electric instruments (including guitar, double bass, piano, and harpsichord), and two percussion; *Eleven Echoes of Autumn (Echoes I)* (1966) for alto flute, clarinet, piano, and violin; *Echoes of Time and the River (Echoes II)* (1967) for orchestra; *Night of the Four Moons* (1969), for alto and four instruments; and *Ancient Voices of Children* (1970) for soprano, boy soprano, oboe, chromatic harmonica, mandolin, harp, electric piano, vibraphone, marimba, and many other conventional as well as nonconventional percussion instruments.

The seemingly incongruous stylistic and timbral elements in Crumb's compositions are exploited for their contrasting dramatic and atmospheric possibilities. At the same time, these elements are absorbed into carefully organized, highly unified musical constructions, which are inextricably associated with the larger dramatic conceptions. In these settings, in which Crumb has "sought musical images that enhance and reinforce the powerful, yet strangely haunting imagery of Lorca's poetry,"[11] large-scale structural associations and interactions of the multiplicity of musical resources provide the basis upon which the composer can express the meaning of the poetry most effectively. Many of Crumb's settings are based on a chiastic arch-form conception, reminiscent of the forms of both Debussy and Bartók. This formal plan serves to identify or associate corresponding elements with each other in the large-scale musico-dramatic design. *Night Music I,* for instance, consists of seven nocturnes organized in a symmetrical arch-form around a central movement, characterized by a dynamic rhythmic energy and constructed in contrasting ABAB sections with coda. The symmetry of the overall form of the seven nocturnes is established by the placement of the two Lorca settings as Movements III, "La Luna Asoma" (The Moon Rises), and V, "Gacela de la terrible Presencia" (Gacela of the Terrible Presence), around the purely instrumental central movement.[12]

The overall chiastic arch-form of *Ancient Voices of Children* provides an appropriate musical shape for the setting of five Lorca fragments, which the composer has "grouped into a sequence that seemed to suggest a 'larger rhythm' in terms of musical continuity." The five poetic fragments, which refer to the lost soul of childhood and the plea to Christ to return to that ancient voice, are set symmetrically in a larger cycle of seven dances and songs (of a hauntingly primitive, ornate non-Western quality): (1) Song I; (2) "Dances of the Ancient Earth"; (3) Song II; (4) Song III and "Dance of the Sacred Life-Cycle";(5) Song IV; (6) "Ghost Dance"; (7) Song V. The second and sixth sections, which are purely instrumental dance interludes, correspond to each other in the large-scale symmetrical form, while the fourth section, both sung and danced, is central both dramatically and musically. The latter section, "Dance of the Sacred Life-Cycle," is symbolized by the use of circular notation (for oboe, piano, mandolin, harp, and soprano) over a bolero drum ostinato, the latter of which contributes to the overall arch shape by its crescendo-decrescendo pattern. (Symbolic use of circular and other notational arrangements is commonly found in the works of Berio, Stockhausen, and others also.) The poetic meaning is heightened by a special structural use of timbre in this section, in which the austere sound of a boy soprano replaces the more brilliant soprano timbre the second time around. It is also significant to the chiastic musical conception that the entire work is framed by the word "niño" ("boy" or "child"): Section I opens with "El niño

---

[11] Ibid.

[12] For a more detailed analysis of this work, see Edith Borroff, *Three American Composers* (Lanham, Maryland: University Press of America, 1986), pp. 217–222.

busca su voz" ("The little boy was looking for his voice") and Section 7 closes with "mi alma antigua de niño" ("my ancient soul of a child"). A sense of emotional freedom is achieved throughout the work, despite the rigid framework for the diverse musical elements. This is manifested in the composer's stylistic indications for the individual movements. As Borroff has aptly observed, "The emotional life of the work is independent of the arch format . . . the finale does not balance the opening, but transcends it, as the emotional form transcends the arch structure."[13]

Other works of Crumb also reveal a highly systematic formal approach to the diverse musical materials, often in connection with an extramusical idea. In *Black Angels* (1970), for electric string quartet, the symmetrical organization is set in three large parts—I. Departure, II. Absence, III. Return—subdivided into thirteen smaller sections. Numbers 7 and 13 are employed structurally throughout to symbolize good and evil, respectively. Sonic resources are distributed symmetrically within the large palindrome to heighten this basic polarity. The overall arrangement of the twelve pieces of *Makrokosmos I,* which is the first of two sets of "fantasy pieces" for piano (1972 and 1973), is also connected inextricably to an extramusical concept, in which each piece is associated with a sign of the zodiac and a particular person born under that sign. The twelve pieces are organized in three sections of four continuous pieces each. The fourth piece in each grouping has a symbolic notation: number 4 is in the shape of a cross, number 8 in a circle, and number 12 in a spiral. Numerous sonic devices, produced on the piano both by traditional and nontraditional techniques, are integrated into the overall structure, but four elements that are presented in the opening three lines are essential in unifying the entire work.[14] An ascending progression of fourteen minor triads, separated between the two hands, is the source for the four basic intervallic elements. These include the tritone and perfect fifth, both of which are derived from special root relationships between adjacent chords in the alternating hands, the minor second, derived from the root adjacencies in each hand, and a three-note motif, A–B–F, exploited in both inversion and transposition. Crumb's aesthetics and philosophy of musical composition are described perceptively by Borroff:

> He is one of the composers that Ross Lee Finney has designated as "American tinkerers," men in the tradition not of erudition but of practical know-how. . . . In these experiments Crumb has used whatever has come to his attention, from the mountain music of his boyhood, from his tool case, or even from the kitchen, from whatever he has heard or read—in short, within the homely tradition of the inventor rather than the erudite speculation of the university scientist.[15]

[13] Ibid., p. 225.

[14] This is discussed by Larry Lusk, in "George Crumb: *Makrokosmos,* Vol. 1. Twelve Fantasy-Pieces After the Zodiac for Amplified Piano," *Notes* 31/1 (September 1974): 158.

[15] See Borroff, *Three American Composers,* n.12, above, p. 256.

LATIN-AMERICAN COMPOSERS AT HOME AND IN THE UNITED STATES

Since the early part of the twentieth century, various Latin American composers had drawn from their regional folk and popular sources, often fusing them with traditional and more modernistic European styles and techniques. Since the 1950s, increasing international mobility and cultural interactions have led many of the younger Latin American composers to assimilate some of the most varied contemporary approaches. Prior to World War II, atonal and twelve-tone techniques had already appeared in the works of Juan Carlos Paz who, rejecting the nationalist movement of his time, had founded with other Argentinian composers the Grupo Renovación in Buenos Aires as early as 1929. In the cosmopolitan environment of postwar Latin America, even those composers who continued to draw from their native sources have transformed them radically by infusion of contemporary elements (serial, aleatoric, and *musique concrète* techniques as well as the electronic medium). For example, the Mexican composer Carlos Chávez moved away from national influences toward more Romantic and Neoclassical styles in subsequent symphonic and chamber works, while the Spanish–Mexican composer Rodolfo Halffter moved toward twelve-tone serialism, as did the Brazilian Cláudio Santoro in the 1960s, who began as a nonnationalist, then turned temporarily toward his folk sources. The Brazilian composer Gilberto Mendes has aimed, since the late 1950s, at establishing a new Brazilian music based on more avant-garde techniques. His use of *musique concrète,* which might include local radio programs as part of his basic "national" materials, has permitted him to absorb modified Brazilian (Portuguese) speech patterns and popular musical sounds into a cosmopolitan approach. The folk sources in works of postwar Latin American composers have been absorbed as part of a more sophisticated and complex process of transformation and stylization.

The stylistic evolution of Alberto Ginastera (1916–1983), the most prominent of postwar Latin American composers, reveals a continuation of several early twentieth-century tendencies, which he was to combine with more recent techniques. Between 1948 and 1954, he moved from an objective use of Argentinian folk elements to a subjective or sublimated nonliteral usage, beginning with the *String Quartet No. 1* (1948) through the orchestral *Pampeana No. 3* (1954). He returned to the subjective approach after 1973. In his works after 1958, he turned to the use of twelve-tone-serial techniques in a somewhat more abstract idiom, in which he still remained faithful to traditional forms. In the early 1960s, he turned to a more complex fusion of traditional and contemporary forms and techniques.

It was in the second and third movements of his *String Quartet No. 2* (1958, revised 1967) that he began to employ twelve-tone serial techniques, while infusing the Argentinian cultural identity so prevalent in his earlier works with a more cosmopolitan Bartókian style as well. The affinity with Berg's approach is suggested in part in Ginastera's incorporation of a secret program into the twelve-tone context of the second movement of his *Quartet,* as Berg had done in his *Lyric Suite* for the same medium, though Ginastera could not have known about Berg's secret program at that time.[16] However, just as Berg had joined his own initials (A–B♭) with those of Hanna Fuchs (B–F) to form a basic cell (B♭–A–F–B) within the twelve-tone row of the third movement of the *Lyric Suite,* Ginastera incorporated the "BACH" motif (B♭–A–C–B) into the twelve-tone row of the second movement of his quartet. The two hexachords of the row, D–G–B♭–F♯–A–C♯ / E–B–F–A♭–C–D♯, are each bounded by a half-step, D–C♯ and E–D♯, respectively, the combination of which gives us a transposition of the BACH motif. The harmonization of these hexachordal terminals with the remaining notes of the hexachords is part of a larger set of programmatic associations. Kuss, who worked closely with Ginastera on his works, points out further that this motif was also to "serve as generative material for post-dodecaphonic works, such as the *String Quartet No. 3* with soprano (1973), the *Cello Sonata* (1979), and its recomposed version, the *Cello Concerto No. 2* (1980–1981)."[17]

The transformation of Ginastera's style, in which he absorbed and synthesized (rather than discarded) certain constant elements thoroughly from earlier works into a personal contemporary idiom, is revealed further in both the *Cantata para América mágica* (1960), for soprano and large percussion group, based on an "apotheosis of the elusive pre-Colombian past that nourished his imagination since the earliest ballet *Panambi* (1934–1937)," and the *First Piano Concerto* (1961).[18] The "magical" element that imbues these and other works since the "Presto magico" of *String Quartet No. 2,* a type of movement that also alludes to the exotic string writing found in the rapid scherzo movements of certain Bartók quartets, is related perhaps to the hallucinatory or imaginary world that the Argentinian writer Jorge Luis Borges builds in his literature.

The synthesis of sublimated national elements with contemporary aesthetic, stylistic, and technical features is epitomized in Ginastera's works of the early 1960s. The virtuoso *Violin Concerto* (1963) is a rare example of the Webernian influence in his works and, at the same time, incorporates such divergent features as quotes from the Paganini *Caprices,* microtonal elements, and other experimental devices, which evoke a hallucinatory quality. The operas *Don Rodrigo* (1964), *Bomarzo* (1967), and *Beatrix Cenci* (1971) are basic to Ginastera's move toward fusion of divergent elements in an intensified expressionistic idiom imbued by a sense of the fantastic. It is only in *Don Rodrigo,* however, that Ginastera follows most closely the twelve-tone-serial principles of Berg's *Lulu,* exploiting all the possibilities of derivative sets and their dramatic associations, whereas *Bomarzo* employs row technique less rigorously.

Don Rodrigo is modelled clearly after both of Berg's operas, its self-

---

[16] Malena Kuss, "Alberto Ginastera," in *Mitteilungen der Paul Sacher Stifung* no. 2 (January 1989): 17–18.

[17] Ibid., p. 18.

[18] Malena Kuss, Preface to *Alberto Ginastera: A Complete Catalogue of his Works* (London: Boosey and Hawkes, 1986), pp. 8–11.

contained traditional forms from *Wozzeck* and its row technique from *Lulu*. Ginastera himself referred to certain stylistic vocal sources in both Berg and Verdi, in which he alternates lyrical melody with *Sprechstimme,* and he also stated that *Don Rodrigo* should be sung "like Othello."[19] Although Ginastera does not use fugues or other clearly identifiable traditional procedures in *Don Rodrigo,* as Berg had done in *Wozzeck,* both the overall and local dramatic and musical structures of his opera reveal his affinity with the Viennese master. The three acts are in the shape of an arch which, like the dramatic structure of *Wozzeck,* corresponds with exposition, crisis, and dénouement, with corresponding poetic-musical differentiations: epic, lyrical, and tragic.[20] This tripartite scheme is reflected in the shape of the three scenes that comprise each of the acts and, as in *Wozzeck,* these scenes are separated by instrumental interludes. The use of traditional musical forms in *Wozzeck* also served as a model for *Don Rodrigo,* though in the latter they appear to have been determined more by free association to the traditional models than by literal adherence. The musical forms of the scenes are: I Rondo (Introduzione alternates with Arioso and Ballata e Recitativo); II Suite in quattro pezzi (Alleluia, Cavatina, Fanfara, Coda); III Melodrama (Recitativo, Imprecazione, Finale); IV Caccia and Scherzo (Musica di caccia, Scherzo pastorale, Madrigale a cinque, Ripresa dallo Scherzo e Coda); V Notturno e Duo (Musica notturna: Preludium, Aria, Duo d'amore); VI Aria in cinque strofe; VII Tripartita (Esposizione, Sviluppo in modo di Madrigale drammatico, Ricapitulazione); VIII Canon ed Aria (Canoni ritmici, Aria e ritornelli); and IX Struttura d'arco (Preludio e Recitativo, Arietta, Arioso I, Aria da Chiesa, Arioso II, Romance, Finale). At the same time, the arch-shape of the nine scenes is established by the pairing of corresponding scenes in the symmetrical organization according to dramatic opposites (Ex. 20–8).[21] The expressionistic context of *Bomarzo* is also based on traditional types, including the use of a madrigal (but only one major aria) as well as interludes, and he employs cinematic techniques such as flashback—the whole set of fifteen scenes based on a circular conception ("death" idea in Scene 1 returns in 15). As a dramaturgical tour de force, "Bomarzo is a surreal conception of the fictional inner life of Pier Francesco Orsini that abrogates dramatic movement as allegory replaces character and a play of sensory ideas replaces action."[22]

[19] John Vincent, "New Opera in Buenos Aires," *Inter-American Music Bulletin* 44 (November 1964): 2–3.

[20] Pola Suárez Urtubey, *Alberto Ginastera* (Buenos Aires: Ediciones Culturales Argentinas, 1967), p. 58.

[21] See Vincent, "New Opera in Buenos Aires," n. 19, above, p. 3; see also Gerard Béhague, *Music in Latin America: An Introduction* (Englewood Cliffs, NJ: Prentice-Hall, 1979), Figure 10–1.

[22] Malena Kuss, "Bomarzo," in Pipers *Enzyklopaedie des Musiktheatres* Vol. 2, ed. Carl Dahlhaus et al. (Munchen: Piper, 1987), p. 385. See also "Symbol und Phantasie in Ginastera's 'Bomarzo' (1967)," *Alberto Ginastera,* ed. Friedrich Spangemacher [*Musik der Zeit,* 4] (London: Boosey and Hawkes, 1984), pp. 88–102.

EXAMPLE 20–8. Alberto Ginastera, *Don Rodrigo,* arch-shape of nine scenes, in three acts, established by pairing of corresponding scenes in symmetrical organization according to dramatic opposites

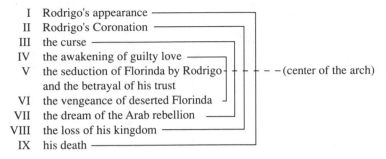

Despite the abstract musical language of *Don Rodrigo,* there is evidence that some of his technical materials in the opera are transformations of folk-music structures. The folk-music element is implied in the structure of the series, which serves as the source for derivative series from which he carves the motifs of the opera. In his earlier nationalistic works, such as the *Danzas argentinas I* (1937) (mm. 78ff.) and the opening of *Malambo* (1940), he employed the tuning of the guitar, E–A–D–G–B–E, from which he frequently derives a chord from the two perfect-fourth boundaries, E–A/B–E.[23] In the *Variaciones concertantes* (1953), Variation III (mm. 11–15), a chromatically compressed form of the two perfect fourths, F♯–B/C–F, outlined in the "Variazione giocosa per flauto" in its original diatonic form (B–E/F♯–[A]–B), appears as the initial harmonic construction (B♭–E♭–E–A) of *Don Rodrigo*—this is the same cell that initiates the opening twelve-tone trope of *Lulu.* Transposed fragments of this chord then overlap against a complete statement of the transposed cell (C♯–F♯–G–C) in the chorus. According to Kuss, "Ginastera's use of it as a purely constructive element in *Don Rodrigo* should not necessarily sever it from the previously established nativistic associations that initially motivated its use."[24]

As in Berg's *Lulu* as well as Dallapiccola's *Il Prigioniero,* in which two of the three rows ("Prayer" and "Hope") are also based prominently on transpositions of the 0–1–6–7 tetrachord (see Ex. 14–5, above), Ginastera's opera is also based on an elaborate interrelation of motifs, which are musically symbolized by a number of derived sets generated from the basic "Heroic" series (Ex. 20–9).[25] For instance, the initial 0–1–6–7 tetrachord (E♭–E–A–

---

[23] Malena Kuss, "Type, Derivation, and Use of Folk Idioms in Ginastera's Don Rodrigo (1964)," *Latin American Music Review* Vol. 1/2 (1980): 178–179.

[24] See ibid., p. 181.

[25] Two of these row forms—the "Serie Heroica" and "Serie Florinda"—are outlined and shown to serve as motivic sources by Suárez Urtubey, *Alberto Ginastera,* n.20, above, pp. 59ff., which according to Kuss came directly from Ginastera himself. Kuss was the first scholar to disclose the dramatic associations not only of the basic series,

EXAMPLE 20–9. Alberto Ginastera, *Don Rodrigo,* (a) basic "Heroic" series, (b) "Florinda" series, and (c) "Rodrigo" series, cellular connections

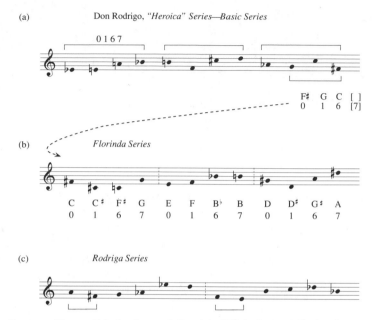

Music: Alberto Genastera; Libretto: Alejandro Casona. © Copyright 1969 by Boosey & Hawkes, Inc. Reprinted by permission.

B♭) of the latter (a), a chordal permutation of which opens the opera, is projected into the entire tetrachordal structure of Florinda's derived series (b). The initial transposition (C–C♯–F♯–G) of her series appears as the second chord of the opera, first as a partial chordal statement, G–C–[　]–F♯ (mm. 2ff.), in overlap with notes 5 and 6 (B–F) of the basic "Heroic" series, then in complete form as the first choral chord (C♯–F♯–G–C). The incomplete form (G–C–[　]–F♯), which appears complete at the opening of the Florinda series (b), also forms the last three notes of the "Heroic" series (a), thereby foreshadowing the interaction of the main characters. This connection is also anticipated at the outset, where the presence of Rodrigo's series (c) is implied in the succession of upper chordal notes (A–F♯–G–A♭) already of both orchestra and chorus (mm. 1–4). It is also striking that the oscillating figure, B–F–G–C♯ (m. 8, lower staff), joins the B–F-tritone adjacency (notes 5–6)

---

but also of the entire network of derivative series and motifs in her 1980 article (ibid.) as well as in "Native Idioms in Twentieth-Century Operas From Argentina, Brazil and Mexico: Towards a Comparative Chronology of Stylistic Change," *Transplanted European Music Cultures Miscellanea Musicologica,* Adelaide Studies in Musicology, Vol. 12 (Adelaide, 1987): 62–65.

of the "Heroic" series linearly with tritone G–C♯ from the initial tetrachord of Florinda's series. This flexible nonserial interaction of 0–1–6–7 cell transpositions, which will develop into the principal serial forms, reveals Ginastera's inclination toward musico-dramatic considerations from the outset. The entire harmonic sonority at this point (m. 8) is based on a fusion of the complete cellular forms (B–C–F–F♯ and G–G♯–C♯–D) to which these two tritones belong.

Rodrigo's motif (Act II, Scene 5, mm. 359–360; see also mm. 523–525) is both symbolized in and derived from Florinda's series (Ex. 20–10). At Florinda's exclamation, "Rodrigo! Rodrigo!," the verticalization of her three 0–1–6–7 tetrachords (G–C–C♯–F♯, B–B♭–F–E, and D♯–A–D–G♯) and their

EXAMPLE 20–10. Alberto Ginastera, *Don Rodrigo,* Act II, Scene 5, mm. 359–360, also mm. 523–525, derivation of Rodrigo motif from upper notes of 0–1–6–7 chords of Florinda series

transposed repeat (B♭–E♭–E–A, D–D♭–A♭–G, and F♯–C–F–B) bring the upper notes of her chords into melodic proximity (F♯–E–G♯–A–G–B) to give us Rodrigo's motif, the same procedure that Berg had used to derive the "Lulu" series from the "Picture" chords. Conversely, Florinda's motif (Act II, Scene 5, mm. 344–346) is both symbolized in and derived from Rodrigo's series. At Rodrigo's exclamation, "Florinda! Florinda!," the composer derives the vocal melodic motif, A–F♯–F–E, from the initial dyads (A–F♯ and F–E) of the two hexachords of Rodrigo's series (Ex. 20–9c). Ginastera's opera therefore reveals the continuation of various tendencies both from Romantic opera and the expressionistic twelve-tone idioms of Berg and Dallapiccola. Earlier works point to the stylistic influence of Bartók as well. Thus, while the opera is removed for the most part from Ginastera's native folk sources, certain elements from the folk idiom are traced from the diatonic guitar tuning of his earlier works to the chromatic 0–1–6–7 cell that generates the first segment of the basic "Heroic" series and the network of derived set-forms.

Ginastera's general evolution away from his native sources toward a more personal synthesis is also reflected in the music of other Latin American composers, who began to broaden their technical bases during their early studies in the United States. Some have absorbed the essence of their native sources into more complex contemporary idioms after having settled in the United States in the 1950s. Among those who have remained less inclined toward infusion of contemporary techniques, the Chilean Juan Orrego-Salas (b. 1919) has incorporated some traditional Spanish features into a neoclassical idiom, while the Uruguayan José Serebrier (b. 1938) has maintained the Latin American flavor in some of his works. Others who also settled in the United States have often absorbed their native folk elements into a more complex atonal idiom. The Panamanian Roque Cordero (b. 1917), who had established a nationalistic style initially in his *Capricho Interiorano* (1939), *Sonatina* (1943), *Obertura Panameña No. 2* (1944), and *Rapsodia Campesina* (1953), absorbed these features and other traditional elements into a flexible twelve-tone language in a more complex rhythmic style in the 1950s and 1960s.[26] His *Second Symphony* (1956) develops three related twelve-tone rows freely within a traditional sonata outline, further synthesizing the national quality and his serial techniques in the *String Quartets Nos. 2* (1968) and *3* (1973), *Permutaciones* (1974), and *Variations and Theme for Five* (1975). The Spanish-Cuban composer Julián Orbón (b. 1925), who had adhered initially to the Spanish neoclassical tradition of Falla and the Halffters in his choral *Suite de Siete Canciones de Juan del Encina* (1947), began to move away from the Spanish sources in his *Cantigas del Rey* (1960) to a less tonal idiom in the 1960s and 1970s.[27]

[26] See Béhague, *Music in Latin America,* n.21, above, p. 261. See also Aurelio de la Vega, "Latin American Composers in the United States," *Latin American Music Review* 1/2 (October 1980): 167.
[27] Béhague, ibid.

The Cuban composer Aurelio de la Vega (b. 1925) has pointed out that "the global melting pot of the music of this era of quick communication is no longer centered exclusively in Europe but now most prominently encompasses the New World. And the Latin American composers in the United States are certainly and decisively contributing to this fascinating process."[28] Among these composers, we may single out both de la Vega, who is among the most prominent Cuban composers of the postwar era, and the Argentinian composer Luis Jorge González (b. 1936) for having synthesized divergent traditional and modernistic tendencies thoroughly into personal contemporary idioms. De la Vega moved from his "postimpressionism and the modernistic Romanticism of Szymanowski" and some use of Afro-Cuban rhythms in his early works of the 1940s to a more chromatic and rhythmic idiom in the 1950s, arriving at a stage of serial development in his *String Quartet in Five Movements* "In Memoriam Alban Berg" (1957).[29] Here, his personal use of twelve-tone technique is set within a dynamic and motoric rhythmic context, after which he returned to a nonserialized chromaticism in the 1960s. De la Vega's more recent development has been based on a fusion of national rhythms and sonorities with some of the most recent contemporary techniques. A complexity of intervallic combinations and contours underlie his intensified personal style of the 1970s and 1980s. At the same time, all of his works were now to incorporate the Cuban *clave* rhythmic formula, despite his expressed opposition to any inclination toward a more pervasive use of his folk sources. With his orchestral *Intrata* (1972), he approached a new level of polyphonic writing and, during this period, also turned to the use of electronic instruments, some adoption of open form and other aleatoric procedures, and a tendency since the mid-1970s toward fusion of the arts, as manifested in his use of visual elements in his graphic scorings.[30] His *Tropimapal* (1983), for an ensemble of winds, percussion, and strings, exemplifies the composer's postserial chromatic idiom.

National elements imbue the contemporary atonal language of Luis Jorge González more pervasively, who has drawn from both Argentinian Indian (Quechuan) melodic and rhythmic styles as well as the tango for his personal and expressive idiom. While Gonzalez's early compositions are permeated by both popular and folkloristic materials, these sources have been absorbed and transformed increasingly into a more abstract style. However, in contrast to many of his Latin American contemporaries, his transformations have enhanced rather than obscured the essence of his native sources. Already, in his early set of five songs, *Cantares de Peregrino* ("Songs of the

---

[28] See de la Vega, "Latin American Composers in the United States," n.26, above, p. 174.

[29] See Béhague, *Music in Latin America: An Introduction,* n.21, above, p. 302.

[30] See ibid., p. 302. See also Mercedes Otero, *Aurelio De la Vega,* program notes for the recording of *Tropimapal* performed by The North/South Consonance Ensemble, Max Lifchitz, conductor (Greenville, Maine: Opus One, 134, Contemporary Music on Records of Distinction).

Pilgrim," 1960), composed while still in Argentina, his use of invented rather than stylized folk tunes led him to incorporate linear chromatic shifts into his otherwise diatonic and tonal folk-like melodic constructions, characterized by linear triadic outlines. Such chromaticized folk-like melodic inventions allowed him the possibility of an elaborated process of harmonization, the chromaticism of which foreshadowed his espousal of free atonality. While he made some use of authentic folk tunes from Argentina, many of which he had arranged before coming to the United States in 1971, all of them were drawn together into a single set of twelve choral songs under the title *Quiero Cantar Una Copla* ("I want to Sing a Copla"), and published in 1981. Thus, he wanted to keep separate what was authentic—he collected one of these from a folk singer—and what were his own inventions, the latter also based on simple folk-like elements (modes, triadic outlines, and symmetrical phrases) to which he could add his own harmonies.

From 1957 to 1959 and again from 1963 to 1964, González studied in Buenos Aires with Erwin Leuchter, who encouraged his studies of the chromatic scores of both Wagner and Brahms. At the same time, Leuchter, who had personal as well as musical associations with Berg and Webern, also introduced González to twelve-tone serial techniques. He had already had his first contact with both nontwelve-tone and twelve-tone serial pieces in 1958, having become aware of the serial idea through Leuchter's explanation of Dallapiccola's *Tre Laudi,* based on small serialized nuclei in chromatic counterpoint. This led to his study of Berg's *Violin Concerto,* in which he was struck by the combination of the twelve-tone serial principle with folk dances (Viennese waltz, etc.). Leuchter's suggestion that he include such chromatic materials into his own folk materials was to have significant results in several of his works, in which he attempted to join dance rhythms with the twelve-tone principle.

González's early contact with atonal and twelve-tone serial procedures in the works of the European masters resulted in his absorption of chromatic materials into the Ravelian style of his *Sonata for Violin and Piano* (1962) and *Sonatina for Piano* (1963). These works reveal his early move toward his more intense fusion of European sources with indigenous stylistic elements (combining his new chromaticism with folk-like rhythms). The latter are expansions of what he had heard in the music of other Argentinian composers and had learned from his studies and research with Argentinian folklorists as well as his travels into his native territories. In these and other works, he also fused Spanish colonial elements with the rhythms of Indian music by means of his own original approach. His typical alternations of motoric 6/8 and 3/4 rhythmic patterns and other irregular combinations are found throughout Latin America. The folk influence is also manifested in his interest in Argentinian literature, for instance, that of Jorge Luis Borges, whose style and subjects are Argentinian and universal simultaneously. Thus, González could use chromatic and atonal techniques for dramatic expression in his instrumental and vocal text settings in combination with certain things he had heard in folk-music performances, including diverse accentuations and shifting meters. All of these features were further developed in the quasiserialistic technique of his *Sonata for Clarinet and Piano* (1965).

González wanted to compose an Argentinian music that would also be entirely contemporary, but Leuchter had said that folk music was too tonal for a modernistic idiom. Therefore, while the essence of his native folk sources can be traced in a number of his more recent compositions, he was to move toward an increasingly abstract development in his search for a thoroughly contemporary chromatic style. In his *Visiones de la Pampa* (1963–1967), for orchestra, he leaned toward a neonationalist approach, attempting to stylize the folk rhythms by creating similar patterns that contain the same rhythmic units as folk music. He thereby expanded the various features of his earlier *Cantares* while evoking its sweeping melodies. However, it was only after González came to the United States in 1971 that he began to establish a thoroughly atonal chromatic idiom, as manifested in his *Voces II* (1973, revised 1987), for nine instruments, and the first pieces of his series of *Soledades Sonoras* ("Sounds of Solitude," 1974–1986), for single instruments. These works represent his first significant development of a new harmonic language, now based more thoroughly on nontertian harmonies and more complex, highly altered tertian constructions.

His increased experimentalism occurred just prior to his studies with Earle Brown at the Peabody Conservatory in the early 1970s. González had already begun to experiment with new timbral combinations and "open form" in his *Mutables,* four studies for vibraphone and piano (1969, rev. 1975). This came not from the influence of Brown's work with this aleatoric structural principle, but rather from certain structural relations suggested in Latin American poetry, where phrases are combined in a more complex organization based on divergent and unrelated figures of speech. His first piece composed in the United States was *Voces I* (1972), for clarinet and piano, which in a special way represents the fusion of his national aesthetics with contemporary techniques. Here, he exploited instrumental possibilities as the basis of the idea of "things" having voices, an aspect of "Magical realism" which "presupposes that the boundaries between dream and reality are blurred and one permeates the other."[31] González has identified this and many of his other works as "exponents of 'Magical realism' in the same way that many literary works written during the twentieth-century by authors such as García-Marquez, Asturias, Carpentier and others are," an aesthetic concept which permeates Latin American literary and artistic thought. Here, the composer had infused his timbral elaborations, in which spaces are to be "discovered and explored . . . as if they were sorcerers," into a context of nontwelve-tone serial techniques and new rhythmic explorations.

Harawi (1980), for flute and guitar, reveals a fusion of the folk-like Quechuan Indian style with more abstract manipulations of atonal pitch cells. While the instrumentation itself is reminiscent of the wooden flute of the Quechuans, the basic atonal cell itself is a combination of the primitive

[31] See ibid., Luis Jorge González, *Voces,* program notes for the recording.

pentatonic scale with chromatic elements. In the first two contour-related phrases, the rhythmically and tonally varied second phrase establishes the principle of *developing variation* common to all of González's music.[32] As part of this principle, the opening establishes the basic "white-key" pentatonic collection, D–F–G–A–C, to which is added a chromatic "black-key" D♭ and a cadential quarter-tone-raised F♯ (Ex. 20–11). These "black-key" intrusions, used as the basis of quarter-tone inflections, point to intonational aspects of authentic folk-music performance and, at the same time, initiate the interactions of the "white-" and "black-key" spheres that result in continuously shifting permutations and transpositions of the basic set, D–F–G–A–C–D♭. As part of the technique of *developing variation,* the set also occurs in complex chromatic chords with superimpositions of it at various pitch levels. The overall direction of the developmental form is determined in part by the "black-key" intrusions into the "white-key" area and the reverse, these interactions serving as the primary means of progression, not only in this but other works as well.

The musical language of *Voces II* (1973), which was revised and published in 1987, represents the more abstract part of González's development in his search for an atonal chromaticism in an idiom no longer tied to folk elements. In his move away from the overt use of folk rhythms and melodies, he tended toward a fusion of diverse cultural elements, including those from the European background. González was aware of the investigations of certain folklorists, such as Rodolfo Hoffmann, who studied folk scales and discussed the possibilities of expanding three-note segments to heptatonic modes. Through his own studies of the influence of Spain on Latin American music, González had fused European influences intuitively with the added-note procedures found in Mestizo music. Thus, based on González's general aesthetic inclination toward *magical realism,* so evident in the literary tradition of Latin American culture, the musical context of *Voces* transcends the coloristic aspects of folklorism and strives toward more essential things, as manifested in his more general rhythmic speculations in a context of continual pitch-set transformation. Thus, in *Voces II,* the composer makes extensive use of the principle of *developing variation,* based on the development of a particular element, the exploration of some possibility (either timbric, melodic, or rhythmic) of an isolated element, a new combination of existing materials, and the addition of a new element to the preexisting ones, each of the variations exploring a diverse timbral combination in addition to aspects of pitch-set manipulation.

The basic seven-note pitch-set, C–C♯–D–F♯–G♯–A–A♯ (0–1–2–6–8–9–10), is partitioned in diverse manners in the different sections. The composer always attempts to maintain some of the main characteristics of the set as the source material for a particular section. In Movement I, "Por los espacios de la voz" ("For the spaces of the voice"), the set is the source for

---

[32] González's concept of *developing variation,* Schoenberg's term originally, reveals some affinity with the musical thought of the Viennese composer.

EXAMPLE 20–11. Luis Jorge González, *Harawi,* opening, basic "white-key" pentatonic collection, D–F–G–A–C, to which is added a chromatic "black-key," D♭ and a cadential quarter-tone-raised F♯, followed by other "black-key" intrusions

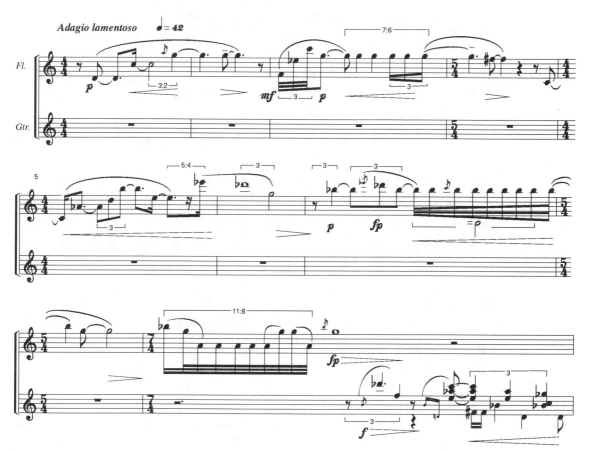

Used by permission of the composer. Composed in 1980, unpublished.

various minisets throughout the diverse sections. While the chromatic construction of this set contrasts with the essentially pentatonic set (i.e., with added chromatic element) in *Harawi,* the developmental principle toward a totally chromatic context is similar. The basic set (Ex. 20–12), established harmonically in the initial dotted-rhythmic figure (1), is expanded immediately at the modified reiteration of the dotted rhythm in the right hand of the piano (2) by the addition of F–G–B (pitches 5–7–11). This is followed by the addition of E (pitch 4) in the open-fifth harmonic of the contrasting violin entry. Then, against the first appearance of basic rhythmic cells a and b (m. 2, in percussion 1), the basic pitch-set (as represented in the opening chord, C♯–G♯–A–C/D–F♯–A♯) is inverted harmonically and reinterpreted regis-

EXAMPLE 20–12. Luis Jorge González, *Voces II*, opening, "developing variation" of basic seven-note set (C–C♯–D–F♯–G♯–A–A♯) in initial dotted-rhythmic figure, introduction of basic rhythmic cells

NORTH/SOUTH EDITIONS (BMI), P.O. Box 698, Cathedral Station, New York, NY 10025-0698; (518) 274-4965. Used by permission.

trally in the piano (4), i.e., in enharmonic spelling, A♯–D–F♯–[G♯]/A–C–C♯–G♯. In the remainder of the first piano phrase (mm. 2–3), individual linear segments, F♯–C♯–F–D (in referential ordering, F♯–C♯–D–F) and A–B–F (or F–A–B), which represent transpositions and permutations of two of the opening rhythmically defined components of the basic set, C♯–G♯–A–C and F–G–B, acquire structural significance within the larger piano statement.

The cadential whole-tone segment, F–A–B (mm. 2–3), belongs to a new rhythmic cell (c), all three rhythmic cells (a, b, and c) of which subsequently undergo only small changes as they are interwoven to produce a sense of continuity within the diversity of foreground materials. The movement evolves an elaborate set of seven continuous variations from the initial piano statement of the main thematic motifs, each variation dealing with a different subset drawn from the basic set (or its inversion) in a characteristic timbral elaboration.[33] An essential subset that emerges as the basis of set identification as well as expansion and transformation is the cadential gapped whole-tone cell, F–A–B, of the opening piano statement. The latter is a literal inversion of the initial cadential cell, F–G–B (m. 1), the two together implying an expanded whole-tone segment (F–G–A–B). This is supported by the prominent reiterations in the percussion of the common cellular tritone boundary, B–F, as well as segment F–G–B. The main cadential segment (F–A–B) is expanded locally by the addition of C#–E♭ (left hand) to produce a larger, timbrally uniform five-note segment of the whole-tone scale, F–[ ]–A–B–C#–E♭, against the contrasting held fifth (A–E) of the violin. In addition, the complementary relation between the two whole-tone cycles is implied in the phrasal structure, a segment from the other whole-tone cycle (D–F#–A#) of which is isolated registrally in the opening chord. The latter is expanded (see 4 in Ex. 20–12) in the harmonically inverted form of the basic set to B♭–D–F#–G#. The opening phrase is thereby bounded temporally by prominently placed segments of the two whole-tone cycles. In each case, these segments appear as components within the larger basic set.

In Movement II, "Tu voz de fuego blanco" ("Your voice of white fire"), developmental technique is also used as the basis for integrating separate sections. In this movement, diverse motifs, made of small sets (three to five pitches), appear in contrasting sections, which are interlocked with variations of the main melodic idea (introduced by the oboe, mm. 8–14). Each of these sections is characterized by a unique coloristic orchestration. Various brief elements, including flutter-tongue and tremolandi, are combined subsequently to produce unity within variety. These motifs converge at the climax of the movement (mm. 64–75).

González has also incorporated the Argentinian tango into his angular and atonal chromaticism since the early 1970s, not by means of any literal usage, but rather by absorbing its essence in a gestural approach to this popular element. He first used the tango in his three pieces for piano, entitled *Calles de Buenos Aires* ("Streets of Buenos Aires," 1972, last piece 1978), then in his *Con Fervor por Buenos Aires* ("With Warmth for Buenos Aires," 1985–1989), a set of songs for voice and chamber ensemble, based on an unorthodox approach to twelve-tone serialism. The essence of the tango has also been employed in his free-atonal *Historias de Orilleros* ("Stories of Outlaws," begun in 1988), for string quartet, and the *Espejismos de la Noche* ("Mirages of the Night," begun in 1989), for piano and chamber orchestra. The latter work also represents González's use of *Magical realism,* which is manifested in various ways. As in his *Qasidah del Alba* ("Poem of the Dawn," 1979–1985), for guitar and orchestra, *Luminescences* (1982–1985), for piano trio, and *Arcosantiana* (1989), his symbolic use of numbers is projected into the deep-level structure, so this aesthetic conception, so prevalent in Latin America, be-

---

[33] The variations are outlined as follows: I (m. 1); II (end of m. 7); III (m. 19); IV (m. 27); V (end of m. 41); VI (m. 51); and VII (m. 70).

comes the basis of an abstract mathematical approach to formal design in a chromatic and also clearly directional atonal musical language.

SUGGESTED READINGS

GERARD BÉHAGUE.   *Music in Latin America: An Introduction* (Englewood Cliffs, NJ: Prentice-Hall, Inc., 1979).

EDITH BORROFF.   *Three American Composers* (Lanham, MD: University Press of America, Inc., 1986) (on Irwin Fischer, Ross Lee Finney, and George Crumb).

PETER EVANS.   *The Music of Benjamin Britten* (Minneapolis: University of Minnesota Press, 1979).

MALENA KUSS.   "Alberto Ginastera," in *Mitteilungen der Paul Sacher Stiftung* no. 2 (January 1989): 17–18.

———.   "Native Idioms in Twentieth-Century Operas From Argentina, Brazil and Mexico: Towards a Comparative Chronology of Stylistic Change," *Transplanted European Music Cultures Miscellanea Musicologica,* Adelaide Studies in Musicology, Vol. 12 (Adelaide, 1987): 54–73.

———.   "Symbol und Phantasic in Ginastera's 'Bomarzo' (1967)," *Alberto Ginastera,* ed. Friedrich Spangemacher [*Musik der Zeit,* 4] (London: Boosey and Hawkes, 1984), pp. 88–102.

———.   "Type, Derivation, and Use of Folk Idioms in Ginastera's Don Rodrigo (1964)," *Latin American Music Review* Vol. 1/2 (1980): 176–195.

———.   Preface to *Alberto Ginastera: A Complete Catalogue of His Works* (London: Boosey & Hawkes, 1986), pp. 8–11.

DONALD MITCHELL.   *Britten and Auden in the Thirties: The Year 1936* (London and Boston: Faber and Faber, 1981).

———.   "The Musical Atmosphere," in *Benjamin Britten: A Commentary on His Works from a Group of Specialists,* ed. Donald Mitchell and Hans Keller (Salisbury Square, London: Rockliff Publishing Corporation Limited, 1952), pp. 9–58.

PRESTON STEDMAN.   *The Symphony* (Englewood Cliffs, NJ: Prentice-Hall, Inc., 1979), pp. 353–366 (on William Schuman).

POLA SUÁREZ URTUBEY.   *Alberto Ginastera* (Buenos Aires: Ediciones Culturales Argentinas, 1967).

AURELIO DE LA VEGA.   "Latin American Composers in the United States," *Latin American Music Review* 1/2 (October 1980): 162–175.

JOHN VINCENT.   "New Opera in Buenos Aires," *Inter-American Music Bulletin* 44 (November 1964): 1–4.

General Index

This index lists, under composers' names, only those compositions that are analyzed in some detail or are referred to with some frequency in the text. This index is also selective regarding historical, stylistic, and technical terms, omitting many of the more common ones which occur pervasively.

541